P9-DHA-591

Leaders and the Leadership Process

Readings, Self-Assessments, and Applications

Jon L. Pierce
John W. Newstrom

University of Minnesota—Duluth

Irwin McGraw-Hill

Boston, Massachusetts   Burr Ridge, Illinois   Dubuque, Iowa
Madison, Wisconsin   New York, New York   San Francisco, California   St. Louis, Missouri

—To the students of leadership—
To those of you who will lead our organizations and
To those of you who will be affected by their leadership practices

Irwin/McGraw-Hill

*A Division of The **McGraw·Hill** Companies*

Copyright   1995 Richard D. Irwin, Inc. in a joint venture with the
Austen Press, a Times Mirror Higher Education Group Inc., company.

All rights reserved. No part of this publication may be reproduced,
stored in a retrieval system, or transmitted, in any form or by any
means, electronic, mechanical, photocopying, or otherwise, without
the prior written permission of the publisher.

Publisher: William Schoof
Acquisitions Editor: Mary Fischer
Production Manager: Bob Lange

Design and project management provided by Elm Street Publishing
Services, Inc.

Compositor: G&S Typesetters
Typeface: 10/12 Palatino
Printer: Malloy Lithographing, Inc.

Library of Congress Cataloging-in-Publication Data
Pierce, Jon L.
    Leaders and the leadership process : readings, self-assessments,
and applications / Jon L. Pierce, John W. Newstrom.
        p.   cm.
    Includes bibliographical references.
    ISBN 0-256-16311-1
    1. Leadership. 2. Leadership—Case studies. 3. Leadership—
Problems, exercises, etc.   I. Newstrom, John W. II. Title.
HM141.P48   1994
303.3′4—dc20   94-16990

Printed in the United States of America
        7   8   9   0   M   L   9   8

Address orders:
Richard D. Irwin, Inc.
1333 Burr Ridge Parkway
Burr Ridge, IL 60521

Richard D. Irwin, Inc.

Cover source: © Oli Tennent/Tony Stone Images

The Book: Leaders and the Leadership Process

Several years ago the Management and Organization faculty at the University of Minnesota–Duluth (Professors Robert Wharton, Linda E. Parry, Kjell R. Knudsen, John W. Newstrom, and Jon L. Pierce) decided that the undergraduate curriculum needed a course in leadership. Claims that many of our organizations were "over managed and under led" and that the crisis facing American organizations was in large part a function of "bad management and inept leadership" led us to believe that it was important for our students to explore the subject of leadership in greater depth and to begin thinking about and looking at themselves within the leadership context. A course in leadership might serve as an important catalyst in fulfilling this objective.

As part of the design process, we consulted several leading leadership scholars around the country, asking for assistance with the construction of the reading list for our new course. We informed these individuals of our decision to conduct an undergraduate seminar in leadership and asked them to help identify important material from the leadership literature. After compiling this list we offered our first course. During the past several years this course has been offered on several occasions, continually refined, and proven to be extremely popular with our students.

Recently Mary Fischer, John Weimeister, and Bill Schoof of The Austen Press approached us about taking our undergraduate course materials in leadership and putting them into book form. Their interest in our leadership class led us to the creation of this book.

Purpose of the Book

Few management and organization topics have generated as much interest and research activity as leadership. "Fads" in the corporate world find their roots in practitioners' fancy for and belief in "quick fixes" for organizational woes, and consultants' desire to make a quick buck. Thus, the corporate desire to search continually for "new bottles for old wine," coupled with academicians' inclination to study and think about what inspires them, creates all the ingredients for a short-lived interest in leadership and the leadership process. However, this has not been the case. Instead, widespread interest in leadership has spanned nearly five decades with significant historical roots stemming from the works of many ancient Greek, Roman, Chinese, and Egyptian philosophers.

Thousands of pages in academic books and journals have been devoted to the topic of leadership. During the past several years, the popular press has published and sold millions of copies of several dozen books written on the topic of leaders and leadership. Organizations frantically search for the magical leader who can pull the firm together and place it back on the competitive path. We frequently hear stories about important historical leaders; we attribute organizational successes and failures to the things that our leaders did or failed to do; and at the national level we commonly resurrect dreams of the way it was when certain charismatic leaders were at the nation's helm.

It is evident that there is a strong interest in leadership. Our university, along with a large number of other institutions of higher education, has in recent years instituted courses in leadership.

This book's development reflects that interest and the obvious need for a greater number of individuals to take the issue of organizational leadership more seriously. *The primary purpose of this book is to serve as a catalyst for the student of leadership's thinking and dialogue about leaders and the leadership process.* This book is intended to give the student a feel for the breadth and richness of this study. This set of readings aims to provide the student with a sense of the complexity associated with organizational leadership as well as an important understanding of some of the pieces that serve to define this complex mosaic called leadership.

What the Book Is and Is Not

This book of readings cannot provide the reader with thorough and complete coverage of the leadership literature. During the past five-plus decades, those leadership scholars who have chosen to observe, study, think, and write about leadership have produced literally thousands of pages of theory and empirical observation. For obvious reasons, this reader provides you with but a sampling of this literature.

While this book does touch on the major themes that have characterized the work done in the realm of leadership, there are many important authors and contributions that could not be included in our work. This omission is not intended to downplay the importance of the scholarship that they have given to our understanding of this very important topic.

While this book does include some of the classic and seminal articles on leadership, there are many classical pieces that could not be included. Once again, this is not intended to suggest that they are less important than the pieces that we ultimately chose to include.

The Book's Organization

This book is organized into two parts. Part One, divided into 12 chapters, presents a set of readings that will help students understand leaders and the leadership process. The majority of the readings included in this reader are taken from academic journals. Our editing has streamlined several readings by removing complex sections, thus making the material more "reader friendly" and appropriate for diverse audiences.

- Chapter One looks at the definition of leadership, suggests that leadership is a process, and provides some insight into the role played by leaders.

- Building upon the suggestion that leadership is, in part, an influence process, Chapter Two looks at the ways leaders exercise social influence and their source of power.

- Chapter Three suggests that effective leaders are individuals who possess the "right stuff." The traits associated with effective leadership are reviewed.

- The argument in Chapter Four suggests that effective leadership is in part a function of what it is that leaders do. The behaviors that can be used to describe leadership and effective leadership are explored.

- Chapter Five suggests that different situations call for different leader behaviors. One leadership style simply does not serve all individuals (followers), nor does it serve all situations within which leaders and their followers find themselves embedded.

- Chapter Six reinforces the notion that the follower plays a powerful role in the leadership process. The follower is not a passive part of the leadership formula, and in fact the attributes and behaviors of the follower frequently serve to shape the leadership process.

- There has been a long-standing interest in participative leadership. Chapter Seven explores issues surrounding the theoretical reasons for the use of participative leadership and provides insight into the relationship between participation and leader effectiveness.

- While it is easy to conclude that leadership is always necessary, the readings in Chapter Eight suggest that there are situational factors that can serve as substitutes for, neutralizers of, and enhancers of leaders and their behaviors.

- Chapter Nine provides insight into the nature and character of the charismatic and transformational leader—the leadership style that today's business world appears to be frantically searching for.

- While it is common to think about leadership at the small group, department, and work-team level, there are organizational leaders as well. Chapter Ten introduces the concept of strategic leadership. The readings in this chapter provide insight into the nature and character of leadership stemming from the upper echelons of the organization.

- Chapter Eleven asks the seemingly strange question—Does leadership really make a difference? The readings in this chapter address both sides of the debate. *Point:* Leadership does *not* make a difference, it is simply the product of a societal love affair and romantic notions that surround leaders. *Counterpoint:* Leadership *does* make a difference in the level of organizational performance, it is not simply a so- cially constructed organizational reality. The third reading in Chapter Eleven pro- vides a reminder that the effects of leadership are not always positive in nature.

- Chapter Twelve invites us to think about the 21st century, the hypercompetitive and turbulent environment, and the emerging organization. The flexible, learning, and self-organizing organization appears to be calling for a new leadership paradigm. In this chapter students will have the opportunity to explore some of the emerging leadership issues.

Self-Assessments

Many of the book chapters include self-assessment exercises, which give readers the opportunity to profile themselves along several different dimensions associated with leaders and the leadership process. These self-assessments provide readers with an op- portunity to take a look at themselves and further understand how they might fit within the realm of this complex mosaic of leadership.

Part Two, Beyond Theory and into the Practice of Leadership, provides readers with addi- tional opportunities to explore leaders and the leadership process. This section of the book is intended to move students beyond the theory of leadership and closer to the world of practice and application. Several popular books that have appeared at local bookstores in recent years have been written by management practitioners, consultants, and observers of leaders at work. We have provided a summary of some of the most recent and popular leadership books.

To facilitate students' ability to apply their understanding of the leadership literature and to work on the development of analytical and problem-solving skills, we have in- cluded several incidents, case studies, and exercises. We firmly believe that active learn- ing contributes more to the overall learning process than passive learning. We therefore encourage students to read, think about, discuss, debate, observe, experiment with, ana- lyze, and solve issues that define leadership and the leadership process. The cases, inci- dents, and exercises are intended to supplement the conceptual material and help readers come to understand leaders and the leadership process more fully.

Acknowledgments

There are many individuals whom we would like to acknowledge for their role in assisting us with the creation of this book. First, there are a myriad of organization scholars who have worked hard at developing the theory of leadership and providing scientific observations of leaders and the leadership process. We thank them for providing us with an understanding of and insight into this very important organizational phenomenon.

Robert J. House, Craig Lundberg, Jerry Hunt, Chet Schreisheim, Warren Bennis, Henry P. Sims, Jr., Peter Frost, Jane M. Howell, Alan C. Filley, Charles C. Manz, Kimberly Boal, Larry L. Cummings, and Bernard M. Bass each provided us with ideas pertaining to important pieces of leadership literature, case studies, and exercises/incidents that could be employed to help communicate the many lessons of leadership. In addition, some of our leadership students took the initiative to read and summarize a popular leadership book for inclusion in this book of readings.

Several individuals, including Brian P. Niehoff, Albert A. Vicere, Morgan McCall, and Martin Schatz, reviewed, critiqued, and offered very helpful suggestions that aided us in strengthening the breadth, inclusiveness, thoroughness, and quality of our edited work. We want to say "thank you" for your assistance.

A special form of recognition must go to the undergraduate students who took the leadership course from us here at the University of Minnesota–Duluth. Your passionate interest in leadership and the understanding of leaders and the leadership process that you derived from this set of readings encouraged us to assemble this book. Consequently, other students can now benefit from this interesting collection of materials taken from the leadership literature.

We benefited greatly from the many hours of assistance that we received from three individuals here at the University of Minnesota–Duluth. Greta Hasskamp, thank you very much for your time, energy, patience, and assistance. Heather Goette and Connie Johnson also provided us with help on a myriad of tasks associated with the preparation of our manuscript.

Finally, we would like to extend our appreciation to Mary Fischer, Bill Schoof, and John Weimeister of Austen Press. We sincerely appreciate the opportunity you provided us to create this leadership book.

Jon L. Pierce
John W. Newstrom
October 1994

Contents

Prologue

Where should a systematic study of leadership begin? The contemporary study of leaders and the leadership process finds its most recent roots stemming from social psychology, sociology, psychology, and organizational behavior. Several noted group and organizational scholars, among them Kurt Lewin, Ronald Lippitt, Ralph White, J. Dowd, Ralph Stogdill, Edwin Fleishman, and G. Spiller, launched their inquiries into leadership during the 1930s and 1940s.

It is, however, possible to start the study of leadership by turning to the classics. Homer's *Iliad* and *The Odyssey* provide detailed biographies of great leaders. Plutarch's *Lives* provides insight into what makes great leaders act the way that they do, while Sophocles' plays, *Ajax* and *Antigone*, depict the psychology of leadership. Shakespeare, in *Othello*, provides a look into the role of intuition and *King Lear* provides clues into the difference that leadership makes by examining the role of succession. The *Republic*, by Plato, examines and expresses reservations about democratic management and leadership, while John Stuart Mill, in his essay *On Liberty*, constructs his arguments for participative management.[1]

Fred A. Kramer (1992), in the first reading, launches our study of leadership with his "Perspectives on Leadership from Homer's *Odyssey*." We concur with his conclusion that "each of us should evaluate our own journey into self-awareness and self-understanding." We hope that the wide variety of readings and other materials in this collection will stimulate you to begin that search into your understanding of leaders and the leadership process. We invite you to study the classic, recent, and emerging perspectives on leadership and reflect on their implications for you, organizations, and our rapidly emerging global community.

[1] For the reader interested in the "classic touch" to the subject of leadership, we recommend as a starting point to your journey into this literature your reading of John K. Clemens and Douglas F. Mayer's *The Classic Touch: Lessons in Leadership from Homer to Hemingway*, Homewood, IL: Dow Jones-Irwin, 1987.

Perspectives on Leadership from Homer's *Odyssey*

Fred A. Kramer
University of Massachusetts-Amherst

*B*usiness and public-administration education and practice can be a harrowing experience. As Warren Bennis has suggested, "The more our work makes us specialists, the more we must strive to remain or become generalists in other matters, to perceive the interconnections among science, esthetics, and ethics, to avoid becoming lopsided. All of humanity's pursuits are connected, after all, and we remain ignorant of those connections at our peril."[1] Classic works of literature can help us overcome parochial tendencies, so we can better deal with our immediate problems and look beyond them.

Homer's epic poem, the *Odyssey*, illuminates truths that have value today. Many of us may look back to our high-school introduction to the *Odyssey* and recall a series of stories that may surface from the mists of our memories. Maybe our memories of the *Odyssey* support Edgar Allen Poe's view of epic poems. To Poe, epic was "the art of being dull in verse."[2] But the *Odyssey* need not be dull if read by more mature minds than the average teenager's. It may even be relevant. Surely modern leaders are not going to confront a Cyclops in a cave or see some of our trusted lieutenants turned into swine by the magical powers of Circe. But on some level, similar things happen in the course of coping with administrative demands today.

There are two levels on which the modern manager who aspires to improve his or her leadership abilities may engage the story of Odysseus. The deeper level is the intensely personal psychological journey toward self-awareness and self-development. As Cedric H. Whitman suggests, "The nature of myth, or folk tale, is to reflect in external form the psyche's subconscious exploration of itself and its experience."[3] In the changing environment of modern business and government, leaders are expected to embark on journeys into the unknown. Perhaps the successful completion of these journeys depends on notions of self-discovery similar to the ones that Odysseus went through.

To deal with this personal level of the *Odyssey*, one must read the tales and reflect deeply on how Homer's metaphors enhance one's personal growth.

On another level, however, one can reinterpret the stories that we first encountered in high school with a special relevance to management or leadership problems. The purpose of this paper is to show the relevance of some of Homer's insights into management with the hope that some readers will be inspired to read more of Homer to develop the arguments on a deeper, more personal level. We will see that many of Homer's key insights on leadership and management are relevant today, but, more importantly, we will see that thinking metaphorically can enhance our own development.

The *Odyssey* is, in part, the story of one man's adventures after the Trojan War. After the successful sack of Troy, Odysseus embarked with several ships and many followers to return to his native Ithaca, off the western coast of the Peloponnesian peninsula. In what should have been a fairly standard trip—there was the usual side trip to sack and pillage Lauchachia en route just to keep certain that standard operating procedures honed by years of planning and maneuvers remained in good order—Odysseus incurred the wrath of Poseidon, the god of earth and sea. Despite Odysseus' efforts to meet his goal on time and within budget, events beyond his control intervened. Instead of a few weeks, Odysseus was gone for ten more years.

During this time, his wife, Penelope, steadfastly remained loyal to him. Although pursued by several dozen suitors from all over the Greek world, she remained virtuous. She also was faced with some budgetary difficulties. In the manner of the times, the suitors who wanted to replace Odysseus in Penelope's bed as well as lay claim to Odysseus' kingdom hung around the palace drinking and feasting—at Penelope's expense. This drain on Ithaca's coffers did not escape the gods. Athena, in particular, took pity on Penelope and successfully argued that the gods should allow Odysseus to return. As part of her plan, she told Telemachus, Odysseus' son, who was a baby when Odysseus went off to war but who was now full grown, to outfit a ship and go looking for his father.

Fed up with the actions of the suitors, who had virtually taken over his father's palace, Telemachus embarked on what he felt would be an impossible mission. He was helped in this effort by the man Odysseus left behind to look after the palace and grounds, Mentor. Athena assumed Mentor's appearance and accompanied Telemachus on the journey. Along the way, "Mentor" gave him encouragement—the encouragement that he needed to develop into a fully functioning, responsible adult. Telemachus was relieved to be doing

Source: Edited and reprinted with permission from *Business and the Contemporary World* (Summer 1992), 168–173.

At the time this article was written, Fred A. Kramer was a professor of political science and director of the MPA Program at the University of Massachusetts (Amherst). He is the author of *Dynamics of Public Bureaucracy* and a variety of articles that have appeared in professional journals. Author affiliation may have changed since article was first published.

something. He was a man of action even though he perceived that the odds were against him.

Like all good mentors, Athena imbued Telemachus with a sense of responsibility. In seeking to master his challenging assignment, Telemachus discovered his inner strength. The babbling teenager became an articulate, courageous adult who impressed others with his leadership potential. With his mentor's help and support, Telemachus gained confidence and achieved a degree of success that he had not previously thought possible. In short, under a mentor's guidance, Telemachus showed leadership qualities similar to those his father had displayed during the Trojan War.

Mentor meets each of the leadership criteria suggested by a current observer of leadership problems, Warren Bennis. In *Why Leaders Can't Lead*, Bennis suggests four "competencies" that leaders must show. These are: management of attention through vision; management of meaning through communication; management of trust through reliability and constancy; and management of self through knowing one's skills and deploying them effectively.[4]

The first three competencies are closely related. To Bennis, having a vision is absolutely essential to leadership. The leader's vision provides a focus and sets the agenda for the organization. Having a clear vision brings about confidence in the followers. To engender confidence in the followers, the leader must be able to communicate that vision. A leader organizes meaning for the members of the organization. "Leadership creates a new audience for its ideas because it alters the shape of understanding by transmitting information in such a way that it 'fixes' and secures tradition. Leadership, by communicating meaning, creates a commonwealth of learning, and that, in turn, is what effective organizations are."[5] The management of trust implies accountability, predictability, and reliability and is based on the kinds of positions that a leader takes.[6] These positions are based on the leader's vision for the organization, which must be clear, attractive, and attainable. According to Bennis and Burt Nanus, his collaborator on an earlier book, vision and position stand in the same relationship to each other as do thought and action.[7]

The management of self is another order of skill—one that may have to precede the others. Deployment of self is based largely on positive self-regard. To Bennis, positive self-regard is not "narcissistic character." Instead, leaders know their worth; they trust themselves without letting their ego or image get in the way.[8] They do this in several ways. First, they recognize their strengths and compensate for their weaknesses. Second, they nurture their own skills with discipline by working on and developing their own talents. And third, leaders have the capacity to discern the fit between their perceived skills and what the job requires. According to Bennis and Nanus, the self-regard that leaders show is "contagious." It empowers subordinates throughout the organization to bring their own skills to bear on issues that affect the organization within the context of the leader's vision.[9]

In the *Odyssey*, Mentor provides a vision—Telemachus must search for his father. Mentor communicates that vision clearly and takes positions that indicate to Telemachus that he, in fact, can succeed in his task. This is possible because, as one of the immortals (remember that Mentor was really Athena, Zeus's daughter), Mentor had a strong sense of self.

What is more important for us, however, is the impact that Mentor has on Telemachus. Mentor's sense of confidence and vision was contagious. This confidence and vision empowered Telemachus to become a leader in his own right.

Not only did Athena get the gods' consent to serve as mentor and protector of Telemachus in his search for his father, but she convinced Zeus to intervene directly with Calypso, the beautiful nymph, who had kept Odysseus prisoner on her island for seven years. Even though Calypso was disappointed at the prospect of losing Odysseus, she helped him build and stock a raft for his sea journey back to Ithaca. All was smooth sailing for Odysseus until his old Nemesis, Poseidon, spotted his raft. Poseidon had not been a party to the gods' discussion about Odysseus. Athena had broached the idea of allowing Odysseus to return to Ithaca at a meeting that took place on Olympus while Poseidon was finishing up a project in Ethiopia. Even though the gods had made a decision regarding the Odysseus matter, Poseidon felt that his interests had not been adequately treated in the deliberations. Upon spotting Odysseus, the "mighty Earthshaker" waved his trident to start an incredible storm. Unanticipated changes in the political environment can upset stated goals.

With some supernatural help, Odysseus managed to swim to shore in the land of the Phaeacians. The Phaeacians were a neutral, peace loving, seafaring people. Because the ruler, Alcinous, claimed to be a direct descendent of Poseidon, Odysseus wisely did not relate the story of his adventures. Initially Odysseus was mistakenly thought to be an immortal, but, without revealing his identity, he convinced his host that he was just an ordinary guy who wanted to get home. Although Odysseus struck a modest, humble pose, he was goaded into participating in some athletic games. Naturally, the self-effacing stranger beat his adversaries at their own games. But Odysseus was a gracious winner, and Alcinous agreed to help him get back to Ithaca. Odysseus, at this point, shows virtually all the aspects that Bennis attributes to leaders.[10] He shows integrity, dedication, magnanimity, humility, and creativity. No wonder he was mistaken for an immortal.

At a feast that preceded his departure, Odysseus, upon hearing a song about his exploits during the Trojan War, broke into tears and admitted that he was the long-suffering subject of the bard's song. He then related his story, which is a metaphoric journey into self-awareness—a journey essential for all leaders.

A brief recapitulation of a few stories will show how interesting and relevant Odysseus's adventures are for today's managers. Odysseus had an early encounter in the land of the lotus-eaters. The lotus-eaters were a peaceful people. They were different from Odysseus and his men, who were the aggressive sackers of cities. What made the lotus-eaters so different was their food—lotus flowers. Bread and meat were the staples of Odysseus and his band. The lotus flowers induced a feeling of well-being in anyone who ate them. Odysseus discovered this when some of his men who were sent out to serve as ambassadors to these people accepted some lotus flower snacks. Perhaps they should have just said, "No." The effect of their tasting the lotus was to deflect them from group goals. One taste and they lost sight of the objective of returning to Ithaca and desired only to "go native"—to stay happily in the land of the lotus-eaters. Odysseus exercised a classical Theory X management technique to cope with this insubordination. He ordered these men dragged back to the ships by force and kept under tight control until the effects of the lotus flowers dissipated. We can interpret this action as a solely managerial, as opposed to a leadership, response. There is no attempt to broaden vision or incorporate new goals or learn from new experiences. Dragging those spaced-out comrades back to the boat was efficient, but was it really the right thing to do?

After the interlude with the lotus-eaters, Odysseus and his band rowed on to the land of the Cyclopes who are described as having had no stable laws, and, by implication, no lawyers. Odysseus, like many modern public and business leaders, was curious as to how such a system could operate. He and a group of twelve followers set off to explore the environment. Their curiosity drew them to the care of Polyphemus, the one-eyed giant who imprisoned them. Of course, the monster did take a couple of men for dinner and breakfast, summarily dashing their heads on the rocks in the cave and devouring them. Clearly Odysseus' leadership was put to the test.

Analyzing the situation and the materials available to him, Odysseus developed a plan while the monster was out tending his flocks of sheep and goats. Essentially it entailed getting the Cyclops drunk and poking his eye out with a burning stake while he slept under the influence of some fortified wine, which Odysseus just happened to have brought with him. While Odysseus gave Polyphemus the wine, he referred to himself as "Nobody." Odysseus, evidently, had a passion for anonymity. This ruse had immediate benefits for Odysseus, because the monster agreed that he would eat Nobody last. Carrying out the plan was dangerous, but Odysseus rallied his men and they successfully blinded Polyphemus.

The pain of the blinding, however, woke the giant and he called for his fellow Cyclopes, who gathered at the mouth of his cave. Polyphemus told his fellows, "Nobody is murdering me by craft." They were puzzled. "If nobody harms you . . . ," they responded before going about their own business. Odysseus managed to get his men out of the angry monster's cave and back to the ships.

Once aboard his ship, Odysseus could not refrain from deriding the blind, miserable monster. Far from keeping in the background and practicing anonymity, Odysseus boasted of his cleverness. Despite the wise words of those in his crew who advised him to keep quiet and get on with the journey, Odysseus continued to make fun of the blinded Cyclops and told Polyphemus his name. Even a vanquished foe may have some power resources that can be brought to bear on future issues. In Polyphemus's case, he prayed to his father Poseidon to make life difficult for Odysseus. His prayers were answered, but perhaps Odysseus became a better person, and leader, because of the trials set up by Poseidon.

This story brings out some leadership attributes of Odysseus as well as some drawbacks. Bennis would applaud the curiosity and vision that took Odysseus and his band to the cave. Although Bennis sees a difference between leadership and problem-solving, the clever way in which Odysseus leads his men to freedom is a positive aspect of leadership potential. Once back on his ship, however, Odysseus shows us that he is not really a true leader yet. His boasting almost

brings disaster immediately. Surely there is little of the magnanimity and humility that Bennis found in some modern leaders.

The adventures of Odysseus go on and on. The story of this journey becomes increasingly metaphorical at ever-deepening levels until he reaches a state of self-awareness that is a key to successful leadership. But we need not get into all the details of Odysseus' adventures on his eventual return to Ithaca and reunion with his wife and son. There are enough interesting stories—the sailors breaking into the bag of winds while Odysseus slept, the dilemma of Scylla and Charibdis, the Sirens' song, and many more—to keep a modern manager engaged with the plot so that he or she may encounter the deeper metaphors that might inspire more creative thinking. If one reacquaints oneself with the rich metaphors of the epic, one will think. One will grow.

Public and business leaders should go beyond literal thinking. Although they certainly have to be concerned with real-world problems, perhaps the solutions to these problems can be found through more creative responses than are routinely tried in both the public and private sectors.

Rosabeth Moss Kanter has admonished her readers to "think across boundaries."[11] A fundamental challenge to leaders in this turbulent world is to expand their own, and others', thinking. They must also engage in integrative, holistic thinking. As Kanter puts it:

To see problems and opportunities integratively is to see them as wholes related to larger wholes, rather than dividing information and experience into discrete bits assigned to distinct, separate categories that never touch one another. Blurring the boundaries and challenging the categories permit new possibilities to emerge, like twisting a kaleidoscope to see the endless patterns that can be created from the same set of fragments.[12]

Think of that metaphor of the kaleidoscope. Those are the same fragments. They have simply been rearranged. Can we train our minds to rearrange the fragments that we work with in business and public-policy problems?

The modern reader generally sees myths to be misconceptions or lies. Indeed, Bennis and Nanus present several leadership "myths" and then dispel them.[13] Myth to Homer, however, is a metaphor for the truth. The teachings about leadership that come from Homer are distilled from myths as metaphors. From these metaphors we find that such attributes as vision, dedication, communication, delegation, openness, creativity, magnanimity, and integrity are important components of leadership. But most important, Homer teaches us that a person should grow and develop. A person should learn from experience.

The main lesson of the *Odyssey* is that each of us should undertake our own journeys into self-awareness and self-understanding. By so doing we can develop our own leadership potential if we so choose. Although Homer does not tell us exactly how to go about our search for self-understanding, a deep reflection on his metaphors might illuminate that search for some people because thinking metaphorically can help us see things in new ways.

Notes

[1] Warren Bennis, *Why Leaders Can't Lead* (San Francisco: Jossey-Bass, 1989), 119.

[2] Quoted in Cedric H. Whitman, *Homer and the Heroic Tradition* (Cambridge, MA: Harvard University Press, 1958), 15.

[3] Ibid., 297.

[4] Bennis, 19–21.

[5] Warren Bennis and Burt Nanus, *Leaders: The Strategies for Taking Charge* (New York: Harper & Row, 1985), 42.

[6] Ibid., 43.

[7] Ibid., 154.

[8] Bennis, 57–58.

[9] Bennis and Nanus, 58–60.

[10] Bennis, 118–20.

[11] Rosabeth Moss Kanter, "Thinking Across Boundaries," *Harvard Business Review* 68 (November-December 1990): 9.

[12] Ibid.

[13] Bennis and Nanus, 222–25.

Note to the Instructor

Austen Press texts are marketed and distributed by Richard D. Irwin, Inc. For assistance in obtaining supplementary material for this and other Austen Press titles, please contact your Irwin sales representative or the customer service division of Richard D. Irwin at (800) 323-4560.

PART I

Readings

Chapter 1

Introduction to Leadership

*T*his journey through the leadership literature starts with a set of readings that helps define leadership. On the surface, leadership would appear to have a simple definition. In fact, arriving at a definition is more complex because of the variety of ways that leadership has been envisioned.

In the first reading in this chapter, Bernard Bass (1990) provides us with a perspective on leadership as seen by ancient Greeks, Egyptians, and Chinese. They tended to focus on some of the key qualities possessed by the leader. For example, Taoism suggests that leaders need to act such that others come to believe that their success was due to their own efforts and not that of the leader. Lao Tzu said, "A leader is best when people barely know he exists, Not so good when people obey and acclaim him, Worse when they despise him. But of a good leader, who talks little, When his task is done, his aim fulfilled, They will all say, We did it ourselves." The Greeks believed that leaders possessed justice and judgment, wisdom and counsel, shrewdness and cunning, and valor and activism. Drawing upon the Egyptians, Bass also suggests that the leadership context consists of the leader and follower. He went on to note that there are nearly as many definitions given to leadership as there have been authors who have written about the concept. Based upon an extensive review of the leadership literature, Bass provides us with an overview to the meaning of leadership by organizing the myriad of definitions around 13 different approaches. Among some of the interesting concepts that have been linked to the definition of leadership has been its role as "the focus of group processes, as a personality attribute, as the art of inducing compliance, as an exercise of influence, as a particular kind of act, as a form of persuasion, as a power relation, as an instrument in the attainment of goals, as an effect of interaction, as a differentiated role, and as the initiation of structure" (Bass, 1990, 20). To these many roles many contemporary writers are suggesting that leaders also coach, facilitate, and nurture.

According to Albert Murphy (1941) in the second reading, leadership is not a psychological phenomenon (something embedded in the traits of the individual); instead, leadership is essentially *sociological* in nature. Situations in which people find themselves create needs, and it is the nature of these demands that serves to define the type of leadership needed and thus who will lead. Leadership, according to Murphy, is said to be a function of the whole situation and not something that resides in a person.

Leadership, when viewed from a sociological perspective, is framed as an interplay between two or more actors (i.e., leader and followers) within a particular context. This interplay between the situation, the needs that it creates for people, and the individual is defined as the leadership process, and it is this process that serves to define who is the leader, group effectiveness, future group (social) needs, and once again who serves as the group's next leader. Thus, the leadership process is fluid and not static in nature.

Today, in the popular world of leadership, the word *vision* is at center stage. The country and many organizations find themselves suffering from a leadership void. As a consequence there is a search for those who have a vision that can unite people in the social system, providing them with a sense of purpose, unity, and a common direction. The third selection in this opening chapter provides a perspective on the leadership phenomenon of *vision.*

Linda Smircich and Gareth Morgan (1982) define the phenomenon of leadership from the perspective of what it is that leaders do for the groups that they are a part of. Leaders, according to Smircich and Morgan provide meaning to events for others. Some individuals emerge as leaders because they "frame experience in a way that provides a viable basis for action. . . ." (258) They are individuals who are capable of taking ambiguous situations, interpreting these situations, and framing for the follower an understanding of the situation and what needs to be done in order to move forward. Smircich and Morgan reinforce Murphy's notion that leadership is a sociological process that is characterized by an interplay between the leader, the followers, and their common situation (context). Finally, their work implies a power and dependency relationship. Followers surrender their power to interpret and define reality, while simultaneously granting this power to someone else. The second chapter of this book takes a closer look at the role of power and influence as a part of the leadership process.

An implicit message derived from this set of readings is that leadership can sometimes be differentiated from management and headship. Leadership, therefore, can be cast as either a formal role, whereby someone is a group's designated leader, or an informal role as in the case of an emergent leader arising from a set of dynamics that are transpiring between members of a group and the context within which they are embedded.

Concepts of Leadership

Bernard M. Bass
State University of New York-Binghamton

*L*eadership is one of the world's oldest preoccupations. The understanding of leadership has figured strongly in the quest for knowledge. Purposeful stories have been told through the generations about leaders' competencies, ambitions, and shortcomings; leaders' rights and privileges; and the leaders' duties and obligations.

The Beginnings

Leaders as prophets, priests, chiefs, and kings served as symbols, representatives, and models for their people in the Old and New Testaments, in the Upanishads, in the Greek and Latin classics, and in the Icelandic sagas. In the *Iliad,* higher, transcendental goals are emphasized: "He serves me most, who serves his country best" (Book X, line 201). The *Odyssey* advises leaders to maintain their social distance: "The leader, mingling with the vulgar host, is in the common mass of matter lost" (Book III, line 297). The subject of leadership was not limited to the classics of Western literature. It was of as much interest to Asoka and Confucius as to Plato and Aristotle.

Myths and legends about great leaders were important in the development of civilized societies. Stories about the exploits of individual heroes (and occasionally heroines) are central to the Babylonian *Gilgamesh, Beowolf,* the *Chanson de Roland,* the Icelandic sagas, and the Ramayana (now they would be called cases). All societies have created myths to provide plausible and acceptable explanations for the dominance of their leaders and the submission of their subordinates (Paige, 1977). The greater the socioeconomic injustice in the society, the more distorted the realities of leadership—its powers, morality, and effectiveness—in the mythology.

The study of leadership rivals in age the emergence of civilization, which shaped its leaders as much as it was shaped by them. From its infancy, the study of history has been the study of leaders—what they did and why they did it. Over the centuries, the effort to formulate principles of leadership spread from the study of history and the philosophy associated with it to all the developing social sciences. In modern psychohistory, there is still a search for generalizations about leadership, built on the in-depth analysis of the development, motivation, and competencies of world leaders, living and dead.

Written philosophical principles emerged early. As can be seen in Figure 1.1, the Egyptian hieroglyphics for leadership (*seshemet*), leader (*seshemu*) and the follower (*shemsu*) were being written 5,000 years ago.

In 2300 B.C. in the Instruction of Ptahhotep, three qualities were attributed to the Pharaoh. "Authoritative utterness is in thy mouth, perception is in thy heart, and thy tongue is the shrine of justice" (Lichtheim, 1973). The Chinese classics, written as early as the sixth century B.C., are filled with hortatory advice to the country's leaders about their responsibilities to the people. Confucius urged leaders to set a moral example and to manipulate rewards and punishments for teaching what was right and good. Taoism emphasized the need for the leader to work himself out of his job by making the people believe that successes were due to their efforts.

Greek concepts of leadership were exemplified by the heroes in Homer's *Iliad.* Ajax symbolized inspirational leadership and law and order. Other qualities that the Greeks admired and thought were needed (and sometimes wanting) in heroic leaders were (1) justice and judgment (Agamemnon), (2) wisdom and counsel (Nestor), (3) shrewdness and cunning (Odysseus), and (4) valor and activism (Achilles) (see Sarachek, 1968). (Shrewdness and cunning are not regarded as highly in contemporary society as they once were.) Later, Greek philosophers, such as Plato in the *Republic,* looked at the requirements for the ideal leader of the ideal state (the philosopher king). The leader was to be the most important element of good government, educated to rule with order and reason. In *Politics,* Aristotle was disturbed by the lack of virtue among those who wanted to be leaders. He pointed to the need to educate youths for such leadership. Plutarch, although he was involved with prosocial ideals about leadership, compared the traits and behavior of actual Greek and Roman leaders to support his point of view in *The Parallel Lives* (Kellerman, 1987).

A scholarly highlight of the Renaissance was Machiavelli's (1513/1962) *The Prince.* Machiavelli's thesis that "there is nothing more difficult to take in hand, more perilous to conduct, or more uncertain in its success, than to take the lead in the introduction of a new order of things" is still a germane description of the risks of leadership and the resistance to it. Machiavelli was the ultimate pragmatist. He believed that leaders needed steadiness, firmness, and concern for the maintenance of authority, power, and order in government. It was best if these objectives could be accomplished by gaining the esteem of the populace, but if they could not, then craft, deceit, threat, treachery, and violence were required (Kellerman, 1987). Machiavelli is still widely quoted as a guide to an effective leadership of sorts, which was the basis for a modern line of investigation with the Mach scale (Chris-

Source: Edited and reprinted with permission of The Free Press, a Division of Macmillian, Inc. from *Bass & Stogdill's Handbook of Leadership: Theory, Research, and Managerial Applications,* Third Edition by Bernard M. Bass. Copyright © 1974, 1981, 1990. Author affiliation may have changed since article was first published.

F I G U R E   1 . 1
Egyptian Hieroglyphics for Leadership, Leader, and Follower

Seshemet-Leadership

Seshemu-Leader

Shemsu-Follower

tie & Geis, 1970). A 1987 survey of 117 college presidents reported that they still found *The Prince* highly relevant.

In the same way, a fundamental principle at West Point today can be traced back to Hegel's (1830/1971) *Philosophy of Mind,* which argued that by first serving as a follower, a leader subsequently can best understand his followers. Hegel thought that this understanding is a paramount requirement for effective leadership.

Universality

Leadership is a universal phenomenon in humans and in many species of animals. . . .

Humans.   Parenthood, a condition that unarguably cuts across cultural lines, makes for ready-made patterns of leadership. Nevertheless, the patterns of behavior that are regarded as acceptable in leaders differ from time to time and from one culture to another. Citing various anthropological reports on primitive groups in Australia, Fiji, New Guinea, the Congo, and elsewhere, H. L. Smith and Krueger (1933) concluded that leadership occurs among all people, regardless of culture, be they isolated Indian villagers, nomads of the Eurasian steppes, or Polynesian fisherfolk. Lewis (1974) concluded, from a more recent anthropological review, that even when a society does not have institutionalized chiefs, rulers, or elected officials, there are always leaders who initiate action and play central roles in the group's decision making. No societies are known that do not have leadership in some aspects of their social life, although many may lack a single overall leader to make and enforce decisions.

Leaders, such as Abraham, Moses, David, Solomon, and the Macabees, were singled out in the Old Testament for a detailed exposition of their behavior and relations with God and their people. God was the supreme leader of his Chosen People who clarified, instructed, and directed what was to be done through the words of his Prophets and arranged for rewards for compliance and punishment for disobedience to the laws and rules He had handed down to Moses. In Islam, the ideal caliphate leadership was based on religious law (Rabi, 1967).

In *The Parallel Lives,* Plutarch (1932), in about A.D. 100, tried to show the similarities between 50 Greek and Roman leaders. Latin authors, such as Caesar, Cicero, and Seneca to name just a few, wrote extensively on the subject of leadership and administration. Their influence was considerable on the medieval and Renaissance periods, which looked back to the classics for guidance. Their influence on Thomas Jefferson and James Madison had an impact on the design of the U.S. government as we know it, as did such Renaissance scholars as Montesquieu in his *The Spirit of Laws* (1748).

Military writings about leadership stretch from the Chinese classics to the present. Napoleon listed 115 qualities that are essentials for a military leader. Meyer (1980) called for a renaissance in the concern for military leadership, in contrast to the focus on the "overmanagement" of logistics. Resources must be managed by the military leader but are no substitute for effective leadership. . . .

The Meaning of Leadership

The word *leadership* is a sophisticated, modern concept. In earlier times, words meaning "head of state," "military commander," "princeps," "proconsul," "chief," or "king" were common in most societies; these words differentiated the ruler from other members of society. A preoccupation with leadership, as opposed to headship based on inheritance, usurpation, or appointment, occurred predominantly in countries with an Anglo-Saxon heritage. Although the *Oxford English Dictionary* (1933) noted the appearance of the word *leader* in the English language as early as the year 1300, the word *leadership* did not appear until the first half of the nineteenth century in writings about the political influence and control of British Parliament. And the word did not appear in the most other modern languages until recent times.

Defining Leadership

There are almost as many different definitions of leadership as there are persons who have attempted to define the concept. Moreover, as Pfeffer (1977) noted, many of the definitions are ambiguous. Furthermore, the distinction between leadership and other social-influence processes is often blurred (Bavelas, 1960; Hollander & Julian, 1969). The many dimensions into which leadership has been cast and their overlapping meanings have added to the confusion. . . .

Leadership as a Focus of Group Processes

Early on, definitions of the leader tended to view the leader as a focus of group change, activity, and process. Cooley (1902) maintained that the leader is always the nucleus of a tendency, and (that) all social movements, closely examined, will be found to consist of tendencies having such nuclei. Mumford (1906–07) observed that "leadership is the preeminence of one or a few individuals in a group in the process of control of societal phenomena." Blackmar (1911) saw leadership as the "centralization of effort in one person as an expression of the power of all." Chapin (1924b) viewed leadership as "a point of polarization for group cooperation." According to L. L. Bernard (1927), leaders are influenced by the needs and wishes of the group members; in turn, they focus the attention and release the energies of group members in a desired direction. Regarding the dominance of the leader's personality, M. Smith (1934) commented that "the social group that expresses its unity in connected activity is always composed of but two essential portions: the center of focal activity, and the individuals who act with regard to the center." For Redl (1942), the leader is a central or focal person who integrates the group.

As a nation develops, it needs a centralized locus for its operation which can only be achieved by a single leader (Babikan, 1981). All important decisions and their implementation center on the cult of the leader even when, as in parliamentary democracies, actual decision making is diffuse. The leader embodies the collective will. This single leader sorts out the essential problems, offers possible solutions, establishes priorities, and launches developmental operations.

J. F. Brown (1936) maintained that "the leader may not be separated from the group, but may be treated as a position of high potential in the field." Following in the same tradition, Krech and Crutchfield (1948) observed that "by virtue of his special position in the group, he serves as a primary agent for the determination of group structure, group atmosphere, group goals, group ideology, and group activities." For Knickerbocker (1948), "when conceived in terms of the dynamics of human social behavior, leadership is a function of needs existing within a given situation, and consists of a relationship between an individual and a group."

This emphasis on the leader as the center, or focus, of group activity directs attention to group structure and group processes in studying leadership. On the one hand, some of the earliest theorists, such as Cooley and Mumford, were sophisticated in their concept of leadership. On the other hand, several of the definitions placed the leader in a particularly fortuitous, if not helpless, position, given the inexorable progress of the group. Leaders were thought to have to stay one pace ahead of the group to avoid being run over. Centrality of location in the group can permit a person to control communications, and hence is likely to place him or her in a position of leadership, but centrality, in itself, is not leadership.

Leadership as Personality and Its Effects

The concept of personality appealed to several early theorists, who sought to explain why some persons are better able than are others to exercise leadership. A. O. Bowden (1926) equated leadership with strength of personality: "Indeed, the amount of personality attributed to an individual may not be unfairly estimated by the degree of influence he can exert upon others." Bingham (1927) defined a leader as a person who possesses the greatest number of desirable traits of personality and character. According to L. L. Bernard (1926), "Any person who is more than ordinarily efficient in carrying psychosocial stimuli to others and is thus effective in conditioning collective responses may be called a leader"; the leader must possess prestige and "must know what stimuli

will condition adequate responses for his purposes and develop a technique for presenting these stimuli." Tead (1929) regarded leadership as a combination of traits that enables an individual to induce others to accomplish a given task.

The personality theorists tended to regard leadership as a one-way effect: Leaders possess qualities that differentiate them from followers. But these theorists did not acknowledge the extent to which leaders and followers have interactive effects by determining which qualities of followers are of consequence in a situation. What theorists now see is that the personal qualities of a would-be leader determine his or her *esteem* in the eyes of potential followers. Some personality traits, such as ascendancy or social boldness, more often than not go hand in hand with being esteemed and attaining leadership, but social boldness is not leadership. At the extreme, in times of crisis, followers *endow* a highly dominant figure who is empathic to their critical needs with charisma. The hero's personality then makes it possible for him or her to perform enormous feats of leadership (Stark, 1970).

Leadership as the Art of Inducing Compliance

Munson (1921) defined leadership as "the ability to handle men so as to achieve the most with the least friction and the greatest cooperation. . . . Leadership is the creative and directive force of morale." According to F. H. Allport (1924), "leadership . . . is personal social control." B. V. Moore (1927) reported the results of a conference at which leadership was defined as "the ability to impress the will of the leader on those led and induce obedience, respect, loyalty, and cooperation." Similarly, Bundel (1930) regarded leadership as "the art of inducing others to do what one wants them to do." According to T. R. Phillips (1939), "leadership is the imposition, maintenance, and direction of moral unity to our ends." Warriner (1955) suggested that "leadership as a form of relationship between persons requires that one or several persons act in conformance with the request of another." For Bennis (1959), "leadership can be defined as the process by which an agent induces a subordinate to behave in a desired manner."

The compliance-induction theorists, perhaps even more than the personality theorists, tended to regard leadership as a unidirectional exertion of influence and as an instrument for molding the group to the leader's will. They expressed little recognition of the rights, desires, and necessities of the group members or of the group's traditions and norms. This disregard for the followers and the group was rejected by various other theorists, who sought to remove, by definition, any possibility of legitimating an authoritarian concept of leadership. Yet, regardless of the sentiments of some behavioral scientists, one cannot ignore that much leadership is authoritarian, directive, and even coercive. Its effects are seen in public compliance but not necessarily in private acceptance.

Leadership as the Exercise of Influence

Use of the concept of influence marked a step in the direction of generality and abstraction in defining leadership. J. B. Nash (1929) suggested that "leadership implies influencing change in the conduct of people." Tead (1935) defined it as "the activity of influencing people to cooperate toward some goal which they come to find desirable." Stogdill (1950) termed it "the process of influencing the activities of an organized group in its efforts toward goal setting and goal achievement."

Shartle (1951a, 1951b) proposed that the leader be considered an individual "who exercises positive influence acts upon others" or "who exercises more important influence acts than any other members of the group or organization." Similarly, Tannenbaum, Weschler, and Massarik (1961) defined leadership as "interpersonal influence, exercised in a situation and directed, through the communication process, toward the attainment of a specified goal or goals." This definition was expanded by Ferris and Rowland (1981), who conceived of the leadership-influence process as a contextual influence that has an impact on subordinates' attitudes and performance through effects on the subordinates' perceptions of their job characteristics.

The interactive aspect became apparent as leadership was linked by definition to influence processes. Haiman (1951) suggested that "direct leadership is an interaction process in which an individual, usually through the medium of speech, influences the behavior of others toward a particular end." According to Gerth and Mills (1953), "leadership . . . is a relation between leader and led in which the leader influences more than he is influenced: because of the leader, those who are led act or feel differently than they otherwise would." For Cartwright (1965), leadership was equated with the "domain of influence." Katz and Kahn (1966) considered "the essence of organizational leadership to be the influential increment over and above mechanical compliance with routine directions of the organization." They observed that although all supervisors at the same level of organization have equal power, they do not use it with equal effectiveness to influence individuals and the organization. In the same way, Hollander and Julian (1969) suggested that "leadership in the broadest sense implies the presence of a particular influence relationship between two or more persons."

According to Hemphill (1949a) and Bass (1960), an individual's effort to change the behavior of others is attempted leadership. When the other members actually change, this creation of change in others is successful leadership. If the others are reinforced or rewarded for changing their behavior, this evoked achievement is effective leadership. The distinctions between attempted, successful, and effective leadership are important because the dynamics of each are quite different.

The concept of influence recognizes the fact that individuals differ in the extent to which their behaviors affect the activities of a group. It implies a reciprocal relationship between the leader and the followers, but one that is not necessarily characterized by domination, control, or induction of compliance by the leader. It merely states that leadership exercises a determining effect on the behaviors of group members and on activities of the group. The definition of influence also recognizes that leaders can influence group members by their own example. The Israeli lieutenant leads with the call, "Follow me." Leaders serve as models for the followers. As Gandhi suggested: "Clean examples have a cu-

rious method of multiplying themselves" (quoted in Paige, 1977, p. 65).

Defining effective leadership as successful influence by the leader that results in the attainment of goals by the influenced followers, that is, defining leadership in terms of goal attainment (to be discussed later in the chapter) is particularly useful for it permits the use of reinforcement theory to understand leader-follower behavior.

Limited to Discretionary Influence.   Numerous theorists wanted to limit leadership to only that influence which is not mandated by the leader's role. As noted before, Katz and Kahn (1966) defined leadership as an influential increment over and above compliance with the routine directives of the organization. J. A. Miller (1973a) saw leaders exerting influence "at the margin" to compensate for what was missing in the specified process and structure. Jacobs and Jaques (1987) conceived and viewed leadership in complex organizations as "discretionary action directed toward dealing with unanticipated events that otherwise would influence outcomes of critical tasks at the actor's level" (as did Osborn, Hunt, & Jauch, 1980). It is influence over and above what is typically invested in the role—influence beyond what is due to formal procedures, rules, and regulations. Thus, managers are leaders only when they take the opportunity to exert influence over activities beyond what has been prescribed as their role requirements.

Leadership as an Act or Behavior

One school of theorists preferred to define leadership in terms of acts or behaviors. For L. F. Carter (1953), "leadership behaviors are any behaviors the experimenter wishes to so designate or, more generally, any behaviors which experts in this area wish to consider as leadership behaviors." Shartle (1956) defined a leadership act as "one which results in others acting or responding in a shared direction."

Hemphill (1949a) suggested that "leadership may be defined as the behavior of an individual while he is involved in directing group activities." Fiedler (1967a) proposed a somewhat similar definition:

> By leadership behavior we generally mean the particular acts in which a leader engages in the course of directing and coordinating the work of his group members. This may involve such acts as structuring the work relations, praising or criticizing group members, and showing consideration for their welfare and feelings.

Leadership as a Form of Persuasion

Both Presidents Eisenhower and Truman emphasized the persuasive aspect of leadership. According to Eisenhower, "leadership is the ability to decide what is to be done, and then to get others to want to do it" (quoted in Larson, 1968, p. 21). According to Truman (1958, p. 139), "a leader is a man who has the ability to get other people to do what they don't want to do, and like it." And for Lippmann (1922), such persuasiveness is long lasting: "The final test of a leader is that he leaves behind him in other men the conviction and the will to carry on." Several theorists defined leadership as successful persuasion without coercion; followers are convinced by the merits of the argument, not by the coercive power of the arguer. Neustadt (1960) concluded, from his study of U.S. presidents, that presidential leadership stems from the power to persuade. Schenk (1928) suggested that "leadership is the management of men by persuasion and inspiration rather than by the direct or implied threat of coercion." Merton (1969) regarded leadership as "an interpersonal relation in which others comply because they want to, not because they have to." According to Cleeton and Mason (1934), "leadership indicates the ability to influence men and secure results through emotional appeals rather than through the exercise of authority." Copeland (1942) maintained that

> leadership is the art of dealing with human nature. . . . It is the art of influencing a body of people by persuasion or example to follow a line of action. It must never be confused with drivership . . . which is the art of compelling a body of people by intimidation or force to follow a line of action.

Odier (1948) differentiated between the value and the valence of a leader. Valence is the power of a person to act on the feeling or value of another person or group of persons, of modifying (strengthening or weakening) it in one fashion or another. Thus, valence is defined not by the value of the leader's personality but by the quality of the influences he or she exerts on the members of a group. Koontz and O'Donnell (1955) regarded leadership as "the activity of persuading people to cooperate in the achievement of a common objective."

Persuasion is a powerful instrument for shaping expectations and beliefs—particularly in political, social, and religious affairs. The definition of leadership as a form of persuasion tended to be favored by students of politics and social movements and by military and industrial theorists who were opposed to authoritarian concepts. It was also the province of rhetoricians and communications theorists. Research on persuasion, persuasibility, and communications has paralleled research on leadership (W. Weiss, 1958). Persuasion can be seen as one form of leadership. Much of what has been learned from studies of persuasion can be incorporated into an understanding of leadership.

Leadership as a Power Relation

Most political theorists, from Machiavelli through Marx to the academic political scientists of the twentieth century, have seen power as the basis of political leadership. Social psychologists J. R. P. French (1956) and Raven and French (1958a, 1958b) defined leadership in terms of differential power relationships among members of a group. For the latter, interpersonal power—referent, expert, reward-based, coercive, or legitimate—is conceived "as a resultant of the maximum force which A can induce on B minus the maximum resisting force which B can mobilize in the opposite direction." Similarly, Janda (1960) defined "leadership as a particular type of power relationship characterized by a group

member's perception that another group member has the right to prescribe behavior patterns for the former regarding his activity as a member of a particular group."

M. Smith (1948) equated leadership with control of the interaction process. Thus, "the initiator of an interaction, A, gives a stimulus to the second participant, B. A asserts his control by interfering with B's original course of action."

Power is regarded as a form of influence relationship. It can be observed that some leaders tend to transform any leadership opportunity into an overt power relationship. In fact, the very frequency of this observation, combined with the often undesirable consequences for individuals and societies, has induced many theorists to reject the notion of authoritarian leadership. Nevertheless, many of those who were most committed at one time to trust building, openness, and participatory approaches, like Bennis (1970), have faced the world as it is, not as they would like it to be, and have come to acknowledge the importance of power relations in understanding leadership.

The power relationship may be subtle or obscure. "As a power relation, leadership may be known to both leader and led, or unknown to either or both" (Gerth & Mills, 1953). For instance, myths and symbols about the master-slave relationship may unconsciously influence superior-subordinate relationships in modern organizations (Denhardt, 1987).

Leadership as an Instrument of Goal Achievement

Numerous theorists have included the idea of goal achievement in their definitions. Several have defined leadership in terms of its instrumental value for accomplishing a group's goals and satisfying its needs. According to Cowley (1928), "a leader is a person who has a program and is moving toward an objective with his group in a definite manner." Bellows (1959) defined leadership as "the process of arranging a situation so that various members of a group, including the leader, can achieve common goals with maximum economy and a minimum of time and work." For Knickerbocker (1948), "the functional relation which is leadership exists when a leader is perceived by a group as controlling means for the satisfaction of their needs."

The classical organizational theorists defined leadership in terms of achieving a group's objectives. R. C. Davis (1942) referred to leadership as "the principal dynamic force that motivates and coordinates the organization in the accomplishment of its objectives." Similarly, Urwick (1953) stated that the leader is "the personal representation of the personification of common purpose not only to all who work on the undertaking, but to everyone outside it." K. Davis (1962) defined leadership as "the human factor which binds a group together and motivates it toward goals."

For Jacobs and Jaques (1987), leaders give purpose to others to expend and mobilize energy to try to compete. Cattell (1951) took the extreme position that leadership is whatever or whoever contributes to the group's performance; it is the group's *syntality*, resulting from its members and the relations among them. To measure each member's leadership, Cattell noted, remove him or her from the group, one at a time, and observe what happens to the group's performance.

In a similar vein, as noted earlier, both Calder (1977) and Pfeffer (1977) stated that leadership is mainly influence and is even attributed to participants after the fact. The attributions may be based on implicit theories of leadership (Rush, Thomas, & Lord, 1977). Outcomes are attributed more readily to the leader; thus, when things go wrong, the leader is likely to be blamed and even removed (Hollander, 1986).

For Burns (1978), Bennis (1983), Bass (1985a), and Tichy and Devanna (1986), leadership transforms followers, creates visions of the goals that may be attained, and articulates for the followers the ways to attain those goals. As Luiz Muñoz Marin, former governor of Puerto Rico, said: "A political leader is a person with the ability to imagine nonexisting states of affairs combined with the ability to influence other people to bring them about" (quoted in Paige, 1977, p. 65).

Envisioning the goals involves intuition, fantasy, and dreaming, not just analytical, systematic, conscious thought processes. For Jack Sparks, the chief executive officer who transformed the Whirlpool Corporation,

> ... the vision came after years of mulling over the kind of organization that Whirlpool could be, and after his constant interaction with people in other organizations and academics. The vision was his; and the strategic planning process became the vehicle for implementing that vision, not its source. (Tichy & Devanna, 1985, p. 138)

Tucker (1981) observed that most current politicians must focus the attention of their constituents on short-term goals and programs. More statesmanlike opinion leaders are necessary to arouse and direct a democracy toward achieving longer-term goals, such as stabilization of the population, improvement of the environment, and arms control.

Leadership as an Emerging Effect of Interaction

Several theorists have viewed leadership not as a cause or control of group action but as an effect of it. Bogardus (1929) stated that "as a social process, leadership is that social inter-stimulation which causes a number of people to set out toward an old goal with new zest or a new goal with hopeful courage—with different persons keeping different places." For Pigors (1935), "leadership is a process of mutual stimulation which, by the successful interplay of individual differences, controls human energy in the pursuit of a common cause." For H. H. Anderson (1940), "a true leader in the psychological sense is one who can make the most of individual differences, who can bring out the most differences in the group and therefore reveal to the group a sounder base for defining common purposes."

This group of theorists was important because they called attention to the fact that emergent leadership grows out of the interaction process itself. It can be observed that leadership truly exists only when it is acknowledged and conferred by other members of the group. Although the authors probably did not mean to imply it, their definitions suggest that this quality amounts to little more than passive acceptance of the importance of one's status. An individual often emerges as leader as a consequence of interactions within the group that arouse expectations that he or she, rather than someone else, can serve the group most usefully by helping it to attain its objectives.

Leadership as a Differentiated Role

According to role theory, each member of a society occupies a position in the community, as well as in various groups, organizations, and institutions. In each position, the individual is expected to play a more or less well-defined role. Different members occupying different positions play different roles. Birth and class may force the differentiation of roles. According to the leader of Ponape, Heinrich Iriarte, some Micronesians are born to rule while others are born to serve (Paige, 1977, p. 65).

Leadership may be regarded as an aspect of role differentiation. H. H. Jennings (1944) observed that "leadership . . . appears as a manner of interaction involving behavior by and toward the individual 'lifted' to a leadership role by other individuals." Similarly, C. A. Gibb (1954) regarded group leadership as a *position* emerging from the interaction process itself. For T. Gordon (1955), leadership was an interaction between a person and a group or, more accurately, between a person and the group members. Each participant in this interaction played a role. These roles differed from each other; the basis for their difference was a matter of influence—that is, one person, the leader, influenced, and the other persons responded.

Sherif and Sherif (1956) suggested that leadership is a role within the scheme of relations and is defined by reciprocal expectations between the leader and other members. The leadership role is defined, as are other roles, by stabilized expectations (norms) that, in most matters and situations of consequence to the group, are more exacting and require greater obligations from the leader than do those for other members of the group.

Newcomb, Turner, and Converse (1965) observed that members of a group make different contributions to the achievement of goals. Insofar as any member's contributions are particularly indispensable, they may be regarded as leaderlike; and insofar as any member is recognized by others as a dependable source of such contributions, he or she is leaderlike. To be so recognized is equivalent to having a role relationship to other members.

Much of the research on the emergence and differentiation of roles pertains equally well to leadership. As Sherif and Sherif (1956) indicated, roles are defined in terms of the expectations that group members develop in regard to themselves and other members. Thus, the theory and research pertaining to the reinforcement, confirmation, and structuring of expectations apply also to the leadership problem. Of all the available definitions, the role conception of leadership is most firmly buttressed by research findings.

The recognition of leadership as an instrument of goal attainment, as a product of interaction processes, and as a differentiated role adds to the development of a coherent theory that fits much of the facts available to date. Leadership as a differentiated role is required to integrate the various other roles of the group and to maintain unity of action in the group's effort to achieve its goals.

Leadership as the Initiation of Structure

Several commentators viewed leadership not as the passive occupancy of a position or as acquisition of a role but as a process of originating and maintaining the role *structure*—the pattern of role relationships. M. Smith (1935a) equated leadership with the management of social differentials through the process of giving stimuli that other people respond to integratively. Lapiere and Farnsworth (1936) observed that situations may be distinguished from one another by the extent to which they are organized by one member of the group. Such organization is usually spoken of as leadership, with its nature and degree varying in different social situations.

Gouldner (1950) suggested that there is a difference in effect between a stimulus from a follower and one from a leader. The difference is in the probability that the stimulus will structure the group's behavior. The stimulus from a leader has a higher probability of structuring a group's behavior because of the group-endowed belief that the leader is a legitimate source of such stimuli. Gouldner disagreed with C. A. Gibb (1947) regarding the notion that once the group's activity is dominated by an established and accepted organization, leadership tends to disappear. Thus, Bavelas (1960) defined organizational leadership as the function of "maintaining the operational effectiveness of decision-making systems which comprise the management of the organization."

Homans (1950) identified the leader of a group as a member who "originates interaction." For Hemphill (1954), "to lead is to engage in an act that initiates a structure in the interaction as part of the process of solving a mutual problem." And Stogdill (1959) defined leadership as "the initiation and maintenance of structure in expectation and interaction."

This group of theorists attempted to define leadership in terms of the variables that give rise to the differentiation and maintenance of role structures in groups. Such a definition has greater theoretical utility than do those that are more concrete and descriptive to a lay person: It leads to a consideration of the basic processes involved in the emergence of the leadership role.

Again, what must be kept in mind is that leadership is more than just the initiation of structure. As Gouldner (1950) noted, we need room for acts of leadership in the completely structured group. Stogdill's (1959) inclusion of maintenance of structure is important. Furthermore, if structure is the consistent pattern of differentiated role relationships within a group, we must be sure also to consider the persons, resources, and tasks within the differentiated roles.

Leadership as a Combination of Elements

Naturally, some scholars combine several definitions of leadership to cover a larger set of meanings. Bogardus (1934) defined leadership as "personality in action under group conditions . . . not only is leadership both a personality and a group phenomenon, it is also a social process involving a number of persons in mental contact in which one person assumes dominance over the others." Previously, Bogardus (1928) described leadership as the creation and setting forth of exceptional behavioral patterns in such a way that other persons respond to them. For Jago (1982), leadership is the exercise of noncoercive influence to coordinate the members of an organized group to accomplishing the group's objectives. Leadership is also a set of properties attributed to those who are perceived to use such influences successfully. Other definitions, such as Barrow's (1977), combine interpersonal influence and collective efforts to achieve goals into the definition of leadership. Dupuy and Dupuy (1959) add to this combination of definitions that leadership also involves obedience, confidence, respect, and loyal cooperation from followers. Still others prefer to discuss leadership as a collection of roles that emerge from an interactional process. For Tichy and Devanna (1986), the combination of power with personality defines the transformational leader as a skilled, knowledgeable change agent with power, legitimacy, and energy. Such a leader is courageous, considerate, value driven, and able to deal with ambiguity and complexity.

The search for the one and only proper and true definition of leadership seems to be fruitless, since the appropriate choice of definition should depend on the methodological and substantive aspects of leadership in which one is interested. For instance, if one is to make extensive use of observation, then it would seem important to define leadership in terms of acts, behavior, or roles played; its centrality to group process; and compliance with the observed performance, rather than in terms of personality traits, perceived power relations, or perceived influence. Contrarily, if extensive examination of the impact of the leadership was the focus of attention, then it would seem more important to define leadership in terms of perceived influence and power relations. . . .

The Handbook Definition

Leadership is an interaction between two or more members of a group that often involves a structuring or restructuring of the situation and the perceptions and expectations of the members. Leaders are agents of change—persons whose acts affect other people more than other people's acts affect them. Leadership occurs when one group member modifies the motivation or competencies of others in the group. Research in the 1970s and 1980s often expressed this idea as the directing of attention of other members to goals and the paths to achieve them. It should be clear that with this broad definition, any member of the group can exhibit some amount of leadership, and the members will vary in the extent to which they do so.

The introduction of the concepts of goal attainment and the solution of problems in certain definitions recognizes the fact that leadership serves a continuing function in a group. But these concepts do not account for the continuation of leadership. The concepts of role, position, reinforcement of behavior, and structuring expectation serve better to account for the persistence of leadership. For the purposes of theory development, it would seem reasonable to include variables in the definition of leadership that account for the differentiation and maintenance of group roles. Finally, room is needed for a conception of leadership as an attribution that is consistent with the implicit theories about it that are held by the individuals and groups who are led. . . .

Summary and Conclusions

The study of leaders and leadership is coterminous with the rise of civilization. It is a universal phenomenon. It is not a figment of the imagination, although there are conditions in which the success or failure of groups and organizations will be incorrectly attributed to the leaders, rather than to environmental and organizational forces over which the leaders have no control. In industrial, educational, and in military settings and in social movements, leadership plays a critical, if not the most critical role, and, as such, is an important subject for study and research.

How to define leadership can be a long-drawn-out discussion that dominates the early portion of deliberations of a scholarly meeting on the subject of leadership. In this chapter, we have seen the rich variety of possibilities, which leads to our conclusion that the definition of leadership should depend on the purposes to be served by the definition. Leadership has been seen as the focus of group processes, as a personality attribute, as the art of inducing compliance, as an exercise of influence, as a particular kind of act, as a form of persuasion, as a power relation, as an instrument in the attainment of goals, as an effect of interaction, as a differentiated role, and as the initiation of structure. Definitions can be broad and include many of these aspects or they can be narrow. A distinction may be made between headship and leadership. One complex definition that has evolved, particularly to help understand a wide variety of research findings, delineates effective leadership as the interaction among members of a group that initiates and maintains improved expectations and the competence of the group to solve problems or to attain goals. Types of leaders can be differentiated according to some of these definitions, more often on the basis of role, functional, or institutional differences.

References

Allee, W. C. (1945). Social biology of subhuman groups. *Sociometry, 8,* 21–29.

Allee, W. C. (1951). *Cooperation among animals with human implications.* New York: Schuman.

Allee, W. C., Emerson, A. E., Park, O., Park, T., & Schmidt, K. P. (1949). *Principles of animal ecology.* Philadelphia: Saunders.

Allport, F. H. (1924). *Social psychology.* Boston: Houghton Mifflin.

Anderson, H. H. (1940). An examination of the concepts of domination and integration in relation to dominance and ascendance. *Psychological Review,* 47, 21–37.

Barrow, J. C. (1977). The variables of leadership: A review and conceptual framework. *Academy of Management Review,* 2, 231–251.

Bass, B. M. (1960). *Leadership, psychology, and organizational behavior.* New York: Harper.

Bass, B. M. (1985a). *Leadership and performance beyond expectations.* New York: Free Press.

Bavelas, A. (1960). Leadership: Man and function. *Administrative Science Quarterly,* 4, 491–498.

Bellows, R. M. (1959). *Creative leadership.* Englewood Cliffs, NJ: Prentice-Hall.

Bennis, W. G. (1970). *American bureaucracy.* Chicago: Aldine.

Bogardus, E. S. (1929). Leadership and attitudes. *Sociology and Social Research,* 13, 377–387.

Burns, J. M. (1978). *Leadership.* New York: Harper & Row.

Calder, B. J. (1977). An attribution theory of leadership. In B. M. Staw and G. R. Salancik (Eds.), *New directions in organizational behavior.* Chicago: St. Clair.

Carter, L. F. (1953). Leadership and small group behavior. In M. Sherif & M. O. Wilson (Eds.), *Group relations at the crossroads.* New York: Harper.

Cartwright, D. (1965). Influence, leadership, control. In J. G. March (Ed.), *Handbook of organizations.* Chicago: Rand McNally.

Cattell, R. B. (1951). New concepts for measuring leadership in terms of group syntality. *Human Relations,* 4, 161–184.

Cleeton, G. U., & Mason, C. W. (1934). *Executive ability—its discovery and development.* Yellow Springs, OH: Antioch Press.

Copeland, N. (1942). *Psychology and the soldier.* Harrisburg, PA: Military Service Publishing.

Cowley, W. H. (1928). Three distinctions in the study of leaders. *Journal of Abnormal and Social Psychology,* 23, 144–157.

Davis, K. (1962). *Human relations at work.* New York: McGraw-Hill.

Davis, R. C. (1942). *The fundamentals of top management.* New York: Harper.

Dupuy, R. E., & Dupuy, T. N. (1959). *Brave men and great captains.* New York: Harper & Row.

Ferris, G. R., & Rowland, K. M. (1981). Leadership, job perceptions, and influence: A conceptual integration. *Human Relations,* 34, 1069–1077.

Fiedler, F. E. (1967a). *A theory of leadership effectiveness.* New York: McGraw-Hill.

French, J. R. P. (1956). A formal theory of social power. *Psychological Review,* 63, 181–194.

Gerth, H., & Mills, C. W. (1953). *Character and social structure.* New York: Harcourt, Brace.

Gibb, C. A. (1947). The principles and traits of leadership. *Journal of Abnormal and Social Psychology,* 42, 267–284.

Gibb, C. A. (1969a). Leadership. In G. Lindzey & E. Aronson (Eds.), *The handbook of social psychology,* 2nd ed. Vol. 4. Reading, MA: Addison-Wesley.

Gordon, T. (1955). *Group-centered leadership—a way of releasing the creative power of groups.* Boston: Houghton-Mifflin.

Gouldner, A. W. (1950). *Studies in leadership.* New York: Harper.

Haiman, F. S. (1951). *Group leadership and democratic action.* Boston: Houghton-Mifflin.

Hegel, G. F. (1830/1971). Philosophy of mind. (Trans. W. Wallace). *Encyclopedia of the philosophical sciences.* Oxford: Clarendon Press.

Hemphill, J. K. (1949a). The leader and his group. *Journal of Educational Research,* 28, 225–229, 245–246.

Hemphill, J. K. (1954). *A proposed theory of leadership in small groups.* (Tech. Rep.). Columbus: Ohio State University, Personnel Research Board.

Hollander, E. P. (1986). On the central role of leadership processes. *International Review of Applied Psychology,* 35, 39–52.

Hollander, E. P., & Julian, J. W. (1969). Contemporary trends in the analysis of leadership processes. *Psychological Bulletin,* 71, 387–397.

Holloman, C. R. (1968). Leadership and headship: There is a difference. *Personnel Administration,* 31(4), 38–44.

Homans, G. C. (1950). *The human group.* New York: Harcourt, Brace.

Iliad of Homer (1720/1943), A. Pope (Trans.). New York: Heritage Press.

Jago, A. G. (1982). Leadership: Perspectives in theory and research. *Management Science,* 28, 315–336.

Janda, K. F. (1960). Towards the explication of the concept of leadership in terms of the concept of power. *Human Relations,* 13, 345–363.

Jennings, H. H. (1944). Leadership—a dynamic redefinition. *Journal of Educational Sociology,* 17, 431–433.

Katz, D., & Kahn, R. L. (1966, 1978). *The social psychology of organizations.* New York: Wiley.

Kellerman, B. (1987). *The politics of leadership in America: Implications for higher education in the late 20th century.* Paper, Invitational Interdisciplinary Colloquium on Leadership in Higher Education, National Center for Postsecondary Governance and Finance, Teachers College, Columbia University, New York.

Knickerbocker, I. (1948). Leadership: A conception and some implications. *Journal of Social Issues,* 4, 23–40.

Kochan, T. A., Schmidt, S. M., & de Cotiis, T. A. (1975). Superior-subordinate relations: Leadership and headship. *Human Relations,* 28, 279–294.

Koontz, H., & O'Donnell, C. (1955). *Principles of management.* New York: McGraw-Hill.

Larson, A. (1968). *Eisenhower: The president nobody knew.* New York: Popular Library.

Lewis, H. S. (1974). Leaders and followers: Some

anthropological perspectives. *Addison-Wesley Module in Anthropology No. 50*. Reading, MA: Addison-Wesley.

Lichtheim, M. (1973). *Ancient Egyptian literature. Vol. 1: The old and middle kingdoms*. Los Angeles: University of California Press.

Lippmann, W. (1922). *Public opinion*. New York: Harcourt, Brace.

Machiavelli, N. (1513/1962). *The prince*. New York: Mentor Press.

Merton, R. K. (1969). The social nature of leadership. *American Journal of Nursing, 69*, 2614–2618.

Meyer, E. C. (1980). Leadership: A return to the basics. *Military Review, 60*(7), 4–9.

Miller, J. A. (1973a). *Structuring/destructuring: Leadership in open systems*. (Tech. Rep. No. 64). Rochester, NY: University of Rochester, Management Research Center.

Murchison, C. (1935). The experimental measurement of a social hierarchy in Gallus Domesticus. *Journal of General Psychology, 12*, 3–39.

Nash, J. B. (1929). Leadership. *Phi Delta Kappan, 12*, 24–25.

Neustadt, R. (1960). *Presidential power*. New York: Wiley.

Newcomb, T. M., Turner, R. H., & Converse, P. E. (1965). *Social psychology*. New York: Holt, Rinehart & Winston.

Odier, C. (1948). Valeur et valence du chef. *Schweizerisches Archiv für Neurologisches Psychiatrie, 61*, 408–410.

Osborn, R. N., Hunt, J. G., & Jauch, L. R. (1980). Organization theory: An integrated approach. New York: Wiley.

Paige, G. D. (1977). *The scientific study of political leadership*. New York: Free Press.

Pigors, P. (1935). *Leadership or domination*. Boston: Houghton Mifflin.

Plutarch. (1932). *Lives of the noble Grecians and Romans*. New York: Modern Library.

Rabi, M. M. (1967). *The political theory of Ibn Khaldun*. Leiden: Brill.

Raven, B. H., & French, J. R. P. (1958a). Group support, legitimate power, and social influence. *Journal of Personality, 26*, 400–409.

Raven, B. H., & French, J. R. P. (1958b). Legitimate power, coercive power, and observability in social influence. *Sociometry, 21*, 83–97.

Smith, H. L., & Krueger, L. M. (1933). *A brief summary of literature on leadership*. Bloomington: Indiana University, School of Education Bulletin.

Smith, M. (1935a). Leadership: The management of social differentials. *Journal of Abnormal and Social Psychology, 30*, 348–358.

Smith, M. (1935b). Comparative study of Indian student leaders and followers. *Social Forces, 13*, 418–426.

Smith, M. (1948). Control interaction. *Journal of Social Psychology, 28*, 263–273.

Stogdill, R. M. (1950). Leadership, membership and organization. *Psychological Bulletin, 47*, 1–14.

Stogdill, R. M. (1959). *Individual behavior and group achievement*. New York: Oxford University Press.

Tannenbaum, R., Weschler, I. R., & Massarik, F. (1961). *Leadership and organization*. New York: McGraw-Hill.

Tichy, N., & Devanna, M. (1986). *Transformational leadership*. New York: Wiley.

Truman, H. S. (1958). *Memoirs*. New York: Doubleday.

Tucker, R. C. (1981). *Politics as leadership*. Columbia: University of Missouri Press.

Urwick, L. F. (1953). *Leadership and morale*. Columbus: Ohio State University, College of Commerce and Administration.

Weiss, W. (1958). The relationship between judgments of communicator's position and extent of opinion change. *Journal of Abnormal and Social Psychology, 56*, 380–384.

A Study of the Leadership Process

Albert J. Murphy
New York University

A fault of most leadership studies is emphasis upon the "individual" rather than upon the individual as a factor in a social situation. Such studies seek to determine the qualities of a person which distinguish him as a leader. They imply that these somehow can be abstracted. Difficulties immediately appear. It is discovered that leadership takes protean forms, that it is unstable, that the qualities necessary at one time are unnecessary at other times, that leaders rise and fall as situations change, that the same individual alternates between leading and following. Consequently, leadership becomes a slippery, ill-defined concept. These are commonplaces, but in spite of them, the authors usually fail to sense the root difficulty, viz., the inadequacy of the personality concept as a means of understanding the problem. Leadership is not a psychologically simple concept.

Leadership study calls for a situational approach; this is fundamentally sociological, not psychological. Leadership does not reside in a person. It is a function of the whole situation. The situation calls for certain types of action; the leader does not inject leadership but is the instrumental factor through which the situation is brought to a solution. The emphasis in the title of this paper is not on "leadership qualities" but on the "leadership process." The word *process* calls attention to the interplay of factors in a total situation. The situation is fundamental and in all cases makes the leader. This is obvious in everyday life and in history. The Hitlers and the Mussolinis are made by situations, and they can be understood only in terms of those situations. Their characteristics are indicative of the times in which they live and the situations of which they are a part. Groups do not act because they have leaders, but they secure leaders to help them to act. In other words, the leader meets a critical need just as a dentist meets a critical need. We go to a dentist because we have a toothache, not the other way around. Skills and abilities of all kinds have a functional relation to the needs of the situation, and these needs are always primary. Leadership comes into being when an individual meets certain social needs, when he releases in the social situation of which he is a part certain ideas and tendencies which are accepted by the group because they indicate solutions of needs which are dimly sensed. Leadership is best understood when it is looked at impersonally as that quality of a complex situation which, when lifted into a place of prominence, composes its conflicts and creates a new and more desirable situation.

The concept of process is important also in that it calls attention to the fluidity of the leadership situation. Leadership is not a static thing; it is an immutable aspect of person-

ality. Many of the components of leadership, such as self-confidence and the confidence of the group, which are so essential, change with the situation. The self-confidence of a work leader or of a boys' gang leader usually disappears as soon as these individuals are put into a parlor. Ascendance, also a leadership component, increases when training is given in handling the materials of a situation. While leadership, self-confidence, ascendancy, and other so-called traits and attitudes, apparently carry over from one situation to another, it is only because the situations have practically identical elements. They are not fixed qualities of a person in any sense, nor are they fixed in the relation of two people, but are functions of a three-cornered relation—between the persons concerned and the job. Shyness often becomes dominance when the situation includes elements in which the individual's skill counts. So-called traits are names of processes; they are fluid; in no strict sense are they "attached" to anybody as "innate" or "acquired" characteristics. While studies of leadership make it appear that leaders usually have certain characteristics which combine under the term leadership ability, this generalization is misleading. Such factors as knowledge, forcefulness, tone of voice, and size are effective components in the solution of many social situations and are, therefore, generally regarded as leadership qualities, especially in unorganized group situations like gangs, but the variety of possible factors is endless. Leadership qualities, so-called, vary indefinitely as the needs of groups vary indefinitely.

A few illustrations will make it obvious that the choice of leaders is dictated by group needs. A group lost in the woods would immediately follow the man who, no matter what his personal qualities, had a knowledge of the woods and the way out. A social group whose needs are conviviality and the pleasant interplay of personalities will be most stimulated by a person who is lively and sociable. The leader of an organization which integrates the functions of other organizations will be a person through whom the leadership drives of others may function; such a person becomes a leader through releasing, channelizing, and integrating the abilities of others. A discussion group leader will be self-effacing, tolerant, critical, and interested in the contributions of others. In the case of the group in the woods, personality, height, weight, and voice count for nothing: the only qualification is a knowledge of the way out. In the case of the social gathering, a personality characterized by pleasing vivacity is of major importance. In the third case, the essential characteristic of the leader is ability to release the activities and ambitions of oth-

Source: Edited and reprinted from *American Sociological Review* 6 (1941), 674–687. Author affiliation may have changed since article was first published.

ers in a way which will promote the interest of all the groups concerned; in this case, height, weight, and voice would be irrelevant and forcefulness might even be disastrous. In the case of the discussion group, where leadership is of a highly integrative type, dominance and self-assertiveness, usually thought of as leadership traits, would be fatal. When the great variety of possible groups is considered, leadership appears clearly as a function of the situation. When the situation is simple, as in the case of the group lost in the woods, the demands on leadership are simple, but in complex situations the demands on leadership are multiple.

In order to bring out the meaning of leadership in terms of the situational processes, we may take a case from the study of leaders in work camps. In response to the request that members of work crews describe the characteristics of leaders whom they regarded as successful, the men mentioned things like these: he gets the work done; he explains things to you and doesn't yell at you; he plays no favorites but treats all men alike; he isn't so easy that you can step all over him; he watches out for the safety of the men in his crew.

These are modes of behavior. They are called for by the situation and are, in fact, responses to it. The young men who mentioned these desirable activities were not thinking of traits. So-called traits are derived by grouping these activities which are responses to the situation under classificatory labels or trait names. The first activity, "He gets the work done," is called the trait of efficiency. The second is called reasonableness; the third is called justice; the fourth is called strictness; the fifth, carefulness. Obviously, the leader is reacting to a total situation which embraces these elements as well as others. The qualities mentioned are simply names for types of activity which meet the needs of a group, which incorporate and make effective the important factors of the situation, emotional and otherwise. The group takes pride in doing a reasonable amount of work; it desires reasonable explanations; it desires fair play in work assignments; it appreciates the need of necessary strictness; it appreciates care for its safety. Does the leader have these traits? The abstractions mentioned and imputed to the leader as qualities are really

descriptions of what most of the members of the work gang desire. The names of the appropriate activities are imputed to him as his characteristics. In short, what has happened is this: (1) the group has certain needs, practical and emotional; (2) the leader responds to the situation as a whole with appropriate activities; (3) those responses are classified and labeled with trait names; (4) these names which are abstractions and summational fictions are imputed to the leader as causal psychological entities.

Confusion in the study of leadership results from endowing abstractions with reality and imputing character qualities to the person who brings the element of control into the situation. We have failed to see the leadership process as an interplay of forces, as an integrative activity. Of course, when types of a leader's integrative activities become habitual, we may call them traits provided we understand that they are activities, and we may try to develop them because these habits of conduct are useful in a large number of situations.

In summary, leadership is the process of securing direction in social activity which otherwise would be blind and disorderly. Leadership activities are resultants of the interplay of the factors which emerge out of a situation and reenter it as controls. Emphasis on so-called traits of personality, which have been shown to be hypostatized summational fictions, therefore, gives way to a study of the integrative factors in the situation. The personality does not stand alone but is a changing element in a total situation. The situation is a concept embracing many elements: the leader with his abilities and drives, the group (including potential leaders), material resources, viewpoints, desires, and needs, and a condition of readiness for leadership. This situational whole is a continuous series of influences and changes. Relativity characterizes every factor. Leading alternates with following. Solutions are new stages in the situation preparing the way for other solutions which in turn call for new types of leadership to secure new ends. Leadership may be defined *as that element in a group situation which, when made conscious and controlling, brings about a new situation that is more satisfying to the group as a whole. . . .*

Leadership: The Management of Meaning

L. Smircich
University of Massachusetts-Amherst
G. Morgan
York University

The concept of leadership permeates and structures the theory and practice of organizations and hence the way we shape and understand the nature of organized action, and its possibilities. In fact, the concept and practice of leadership, and variant forms of direction and control, are so powerfully ingrained into popular thought that the absence of leadership is often seen as an absence of organization. Many organizations are paralyzed by situations in which people appeal for direction, feeling immobilized and disorganized by the sense that they are not being led. Yet other organizations are plagued by the opposite situation characterized in organizational vernacular as one of "all chiefs, no Indians"—the situation where the majority aspire to lead and few to follow. Thus, successful acts of organization are often seen to rest in the synchrony between the initiation of action and the appeal for direction; between the actions of leaders and the receptivity and responsiveness of followers. . . .

The Phenomenon of Leadership

Leadership is realized in the process whereby one or more individuals succeeds in attempting to frame and define the reality of others. Indeed, leadership situations may be conceived as those in which there exists an *obligation* or a perceived *right* on the part of certain individuals to define the reality of others.

This process is most evident in unstructured group situations where leadership emerges in a natural and spontaneous manner. After periods of interaction, unstructured leaderless groups typically evolve common modes of interpretation and shared understandings of experience that allow them to develop into a social organization (Bennis & Shepard, 1965). Individuals in groups that evolve this way attribute leadership to those members who structure experience in meaningful ways. Certain individuals, as a result of personal inclination or the emergent expectations of others, find themselves adopting or being obliged to take a leadership role by virtue of the part they play in the definition of the situation. They emerge as leaders because of their role in framing experience in a way that provides a viable basis for action, e.g., by mobilizing meaning, articulating and defining what has previously remained implicit or unsaid, by inventing images and meanings that provide a focus for new attention, and by con-

solidating, confronting, or changing prevailing wisdom (Peters, 1978; Pondy, 1976). Through these diverse means, individual actions can frame and change situations, and in so doing enact a system of shared meaning that provides a basis for organized action. The leader exists as a formal leader only when he or she achieves a situation in which an obligation, expectation, or right to frame experience is presumed, or offered and accepted by others.

Leadership, like other social phenomena, is socially constructed through interaction (Berger & Luckmann, 1966), emerging as a result of the constructions and actions of both leaders and led. It involves a complicity or process of negotiation through which certain individuals, implicitly or explicitly, surrender their power to define the nature of their experience to others. Indeed, leadership depends on the existence of individuals willing, as a result of inclination or pressure, to surrender, at least in part, the powers to shape and define their own reality. If a group situation embodies competing definitions of reality, strongly held, no clear pattern of leadership evolves. Often, such situations are characterized by struggles among those who aspire to define the situation. Such groups remain loosely coupled networks of interaction, with members often feeling that they are "disorganized" because they do not share a common way of making sense of their experience.

Leadership lies in large part in generating a point of reference, against which a feeling of organization and direction can emerge. While in certain circumstances the leader's image of reality may be hegemonic, as in the case of charismatic or totalitarian leaders who mesmerize their followers, this is by no means always the case. For the phenomenon of leadership in being interactive is by nature dialectical. It is shaped through the interaction of at least two points of reference, i.e., of leaders and of led.

This dialectic is often the source of powerful internal tensions within leadership situations. These manifest themselves in the conflicting definitions of those who aspire to define reality and in the fact that while the leader of a group may forge a unified pattern of meaning, that very same pattern often provides a point of reference for the negation of leadership (Sennett, 1980). While individuals may look to a leader to frame and concretize their reality, they may also react against, reject, or change the reality thus defined. While leadership often emerges as a result of expectations projected

Source: Edited and reprinted with permission from NTL Institute, "Leadership: The management of meaning" by L. Smircich and G. Morgan, pp. 257–273, *Journal of Applied Behavioral Science* 18, 3, copyright 1982. Author affiliation may have changed since article was first published.

on the emergent leader by the led, the surrender of power involved provides the basis for negation of the situation thus created. Much of the tension in leadership situations stems from this source. Although leaders draw their power from their ability to define the reality of others, their inability to control completely provides seeds of disorganization in the organization of meaning they provide.

The emergence of leadership in unstructured situations thus points toward at least four important aspects of leadership as a phenomenon. First, leadership is essentially a social process defined through interaction. Second, leadership involves a process of defining reality in ways that are sensible to the led. Third, leadership involves a dependency relationship in which individuals surrender their powers to interpret and define reality to others.[1] Fourth, the emergence of formal leadership roles represents an additional stage of institutionalization, in which rights and obligations to define the nature of experience and activity are recognized and formalized.

Leadership in Formalized Settings

The main distinguishing feature of formal organization is that the way in which experience is to be structured and defined is built into a stock of taken-for-granted meanings, or "typifications" in use (Schutz, 1967) that underlie the everyday definition and reality of the organization. In particular, a formal organization is premised upon shared meanings that define roles and authority relationships that institutionalize a pattern of leadership. In essence, formal organization truncates the leadership process observed in natural settings, concretizing its characteristics as a mode of social organization into sets of predetermined roles, relationships, and practices, providing a blueprint of how the experience of organizational members is to be structured.

Roles, for example, institutionalize the interactions and definitions that shape the reality of organizational life. Rules, conventions, and work practices present ready-made typifications through which experience is to be made sensible. Authority relationships legitimize the pattern of dependency relations that characterize the process of leadership, specifying who is to define organizational reality, and in what circumstances. Authority relationships institutionalize a hierarchical pattern of interaction in which certain individuals are expected to define the experience of others—to lead, and others to have their experience defined—to follow. So powerful is this process of institutionalized leadership and the expectation that someone has the right and obligation to define reality, that leaders are held to account if they do not lead "effectively." . . .

Leadership as the Management of Meaning

A focus on the way meaning in organized settings is created, sustained, and changed provides a powerful means of understanding the fundamental nature of leadership as a social process. In understanding the way leadership actions attempt to shape and interpret situations to guide organizational members into a common interpretation of reality, we are able to understand how leadership works to create an important foundation for organized activity. This process can be most easily conceptualized in terms of a relationship between figure and ground. Leadership action involves a moving figure—a flow of actions and utterances (i.e., what leaders do) within the context of a moving ground—the actions, utterances, and general flow of experience that constitute the situation being managed. Leadership as a phenomenon is identifiable within its wider context as a form of action that seeks to shape its context.

Leadership works by influencing the relationship between figure and ground, and hence the meaning and definition of the context as a whole. The actions and utterances of leaders guide the attention of those involved in a situation in ways that are consciously or unconsciously designed to shape the meaning of the situation. The actions and utterances draw attention to particular aspects of the overall flow of experience, transforming what may be complex and ambiguous into something more discrete and vested with a specific pattern of meaning. This is what Schutz (1967) has referred to as a "bracketing" of experience, and Goffman (1974) as a "framing" of experience, and Bateson (1972) and Weick (1979) as the "punctuation of contexts." The actions and utterances of leaders frame and shape the context of action in such a way that the members of that context are able to use the meaning thus created as a point of reference for their own action and understanding of the situation.

This process can be represented schematically in terms of the model presented in Figure 1. When leaders act, they punctuate contexts in ways that provide a focus for the creation of meaning. Their action isolates an element of experience, which can be interpreted in terms of the context in which it is set. Indeed, its meaning is embedded in its relationship with its context. Consider, for example, the simple situation in which someone in a leadership role loses his or her temper over the failure of an employee to complete a job on time. For the leader this action embodies a meaning that links the event to context in a significant way—e.g., "This employee has been asking for a reprimand for a long time";

FIGURE 1

Leadership: A Figure-Ground Relationship Which Creates Figure-Ground Relationships

Framing Experience $\longrightarrow$	Interpretation $\longrightarrow$	Meaning and Action
Leadership action creates a focus of attention within the ongoing stream of experience which characterizes the total situation. Such action "brackets" and "frames" an element of experience for interpretation and meaningful action.	The action assumes significance, i.e., is interpreted within its wider context. The leader has a specific figure-ground relation in mind in engaging in action; other members of the situation construct their own interpretation of this action.	Action is grounded in the interpretive process which links figure and ground.

"This was an important job"; "This office is falling apart." For the employees in the office, the event may be interpreted in similar terms, or a range of different constructions placed upon the situation—e.g., "Don't worry about it; he always loses his temper from time to time"; "She's been under pressure lately because of problems at home."

The leader's action may generate a variety of interpretations that set the basis for meaningful action. It may serve to redefine the context into a situation where the meeting of deadlines assumes greater significance, or merely serves as a brief interruption in daily routine, soon forgotten. As discussed earlier, organized situations are often characterized by complex patterns of meaning, based on rival interpretations of the situation. Different members may make sense of situations with the aid of different interpretive schemes, establishing "counter-realities," a source of tension in the group situation that may set the basis for change of an innovative or disintegrative kind. These counterrealities underwrite much of the political activities within organizations, typified by the leader's loyal lieutenants—the "yes men" accepting and reinforcing the leader's definition of the situation and the "rebels" or "out" groups forging and sustaining alternative views.

Effective leadership depends upon the extent to which the leader's definition of the situation (e.g., "People in this office are not working hard enough.") serves as a basis for action by others. It is in this sense that effective leadership rests heavily on the framing of the experience of others, so that action can be guided by common conceptions as to what should occur. The key challenge for a leader is to manage meaning in such a way that individuals orient themselves to the achievement of desirable ends. In this endeavor the use of language, ritual, drama, stories, myths, and symbolic construction of all kinds may play an important role (Pfeffer, 1981; Pondy, Frost, Morgan & Dandridge, 1982; Smircich, 1982). They constitute important tools in the management of meaning. Through words and images, symbolic actions and gestures, leaders can structure attention and evoke patterns of meaning that give them considerable control over the situation being managed. These tools can be used to forge particular kinds of figure-ground relations that serve to create appropriate modes of organized action. Leadership rests as much in these symbolic modes of action as in those instrumental modes of management, direction, and control that define the substance of the leader's formal organizational role. . . .

Implications for the Theory and Practice of Contemporary Organization

. . . Leaders symbolize the organized situation in which they lead. Their actions and utterances project and shape imagery in the minds of the led, which is influential one way or another in shaping actions within the setting as a whole. This is not to deny the importance of the voluntary nature of the enactments and sense-making activities initiated by members of the situation being managed. Rather, it is to recognize and emphasize the special and important position accorded to the leader's view of the situation in the frame of reference of others. Leaders, by nature of their leadership role, are pro-

vided with a distinctive opportunity to influence the sense making of others. Our case study illustrates the importance of the leader recognizing the nature of his or her influence and managing the meaning of situations in a constructive way. At a minimum this involves that he or she (a) attempt to deal with the equivocality that permeates many interactive situations; (b) attend to the interpretive schemes of those involved; and (c) embody, through use of appropriate language, rituals, and other forms of symbolic discourse, the meanings and values conducive to desired modes of organized action. A focus on leadership as the management of meaning encourages us to develop a theory for the practice of leadership in which these three generalizations are accorded a central role.

Our analysis also draws attention to the role of power as a defining feature of the leadership process. We see the way the power relations embedded in a leadership role oblige others to take particular note of the sense-making activities emanating from that role. We have characterized this in terms of a dependency relation between leaders and led, in which the leader's sense-making activities assume priority over the sense-making activities of others.

The existence of leadership depends on and fosters this dependency, for insofar as the leader is expected to define the situation, others are expected to surrender that right. As we have noted, leadership as a phenomenon depends upon the existence of people who are prepared to surrender their ability to define their reality to others. Situations of formal leadership institutionalize this pattern into a system of rights and obligations whereby the leader has the prerogative to define reality, and the led to accept that definition as a frame of reference for orienting their own activity.

Organized action in formal settings constitutes a process of enactment and sense making on the part of those involved, but one shaped in important ways by the power relations embedded in the situation as a whole. Leadership and the organizational forms to which it gives rise enact a reality that expresses a power relationship. An understanding of the power relationship embedded in all enactment processes is thus fundamental for understanding the nature of organization as an enacted social form, for enactments express power relationships.

Thus our analysis of the leadership process tells us much about the nature of organization as a hierarchical phenomenon. Most patterns of formal organization institutionalize the emergent characteristics of leadership into roles, rules, and relations that give tangible and enduring form to relationships between leaders and led. Our analysis of leadership as a social phenomenon based on interaction, sense making, and dependency implies a view of much modern organization in which these factors are seen as defining features. To see leadership as the management of meaning is to see organizations as networks of managed meanings, resulting from those interactive processes through which people have sought to make sense of situations.

This view of leadership and organization provides a framework for reconsidering the way leadership has been treated in organizational research. By viewing leadership as a relationship between traits, roles, and behaviors and the situations in which they are found, or as a transactional process involving the exchange of rewards and influence, most leadership research has focused upon the dynamics and surface features of leadership as a tangible social process. The way leadership as a phenomenon involves the structuring and transformation of reality has with notable exceptions (e.g., Burns, 1978), been ignored, or at best approached tangentially. The focus on the exchange of influence and rewards has rarely penetrated to reveal the way these processes are embedded in, and reflect a deeper structure of power-based meaning and action. Leadership is not simply a process of acting or behaving, or a process of manipulating rewards. It is a process of power-based reality construction and needs to be understood in these terms.

The concept of leadership is a central building block of the conventional wisdom of organization and management. For the most part the idea that good organization embodies effective leadership practice passes unquestioned. Our analysis here leads us to question this wisdom and points toward the unintended consequences that leadership situations often generate.

The most important of these stem from the dependency relations that arise when individuals surrender their power and control over the definition of reality to others. Leaders may create situations in which individuals are crippled by purposelessness and inaction when left to guide efforts on their own account. Leadership may actually work against the development of self-responsibility, self-initiative, and self-control, in a manner that parallels Argyris's (1957) analysis of the way the characteristics of bureaucratic organization block potentialities for full human development. These blocks arise whenever leadership actions divert individuals from the process of defining and taking responsibility for their own action and experience.

Leadership situations may generate a condition of "trained inaction" in the led, a variant form of Veblen's (1904) "trained incapacity," observed by Merton (1968) as a dominant characteristic of the bureaucratic personality. . . .

The conventional wisdom that organization and leadership are by definition intertwined has structured the way we see and judge alternative modes of organized action. Approaching this subject from a perspective that treats organization as a phenomenon based on the management of meaning, we can begin to see and understand the importance of developing and encouraging alternative means through which organized action can be generated and sustained.

Notes

[1] A minor qualification is appropriate here in that certain charismatic leaders may inspire others to restructure their reality in creative ways. The dependency relation is evident, however, in that the individual takes the charismatic leader as a point of reference in this process.

Reference Notes

[1] Bougon, M. *Schemata, leadership, and organizational behavior.* Doctoral dissertation, Cornell University, 1980.

References

Argyris, C. *Personality and organization.* New York: Harper, 1957.

Barnard, C. *The functions of the executive.* Cambridge, Mass.: Harvard University Press, 1938.

Bateson, G. *Steps to an ecology of mind.* New York: Ballantine Books, 1972.

Bennis, W. G., & Shepherd, H. A. A theory of group development. *Human Relations,* 1965, 9, 415–457.

Berger, P., & Luckmann, T. *The social construction of reality.* New York: Anchor Books, 1966.

Bogdan, R., & Taylor, S. J. *Introduction to qualitative methods.* New York: Wiley, 1975.

Burns, J. M. *Leadership.* New York: Harper & Row, 1978.

Emery, F. E., & Trist, E. L. *Towards a social ecology.* Harmondsworth: Penguin, 1973.

Fiedler, F. E. *A theory of leadership effectiveness.* New York: McGraw-Hill, 1967.

Goffman, E. *Frame analysis.* New York: Harper Colophon Books, 1974.

Jacobs, T. O. *Leadership and exchange in formal organizations.* Alexandria, Va.: Human Resources Organization, 1971.

Katz, D., & Kahn, R. L. *The social psychology of organizations.* New York: Wiley, 1966.

Mann, R. D. A review of the relationships between personality and performance in small groups. *Psychological Bulletin,* 1959, 56, 241–270.

Merton, R. K. *Social theory and social structure.* (enlarged ed.). New York: Free Press, 1968.

Mintzberg, H. *The nature of managerial work.* Englewood Cliffs, NJ: Prentice-Hall, 1973.

Peters, T. J. Symbols, patterns and settings: An optimistic case for getting things done. *Organizational Dynamics,* 1978, 3–22.

Pfeffer, J. Management as symbolic action: The creation and maintenance of organizational paradigms. *Research in Organizational Behavior,* 1981, 3, 1–52.

Pondy, L. R. Leadership is a language game. In M. McCall & M. Lombardo (Eds.), *Leadership: Where else can we go?* Durham, N.C.: Duke University Press, 1976.

Pondy, L. R., Frost, P., Morgan, G., & Dandridge, T. (Eds.). *Organizational symbolism.* Greenwich, Conn.: JAI Press, 1982.

Quinn, J. B. *Strategies for change.* New York: Irwin, 1980.

Roethlisberger, F. J., & Dickson, W. J. *Management and the worker.* Cambridge, Mass.: Harvard University Press, 1939.

Schatzman, L., & Strauss, A. *Fieldwork.* Englewood Cliffs, N.J.: Prentice-Hall, 1973.

Schutz, A. *Collected papers I: The problem of social reality.* (2nd ed.). The Hague: Martinus Nijhoff, 1967.

Selznick, P. *Leadership in administration.* New York: Harper & Row, 1957.

Sennett, R. *Authority.* New York: Knopf, 1980.

Smircich, L. Organizations as shared meanings. In Pondy, L. R., Frost, P., Morgan, G., & Dandridge, T. (Eds.), *Organizational symbolism.* Greenwich, Conn.: JAI Press, 1982.

Stogdill, R. M. *Handbook of leadership: A survey of theory and research.* New York: The Free Press, 1974.

Veblen, T. *The theory of business enterprise.* Clifton, N.J.: Augustus M. Kelly, 1975 (originally published 1904).

Weick, K. *The social psychology of organizing.* Reading, Mass.: Addison-Wesley, 1979.

Chapter Two

Leadership as an Influence Process

C hapter One portrayed leadership as an interpersonal process that involves the exercise of influence. Leaders, for example, frame reality, provide direction, initiate structure, facilitate, induce compliance, support, remove barriers, and control the behavior(s) of others. This chapter asks "*How* do leaders influence others?" and "*What* are their sources of power?"

The reading in this chapter is John R. P. French and Bertram Raven's (1959) classic perspective on "the bases of social power." The authors seek to identify the major types of power and articulate the source from which each type of power stems. According to French and Raven, *power* is the ability to exercise influence, and *influence* is the ability to bring about change (i.e., a "change in behavior, opinions, attitudes, goals, needs, values, and all other aspects of the person's psychological field" (pp. 150–151). Power, therefore, can be seen as the ability to induce change in one's environment.

The work of French and Raven suggests that part of the leadership process consists of the exercise of influence. A leader's ability to influence others stems from his or her ability (or perceived ability) to exercise reward, coercive, referent, expert, and/or legitimate power. The nature of each of these types of power is defined in their article. You can develop a profile of your own "style of influence" by completing the self-assessment on power presented at the end of this introduction to Chapter Two.

A leader's power base is not the simple sum of the various sources of power that he or she is capable of exercising. There appears to be a synergistic effect that stems from some combinations of power. For example, referent power, because it stems from a valued and respected person, tends to magnify the impact of other sources of power, especially legitimate, resource, and expert power. The opposite effect can also be produced. High coercive power may well dilute the impact of referent power. As might be suspected, therefore, not all forms of power are equally effective. Hinkin and Schriesheim (1990) found that "rationality" was the most commonly used influence tactic by effective leaders and that rationality was positively related to referent, expert, and legitimate power.[1] According to Podsakoff and Schriesheim's (1985) literature review, follower performance and satisfaction are commonly associated with the leader's use of expert and referent power, while at times the use of legitimate, reward, and coercive power have a negative relationship with these two dimensions of leader effectiveness. These results suggest that effective leaders rely more upon some forms of power than others.[2] These observations are not surprising, according to sociologist Amitai Etzioni,

---

[1] T. R. Hinkin and C. A. Schriesheim, "Relationships Between Subordinate Perceptions of Supervisor Influence Tactics and Attributed Bases of Supervisory Power," *Human Relations* 43 (1940) 221–237.

[2] P. M. Podsakoff & C. A. Schriesheim, "Field Studies of French and Raven's Bases of Power: Critique, Reanalysis, and Suggestions for Future Research," *Psychological Bulletin* 97 (1985), 387–411.

FIGURE 2.1
The Leader Power-Follower Response Relationship

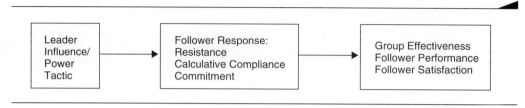

who suggested that different forms of power produce different forms of compliance.[3] Coercive power commonly produces resistance, which eventually leads to alienation. Remunerative or reward power frequently produces an instrumental or calculative response. The level and type of subordinate compliance is based upon the attractiveness of the benefits offered relative to the cost incurred. Finally, reliance upon rationality, moralistic appeal, expert and/or referent power frequently elicits follower commitment. As illustrated in Figure 2.1, it is this level/type of compliance that mediates the impact of a leader's power upon the group's performance, member performance, and follower satisfaction with the leader.

Power often plays a role in the determination of an emergent leader. Hollander (1961) advanced *idiosyncrasy credit theory* in an attempt to explain the emergence of leadership as well as the determinants of leader effectiveness.[4] According to the idiosyncrasy model, group members evaluate other members in terms of the degree to which they conform to expectations and help the group move toward goal attainment. The result of these evaluations serves to define an individual's status and role in the group. Group status is defined in terms of idiosyncrasy credits, which represent the accumulation of positive impressions that others hold toward members of the group. These credits allow a group member to deviate from the group's norms of accepted behavior. For an individual to emerge as a group leader, he/she must deviate from expected member behavior, and, in the process, display behaviors that are both unique and perceived as helping the group move toward the attainment of its goals.

As suggested by Hollander's reference to idiosyncrasy credits and the emergence of a group leader, power does not automatically flow to just anyone, nor is one guaranteed that once one has power that one will be able to retain that power. Salancik and Pfeffer (1977) provided an interesting insight into these two issues—who gets power and how they hold on to it.[5] The answer to these two questions provides an additional insight into who is the group's leader, leader influence, and the leadership process.

Power—according to Salancik and Pfeffer—derives from activities rather than individuals, and the power possessed by a leader is never absolute. As the situation in which a leader and his or her followers are embedded changes, so too may the amount of power held by the leader change as well as the person in the leadership position.

As the situation facing a group of individuals (e.g., a project team, work group, organization) changes so too do the "critical" issues facing the group. Power in social systems tends to flow to those individuals who possess the resources, especially if those resources that the group needs to solve its critical issues are scarce. The individual in a group, therefore, who is capable of contributing the scarce resources needed by the group to solve its most pressing problems tends to define leadership, the nature of the leader's power, and the amount of influence that he or she is capable of exercising.

---

[3] A. Etzioni, *A Comparative Analysis of Complex Organizations, on Power, Involvement, and Their Correlates* (New York: Free Press of Glencoe, 1961).

[4] E. P. Hollander, "Emergent Leadership and Social Influence." In L. Petrullo and J. C. Brengelmann, eds., *Leadership and Interpersonal Behavior* (New York: Holt, Rinehart, & Winston, 1961), 30–47.

[5] G. R. Salancik & J. Pfeffer. (1977). Who Gets Power—And How They Hold on to it: A Strategic Contingency Model of Power. *Organizational Dynamics*, (Winter), 3–21.

FIGURE 2.2
The Leadership Process

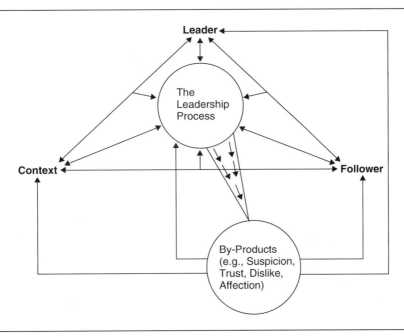

Source: R. B. Dunham & J. L. Pierce, (1989) *Management*. Glenview, IL: Scott, Foresman, 556.

Figure 2.2 provides a visual and conceptual framework around which you can organize your understanding of leadership and the leadership process.

The leadership process can be envisioned as a complex and dynamic exchange. There are four key components that take part in this interactive process (i.e., leader, follower[s], the context, and the resulting by-product) that can be employed to articulate the meaning of leadership and the leadership process:

- The *leader* is the person who takes charge and guides the performance or activity.
- The *follower*(s) is a person who performs under the guidance and instructions of a leader.
- The *context* is the situation—formal or informal, social or work, dynamic or static, emergency or routine, complex or simple, and so on—surrounding a leader-follower relationship.
- *By-products* can include nearly anything arising from interplay between the leader-follower and leader-situation, such as respect for an able leader's decisions, goal attainment, customer satisfaction, high-quality products, or animosity resulting from a punitive leader's actions.

The leadership process is both interactive and dynamic. Leaders influence followers, followers influence leaders, and all parties are influenced by the context in which the exchange takes place. In turn, by-products of a leader-follower exchange can influence future interactions as they may produce a change in the context, in the followers, and/or in the leader.

According to this model, understanding of leadership and the leadership process necessitates developing an understanding of the leader, the follower(s), the context, the influence processes (e.g., follower → leader; situation → follower; situation → leader; leader → situation; leader → follower), and the resulting by-products. The figure reveals that leadership (according to Murphy, 1941) is a sociological phenomenon and that it is dynamic (fluid) in nature. As suggested by Murphy (1941), Smircich and Morgan (1982), and Salancik and Pfeffer (1977), *leadership is a process, interactive and interpersonal (social)*

FIGURE 2.3
The Expanded Leadership Process

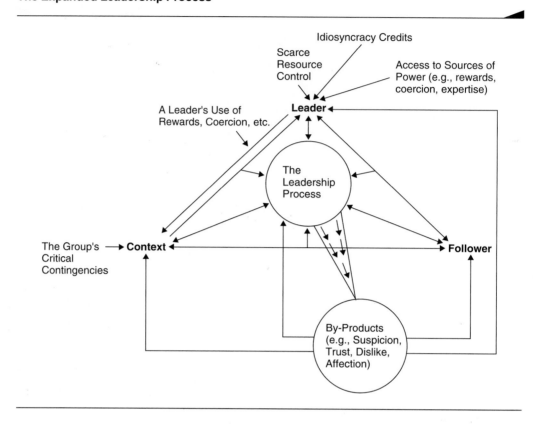

in nature, in which elements embedded in the situation, followers, and the leader influence the exercise of power that provides direction and meaning for the group's activities.

As illustrated by Figure 2.3, the work of Salancik and Pfeffer suggests that critical contingencies play a role defining the situation facing the group, which in turn influences "who will be the leader" (critical contingencies → situation → leader) and in part defines and shapes the leader's power. Also playing a role in giving definition to "who will be the leader" is who controls scarce resources (scarce resource control → leader) that are critical to helping the group overcome its most pressing issues. French and Raven's work suggests that people's ability to administer rewards and coercion, for example, enables them to serve as a leader and provides further insight into the leader-follower, and the leader-situation relationship.

The next chapter looks at attributes of the individual that play a role in defining who is the leader. Identifying and understanding the significant traits that define leaders will expand our understanding of the leadership process by understanding "the leader."

Personal Power Profile

Instructions: Below is a list of statements that may be used in describing behaviors that supervisors (leaders) in work organizations can direct toward their subordinates (followers). First, carefully read each descriptive statement, thinking in terms of *how you prefer to influence others*. Mark the number that most closely represents how you feel. Use the following numbers for your answers.

5 = Strongly agree
4 = Agree
3 = Neither agree nor disagree
2 = Disagree
1 = Strongly disagree

	Strongly Disagree	Disagree	Neither Agree nor Disagree	Agree	Strongly Agree
To influence others, I would prefer to:					
1. increase their pay level	1	2	3	4	5
2. make them feel valued	1	2	3	4	5
3. give undesirable job assignments	1	2	3	4	5
4. make them feel like I approve of them	1	2	3	4	5
5. make them feel that they have commitments to meet	1	2	3	4	5
6. make them feel personally accepted	1	2	3	4	5
7. make them feel important	1	2	3	4	5
8. give them good technical suggestions	1	2	3	4	5
9. make the work difficult for them	1	2	3	4	5
10. share my experience and/or training	1	2	3	4	5
11. make things unpleasant here	1	2	3	4	5
12. make being at work distasteful	1	2	3	4	5
13. influence their getting a pay increase	1	2	3	4	5

(continued)

	Strongly Disagree	Disagree	Neither Agree nor Disagree	Agree	Strongly Agree
14. make them feel like they should satisfy their job requirements	1	2	3	4	5
15. provide them with sound job-related advice	1	2	3	4	5
16. provide them with special benefits	1	2	3	4	5
17. influence their getting a promotion	1	2	3	4	5
18. give them the feeling that they have responsibilities to fulfill	1	2	3	4	5
19. provide them with needed technical knowledge	1	2	3	4	5
20. make them recognize that they have tasks to accomplish	1	2	3	4	5

Scoring: Using the grid below, insert your scores from the 20 questions and proceed as follows: *Reward power*—sum your response to items 1, 13, 16, and 17, and divide by 4. *Coercive power*—sum your response to items 3, 9, 11, and 12, and divide by 4. *Legitimate power*—sum your response to questions 5, 14, 18, and 20, and divide by 4. *Referent power*—sum your response to questions 2, 4, 6, and 7, and divide by 4. *Expert power*—sum your response to questions 8, 10, 15, and 19, and divide by 4.

Reward	Coercive	Legitimate	Referent	Expert
1 _____	3 _____	5 _____	2 _____	8 _____
13 _____	9 _____	14 _____	4 _____	10 _____
16 _____	11 _____	18 _____	6 _____	15 _____
17 _____	12 _____	20 _____	7 _____	19 _____
Total _____	_____	_____	_____	_____
Divide by 4 _____	_____	_____	_____	_____

Interpretation: A high score (4 and greater) on any of the five dimensions of power implies that you prefer to influence others by employing that particular form of power. A low score (2 and less) implies that you prefer not to employ this particular form of power to influence others. This represents your power profile. Your overall power position is not reflected by the simple sum of the power derived from each of the five sources. Instead, some combinations of power are synergistic in nature—they are greater than the simple sum of their parts. For example, referent power tends to magnify the impact of other power sources because these other influence attempts are coming from a "respected" person. Reward power often increases the impact of referent power, because people generally tend to like those who give them things that they desire. Some power combinations tend to produce the opposite of synergistic effects, such that the total is less than the sum of the parts. Power dilution frequently accompanies the use of (or threatened use of) coercive power.

Source: Modified version of T. R. Hinken and C. A. Schriesheim, "Development and Application of New Scales to Measure the French and Raven (1959) Bases of Social Power." *Journal of Applied Psychology* 74, 1989, 561–567.

The Bases of Social Power

J. R. P. French, Jr. and B. Raven
University of Michigan

The processes of power are pervasive, complex, and often disguised in our society. Accordingly, one finds in political science, in sociology, and in social psychology a variety of distinctions among different types of social power or among qualitatively different processes of social influence (1, 6, 14, 20, 23, 29, 30, 38, 41). Our main purpose is to identify the major types of power and to define them systematically so that we may compare them according to the changes which they produce and the other effects which accompany the use of power. The phenomena of power and influence involve a dyadic relation between two agents which may be viewed from two points of view: (a) What determines the behavior of the agent who exerts power? (b) What determines the reactions of the recipient of this behavior? We take this second point of view and formulate our theory in terms of the life space of P, the person upon whom power is exerted. In this way we hope to define basic concepts of power which will be adequate to explain many of the phenomena of social influence, including some which have been described in other less genotypic terms.

Recent empirical work, especially on small groups, has demonstrated the necessity of distinguishing different types of power in order to account for the different effects found in studies of social influence. Yet there is no doubt that more empirical knowledge will be needed to make final decisions concerning the necessary differentiations, but this knowledge will be obtained only by research based on some preliminary theoretical distinctions. We present such preliminary concepts and some of the hypotheses they suggest.

Power, Influence, and Change

Psychological Change

Since we shall define power in terms of influence, and influence in terms of psychological change, we begin with a discussion of change. We want to define change at a level of generality which includes changes in behavior, opinions, attitudes, goals, needs, values, and all other aspects of the person's psychological field. We shall use the word *system* to refer to any such part of the life space.[1] Following Lewin (26, p. 305) the state of a system at time 1 will be denoted $s_1(a)$.

Psychological change is defined as any alteration of the state of some system a over time. The amount of change is measured by the size of the difference between the states of the system *at* time 1 and at time 2: $ch(a) = s_2(a) - s_1(a)$.

Change in any psychological system may be conceptualized in terms of psychological forces. But it is important to note that the change must be coordinated to the resultant force of all the forces operating at the moment. Change in an opinion, for example, may be determined jointly by a driving force induced by another person, a restraining force corresponding to anchorage in a group opinion, and an own force stemming from the person's needs. . . .

The Bases of Power

By the basis of power, we mean the relationship between O and P, which is the source of that power. It is rare that we can say with certainty that a given empirical case of power is limited to one source. Normally, the relation between O and P will be characterized by several qualitatively different variables which are bases of power (30, Chapter 11). Although there are undoubtedly many possible bases of power which may be distinguished, we shall here define five which seem especially common and important. These five bases of O's power are: (1) reward power, based on P's perception that O has the ability to mediate rewards for him; (2) coercive power, based on P's perception that O has the ability to mediate punishments for him; (3) legitimate power, based on the perception by P that O has a legitimate right to prescribe behavior for him; (4) referent power, based on P's identification with O; (5) expert power, based on the perception that O has some special knowledge or expertness. . . .

Reward Power

Reward power is defined as power whose basis is the ability to reward. The strength of the reward power of O/P increases with the magnitude of the rewards which P perceives that O can mediate for him. Reward power depends on O's ability to administer positive valences and to remove or decrease negative valences. The strength of reward power also depends upon the probability that O can mediate the reward, as perceived by P. A common example of reward power is the addition of a piecework rate in the factory as an incentive to increase production.

The new state of the system induced by a promise of reward (for example the factory worker's increased level of production) will be highly dependent on O. Since O mediates the reward, he controls the probability that P will receive it. Thus P's new rate of production will be dependent on his subjective probability that O will reward him for conformity

Source: Edited and reprinted with permission from D. Cartwright, *Studies in Social Power* (Ann Arbor, MI: Institute for Social Research, University of Michigan 1959), 150–67. Author affiliation may have changed since article was first published.

minus his subjective probability that O will reward him even if he returns to his old level. Both probabilities will be greatly affected by the level of observability of P's behavior. Incidentally, a piece rate often seems to have more effect on production than a merit rating system because it yields a higher probability of reward for conformity and a much lower probability of reward for nonconformity.

The utilization of actual rewards (instead of promises) by O will tend over time to increase the attraction of P toward O and therefore the referent power of O over P. As we shall note later, such referent power will permit O to induce changes which are relatively independent. Neither rewards nor promises will arouse resistance in P, provided P considers it legitimate for O to offer rewards.

The range of reward power is specific to those regions within which O can reward P for conforming. The use of rewards to change systems within the range of reward power tends to increase reward power by increasing the probability attached to future promises. However, unsuccessful attempts to exert reward power outside the range of power would tend to decrease the power; for example if O offers to reward P for performing an impossible act, this will reduce for P the probability of receiving future rewards promised by O.

Coercive Power

Coercive power is similar to reward power in that it also involves O's ability to manipulate the attainment of valences. Coercive power of O/P stems from the expectation on the part of P that he will be punished by O if he fails to conform to the influence attempt. Thus negative valences will exist in given regions of P's life space, corresponding to the threatened punishment by O. The strength of coercive power depends on the magnitude of the negative valence of the threatened punishment multiplied by the perceived probability that P can avoid the punishment by conformity, i.e., the probability of punishment for nonconformity minus the probability of punishment for conformity (**11**). Just as an offer of a piece-rate bonus in a factory can serve as a basis for reward power, so the ability to fire a worker if he falls below a given level of production will result in coercive power.

Coercive power leads to dependent change also; and the degree of dependence varies with the level of observability of P's conformity. An excellent illustration of coercive power leading to dependent change is provided by a clothes presser in a factory observed by Coch and French (**3**). As her efficiency rating climbed above average for the group the other workers began to "scapegoat" her. That the resulting plateau in her production was not independent of the group was evident once she was removed from the presence of the other workers. Her production immediately climbed to new heights.[5]

At times, there is some difficulty in distinguishing between reward power and coercive power. Is the withholding of a reward really equivalent to a punishment? Is the withdrawal of punishment equivalent to a reward? The answer must be a psychological one—it depends upon the situation as it exists for P. But ordinarily we would answer these questions in the affirmative; for P, receiving a reward is a positive valence as is the relief of suffering. There is some evidence that conformity to group norms in order to gain acceptance

(reward power) should be distinguished from conformity as a means of forestalling rejection (coercive power) (**5**).

The distinction between these two types of power is important because the dynamics are different. The concept of "sanctions" sometimes lumps the two together despite their opposite effects. While reward power may eventually result in an independent system, the effects of coercive power will continue to be dependent. Reward power will tend to increase the attraction of P toward O; coercive power will decrease this attraction (**11, 12**). The valence of the region of behavior will become more negative, acquiring some negative valence from the threatened punishment. The negative valence of punishment would also spread to other regions of the life space. Lewin (**25**) has pointed out this distinction between the effects of rewards and punishment. In the case of threatened punishment, there will be a resultant force on P to leave the field entirely. Thus, to achieve conformity, O must not only place a strong negative valence in certain regions through threat of punishment, but O must also introduce restraining forces, or other strong valences, so as to prevent P from withdrawing completely from O's range of coercive power. Otherwise the probability of receiving the punishment, if P does not conform, will be too low to be effective.

Legitimate Power

Legitimate power is probably the most complex of those treated here, embodying notions from the structural sociologist, the group-norm and role-oriented social psychologist, and the clinical psychologist.

There have been considerable investigation and speculation about socially prescribed behavior, particularly that which is specific to a given role or position. Linton (**29**) distinguishes group norms according to whether they are universals for everyone in the culture, alternatives (the individual having a choice as to whether or not to accept them), or specialties (specific to given positions). Whether we speak of internalized norms, role prescriptions and expectations (**34**), or internalized pressures (**15**), the fact remains that each individual sees certain regions toward which he should locomote, some regions toward which he should not locomote, and some regions toward which he may locomote if they are generally attractive for him. This applies to specific behaviors in which he may, should, or should not engage; it applies to certain attitudes or beliefs which he may, should, or should not hold. The feeling of "oughtness" may be an internalization from his parents, from his teachers, from his religion, or may have been logically developed from some idiosyncratic system of ethics. He will speak of such behaviors with expressions like "should," "ought to," or "has a right to." In many cases, the original source of the requirement is not recalled.

Though we have oversimplified such evaluations of behavior with a positive-neutral-negative trichotomy, the evaluation of behaviors by the person is really more one of degree. This dimension of evaluation, we shall call "legitimacy." Conceptually, we may think of legitimacy as a valence in a region which is induced by some internalized norm or value. This value has the same conceptual property as power, namely an ability to induce force fields (**26**, p. 40–41). It may or may not be correct that values (or the superego) are internalized parents, but at least they can set up force fields which have a phenomenal "oughtness" similar to a parent's prescription. Like a value, a need can also induce valences (i.e., force fields) in P's psychological environment, but these valences have more the phenomenal character of noxious or attractive properties of the object or activity. When a need induces a valence in P—for example, when a need makes an object attractive to P—this attraction applies to P but not to other persons. When a value induces a valence, on the other hand, it not only sets up forces on P to engage in the activity, but P may feel that all others ought to behave in the same way. Among other things, this evaluation applies to the legitimate right of some other individual or group to prescribe behavior or beliefs for a person even though the other cannot apply sanctions.

Legitimate power of O/P is here defined as that power which stems from internalized values in P which dictate that O has a legitimate right to influence P and that P has an obligation to accept this influence. We note that legitimate power is very similar to the notion of legitimacy of authority which has long been explored by sociologists, particularly by Weber (**42**), and more recently by Goldhammer and Shils (**14**). However, legitimate power is not always a role relation: P may accept an induction from O simply because he had previously promised to help O and he values his word too much to break the promise. In all cases, the notion of legitimacy involves some sort of code or standard accepted by the individual by virtue of which the external agent can assert his power. We shall attempt to describe a few of these values here.

Bases for Legitimate Power. Cultural values constitute one common basis for the legitimate power of one individual over another. O has characteristics which are specified by the culture as giving him the right to prescribe behavior for P, who may not have these characteristics. These bases, which Weber (**42**) has called the authority of the "eternal yesterday," include some things as age, intelligence, caste, and physical characteristics. In some cultures, the aged are granted the right to prescribe behavior for others in practically all behavior areas. In most cultures, there are certain areas of behavior in which a person of one sex is granted the right to prescribe behavior for the other sex.

Acceptance of the social structure is another basis for legitimate power. If P accepts as right the social structure of his group, organization, or society, especially the social structure involving a hierarchy of authority, P will accept the legitimate authority of O who occupies a superior office in the hierarchy. Thus legitimate power in a formal organization is largely a relationship between offices rather than between persons. And the acceptance of an office as *right* is a basis for legitimate power—a judge has a right to levy fines; a foreman should assign work; a priest is justified in prescribing religious beliefs; and it is the management's prerogative to make certain decisions (**10**). However, legitimate power also involves the perceived right of the person to hold the office.

Designation by a legitimizing agent is a third basis for legitimate power. An influencer O may be seen as legitimate in prescribing behavior for P because he has been granted such power by a legitimizing agent whom P accepts. Thus, a department head may accept the authority of his vice president in a certain area because that authority has been specifically delegated by the president. An election is perhaps the most common example of a group's serving to legitimize the authority of one individual or office for other individuals in the group. The success of such legitimizing depends upon the acceptance of the legitimizing agent and procedure. In this case it depends ultimately on certain democratic values concerning election procedures. The election process is one of legitimizing a person's right to an office which already has a legitimate range of power associated with it.

Range of Legitimate Power of O/P. The areas in which legitimate power may be exercised are generally specified along with the designation of that power. A job description, for example, usually specifies supervisory activities and also designates the person to whom the jobholder is responsible for the duties described. Some bases for legitimate authority carry with them a very broad range. Culturally derived bases for legitimate power are often especially broad. It is not uncommon to find cultures in which a member of a given caste can legitimately prescribe behavior for all members of lower castes in practically all regions. More common, however, are instances of legitimate power where the range is specifically and narrowly prescribed. A sergeant in the army is given a specific set of regions within which he can legitimately prescribe behavior for his men.

The attempted use of legitimate power which is outside of the range of legitimate power will decrease the legitimate power of the authority figure. Such use of power which is not legitimate will also decrease the attractiveness of O (**11, 12, 36**).

Legitimate Power and Influence. The new state of the system which results from legitimate power usually has high dependence on O though it may become independent. Here, however, the degree of dependence is not related to the level of observability. Since legitimate power is based on P's values, the source of the forces induced by O include both these internal values and O. O's induction serves to activate the values and to relate them to the system which is influenced, but thereafter the new state of the system may become directly dependent on the values with no mediation by O. Accordingly, this new state will be relatively stable and consistent across varying environmental situations, since P's values are more stable than his psychological environment.

We have used the term *legitimate* not only as a basis for the power of an agent, but also to describe the general behaviors of a person. Thus, the individual P may also consider the legitimacy of the attempts to use other types of power by O. In certain cases, P will consider that O has a legitimate right to threaten punishment for nonconformity; in other cases, such use of coercion would not be seen as legitimate. P might change in response to coercive power of O, but it will make a considerable difference in his attitude and conformity if O is not seen as having a legitimate right to use such coercion. In such cases, the attraction of P for O will be particularly diminished, and the influence attempt will arouse more resistance (**11**). Similarly the utilization of reward power may vary in legitimacy; the word *bribe*, for example, denotes an illegitimate reward.

Referent Power

The referent power of O/P has its basis in the identification of P with O. By identification, we mean a feeling of oneness of P with O, or a desire for such a identity. If O is a person toward whom P is highly attracted, P will have a desire to become closely associated with O. If O is an attractive group, P will have a feeling of membership or a desire to join. If P is already closely associated with O, he will want to maintain this relationship (39, 41). P's identification with O can be established or maintained if P behaves, believes, and perceives as O does. Accordingly, O has the ability to influence P, even though P may be unaware of this referent power. A verbalization of such power by P might be, "I am like O, and therefore I shall behave or believe as O does," or "I want to be like O, and I will be more like O if I behave or believe as O does." The stronger the identification of P with O the greater the referent power of O/P.

Similar types of power have already been investigated under a number of different formulations. Festinger (7) points out that in an ambiguous situation, the individual seeks some sort of "social reality" and may adopt the cognitive structure of the individual or group with which he identifies. In such a case, the lack of clear structure may be threatening to the individual, and the agreement of his beliefs with those of a reference group will both satisfy his need for structure and give him added security through increased identification with his group (16, 19).

We must try to distinguish between referent power and other types of power which might be operative at the same time. If a member is attracted to a group and he conforms to its norms only because he fears ridicule or expulsion from the group for nonconformity, we would call this coercive power. On the other hand, if he conforms in order *to obtain praise* for conformity, it is a case of reward power. The basic criterion for distinguishing referent power from both coercive and reward power is the mediation of the punishment and the reward by O: to the extent that O mediates the sanctions (i.e., has means control over P), we are dealing with coercive and reward power; but to the extent that P avoids discomfort or gains satisfaction by conformity based on identification, regardless of O's responses, we are dealing with referent power. *Conformity with majority opinion* is sometimes based on a respect for the collective wisdom of the group, in which case it is expert power. It is important to distinguish these phenomena, all grouped together elsewhere as "pressures toward uniformity," since the type of change which occurs will be different for different bases of power.

The concepts of "reference group" (40) and "prestige suggestion" may be treated as instances of referent power. In this case, O, the prestigeful person or group, is valued by P; because P desires to be associated or identified with O, he will assume attitudes or beliefs held by O. Similarly a negative reference group which O dislikes and evaluates negatively may exert negative influence on P as a result of negative referent power.

It has been demonstrated that the power which we designate as referent power is especially great when P is attracted to O (2, 7, 8, 9, 13, 23, 30). In our terms, this would mean that the greater the attraction, the greater the identification, and consequently the greater the referent power. In some cases,

attraction or prestige may have a specific basis, and the range of referent power will be limited accordingly: a group of campers may have great referent power over a member regarding campcraft, but considerably less effect on other regions (30). However, we hypothesize that the greater the attraction of P toward O, the broader the range of referent power of O/P.

The new state of a system produced by referent power may be dependent on or independent of O; but the degree of dependence is not affected by the level of observability to O (6, 23). In fact, P is often not consciously aware of the referent power which O exerts over him. There is probably a tendency for some of these dependent changes to become independent of O quite rapidly.

Expert Power

The strength of the expert power of O/P varies with the extent of the knowledge or perception which P attributes to O within a given area. Probably P evaluates O's expertness in relation to his own knowledge as well as against an absolute standard. In any case expert power results in primary social influence on P's cognitive structure and probably not on other types of systems. Of course changes in the cognitive structure can change the direction of forces and hence of locomotion, but such a change of behavior is secondary social influence. Expert power has been demonstrated experimentally (8, 33). Accepting an attorney's advice in legal matters is a common example of expert influence; but there are many instances based on much less knowledge, such as the acceptance by a stranger of directions given by a native villager.

Expert power, where O need not be a member of P's group, is called "informational power" by Deutsch and Gerard (4). This type of expert power must be distinguished from influence based on the content of communication as described by Hovland et al. (17, 18, 23, 24). The influence of the content of a communication upon an opinion is presumably a secondary influence produced after the *primary* influence (i.e., the acceptance of the information). Since power is here defined in terms of the primary changes, the influence of the content on a related opinion is not a case of expert power as we have defined it, but the initial acceptance of the validity of the content does seem to be based on expert power or referent power. In other cases, however, so-called facts may be accepted as self-evident because they fit into P's cognitive structure; if this impersonal acceptance of the truth of the fact is independent of the more or less enduring relationship between O and P, then P's acceptance of the fact is not an actualization of expert power. Thus we distinguish between expert power based on the credibility of O and informational influence which is based on characteristics of the stimulus such as the logic of the argument or the "self-evident facts."

Wherever expert influence occurs, it seems to be necessary both for P to think that O knows and for P to trust that O is telling the truth (rather than trying to deceive him).

Expert power will produce a new cognitive structure which is initially relatively dependent on O, but informational influence will produce a more independent structure. The former is likely to become more independent with the passage of time. In both cases the degree of dependence on O is not affected by the level of observability.

The "sleeper effect" (**18, 24**) is an interesting case of a change in the degree of dependence of an opinion on O. An unreliable O (who probably had negative referent power but some positive expert power) presented "facts" which were accepted by the subjects and which would normally produce secondary influence on their opinions and beliefs. However, the negative referent power aroused resistance and resulted in negative social influence on their beliefs (i.e., set up a force in the direction opposite to the influence attempt), so that there was little change in the subjects' opinions. With the passage of time, however, the subjects tended to forget the identity of the negative communicator faster than they forgot the contents of his communication, so there was a weakening of the negative referent influence and a consequent delayed positive change in the subjects' beliefs in the direction of the influence attempt ("sleeper effect"). Later, when the identity of the negative communicator was experimentally reinstated, these resisting forces were reinstated, and there was another negative change in belief in a direction opposite to the influence attempt (**24**).

The range of expert power, we assume, is more delimited than that of referent power. Not only is it restricted to cognitive systems, but the expert is seen as having superior knowledge or ability in very specific areas, and his power will be limited to these areas, though some "halo effect" might occur. Recently, some of our renowned physical scientists have found quite painfully that their expert power in physical sciences does not extend to regions involving international politics. Indeed, there is some evidence that the attempted exertion of expert power outside of the range of expert power will reduce that expert power. An undermining of confidence seems to take place.

Summary

We have distinguished five types of power: referent power, expert power, reward power, coercive power, and legitimate power. These distinctions led to the following hypotheses.

1. For all five types, the stronger the basis of power, the greater the power.

2. For any type of power, the size of the range may vary greatly, but, in general, referent power will have the broadest range.

3. Any attempt to utilize power outside the range of power will tend to reduce the power.

4. A new state of a system produced by reward power or coercive power will be highly dependent on O, and the more observable P's conformity, the more dependent the state. For the other three types of power, the new state is usually dependent, at least in the beginning, but in any case the level of observability has no effect on the degree of dependence.

5. Coercion results in decreased attraction of P toward O and high resistance; reward power results in increased attraction and low resistance.

6. The more legitimate the coercion, the less it will produce resistance and decreased attraction.

Notes

[5]Though the primary influence of coercive power is dependent, it often produces secondary changes which are independent. Brainwashing, for example, utilizes coercive power to produce many primary changes in the life space of the prisoner, but these dependent changes can lead to identification with the aggressor and hence to secondary changes in ideology which are independent.

References

[1]Asch, S. E. *Social psychology.* New York: Prentice-Hall, 1952.

[2]Back, K. W. Influence through social communication. *J. abnorm. soc. Psychol.,* 1951, **46,** 9–23.

[3]Coch, L., & French, J. R. P., Jr. Overcoming resistance to change. *Hum. Relat.,* 1948, **1,** 512–32.

[4]Deutsch, M., & Gerard, H. B. A study of normative and informational influences upon individual judgment. *J. abnorm. soc. Psychol.,* 1955, **51,** 629–36.

[5]Dittes, J. E., & Kelley, H. H. Effects of different conditions of acceptance upon conformity to group norms. *J. abnorm. soc. Psychol.,* 1956, **53,** 100–107.

[6]Festinger, L. An analysis of compliant behavior. In Sherif, M., & Wilson, M. O., (Eds.). *Group relations at the crossroads.* New York: Harper, 1953, 232–56.

[7]Festinger, L. Informal social communication. *Psychol. Rev.,* 1950, **57,** 271–82.

[8]Festinger, L., Gerard, H. B., Hymovitch, B., Kelley, H. H., & Raven, B. H. The influence process in the presence of extreme deviates. *Hum. Relat.,* 1952, **5,** 327–346.

[9]Festinger, L., Schacter, S., & Back, K. The operation of group standards. In Cartwright, D., & Zan-der, A. *Group dynamics: research and theory.* Evanston: Row, Peterson, 1953, 204–23.

[10]French, J. R. P., Jr., Israel, Joachim & Ås, Dagfinn "Arbeidernes medvirkning i industribedriften. En eksperimentell undersøkelse." Institute for Social Research, Oslo, Norway, 1957.

[11]French, J. R. P., Jr., Levinger, G., & Morrison, H. W. The legitimacy of coercive power. In preparation.

[12]French, J. R. P., Jr., & Raven, B. H. An experiment in legitimate and coercive power. In preparation.

[13]Gerard, H. B. The anchorage of opinions in face-to-face groups. *Hum. Relat.,* 1954, **7,** 313–325.

[14]Goldhammer, H., & Shils, E. A. Types of power and status. *Amer. J. Sociol.,* 1939, **45,** 171–178.

[15]Herbst, P. G. Analysis and measurement of a situation. *Hum. Relat.,* 1953, **2,** 113–140.

[16]Hochbaum, G. M. Self-confidence and reactions to group pressures. *Amer. soc. Rev.,* 1954, **19,** 678–687.

[17]Hovland, C. I., Lumsdaine, A. A., & Sheffield, F. D. *Experiments on mass communication.* Princeton: Princeton Univer. Press, 1949.

[18]Hovland, C. I., & Weiss, W. The influence of source credibility on communication effectiveness. *Publ. Opin. Quart.,* 1951, **15,** 635–650.

[19]Jackson, J. M., & Saltzstein, H. D. The effect of person-group relationships on conformity processes. *J. abnorm. soc. Psychol.,* 1958, **57,** 17–24.

[20]Jahoda, M. Psychological issues in civil liberties. *Amer. Psychologist,* 1956, **11,** 234–240.

[21]Katz, D., & Schank, R. L. *Social psychology.* New York: Wiley, 1938.

[22]Kelley, H. H., & Volkart, E. H. The resistance to change of group-anchored attitudes. *Amer. Soc. Rev.,* 1952, **17,** 453–465.

[23]Kelman, H. Three processes of acceptance of social influence: compliance, identification and internalization. Paper read at the meetings of the American Psychological Association, August 1956.

[24]Kelman, H., & Hovland, C. I. "Reinstatement" of the communicator in delayed measurement of opinion change. *J. abnorm. soc. Psychol.,* 1953, **48,** 327–335.

[25]Lewin, K. *Dynamic theory of personality.* New York: McGraw-Hill, 1935, 114–170.

26 Lewin, K. *Field theory in social science.* New York: Harper, 1951.

27 Lewin, K., Lippitt, R., & White, R. K. Patterns of aggressive behavior in experimentally created social climates. *J. soc. Psychol.,* 1939, **10,** 271–301.

28 Lasswell, H. D., & Kaplan, A. *Power and society: A framework for political inquiry.* New Haven: Yale Univer. Press, 1950.

29 Linton, R. *The cultural background of personality.* New York: Appleton-Century-Crofts, 1945.

30 Lippitt, R., Polansky, N., Redl, F., & Rosen, S. The dynamics of power. *Hum. Relat.,* 1952, **5,** 37–64.

31 March, J. G. An introduction to the theory and measurement of influence. *Amer. polit. Sci. Rev.,* 1955, **49,** 431–451.

32 Miller, J. G. Toward a general theory for the behavioral sciences. *Amer. Psychologist,* 1955, **10,** 513–531.

33 Moore, H. T. The comparative influence of majority and expert opinion. *Amer. J. Psychol.,* 1921, **32,** 16–20.

34 Newcomb, T. M. *Social psychology.* New York: Dryden, 1950.

35 Raven, B. H. The effect of group pressures on opinion, perception, and communication. Unpublished doctoral dissertation, University of Michigan, 1953.

36 Raven, B. H., & French, J. R. P., Jr. Group support, legitimate power, and social influence. *J. Person.,* 1958, **26,** 400–409.

37 Rommetveit, R. *Social norms and roles.* Minneapolis: Univer. Minnesota Press, 1953.

38 Russell, B. *Power: A new social analysis.* New York: Norton, 1938.

39 Stotland, E., Zander, A., Burnstein, E., Wolfe, D., & Natsoulas, T. Studies on the effects of identification. University of Michigan, Institute for Social Research. Forthcoming.

40 Swanson, G. E., Newcomb, T. M., & Hartley, E. L. *Readings in social psychology.* New York: Henry Holt, 1952.

41 Torrance, E. P., & Mason, R. Instructor effort to influence: an experimental evaluation of six approaches. Paper presented at USAF-NRC Symposium on Personnel, Training, and Human Engineering. Washington, D.C., 1956.

42 Weber, M. *The theory of social and economic organization.* Oxford: Oxford Univer. Press, 1947.

Chapter Three

Leaders and the Role of Personal Traits

*A*t one point in time "great person" theories of leadership were popular. It was commonly assumed that certain individuals, when born, were destined to lead. Julius Caesar, Joan of Arc, Catherine II the Great, and Napoleon are cited as naturally great leaders, individuals supposedly born with a set of personal qualities that enabled them to be effective leaders.

Early in the 20th century, students of leadership raised a critical question: "Do leaders tend to possess a set of traits (i.e., physical, demographic, intellective, and personality characteristics) that equip them to be leaders?" as assumed by the great person theories. For some, leadership began to be seen as a psychological phenomenon, with individuals inherently possessing capacities, motives, and patterns of behavior that distinguished them from others (i.e., nonleaders).

Ralph Stogdill (1948) conducted an extensive review of the literature and attempted to identify and summarize the personal factors that are associated with leadership. His review produced an identification of several categories of important leader traits. Among them are:

- Capacity (intelligence, alertness, verbal facility, originality, judgment).
- Achievement (scholarship, knowledge, athletic accomplishments).
- Responsibility (dependability, initiative, persistence, aggressiveness, self-confidence, desire to excel).
- Participation (activity, sociability, cooperation, adaptability, humor).
- Status (socio-economic position, popularity).

Stogdill's work also provided additional insight into the process of leadership. He suggested that leadership is a relationship; that it is associated with the attainment of group objectives, implying that leadership is an activity, consisting of movement and getting work accomplished; and that it is evolutionary and interactive in nature.

Again in 1974 Stogdill reviewed 163 studies published between 1949 and 1970 that provided additional insight into leader traits. This body of evidence reinforced the observations that he drew in 1948 and identified some additional traits and skills. Stogdill (1974) provided the following trait profile of the successful leaders:

> *The leader is characterized by a strong drive for responsibility and task completion, vigor and persistence in pursuit of goals, venturesomeness and originality in problem solving, drive to exercise initiative in social situations, self-confidence and sense of personal identity, willingness to accept consequences of decision and action, readiness to absorb interpersonal stress, willingness to tolerate frustration and delay, ability to influence other persons' behavior, and capacity to structure social interaction systems to the purpose at hand (p. 81).*[1]

[1]R. M. Stogdill, *Handbook of leadership: A survey of the literature* (New York: Free Press, 1974).

Certain individuals (i.e., those possessing a unique configuration of personal factors—ideas, initiative, persistence, knowledge of how to get things done, responsibility, status—relative to the other members of the group) come to occupy a special position in the group. Through their orchestration of group activity (e.g., providing meaning, information, judgment, activity), they emerge as leaders, and in this capacity they continue to provide orchestration to group activities. Reference to the orchestration of group activity suggests that leadership can be seen as a working relationship among members of a group. Through this working and interactive process, the leader makes contributions that are important to the group, acquires a status within the group, and comes to fulfill a leadership role. Verbal fluency, popularity, cooperativeness, self-confidence, initiative, and persistence, for example, tend to contribute to the individual's emergence into this leadership role and subsequently tend to reinforce the person's legitimacy as the group's leader.

Stogdill also highlighted the importance of the situation. He notes that a person does not emerge as a leader simply by possessing these key traits. The pattern of traits possessed must achieve some semblance of fit with the situation in which the followers find themselves as well as the characteristics, goals, and activities of the followers. Thus, according to Stogdill, the person who is a leader in one group may not be a leader in the next situation.

Between the mid-1940s and the early 1990s, there has been a continued interest in the role of individual traits in the leadership equation. Edwin A. Locke and several of his students conducted an extensive review of the leadership trait literature resulting in the publication of *The Essence of Leadership* (1991). Part of their work is summarized in the second reading in this chapter. Shelley A. Kirkpatrick and Edwin A. Locke (1991) provide a contemporary answer to the question "Do leadership traits really matter?"

According to Kirkpatrick and Locke, there appears to be a set of traits that endows an individual with "the right stuff" to be an effective leader. These traits are important "preconditions" giving an individual the *potential* to be an effective leader. Possessing these traits, however, does not guarantee leadership success. Among the key traits that appear to differentiate leaders from nonleaders, according to Kirkpatrick and Locke are drive, the desire to lead, honesty/integrity, self-confidence, cognitive ability, and knowledge of the business. Several other traits identified as possible characteristics of effective leaders included charisma, creativity/originality, and flexibility/adaptiveness. In their article the authors provide us with insight into the meaning of and leadership role played by each of these attributes.

Energy and drive as it characterizes an individual's disposition has been the focus of recent research. Evidence suggests that individuals whose personality can be characterized by positive affectivity (i.e., a positive mood state, high levels of energy and drive) tend to be more competent interpersonally, to contribute more to group activities, and therefore are able to function more effectively in their leadership role.[2] By virtue of their energetic personalities, these individuals infuse excitement and energy into group activity. The self-assessment presented at the end of this chapter opener provides you with an opportunity to profile your own level of positive and negative affectivity.

According to Kirkpatrick and Locke, people who possess these traits are more likely to engage in the behaviors associated with effective leadership. These traits help leaders acquire the necessary skills (i.e., capacities for action such as decision making and problem solving) needed for effective leadership. In addition, they have the ability to create vision, and they possess the capacity to design a strategy that leads to vision implementation (e.g., structure activities, motivate others, manage information, build teams, and promote change and innovation). Those who possess these traits are simply more likely to engage in the behaviors associated with effective leadership than individuals who are not endowed with these characteristics.

During the past few years, accompanying societal efforts to break the glass ceiling

---

[2]B. M. Staw and S. G. Barsade, "Affect and Managerial Performance: A Test of the Sadder-but-Wiser vs. Happier-and-Smarter Hypothesis," *Administrative Science Quarterly* 38 (1993), 304–331.

F I G U R E 3 . 1
The Leadership Process: Leader Traits

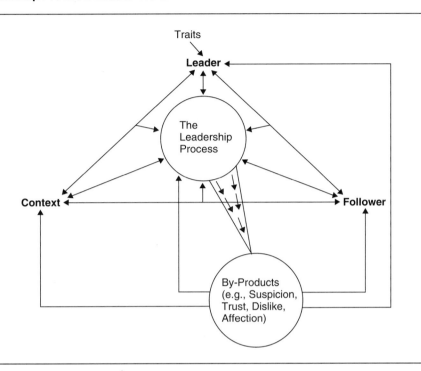

(i.e., artificial barriers to the promotion of females), there has been an interest in issues pertaining to gender and leadership style. In the third reading, Alice H. Eagly and Blair T. Johnson (1990) review the arguments addressing the reasons to expect an absence (and presence) of sex differences in leadership style. They also conduct a statistical (meta) analysis of a number of research studies that have attempted to address the question "Is there a difference in the leadership style of men and women?" Although gender-related leadership style patterns were uncovered, it is yet unclear whether the behaviors observed were primarily caused by different sex-based traits, perceived role requirements, or other task and environmental factors.

Returning to our leadership process model, the discussion of traits provides further insight into the leadership process through an expanded understanding of the leader.

In this chapter, Stogdill suggested that leadership unfolds in a working relationship, and Kirkpatrick and Locke concluded that those with the key leadership traits are more likely to engage in the behaviors associated with effective leadership. This leads to a new question—"What are the behaviors associated with effective leadership?" The readings in the next chapter look at what it is that effective leaders "do."

Self-Assessment

Positive and Negative Affectivity

Instructions: For each of the following items, please indicate how you felt at work during the past week.

	Very Slightly or Not at All				Very Much
1. Active	1	2	3	4	5
2. Calm	1	2	3	4	5
3. Distressed	1	2	3	4	5
4. Sleepy	1	2	3	4	5
5. Strong	1	2	3	4	5
6. Excited	1	2	3	4	5
7. Scornful	1	2	3	4	5
8. Hostile	1	2	3	4	5
9. Enthusiastic	1	2	3	4	5
10. Dull	1	2	3	4	5
11. Fearful	1	2	3	4	5
12. Relaxed	1	2	3	4	5
13. Peppy	1	2	3	4	5
14. At rest	1	2	3	4	5
15. Nervous	1	2	3	4	5
16. Drowsy	1	2	3	4	5
17. Elated	1	2	3	4	5
18. Placid	1	2	3	4	5
19. Jittery	1	2	3	4	5
20. Sluggish	1	2	3	4	5

Source: M. J. Burke, A. P. Brief, J. M. George, L. Roberson, and J. Webster, Measuring Affect at Work: Confirmatory Analyses of Competing Mood Structures with Conceptual Linkage to Cortical Regulatory Systems, *Journal of Personality and Social Psychology* 57 (1989) 1091—1102.

Scoring:

1. Subtract your response to each of the following items from 6: 2 (calm), 4 (sleepy), 10 (dull), 12 (relaxed), 14 (at rest), 16 (drowsy), 18 (placid), and 20 (sluggish).

2. *Positive Affectivity* is reflected with two scores, the first signaling general and positive affectivity and the second denoting "high positive affectivity."

    a. Positive Affectivity—Where appropriate, employing your adjusted response scores, sum your response scores to the following items: 1, 4, 5, 6, 9, 10, 13, 16, 17, and 20, divide by 10, and enter that score here _____.

    b. High Positive Affectivity—Where appropriate, employing your adjusted response scores, sum your response scores to the following items: 1, 5, 6, 9, 13, and 17, divide by 6, and enter that score here _____.

3. *Negative Affectivity* is reflected with two scores, the first signaling general and negative affectivity and the second denoting "high negative affectivity."

    a. Negative Affectivity—Where appropriate, employing your adjusted response scores, sum your response scores to the following items: 2, 3, 7, 8, 11, 12, 14, 15, 18, and 19, divide by 10, and enter that score here _____.

    b. High Negative Affectivity—Where appropriate, employing your adjusted response scores, sum your response scores to the following items: 3, 7, 8, 11, 15, and 19, divide by 6, and enter that score here _____.

Interpretation: A high score (4 and greater) implies a high level of affectivity (i.e., positive, negative, high positive, and high negative). A low score (2 or less) implies a low level of affectivity (i.e., positive, negative, high positive, and high negative). Some people have a "sunny" disposition—seeing the glass as almost full as opposed to almost empty. Others nearly always appear gloomy. Affectivity essentially reflects an individual's *pervasive mood state.* Negative affectivity and high negative affectivity reflect negative emotionality. Those people are distressed, scornful, hostile, fearful, nervous, and jittery. Positive affectivity and high positive affectivity reflect positive emotionality. These individuals tend to feel active, excited, enthusiastic, peppy, and strong. Leaders who have strong positive affectivity are characterized as possessing an air of confidence, competency, and optimism. They tend to transfer their energy to others and tend to be characterized as leaders of cohesive, productive work groups.

Personal Factors Associated with Leadership: A Survey of the Literature[1]

R. M. Stogdill
Ohio State University

S mith and Krueger (100) have surveyed the literature on leadership to 1933. Recent developments in leadership methodology, as related especially to military situations, were reviewed in 1947 by Jenkins (54). The present survey is concerned only with those studies in which some attempt has been made to determine the traits and characteristics of leaders. In many of the studies surveyed, leadership was not defined. In others the methods used in the investigation appeared to have little relationship to the problem as stated. An attempt has been made to include all studies bearing on the problem of traits and personal factors associated with leadership. In all except four cases, the original book or article has been read and abstracted in detail. The data from one American and three German publications have been derived from competent abstracts.

The present survey lists only those factors which were studied by three or more investigators. Evidence reported by fewer investigators has not been regarded as providing a satisfactory basis for evaluation. It is realized that the number of investigations in which a factor was studied is not necessarily indicative of the importance of the factor. However, the frequency with which a factor was found to be significant appears to be the most satisfactory single criterion for evaluating the data accumulated in this survey, but other criteria, such as the competency of the experimental methods employed and the adequacy of the statistical treatment of data, have also been regarded in evaluating the results of a particular study.

In analyzing data obtained from various groups and by various methods, the question arises as to the extent to which results may be influenced by differences in social composition of the groups, differences in methodology, and differences in leadership criteria. There is no assurance, for example, that the investigator who analyzes the biographies of great men is studying the same kind of leadership behavior that is revealed through observation of children's leadership activities in group situations. It is of interest, however, that some of the studies employing the two different methods yield remarkably similar results. On the other hand, there are some factors that appear only in certain age and social groups or only when certain methods are employed. . . .

Summary

1. The following conclusions are supported by uniformly positive evidence from 15 or more of the studies surveyed:

   a. The average person who occupies a position of leadership exceeds the average member of his group in the following respects: (1) intelligence, (2) scholarship, (3) dependability in exercising responsibilities, (4) activity and social participation, and (5) socioeconomic status.

   b. The qualities, characteristics, and skills required in a leader are determined to a large extent by the demands of the situation in which he is to function as a leader.

2. The following conclusions are supported by uniformly positive evidence from 10 or more of the studies surveyed:

   a. The average person who occupies a position of leadership exceeds the average member of his group to some degree in the following respects: (1) sociability, (2) initiative, (3) persistence, (4) knowing how to get things done, (5) self-confidence, (6) alertness to, and insight into, situations, (7) coöperativeness, (8) popularity, (9) adaptability, and (10) verbal facility.

3. In addition to the above, a number of factors have been found which are specific to well-defined groups. For example, athletic ability and physical prowess have been found to be characteristics of leaders in boys' gangs and play groups. Intellectual fortitude and integrity are traits found to be associated with eminent leadership in maturity.

4. The items with the highest overall correlation with leadership are originality, popularity, sociability, judgment, aggressiveness, desire to excel, humor, coöperativeness, liveliness, and athletic ability, in approximate order of magnitude of average correlation coefficient.

5. In spite of considerable negative evidence, the general trend of results suggests a low positive correlation be-

Source: Edited and reprinted from *The Journal of Psychology* 28, 35–71, 1948, with the permission of Helen Dwight Reid Educational Foundation. Published by Heldref Publications, 1319 Eighteenth St., N. W. Washington, D. C. 20036-1802. Copyright 1948. Author affiliation may have changed since article was first published.

[1] Received in the Editorial Office on September 1, 1947, and published immediately at Provincetown, Massachusetts. Copyright by The Journal Press, a coöperative contribution of the U.S. Navy, Office of Naval Research, and the Ohio State University Research Foundation. This study represents one aspect of a program of research on leadership being conducted by the Personnel Research Board of the Ohio State University, under the direction of Dr. C. L. Shartle. The opinions expressed herein are not to be regarded as representing the opinion of, or having the endorsement of, the Navy Department.

tween leadership and such variables as chronological age, height, weight, physique, energy, appearance, dominance, and mood control. The evidence is about evenly divided concerning the relation to leadership of such traits as introversion-extroversion, self sufficiency, and emotional control.

6. The evidence available suggests that leadership exhibited in various school situations may persist into college and into later vocational and community life. However, knowledge of the facts relating to the transferability of leadership is very meager and obscure.

7. The most fruitful studies, from the point of view of understanding leadership, have been those in which leadership behavior was described and analyzed on the basis of direct observation or analysis of biographical and case history data.

Discussion

The factors which have been found to be associated with leadership could probably all be classified under the general headings of *capacity, achievement, responsibility, participation,* and *status:*

1. *Capacity* (intelligence, alertness, verbal facility, originality, judgment).

2. *Achievement* (scholarship, knowledge, athletic accomplishments).

3. *Responsibility* (dependability, initiative, persistence, aggressiveness, self-confidence, desire to excel).

4. *Participation* (activity, sociability, coöperation, adaptability, humor).

5. *Status* (socio-economic position, popularity).

These findings are not surprising. It is primarily by virtue of participating in group activities and demonstrating his capacity for expediting the work of the group that a person becomes endowed with leadership status. A number of investigators have been careful to distinguish between the leader and the figure-head, and to point out that leadership is always associated with the attainment of group objectives. Leadership implies activity, movement, getting work done. The leader is a person who occupies a position of responsibility in coördinating the activities of the members of the group in their task of attaining a common goal. This leads to consideration of another significant factor.

6. *Situation* (mental level, status, skills, needs and interests of followers, objectives to be achieved, etc.).

A person does not become a leader by virtue of the possession of some combination of traits, but the pattern of personal characteristics of the leader must bear some relevant relationship to the characteristics, activities, and goals of the followers. Thus, leadership must be conceived in terms of the interaction of variables which are in constant flux and change. The factor of change is especially characteristic of the situation, which may be radically altered by the addition or loss of members, changes in interpersonal relationships, changes in goals, competition of extra-group influences, and the like. The personal characteristics of leader and of the fol-

lowers are, in comparison, highly stable. The persistence of individual patterns of human behavior in the face of constant situational change appears to be a primary obstacle encountered not only in the practice of leadership, but in the selection and placement of leaders. It is not especially difficult to find persons who are leaders. It is quite another matter to place these persons in different situations where they will be able to function as leaders. It becomes clear that an adequate analysis of leadership involves not only a study of leaders, but also of situations.

The evidence suggests that leadership is a relation that exists between persons in a social situation, and that persons who are leaders in one situation may not necessarily be leaders in other situations. Must it then be assumed that leadership is entirely incidental, haphazard, and unpredictable? Not at all. The very studies which provide the strongest arguments for the situational nature of leadership also supply the strongest evidence indicating that leadership patterns as well as nonleadership patterns of behavior are persistent and relatively stable. Jennings (55) observes that "the individual's choice behavior, in contrast to his social expansiveness, appears as an expression of needs which are, so to speak, so 'central' to his personality that he must strive to fulfill them whether or not the possibility of fulfilling them is at hand." A somewhat similar observation is made by Newstetter, Feldstein, and Newcomb (78), who report that:

Being accepted or rejected is not determined by the cordiality or antagonism of the individual's treatment of his fellows, nor evidently is the individual's treatment of his fellows much affected by the degree to which he is already being accepted or rejected by them. Their treatment of him is related to their acceptance or rejection of him. Their treatment of him is, of course, a reaction to some or all of his behaviors, but we have been completely unsuccessful in attempting to measure what these behaviors are.

The authors conclude that these findings provide "devastating evidence" against the concept of the operation of measurable traits in determining social interactions. The findings of Newstetter and his associates do not appear to provide direct evidence either for or against a theory of traits, but they do indicate that the complex of factors that determines an individual's status in a group is most difficult to isolate and evaluate.

The findings of Jennings and Newstetter suggest that the problem of selecting leaders should be much less difficult than that of training nonleaders to become leaders. The clinician or group worker who has observed the fruitless efforts of socially isolated individuals to gain group acceptance or leadership status is aware of the real nature of the phenomena described by Jennings and Newstetter. Some individuals are isolates in almost any group in which they find themselves, while others are readily accepted in most of their social contacts.

A most pertinent observation on this point is made by Ackerson (1), who reports that "the correlation for 'leaders' and 'follower' are not of opposite sign and similar magnitude as would be expected of traits supposed to be antithetical."

These may not be the opposite poles of a single underlying trait. "It may be that the true antithesis of 'leader' is not 'follower,' but 'indifference,' i.e., the incapacity or unwillingness either to lead or to follow. Thus it may be that some individuals who under one situation are leaders may under other conditions take the role of follower, while the true 'opposite' is represented by the child who neither leads nor follows."

The findings suggest that leadership is not a matter of passive status, or of the mere possession of some combination of traits. It appears rather to be a working relationship among members of a group, in which the leader acquires status through active participation and demonstration of his capacity for carrying coöperative tasks through to completion. Significant aspects of this capacity for organizing and expediting coöperative effort appear to be intelligence, alertness to the needs and motives of others, and insight into situations, further reinforced by such habits as responsibility, initiative, persistence, and self-confidence. The studies surveyed offer little information as to the basic nature of these personal qualifications. Cattell's (19) studies suggest that they may be founded to some degree on basic intelligence, but Cattell and others also suggest that they are socially conditioned to a high degree. Problems which appear to be in need of thorough investigation are those relating to factors which condition social participation, insight into situations, mood control, responsibility, and transferability of leadership from one situation to another. Answers to these questions seem basic not only to any adequate understanding of the personal qualifications of leaders, but also to any effective training for leadership.

References

[1] Ackerson, L. Children's Behavior Problems: Relative Importance and Intercorrelation among Traits. Chicago: Univ. Chicago Press, 1942.

[2] Arrington, R. E. Time sampling in studies of social behavior: A critical review of techniques and results with research suggestions. *Psychol. Bull.,* 1943, **40,** 81–124.

[3] Baldwin, L. E. A study of factors usually associated with high school male leadership. Unpublished Master's thesis, Ohio State Univ., 1932.

[4] Barker, R. G. The social interrelations of strangers and acquaintances. *Sociometry,* 1942, **5,** 169–179.

[5] Bellingrath, G. C. Qualities associated with leadership in extra-curricular activities of the high school. *Teach. Coll. Contr. Educ.,* 1930, No. 399.

[6] Bernard, J. Political leadership among North American Indians. *Amer. J. Sociol.,* 1928, **34,** 296–315.

[7] Bonney, M. E. The constancy of sociometric scores and their relationship to teacher judgments of social success and to personality self-ratings. *Sociometry,* 1943, **6,** 409–424.

[8] Bowden, A. O. A study of the personality of student leaders in colleges in the United States. *J. Abn. & Soc. Psychol.,* 1926, **21,** 149–160.

[9] Brogden, H. E., & Thomas, W. F. The primary traits in personality items purporting to measure sociability. *J. of Psychol.,* 1943, **16,** 85–97.

[10] Broich, H. Führeranforderungen in der Kindergruppe. *Z. angew. Psychol.,* 1929, **32,** 164–212.

[11] Brown, M. Leadership among high school pupils. *Teach. Coll. Contr. Educ.,* 1933, No. 559.

[12] ———. Leadership among high school pupils. *Teach. Coll. Rec.,* 1934, **35,** 324–326.

[13] Brown, S. C. Some case studies of delinquent girls described as leaders. *Brit. J. Educ. Psychol.,* 1931, **1,** 162–179.

[14] Burks, F. W. Some factors related to social success in college. *J. Soc. Psychol.,* 1938, **9,** 125–140.

[15] Buttgereit, H. Führergestalten in der Schulklasse. *Z. angew. Psychol.,* 1932, **43,** 369–413.

[16] Caldwell, O. W. Some factors in training for leadership. *Nat. Ass. Sec. Sch. Prin., Fourth Yearb.,* 1920, 2–13.

[17] Caldwell, O. W., & Wellman, B. Characteristics of school leaders. *J. Educ. Res.,* 1926, **14,** 1–15.

[18] Carlson, H. B., & Harrell, W. An analysis of Life's "Ablest Congressman" poll. *J. Soc. Psychol.,* 1942, **15,** 153–158.

[19] Cattell, R. B. Description and Measurement of Personality. New York: World Book, 1946.

[20] Chapin, F. S. Community Leadership and Opinion in Red Wing. Minneapolis: Univ. Minnesota Press, 1945.

[21] Chapple, E. D., & Donald, G., Jr. A method of evaluating supervisory personnel. *Harvard Bus. Rev.,* 1946, **24,** 197–214.

[22] Chevaleva-Ianovskaia, E., & Sylla, D. Essai d'une étude sur les enfants meneurs. *J. de Psychol.,* 1929, **26,** 604–612.

[23] Clem, O. M., & Dodge, S. B. The relation of high school leadership and scholarship to post-school success. *Peabody J. Educ.* 1933, **10,** 321–329.

[24] Courtenay, M. E. Persistence of leadership. *Sch. Rev.,* 1938, **46,** 97–107.

[25] Cowley, W. H. Three distinctions in the study of leaders. *J. Abn. & Soc. Psychol.,* 1928, **23,** 144–157.

[26] ———. Traits of face-to-face leaders. *J. Abn. & Soc. Psychol.,* 1931, **26,** 304–313.

[27] Cox, C. M. The Early Mental Traits of Three Hundred Geniuses. Stanford University: Stanford Univ. Press, 1926.

[28] Crawford, A. B. Extra-curriculum activities and academic work. *Person. J.,* 1928, **7,** 121–129.

[29] Dashiell, J. F. Personality traits and the different professions. *J. Appl. Psychol.,* 1930, **14,** 197–201.

[30] Davis, J. A study of one hundred sixty-three outstanding communist leaders. *Publ. Amer. Sociol. Soc.,* 1930, **24,** 42–55.

[31] Detroit Teachers College. How Children Choose Friends. Detroit: Detroit Teachers College, 1929.

[32] Drake, R. M. A study of leadership. *Charac. & Pers.,* 1944, **12,** 285–289.

[33] Dunkerley, M. D. A statistical study of leadership among college women. *Stud. Psychol. & Psychiat.,* 1940, **4,** 1–65.

[34] Eichler, G. A. Studies in student leadership. *Penn. St. Coll. Stud. Educ.,* 1934, No. 10.

[35] Fauquier, W., & Gilchrist, T. Some aspects of leadership in an institution. *Child Devel.,* 1942, **13,** 55–64.

[36] Fay, P. J., & Middleton, W. C. Judgment of leadership from the transmitted voice. *J. Soc. Psychol.,* 1943, **17,** 99–102.

[37] Finch, F. H., & Carroll, H. A. Gifted children as high school leaders. *J. Genet. Psychol.,* 1932, **41,** 476–481.

[38] Flemming, E. G. A factor analysis of the personality of high school leaders. *J. Appl. Psychol.,* 1935, **19,** 596–605.

[39] Garrison, K. C. A study of some factors related to leadership in high school. *Peabody J. Educ.,* 1935, **11,** 11–17.

[40] Goodenough, F. L. Inter-relationships in the behavior of young children. *Child Devel.,* 1930, **1,** 29–48.

[41] Gowin, E. B. The Executive and His Control of Men. New York: Macmillan, 1915.

[42] ———. The Selection and Training of the Business Executive. New York: Macmillan, 1918.

[43] Guilford, J. P., & Guilford, R. B. Personality factors, *D, R, T,* and *A. J. Abn. & Soc. Psychol.,* 1939, **34,** 21–36.

[44] Hanawalt, N. G., Hamilton, C. E., & Morris, M. L. Level of aspiration in college leaders and non-leaders. *J. Abn. & Soc. Psychol.,* 1934, **38,** 545–548.

[45] Hanawalt, N. G., Richardson, H. M., & Hamilton, R. J. Leadership as related to Bernreuter personality measures: II. An item analysis of responses of college leaders and non-leaders. *J. Soc. Psychol.,* 1943, **17,** 251–267.

[46] Hanawalt, N. G., & Richardson, H. M. Leadership as related to the Bernreuter personality measures: IV. An item analysis of responses of adult leaders and non-leaders. *J. Appl. Psychol.,* 1944, **28,** 397–411.

[47] Hanfmann, E. Social structure of a group of kindergarten children. *Amer. J. Orthopsychiat.,* 1935, **5,** 407–410.

[48] Heath, C. W., & Gregory, L. W. What it takes to be an officer. *Infantry J.,* 1946, **58,** 44–45.

[49] Henning, H. Ziele und Möglichkeiten der experimentellen charakterprüfung *Jarbuch d. Charakterol.,* 1929, **6,** 213–273.

[50] Hollingworth, L. S. Gifted Children. New York: Macmillan, 1926.

[51] Hooker, E. R. Leaders in village communities. *Soc. For.,* 1928, **6,** 605–614.

52 Howell, C. E. Measurement of leadership. *Sociometry*, 1942, **5**, 163–168.

53 Hunter, E. C., & Jordan, A. M. An analysis of qualities associated with leadership among college students. *J. Educ. Psychol.*, 1939, **30**, 497–509.

54 Jenkins, W. O. A review of leadership studies with particular reference to military problems. *Psychol. Bull.*, 1947, **44**, 54–79.

55 Jennings, H. H. Leadership and Isolation. New York: Longmans Green, 1943.

56 Jones, A. J. The Education of Youth for Leadership. New York: McGraw-Hill, 1938.

57 Kohs, S. C., & Irle, K. W. Prophesying Army promotion. *J. Appl. Psychol.*, 1920, **4**, 73–87.

58 Lehman, H. C. The creative years in science and literature. *Sci. Mon.*, 1937, **45**, 65–75.

59 ———. Optimum ages for eminent leadership. *Sci. Mon.*, 1942, **54**, 162–175.

60 Leib, A. Vorstellungen und Urteile von Schülern über Fuhrer in der Schulklasse. *Z. angew. Psychol.*, 1928, **30**, 241–346.

61 Levi, I. J. Student leadership in elementary and junior high school, and its transfer into senior high school. *J. Educ. Res.*, 1930, **22**, 135–139.

62 Link, H. C. The definition of social effectiveness and leadership through measurement. *Educ. & Psychol. Meas.*, 1944, **4**, 57–67.

63 Luithlen, W. F. Zur Psychologie der Initiative und der Führereigenschaften. *Z. angew. Psychol.*, 1931, **39**, 56–122.

64 Maller, J. B. Coöperation and competition: An experimental study in motivation. *Teach. Coll. Contr. Educ.*, 1925, No. 384.

65 Malloy, H. Study of some of the factors underlying the establishment of successful social contacts at the college level. *J. Soc. Psychol.*, 1936, **7**, 205–228.

66 McCandless, B. R. Changing relationships between dominance and social acceptability during group democratization. *Amer. J. Orthopsychiat.*, 1942, **12**, 529–535.

67 McCuen, T. L. Leadership and intelligence. *Education*, 1929, **50**, 89–95.

68 McGahan, F. E. Factors associated with leadership ability. *Texas Outlook*, 1941, **25**, 37–38.

69 Merriam, C. E. Four American Party Leaders. New York: Macmillan, 1926.

70 Merriam, C. E., & Gosnell, H. E. The American Party System. New York: Macmillan, 1929.

71 Michels, R. Political Parties. New York: Macmillan, 1915.

72 Middleton, W. C. Personality qualities predominant in campus leaders. *J. Soc. Psychol.*, 1941, **13**, 199–201.

73 Miller, N. E., & Dollard, J. Social Learning and Imitation. New Haven: Yale Univ. Press, 1941.

74 Moore, L. H. Leadership traits of college women. *Sociol. & Soc. Res.*, 1932, **17**, 44–54.

75 ———. Leadership traits of college women. *Sociol. & Soc. Res.*, 1935, **20**, 136–139.

76 Nafe, R. W. A psychological description of leadership. *J. Soc. Psychol.*, 1930, **1**, 248–266.

77 Newcomb, T. M. Personality and Social Change. New York: Dryden Press, 1943.

78 Newstetter, W. I., Feldstein, M. J., & Newcomb, T. M. Group Adjustment: A Study in Experimental Sociology. Cleveland: Western Reserve Univ., 1938.

79 Nutting, R. L. Some characteristics of leadership. *Sch. & Soc.*, 1923, **18**, 387–390.

80 Page, D. P. Measurement and prediction of leadership. *Amer. J. Sociol.*, 1935, **41**, 31–43.

81 Parten, M. B. Leadership among preschool children. *J. Abn. & Soc. Psychol.*, 1933, **27**, 430–440.

82 Partridge, E. D. Leadership among adolescent boys. *Teach. Coll. Contr. Educ.*, 1934, No. 608.

83 Peck, E. M. A study of the personalities of five eminent men. *J. Abn. & Soc. Psychol.*, 1931, **26**, 37–57.

84 Pigors, P. Leadership and domination among children. *Sociologus*, 1933, **9**, 140–157.

85 Pinard, J. W. Tests of perseveration. *Brit. J. Psychol.*, 1932, **32**, 5–19.

86 Prosh, F. The basis on which students choose their leaders. *Amer. Phys. Educ. Rev.*, 1928, **33**, 265–267.

87 Puffer, J. A. Boys gangs. *Ped. Sem.*, 1905, **12**, 175–213.

88 Reals, W. H. Leadership in the high school. *Sch. Rev.*, 1938, **46**, 523–531.

89 Reininger, K. Das soziale Verhalten von Schulneulingen. *Wien Arb. pädag. Psychol.*, 1927, **7**, 14.

90 Remmelin, M. K. Analysis of leaders among high school seniors. *J. Exp. Educ.*, 1938, **6**, 413–422.

91 Reynolds, F. J. Factors of leadership among seniors of Central High School, Tulsa, Oklahoma. *J. Educ. Res.*, 1944, **37**, 356–361.

92 Richardson, H. M., & Hanawalt, N. G. Leadership as related to Bernreuter personality measures: I. College leadership in extra-curricular activities. *J. Soc. Psychol.*, 1943, **17**, 237–249.

93 ———. Leadership as related to the Bernreuter personality measures: III. Leadership among adult men in vocational and social activities. *J. Appl. Psychol.*, 1944, **28**, 308–317.

94 Roslow, S. Nation-wide and local validation of the *PQ* or Personality Quotient test. *J. Appl. Psychol.*, 1940, **24**, 529–539.

95 Schuler, E. A. A study of the consistency of dominant and submissive behavior in adolescent boys. *J. Genet. Psychol.*, 1935, **46**, 403–432.

96 Shannon, J. R. The post-school careers of high school leaders and high school scholars. *Sch. Rev.*, 1929, **37**, 656–665.

97 Sheldon, W. H. Social traits and morphologic type. *Person. J.*, 1927, **6**, 47–55.

98 Simpson, R. H. A study of those who influence and of those who are influenced in discussion. *Teach. Coll. Contr. Educ.*, 1938, No. 748.

99 Smith, C. Social selection in community leadership. *Soc. For.*, 1937, **15**, 530–545.

100 Smith, H. L., & Krueger, L. M. A brief summary of literature on leadership. *Bull. Sch. Educ., Indiana Univ.*, 1933, **9**, No. 4.

101 Smith, M. Comparative study of Indian student leaders and followers. *Soc. For.*, 1935, **13**, 418–426.

102 Smith, M., & Nystrom, W. C. A study of social participation and of leisure time of leaders and non-leaders. *J. Appl. Psychol.*, 1937, **21**, 251–259.

103 Sorokin, P. A. Social Mobility. New York: Harper, 1927.

104 ———. Leaders of labor and radical movements in the United States and foreign countries. *Amer. J. Sociol.*, 1927, **33**, 382–411.

105 Sorokin, P. A., & Zimmerman, C. C. Farmer leaders in the United States. *Soc. For.*, 1928, **7**, 33–46.

106 Spaulding, C. B. Types of junior college leaders. *Sociol. & Soc. Res.*, 1934, **18**, 164–168.

107 Starch, D. How to Develop Your Executive Ability. New York: Harper, 1943.

108 Stray, H. F. Leadership traits of girls in girls' camps. *Sociol. & Soc. Res.*, 1934, **18**, 241–250.

109 Sward, K. Temperament and direction of achievement. *J. Soc. Psychol.*, 1933, **4**, 406–429.

110 Swigart, J. S. A study of the qualities of leadership and administrative qualifications of thirty-eight women executives. Master's thesis, Ohio State Univ., 1936.

111 Taussig, F. W., & Joslyn, C. S. American Business Leaders. New York: Macmillan, 1932.

112 Terman, L. M. A preliminary study in the psychology and pedagogy of leadership. *Ped. Sem.*, 1904, **11**, 413–451.

113 Terman, L. M., *et al.* Genetic Studies of genius: I. Mental and Physical Traits of a Thousand Gifted Children. Stanford: Stanford Univ. Press, 1925.

114 Thorndike, E. L. The relation between intellect and morality in rulers. *Amer. J. Sociol.*, 1936, **42**, 321–334.

115 Thrasher, F. The Gang: A Study of 1,313 Gangs in Chicago. Chicago: Univ. Chicago Press, 1927.

116 Thurstone, L. L. A Factorial Study of Perception. Chicago: Univ. Chicago Press, 1944.

117 Tryon, C. M. Evaluations of adolescent personality by adolescents. *Monog. Soc. Res. Child Devel.*, 1939, **4**, No. 4.

118 Warner, M. L. Influence of mental level in the formation of boys' gangs. *J. Appl. Psychol.*, 1923, **7**, 224–236.

119 Webb, U. Character and intelligence. *Brit. J. Psychol. Monog.*, 1915, No. 20.

120 Wetzel, W. A. Characteristics of pupil leaders. *Sch. Rev.*, 1932, **40**, 532–534.

121 Wilkins, E. H. On the distribution of extra-curricular activities. *Sch. & Soc.*, 1940, **51**, 651–656.

122 Winston, S. Studies in negro leadership: Age and occupational distribution of 1,608 negro leaders. *Amer. J. Sociol.*, 1932, **37**, 595–602.

123 Winston, S. Bio-social characteristics of American inventors. *Amer. Soc. Rev.*, 1937, **2**, 837–849.

124 Zeleny, L. Characteristics of group leaders. *Sociol. & Soc. Res.*, 1939, **24**, 140–149.

Leadership: Do Traits Matter?

S. A. Kirkpatrick and E. A. Locke
University of Maryland

*F*ew issues have a more controversial history than leadership traits and characteristics. In the 19th and early 20th centuries, "great man" leadership theories were highly popular. These theories asserted that leadership qualities were inherited, especially by people from the upper class. Great men were born not made (in those days, virtually all business leaders were men). Today, great man theories are a popular foil for so-called superior models. To make the new models plausible, the "great men" are endowed with negative as well as positive traits. In a recent issue of the *Harvard Business Review*, for example, Slater and Bennis write,

> *The passing years have . . . given the coup de grace to another force that has retarded democratization—the "great man" who with brilliance and farsightedness could preside with dictatorial powers as the head of a growing organization.*[1]

Such great men, argue Slater and Bennis, become "outmoded" and dead hands on "the flexibility and growth of the organization." Under the new democratic model, they argue, "the individual *is* of relatively little significance."

Early in the 20th century, the great man theories evolved into trait theories. ("Trait" is used broadly here to refer to people's general characteristics, including capacities, motives, or patterns of behavior.) Trait theories did not make assumptions about whether leadership traits were inherited or acquired. They simply asserted that leaders' characteristics are different from nonleaders'. Traits such as height, weight, and physique are heavily dependent on heredity, whereas others such as knowledge of the industry are dependent on experience and learning.

The trait view was brought into question during the mid-century when a prominent theorist, Ralph Stogdill, after a thorough review of the literature concluded that "a person does not become a leader by virtue of the possession of some combination of traits."[2] Stogdill believed this because the research showed that no traits were universally associated with effective leadership and that situational factors were also influential. For example, military leaders do not have traits identical to those of business leaders.

Since Stogdill's early review, trait theory has made a comeback, though in altered form. Recent research, using a variety of methods, has made it clear that successful leaders are not like other people. The evidence indicates that there are certain core traits which significantly contribute to business leaders' success.

Traits *alone*, however, are not sufficient for successful business leadership—they are only a precondition. Leaders who possess the requisite traits must take certain *actions* to be successful (e.g. formulating a vision, role modeling, setting goals). Possessing the appropriate traits only makes it more likely that such actions will be taken and be successful. After summarizing the core leadership traits, we will discuss these important actions and the managerial implications.

The Evidence: Traits Do Matter

The evidence shows that traits do matter. Six traits on which leaders differ from nonleaders include drive, the desire to lead, honesty/integrity, self-confidence, cognitive ability, and knowledge of the business.[3] These traits are shown in Exhibit 1.

Drive

The first trait is labeled "drive," which is not to be confused with physical need deprivation. We use the term to refer to a constellation of traits and motives reflecting a high-effort level. Five aspects of drive include achievement motivation, ambition, energy, tenacity, and initiative.

Achievement. Leaders have a relatively high desire for achievement. The need for achievement is an important motive among effective leaders and even more important among successful entrepreneurs. High achievers obtain satisfaction from successfully completing challenging tasks, attaining standards of excellence, and developing better ways of doing things. To work their way up to the top of the organization, leaders must have a desire to complete challenging assignments and projects. This also allows the leader to gain technical expertise, both through education and work experience, and to initiate and follow through with organizational changes. . . .

Ambition. Leaders are very ambitious about their work and careers and have a desire to get ahead. To advance, leaders actively take steps to demonstrate their drive and determination. Ambition impels leaders to set hard, challenging goals for themselves and their organizations. Walt Disney, founder of Walt Disney Productions, had a "dogged determination to succeed," and C.E. Woolman of Delta Air Lines had "inexhaustible ambition."

Effective leaders are more ambitious than nonleaders. In

Source: Edited and reprinted with permission from *Academy of Management Executive* 5, 2 (1991), 48–60. Author affiliation may have changed since article was first published.

their 20-year study, psychologists Ann Howard and Douglas Bray found that among a sample of managers at AT&T, ambition, specifically the desire for advancement, was the strongest predictor of success twenty years later. . . .

Energy.   To sustain a high achievement drive and get ahead, leaders must have a lot of energy. Working long, intense work weeks (and many weekends) for many years requires an individual to have physical, mental, and emotional vitality.

Leaders are more likely than nonleaders to have a high level of energy and stamina and to be generally active, lively, and often restless. Leaders have been characterized as "electric, vigorous, active, full of life" as well as possessing the "physical vitality to maintain a steadily productive work pace."[7] Even at age 70, Sam Walton, founder of Wal-Mart discount stores, still attended Wal-Mart's Saturday morning meeting, a whoop-it up 7:30 a.m. sales pep rally for 300 managers.

The need for energy is even greater today than in the past, because more companies are expecting all employees, including executives, to spend more time on the road visiting the organization's other locations, customers, and suppliers.

Tenacity.   Leaders are better at overcoming obstacles than nonleaders. They have the "capacity to work with distant objects in view" and have a "degree of strength of will or perseverance."[8] Leaders must be tirelessly persistent in their activities and follow through with their programs. Most organizational change programs take several months to establish and can take many years before the benefits are seen. Leaders must have the drive to stick with these programs, and persistence is needed to ensure that changes are institutionalized. . . .

Persistence, of course, must be used intelligently. Dogged pursuit of an inappropriate strategy can ruin an organization. It is important to persist in the right things. But what are the right things? In today's business climate, they may include the following: satisfying the customer, growth, cost control, innovation, fast response time, and quality, or, in Tom Peters' terms, a constant striving to improve just about everything.

Initiative.   Effective leaders are proactive. They make choices and take action that leads to change instead of just reacting to events or waiting for things to happen; that is, they show a high level of initiative. . . .

Instead of sitting "idly by or [waiting] for fate to smile upon them," leaders need to "challenge the process."

Leaders are achievement-oriented, ambitious, energetic, tenacious, and proactive. These same qualities, however, may result in a manager who tries to accomplish everything alone, thereby failing to develop subordinate commitment and responsibility. Effective leaders must not only be full of drive and ambition, they must *want to lead others.*

Leadership Motivation

Studies show that leaders have a strong desire to lead. Leadership motivation involves the desire to influence and lead others and is often equated with the need for power. People with high leadership motivation think a lot about influencing other people, winning an argument, or being the greater authority. They prefer to be in a leadership rather than subordinate role. The willingness to assume responsibility, which seems to coincide with leadership motivation, is frequently found in leaders. . . .

Sears psychologist Jon Bentz describes successful Sears executives as those who have a "powerful competitive drive for a position of . . . authority . . . [and] the need to be recognized as men of influence."[11] Astronauts John Glenn and Frank Borman built political and business careers out of their early feats as space explorers, while other astronauts did not. Clearly, all astronauts possessed the same opportunities, but it was their personal makeup that caused Glenn and Borman to pursue their ambitions and take on leadership roles.

Psychologist Warren Bennis and colleague Burt Nanus state that power is a leader's currency, or the primary means through which the leader gets things done in the organization. A leader must want to gain the power to exercise influence over others. Also, power is an "expandable pie," not a fixed sum; effective leaders give power to others as a means of increasing their own power. Effective leaders do not see power as something that is competed for but rather as something that can be created and distributed to followers without detracting from their own power. . . .

A manager who was not as successful completed the sentence fragment "Taking orders . . ." with the ending "is easy, for it removes the danger of a bad decision."

Successful leaders must be willing to exercise power over subordinates, tell them what to do, and make appropriate use of positive and negative sanctions. Previous studies have shown inconsistent results regarding dominance as a leadership trait. According to Harvard psychologist David McClelland, this may be because there are two different types of dominance: a personalized power motive, or power lust, and a socialized power motive, or the desire to lead.[13]

Personalized Power Motive.   Although a need for power is desirable, the leader's effectiveness depends on what is behind it. A leader with a personalized power motive seeks power as an end in itself. These individuals have little self-control, are often impulsive, and focus on collecting symbols of personal prestige. Acquiring power solely for the sake of dominating others may be based on profound self-doubt. The personalized power motive is concerned with domination of others and leads to dependent, submissive followers.

Socialized Power Motive.   In contrast, a leader with a socialized power motive uses power as a means to achieve desired goals, or a vision. Its use is expressed as the ability to develop networks and coalitions, gain cooperation from others, resolve conflicts in a constructive manner, and use role modeling to influence others.

Individuals with a socialized power motive are more emotionally mature than those with a personalized power motive. They exercise power more for the benefit of the whole organization and are less likely to use it for manipulation. These leaders are also less defensive, more willing to take advice from experts, and have a longer-range view. They use their power to build up their organization and make it successful. The socialized power motive takes account of followers' needs and results in empowered, independent followers.

Honesty and Integrity

Honesty and integrity are virtues in all individuals, but have special significance for leaders. Without these qualities, leadership is undermined. Integrity is the correspondence between word and deed, and honesty refers to being truthful or nondeceitful. The two form the foundation of a trusting relationship between leader and followers.

In his comprehensive review of leadership, psychologist Bernard Bass found that student leaders were rated as more trustworthy and reliable in carrying out responsibilities than followers. Similarly, British organizational psychologists Charles Cox and Cary Cooper's "high flying" (successful) managers preferred to have an open style of management, where they truthfully informed workers about happenings in the company. Morgan McCall and Michael Lombardo of the Center for Creative Leadership found that managers who reached the top were more likely to follow the following formula: "I will do exactly what I say I will do when I say I will do it. If I change my mind, I will tell you well in advance so you will not be harmed by my actions."[14]

Successful leaders are open with their followers, but also discreet and do not violate confidences or carelessly divulge potentially harmful information. One subordinate in a study by Harvard's John Gabarro made the following remark about his new president: "He was so consistent in what he said and did, it was easy to trust him." Another subordinate remarked about an unsuccessful leader, "How can I rely on him if I can't count on him consistently?"[15]

Professors James Kouzes, Barry Posner, and W.H. Schmidt asked 1500 managers "What values do you look for and admire in your supervisors?" Integrity (being truthful and trustworthy, and having character and conviction) was the most frequently mentioned characteristic. Kouze and Posner conclude:

> Honesty is absolutely essential to leadership. After all, if we are willing to follow someone, whether it be into battle or into the boardroom, we first want to assure ourselves that the person is worthy of our trust. We want to know that he or she is being truthful, ethical, and principled. We want to be fully confident in the integrity of our leaders.

Effective leaders are credible, with excellent reputations, and high levels of integrity. The following description (from Gabarro's study) by one subordinate of his boss exemplifies the concept of integrity: "By integrity, I don't mean whether he'll rob a bank, or steal from the till. You don't work with people like that. It's whether you sense a person has some basic principles and is willing to stand by them."

Bennis and Nanus warn that today credibility is at a premium, especially since people are better informed, more cautious, and wary of authority and power. Leaders can gain trust by being predictable, consistent, and persistent and by making competent decisions. An honest leader may even be able to overcome lack of expertise, as a subordinate in Gabarro's study illustrates in the following description of his

superior: "I don't like a lot of the things he does, but he's basically honest. He's a genuine article and you'll forgive a lot of things because of that. That goes a long way in how much I trust him."

Self-Confidence

There are many reasons why a leader needs self-confidence. Being a leader is a very difficult job. A great deal of information must be gathered and processed. A constant series of problems must be solved and decisions made. Followers have to be convinced to pursue specific courses of action. Setbacks have to be overcome. Competing interests have to be satisfied. Risks have to be taken in the face of uncertainty. A person riddled with self-doubt would never be able to take the necessary actions nor command the respect of others.

Self-confidence plays an important role in decision making and in gaining others' trust. Obviously, if the leader is not sure of what decision to make, or expresses a high degree of doubt, then the followers are less likely to trust the leader and be committed to the vision.

Not only is the leaders' self-confidence important, but so is others' perception of it. Often, leaders engage in impression management to bolster their image of competence; by projecting self-confidence they arouse followers' self-confidence. Self-confident leaders are also more likely to be assertive and decisive, which gains others' confidence in the decision. This is crucial for effective implementation of the decision. Even when the decision turns out to be a poor one, the self-confident leader admits the mistake and uses it as a learning opportunity, often building trust in the process. . . .

Emotional Stability. Self-confidence helps effective leaders remain even-tempered. They do get excited, such as when delivering an emotionally charged pep talk, but generally do not become angry or enraged. For the most part, as long as the employee did his/her homework, leaders remain composed upon hearing that an employee made a costly mistake. For example, at PepsiCo, an employee who makes a mistake is "safe . . . as long as it's a calculated risk."

Emotional stability is especially important when resolving interpersonal conflicts and when representing the organization. A top executive who impulsively flies off the handle will not foster as much trust and teamwork as an executive who retains emotional control. Describing a superior, one employee in Gabarro's study stated, "He's impulsive and I'm never sure when he'll change signals on me."

Researchers at the Center for Creative Leadership found that leaders are more likely to "derail" if they lack emotional stability and composure. Leaders who derail are less able to handle pressure and more prone to moodiness, angry outbursts, and inconsistent behavior, which undermines their interpersonal relationships with subordinates, peers, and superiors. In contrast, they found the successful leaders to be calm, confident, and predictable during crisis.

Psychologically hardy, self-confident individuals consider stressful events interesting, as opportunities for development, and believe that they can influence the outcome. K. Labich in *Fortune* magazine argued that "By demonstrating grace under pressure, the best leaders inspire those around them to stay calm and act intelligently."[17]

Cognitive Ability

Leaders must gather, integrate, and interpret enormous amounts of information. These demands are greater than ever today because of rapid technological change. Thus, it is not surprising that leaders need to be intelligent enough to formulate suitable strategies, solve problems, and make correct decisions.

Leaders have often been characterized as being intelligent, but not necessarily brilliant and as being conceptually skilled. Kotter states that a "keen mind" (i.e., strong analytical ability, good judgement, and the capacity to think strategically and multidimensionally) is necessary for effective leadership, and that leadership effectiveness requires "above average intelligence," rather than genius.

An individual's intelligence and the perception of his or her intelligence are two highly related factors. Professors Lord, DeVader, and Alliger concluded that "intelligence is a key characteristic in predicting leadership perceptions."[18] Howard and Bray found that cognitive ability predicted managerial success twenty years later in their AT&T study. Effective managers have been shown to display greater ability to reason both inductively and deductively than ineffective managers.

Intelligence may be a trait that followers look for in a leader. If someone is going to lead, followers want that person to be more capable in *some* respects than they are. Therefore, the follower's perception of cognitive ability in a leader is a source of authority in the leadership relationship.

Knowledge of the Business

Effective leaders have a high degree of knowledge about the company, industry, and technical matters. For example, Jack Welsh, president of GE has a PhD in engineering; Geroge Hatsopolous of Thermo Electron Corporation, in the years preceding the OPEC boycott, had both the business knowledge of the impending need for energy-efficient appliances and the technical knowledge of thermodynamics to create more efficient gas furnaces. Technical expertise enables the leader to understand the concerns of subordinates regarding technical issues. Harvard Professor John Kotter argues that expertise is more important than formal education.

Effective leaders gather extensive information about the company and the industry. Most of the successful general managers studied by Harvard's Kotter spent their careers in the same industry, while less successful managers lacked industry-specific experiences. Although cognitive ability is needed to gain a thorough understanding of the business, formal education is not a requirement. Only forty percent of the business leaders studied by Bennis and Nanus had business degrees. In-depth knowledge of the organization and industry allows effective leaders to make well-informed decisions and to understand the implications of those decisions.

Other Traits

Charisma, creativity/originality, and flexibility are three traits with less clear-cut evidence of their importance to leadership.[19] Effective leaders may have charisma; however, this trait may only be important for political leaders. Effective leaders also may be more creative than nonleaders, but there is no consistent research demonstrating this. Flexibility or adaptiveness may be important traits for a leader in today's turbulent environment. Leaders must be able to make decisions and solve problems quickly and initiate and foster change.

There may be other important traits needed for effective leadership; however, we believe that the first six that we discussed are the core traits. . . .

Management Implications

Individuals can be *selected* either from outside the organization or from within non- or lower-managerial ranks based on their possession of traits that are less changeable or trainable. Cognitive ability (not to be confused with knowledge) is probably the least trainable of the six traits. Drive is fairly constant over time although it can change; it is observable in employees assuming they are given enough autonomy and responsibility to show what they can do. The desire to lead is more difficult to judge in new hires who may have had little opportunity for leadership early in life. It can be observed at lower levels of management and by observing people in assessment center exercises.

Two other traits can be developed through experience and *training*. Knowledge of the industry and technical knowledge come from formal training, job experience, and a mentally active approach toward new opportunities for learning. Planned job rotation can facilitate such growth. Self-confidence is both general and task specific. People differ in their general confidence in mastering life's challenges, but task-specific self-confidence comes from mastering the various skills that leadership requires as well as the technical and strategic challenges of the industry. Such confidence parallels the individual's growth in knowledge.

Honesty does not require skill building; it is a virtue one achieves or rejects by choice. Organizations should look with extreme skepticism at any employee who behaves dishonestly or lacks integrity, and should certainly not reward dishonesty in any form, especially not with a promotion. The key role models for honest behavior are those at the top. On this issue, organizations get what they model, not what they preach.

Conclusions

Regardless of whether leaders are born or made or some combination of both, it is unequivocally clear that *leaders are not like other people.* Leaders do not have to be great men or women by being intellectual geniuses or omniscient prophets to succeed, but they do need to have the "right stuff," and this stuff is not equally present in all people. Leadership is a demanding, unrelenting job with enormous pressures and grave responsibilities. It would be a profound disservice to leaders to suggest that they are ordinary people who happened to be in the right place at the right time. Maybe the place matters, but it takes a special kind of person to master the challenges of opportunity. Let us not only give credit, but also use the knowledge we have to select and train our future leaders effectively. We believe that in the realm of leadership (and in every other realm), the individual *does* matter.

Notes

This article is based on a chapter of a forthcoming book by Edwin A. Locke, Shelley A. Kirkpatrick, Jill K. Wheeler, Jodi Schneider, Kathryn Niles, Harold Goldstein, Kurt Welsh, & Dong-OK Chah, entitled *The Essence of Leadership*. We would like to thank Dr. Kathryn Bartol for her helpful comments on this manuscript.

[1] P. Slater and W.G. Bennis, "Democracy is Inevitable," *Harvard Business Review*, Sept-Oct, 1990, 170 and 171. For a summary of trait theories, see R.M. Stogdill's *Handbook of Leadership*, (New York: Free Press, 1974). For reviews and studies of leadership traits, see R.E. Boyatzis, *The Competent Manager* (New York: Wiley & Sons, 1982); C.J. Cox and C.L. Cooper, *High Flyers: An Anatomy of Managerial Success* (Oxford: Basil Blackwell); G.A. Yukl, *Leadership in Organizations* (Englewood Cliffs, NJ: Prentice Hall, 1989), Chapter 9.

[2] R.M. Stogdill, "Personal Factors Associated with Leadership: A Survey of the Literature," *Journal of Psychology*, 1948, *25*, 64.

[3] See the following sources for evidence and further information concerning each trait: 1) drive: B.M. Bass's *Handbook of Leadership* (New York: The Free Press, 1990); K.G. Smith and J.K. Harrison, "In Search of Excellent Leaders" (in W.D. Guth's *The Handbook of Strategy*, New York: Warren, Gorham, & Lamont, 1986). 2) desire to lead: V.J. Bentz, "The Sears Experience in the Investigation, Description, and Prediction of Executive Behavior," (In F.R. Wickert and D.E. McFarland's *Measuring Executive Effectiveness*, (New York: Appleton-Century-Crofts, 1967); J.B. Miner, "Twenty Years of Research on Role-Motivation Theory of Managerial Effectiveness," *Personnel Psychology*, 1978, *31*, 739–760. 3) honesty/integrity: Bass, op cit.; W.G. Bennis and B. Nanus, *Leaders: The Strategies for Taking Charge* (New York: Harper & Row, 1985); J.M. Kouzes and B.Z. Posner. *The Leadership Challenge: How to Get Things Done in Organizations* (San Francisco: Jossey-Bass); T. Peters, *Thriving on Chaos* (New York: Harper & Row, 1987); A. Rand, *For the New Intellectual* (New York: Signet, 1961). 4) self-confidence: Bass, op cit. and A. Bandura, *Social Foundations of Thought and Action: A Social Cognitive Theory*, (Englewood Cliffs, NJ: business: Bennis and Nanus, op. cit.; J.P. Prentice-Hall). Psychological hardiness is discussed by S.R. Maddi and S.C. Kobasa, *The Hardy Executive: Health under Stress* (Chicago: Dorsey Professional Books, 1984); M.W. McCall Jr. and M.M. Lombardo, *Off The Track: Why and How Successful Executives get Derailed* (Technical Report No. 21, Greensboro, NC: Center for Creative Leadership, 1983). 5) cognitive ability: R.G. Lord, C.L. DeVader, and G.M. Alliger, "A Meta-Analysis of the Relation between Personality Traits and Leadership Perceptions: An Application of Validity Generalization Procedures," *Journal of Applied Psychology*, 1986; *61*, 402–410; A. Howard and D.W. Bray, *Managerial Lives in Transition: Advancing Age and Changing Times* (New York: Guilford Press, 1988). 6) knowledge of the business: Bennis and Nanus, op. cit.; J.P. Kotter, *The General Managers* (New York: MacMillan); Smith and Harrison, op. cit. . . .

[7] From Kouzes and Posner, op. cit., pp. 122 and V.J. Bentz, op cit. The Sam Walton quote is from J. Huey, "Wal-Mart: Will it take over the world?," *Fortune*, January 30, 1989, 52–59.

[8] From Bass, op. cit. . . .

[11] From Bentz, op. cit. . . .

[13] The distinction between a personalized and a socialized power motive is made by D.C. McClelland, "N-achievement and entrepreneurship: A longitudinal study," Journal of Personality and Social Psychology, 1965, *1*, 389–392. These two power motives are discussed further by Kouzes and Posner, op. cit.

[14] From McCall and Lombardo, op cit.

[15] From Gabarro, op. cit.

[16] K.F. Girard examines Manor Care in "To the Manor Born," *Warfield's*, March, 1989, 68–75.

[17] From K. Labich, "The Seven Keys to Business Leadership," *Fortune*, October 24, 1988, 58–66.

[18] From Lord, DeVader, and Alliger, op. cit.

[19] For research on charisma, see Bass, op. cit. and R.J. House, W.D. Spangler, and J. Woycke, "Personality and charisma in the U.S. presidency: A psychological theory of leadership effectiveness (Wharton School, University of Pennsylvania, 1989, unpublished manuscript), on creativity/originality, see Howard and Bray, op. cit. and A. Zaleznik, *The Managerial Mystique* (New York: Harper and Row, 1989); on flexibility, see Smith and Harrison, op. cit.

[20] From Bennis and Nanus, op. cit.

[21] From J.A. Conger, *Charismatic Leadership: The Elusive Factor in Organizational Effectiveness* (San Francisco: Jossey-Bass, 1988).

[22] C. Manz and H.P. Sims, *Superleadership: Leading Others to Lead Themselves* (New York: Prentice Hall, 1989).

[23] See E.A. Locke and G.P. Latham. *A Theory of Goal Setting & Task Performance* (Englewood Cliffs, NJ: Prentice Hall, 1990).

[24] See Bandura, op. cit.

[25] See D.C. Hambrick, "The top management team: Keys to strategic success," *California Management Review*, 1987, *30*, 1–20.

Gender and Leadership Style: A Meta-Analysis

A. H. Eagly and B. T. Johnson
Purdue University

*I*n recent years many social scientists, management consultants, and other writers have addressed the topic of gender and leadership style. Some authors with extensive experience in organizations who write nontechnical books for management audiences and the general public have argued for the presence of sex differences in leadership style. For example, Loden (1985) maintained that there is a masculine mode of management characterized by qualities such as competitiveness, hierarchical authority, high control for the leader, and unemotional and analytic problem solving. Loden argued that women prefer and tend to behave in terms of an alternative feminine leadership model characterized by cooperativeness, collaboration of managers and subordinates, lower control for the leader, and problem solving based on intuition and empathy as well as rationality. Loden's writing echoes the androgynous manager theme developed earlier by Sargent (1981), who accepted the idea that women and men, including those who are managers in organizations, behave stereotypically to some extent. Sargent advocated that managers of each sex adopt "the best" of the other sex's qualities to become more effective, androgynous managers. In a somewhat different rendition of this sex-difference theme, Hennig and Jardin (1977) also acknowledged sex-differentiated managerial behavior, which they ascribed to personality traits acquired in early socialization, particularly through differing male and female resolutions of the Oedipus complex.

In contrast to these generalizations about gender-stereotypic leadership styles promulgated in books written primarily for practicing managers and the general public, social scientists have generally maintained that there are in fact no reliable differences in the ways that women and men lead. Although a few social scientists have acknowledged that there is some evidence for sex differences in leadership style among research participants who have not been selected for occupancy of leadership roles in natural settings (e.g., Brown, 1979; Hollander, 1985), most have agreed that women and men who occupy leadership roles in organizations do not differ (but see Shakeshaft, 1987, for a contrasting opinion). Illustrating this consensus among social scientists are the following representative statements summarizing research comparing the styles of female and male leaders: "The preponderance of available evidence is that no consistently clear pattern of differences can be discerned in the supervisory style of female as compared to male leaders" (Bass, 1981, p. 499); "Contrary to notions about sex specialization in leadership styles, women leaders appear to behave in similar fashion to their male colleagues" (Nieva & Gutek, 1981, p. 91); "There is as yet no research evidence that makes a case for sex differences in either leadership aptitude or style" (Kanter, 1977a, p. 199); "In general, comparative research indicates that there are few differences in the leadership styles of female and male designated leaders" (Bartol & Martin, 1986, p. 278).

Underlying this divergence in the opinions voiced in popular and social scientific writings is the fact that authors in these two camps have based their conclusions on quite different kinds of data. Authors such as Loden (1985) who have written books for managers and the general public based their conclusions primarily on their own experience in organizations as well as on the impressions they gleaned from interviews with practicing managers. Social scientists typically based their conclusions on more formal studies of managerial behavior in which data were gathered via questionnaires or behavioral observations and then analyzed quantitatively. In view of these contrasting methods, it is tempting for social scientists to dismiss the generalizations that are based on personal experience and interviews and to accept as valid only those conclusions that stem from more formal empirical research on leadership. However, the generalizations that social scientists appear to have accepted in this area, which stem from reviews of empirical research (e.g., Bartol & Martin, 1986), are quite vulnerable to error because of the relatively informal methods by which reviewers have drawn conclusions from the available research. With only one exception,[1] these reviews were traditional, narrative reviews and, therefore, were not based on any clear rules about how one derives conclusions from research findings. Moreover, none of the existing reviews was based on more than a small proportion of the available studies. For example, both Bartol and Martin (1986) and Dobbins and Platz (1986) based their generalizations on eight studies that compared the leadership styles of men and women, yet we located 162 studies pertaining only to the four types of leadership style

Source: Edited and reprinted with permission from *Psychological Bulletin* 108 (1990), 223–256. Copyright (1990) by the American Psychological Association. Author affiliation may have changed since article was first published.

This research was supported by National Science Foundation Grants BNS–8605256 and BNS–8807495. Preliminary reports of this research were presented at the Annual Meetings of the Eastern Psychological Association, April 1988; the Midwestern Psychological Association, April 1988; the International Congress of Psychology, September 1988; and the American Psychological Association, August 1989. A table showing the effect sizes and study characteristics for each study included in the meta-analysis is available from the first author.

we included in our meta-analysis (see *Method*). Moreover, prior reviewers did not state the criteria by which they selected their small samples of studies. As we became aware of these selection problems and of the severe underuse of available research on gender and leadership style, we decided that a thorough survey of this domain was long overdue. Our meta-analysis thus provides a systematic, quantitative integration of the available research in which the leadership styles of men and women were compared and statistical analyses were performed on the resulting data.

Theoretical Analysis of Sex Differences in Leadership Styles

Leaving aside the claims of both the social scientists and the management experts who have written about gender and leadership style, we face a topic of considerable complexity that we analyze from several perspectives. One of our perspectives takes into account existing knowledge about sex differences in social behaviors such as aggression, helping, and conformity as well as numerous nonverbal and communicative behaviors. Large numbers of laboratory and field studies have been performed on such behaviors, primarily by social psychologists, and in many of these studies female and male behavior has been compared. Quantitative reviews of this research have established the presence rather than the absence of overall sex differences (see overviews by Eagly, 1987; Eagly & Wood, in press; Hall, 1984). These differences, although typically not large, tend to be comparable in magnitude to most other findings reported in social psychological research. On the average, sex appears to be a variable that has neither especially impactful nor especially weak effects on social behavior and that produces findings consistent with laypeople's ideas about how the sexes differ (see Eagly, 1987).

Reasons to Expect the Absence of Sex Differences in Leadership Style. Despite the gender-stereotypic findings generally produced in studies of social behavior, similar results would not necessarily be obtained for leaders and managers because of important differences between leadership research and typical research in social psychology. In particular, the majority of leadership studies have been performed in organizations. In contrast, most social psychological research has been carried out in experimental laboratories and to a lesser extent in field settings not embedded within organizations (e.g., on street corners). In such environments, subjects interact with strangers on a short-term basis, and the constraints of organizational and familial roles are generally minimal or absent. Consequently, there is often considerable ambiguity about how one should behave, and people may react in terms of quite global and readily observable attributes of themselves and others (e.g., sex, age, race, and general physical appearance). In situations of this type, gender roles, which are rules about how one should behave as a male or female, may provide more guidance than they otherwise would and thus produce gender-stereotypic behavior.

Behavior may be less stereotypic when women and men who occupy the same managerial role are compared because these organizational leadership roles, which typically are paid jobs, usually provide fairly clear guidelines about the conduct of behavior. Managers become socialized into their roles in the early stages of their experience in an organization (see Feldman, 1976; Graen, 1976; Terborg, 1977; Wanous, 1977). In addition, male and female managers have presumably been selected by organizations (and have selected themselves into these roles) according to the same set of organizationally relevant criteria. further decreasing the likelihood that the men and women who occupy these roles differ substantially in their style. Thus, reasonable assumptions about socialization into leadership roles and selection for these roles suggest that male and female leaders *who occupy the same organizational role* should differ very little. Managers of both sexes are presumably more concerned about managing effectively than about representing sex-differentiated features of societal gender roles.

This argument that organizational roles should override gender roles is consistent with Kantor's (1977a) structural interpretation of organizational behavior. Kanter argued that apparent sex differences in the behavior of organizational leaders are in fact a product of the differing structural positions of the sexes within organizations. Because women are more often in positions of little power or opportunity for advancement, they behave in ways that reflect their lack of power. Kanter's reasoning thus suggests that women and men who are equivalent in terms of status and power would behave similarly, even though sex differences may appear to be substantial when women and men are compared without control of their organizational status.

Reasons to Expect the Presence of Sex Differences in Leadership Style. Despite these reasons for arguing that differences between female and male organizational leaders should be minimal, other perspectives suggest that sex differences may be common, especially in some types of leadership research. As our reasoning has already implied, the social structural rationale for the absence of differences between occupants of the same managerial role within organizations is fully consistent with the presence of differences in leadership studies that compare women and men in other circumstances. In the leadership literature, there are two major types of studies that did not examine organizational leaders—namely, laboratory experiments, usually conducted with college students, and assessment studies, which we defined as research assessing the styles of people who were not selected for occupancy of leadership positions. Because the social structural rationale for the absence of differences between women and men in the same organizational role is not relevant to studies of these two types, sex-differentiated leadership styles are likely to be prevalent in such research, just as gender-stereotypic behavior is commonly found in social psychological research more generally.

There are, in addition, several reasons to suggest that male and female organizational leaders, even those who occupy the same positions, may differ to some extent in their leadership style despite the structural forces for minimizing differences that we have already noted. One such reason acknowledges the possibility of ingrained sex differences in personality traits and behavioral tendencies, differences that are not nullified by organizational selection or socialization. For example, some psychologists have maintained that sex differences in adult social behavior are in part a product of biological influences such as the greater prenatal androgynization of males (e.g., Money & Ehrhardt, 1972). Other psychologists have emphasized the importance of childhood events that are different for the sexes such as experiences that occur in sex-segregated play groups in which girls and boys play in different styles and use different methods of influencing one another (Maccoby, 1988). Thus, it is possible that biological sex differences and sex-differentiated prior experiences cause men and women to be somewhat different kinds of people, even if they do occupy the same managerial role. It may not be possible to find men and women who are so nearly equivalent that trait-level differences disappear entirely, even though sex differences in the behavior of organizational leaders may be smaller than those in the general population. In particular, men and women may come to managerial roles with a somewhat different set of skills. Especially relevant is the evidence meta-analyses have provided for women's social skills: Women as a group, when compared with men as a group, can be described as friendly, pleasant, interested in other people, expressive, and socially sensitive (see Eagly, 1987; Hall, 1984). To the extent that such findings reflect ingrained sex differences that are not leveled by organizational selection or socialization, male and female managers may behave differently, despite structural forces toward sameness.

Another perspective suggesting that leader behavior may be somewhat sex differentiated in organizations postulates *gender-role spillover,* which is "a carryover into the workplace of gender-based expectations for behavior" (Gutek & Morasch, 1982, p. 58; see also Nieva & Gutek, 1981). The spillover concept suggests that gender roles may contaminate organizational roles to some extent and cause people to have different expectations for female and male managers. In support of this idea, Russell, Rush, and Herd (1988) found that university women described an effective female (vs. male) leader as exhibiting higher levels of both the interpersonally oriented and the task-oriented aspects of leadership (i.e., higher in consideration and initiation of structure, see discussion of these variables in next subsection).[2]

Consistent with the idea that gender roles spill over to organizational roles, several social scientists have claimed that female leaders and managers experience conflict between their gender role and their leadership role (see Bass, 1981; Bayes & Newton, 1978; Kruse & Wintermantel, 1986; O'Leary, 1974). This conflict arises for female leaders because the stereotype of manager and the normative expectations associated with being a good manager include more masculine than feminine qualities (see Powell, 1988). The idea that women are subjected to incompatible expectations from the managerial and the female role thus presumes that gender roles are important within organizations.

Another manifestation of the spillover of gender roles onto organizational roles is that people who hold positions in organizations tend to have negative attitudes about women occupying managerial roles. Reflecting the subordinate status of women in the society, numerous studies have shown that people are often reluctant to have a female supervisor and think that women are somewhat less qualified for leadership and that female managers would have negative effects on morale (see reviews by O'Leary, 1974; Riger & Galligan, 1980; Terborg, 1977). Because these attitudes and beliefs raise questions about women's competence, ability to lead, and potential for advancement, female managers often

face a less supportive environment than male managers. Sex differences in leadership style might result from this aspect of gender-role spillover as well as from the other aspects we have noted.

Finally, some of the fine-grained features of the structural interpretation of organizational behavior suggest other possible sources of sex differences in the behavior of organizational leaders. One such consideration is that, as Kanter (1977b) pointed out, women in managerial roles often have the status of *token* because of their rarity in such positions. Thus, female managers commonly are members of a numerically small minority, whereas their male counterparts are members of a majority group. As Kanter and others argued, token status increases one's visibility (Taylor, Fiske, Etcoff, & Ruderman, 1978) and can have a number of negative implications for how one is perceived and treated, especially when the token is a woman (Crocker & McGraw, 1984; Ott, 1989; Yoder & Sinnett, 1985). In addition, even those female and male leaders who occupy the same organizational role may differ systematically in seniority, salary, the availability of mentoring and informal collegial support, and other characteristics that convey some of the subtleties of organizational status. Women, especially as relative newcomers in many managerial roles, tend to have less status in these ways, and this difference may be reflected in their behavior.

In summary, ingrained sex differences in traits and behavioral tendencies, a spillover of gender roles onto organizational roles, and subtle differences in the structural position of women and men could cause leadership behavior to be somewhat sex-differentiated even when occupants of the same organizational role are compared. Therefore, some evidence of sex differences in leadership style in organizational studies would not be surprising. Nonetheless, our reasoning that organizational roles are more important than gender roles led us to predict that differences between men and women occupying the same leadership role in organizations would be smaller than differences between men and women observed in other types of leadership research, namely laboratory experiments and assessment studies.

Design of the Meta-Analysis

Types of Leadership Style.   The fact that investigators have examined many facets of leadership style (see Bass, 1981) requires that reviewers decide which facets to include and how to organize them into types. In examining this issue, we found that the majority of the studies had assessed the extent to which leaders or managers were concerned with two aspects of their work. The first of these aspects we termed *task accomplishment* (or, for brevity, task style)—that is, organizing activities to perform assigned tasks. The second aspect we termed *maintenance of interpersonal relationships* (or, for brevity, interpersonal style)—that is, tending to the morale and welfare of the people in the setting.

This distinction between task and interpersonal styles was first represented in leadership research by Bales (1950), who proposed two categories of leaders, those with an orientation to task accomplishment and those with a socioemotional orientation indicative of concern for morale and relationships among group members. This distinction was developed further in the Ohio State studies on leadership (e.g., Halpin,

1957; Halpin & Winer, 1957; Hemphill & Coons, 1957; Stogdill, 1963). In this research, task orientation, labeled *initiation of structure,* included behavior such as having subordinates follow rules and procedures, maintaining high standards for performance, and making leader and subordinate roles explicit. Interpersonal orientation, labeled *consideration,* included behavior such as helping and doing favors for subordinates, looking out for their welfare, explaining procedures, and being friendly and available. Task and interpersonal orientations are typically regarded as separate, relatively orthogonal dimensions (e.g., in the Leader Behavior Description Questionnaire [LBDQ] constructed by the Ohio State researchers; Halpin & Winer, 1957). Less commonly, these orientations are treated as two ends of a single continuum (e.g., in the Least Preferred Co-Worker [LPC] instruments; Fiedler, 1967).[3]

Task and interpersonal styles in leadership research are obviously relevant to gender because of the stereotypes people have about sex differences in these aspects of behavior (see Ashmore, Del Boca, & Wohlers, 1986; Eagly & Steffen, 1984). Men are believed to be more self-assertive and motivated to master their environment (e.g., more aggressive, independent, self-sufficient, forceful, dominant). In contrast, women are believed to be more selfless and concerned with others (e.g., more kind, helpful, understanding, warm, sympathetic, aware of others' feelings). In research on gender, these two orientations have been labeled *masculine* and *feminine, instrumental* and *expressive,* and *agentic* and *communal.* Although the task and interpersonal dimensions studied in leadership research are not as broad as these very general tendencies examined in gender stereotype research, the ideas are quite similar. Therefore, leadership research provides an excellent opportunity to determine whether the behavior of leaders is gender stereotypic.

The only other aspect of leadership style studied frequently enough to allow us to represent it in our meta-analysis is the extent to which leaders (a) behave democratically and allow subordinates to participate in decision making, or (b) behave autocratically and discourage subordinates from participating in decision making.[4] The dimension of *democratic* versus *autocratic* leadership (or participative vs. *directive* leadership) follows from early experimental studies of leadership style (e.g., Lewin & Lippitt, 1938) and has been developed since that time by a number of researchers (e.g., Likert, 1961; Vroom & Yetton, 1973). Although democratic versus autocratic style is a different (and narrower) aspect of leader behavior than task-oriented and interpersonally oriented styles (see Bass, 1981), the democratic–autocratic dimension also relates to gender stereotypes, because one component of the agentic or instrumental aspect of these stereotypes is that men are relatively dominant and controlling (i.e., more autocratic and directive than women).

Methods of Assessing Leadership Style.   The diversity of the methods that have been used to assess style complicates the task of integrating research in this area. Moreover, a substantial methodological literature criticizes and compares these measures (see Bass, 1981). Because the methodological issues that have been raised remain largely unresolved by leadership researchers, we did not attempt to settle these issues in order to base our meta-analytic generalizations on only those measures that we or other investigators might regard as most valid. Instead, we included all measures that researchers regarded as assessing task-oriented and interpersonally oriented styles or autocratic versus democratic style. We coded our studies on a number of these measures' features, many of which may be regarded as having implications for the quality of the measures. For example, measures differed in how directly or indirectly they assessed leadership style; the most direct measures were based on observers' coding of ongoing leadership behavior, and the most indirect measures were based on leaders' responses to questionnaire measures of attitudes or personality. Representing such features in our coding scheme (see *Method*) allowed us to determine whether they covaried with sex differences in leadership style.

Congeniality of Leadership Roles for Men and Women. When we thought about gender in relation to the available studies of leadership style, we were struck by the variation in the extent to which the leadership roles investigated in this research (e.g., elementary school principal, nursing supervisor, military officer) would be perceived as congenial mainly for women or men. For leadership roles that are typically regarded as especially suitable for women, negative attitudes toward female leaders presumably would not be prevalent, nor would conflict between the female and the leader role be an issue. Presumably women would be under less pressure to adopt male-stereotypic styles of leadership in such positions.

To enable us to take account of the gender congeniality of leadership roles, we conducted a questionnaire study to obtain judgments of each role and analyzed these judgments to estimate the extent to which women or men were more interested in each role and believed themselves more competent to perform it. In addition, because people associate task-oriented qualities with men and interpersonally oriented qualities with women, we also determined the extent to which each role was judged to require each set of these gender-stereotypic qualities. These features of our meta-analysis allowed us to determine whether the ascription of gender-stereotypic qualities to leadership roles related to sex differences in the styles by which people carry out these roles.

Predictions for Meta-Analysis.   As we have already stated, our major prediction is that gender-stereotypic sex differences in leadership style are less pronounced in organizational studies comparing occupants of the same managerial role than in leadership studies of other types. Beyond this prediction, our purposes as reviewers are primarily descriptive and exploratory, even though other predictions might follow from the issues we have discussed. For example, if, as we suggested, female managers often face a less supportive environment than do male managers, these women might strive so hard to overcome antifemale prejudices that they behave counterstereotypically as a result. Additional complexities enter if we reason that ratings of leaders' behavior could produce findings that are more stereotypic than those produced by measures grounded more firmly in behavior. Rather than set forth a series of speculative hypotheses that take these and other considerations into account, we prefer to present our review and to discuss such issues as they become relevant to interpreting our meta-analytic findings. . . .

Discussion

Interpersonal and Task Styles

Our major hypothesis was that stereotypic sex differences would be less pronounced in organizational studies than in assessment or laboratory studies. Indeed, this hypothesis was confirmed for both interpersonal and task styles. These findings support our arguments that the criteria organizations use for selecting managers and the forces they maintain for socializing managers into their roles minimize tendencies for the sexes to lead or manage in a stereotypic manner. Yet these data also suggest that people not selected or trained for leadership roles do manifest stereotypic leadership behavior when placed in these roles, as shown by the data from the assessment and the laboratory studies. Moreover, our claim that selection criteria lessen sex differences is strengthened by the finding that those few laboratory leaders who gained their positions through emergence did not manifest the stereotypic styles of laboratory leaders who were appointed. Evidently sex differences were leveled even by the implicit leader selection criteria of initially leaderless groups.

When we ignored whether the sex comparisons were from organizational, assessment, or laboratory studies (see Table 4), sex differences in interpersonal and task styles were quite small, with overall trends toward women being more concerned about both maintenance of interpersonal relationships and task accomplishment. In view of these trends, it is not surprising that measures placing interpersonal and task orientation on the ends of a single dimension produced no sex difference in any of the overall summaries. On such bipolar measures, the stereotypic interpersonal sex difference and the counterstereotypic task difference would cancel one another, resulting in no difference.

Given the variety of settings, roles, and measures encountered in this research, the sex comparisons for the task and interpersonal styles were expected to be inconsistent across the studies. Yet the removal of relatively small numbers of the effect sizes (10% to 13%) produced homogeneous sets of effect sizes consistent with description in terms of single means. This aspect of the findings lends some confidence to our statements that if we take the entire research literature into account, women's leadership styles emphasize both interpersonal relations and task accomplishment to a slightly greater extent than men's styles.

Democratic versus Autocratic Style

The strongest evidence we obtained for a sex difference in leadership style occurred on the tendency for women to adopt a more democratic or participative style and for men to adopt a more autocratic or directive style. Moreover, this sex difference did *not* become smaller in the organizational studies, as did the differences in the interpersonal and task styles. Although the overall mean weighted effect size ($d_+ = 0.22$) was not large, the mean became larger once outliers were removed ($d_+ = 0.27$), and 92% of the available comparisons went in the direction of more democratic behavior from women than men. Despite this impressive consistency in the direction of the sex difference, the effect sizes themselves were quite heterogeneous, requiring the removal of 22% to obtain a set that did not reject the hypothesis of homogeneity.

Yet substantial inconsistency across the studies is not unexpected for this type of style in view of the tendency for investigators to construct unique measures and not to rely on standard instruments, as did most investigators of the other types of leadership style that we reviewed.

Our interpretation of the sex difference in the extent to which leaders behave democratically versus autocratically is necessarily speculative, but follows from some of the considerations that we presented early in this article (see *Reasons to Expect the Presence of Sex Differences in Leadership Style*). We thus argued that women and men recruited into leadership roles in organizations may not be equivalent in personality and behavioral tendencies, even though they satisfy the same selection criteria. In particular, we noted that women's social skills might enable them to perform managerial roles differently than men. Interpersonal behavior that is skillful (e.g., in terms of understanding others' feelings and intentions) should facilitate a managerial style that is democratic and participative. Making decisions in a collaborative style requires not only the soliciting of suggestions from one's peers and subordinates, but also the preservation of good relationships with them when evaluating and perhaps rejecting their ideas. The give-and-take of collaborative decision making introduces interpersonal complexity not encountered by leaders who behave in an autocratic or directive manner. This interpretation is supported by research showing that teachers who lacked social skills, as indexed by their relative inability to decode nonverbal cues, had more autocratic attitudes and were generally more dogmatic (Rosenthal, Hall, DiMatteo, Rogers, & Archer, 1979).

Another perspective on the democratic–autocratic sex difference acknowledges the attitudinal bias against female leaders that we considered in the beginning of the article. The skepticism that many people have expressed concerning women's capabilities in managerial and leadership roles may be exacerbated by any tendency for women in these roles to take charge in an especially authoritative manner. Placating subordinates and peers so that they accept a woman's leadership may to some extent require that she give them input into her decisions and allow some degree of control over these decisions. Moreover, to the extent that women leaders have internalized to some degree the culture's reservations about their capability for leadership, they may gain confidence as leaders by making collaborative decisions that they can determine are in line with their associates' expectations. Thus, proceeding in a participative and collaborative mode may enable many female leaders to win acceptance from others, gain self-confidence, and thereby be effective. Because men are not so constrained by attitudinal bias, they are freer to lead in an autocratic and nonparticipative manner should they so desire.[20]

The Impact of Gender Congeniality of Leadership Roles and Sex Distribution of Role Occupants

Our findings suggested that leaders of each sex emphasized task accomplishment when they were in a leadership role regarded as congruent with their gender. Thus, only the sex differences in task style were significantly correlated with the tendency for the leadership roles to be regarded as more congenial for men or women, as indexed by our questionnaire respondents' judgments (see Table 6). Male leaders tended to be more task oriented than female leaders to the extent that a leadership role was more congenial to men; female leaders tended to be more task oriented than male leaders to the extent that a leadership role was more congenial to women. Furthermore, women tended to be more task oriented than men in leadership roles that are feminine in the sense that our respondents judged they require considerable interpersonal ability.[21]

These findings suggest that being out of role in gender-relevant terms has its costs for leaders in terms of some decline in their tendency to organize activities to accomplish relevant tasks. Because our meta-analytic data are not informative concerning the mediation of these effects, these provocative findings should be explored in primary research. Perhaps people who are out of role lack (or are perceived to lack) the skills necessary to organize the task-relevant aspects of their environment. Out-of-role leaders may be somewhat deficient in the knowledge and authority required to organize people and resources to accomplish task-relevant goals.

The extent to which leadership roles were male dominated numerically also related to sex differences in leadership style. Specifically, the tendencies for female leaders to be more interpersonally oriented and more democratic than male leaders weakened to the extent that a role was male dominated. Thus, when women were quite rare in leadership roles and therefore tended to have the status of token in organizations or groups, they abandoned stereotypically feminine styles characterized by concern for the morale and welfare of people in the work setting and consideration of these people's views when making decisions. These findings suggest that women may tend to lose authority if they adopt distinctively feminine styles of leadership in extremely male-dominated roles. Women who survive in such roles probably have to adopt the styles typical of male role occupants.

Conclusion

The view, widely accepted by social scientists expert on leadership, that women and men lead in the same way should be very substantially revised. Similarly, the view, proclaimed in some popular books on management, that female and male leaders have distinctive, gender-stereotypic styles also requires revision. Our quantitative review has established a more complex set of findings. Although these findings require further scrutiny before they should be taken as definitive, the agreement of these findings with our role theory framework substantiates our interpretation of them. Thus, consistent with research on sex differences in numerous social behaviors (Eagly, 1987; Hall, 1984), we have established that leadership style findings generated in experimental settings tend to be gender stereotypic. Indeed, these findings concur with the generalizations of those narrative reviewers who noted that male and female leaders often differ in laboratory experiments (Brown, 1979; Hollander, 1985). In such settings, people interact as strangers without the constraints of long-term role relationships. Gender roles are moderately important influences on behavior in such contexts and tend to produce gender-stereotypic behavior (see Eagly, 1987). In addition, somewhat smaller stereotypic sex differences were obtained in assessment studies, in which people not selected for leadership responded to instruments assessing their lead-

ership styles. Because respondents not under the constraints of managerial roles completed questionnaires in these studies, some tendency for leadership styles to appear stereotypic was expected from the perspective of our social role framework.

When social behavior is regulated by other, less diffuse social roles, as it is in organizational settings, behavior should primarily reflect the influence of these other roles and therefore lose much of its gender-stereotypic character. Indeed, the findings of this meta-analysis for interpersonal and task styles support this logic. Nonetheless, women's leadership styles were more democratic than men's even in organizational settings. This sex difference may reflect underlying differences in female and male personality or skills (e.g., women's superior social skills) or subtle differences in the status of women and men who occupy the same organizational role. Deciding among the various causes that we have discussed would require primary research targeted to this issue.

The magnitude of the aggregate effect sizes we obtained in this meta-analysis deserves comment. When interpreting effect sizes, reviewers should take the methods of the studies into account, and, as Glass, McGaw, and Smith (1981) argued, they should avoid applying numerical guidelines to identify effect sizes as small or large. One feature of research on leadership style that is especially relevant to interpreting the magnitude of our aggregate effect sizes is that investigators face many barriers to achieving well-controlled studies. In organizational studies, the environments in which managers carry out their roles are quite diverse, even within a single organization. Because managers' leadership styles are evaluated either by themselves or by their associates, the various managers in a study are not necessarily evaluated by the same standard. Although more control of environmental influences can be achieved in laboratory studies of leadership (e.g., all leaders can be observed in a similar social setting), even these studies are relatively uncontrolled because each leader interacts with a unique group of followers. Counterbalancing the greater control of environmental factors in laboratory than organizational studies is the less rigorous selection of research participants for laboratory research and the resulting greater variability of leadership style within each sex. In general, uncontrolled variability in both organizational and laboratory studies of leadership would inflate the standard deviations that are the denominators of the effect sizes and thereby decrease the magnitude of these effect sizes. As a consequence, neither sex nor other variables would ordinarily produce large effect sizes in studies of leadership style. Therefore, we believe that effect sizes of the magnitude we obtained are considerably more consequential than effect sizes of the same magnitude obtained in more controlled forms of research.

Our review has not considered the extent to which the sex differences in leadership style that we have documented might produce differences in the effectiveness of leaders. Whether men or women are more effective leaders as a consequence of their differing styles is a complex question that could be addressed meta-analytically only by taking measures of group and organizational outcomes into account along with measures of leadership style. Because experts on leader effectiveness ordinarily maintain that the effectiveness of leadership styles is contingent on features of the group or organizational environment (e.g., Fiedler, 1967; Vroom & Yetton, 1973), we are unwilling to argue that women's relatively democratic and participative style is either an advantage or disadvantage. No doubt a relatively democratic style enhances a leader's effectiveness under some circumstances.[22] Nonetheless, we note that in recent years many management and organizational consultants have criticized traditional management practices for what they believe are overly hierarchical and rigidly bureaucratic forms (Foy, 1980; Heller & Van Til, 1986; Kanter, 1983; Naisbett, 1982; Ouchi, 1981; Peters & Waterman, 1982). Moreover, it is consistent with many feminist theorists' descriptions of hierarchy and domination (e.g., Elshtain, 1981; Miller, 1976) to argue that employment would be less alienating if forms of interaction in the workplace were less hierarchical and instead characterized by cooperation and collaboration between collegial groups of coworkers. Indeed, both consultants and feminists have advocated organizational change toward the more democratic and participative leadership styles that our meta-analysis suggests are more prevalent among women then men.

Notes

[1] The one available quantitative review of sex differences in leadership style (Dobbins & Platz, 1986) unfortunately included studies with designs not suited for examining these differences. These inappropriate studies investigated bias in subjects' perceptions of leaders by equalizing the behavior of male and female leaders and varying only the leader's sex (Butterfield & Powell, 1981; Lee & Alvares, 1977). Because equivalence of male and female behavior was ensured in these studies, they cannot be regarded as assessing sex differences in leadership style.

[2] Whereas the belief that effective female managers are especially concerned about relationships may reflect stereotypic beliefs about women in general, the belief that effective female managers are especially concerned about task accomplishment may reflect a more complex theory about women having to perform extremely well to succeed as managers.

[3] Although the Least Preferred Co-Worker Scale has been given a variety of interpretations, the view that low-LPC people are task oriented and high-LPC people are relationship oriented seems to be the most widely accepted of these interpretations (see Rice, 1978).

[4] Although Bass (1981) distinguished between (a) democratic versus autocratic leadership and (b) participative versus directive leadership, we treated these measures as a single class because we found this distinction difficult to maintain when categorizing measures. We refer to this single class as *democratic versus autocratic* style. Researchers have treated this style as a single, bipolar dimension because democratic and autocratic styles presumably are incompatible. In contrast, interpersonal and task styles apparently are not incompatible, as suggested by the preference of most researchers for treating these styles as separate, relatively orthogonal dimensions.

[20] A subsequent meta-analysis by Eagly, Makhijani, and Klonsky (1990) showed that subjects evaluate autocratic behavior by female leaders more negatively than they evaluate the equivalent behavior by male leaders. An additional consideration in interpreting the democratic–autocratic sex difference is that measures of this type were based primarily on leaders' self-reports (see Table 1), and, at least for task and interpersonal styles, leaders' self-reports were more stereotypic than subordinates' reports on leaders (see *Results*). Thus, it is possible that the tendency for women to be more democratic than men was exaggerated somewhat by the reliance on leaders' self-reports in these studies. Yet, because the sex comparisons for the democratic versus autocratic style were more stereotypic than the subset of sex comparisons for the interpersonal and task styles that were based on self-reports, it is very unlikely that this methodological feature of the democratic–autocratic studies fully accounts for the sex difference in this type of style.

[21] We explored whether a tendency for laboratory leadership roles to be more congenial for men might have contributed to the more stereotypic task styles found in laboratory (vs. organizational) studies (see Table 4). Indeed, our questionnaire respondents judged the laboratory (vs. organizational) roles as somewhat more congenial to men on the measures of sex differences in competence and interest and on the measure of stereotypic sex differences in interest ($ps < .05$ or smaller). In addition, the laboratory roles were judged to require less interpersonal ability than organizational roles but, contrary to the idea that the laboratory roles were relatively masculine, they were also judged to require less task ability ($ps < .001$). Thus, there was some degree of confounding between the type of study and the gender congeniality of the roles. Nonetheless, the significant relations between the congeniality measures and sex differences in task style reported in Table 6 remained significant when examined within the set of organizational studies.

[22] Consistent with the position that effectiveness of leadership styles depends on a group's task and other considerations, Wood (1987) argued, based on her meta-analysis of sex differences in group performance, that women's distinctive style of social interaction facilitated group performance at tasks requiring positive social activities such as cooperation but lacked this facilitative effect for other types of tasks.

References

Alpren, M. (1954). The development and validation of an instrument used to ascertain a school principal's pattern of behavior (Doctoral dissertation, University of Florida). *Dissertation Abstracts International, 33,* 1579A.

Arcy, J. A. B. (1980). Self-perceptions of leader behavior of male and female elementary school principals in selected school districts in the midwest United States (Doctoral dissertation, Iowa State University, 1979). *Dissertation Abstracts International, 40,* 3638A.

Ashmore, R. D., Del Boca, F. K., & Wohlers, A. J. (1986). Gender stereotypes. In R. D. Ashmore & F.K. Del Boca (Eds.), *The social psychology of female-male relations: A critical analysis of central concepts* (pp. 69–119). Orlando, FL: Academic Press.

Bales, R. F. (1950). *Interaction process analysis: A method for the study of small groups.* Reading, MA: Addison-Wesley.

Barone, F. J. (1982). A comparative study of Theory X–Theory Y attitudes among managers and OD agents. *Dissertation Abstracts International, 42,* 4260A. (University Microfilms No. 82-07, 156)

Bartol, K. M., & Martin, D. C. (1986). Women and men in task groups. In R. D. Ashmore & F. K. Del Boca (Eds.), *The social psychology of female-male relations: A critical analyses of central concepts* (pp. 259–310). Orlando, FL: Academic Press.

Bass, B. M. (1981). *Stodgill's handbook of leadership: A survey of theory and research* (rev. ed.). New York: Free Press.

Baugher, S. L. (1983). Sex-typed characteristics and leadership dimensions of vocational education administrators in a midwest region of the United States (Doctoral dissertation, University of Missouri–Columbia, 1982). *Dissertation Abstracts International, 44,* 22A.

Bayes, M., & Newton, P. M. (1978). Women in authority: A sociopsychological analysis. *Journal of Applied Behavioral Science, 14,* 7–20.

Birdsall, P. (1980). A comparative analysis of male and female managerial communication style in two organizations. *Journal of Vocational Behavior, 16,* 183–196.

Blake, R. R., & Mouton, J. S. (1964). *The managerial grid.* Houston, TX: Gulf.

Blake, R. R., & Mouton, J. S. (1978). *The new managerial grid.* Houston, TX: Gulf.

Brown, S. M. (1979). Male versus female leaders: A comparison of empirical studies. *Sex Roles, 5,* 595–611.

Butterfield, D. A., & Powell, G. N. (1981). Effect of group performance, leader sex, and rater sex on ratings of leader behavior. *Organizational Behavior and Human Performance, 28,* 129–141.

Carli, L. L. (1989). Gender differences in interaction style and influence. *Journal of Personality and Social Psychology, 56,* 565–576.

Coleman, D. G. (1979). *Barnard's effectiveness and efficiency applied to a leader style model.* Unpublished manuscript, Northeast Missouri State University, Kirksville, MO.

Crocker, J., & McGraw, K. M. (1984). What's good for the goose is not good for the gander: Solo status as an obstacle to occupational achievement for males and females. *American Behavioral Scientist, 27,* 357–369.

Crudge, J. (1983). The effect of leadership styles on the rehabilitation training of student-workers (Doctoral dissertation, United States International University, 1982). *Dissertation Abstracts International, 43,* 3300A.

Dobbins, G. H. (1986). Equity vs. equality: Sex differences in leadership. *Sex Roles, 15,* 513–525.

Dobbins, G. H., Pence, E. C., Orban, J. A., & Sgro, J. A. (1983). The effects of sex of the leader and sex of the subordinate on the use of organizational control policy. *Organizational Behavior and Human Performance, 32,* 325–343.

Dobbins, G. H., & Platz, S. J. (1986). Sex differences in leadership: How real are they? *Academy of Management Review, 11,* 118–127.

Eagly, A. H. (1987). *Sex differences in social behavior: A social-role interpretation.* Hillsdale, NJ: Erlbaum.

Eagly, A. H., & Carli, L. L. (1981). Sex of researchers and sex-typed communications as determinants of sex differences in influence-ability: A meta-analysis of social influence studies. *Psychological Bulletin, 90,* 1–20.

Eagly, A. H., Makhijani, M. G., & Klonsky, B. G. (1990). *Gender and the evaluation of leaders: A meta-analysis.* Manuscript submitted for publication.

Eagly, A. H., & Steffen, V. J. (1984). Gender stereotypes stem from the distribution of women and men into social roles. *Journal of Personality and Social Psychology, 46,* 735–754.

Eagly, A. H., & Wood, W. (in press). Explaining sex differences in social behavior: A meta-analytic perspective. *Personality and Social Psychology Bulletin.*

Elshtain, J. (1981). *Public man, private woman: Women in social and political thought.* Princeton, NJ: Princeton University Press.

Feldman, D. C. (1976). A contingency theory of socialization. *Administrative Science Quarterly, 21,* 433–452.

Fiedler, F. E. (1967). *A theory of leadership effectiveness.* New York: McGraw-Hill.

Fleishman, E. A. (1953). The management of leadership attitudes in industry. *Journal of Applied Psychology, 36,* 153–158.

Fleishman, E. A. (1957). The Leadership Opinion Questionnaire. In R. M. Stogdill & A. E. Coons (Eds.), *Leader behavior: Its description and measurement* (pp. 120–133). Columbus, OH: Bureau of Business Research, Ohio State University.

Fleishman, E. A. (1960). *Manual for the Leadership Opinion Questionnaire.* Chicago: Science Research Associates.

Fleishman, E. A. (1970). *Manual for the Supervisory Behavior Description Questionnaire.* Washington, DC: American Institutes for Research.

Foy, N. (1980). *The yin and yang of organizations.* New York: Morrow.

Ghiselli, E. E. (1964). *Theory of psychological measurement.* New York: McGraw-Hill.

Glass, G. V., McGaw, B., & Smith, M. L. (1981). *Meta-analysis in social research.* Beverly Hills, CA: Sage.

Graen, G. (1976). Role-making processes within complex organizations. In M. D. Dunnette (Ed.), *Handbook of industrial and organizational psychology* (pp. 1201–1245). Chicago: Rand McNally.

Grobman, H., & Hines, V. A. (1956). What makes a good principal? *National Association of Secondary School Principals Bulletin, 40,* 5–16.

Gupta, N., Jenkins, G. D., Jr., & Beehr, T. A. (1983). Employee gender, gender similarity, and supervisor-subordinate cross-evaluations. *Psychology of Women Quarterly, 8,* 174–184.

Gustafson, L. C. (1982). The leadership role of the public elementary school media librarian as perceived by the principal and its relationship to the factors of the sex, educational background, and the work experience of the media librarian (Doctoral dissertation, University of Maryland). *Dissertation Abstracts International, 43,* 2206A.

Gutek, B. A., & Morasch, B. (1982). Sex-ratios, sex-role spillover, and sexual harassment of women at work. *Journal of Social Issues, 38,* 55–74.

Hall, A. H. (1983). The influence of a personal planning workshop on attitudes toward managerial style (Doctoral dissertation, University of Maryland, 1983). *Dissertation Abstracts International, 44,* 2953A.

Hall, J. A. (1984). *Nonverbal sex differences: Communication accuracy and expressive style.* Baltimore, MD: Johns Hopkins University Press.

Halpin, A. W. (1957). *Manual for the Leader Behavior Description Questionnaire.* Columbus, OH: Bureau of Business Research, Ohio State University.

Halpin, A. W. (1966). *Theory and research in administration.* New York: Macmillan.

Halpin, A. W., & Winer, B. J. (1957). A factorial study of the leader behavior descriptions. In R. M. Stogdill & A. E. Coons (Eds.), *Leader behavior: Its description and measurement* (pp. 39–51). Columbus, OH: Bureau of Business Research, Ohio State University.

Hedges, L. V. (1981). Distribution theory for Glass's estimator of effect size and related estimators. *Journal of Educational Statistics, 6,* 107–128.

Hedges, L. V. (1982a). Fitting categorical models to effect sizes from a series of experiments. *Journal of Educational Statistics, 7,* 119–137.

Hedges, L. V. (1982b). Fitting continuous models to effect size data. *Journal of Educational Statistics, 7,* 245–270.

Hedges, L. V. (1987). How hard is hard science, how soft is soft science? The empirical cumulativeness of research. *American Psychologist, 42,* 443–455.

Hedges, L. V., & Becker, B. J. (1986). Statistical methods in the meta-analysis of research on gender differences. In J. S. Hyde & M. C. Linn (Eds.), *The psychology of gender: Advances through meta-analysis* (pp. 14–50). Baltimore, MD: Johns Hopkins University Press.

Hedges, L. V., & Olkin, I. (1985). *Statistical methods for meta-analysis.* Orlando, FL: Academic Press.

Heft, M., & Deni, R. (1984). Altering preferences for leadership style of men and women undergraduate residence advisors through leadership training. *Psychological Reports, 54,* 463–466.

Heller, T., & Van Til, J. (1986). Leadership and followership: Some summary propositions. In T. Heller, J. Van Til, & L. A. Zurcher (Eds.), *Contemporary studies in applied behavioral science: Vol. 4. Leaders and followers: Challenges for the future* (pp. 251–263). Greenwich, CT: JAI Press.

Hemphill, J. K., & Coons, A. E. (1957). Development of the Leader Behavior Description Questionnaire. In R. M. Stogdill & A. E. Coons (Eds.), *Leader behavior: Its description and measurement* (pp. 6–38). Columbus, OH: Bureau of Business Research, Ohio State University.

Hennig, M., & Jardin, A. (1977). *The managerial woman.* New York: Anchor Press.

Hersey, P., & Blanchard, K. H. (1977). *Management of organizational behavior: Utilizing human resources* (3rd ed.). Englewood Cliffs, NJ: Prentice-Hall.

Hersey, P., & Blanchard, K. H. (1982). *Management of organizational behavior: Utilizing human resources* (4th ed.). Englewood Cliffs, NJ: Prentice-Hall.

Hollander, E. P. (1985). Leadership and power. In G. Lindzey & E. Aronson (Eds.), *Handbook of social psychology* (3rd ed., Vol. 2, pp. 485–537). New York: Random House.

Hughes, H., Jr., Copeland, D. R., Ford, L. H., & Heidt, E. A. (1983). *Leadership and management education and training (LMET) course requirements for recruit company and "A" school instructors* (Tech. Rep. No. 154, Report No. AD-A137306). Orlando, FL: Department of the Navy.

Hurst, A. G., Stein, K. B., Korchin, S. J., & Soskin, W. F. (1978). Leadership style determinants of cohesiveness in adolescent groups. *International Journal of Group Psychotherapy, 28,* 263–277.

Jacoby, J., & Terborg, J. R. (1975). *Managerial Philosophies Scale.* Conroe, TX: Teleometrics International.

Kanter, R. M. (1977a). *Men and women of the corporation.* New York: Basic Books.

Kanter, R. M. (1977b). Some effects of proportions on group life: Skewed sex ratios and responses to token women. *American Journal of Sociology, 82,* 965–990.

Kanter, R. M. (1983). *The change masters: Innovations for productivity in the American corporation.* New York: Simon and Schuster.

Koberg, C. S. (1985). Sex and situational influences on the use of power: A follow-up study. *Sex Roles, 13,* 625–639.

Kruse, L., & Wintermantel, M. (1986). Leadership Ms.-qualified: I. The gender bias in everyday and scientific thinking. In C. F. Graumann & S. Moscovici (Eds.), *Changing conceptions of leadership* (pp. 171–197). New York: Springer-Verlag.

Lanning, G. E., Jr. (1982). A study of relationships and differences between management styles and staff morale as perceived by personnel in the colleges of the Ventura County community district. *Dissertation Abstracts International, 43,* 996A. (University Microfilms No. 82-20, 739).

Lee, D. M., & Alvares, K. M. (1977). Effects of sex on descriptions and evaluations of supervisory behavior in a simulated industrial setting. *Journal of Applied Psychology, 62,* 405–410.

Lewin, K., & Lippitt, R. (1938). An experimental approach to the study of autocracy and democracy: A preliminary note. *Sociometry, 1,* 292–300.

Likert, R. (1961). *New patterns of management.* New York: McGraw-Hill.

Loden, M. (1985). *Feminine leadership or how to succeed in business without being one of the boys.* New York: Times Books.

Maccoby, E. E. (1988). Gender as a social category. *Developmental Psychology, 24,* 755–765.

Marnani, E. B. (1982). Comparison of preferred leadership styles, potential leadership effectiveness, and managerial attitudes among black and white, female and male management students (Doctoral dissertation, United States International University, 1981). *Dissertation Abstracts International, 43,* 1271A.

Martinez, M. R. (1982). A comparative study on the relationship of self-perceptions of leadership styles between Chicano and Anglo teachers (Doctoral dissertation, Bowling Green State University). *Dissertation Abstracts International, 43,* 766A.

McGregor, D. (1960). *The human side of enterprise.* New York: McGraw-Hill.

McNemar, Q. (1962). *Psychological statistics* (3rd ed.). New York: Wiley.

Miller, J. B. (1976). *Toward a new psychology of women.* Boston: Beacon Press.

Money, J., & Ehrhardt, A. A. (1972). *Man & woman, boy & girl.* Baltimore, MD: Johns Hopkins University Press.

Moore, S. F., Shaffer, L., Goodsell, D. A., & Baringoldz, G. (1983). Gender or situationally determined spoken language differences? The case of the leadership situation. *International Journal of Women's Studies, 6,* 44–53.

Myers, M. S. (1970). *Every employee a manager.* New York: McGraw-Hill.

Naisbitt, J. (1982). *Megatrends: Ten new directions transforming our lives.* New York: Warner Books.

Nieva, V. F., & Gutek, B. A. (1981). *Women and work: A psychological perspective.* New York: Praeger.

O'Leary, V. E. (1974). Some attitudinal barriers to occupational aspirations in women. *Psychological Bulletin, 81,* 809–826.

Ott, E. M. (1989). Effects of the male-female ratio at work: Policewomen and male nurses. *Psychology of Women Quarterly, 13,* 41–57.

Ouchi, W. G. (1981). *Theory Z: How American business can meet the Japanese challenge.* Reading, MA: Addison-Wesley.

Peters, T. J., & Waterman, R. H., Jr. (1982). *In search of excellence: Lessons from America's best-run companies.* New York: Harper & Row.

Powell, G. N. (1988). *Women & men in management.* Newbury Park, CA: Sage.

Reddin, W. J., & Reddin, M. K. (1979). *Educational Administrative Style Diagnosis Test (EASDT).* Fredericton, New Brunswick, Canada: Organizational Tests.

Renwick, P. A. (1977). The effects of sex differences on the perception and management of superior-subordinate conflict: An exploratory study. *Organizational Behavior and Human Performance, 19,* 403–415.

Rice, R. W. (1978). Construct validity of the Least Preferred Co-Worker score. *Psychological Bulletin, 85,* 1199–1237.

Rice, R. W., Instone, D., & Adams, J. (1984). Leader sex, leader success, and leadership process: Two field studies. *Journal of Applied Psychology, 69,* 12–31.

Riger, S., & Galligan, P. (1980). Women in management: An exploration of competing paradigms. *American Psychologist, 35,* 902–910.

Rosenthal, R., Hall, J. A., DiMatteo, M. R., Rogers, P. L., & Archer, D. (1979). *Sensitivity to nonverbal communication: The PONS test.* Baltimore, MD: Johns Hopkins University Press.

Rosenthal, R., & Rubin, D. B. (1986). Meta-analytic procedures for combining studies with multiple effect sizes. *Psychological Bulletin, 99,* 400–406.

Russell, J. E. A., Rush, M. C., & Herd, A. M. (1988). An exploration of women's expectations of effective male and female leadership. *Sex Roles, 18,* 279–287.

Sargent, A. G. (1981). *The androgynous manager.* New York: Amacom.

Sargent, J. F., & Miller, G. R. (1971). Some differences in certain communication behaviors of autocratic and democratic group leaders. *Journal of Communication, 21,* 233–252.

Shakeshaft, C. (1987). *Women in educational administration.* Newbury Park, CA: Sage.

Sirianni-Brantley, K. (1985). The effect of sex role orientation and training on leadership style (Doc-

toral dissertation, University of Florida, 1984). *Dissertation Abstracts International, 45,* 3106B.

Stake, J. E. (1981). Promoting leadership behaviors in low performance-self-esteem women in task-oriented mixed-sex dyads. *Journal of Personality, 49,* 401–414.

Stogdill, R. M. (1963). *Manual for the Leader Behavior Description Questionnaire-Form XII.* Columbus, OH: Bureau of Business Research, Ohio State University.

Stogdill, R. M., Goode, O. S., & Day, D. R. (1962). New leader behavior description subscales. *Journal of Psychology, 54,* 259–269.

Tanner, J. R. (1982). Effects of leadership, climate and demographic factors on school effectiveness: An action research project in leadership development (Doctoral dissertation, Case Western Reserve University, 1981). *Dissertation Abstracts International, 43,* 333A.

Taylor, S. E., Fiske, S. T., Etcoff, N., & Ruderman, A. (1978). The categorical and contextual bases of person memory and stereotyping. *Journal of Personality and Social Psychology, 36,* 778–793.

Terborg, J. R. (1977). Women in management: A research review. *Journal of Applied Psychology, 62,* 647–664.

Van Aken, E. W. (1954). An analysis of the methods of operation of principals to determine working patterns (Doctoral dissertation, University of Florida). *Dissertation Abstracts International, 14,* 1983.

Vroom, V. H., & Yetton, P. W. (1973). *Leadership and decision-making.* Pittsburgh, PA: University of Pittsburgh Press.

Wanous, J. P. (1977). Organizational entry: Newcomers moving from outside to inside. *Psychological Bulletin, 84,* 601–618.

Wood, W. (1987). Meta-analytic review of sex differences in group performance. *Psychological Bulletin, 102,* 53–71.

Yoder, J. D., & Sinnett, L. M. (1985). It is all in the numbers? A case study of tokenism. *Psychology of Women Quarterly, 9,* 413–418.

Chapter Four

Leadership and Leader Behaviors

T he studies of leader traits reported in Chapter Three successfully identified a number of personal attributes that endow an individual with the *potential* to be a successful leader. However, while there are important traits, the characteristics that an individual possesses do not provide a complete picture of "who is the effective leader," nor an answer to the question "what determines leadership success." In the last chapter Ralph Stogdill (1948) suggested that leadership consists of movement and getting work accomplished. He noted that the leader-follower relationship could be seen as a working relationship, one in which the leader orchestrates group activity. Kirkpatrick and Locke (1991) also suggested that leadership can be seen as an activity, noting that people who possess a key set of traits are more likely to engage in the behaviors associated with effective leadership.

Following the inability to explain the "totality" of leadership and effective leadership by employing the traits that individuals carry with them into leadership situations, an interest in understanding what it is that effective leaders actually "do" emerged. Students of leadership began to focus on the *behaviors* that leaders engage in, and whether or not effective leadership was a function of the actual behaviors engaged in by leaders. David G. Bowers and Stanley E. Seashore (1966) defined leadership as "organizationally useful behavior by one member of an organizational family toward another member or members of that same organizational family" (p. 240).

During the late 1940s, major research efforts looking into leader behavior were launched at the University of Michigan and The Ohio State University. These initiatives resulted in the identification of a number of different leader behaviors and accompanying categorization schemes.

Some of the more popular typologies employed to categorize leader behavior have focused on the amount of control exercised (or closeness of supervision), employee- versus job-orientation, as well as some very specific behaviors (e.g., communication, representation, fraternization, and organization[1]). Theoretically, it has been reasoned that leader behaviors have an impact upon follower attitudes (e.g., satisfaction with the leader and the job), motivation, work-related behaviors (e.g., performance), and group properties (e.g., group cohesiveness), each of which ultimately has an impact upon work group effectiveness. (You might find it interesting to profile your own level of satisfaction with your leader by completing the self-assessment at the end of this chapter opener.)

The first reading in this chapter by Bowers and Seashore (1966) highlights the fact that the work conducted at the University of Michigan resulted in the identification of a number of different leader behaviors and leader behavior classification schemes. Four dimensions of leader behavior (i.e., support, interaction facilitation, goal emphasis, and work facilitation) emerged as "the basic structure of what one may term 'leadership'" (Bowers and Seashore, p. 247). (The second self-assessment, appearing at the end of this chapter opener, provides you with the opportunity to profile your own leadership style as it pertains to several of these important leader behaviors.) Accompanying their re-

---

[1] E. A. Fleishman, The Description of Supervisory Behavior, *Journal of Applied Psychology,* 37 (1953), 1–6.

view of significant leader behaviors, Bowers and Seashore provide an interesting perspective on leadership. They note that effective work groups tend to require the presence of *each* of these four behaviors, yet they go on to note that *anyone* in a group may provide these behaviors and that they need not be directly infused into the group by the leader. The formal leader's role may be one of making sure that the necessary behaviors are present and in sufficient degree.

Under the direction of Ralph Stogdill, a group of researchers at The Ohio State University began an extensive and systematic study directed toward the identification of the behaviors that were associated with effective group performance. This work identified several behaviors engaged in by leaders (e.g., integration, production emphasis, evaluation, domination, initiation), which eventually resulted in an almost exclusive focus on two specific leader behaviors—consideration and initiating structure behaviors.

Andrew W. Halpin (1957) examined the role of these two leader behaviors (i.e., initiating structure and consideration) and their relationship to leader effectiveness, the level of satisfaction of the leader's group members, and member ratings of confidence and proficiency, friendship and cooperation, and morale in association with their leader. While this study was conducted in a military context, findings similar to these have been observed in numerous settings. Halpin's work highlights leader behavior as an important part of the leadership process, making a difference in terms of morale, satisfaction, and effectiveness.

In the next set of readings, Edwin A. Fleishman (1962, 1970) and his colleagues (Edwin F. Harris and J. Simmons) investigate the effect of leader initiating structure and consideration behavior on member grievances, turnover, and group effectiveness. Their findings reinforce Halpin's observations suggesting the usefulness of employing these two behavioral dimensions in organization settings and across relatively divergent cultures (i.e., Japan, United States, and Israel).

Taken together, these studies provide a useful framework suggesting that leaders and leadership can be studied from the perspective of leader behaviors. In addition, their evidence suggested that what leaders do can make a difference. Meaningful effects of leader behavior have been found in the areas of employee behavior (e.g., grievances, turnover) and attitudes (e.g., satisfaction, morale, group culture), as well as assessments of leader performance and group effectiveness.

An overview of the leader behavior literature highlights the fact that the consequences associated with leader behaviors are not always consistent.[2] While consideration is commonly associated with follower satisfaction, the effects associated with initiating structure behavior are more volatile across situations. At times initiating structure is positively associated with satisfaction, while at other times its effects are negative. While leader consideration behavior is seldom associated with positive performance effects, the relationship between initiating structure and performance produces a mixed picture. Sometimes the effects are positive, sometimes there is no meaningful relationships, and at other times the effects are in fact negative.

It has been argued on numerous occasions, especially by Robert R. Blake and Jane S. Mouton in the presentation of their *managerial grid*,[3] that leaders who simultaneously display high degrees of both structuring and consideration behavior are likely to be the most effective in terms of follower satisfaction and performance. Larson, Hunt, and Osborn (1976), after reviewing the literature concluded that the "hi-hi paradigm" is still open to question.[4] While consideration and initiating structure are positively related,

---

[2] A. K. Korman, "Consideration, Initiating Structure, and Organizational Criteria—A Review," *Personnel Psychology* 19 1966, 349–361; S. Kerr and C. Schriesheim, "Consideration, Initiating Structure, and Organizational Criteria—An Update of Korman's 1966 Review," *Personnel Psychology* 27 1974, 555–568.

[3] R. R. Blake and J. S. Mouton, *The Managerial Grid* (Houston: Gulf, 1964); *The New Managerial Grid* (Houston: Gulf, 1978); *The Versatile Manager: A Grid Profile* (Homewood, IL: Dow Jones–Irwin, 1980); "Management by Grid Principles or Situationalism: Which?" *Group & Organization Studies* 6, (1981), 4 439–455.

[4] L. L. Larson, J. G. Hunt, and R. N. Osborn, The Great Hi-Hi Leader Behavior Myth: A Lesson from Occam's Razor," *Academy of Management Journal* 19 (1976), 628–641.

FIGURE 4.1
The Leadership Process: Leader Behaviors

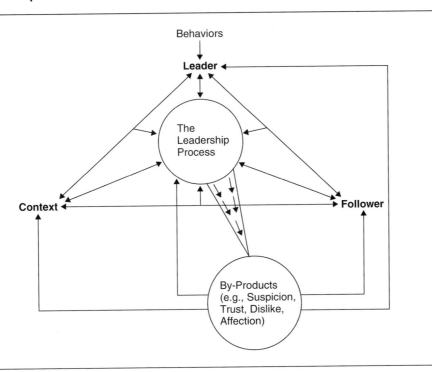

they observed support for the hi-hi paradigm in only 4 of 14 samples that examined the interactive effects of consideration and structure on satisfaction. There was no support found for the hi-hi paradigm in terms of its prediction of performance. Larson and his colleagues noted that in many situations "models involving structure only or consideration only were found to predict satisfaction as well as the more complex models" (p. 628) reflecting the "hi-hi paradigm."

Figure 4.1 provides a perspective on where leader behavior fits into the model of the leadership process. This set of readings suggests strongly that *leader behavior is important.* It provides additional insight into leadership and the leadership process. Leader behaviors reflect part of the process of leadership—goals are set, roadblocks are removed, people are provided encouragement—and at the same time these behaviors have an impact upon the attitudes, motivation, and behaviors of the members of the group.

The next chapter will address the question of how different situations in which leaders and followers find themselves operating affect the style (behaviors) of the leader and the effects that are produced by these behaviors. Blake and Mouton suggest that there is a "one best style" of leadership that fits and works best in *all* situations (i.e., 9,9 or the team leader who simultaneously shows a strong regard for employees and a strong production emphasis). They envision a unique interaction that gets produced by the simultaneous display of a concern for people and production. By contrast, the readings presented in the next chapter will focus on situational demands and the shaping effects that these forces have on leader behaviors and leader effectiveness. Chapter Five, then, calls into question the argument that a single "best" model can be employed to define what it is that "effective leaders do."

Leader Satisfaction

Instructions: Consider your leader and his/her leadership. Identify the face that best expresses how you *feel* about the leadership that he/she provides. (Circle the appropriate number on the scale below.)

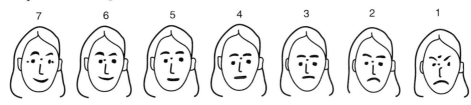

Scoring: Your satisfaction with your leader score is reflected by the numerical response given to the above question.

Interpretation: Leadership satisfaction is a reflection of how positive or negative you feel about the leadership that you receive from your leader. A score of 6 and above would indicate a relatively high level of leadership satisfaction. A score of 2 and below would reflect a relatively high level of leadership dissatisfaction.

Source: Adapted from R. B. Dunham and J. B. Herman, "Development of a Female Faces Scale for Measuring Job Satisfaction," *Journal of Applied Psychology* 60 (1975), 629–631. Copyright (1975) by the American Psychological Association.

Self-Assessment

Leadership—Michigan Organizational Assessment

Instructions: This self-assessment asks about your leadership behaviors. The following statements describe the way you as a supervisor/leader might perform your job. Please indicate whether or not you AGREE with each of the statements as a description of YOUR leader behavior.

	Strongly Disagree	Disagree	Slightly Disagree	Neither Agree nor Disagree	Slightly Agree	Agree	Strongly Agree
As a Leader (Supervisor/ Manager) I would . . .							
1. . . . help subordinates with their personal problems.	. . . 1	. . . 2	. . . 3	. . . 4	. . . 5	. . . 6	. . . 7
2. . . . make sure subordinates have clear goals to achieve.	. . . 1	. . . 2	. . . 3	. . . 4	. . . 5	. . . 6	. . . 7
3. . . . keep people informed about the work which is being done.	. . . 1	. . . 2	. . . 3	. . . 4	. . . 5	. . . 6	. . . 7
4. . . . make sure subordinates know what has to be done.	. . . 1	. . . 2	. . . 3	. . . 4	. . . 5	. . . 6	. . . 7
5. . . . be concerned about them as people.	. . . 1	. . . 2	. . . 3	. . . 4	. . . 5	. . . 6	. . . 7
6. . . . make it clear how they should do their job.	. . . 1	. . . 2	. . . 3	. . . 4	. . . 5	. . . 6	. . . 7
7. . . . help them discover problems before they get too bad.	. . . 1	. . . 2	. . . 3	. . . 4	. . . 5	. . . 6	. . . 7
8. . . . feel each subordinate is important as an individual.	. . . 1	. . . 2	. . . 3	. . . 4	. . . 5	. . . 6	. . . 7
9. . . . help them solve work-related problems.	. . . 1	. . . 2	. . . 3	. . . 4	. . . 5	. . . 6	. . . 7

Source: Institute for Social Research, *Michigan Assessment of Organizations II* (Ann Arbor, MI: Institute for Social Research, 1975).

Scoring: *Personal Support*—Sum your answer to the following items: 1, 5, and 8, and then divide by 3. *Goal emphasis*—Sum your response to the following items: 2, 4, and 6, and divide by 3. *Work facilitation*—Sum your responses to the following items: 3, 7, and 9, and divide by 3.

Interpretation: This profile identifies the extent to which you perceive yourself engaging in three different behaviors as you carry out your leadership role: (1) *support*—you would likely engage in behaviors that enhance someone else's feelings of personal worth and importance; (2) *goal emphasis*—you would likely engage in behaviors that stimulate an enthusiasm for meeting the group's goal or achieving excellent performance; and (3) *work facilitation*—you would likely engage in behaviors that help achieve goal attainment by such activities as scheduling, coordinating, planning, and by providing resources such as tools, materials, and technical knowledge. A score of 5.5 and higher suggests that your leadership style would be strong on that particular dimension of leader behavior. A score of 2.5 and less suggests that your leadership style would not likely be characterized by this particular dimension of leader behavior.

Predicting Organizational Effectiveness with a Four-Factor Theory of Leadership

D. G. Bowers and S. E. Seashore
University of Michigan

*F*or centuries writers have been intrigued with the idea of specifying predictable relationships between what an organization's leader does and how the organization fares. In our own time, behavioral science has looked extensively at this question, yet incongruities and contradictory or unrelated findings seem to crowd the literature. It is the intent in this paper to locate and integrate the consistencies, to explore some neglected issues, and, finally, to generate and use a network of variables for predicting outcomes of organizational effectiveness.

Leadership has been studied informally by observing the lives of great men and formally by attempting to identify the personality traits of acknowledged leaders through assessment techniques. Review of the research literature from these studies, however, reveals few consistent findings.[1] Since the Second World War, research emphasis has shifted from a search for personality traits to a search for behavior that makes a difference in the performance or satisfaction of the followers. The conceptual scheme to be outlined here is an example of this approach.

In this paper, the primary concern is with leadership in businesses or industrial enterprises, usually termed "supervision" or "management," although most of the constructs of leadership to be used here apply equally well to social groups, clubs, and voluntary associations.

Work situations in business organizations in a technologically advanced society typically involve a comparatively small number of persons who receive direction from one person. This is the basic unit of industrial society and has been called the "organizational family."[2] In this modern organizational family, there is usually task interdependence and there is frequently social interdependence as well. The ideal is that of a group of people working effectively together toward the accomplishment of some common aim.

This paper presents a review of the conceptual structure resulting from several programs of research in leadership practices, followed by a reconceptualization that attempts to take into consideration all of these earlier findings. In an attempt to assess the usefulness of the reconceptualization, it is then applied to leadership and effectiveness data from a recent study.

Dimensions of Leadership

It seems useful at the outset to isolate on a common-sense basis certain attributes of "leadership." First, the concept of leadership is meaningful only in the context of two or more people. Second, leadership consists of behavior; more specifically, it is behavior by one member of a group toward another member or members of the group, which advances some joint aim. Not all organizationally useful behavior in a work group is leadership; leadership behavior must be distinguished from the performance of noninterpersonal tasks that advance the goals of the organization. On a common-sense basis, then, leadership is organizationally useful behavior by one member of an organizational family toward another member or members of that same organizational family.

Defined in this manner, leadership amounts to a large aggregation of separate behaviors, which may be grouped or classified in a great variety of ways. Several classification systems from previous research have achieved considerable prominence, and are briefly described here.

Ohio State Leadership Studies

In 1945, the Bureau of Business Research at Ohio State University undertook the construction of an instrument for describing leadership. From extended conversations and discussions among staff members who represented various disciplines, a list of nine dimensions or categories of leadership behavior were postulated. Descriptive statements were then written and assigned to one or another of the nine dimensions, and after further refinement, 150 of these were selected as representing these nine dimensions and were incorporated into the Leader Behavior Description Questionnaire.

Two factor analyses attempted to simplify its conceptual framework further. Hemphill and Coons[3] intercorrelated and factor-analyzed group mean scores for 11 dimensions for a sample composed largely of educational groups,[4] and obtained three orthogonal factors.

1. *Maintenance of membership character.* Behavior of a leader which allows him to be considered a "good fellow" by his subordinates; behavior which is socially agreeable to group members.

2. *Objective attainment behavior.* Behavior related to the output of the group: for example, taking positive action in establishing goals or objectives, structuring group activities in a way that members may work toward an objective, or serving as a representative of group accomplishment in relation to outside groups, agencies, forces, and so on.

Source: Edited and reprinted with permission from *Administrative Science Quarterly* 2, 2 (1966), 238–263. Author affiliation may have changed since article was first published.

3. *Group interaction facilitation behavior.* Behavior that structures communication among group members, encouraging pleasant group atmosphere, and reducing conflicts among members.

Halpin and Winer[5] made an analysis using data collected from air-force crews, revising the original measuring instrument to adapt it to the respondent group. Only 130 items were used, with appropriate rewording, and the number of dimensions was reduced to eight. Treatment of the data indicated that five of the eight were sufficient for describing the entire roster, and the correlation of the 130 items with these five dimensions was regarded as a matrix of oblique factor loadings. These item loadings were then factor analyzed and the results rotated, producing four orthogonal factors.

1. *Consideration.* Behavior indicative of friendship, mutual trust, respect, and warmth.

2. *Initiating structure.* Behavior that organizes and defines relationships or roles, and establishes well-defined patterns of organization, channels of communication, and ways of getting jobs done.

3. *Production emphasis.* Behavior which makes up a manner of motivating the group to greater activity by emphasizing the mission or job to be done.

4. *Sensitivity (social awareness).* Sensitivity of the leader to, and his awareness of, social interrelationships and pressures inside or outside the group.

The Halpin and Winer analysis has been the more widely known and used. Because the investigators dropped the third and fourth factors as accounting for too little common variance, "consideration" and "initiating structure" have become to some extent identified as "the Ohio State" dimensions of leadership.

Early Survey Research Center Studies

Concurrent with the Ohio State studies was a similar program of research in human relations at the University of Michigan Survey Research Center. Approaching the problem of leadership or supervisory style by locating clusters of characteristics which (a) correlated positively among themselves and (b) correlated with criteria of effectiveness, this program developed two concepts called "employee orientation" and "production orientation."[6]

Employee orientation is described as behavior by a supervisor, which indicates that he feels that the "human relations" aspect of the job is quite important; and that he considers the employees as human beings of intrinsic importance, takes an interest in them, and accepts their individuality and personal needs. Production-orientation stresses production and the technical aspects of the job, with employees as means for getting work done; it seems to combine the Ohio State dimensions of initiating structure and production emphasis. Originally conceived to be opposite poles of the same continuum, employee-orientation and production-orientation were later reconceptualized,[7] on the basis of further data, as representing independent dimensions.

Katz and Kahn,[8] writing from a greater accumulation of findings, presented another conceptual scheme, with four dimensions of leadership.

1. *Differentiation of supervisory role.* Behavior by a leader that reflects greater emphasis upon activities of planning and performing specialized skilled tasks; spending a greater proportion of time in actual supervision, rather than performing the men's own tasks himself or absorption in impersonal paperwork.

2. *Closeness of supervision.* Behavior that delegates authority, checks upon subordinates less frequently, provides more general, less frequent instructions about the work, makes greater allowance for individuals to perform in their own ways and at their own paces.

3. *Employee orientation.* Behavior that gives major emphasis to a supportive personal relationship, and that reflects a personal interest in subordinates; being more understanding, less punitive, easy to talk to, and willing to help groom employees for advancement.

4. *Group relationships.* Behavior by the leader that results in group cohesiveness, pride by subordinates in their work group, a feeling of membership in the group, and mutual help on the part of those subordinates.

Differentiation of supervisory role corresponds in part to what the Ohio State studies refer to as initiating structure or objective attainment behavior, and clearly derives from the earlier concept of production orientation. Closeness of supervision, on the other hand, has something in common with maintenance of membership character, consideration, and employee-orientation, but also with objective attainment behavior, initiating structure, and production orientation. Employee orientation clearly corresponds to the earlier concept by the same name, while group relationships is to some extent similar to the interaction facilitation behavior and social sensitivity of the Ohio State studies.

In still another conceptualization, combining theory with review of empirical data, Kahn[9] postulated four supervisory functions.

1. *Providing direct need satisfaction.* Behavior by a leader, not conditional upon behavior of the employee, which provides direct satisfaction of the employee's ego and affiliative needs.

2. *Structuring the path to goal attainment.* Behavior that cues subordinates toward filling personal needs through attaining organizational goals.

3. *Enabling goal achievement.* Behavior that removes barriers to goal achievement, such as eliminating bottlenecks, or planning.

4. *Modifying employee goals.* Behavior that influences the actual personal goals of subordinates in organizationally useful directions.

Direct need satisfaction clearly resembles consideration and employee-orientation; enabling goal achievement seems similar to initiating structure or objective attainment behavior; structuring the path to goal attainment and modifying employee goals are probably closer to the Ohio State production emphasis factor.

Studies at the Research Center for Group Dynamics

Cartwright and Zander,[10] at the Research Center for Group Dynamics, on the basis of accumulated findings, described leadership in terms of two sets of group functions.

1. *Group maintenance functions.* Behavior that keeps interpersonal relations pleasant, resolves disputes, provides encouragement, gives the minority a chance to be heard, stimulates self-direction, and increases interdependence among members.

2. *Goal achievement functions.* Behavior that initiates action, keeps members' attention on the goal, develops a procedural plan, evaluates the quality of work done, and makes expert information available.

These descriptive terms clearly refer to broader constructs than consideration or initiating structure. Group maintenance functions, for example, include what has been termed consideration, maintenance of membership character, or employee-orientation, but they also include functions concerned with relationships among group members not in formal authority positions. This concept is in some ways similar to group interaction facilitation behavior in the Ohio State factor analysis of Hemphill and Coons.[11] Goal achievement functions seem to encompass what the Ohio State studies referred to as initiating structure and production emphasis or objective attainment behavior, and what early Survey Research Center studies called production orientation.

Mann's Three Skills

In subsequent work at the Survey Research Center built upon earlier findings, a recent classification, proposed by several writers and developed and operationalized by Floyd Mann,[12] treats leadership in terms of a trilogy of skills required of supervisors or managers. Although behaviors requiring particular skills and those skills themselves are not necessarily perfectly parallel, it seems reasonable to assume at least an approximate correspondence between the two. The three skills are:

1. *Human relations skill.* Ability and judgment in working with and through people, including knowledge of principles of human behavior, interpersonal relations, and human motivation.

2. *Technical skill.* Ability to use knowledge, methods, techniques, and equipment necessary for the performance of specific tasks.

3. *Administrative skill.* Ability to understand and act according to the objectives of the total organization, rather than only on the basis of the goals and needs of one's own immediate group. It includes planning, organizing the work, assigning the right tasks to the right people, inspecting, following up, and coordinating the work.

Likert's New Patterns of Management

Rensis Likert of the University of Michigan Institute for Social Research, building upon many of the findings of the Survey Research Center and the Research Center for Group Dynamics as well as upon his own early work in the same area for the Life Insurance Agency Management Association, describes five conditions for effective supervisory behavior.

1. *Principle of supportive relations.* The leadership and other processes of the organization must be such as to ensure a maximum probability that in his interactions and his relationships with the organization, each member will, in the light of his background, values, and expectations, view the experience as supportive, and as one that builds and maintains his sense of personal worth and importance.[13]

2. *Group methods of supervision.* Management will make full use of the potential capacities of its human resources only when each person in an organization is a member of one or more effectively functioning work groups that have a high degree of group loyalty, effective skills of interaction, and high performance goals.[14]

3. *High performance goals.* If a high level of performance is to be achieved, it appears to be necessary for a supervisor to be employee-centered, and at the same time to have high performance goals and a contagious enthusiasm as to the importance of achieving these goals.[15]

4. *Technical knowledge.* The (effective) leader has adequate competence to handle the technical problems faced by his group, or he sees that access to this technical knowledge is fully provided.[16]

5. *Coordinating, scheduling, planning.* The leader fully reflects and effectively represents the views, goals, values, and decisions of his group in those other groups where he is performing the function of linking his group to the rest of the organization. He brings to the group of which he is the leader the views, goals, and decisions of those other groups. In this way, he provides a linkage whereby communication and the exercise of influence can be performed in both directions.[17]

Comparison and Integration

These various research programs and writings make it clear that a great deal of conceptual content is held in common. In fact, four dimensions emerge from these studies, which seem to comprise the basic structure of what one may term "leadership":

1. *Support.* Behavior that enhances someone else's feeling of personal worth and importance.

2. *Interaction facilitation.* Behavior that encourages members of the group to develop close, mutually satisfying relationships.

3. *Goal emphasis.* Behavior that stimulates an enthusiasm for meeting the group's goal or achieving excellent performance.

4. *Work facilitation.* Behavior that helps achieve goal attainment by such activities as scheduling, coordinating, planning, and by providing resources such as tools, materials, and technical knowledge.

This formulation is obviously very close, except in terminology, to that expressed by Rensis Likert and was, in fact,

TABLE 1
Correspondence of Leadership Concepts of Different Investigators.

Bowers and Seashore (1964)	Hemphill and Coons (1957)	Halpin and Winer (1957)	Katz et al. (1950)	Katz and Kahn (1951)	Kahn (1958)	Mann (1962)	Likert (1961)	Cartwright and Zander (1960)
Support	Maintenance of member-ship character	Consideration	Employee orientation	Employee orientation / Closeness of supervision	Providing direct need satisfaction	Human relations skills	Principle of supportive relationships	Group maintenance functions
Interaction facilitation	Group interaction facilitation behavior	Sensitivity		Group relationships		Human relations skills	Group methods of supervision	Group maintenance functions
Goal emphasis	Objective attainment behavior	Production emphasis	Production orientation		Structuring path to goal attainment / Modifying employee goals	Administrative skills	High-performance goals	Goal-achievement functions
Work facilitation	Objective attainment behavior	Initiating structure	Production orientation	Differentiation of supervisory role / Closeness of supervision	Enabling goal achievement	Technical skills	Technical knowledge, planning, scheduling	Goal-achievement functions

stimulated by it. Table 1 indicates how concepts from the various research programs relate to these four basic concepts of leadership. More important, however, is the fact that each of these four concepts appears, sometimes separately, sometimes in combination, in all but two (Katz, et al., 1950; Kahn, 1958) of the previous formulations listed. These four dimensions are not considered indivisible, but capable of further subdivision according to some regularity of occurrence in social situations or according to the conceptual preferences of investigators.

Independence of Leadership and Position

Traditional leadership research has focused upon the behavior of formally designated or recognized leaders. This is probably due, at least in part, to the historical influence of the hierarchical models of the church and the army. As a result, it has until recently been customary to study leadership either as an attribute of the person of someone who is authority-vested, or as an attribute of his behavior. More recently, attention has been paid to leadership in groups less formally structured, as illustrated by the work of Bass with leaderless group discussion, the work of Sherif, as well as some of the work of other researchers in the area of group dynamics.[18]

In the previous section, leadership was conceptualized in terms of four social-process functions, four kinds of behavior that must be present in work groups if they are to be effective. The performance of these functions was deliberately not limited to formally designated leaders. Instead, it was proposed that leadership, as described in terms of support, goal emphasis, work facilitation, and interaction facilitation, may be provided by anyone in a work group for anyone else in that work group. In this sense, leadership may be either "supervisory" or "mutual"; that is, a group's needs for support may be provided by a formally designated leader, by members for each other, or both; goals may be emphasized by the formal leader, by members to each other, or by both; and similarly for work facilitation and interaction facilitation.

This does not imply that formally designated leaders are unnecessary or superfluous, for there are both common-sense and theoretical reasons for believing that a formally acknowledged leader through his supervisory leadership behavior sets the pattern of the mutual leadership which subordinates supply each other.

Leadership and Organizational Effectiveness

Leadership in a work situation has been judged to be important because of its connection, to some extent assumed and to some extent demonstrated, to organizational effectiveness. Effectiveness, moreover, although it has been operationalized in a variety of ways, has often been assumed to be a unitary characteristic. These assumptions define a commonly accepted theorem that leadership (if not a unitary characteristic, then a limited roster of closely related ones) is always salutary in its effect and that it always enhances effectiveness. . . .

Research Methods

Research Site

This study as conducted in 40 agencies of a leading life insurance company. These agencies are independently owned businesses, performing identical functions in their separate parts of the country. Only one or two hierarchical levels intervene between the regional manager, at the top of the hierarchy, and the sales agents at the bottom. The typical agency consists of an exclusive territory comprising a number of counties of a state or states. The regional manager ordinarily has headquarters in some principal city of his territory, and contracts with individuals to service the area as sales agents. He receives an "override" upon the commissions of policies sold by these agents, in addition to the full commissions from whatever policies he sells personally.

If geographical distance or volume of business is great enough, he may contract with individuals to serve as district managers. The district manager is given territorial rights for some subportion of the regional manager's territory, is permitted to contract agents to service the area, subject to the approval of the regional manager, and receives a portion of what would otherwise be the regional manager's override upon sales within his territory.

Although this is the usual arrangement, variations occur. Occasionally, for example, a territory will be so constituted as to prevent subdivision into districts. In these cases, the regional manager contracts directly with sales agents throughout his territory. In other cases, the territory is almost entirely urban, in which case the regional manager may substitute salaried or partially salaried supervisory personnel for district managers. In all cases, however, there are at least a regional manager and sales agents, and frequently, in addition, a district manager between these two parties.

In all, the company's field force comprises nearly 100 agencies. Of these, 40 were selected as being roughly representative of them all. Selection was made by company personnel, with an effort to select half of the 40 from the topmost part of the list of agencies ordered by performance, and the

other half from among poorer performing agencies, omitting any having recent organizational disruption or change. Questionnaires were mailed out in April, 1961, to all contracted regional managers, district managers, sales agents, and supervisory personnel on full or part salary in these agencies; 83 percent were returned by June, 1961, for a total of 873 respondents. . . .

Results

Relation of Leadership to Effectiveness

Table 3 presents the correlation coefficients of leadership measures with measures of satisfaction. Table 4 presents similar correlations of leadership measures to performance factors. These data indicate first, that the incidence of significant relationships of leadership to effectiveness is well above the chance level. Of 40 satisfaction-leadership coefficients, 30 are significant beyond the 5 percent level of confidence. Of 56 performance-leadership coefficients, 13 are significant beyond the 5 percent level of confidence. Second, the significant coefficients are not uniformly distributed throughout the matrix; instead, certain effectiveness criteria (e.g., satisfaction with income) and certain leadership measures (e.g., peer work facilitation) have many significant relationships, whereas others have few or none (e.g., performance factor VI). Third, significant coefficients are as often found in relation to peer as to managerial leadership characteristics. . . .

Relation of Peer to Managerial Leadership

Before assessing the adequacy of leadership as a predictor of effectiveness, it seems advisable to answer the question posed earlier about the relationship between peer and managerial leadership. There is a close relationship between all managerial characteristics, on the one hand, and all peer characteristics on the other. Following the same method as that used for effectiveness, it appears that the best predictor of peer support is managerial support; of peer goal emphasis, managerial interaction facilitation; of peer work

TABLE 3
Correlation of Leadership with Satisfactions.

Leadership Measure	Satisfaction with				
	Company	Fellow Agents	Job	Income	Manager
Peer					
Support	.03*	.68	.39	.29*	.47
Goal emphasis	.37	.77	.26*	.42	.62
Work facilitation	.29*	.68	.34	.51	.45
Interaction facilitation	.31	.72	.30*	.42	.55
Manager					
Support	.31	.65	.35	.45	.86
Goal emphasis	.11*	.71	.09*	.43	.31
Work facilitation	.31	.61	.24*	.36	.41
Interaction facilitation	.30*	.67	.10*	.53	.78

*All others significant beyond .05 level of confidence, 2-tail.

T A B L E   4
Correlation of Leadership with Performance Factors.

Leadership Measure	Performance Factor						
	I	**II**	**III**	**IV**	**V**	**VI**	**VII**
Peer							
Support	.26	− .02	− .27	− .21	.23	− .12	.27
Goal emphasis	.49*	− .05	− .45*	− .27	.15	.04	.04
Work facilitation	.33*	.14	− .41*	− .41*	.18	.00	.04
Interaction facilitation	.44*	− .13	− .44*	− .24	.11	.14	.05
Manager							
Support	.28	− .24	− .26	− .12	.25	.16	.10
Goal emphasis	.31*	.11	− .27	− .18	.41*	.03	− .19
Work facilitation	.43*	.13	− .37*	− .33*	.21	.16	− .12
Interaction facilitation	.42*	− .29	− .30	− .21	.13	.20	.01

*Significant beyond .05 level of confidence, 2-tail.

facilitation, managerial interaction facilitation. With one exception, therefore, the best predictor of the peer characteristic is its managerial opposite number. Table 7 indicates that three predictions are improved by related managerial characteristics.

Assuming causation, one may say that if a manager wishes to increase the extent to which his subordinates support one another, he must increase his own support and his own emphasis upon goals. If he wishes to increase the extent to which his subordinates emphasize goals to one another, he must first increase his own facilitation of interaction and his emphasis upon goals. By increasing his facilitation of the work, he will increase the extent to which his subordinates do likewise, and if, in addition, he increases his facilitation of interaction, his subordinates will in turn facilitate interaction among themselves.

These data appear to confirm that there is in fact a significant and strong relationship between managerial and peer leadership characteristics. In general, the statement may be made that a forerunner of each peer variable is its managerial opposite number, and that substantial improvement is in most cases made by combining with this another managerial characteristic. . . .

Figure 1*a* presents the relationships of leadership and nonleadership variables to satisfaction with the company and with income. This diagram indicates that supportive managers make more satisfactory arrangements about the office expenses of their agents and that these arrangements, in part, lead to greater satisfaction with the company as a whole. In addition, as managers facilitate the interaction of their agents, the goals of the company and needs or aspirations of the people who work for it come to be more compatible, which also leads to satisfaction with the company and with income.

Figure 1*b* presents a similar chain of relationships to satisfaction with the job itself. This diagram is interpreted to mean that as agents facilitate the work for each other, less time is spent by agents in paperwork for specific clients. When this happens, when agents behave more supportively toward each other, and when the agents are, on the whole, higher in need for affiliation, there is greater job satisfaction. Figure 1*c* presents relationships to two criteria: satisfaction with fellow agents and volume of business. When agents emphasize goals among themselves, they become more satisfied with each other; and when this condition exists, an agency does a greater volume of business. Figure 1*d* shows very succinctly that agents are satisfied with their manager if he is supportive and knowledgeable. Figure 1*e* presents relationship to business costs in diagram form. Earlier diagrams showed the network of relationships associated with satisfaction with the company and with the job; here, these two satisfaction states are associated with lower business costs. In

T A B L E   7
Improvement of Prediction of Peer Leadership Characteristics by Addition of Other Managerial Leadership Characteristics.

Peer Measure	Managerial Best Predictor	Other Managerial Measures Improving Prediction
Support	Support	Goal emphasis
Goal emphasis	Interaction facilitation	Goal emphasis
Work facilitation	Work facilitation	None
Interaction facilitation	Interaction facilitation	Work facilitation

F I G U R E   1
Predicted measures: (a) satisfaction with company and with income; (b) satisfaction with job; (c) satisfaction with fellow agents; business volume; (d) satisfaction with manager; (e) business costs; (f) business growth.

†Multiple correlation of variables listed against the effectiveness measure.

addition, as agents facilitate the work for each other, they spend a smaller proportion of their time in miscellaneous activities. When this occurs, and when agents emphasize goals to one another, costs are also lower.

Figure 1f diagrams relationships to business growth. The relationships presented in this diagram are less reliable than those presented in earlier figures. They are, as a group, somewhat smaller in size than those found in relation to other criteria already described. With this caution in mind, however, they can be interpreted as follows: business growth is high when the agent force does *not* hold to a classical business ideology; when regional managers, by accepting the opinions

and ideas of their agents, encourage professional development; and when managers reduce rivalries among agents by encouraging their interaction. Far from stressing growth attained by competitive effort, this paradigm presents a picture of growth through cooperative professionalism.

Two additional performance measures of effectiveness present one significant, reasonable "causal" relationship each: staff-clientele maturity is greater when agents have a higher level of aspiration, and more advanced underwriting occurs when agents have a higher level of education. Although significant correlations were presented earlier in relation to these two factors, the reasonable interpretation of them is that the leadership measures are either effects or co-ordinates, not causes, of these descriptive rather than evaluative performance factors.

That no reasonable, significant relationships to manpower turnover are to be found is extremely puzzling. In most investigations of the effect of social-psychological variables upon organizational behavior, it is assumed that performance measures which are more "person" than "production" oriented will show the highest relationships to questionnaire measurements. In the present case this assumption is not supported. No variations of analysis that were attempted produced any noticeable change. An attempt was made to assess curvilinear correlations, but no improvement over linear correlation resulted. It was also thought that the factorial measure of turnover might be too complicated and that a simpler measure of proportion of terminations might be more productive. This also produced no noticeable effect. Apparently, manpower turnover in this particular company or industry is related to forces in the individual, the environment, or perhaps the organizational situation not tapped by the questionnaire measurement used.

It is not surprising that no correlations are found with the regional manager's personal performance. It is, as explained earlier, the weakest factor, and differs from the other factors in being descriptive of a single individual rather than of the agency as a whole. It may well be affected more by variables such as the regional manager's distance from retirement than by factors assessed here.

Discussion and Conclusions

To what extent have the data demonstrated the usefulness of the conceptualization presented at the beginning of this article? It seems reasonable to state the following:

1. Seven of the eight leadership characteristics outlined above in fact play some part in the predictive model generated from the data; only peer interaction facilitation seems to play no unique role.

2. Both managerial and peer leadership characteristics seem important.

3. There are plausible relationships of managerial to peer leadership characteristics.

4. The model is not a simple one of managerial leadership leading to peer leadership, which in turn leads to outcomes separately; instead, different aspects of performance are associated with different leadership characteristics, and, in some cases, satisfaction outcomes seem related to performance outcomes.

5. Some effectiveness measures are related to causal factors other than those tapped in this instrument.

6. The ability to predict outcomes with the variables selected varies from .95 to .00.

7. The role of leadership characteristics in this prediction varies in importance from strong, direct relationships in some cases (e.g., satisfaction with manager) to indirect relationships (e.g., business volume) to no relationship (e.g., advanced underwriting).

8. Leadership, as conceived and operationalized here, is not adequate alone to predict effectiveness; instead, additional and, in some cases, intervening constructs must be included to improve prediction. These "other" constructs are of several distinct types:

   a. *Leadership-related.* Regional manager's expert power, regional manager's influence acceptance, and rivalry among agents.

   b. *Work Patterns.* Percentage of time in miscellaneous activities, in paperwork for clients, in professional development.

   c. *Personal and Motivational.* Education, level of aspiration, need for affiliation, goal compatibility of individual and organization, and classical business ideology.

Notes

[1] C. A. Gibb, "Leadership," in G. Lindzey, *Handbook of Social Psychology* (Cambridge, Mass.: Addison-Wesley Publishing Co., Inc., 1954), II, 877–917; R. M. Stogdill, Personal Factors Associated with Leadership: A Survey of the Literature, *Journal of Psychology*, 25 (1948), 35–71.

[2] F. C. Mann, "Toward an Understanding of the Leadership Role in Formal Organization," in R. Dubin, G. C. Homans, F. C. Mann, and D. C. Miller, *Leadership and Productivity* (San Francisco, Calif.: Chandler Publishing Company, 1965), pp. 68–103.

[3] J. K. Hemphill and A. E. Coons, "Development of the Leader Behavior Description Questionnaire," in R. M. Stogdill and A. E. Coons (eds.) *Leader Behavior: Its Description and Measurement* (Research Monograph No. 88, Columbus, Ohio: Bureau of Business Research, the Ohio State University, 1957), pp. 6–38.

[4] The 11 dimensions were made up of the original 9, one of which (communication) had been subdivided, plus an overall leadership evaluation.

[5] A. W. Halpin and J. Winer, "A Factorial Study of the Leader Behavior Description Questionnaire," in R. M. Stogdill and A. E. Coons, *Leader Behavior, op. cit.*, pp. 39–51.

[6] D. Katz, N. Maccoby, and Nancy C. Morse, *Productivity, Supervision, and Morale in An Office Situation* (Detroit, Mich.: The Darel Press, Inc., 1950); D. Katz, N. Maccoby, G. Gurin, and Lucretia G. Floor, *Productivity, Supervision, and Morale Among Railroad Workers* (Ann Arbor, Mich.: Survey Research Center, 1951).

[7] R. L. Kahn, The Prediction of Productivity, *Journal of Social Issues*, 12 (1956), 41–49.

[8] D. Katz and R. L. Kahn, "Human Organization and Worker Motivation," in L. R. Tripp (ed.), *Industrial Productivity* (Madison, Wisc.: Industrial Relations Research Association, 1951), pp. 146–171.

[9] R. L. Kahn, "Human Relations on the Shop Floor," in E. M. Hugh-Jones (ed.), *Human Relations and Modern Management* (Amsterdam, Holland: North-Holland Publishing Co., 1958), pp. 43–74.

[10] D. Cartwright and A. Zander, *Group Dynamics Research and Theory* (Evanston, Ill.: Row, Peterson & Co., 1960).

[11] Hemphill and Coons, *op. cit.*

[12] Mann, *op. cit.*

[13] R. Likert, *New Patterns of Management* (New York: McGraw-Hill Book Co., 1961), p. 103.

[14] *Ibid.*, p. 104.

[15] *Ibid.*, p. 8.

[16] *Ibid.*, p. 171.

[17] *Ibid.*, p. 171.

[18] B. M. Bass, *Leadership, Psychology, and Organizational Behavior* (New York: Harper & Bros., 1960); Cartwright and Zander, *op. cit.*; M. and Carolyn W. Sherif, *An Outline of Social Psychology* (New York: Harper & Bros., 1956).

The Leader Behavior and Effectiveness of Aircraft Commanders [1]

A. W. Halpin
University of Chicago

What aspects of leader behavior are most important for the effective combat performance of aircraft commanders? That the commanders of medium bombardment aircraft vary in their leadership style is evident from even casual observation. But to note differences in leadership style is of doubtful practical value unless we can identify meaningful dimensions by which such differences may be reliably described. Furthermore, it behooves us to demonstrate that such differences have a bearing upon the commander's combat performance. In other words, we should seek to discover the relationship between *descriptions* of what the leader does and independent *evaluations* of the effectiveness of his leadership.

The source of such evaluations is determined by the aircraft commander's position within a larger organizational structure. He is the leader of a primary, face-to-face group—the crew, but is at the same time responsible to squadron and wing superiors. His position, therefore, confronts him with two sets of obligations: responsibility to his administrative superiors for the accomplishment of the crew's mission, and responsiveness to the crew in respect to the means by which this end is achieved. As the leader of a primary group imbedded within a larger hierarchical organization, the aircraft commander's performance is thus under double scrutiny—by his superiors and by his crew. The expectations imposed upon him from these two sources are not necessarily the same. Accordingly, in examining the pertinence of differences in leadership style, we must be careful to take into account evaluations of the commander's performance derived from both these sources.

The design is straightforward, and involves three kinds of variables: (1) descriptions of the aircraft commander's behavior by the members of his crew, (2) evaluations of his performance by his administrative superiors, and (3) evaluations of the commander in terms of sociometric ratings secured from his crew. The procedure is to determine the relationship between the descriptions (1) and the two sets of evaluations (2 and 3).

Hypotheses

In order to facilitate and insure the fulfillment of role requirements, there is developed within every formal and hierarchical organization some system of rewards and punishments. The larger the organization and the greater the demand for the interchangeability of the incumbents of any given position, the less can the institution tolerate deviations from specified role requirements. If Initiating Structure behavior be viewed as an index of the degree to which any given commander is successful in fulfilling the institutionally established requirements of his role, then one might expect that this behavior would be rewarded. *Specifically, we would expect squadron and wing superiors to rate favorably the performance of those commanders who show high Initiating Structure behavior. This is the first hypothesis to be tested in the present investigation.*

But we have noted at the outset that the leader of any primary group imbedded within a larger organizational structure is confronted by two sets of obligations: to his superiors and to his crew. Responsiveness to the crew refers to responsiveness in terms of interpersonal relations. The dimension of Consideration would appear to be an index of the degree to which the commander is responsive to his crew, in terms not of institutional roles or goals, but rather in regard to interpersonal needs. *This leads to the second hypothesis to be tested: that crews will prefer as aircraft commanders those leaders who are high in Consideration behavior.* The two dimensions may be viewed as contributing primarily to two different kinds of group objectives. Initiating Structure is directed principally at the achievement of the formal goals of the group, i.e., success on missions, whereas Consideration behavior is related essentially to the maintenance or strengthening of the group itself.

Inasmuch as *both* group achievement and group maintenance are important, it is not sufficient for us to examine singly the relationship of each of the two leader behavior dimensions to performance criteria. We may assume that the more effective leader is the commander who simultaneously can contribute to both group objectives. *From this we posit our third hypothesis—that commanders who are rated highest by their superiors on "Overall Effectiveness in Combat" are those who score above the mean on both leader behavior dimensions, and that the commanders who are rated lowest by their superiors on this same criterion are those who score below the mean on both dimensions.*

If these hypotheses are supported by the data, we shall be provided with a firmer basis upon which to build our leader selection and training programs.

The Sample and Primary Data

The sample is comprised of 89 commanders of B-29 aircraft assigned to the Far East Air Force and engaged in flying com-

Source: Edited and reprinted with permission from R. M. Stogdill and A. E. Coons, eds., *Leader Behavior: Its Description and Measurement*, Bureau of Business Research, College of Commerce and Administration, The Ohio State University, Columbus, Ohio (1957), 52–64. Author affiliation may have changed since article was first published.

[1] This study was sponsored jointly by the Human Resources Research Laboratories, Department of the Air Force, and The Ohio State University Research Foundation.

bat missions over Korea. Data were gathered on these commanders in Japan during the summer of 1951. There are three sets of data pertinent to the present study: (1) scores on the Air Force adaptation of the Leader Behavior Description Questionnaire on which the crew members described the behavior of their respective commanders, (2) ratings of the commander's performance secured from his squadron and wing administrative superiors, and (3) sociometric ratings of the commanders by their respective crews. Hemphill and Sechrest (4) have described the collection of the data and the analysis of the criterion data. The data for the present study are described in greater detail by Halpin (2, 3). . . .

Ratings by Administrative Superiors

An Individual Criterion Rating Form was developed for the evaluation of individual crew members including commanders. To obtain these ratings, staff officers at the squadron and wing level were interviewed individually. Each rater was asked to select from a roster those persons with whom he was sufficiently well acquainted to make an equitable rating. The interviewer than asked the rater to evaluate each man on a nine-point scale in respect to seven different characteristics. The ratings were recorded along with a verbatim record of comments made by the rater about the performance of the ratee. No rater was requested to evaluate any men with whose performance he was only vaguely familiar.

Ratings were obtained on 87 of the 89 aircraft commanders in the sample. Fourteen of these 87 were evaluated by one superior, 48 by two, and 25 by three. Each commander was evaluated in respect to the following characteristics:

1. *Technical competence:* The degree of competence in performing his crew duties.

2. *Effectiveness in working with other crew members:* The degree to which the individual is effective in coordinating his work with other crew members, or the degree to which he works as an effective team member.

3. *Conformity to Standard Operating Procedure (SOP):* The degree to which he performs his duties in the prescribed manner.

4. *Performance under stress:* The degree to which he is able to maintain a high level of performance under high stress conditions, i.e., in the face of enemy opposition, or when called upon for long hours of duty.

5. *Attitude and motivation:* The degree to which the crew as a unit displays enthusiasm or eagerness for effective combat performance.

6. *Overall effectiveness:* The degree to which the individual displays an overall effectiveness as a member of a combat crew. . . .

Sociometric Ratings by the Crew

In order to obtain an evaluation of the aircraft commander as perceived by the members of his crew, two kinds of measures have been used: three scores derived from a set of five sociometric rating scales; and a Satisfaction Index indicating the crew's satisfaction with the incumbent aircraft commander. These measures will be discussed in turn.

The five sociometric rating questions were incorporated within a larger Crew Rating Form administered to all crew members including the commander. For each question, a 9-point scale was used, with 5 of the points anchored by brief verbal descriptions. These sociometric questions are listed below:

1. How much confidence do you have in each member of your crew?

1	2	3	4	5	6	7	8	9
None		Little		Average		Great Deal		Highest

2. How would you rate each crew member as your friend or possible friend?

1	2	3	4	5	6	7	8	9
I can't stand to be around him		I would rather not associate		At present he is just another guy		I enjoy being with him		I try to be with him more often

3. How proficient do you think each member of your crew is?

1	2	3	4	5	6	7	8	9
Very poor		Poor		Fair		Good		Very good

4. Rate the morale of each man in this crew.

1	2	3	4	5	6	7	8	9
Very poor		Poor		Average		Good		Excellent

5. To what extent will each crew member go out of his way to help another crew member in performing his duties?

1	2	3	4	5	6	7	8	9
Never goes out of his way		Seldom goes out of his way to help another		Sometimes will go out of his way and sometimes won't		Will generally go out of his way to help another		Always goes out of his way

These five scales will be referred to as ratings of: (1) Confidence, (2) Friendship, (3) Proficiency, (4) Morale, and (5) Cooperation.

Each crew member rated each other member of the crew except himself. For any given man, the rating assigned to him is the average of the ratings he received from his fellow crew members. For the purpose of the present study, we shall be concerned only with the mean ratings received by the aircraft commanders.

As might have been expected, these ratings were highly intercorrelated. Upon factor analysis of the matrix, two factors were identified as sufficiently independent to permit a meaningful interpretation. In this solution, only 16 per cent communality was obtained for the ratings on morale. Consequently, the morale ratings are treated separately. The interrelationships among the other four ratings were such as to suggest the advisability of a straightforward combining of the scores into two groups. Accordingly, we have computed mean scores for each of the five ratings and have then reduced the five scores to the following three:

- Score I—Confidence and Proficiency
- Score II—Friendship and Cooperation
- Score III—Morale

Each of these represents the crew's pooled evaluation of the aircraft commander in respect to these particular characteristics.

Satisfaction Index

The second kind of sociometric rating of the commander secured from the crew was the Satisfaction Index. On one of the questions of the Crew Rating Form, the respondents were asked: "If you could make up a crew from among the crew members in your squadron, whom would you choose for each crew position?" The ratio between the number of choices the incumbent commander received and the number of choices possible was used as an index of the crew's satisfaction with his leadership.

An index of 100 means that in response to this question, all the crew members chose their present aircraft commander. Conversely, an index of 0 means that none of the members chose the incumbent commander. For 88 commanders, the scores on this crew Satisfaction Index ranged from 0 to 100, with a mean of 75 and a standard deviation of 29.

Initiating Structure Scores and Superiors' Ratings

The correlations between the Consideration and the Initiating Structure scores ascribed to the aircraft commanders and their ratings on the other variables are presented in Table 1. One notes, in general, that none of the ratings by superiors, whether in the form of individual ratings or of factor scores correlates significantly with the Consideration scores, but that conversely all the ratings on individual criteria by superiors yield correlations significant at the .01 level with the Initiating Structure scores. The consistency in the magnitude of these correlations is probably a function of a general rater halo, for the only one of the three factor scores derived from these ratings by superiors which correlates significantly with the Initiating Structure scores is Factor I—Overall Effectiveness. This correlation of .25 is significant at the .05 level. On

T A B L E 1

Correlations between Ascribed Consideration and Initiating Structure Scores and Ratings of Commanders by Superiors, and by Crew Members with Means and Standard Deviations for the Respective Variables

Ratings by Superiors and Crew Members	N	Dimension		Mean	SD
		Consideration	Initiating Structure		
Ratings by Superiors		r	r		
Technical Competence	87	.09	.30	5.5	2.5
Effectiveness in Working with Others	87	.18	.28	5.2	2.3
Conformity to Standard Procedures	87	−.03	.32	4.7	2.3
Performance under Stress	87	.18	.32	6.3	1.9
Attitude and Motivation	87	.03	.29	5.1	2.1
Overall Effectiveness	87	.17	.30	5.3	2.4
Factor I: Overall Effectiveness	86	.17	.25	5.5	2.3
Factor II: Lack of Motivation	86	.14	.14	5.1	2.2
Factor III: Conformity to Administrative Requirements	86	−.18	.10	3.6	1.5
Ratings by Crew					
Score I: Confidence and Proficiency	84	.69	.68	7.7	1.5
Score II: Friendship and Cooperation	84	.84	.51	5.7	1.9
Score III: Morale	84	.27	.28	5.2	1.9
Satisfaction Index	88	.75	.47	75.0	28.7

r = .21 is significant at the .05 level.
r = .27 is significant at the .01 level.

the whole, therefore, the superiors rate favorably those aircraft commanders who are perceived by their crews as high in Initiating Structure. This supports the first of the two hypotheses which provided the impetus for the present study.

Consideration Scores and Ratings by Crew Members

The second hypothesis, that the Consideration scores would be correlated with favorable ratings of the commander by the members of his own crew, is also supported. This is especially the case in two instances: The correlation of .75 with the Satisfaction index, and the correlation of .84 with Score II derived from the sociometric ratings on "Friendship and Cooperation." One observes, however, that correlations significant at the .01 level are also obtained with the Initiating Structure scores. In the case of Scores I and III, for example, the correlations are of the same magnitude for each of the leader behavior dimensions. But with the other two variables, the Satisfaction Index and Score II, the difference between the Consideration correlation and the correlation with the Initiating Structure scores is statistically significant. The magnitude of these two correlations and the size of the difference between each of these and the corresponding Initiating Structure correlations is sufficient, however, to support the hypotheses of a high positive relationship between the Consideration scores and the ratings by the crew. . . .

"Crew Acceptance" Cluster

The two highest correlations in Table 1 are those of the Consideration scores with the "Friendship and Cooperation" scores (.84), and with the Satisfaction Index (.75). The correlation between the Satisfaction Index and the "Friendship and Cooperation" scores is, in turn, .81. Here, then, is a consistent cluster of relationships. *The aircraft commanders whom the men perceive as most considerate are those whom they rate highest on "Friendship and Cooperation," and whom they clearly prefer as their aircraft commanders.* In general, the three variables in this cluster appear to measure the crew's acceptance of the aircraft commander as a person. It therefore is of some interest to examine the relationships between the variables in this cluster and the three factor scores derived from the rat-

ings of the commander by his superiors. These correlations are presented in Table 2.

Only one of these correlations is significant, that between the superiors' ratings of the commanders' over-all effectiveness and the index we have used to express the crew's satisfaction with its commander. Apart from this single correlation indicating only approximately 5 per cent of variance common to the two variables, there are only chance relationships between the measures of the commander's acceptance by his crew and the ratings he receives from his superiors.

Up to this point of our analysis, we have examined the relationship between the criteria and each leader behavior dimension taken separately. In general, we found that high Initiating Structure behavior is associated with favorable ratings by administrative superiors, and that high Consideration is associated with acceptance by the crew members. These findings support the first two hypotheses which we have set out to test.

High vs. Low Scores on Both Dimensions

The third hypothesis proposed was that the aircraft commanders rated highest by their superiors on "Overall Effectiveness in Combat" would be those scoring above the mean on both leader behavior dimensions, and that the commanders rated lowest by their superiors on this same criterion would be those scoring below the mean on both dimensions. To test this hypothesis, we first determined appropriate cutting points in the distribution of the ratings the aircraft commanders received from their superiors on "Overall Effectiveness in Combat." It was decided that the upper and lower 15 per cent of the distribution clearly identified two groups of commanders: those rated high on Overall Effectiveness (N=13) and those rated low (N=12). For each of these groups taken separately, the Consideration and the Initiating Structure scores were plotted into the four quadrants defined by coordinates corresponding to the means of the two leader behavior dimensions. These scatterplots for the high and low groups on Overall Effectiveness are presented in Table 3.

The cell entries in the upper left hand quadrant of the table do not differ significantly from each other. Nor do the entries in the two respective lower right hand quadrants. On the other hand, when we compare the two groups of com-

TABLE 2

Correlations of Variables in Crew Acceptance Cluster with Factor Scores Derived from Superiors' Ratings of Aircraft Commanders

Variables in Crew Acceptance Cluster	N	Superior's Ratings		
		I Overall Effectiveness	II Lack of Motivation	III Conformity to Administrative Requirements
		r	*r*	*r*
Consideration	86	.17	.14	−.18
Satisfaction Index	85	.23	.17	−.13
Friendship and Cooperation	89	.14	.16	.10

r = .21 is significant at the .05 level.

T A B L E   3

Relation between Consideration and Initiating Structure Scores of Aircraft Commanders Rated High or Low in Effectiveness by Superiors

Initiating Structure	Consideration			
	Below Mean	**N**	**Above Mean**	**N**
Above Mean	Effectiveness High Low	 4 2	Effectiveness High Low	 8 2
Below Mean	Effectiveness High Low	 1 6	Effectiveness High Low	 0 2

manders with respect to those high on *both* leader behavior dimensions and those low on *both* dimensions, we obtain the relationship summarized in Table 4.

Fisher's (1) method for the exact treatment of 2 x 2 tables was applied to the data in Table 4. The probability of occurrence of frequencies as deviant or more deviant from the null hypothesis than those obtained is less than .03. This indicates that aircraft commanders who are rated high by their superiors on Overall Effectiveness tend to score above the mean on both leader behavior dimensions, whereas the commanders rated low by their superiors tend to score below the mean on *both* dimensions. Here, then, is support for the third hypothesis. The evidence thus indicates that the effective aircraft commander is not the one who engages in one form of

leader behavior at the expense of the other, but rather is the leader whose behavior is above average in respect to both the Consideration and the Initiating Structure dimensions.

Discussion

Two dimensions of the leader behavior of aircraft commanders have been studied. For the sample of 89 aircraft commanders studied, the correlation between these two dimensions is .51. Recognizing that the crux of leadership behavior lies in how it is evaluated by the men with whom the leader must deal, we have determined the relationship between the commanders' behavior in respect to these two dimensions and the evaluation of his combat performance by his superiors and his crew members. In general, we find that the ratings of the commander by his superiors are correlated significantly with the Initiating Structure scores, and that his ratings by his crew members are correlated highest with the Consideration scores.

Both dimensions are integral components of a leader's behavior. But in evaluating the aircraft commander's performance, his superiors and his crew each selectively perceives one dimension as more important than the other. Yet in neither case is the second of the dimensions viewed adversely. For the crew, if the commander is Considerate, then a moderately high degree of Initiating Structure behavior is acceptable. For the superiors, although the prime requirement is that the aircraft commander be strong in Initiating Structure, a moderately high degree of Consideration behavior is acceptable. *In short, our findings suggest that to select a leader who is likely to satisfy both his crew and his superiors, we do best by choosing an aircraft commander who is above average on both leader behavior dimensions.*

T A B L E   4

Number of Aircraft Commanders Scoring High or Low in Effectiveness and Scoring Above the Mean or Below the Mean in Both Leader Behavior Dimensions

Effectiveness Rating	Number below Mean on Both Consideration and Structure	Number above Mean on Both Consideration and Structure
Upper 15 per cent	1	8
Lower 15 per cent	6	2

Patterns of Leadership Behavior Related to Employee Grievances and Turnover

E. A. Fleishman
Yale University

E. F. Harris
Chrysler Corporation

This study investigates some relationships between the leader behavior of industrial supervisors and the behavior of their group members. It represents an extension of earlier studies carried out at the International Harvester Company, while the authors were with the Ohio State University Leadership Studies.

Briefly, these previous studies involved three primary phases which have been described elsewhere (Fleishman, 1951, 1953a, 1953b, 1953c; Fleishman, Harris & Burtt, 1955; Harris & Fleishman, 1955). In the initial phase, independent leadership patterns were defined and a variety of behavioral and attitude instruments were developed to measure them. This phase confirmed the usefulness of the constructs "Consideration" and "Structure" for describing leader behavior in industry.

Since the present study, as well as the previous work, focused on these two leadership patterns, it may be well to redefine them here:

Consideration includes behavior indicating mutual trust, respect, and a certain warmth and rapport between the supervisor and his group. This does not mean that this dimension reflects a superficial "pat-on-the-back," "first name calling" kind of human relations behavior. This dimension appears to emphasize a deeper concern for group members' needs and includes such behavior as allowing subordinates more participation in decision making and encouraging more two-way communication.

Structure includes behavior in which the supervisor organizes and defines group activities and his relation to the group. Thus, he defines the role he expects each member to assume, assigns tasks, plans ahead, establishes ways of getting things done, and pushes for production. This dimension seems to emphasize overt attempts to achieve organizational goals.

Since the dimensions are independent, a supervisor may score high on both dimensions, low on both, or high on one and low on the other.

The second phase of the original Harvester research utilized measures of these patterns to evaluate changes in foreman leadership attitudes and behavior resulting from a management training program. The amount of change was evaluated at three different times—once while the foremen were still in the training setting, again after they had returned to the plant environment, and still later in a "refresher" training course. The results showed that while still in the training situation there was a distinct increase in Consideration and an unexpected decrease in Structure attitudes. It was also found that leadership attitudes became more *dissimilar* rather than similar, despite the fact that all foremen had received the same training. Furthermore, when behavior and attitudes were evaluated back in the plant, the effects of the training largely disappeared. This pointed to the main finding, i.e., the overriding importance of the interaction of the training effects with certain aspects of the social setting in which the foremen had to operate in the plant. Most critical was the "leadership climate" supplied by the behavior and attitudes of the foreman's own boss. This was more related to the foreman's own Consideration and Structure behavior than was the fact that he had or had not received the leadership training.

The third phase may be termed the "criterion phase," in which the relationships between Consideration and Structure and indices of foremen proficiency were examined. One finding was that production supervisors rated high in "proficiency" by plant management turned out to have leadership patterns high in Structure and low in Consideration. (This relationship was accentuated in departments scoring high on a third variable, "perceived pressure of deadlines.") On the other hand, this same pattern of high Structure and low Consideration was found to be related to high labor turnover, union grievances, worker absences and accidents, and low worker satisfaction. There was some indication that these relationships might differ in "nonproduction" departments. An interesting sidelight was that foremen with low Consideration *and* low Structure were more often bypassed by subordinates in the informal organizational structure. In any case, it was evident that "what is an effective supervisor" is a complex question, depending on the proficiency criterion emphasized, management values, type of work, and other situational variables.

The present study examines some of the questions left unanswered by this previous work.

Source: Edited and reprinted with permission from *Personnel Psychology* 15 (1962), 43–56. Author affiliation may have changed since article was first published.

Purpose

The present study focused on two main questions. First, what is the *form* of the relationship between leader behavior and indices of group behavior? Is it linear or curvilinear? As far as we know, no one has really examined this question. Rephrased, this question asks if there are critical levels of Consideration and/or Structure beyond which it does or does not make a difference in group behavior? Is an "average" amount of Structure better than a great deal or no Structure at all? Similarly, is there an optimum level of Consideration above and below which worker grievances and/or turnover rise sharply?

The second question concerns the interaction effects of different combinations of Consideration and Structure. Significant correlations have been found between each of these patterns and such indices as rated proficiency, grievances, turnover, departmental reputation, subordinate satisfactions, etc. (e.g., Fleishman, Harris & Burtt, 1955; Halpin, 1954; Hemphill, 1955; Stogdill & Coons, 1957). These studies present some evidence that scoring low on both dimensions is not desirable. They also indicate that some balance of Consideration and Structure may be optimal for satisfying both proficiency and morale criteria. The present study is a more intensive examination of possible optimum combinations of Consideration and Structure.

The present study investigates the relationships between foreman behavior and two primary indices of group behavior: labor grievances and employee turnover. Both of these may be considered as partial criteria of group effectiveness.

Procedure

Leader Behavior Measures

The study was conducted in a motor truck manufacturing plant. Fifty-seven production foremen and their work groups took part in the study. They represented such work operations as stamping, assembly, body assembly, body paint, machinery, and export. At least three workers, drawn randomly from each foreman's department, described the leader behavior of their foreman by means of the *Supervisory Behavior Description Questionnaire* (described elsewhere, Fleishman, 1953, 1957). Each questionnaire was scored on Consideration and Structure, and a mean Consideration score and a mean Structure score was computed for each foreman. The correlation between Consideration and Structure among foremen in this plant was found to be −.33. The correlation between these scales is usually around zero (Fleishman, 1957), but in this plant foremen who are high in Structure are somewhat more likely to be seen as lower in Consideration and vice versa. However, the relationship is not high. . . .

Results

Leader Behavior and Grievances

Figure 1 plots the average employee grievance rates for departments under foremen scoring at different levels of Consideration. From the curve fitted to these points, it can be seen clearly that the relationship between the foremen's behavior and grievances from their work groups is negative and curvilinear. For most of the range increased Consideration goes with reduced grievance rates. However, increased Consideration above a certain critical level (approximately 76 out of a possible 112) is not related to further decreases in grievances. Furthermore, the curve appears to be negatively accelerated. A given decrease in Consideration just below the critical point (76) is related to a small increase in grievances, but, as Consideration continues to drop, grievance rates rise sharply. Thus, a five-point drop on the Consideration scale, just below a score of 76, is related to a small grievance increase, but a five-point drop below 61 is related to a large rise in grievances. The correlation ratio (eta) represented by this curve is −.51.

FIGURE 1
Relation between Consideration and Grievance Rates

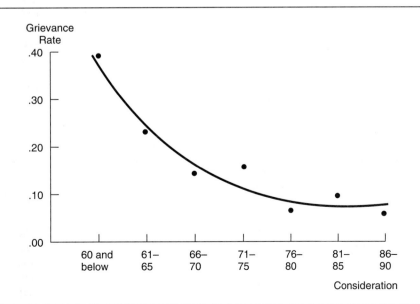

FIGURE 2
Relation between Structure and Grievance Rates

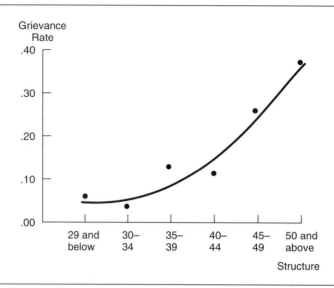

Figure 2 plots grievances against the foremen's Structure scores. Here a similar curvilinear relationship is observed. In this case the correlation is positive (eta = .71). Below a certain level (approximately 36 out of a possible 80 on our scale) Structure is unrelated to grievances, but above this point increased Structure goes with increased grievances. Again we see that a given increase in Structure just above this critical level is accompanied by a small increase in grievances, but continued increases in Structure are associated with increasingly disproportionately large increases in grievances rates.

Both curves are hyperbolic rather than parabolic in form. Thus, it appears that for neither Consideration nor Structure is there an "optimum" point in the middle of the range below and above which grievances rise. Rather there seems to be a range within which increased Consideration or decreased Structure makes no difference. Of course, when one reaches these levels, grievances are already at a very low level and not much improvement can be expected. However, the important point is that this low grievance level is reached before one gets to the extremely high end of the Consideration scale or to the extremely low end of the Structure scale. It is also clear that extremely high Structure and extremely low Consideration are most related to high grievances.

Different Combinations of Consideration and Structure Related to Grievances

The curves described establish that a general relationship exists between each of these leadership patterns and the frequency of employee grievances. But how do *different combinations* of Consideration and Structure relate to grievances? Some foremen score high on both dimensions, some score low on both, etc.

Figure 3 plots the relation between Structure (low, medium, and high) and grievances for groups of foremen who were either low, medium, or high on Consideration. The curves show that grievances occur most frequently among groups whose foremen are low in Consideration, regardless of the amount of emphasis on Structure. The most interesting finding relates to the curve for the high Consideration foremen. This curve suggests that, for the high Considera-

FIGURE 3
Combinations of Consideration and Structure Related to Grievances.

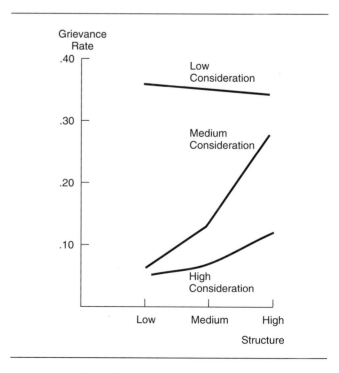

FIGURE 4
Relation between Consideration and Turnover Rates

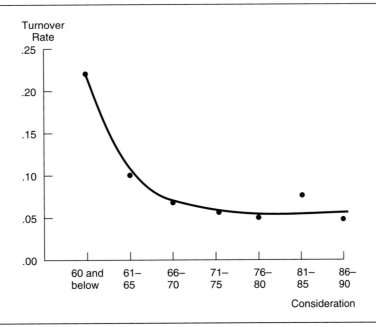

---

tion foremen, Structure could be increased without any appreciable increase in grievances. However, the reverse is not true; that is, foremen who were low in Consideration could not reduce grievances by easing up on Structure. For foremen average on Consideration, grievances were lowest where Structure was lowest and increased in an almost linear fashion as Structure increased. These data show a definite interaction between Consideration and Structure. Apparently, high Consideration can compensate for high Structure. But low Structure will not offset low Consideration.

Before we speculate further about these relationships, let us examine the results with employee turnover.

Leader Behavior and Turnover

Figures 4 and 5 plot the curves for the *Supervisory Behavior Description* scores of these foremen against the turnover criteria. Again, we see the curvilinear relationships. The correlation (eta) of Consideration and turnover is −.69; Structure and turnover correlate .63. As in the case with grievances, below a certain critical level of Consideration and above a certain level of Structure, turnover goes up. There is, however, an interesting difference in that the critical levels differ from those related to grievances. The flat portions of each of these curves are more extended and the rise in turnover beyond the point of inflection is steeper. The implication of this is quite sensible and indicates that "they gripe before they leave." In other words, a given increase in Structure (to approximately 39) or decrease in Consideration (to 66) may result in increased grievances, but not turnover. It takes higher Structure and lower Consideration before turnover occurs.

Different Combinations of Consideration and Structure Related to Turnover

Figure 6 plots the relation between Structure (low, medium, and high) and turnover for groups of foremen who were also either low, medium, or high on Consideration. As with grievances, the curves show that turnover is highest for the work groups whose foremen combine low Consideration with high Structure; however, the amount of Consideration is the dominant factor. The curves show that turnover is highest among those work groups whose foremen are low in Consideration, regardless of the amount of emphasis these same foremen show on Structure. There is little distinction between the work groups of foremen who show medium and high Consideration since both of these groups have low turnover among their workers. Furthermore, increased Structure does not seem related to increased turnover in these two groups.[1]

Conclusions

1. This study indicates that there are significant relationships between the leader behavior of foremen, and the labor grievances and employee turnover in their work groups. In general, low Consideration and high Structure go with high grievances and turnover.

2. There appear to be certain critical levels beyond which increased Consideration or decreased Structure have no effect on grievance or turnover rates. Similarly grievances and turnover are shown to increase most markedly at the extreme ends of the Consideration (low end)

---

[1] This, of course, is consistent with our earlier finding that for increased turnover it takes a bigger drop in Consideration and a bigger increase in Structure to make a difference. Thus, our high and medium Consideration groups separate for grievances, but overlap for turnover.

FIGURE 5
Relation between Structure and Turnover Rates

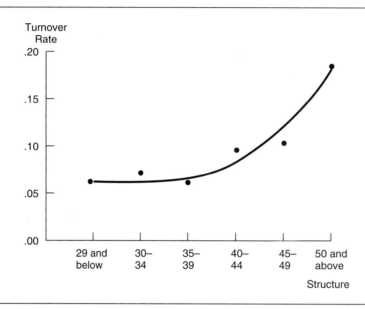

and Structure (high end) scales. Thus, the relationship is curvilinear, not linear, and hyperbolic, not parabolic.

3. The critical points at which increased Structure and decreased Consideration begin to relate to group behavior is not the same for grievances and turnover. Increases in turnover do not occur until lower on the Consideration scale and higher on the Structure scale, as compared with increases in grievances. For example, if Consideration is steadily reduced, higher grievances appear before

FIGURE 6
Combinations of Consideration and Structure Related to Turnover

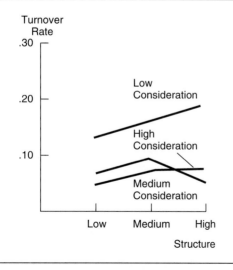

increased turnover occurs. It appears that there may be different "threshold levels" of Consideration and Structure related to grievances and turnover.

4. Other principal findings concern the interaction effects found between different combinations of Consideration and Structure. Taken in combination, Consideration is the dominant factor. For example, both grievances and turnover were highest in groups having low Consideration foremen, regardless of the degree of Structuring behavior shown by these same foremen.

5. Grievances and turnover were lowest for groups with foremen showing medium to high Consideration together with low Structure. However, one of the most important results is the finding that high Consideration foremen could increase Structure with very little increase in grievances and no increase in turnover. High Consideration foremen had relatively low grievances and turnover, regardless of the amount of Structuring engaged in.

Thus, with regard to grievances and turnover, leader behavior characterized by low Consideration is more critical than behavior characterized by high Structure. Apparently, foremen can compensate for high Structure by increased Consideration, but low Consideration foremen cannot compensate by decreasing their Structuring behavior.

One interpretation is that workers under foremen who establish a climate of mutual trust, rapport, and tolerance for two-way communication with their work groups are more likely to accept higher levels of Structure. This might be because they perceive this Structure differently from employees in "low Consideration" climates. Thus, under "low Consideration" climates, high Structure is seen as threatening and restrictive, but under "high Consideration" climates, this same Structure is seen as supportive and helpful. A related interpretation is that foremen who establish such an atmosphere can more easily solve the problems resulting from high Structure. Thus, *grievances* may be solved at this level before they get into the official records. Similarly, *turnover* may reflect escape from a problem situation which cannot be resolved in the absence of mutual trust and two-way communication. In support of this interpretation, we do have evidence that leaders high in Consideration are also better at predicting subordinates' responses to problems (Fleishman & Salter, 1961).

One has to be careful in making cause and effect inferences here. A possible limitation is that our descriptions of foremen behavior came from the workers themselves. Those workers with many grievances may view their foremen as low in Consideration simply because they have a lot of grievances. However, the descriptions of foreman behavior were obtained from workers drawn randomly from each foreman's group; the odds are against our receiving descriptions from very many workers contributing a disproportionate share of grievances. In the case of turnover, of course, our descriptions could not have been obtained from people who had left during the previous 11 months. Yet substantial correlations were obtained between foremen descriptions, supplied by currently employed workers, with the turnover rates of their work groups. Furthermore, we do have evidence that leader behavior over a year period tends to be quite stable. Test-retest correlations for Consideration, as well as for Structure, tend to be high even when different workers do the describing on the retest (Harris & Fleishman, 1955). Our present preference is to favor the interpretation that high turnover and grievances result, at least in part, from the leader behavior patterns described.

The nonlinear relations between leader behavior and our criteria of effectiveness have more general implications for leadership research. For one thing, it points up the need for a more careful examination of the *form* of such relationships before computing correlation coefficients. Some previously obtained correlations with leadership variables may be underestimates because of linearity assumptions. Similarly, some previous negative or contradictory results may be "explained" by the fact that (a) inappropriate coefficients were used or (b) these studies were dealing with only the flat portions of these curves. If, for example, all the foremen in our study had scored over 76 on Consideration and under 36 on Structure, we would have concluded that there was no relation between these leadership patterns and grievances and turnover. Perhaps in comparing one study with another, we need to specify the range of leader behavior involved in each study.

There is, of course, a need to explore similar relationships with other criteria. There is no assurance that similar curvilinear patterns and interaction effects will hold for other indices (e.g., group productivity). Even the direction of these relationships may vary with the criterion used. We have evidence (Fleishman, Harris & Burtt, 1955), for example, that Consideration and Structure may relate quite differently to another effectiveness criterion: management's perceptions of foremen proficiency. However, research along these lines may make it possible to specify the particular leadership patterns which most nearly "optimize" these various effectiveness criteria in industrial organizations.

References

Fleishman, E. A. *"Leadership Climate" and Supervisory Behavior.* Columbus, Ohio: Personnel Research Board, Ohio State University, 1951.

Fleishman, E. A. "Leadership Climate, Human Relations Training, and Supervisory Behavior." *Personnel Psychology,* VI (1953) 205–222. (a)

Fleishman, E. A. "The Description of Supervisory Behavior." *Journal of Applied Psychology,* XXXVII (1953) 1–6. (b).

Fleishman, E. A. "The Measurement of Leadership Attitudes in Industry." *Journal of Applied Psychology,* XXXVII (1953) 153–158. (c)

Fleishman, E. A. "A Leader Behavior Description for Industry." In Stogdill, R. M. and Coons, A. E. (Editors) *Leader Behavior: Its Description and Measurement.* Columbus, Ohio: Bureau of Business Research, 1957.

Fleishman, E. A., Harris, E. F., and Burtt, H. E. *Leadership and Supervision in Industry.* Columbus, Ohio: Bureau of Educational Research, Ohio State University, 1955.

Fleishman, E. A., and Salter, J. A. "The Relation Between the Leader's Behavior and His Empathy toward Subordinates." *Advanced Management,* March, 1961, 18–20.

Harris, E. F., and Fleishman, E. A. "Human Relations Training and the Stability of Leadership Patterns." *Journal of Applied Psychology,* XXXIX (1955), 20–25.

Halpin, A. W. "The Leadership Behavior and Combat Performance of Airplane Commanders." *Journal of Abnormal and Social Psychology,* XLIX (1954), 19–22.

Hemphill, J. K. "Leadership Behavior Associated with the Administrative Reputation of College Departments." *Journal of Educational Psychology,* XLVI (1955), 385–401.

Stogdill, R. M. and Coons, A. E. (Editors). *Leader Behavior: Its Description and Measurement.* Columbus, Ohio: Bureau of Business Research, Ohio State University. 1957.

Relationship between Leadership Patterns and Effectiveness Ratings among Israeli Foremen

E. A. Fleishman[1]
American Institutes for Research
Washington, D. C.

J. Simmons
Israel Institute of Productivity

T his note describes some relationships between descriptions of leader behavior and effectiveness evaluations of foremen in Israeli industry. The data were collected as part of a larger study of Israeli foremen conducted by the Israel Institute of Productivity in cooperation with the Israel Management Training Center (Israel Institute of Productivity, 1962).

Specifically, the objective of the present analysis was to examine the relationship between the leadership patterns of "Consideration" and "Structure" and the proficiency of foremen as rated by the management in their plants.

Procedure

The dimensions of leader behavior investigated were *Consideration* and *Structure* as measured by a modified form of the Supervisory Behavior Description (Fleishman, 1953, 1957). These dimensions have most recently (Fleishman, 1969) been defined as follows:

Consideration (C). Reflects the extent to which an individual is likely to have job relationships with his subordinates characterized by mutual trust, respect for their ideas, consideration of their feelings, and a certain warmth between himself and them. A high score is indicative of a climate of good rapport and two-way communication. A low score indicates the individual is likely to be more impersonal in his relations with group members. *Structure (S).* Reflects the extent to which an individual is likely to define and structure his own role and those of his subordinates toward *goal attainment*. A high score on this dimension characterizes individuals who play a very active role in directing group activities through planning, communicating information, scheduling, criticizing, trying out new ideas, and so forth. A low score characterizes individuals who are likely to be relatively inactive in giving direction in these ways. . . .

The foremen in the study were 318 foremen drawn from 100 factories throughout Israel. The foremen averaged 42 years of age, 11.3 years in length of employment time, 2 years as foremen, 10 years in education, and 18 workers supervised.

The questionnaires were filled out by the managers of each foreman, who utilized the questionnaire to describe the behavior of the foreman reporting to him. The managers were unaware of the underlying scales by which the questionnaire was scored.

Independently, at a later date and in connection with another phase of the project, all foremen were rated by their managers into three levels of "proficiency as a foreman." These levels were "very satisfactory," "satisfactory," and "unsatisfactory." . . .

Conclusions

These Israeli data extend findings in the U.S. (e.g., Anderson, 1966; Fleishman, 1969; Fleishman & Harris, 1962; Fleishman & Ko, 1962; Hemphill, 1955; Halpin, 1955; Sergiovanni, Metzcus & Burden, 1969) and in Japan (Misumi & Tosaki, 1965) that the leadership pattern which *combines* higher consideration and structure is likely to optimize a number of effectiveness criteria for a variety of supervisory jobs.

The evidence is consistent with the notion advanced elsewhere (Fleishman & Harris, 1962) that higher Consideration on the part of the supervisor acts as a moderator variable which allows the supervisor to exercise higher structuring behavior to achieve organizational goals. With low consideration, the same amount of structure is less effective and may be counterproductive.

Limitations of the present study are that the criterion of foreman performance was restricted to management ratings of success and that the ratings were made by those who also described the foreman's leadership behavior on the job. The main values of the study are (a) in showing what perceived leader behaviors tend to be related to perceived effectiveness by management in the Israeli culture, and (b) in offering additional evidence of the generality of some previously-established principles of leader behavior.

Source: Edited and reprinted with permission from *Personnel Psychology* 23 (1970), 169–172. Author affiliation may have changed since article was first published.

[1] In 1962–63, the first author was a Guggenheim Fellow and Visiting Professor in the Department of Industrial and Management Engineering at the Israel Institute of Technology (Technion). The study was conducted by the Israel Institute of Productivity.

References

Anderson, L. R. "Leader Behavior, Member Attitudes, and Task Performance of Intercultural Discussion Groups." *The Journal of Social Psychology,* LXVI (1966), 305–319.

Fleishman, E. A. "The Description of Supervisory Behavior." *Journal of Applied Psychology,* XXXVI (1953) 1–6. (a)

Fleishman, E. A. "A Leader Behavior Description for Industry." In *Leader Behavior: Its Description and Measurement,* R. M. Stogdill and A. E. Coons (Editors). Columbus, Ohio: Bureau of Business Research, Ohio State University, 1957. (a)

Fleishman, E. A. *Manual for Leadership Opinion Questionnaire.* Chicago: Science Research Associates, 1969 Revision.

Fleishman, E. A. and Harris, E. F. "Patterns of Leadership Behavior Related to Employee Grievances and Turnover." *Personnel Psychology,* XV (1962), 43–56.

Fleishman, E. A. and Ko, I. "Leadership Patterns Associated with Managerial Evaluations of Effectiveness." Unpublished report, Yale University, 1962.

Halpin, A. W. "The Leader Behavior and Leadership Ideology of Educational Administrators and Aircraft Commanders." *Harvard Educational Review,* XXV (1955), 18–32.

Hemphill, J. K. "Leadership Behavior Associated with the Administrative Reputation of College Departments." *Journal of Educational Psychology,* XLVI (1955), 385–401.

Israel Institute of Productivity. "A Study of Foremen in Israeli Industry." Mimeographed Report (in Hebrew), Tel Aviv, 1962.

Misumi, J. and Tosaki, T. "A Study of the Effectiveness of Supervisory Patterns with Japanese Hierarchial Organization." *Japanese Psychological Research,* VII (1965), 151–62.

Sergiovanni, T. J., Metzcus, R. and Burden, L. "Toward a Particularistic Approach to Leadership Style: Some Findings." *American Educational Research Journal,* VI (1969), 62–79.

Chapter Five

Leadership and Situational Differences

*T*his chapter addresses the *situation* in the leadership process. The evolving leadership model from the earlier chapters suggests that the situation in part defines the leadership process and that it influences the leader and interacts with the leader's attempts to influence his or her followers. Three key questions that will be addressed are:

- Does the situation in which the leader and follower are embedded make a difference?
- What leader behavior works and when?
- What is the process through which the situation produces its effects?

The importance of the situation has already been alluded to on numerous occasions through the first four chapters. Murphy (1941), for example, noted that situations in which people find themselves create needs, and it is the nature of these needs that defines the type of leadership that best serves the group. Accordingly, Murphy saw leadership as a function (interaction) of (a) what it is that an individual has to offer and (b) the nature of the demands placed upon followers by the situation in which they are embedded. In a similar fashion, Stogdill (1948) suggested that leadership is a working relationship—one in which different contexts create a unique set of group needs, and a group's emerging leader is that individual who is capable of making meaningful contributions to the group.

Leaders, according to Smircich and Morgan (1982), are those individuals who are capable of taking an ambiguous situation and framing it in a meaningful and acceptable way for the followers. Smircich and Morgan also defined leadership as a product of an interaction between the situation, the leader, and the followers.

In Salancik and Pfeffer's (1977) strategic contingencies model of leadership, the leader is a person who brings scarce resources to assist a group of individuals overcome a critical problem that they are facing. As the problems facing a group change, their leader may also change because of his or her access to critical and scarce resources. Thus, Salancik and Pfeffer's work also serves to highlight the importance of the situation in defining leadership and the leadership process.

Chapter Four's overview of the leader behavior literature highlighted the fact that there are inconsistent relationships between the behaviors that leaders engage in and the effects of these behaviors on member attitudes, behavior, and group effectiveness. While these inconsistent observations (e.g., the relationship between initiating structure and performance is sometimes positive, while at other times there is no significant relationship, or the relationship is negative in nature) can be frustrating, they underscore two very important facts. First, these behaviors (e.g., initiating structure and consideration) are *important* as witnessed by their occasionally significant relationship with follower attitudes and behavior. Second, the observation that these behaviors do not always produce significant and positive effects suggests that *something else is transpiring,* such that in one situation the particular leader behavior produces significant effects, and in another situation that behavior is relatively unimportant. The question that these observations raise is, "What effects do situational differences produce in the leader-follower relationship?"

Many decades ago Ralph Stogdill (1948) stated that "the qualities, characteristics, and skills required in a leader are determined to a large extent by the demands of the situation in which he [she] is to function as a leader" (p. 63). Chapter Five provides an understanding of situational differences in the leadership process.

The simple theme of this chapter might well be "different strokes for different folks" and/or "different strokes for the same folks at different points in time." Put more directly, as conditions change, so do the leadership needs that are created and the leader behaviors that will prove effective. If team members know, for example, exactly what needs to be done, when, how, and why, it is unlikely that initiating structure will prove to be needed, or effective if used. In contrast, when team members are operating under conditions of high levels of uncertainty—not knowing what, when, or how to execute the task—a leader who is capable of initiating some structure will make a meaningful contribution.

Influenced by Stogdill's (1948, 1974) reviews of the leader behavior literature and the emerging recognition of the importance of the leadership context, Steven Kerr, Chester A. Schriesheim, Charles J. Murphy, and Ralph M. Stogdill (1974), in the first reading in this chapter, advanced a number of situational propositions linking leader initiation of structure and consideration to leader effectiveness. They note that accumulated evidence suggests that leader effectiveness is not always associated with those who behave in a highly considerate and structuring manner. Among some of the situational factors that influence the effectiveness of leader consideration and initiating structure behavior are, for example, time urgency, amount of physical danger, presence of external stress, degree of autonomy, degree of job scope, importance and meaningfulness of work.

Robert J. House (1971) contends that leader effectiveness is most appropriately examined in terms of the leader's *impact* upon the performance of his or her followers.[1] In the second reading in this chapter, House and Terence R. Mitchell (1974) assert that a leader's behavior will be motivational and subsequently have an impact upon the attitudes and performance behavior of the follower to the extent that it makes the satisfaction of a subordinate's needs contingent upon his or her performance. The strategic functions of a leader, according to House and Mitchell, consist of "(1) recognizing and/or arousing subordinates' needs for outcomes over which the leader has some control, (2) increasing personal payoffs to subordinates for work-goal attainment, (3) making the path to those payoffs easier to travel by coaching and direction, (4) helping subordinates clarify expectancies, (5) reducing frustrating barriers, and (6) increasing the opportunities for personal satisfaction contingent on effective performance" (p. 229). Characteristics of the follower and the situation in which the leader and follower are embedded tend to alter the nature of the leader-follower relationship. Thus, the effectiveness of a leader's behavior is a function of the influence that the leader exercises over the follower in interaction with attributes of the work environment.

According to House and Mitchell, there are four important dimensions to leader behavior—supportive (consideration), directive (initiating structure), participative, and achievement-oriented leadership—that are important under different situational (i.e., task-based) conditions. Their path-goal model addresses the leader's unique need to provide for follower satisfaction, motivation, and performance under four different task conditions: boring, ambiguous, unstructured, and lack of challenge. Role ambiguity, for example, calls for directive leadership to clarify the path to performance. The reduction of role ambiguity enables followers to see their way more clearly toward performance accomplishment. This role clarification, coupled with directive leadership, should prove to be motivating and satisfying for the employee, ultimately producing positive performance consequences.

The third reading in this section presents Fred E. Fiedler's (1974) contingency theory of leadership. Fiedler argues that situations vary in the degree to which they are favorable to the leader. Some situations are simply more favorable for a leader than other situations. Three factors that have a major influence on situation favorability are *leader-*

---

[1] R. J. House, "A Path-Goal Theory of Leader Effectiveness," *Administrative Science Quarterly* 16(1971), 321–38.

member relations (i.e., the quality of the relationship between the leader and followers as might be reflected by the degree to which the group accepts the leader, and member loyalty to the leader), *task structure* (i.e., the degree of structure of the task to be performed as might be reflected by the presence of a clear and unambiguous goal and a well-defined procedure that details how to proceed), and *position power* (i.e., the leader's ability to influence the followers as might be achieved through the exercise of legitimate, reward, coercive, expert, and/or referent power).

An important part of the leadership process, according to Fiedler, is the interaction of the leader's orientation toward others and the favorability of the leadership situation. Some leaders have a strong interpersonal orientation. These individuals need to develop and maintain close interpersonal relationships. Task accomplishment is of secondary importance and becomes important only after their relationship needs have been reasonably well satisfied. Other leaders have a strong task orientation. Their first motivational concern centers on task accomplishment with the development of good interpersonal relationships being a secondary interest. According to the contingency theory of leadership, leaders' motivational orientation toward others can be captured by the attitudes they express about their *least preferred co-worker (LPC)*. (The self-assessment presented at the end of this chapter opener enables you to profile yourself according to your own "least preferred co-worker.")

Leaders with a high LPC score tend to see their least preferred co-workers in fairly favorable terms. These leaders tend to be relationship-oriented, and they are most effective as leaders in situations of intermediate favorability. Leaders with a low LPC score are more task-oriented, and they tend to evaluate their least preferred co-worker fairly negatively. These individuals and their directive leadership styles tend to be associated with effective group performance under highly favorable and unfavorable situations.

Paul Hersey and Kenneth Blanchard's (1976) situational leadership model has received a high level of visibility among management practitioners. Hersey and Blanchard tend to see both the situation facing the leader and follower, and the follower, as significant components of the context facing the leader and his or her choice as to the appropriate style of leadership. According to their situational theory of leadership, appropriate leader behavior is defined by (a) situational demands for direction (task behavior) and socioemotional support (relationship behavior) and (b) the level of "maturity" of the follower or group relative to the task or objective that the leader is attempting to accomplish through the follower's efforts.

It should be noted that there are inconsistent views as to whether or not there is a "one best style" of leadership. Blake and Mouton (1981), discussed in the last chapter, advocate (in their "managerial grid") that the "ideal" is a leader who exhibits high levels of task- and relationship-oriented behavior. Several of the authors presented in this chapter, including Hersey and Blanchard, essentially argue that any one of a number of different styles of leadership is effective, so long as it is appropriately matched with the task (situation) facing the group.

Jan P. Muczyk and Bernard C. Reimann (1987), in the fifth reading, offer a situational view of leadership that revolves around involvement and the exercise of power in the context of decision making and decision execution. Their work defines four different styles of leadership as reflected by the amount of follower participation in the decision-making process and the amount of leader-imposed direction used in the execution of decisions.

Participative leader behavior refers to the degree to which the leader allows his or her followers to become involved in the decision-making *process.* "Autocratic leaders" use their position power to make decisions, while the "democratic (participative) leader" endorses employee involvement at each stage of the decision-making process. *Directive leader behavior* refers to the degree to which the leader allows subordinates to *execute* decisions once they have been made. At one extreme the "permissive leader" allows his or her followers to carry out decisions any way they see fit, and at the other extreme the "directive leader" specifies how activities are to be executed. This classification scheme enables Muczyk and Reimann to identify four different "styles of leadership"—

F I G U R E   5 . 1
The Leadership Process: Critical Contextual Factors

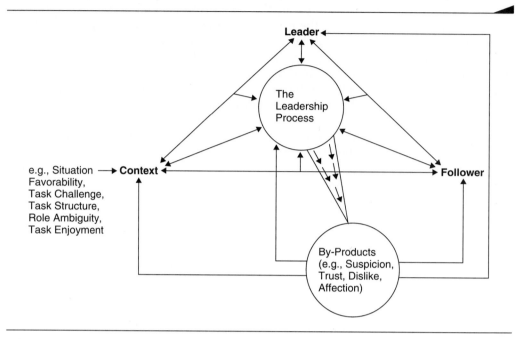

directive/autocrat, permissive/autocrat, directive/democrat, and permissive/democrat—each of which they believe to be an appropriate style dependent upon the nature of the situation facing the leader.

Muczyk and Reimann's situation-based leadership model revolves around several situational factors. The level of expertise/experience possessed by followers, as well as their ability to exercise self-direction and self-control, plays a major role shaping what might be an appropriate leader behavior. In addition to these individual attributes, coordination needs, the availability of time, and the routineness of the tasks also play a major role influencing what might be an appropriate leader behavior.

Figure 5.1 highlights several important components that now contribute to the leadership mosaic. Situational conditions (i.e., attributes of the task being performed) and follower attributes (e.g., task frustration, experienced ambiguity, expertise, ability to exercise self-direction and self-control) interact with the leader, shaping what might be capable of producing effective leadership.

The next chapter continues to look at the situation facing the leader. It focuses, in part, on the role played by the followers. As suggested by figure 5.1, followers influence the leader, they help define the nature of the situation facing the leader, and they shape the effects of the leader's influence attempts.

Self-Assessment

Least Preferred Co-Worker (LPC)

Instructions: Think of the person with whom you can work least well. This may be someone you work with now or someone you knew in the past. It does not have to be the person you like least well, but should be the person with whom you had the most difficulty in getting a job done. Describe this person as he or she appears to you, by circling a number for each scale.

Pleasant	8	7	6	5	4	3	2	1	Unpleasant
Friendly	8	7	6	5	4	3	2	1	Unfriendly
Rejecting	1	2	3	4	5	6	7	8	Accepting
Helpful	8	7	6	5	4	3	2	1	Frustrating
Unenthusiastic	1	2	3	4	5	6	7	8	Enthusiastic
Tense	1	2	3	4	5	6	7	8	Relaxed
Distant	1	2	3	4	5	6	7	8	Close
Cold	1	2	3	4	5	6	7	8	Warm
Cooperative	8	7	6	5	4	3	2	1	Uncooperative
Supportive	8	7	6	5	4	3	2	1	Hostile
Boring	1	2	3	4	5	6	7	8	Interesting
Quarrelsome	1	2	3	4	5	6	7	8	Harmonious
Self-Assured	8	7	6	5	4	3	2	1	Hesitant
Efficient	8	7	6	5	4	3	2	1	Inefficient
Gloomy	1	2	3	4	5	6	7	8	Cheerful
Open	8	7	6	5	4	3	2	1	Guarded

Scoring: Your LPC score is the sum of the answers to these 16 questions. A high score (greater than 76) reflects a relationship orientation, while a low score (less than 62) signals a task orientation.

Interpretation: According to Fiedler's work a person with a high LPC tends to be relationship-oriented. These leaders generally tend to perform best under conditions of intermediate favorability. Leaders with a low LPC score are more task-oriented, and they tend to function best under conditions of high and low favorability. Work by John K. Kennedy, Jr. (1982) indicates that "the performance of middle LPC leaders is generally superior to that of the high and low LPC leaders. . . ." (p. 1)[2]

Source: F. E. Fiedler and M. M. Chemers, *Leadership and Effective Management* (Glenview, IL: Scott, Foresman, 1974).

[2]J. K. Kennedy, Jr., "Middle LPC Leaders and the Contingency Model of Leadership Effectiveness," *Organizational Behavior and Human Performance* 31(1982), 1–14.

Toward a Contingency Theory of Leadership Based upon the Consideration and Initiating Structure Literature

S. Kerr, C. A. Schriesheim, C. J. Murphy, and R. M. Stogdill
The Ohio State University

Introduction

The Ohio State Leadership Studies comprise one of the most comprehensive research programs in the fields of industrial psychology and organizational behavior, and the leader behavior scales derived from these studies have been utilized by literally hundreds of researchers during the last quarter century. Through the years the Ohio State research has sustained its share of criticisms, perhaps the most serious of which is the contention that the studies fail to take situational variables into account (Korman, 1966; Bobbitt, Breinholt, Doktor & McNaul, Chap. 6, in press) and lack a conceptual base. Critics have argued that the effect of the studies has been to support a behavioral theory in which optimality is achieved by combining high Consideration with high Initiating Structure, regardless of situation, in a way that is analogous to the 9–9 leadership style on the Managerial Grid (Blake, Mouton & Bidwell, 1962).

There is some irony in these criticisms, in that a number of those who participated in the Ohio State studies have evidenced a keen awareness of the importance of such situational variables. For example, Fleishman wrote that "research has indicated that leadership is to a great extent situational, and that what is effective leadership in one situation may be ineffective in another." That statement was published in 1953 (a), and was preceded by similar remarks by Stogdill (1948) and by Hemphill (1950).

It is true that many researchers have found a high-Consideration high-Initiating Structure combination to be related to maximal satisfaction and performance (Halpin, 1957a; Keeler & Andrews, 1963; Cunningham, 1964; Misumi & Toshiaki, 1965; Hooper, 1968; Pacinelli, 1968; Fleishman & Simmons, 1970; Yukl, 1971). However, arguments for a high-high style of leadership overlook several important considerations. First, it is known that Consideration and Structure often fail to be independent, and may in fact be negatively correlated (Lowin, Hrapchak & Kavanagh, 1969; Weissenberg & Kavanagh, 1972; Hammer & Dachler, 1973). This may reflect "realities" of the environment being studied, or may result instead from respondent inability to consider the two dimensions separately. In either case, it is often extremely difficult for a leader to behave in such a way that his subordinates will perceive him to be simultaneously high in both Consideration and Structure.

It is also true that while in general high scores on both dimensions may relate positively to satisfaction, morale, and performance, dysfunctional consequences often accompany such scores as well. For example, Consideration has sometimes been found to vary negatively with proficiency ratings by higher management (Harris, 1952; Fleishman, Harris & Burtt, 1955; Graen, Dansereau & Minami, 1972), and Structure often correlates negatively with subordinate satisfaction, grievances, and turnover (Fleishman & Harris, 1962) as well as adversely affecting performance (Cummins, 1971, 1972). Thus, while positive consequences may *generally* result from highly considerate and structuring behavior, this may prove scant consolation to a *particular* supervisor whose job security is low, and whose manager expects low Consideration.

Finally, it should be pointed out that researchers have discovered a number of exceptions to the general rule that a high-high leadership style is the most effective one. Preferences for and attitudes toward Consideration and Structure have been found to vary considerably as a function of both the individual and the situation (Hunt & Liebscher, 1973).

For these reasons it seems an oversimplifcation to claim that the effective leader needs "merely" to behave in a highly considerate and structuring manner. The research literature suggests much more subtlety. . . .

Important Moderating Variables

In the discussion which follows, reference will be made to variables which moderate between the leader behavior "predictors" and various organizational "criteria." These terms are employed in this review because the great majority of the reviewed studies established their designs in this way. In fact, however, there is considerable validity to the criticisms raised by Korman (1966), Lowin and Craig (1968), Yukl (1971), and others, to the effect that the direction of causality between leader behavior and subordinate attitudes and work group performance has not been firmly established. A full treatment of this issue is provided elsewhere (Kerr & Schriesheim, 1974). In general, it seems safe to say that under some conditions subordinate performance *causes* subsequent leader behaviors (Lowin & Craig, 1968; Farris & Lim, 1969) while in other instances subordinate performance *is caused by* leader behavior (Lowin *et al.*, 1969; Hand & Slocum, 1972; Dawson, Messe & Phillips, 1972). It may turn out that the relationship is often one of extensive interdependency. . . .

Source: Edited and reprinted with permission from *Organizational Behavior and Human Performance*, 12(1974), 62–82. Copyright © 1974, Academic Press, Inc. Author affiliation may have changed since article was first published. Results section and corresponding table in this article appear in the *Instructor's Manual*.

The following variables, then, have been found to exert a strong influence between the leader behavior "predictors" Consideration and Initiating Structure and various satisfaction, morale, and performance "criteria."

Pressure

This can take the form of time urgency, task demands, interunit stress, or physical danger. For example, Halpin (1954) found that Initiating Structure was negatively related to platoon members' satisfaction in training, but was positively related to their satisfaction in combat. Halpin (1953) obtained results showing that combat air crews working under threatening situations preferred high Structure, and Holloman (1967) found that military supervisors were expected to be higher in Structure and lower in Consideration than were civilian supervisors.

Attempting to explain similar findings, Oaklander and Fleishman (1964) suggested that when a threat is seen as stemming from external sources (such as interunit stress), Initiating Structure may act as a protective shield. On the other hand, when intraunit stress was involved, Consideration (as measured by the LOQ) was found to be more helpful.

The above studies were affected by pressure which was clearly from external sources. However, other studies which involved pressure arising from urgency of time demands have yielded consistent data. For example, Dawson *et al.* (1972) used an altered version of the Supervisory Behavior Description Questionnaire (SBDQ), and obtained data supportive of the conclusion of Fleishman *et al.* (1955), that correlations between proficiency ratings and Structure were significantly positive only in cases when there was a high degree of time pressure. Fleishman *et al.* also found that departments subject to extensive time demands had leaders who were rated more proficient when they exhibited high-Structure low-Consideration behavior. In departments where such time demands were less common, higher performance ratings were associated with more considerate and less structuring behavior.

Task-Related Satisfaction

Based on data gathered from three firms, House, Filley, and Kerr (1971) concluded that when work was not intrinsically satisfying, increased resentment and dissatisfaction seemed likely to occur as the imposition of deadlines and Structure increased. Reviewing the literature relevant to this point, and citing new data as well, House (1971) elaborated upon this conclusion by stating that relationships between Consideration and subordinate satisfaction and performance tended to be less positive when the task was intrinsically satisfying. In instances when the task failed to provide intrinsic satisfaction, Structure-satisfaction relationships tended to be more negative, but Structure-performance relationships were likely to be more positive.

This conclusion is consistent with Fleishman's (1973) review of the literature and is supported by more recent work by Hunt and Liebscher (1973) as well.

In general, intrinsic satisfaction may often be increased by providing high autonomy and broad job scope, and the studies presented by House (1971) examined the moderating effects of both these dimensions.

Subordinate Need for Information

In general, such needs may result either from characteristics of the individual or from the nature of the task. For example, Soliman, Hartman and Olinger (1972) found that engineers who had low job knowledge perceived Structure as more important than Consideration, while for those whose knowledge was at least adequate, Consideration was most important. In the same vein, Kavanagh (1972) used selected items from the SBDQ on a student sample, and found that "when the subordinate is competent, the supervisor's behavior (relative to task structuring) is more frequently judged to be too much than when the subordinate's competence is low" (p. 597).

An important task-related determinant of need for information is high role ambiguity, and so House's (1971) finding that "the more ambiguous the task the more positive the relationship between leader initiating structure and subordinate satisfaction" (p. 325) is consistent with the studies cited above, and is at least partially supported by more recent work by Dessler (1972; 1973), House and Dessler (in press), and Greene (in press). Stinson and Johnson (1973) found, however, that Structure-satisfaction relationships were positive under conditions of high task certainty and negative under low task certainty.

There has also been some support for House's (1971) conclusion that relationships between leader Consideration and subordinate satisfaction tended to decrease as task certainty decreased. Similar results have recently been described by Dessler (1972), House and Dessler (in press), and Stinson and Johnson (1973).

Job Level

Nealey and Blood (1968) found selected items of the Initiating Structure scale to be positively related to satisfaction at a low supervisory level, but negatively related to satisfaction at a higher level. This is consistent with Stogdill and Coons (1957), with Hill and Hunt (1973), and with Bradshaw (1970), whose data showed respondent preference for Structure (measured by the ideal LBDQ) to diminish at higher organizational levels.

On the other hand, several studies (House, Wigdor & Shulz, 1970; House *et al.*, 1971b; House, Filley & Gujarati, 1971) have obtained strong positive correlations between Structure and satisfaction of high-level subjects. Comparing these results to negative relationships found at lower levels by Fleishman and Harris (1962), House (1971) concluded that Structure seems to clarify path-goal relationships for higher occupational level jobs, while increasing both productivity and dissatisfaction at the lower levels.

House also found in his review of earlier research that Consideration tended to have positive associations with satisfaction for low-level respondents, while having less important associations with higher level subjects. This is consistent with Hemphill (1959), who stated that Consideration was more important among workers at low levels. However, Stogdill and Coons (1957) found Consideration to be important at both the first and second supervisory levels, and Nealey and Blood (1968) and Bradshaw (1970) found preference for Consideration to be relatively constant across different organizational levels.

Finally, several studies (Rambo, 1958, using a "yes" and "no" response choice version of the LBDQ; Hunt & Liebscher, 1971; Hunt, Hill & Reaser, 1971) revealed few or no important differences attributable to job level. Overall, then, while the majority of studies which considered job level as a moderating variable are in agreement about its importance, no clear consensus yet exists concerning the nature of its moderating effects. Since job level cannot be said to be independent of other variables discussed earlier, such as task-related satisfaction and subordinate need for information, research designs which control for these other variables will probably be necessary if more precise information is to be obtained. Notice should also be taken of Rice and Mitchell's (1973) contention that future researchers will do better to examine "factors which an individual himself is likely to perceive about his place in the organization" (p. 56) rather than to focus solely upon empirical relationships between structural properties and behavior. It is usually easy to obtain phenotypic information about organizational structure (in this case, merely by counting job levels), but such an approach is likely to mask more important genotypic differences, such as those concerning status, authority, etc.

Subordinate Expectations

Several studies have produced substantial agreement concerning the importance of subordinate expectations of leader Consideration and Structure as a moderator between such leader behaviors and satisfaction performance criteria. For example, it has been found (Hemphill, Siegel & Westie, 1951; Hemphill, 1955) that discrepancies between observed and expected Consideration and Structure are more closely and negatively related to performance than are either observed or expected behavior scores alone. Stogdill, Scott, and Jaynes (1956) reported that such discrepancies exerted important dysfunctional effects upon both follower performance and leader behavior. Fast (1964) obtained data showing that the greater the disparity between observed and expected Consideration and Structure scores, the lower were respondent (teachers) satisfaction scores. Similarly, Beer (1966) found that subjects whose expectations of emphasis on production (but not Initiating Structure) were high produced significantly higher relationships between perceived leader Structure and subordinate motivation.

The Beer study also found, however, that such expectations failed to moderate relationships between Consideration and motivation, and other studies have indicated that the moderating effects of expectations may themselves be situational. Thus Mannheim, Rim, and Grinberg (1967) reported that, while clerical workers who expect low Structure will reject a leader exhibiting high Structure, manual workers will not. Clerical workers will also reject a leader who is low in Consideration, even when low Consideration is expected. Again, manual workers will not. Given a choice, however, both clerical and manual workers will choose a leader high in Consideration, providing high Consideration is expected.

Congruence of Leadership Styles

Some researchers have found that Consideration and Initiating Structure scores of low-level supervisors were positively and significantly related to the scores of their higher-level superiors (Fleishman, 1951, 1953b; Fleishman *et al.*, 1955; Rambo, 1958). It has further been shown that the less foremen perceive Consideration to be desired by their supervisors, the higher the grievance rates supervised by the foremen (Fleishman, 1951, 1953c). It also seems that a superior's leader behavior may be more highly conditioned by the behavior of higher management than by training received (Fleishman *et al.*, 1955).

Furthermore, it has been found that knowing higher management's Consideration score added to the ability to predict relationships between lower management Consideration and subordinate satisfaction (Hunt *et al.*, 1971). The same study showed, however, that knowing the boss's boss Structure score added nothing to the ability to predict subordinate satisfaction. It was also found that even if the low-level boss is low in Consideration, subordinate satisfaction and performance relationships would increase if higher level management scored high in Consideration. It therefore seems that congruence of leadership style may not be as important a variable as is Consideration. That is, high Consideration by second-level supervisors may reinforce high Consideration by the first-level boss, and may therefore be associated with increased subordinate satisfaction and performance. If the first-level boss is *low* in Consideration, however, it appears preferable for the second-level supervisor to be *high* in Consideration anyway.

More recently, a comprehensive study by Hunt, Osborne and Larson (1973) obtained data which failed to show that congruency exerted any important influence. While it therefore seems safe to say that congruency of leadership style often acts as a significant moderator, its usefulness may be limited to certain situations. More needs to be known, for example, about the benefits of congruency in organizations which require rigid adherence to the chain of command, as compared with others which encourage direct contact between subordinates and management levels above that of the immediate supervisor.

It is also interesting that the studies by Fleishman and Rambo, which found congruency to be an important moderator, employed one measure (basically the SBDQ), while those which found congruency to be relatively unimportant (by Hunt *et al.*) utilized the LBDQ. It is possible that differences in the measuring instruments may account for the apparent inconsistency in findings.

Subordinate's Organizational Independence

Studies have shown that subordinate's perceived independence from the organization, measured essentially in terms of ability to leave, systematically moderates relationships between Consideration and Structure predictors and satisfaction criteria. In general, the greater the perceived independence, the more positive and significant are the relationships (House & Wigdor, 1969; Kerr, House & Wigdor, 1971; House & Kerr, 1973). Herold (1972) found, however, that for employees whose supervisors had high upward influence, organizational independence significantly moderated between Consideration and satisfaction in the opposite direction to the above studies.

More recent work by Kerr (1973) expanded the organizational independence measure to include both ability and willingness to leave, and studied the relationships between leader behavior and satisfaction. He found that independence significantly moderated with respect to Consideration, but not for Structure. In common with most of the above studies, the data showed that for those whose perceived independence is small, relationships between Consideration and satisfaction are often insignificant. Subjects high in independence, however, did not provide data consistent with the earlier studies.

Leader Upward Influence

There is some evidence that this variable significantly moderates between leader predictors and satisfaction criteria, but the nature of its moderating effect is not yet clear. It has already been mentioned that Herold (1972) found positive and significant effects of organizational independence upon Consideration-satisfaction relationships, for workers whose boss had high upward influence. House *et al.* (1971a) found upward influence to be of little importance in one firm studied, but to significantly moderate relationships between Consideration and some measures of satisfaction in another firm.

Miscellaneous Factors

There are several other variables which may well prove to be important moderators, but for which evidence is still limited. Hemphill (1950) found, for example, that as size of the work group increases, so does subordinate acceptance of Initiating Structure. His data revealed that "superior" leaders of large groups generally exhibited high Structure and low Consideration.

Another study which focused upon the work group was done by Cummins (1972), who found that attitudes toward Initiating Structure (as measured by the LOQ) were significantly more negatively related to performance when the group's leader-member relations were poor.

Several findings also exist which indicate that psychological characteristics of the subordinate may be important moderators of leader behavior-criteria relationships. For example, Beer (1966) reported that subjects with greater high-order needs (esteem, autonomy, and self-actualization) are more highly motivated by Structure and are less motivated by Consideration than subjects whose low-order needs are more important. Evans (1973) found that people with a high internal orientation (on the I–E scale, Rotter, 1966) have stronger Consideration-motivation relationships than do people whose orientation is external. Finally, Dessler (1973) obtained data showing that, for highly authoritarian subordinates, Initiating Structure-satisfaction relationships are always positive (regardless of the extent to which task certainty exists).

Consideration as a Moderator

It was first reported by Fleishman and Harris (1962) that Consideration may act as a moderator between Initiating Structure and various criteria. They stated that under conditions of high Consideration, Structure may be perceived by subordinates as supportive and helpful, whereas under low Consideration the same structuring behavior may be seen as restrictive and threatening. This interpretation has been shown to be consistent with data from many other studies (Fleish-

man & Ko, 1962; Misumi & Toshiaki, 1965; Beer, 1966; Skinner, 1969; Fleishman & Peters, 1970; Hunt & Hill, 1971; Dessler, 1972, 1973) for such criteria as motivation, satisfaction, grievances, turnover, and overall performance. A recent discovery of such a moderating effect was made by Cummins (1971, 1972), who found that Initiating Structure (as measured by both the LOQ and higher management's ratings) had a greater effect upon quality of work when the leader believed that he should be high in Consideration. Another study by Dawson *et al.* (1972) reported that when Consideration was perceived to be high, all levels of Initiating Structure were associated with high performance. When Consideration was low, all Structure levels were related to low performance. Under conditions of medium Consideration, increasing Structure was associated with decreasing performance.

On the other hand, some samples of subjects at high occupational levels (House *et al.*, 1970; House *et al.*, 1971b) generated data where Consideration failed to exert an important moderating influence. House (1972) therefore concluded from these data that Consideration may be an important moderator of Structure-satisfaction relationships only for low-level subjects. . . .

Situational Propositions

Utilizing the situational elements listed above, a set of testable propositions follow from the literature reviewed earlier. In particular, many bear close resemblance to the hypotheses advanced in House's (1971) presentation of the Path-Goal theory. In fact it may be said that, while House selected studies from the literature to be illustrative of the points he was making, the more comprehensive review which forms the basis of this paper serves to confirm the representativeness of House's illustrations, particularly concerning his (1971) hypotheses 3, 5, 6, 7, and 8.

The propositions are presented below, in the order that each was previously discussed.

1. The greater the amount of pressure, the greater will be subordinate tolerance of leader Initiating Structure, and the greater will be the (positive) relationships between Structure and satisfaction and performance criteria. Pressure may stem from the nature of the task (degree of time urgency, uncertainty, permissible error rate) or from some threatening source external to the task.

2. The greater the intrinsic satisfaction provided by the task, the less positive will be relationships between Consideration and satisfaction and performance criteria. Intrinsic satisfaction may be derived from high job autonomy, broad job scope, or the opportunity to do interesting and meaningful work.

3. The greater the intrinsic satisfaction provided by the task, the less negative will be relationships between Structure and subordinate satisfaction.

4. The greater the intrinsic satisfaction provided by the task, the less positive will be relationships between Structure and performance.

5. The smaller the informational needs of subordinates, the lower will be their tolerance for Initiating Structure, and the less positive will be relationships between Structure and satisfaction criteria. Need for information may stem

from characteristics of the individual (caused by personality factors or lack of expertise, competence, general experience, or specific job knowledge) or of the task (caused by high task or role ambiguity).

6. The greater the amount of task certainty, the greater will be the (positive) relationships between leader Consideration and subordinate satisfaction.

7. The less the agreement between subordinate expectations of leader Consideration and Structure and their observations of these behaviors, the lower will be the levels of satisfaction and performance of subordinates. Such expectations typically result from a host of cultural, experiential, and informational sources.

8. The less higher management is perceived to exhibit Consideration; the lower will be the (positive) relationships between lower-level supervisors' Consideration and subordinate satisfaction.

9. The greater the perceived organizational independence of subordinates, the greater will be the (positive) relationships between leader behavior variables and satisfaction and performance criteria. Particularly when perceived independence is low, Consideration-satisfaction and Structure-satisfaction relationships will be relatively insignificant. The pattern may be very different, however, for employees whose supervisors are believed to have high upward influence.

10. The greater the perceived upward influence of the supervisor, the greater will be the (positive) relationships between Consideration and subordinate satisfaction. This will be especially true for subordinates who are highly dependent on their boss for such things as recognition, freedom, and physical and financial resources.

Two caveats concerning these propositions are probably in order. First, it seems worth repeating that many of the moderating variables are themselves interrelated, and the propositions cannot therefore be considered to be independent of one another. It will be necessary in the future to control somehow for those potential moderators not under investigation, in order to obtain more precise information about the effects of those which are.

Second, it has already been mentioned that most of the reviewed studies failed to establish research designs adequate to permit cause-effect relationships to be ascertained. The propositions cannot therefore be taken to signify that any consensus yet exists about the direction of causality. More rigorous research than has generally been done in the past will be necessary to learn under what conditions leader behavior is the *cause,* and under what conditions the *result,* of subordinate attitudes and behaviors.

These caveats notwithstanding, the propositions above can be combined to form two postulates which, although extremely general, are nevertheless useful in synthesizing much of the Consideration-Initiating Structure literature. These postulates are also supported by the theoretical tenets of the Path-Goal Theory (House, 1972) and the Exchange Model (Jacobs, 1970), and by many studies which measured leader behavior in ways other than through use of the Ohio State scales. These general postulates are as follows.

1. The more that subordinates are dependent upon the leader for provision of valued or needed services, the higher the positive relationships will be between leader behavior measures and subordinate satisfaction and performance.

There are many instances where "substitutes for leadership" exist, which act to reduce subordinate dependency upon the leader, and consequently impair the leader's ability to influence criteria relationships very much for either better or worse. Thus the existence of extensive government contracts, or rigid bureaucratic rules and regulations, can reduce subordinates' structuring-information needs almost to zero. In other instances the task may be totally specified by technology, or "professional standards" and methodology may render the leader superfluous (Kerr, in press b). In such cases attempts by the leader to impose Structure would tend to be viewed by subordinates as redundant, or "merely as unnecessary to clarify the requirements that subordinates were expected to meet" (House *et al.,* 1971b). Thus, Proposition 5 above is obviously consistent with this postulate.

If it can be hypothesized that intrinsic and extrinsic satisfaction may act as substitutes for one another (as is indicated by Deci, 1972), then Propositions 2 through 4 above can also be viewed as supportive of the postulate. To the extent that intrinsic satisfaction is provided the subordinate by the task itself, his dependency upon the leader for extrinsic satisfaction (through Consideration) is reduced (Proposition 2), and his need for externally imposed Structure to mandate performance is also reduced (Proposition 4). At the same time, he is less likely to view such Structure as dissatisfying, since its effect is to focus attention on a task which is, after all, intrinsically satisfying (Proposition 3).

If we further hypothesize that tasks which are highly certain are less likely to prove intrinsically satisfying, then subordinates who perform such tasks are more apt to be responsive to extrinsic satisfiers. Proposition 6 suggests that under such circumstances leader Consideration can be effective.

The only proposition which appears contrary to the general postulate stated above is number 9, which claims that organizational *independents* rather than *dependents* will yield the highest positive relationships between leader behavior variables and satisfaction and performance criteria. One would expect from the postulate that those least able to abandon an unfavorable employment situation would be most dependent upon their supervisor and upon organizational rewards. Further research is clearly necessary to reconcile this apparent inconsistency, although it should be noted in this regard that Herold's (1972) data did show that, for employees whose boss was perceived to have high upward influence (and who therefore could probably best provide promotions, raises, and other intrinsic and extrinsic rewards), Consideration-satisfaction relationships were *highest* for those low in organizational independence.

2. The more the leader is able to provide subordinates with valued, needed, or expected services, the higher the positive relationships will be between leader behavior measures and subordinate satisfaction and performance.

It has already been suggested that when supervisors

are perceived by subordinates to have high upward influence, they will tend to be viewed by those subordinates as being able to provide organizational rewards. Under these conditions it is logical, as Proposition 10 suggests, that leader Consideration will be more positively associated with subordinate satisfaction. In the same vein, when higher-level management appears to itself exhibit and encourage high Consideration, lower-level leader Consideration will be more positively associated with subordinate satisfaction (Proposition 8). Finally, Proposition 7 provides clear support for this postulate, by stating that, to the extent that leader behavior reflects subordinate expectations, such leader behavior will be more positively associated with both subordinate satisfaction and performance.

Toward a Contingency Theory of Leadership

The intent of this paper has been to derive some situational propositions from the voluminous literature on Consideration and Initiating Structure, and to provide some theoretical linkage among these propositions. No claim is made that such propositions and linkages are adequate to constitute a full theory of leadership. The current state of knowledge is simply not sufficient to permit the full specification of variables, relationships, and explanations necessary for such a theory. The effort presented here fails to meet a number of criteria of theoretical adequacy which is, incidentally, a dilemma shared by other current leadership "theories" (Schriesheim & Bish, 1974). For example:

1. The propositions fail to include all relevant variables necessary for a full explanation of the leadership process. For example, personal characteristics which condition both leader and subordinate behavior are not fully

included. Furthermore, the research reviewed in this paper, in common with leadership research in general, suffers from a lack of concern for group drive, arousal, and freedom of action. Thus, the major contributions made by leader Consideration to group functioning are generally ignored.

2. The propositions are not a set of lawlike statements. Taken together, they do not fully and precisely specify relationships among all variables.

3. No strict procedure for determining the consistency of each proposition with all others is provided.

4. Explanations for the observed relationships described in the propositions are for the most part inadequate. They may largely be considered to be atheoretical empiric generalizations.

These deficiencies, endemic to the field of leadership, must be overcome before the propositions advanced in this paper can be developed into a theory of leadership. Conceptualization of the leadership literature is continuously being attempted (e.g., Stodghill, 1974), but additional research will undoubtedly be needed.

Finally, the authors would like to state their belief that the situational approach undertaken in this paper more accurately reflects the character of the Ohio State research than do efforts to label the studies as behavioral theory dinosaurs, whose importance to the field is merely historical. We should probably also underscore the obvious fact that we have not invented the idea of treating the Consideration-Initiating Structure literature in a situational way. We have clearly drawn heavily upon material pertaining to the Path-Goal Theory, the Southern Illinois University research, and others. Our contribution has simply been one of synthesis and integration, in the hope of bringing us one step closer toward a contingency theory of leadership based upon the Consideration and Initiating Structure literature.

References

Beer, M. *Leadership, employee needs, and motivation.* Columbus: Bureau of Business Research, Ohio State University, Monograph No. 129, 1966.

Blake, R. R., Mouton, J. S., & Bidwell, A. C. Managerial grid. *Advanced Management—Office Executive,* 1962. 1, 12–15 & 36.

Bobbitt, H. R., Breinholt, R. H., Doktor, R. H., & McNaul, J. P. *Organizational behavior: understanding and prediction.* Englewood Cliffs. N.J.: Prentice-Hall. In press.

Bradshaw, H. H. Need satisfaction, management style and job level in a professional hierarchy. *Experimental Publication System,* 1970. 8, Ms. #289-1.

Cummins, R. C. Reliability of initiating structure and job performance as moderated by consideration. *Journal of Applied Psychology,* 1971, 55, 489–490.

Cummins, R. C. Leader-member relations as a moderator of the effects of leader behavior and attitude. *Personnel Psychology,* 1972, 25, 655–660.

Cunningham, C. J. Measures of leader behavior and their relation to performance levels of county extension agents. Unpublished doctoral dissertation. Ohio State University, 1964.

Dawson, J. A., Messe, L. A., & Phillips, J. I. Effects of instructor-leader behavior on student performance. *Journal of Applied Psychology,* 1972, 56, 369–376.

Deci, E. L. The effects of contingent and noncontingent rewards and controls on intrinsic motivation. *Organizational Behavior and Human Performance,* 1972, 8, 217–229.

Dessler, G. A test of a path-goal motivational theory of leadership. *Academy of Management Proceedings,* 1972, 178–181.

Dessler, G. A test of the path-goal theory of leadership. Unpublished doctoral dissertation. Baruch College, City University of New York, 1973.

Evans, M. G. Extensions to a path-goal theory of motivation. Unpublished paper, 1973.

Farris, G. F., & Lim, F. G. Effects of performance on leadership cohesiveness, influence, satisfaction and subsequent performance. *Journal of Applied Psychology,* 1969, 53, 490–497.

Fast, R. G. Leader behavior of principals as it relates to teacher satisfaction. Unpublished master's thesis. University of Alberta, 1964.

Fiedler, F. *A theory of leadership effectiveness.* New York: McGraw–Hill, 1967.

Fleishman, E. A. The relationship between leadership climate and supervisory behavior. Unpublished doctoral dissertation. Ohio State University, 1951.

Fleishman, E. A. The description of supervisory behavior. *Journal of Applied Psychology,* 1953 37, 1–6. (a)

Fleishman, E. A. Leadership climate, human relations training, and supervisory behavior. *Personnel Psychology,* 1953, 6, 205–222. (b)

Fleishman, E. A. Measurement of leadership attitudes in industry. *Journal of Applied Psychology,* 1953, 37, 153–158. (c)

Fleishman, E. A. The leadership opinion questionnaire. In R. M. Stodgill & A. E. Coons (Eds.), *Leader behavior: its description and measurement.* Columbus: The Bureau of Business Research, The Ohio State University, 1957, 120–133.

Fleishman, E. A. Twenty years of consideration and structure. In E. A. Fleishman and J. G. Hunt (Eds.), *Current developments in the study of leadership.* Carbondale: Southern Illinois University Press, 1973.

Fleishman, E. A., & Harris, E. F. Patterns of leadership behavior related to employee grievances and turnover. *Personnel Psychology*, 1962, 15, 43–56.

Fleishman, E. A., Harris, E. F., & Burtt, H. E. *Leadership and supervision in industry.* Columbus: Bureau of Education Research, Ohio State University, Research monograph No. 33, 1955.

Fleishman, E. A. & Ko. Unpublished paper, 1962. Cited in Fleishman. E. A., Twenty years of consideration and structure, 1973.

Fleishman, E. A., & Peters, D. R. Interpersonal values, leadership attitudes and managerial success. *Personnel Psychology*, 1962, 15, 127–143.

Fleishman, E. A., & Simmons, J. Relationship between leadership patterns and effectiveness ratings among Israeli foremen. *Personnel Psychology*, 1970, 23, 169–172.

Graen, G., Dansereau, F., & Minami, T. An empirical test of the man-in-the-middle hypothesis among executives in a hierarchical organization employing a unit-set analysis. *Organizational Behavior and Human Performance*, 1972, 8, 262–285.

Greene, C. N. A longitudinal analysis of relationships among leader behavior and subordinate performance and satisfaction. *Academy of Management Proceedings*. In press.

Halpin, A. W. The leadership behavior and combat performance of airplane commanders. *Journal of Abnormal and Social Psychology*, 1954, 49, 19–22.

Halpin, A. W. Studies in aircrew composition III, 1953. Cited in A. W. Halpin, *The leadership behavior of school superintendents.* Columbus: College of Education, The Ohio State University, 1956.

Halpin, A. W. *Manual for the leader behavior description questionnaire.* Columbus: Bureau of Business Research, Ohio State University, 1957.

Hammer, T. H., & Dachler, H. P. *The process of supervision in the context of motivation theory.* College Park: Department of Psychology, University of Maryland, Research Report No. 3, 1973.

Hand, H., & Slocum, J. A longitudinal study of the effect of a human relations training program on managerial effectiveness. *Journal of Applied Psychology*, 1972, 56, 412–418.

Harris, E. F. Measuring industrial leadership and its implications for training supervisors. Unpublished doctoral dissertation, Ohio State University, 1952.

Hemphill, J. K. Relations between the size of the group and the behavior of superior leaders. *Journal of Social Psychology*, 1950, 32, 11–22.

Hemphill, J. K. Leadership behavior associated with the administrative reputation of college departments. *Journal of Educational Psychology*, 1955, 46, 385–401.

Hemphill, J. K. Job descriptions for executives. *Harvard Business Review*, 1959, 37, 55–67.

Hemphill, J. K., Siegel, A., & Westie, C. W. An explanatory study of relations between perceptions of leader behavior, group characteristics, and expectations concerning the behavior of ideal leaders. Unpublished paper. Columbus: Personnel Research Board, Ohio State University, 1951.

Herold, D. M. Leader's hierarchical influence and subordinate's influence as moderators of considerate leadership style. In J. W. Slocum (Ed.), *Research in organizations.* Proceedings of the Ninth Annual conference of the Eastern Academy of Management, 1972, 139–149.

Hill, J. W., & Hunt, J. G. Managerial level, leadership, and employee need satisfaction. In E. A. Fleishman and J. G. Hunt (Eds.), *Current developments in the study of leadership.* Carbondale: Southern Illinois University Press, 1973.

Holloman, C. R. The perceived leadership role of military and civilian supervisors in a military setting. *Personnel Psychology*, 1967, 20, 199–210.

Hooper, D. B. Differential utility of leadership opinions in classical and moderator models for the prediction of leadership effectiveness. Unpublished doctoral dissertation, Ohio State University, 1968.

House, R. J. A path goal theory of leader effectiveness. *Administrative Science Quarterly*, 1971, 16, 321–338.

House, R. J. Some new applications and tests of the path-goal theory of leadership. Unpublished paper, 1972.

House, R. J. Leader initiating structure and subordinate performance, satisfaction and motivation: a review and a theoretical interpretation. Unpublished paper, 1973.

House, R. J., & Dessler, G. The path-goal theory of leadership: some post hoc and a priori tests. In J. G. Hunt and L. L. Larson (Eds.), *Contingency Approaches to leadership.* Carbondale: Southern Illinois University Press. In press.

House, R. J., Filley, A. C., & Gujarati, D. N. Leadership style, hierarchical influence, and the satisfaction of subordinate role expectations: a test of Likert's influence proposition. *Journal of Applied Psychology*, 1971, 55, 422–432. (a)

House, R. J., Filley, A. C., & Kerr, S. Relation of leader consideration and initiating structure to R & D subordinates' satisfaction. *Administrative Science Quarterly*, 1971, 16, 19–30 (b).

House, R. J., & Kerr, S. Organizational independence, leader behavior, and managerial practices: a replicated study. *Journal of Applied Psychology*, 1973, 58, 173–180.

House, R. J., & Wigdor, L. A Cosmopolitans and locals: some differential correlations between leader behavior, organizational practices, and employee satisfaction and performance. *Academy of Management Proceedings*, 1969, 135–137.

House, R. J., Wigdor, L. A., & Schulz, K. Psychological participation, leader behavior, performance and satisfaction: an extension of prior research and a motivation theory interpretation. *Proceedings of the Eastern Academy of Management*, 1970.

Hunt, J. G., & Hill, J. W. Improving mental hospital effectiveness: a look at managerial leadership. Technical report 71-4, Southern Illinois University, 1971.

Hunt, J. G., Hill, J. W., & Reaser, J. M. Consideration and Structure effects in mental institutions: an examination of two managerial levels. Technical report 71-1. Southern Illinois University, 1971. In *Proceedings of the Midwestern Academy of Management*, 1971.

Hunt, J. G., & Liebscher, V. K. C. Leadership and satisfaction at multiple levels in a highway department. Unpublished paper. Presented at the Institute for Management Sciences, 1971.

Hunt, J. G., & Liebscher, V. K. C. Leadership preference, leadership behavior, and employee satisfaction. *Organizational Behavior and Human Performance*, 1973, 9, 59–77.

Hunt, J. G., Osborne, R. N., & Larson, L. L. *Leadership effectiveness in mental institutions.* Carbondale: Southern Illinois University Technical Report, 1973.

Jacobs, T. O. *Leadership and exchange in formal organizations.* Alexandria, Virginia: Human Resources Research Organization, 1970.

Kavanagh, M. J. Leadership behavior as function of subordinate competence and task complexity. *Administrative Science Quarterly*, 1972, 17, 591–600.

Keeler, B. T., & Andrews, J. H. M. The leader behavior of principals, staff morale and productivity. *Alberta Journal of Educational Research*, 1963, 9, 179–191.

Kerr, S. Ability and willingness to leave as a moderator of relationships between task and leader variables and satisfaction. *Journal of Business Research*. In press. (a)

Kerr, S. Substitutes for leadership. In J. G. Hunt and L. L. Larson (Eds.), *Contingency approaches to leadership.* Carbondale: Southern Illinois University Press. In press. (b)

Kerr, S., House, R. J., & Wigdor, L. A. Some moderating effects of organizational independence. In M. W. Frey (Ed.). *New developments in management and organization theory.* Proceedings of the Eighth Annual Conference of the Eastern Academy of Management. 1971.

Kerr, S., & Schriesheim, C. Causality and stability in leader behavior description. *Proceedings of the Eastern Academy of Management Conference*, 1974.

Korman, A. K. "Consideration," "initiating structure," and organizational criteria—a review. *Personnel Psychology*, 1966, 19, 349–361.

Lowin, A., & Craig, J. R. The influence of level of performance on managerial style: an experimental object-lesson in the ambiguity of correlational data. *Organizational Behavior and Human Performance*, 1968, 3, 440–458.

Lowin, A., Hrapchak, W. J., & Kavanagh, M. J. Consideration and initiating structure: an experimental investigation of leadership traits. *Administrative Science Quarterly*, 1969, 14, 238–253.

Mannheim, B., Rim, Y., & Grinberg, G. Instrumental status of supervisors as related to workers' expectations. *Human Relations*, 1967, 20, 387–397.

Misumi, G., & Toshiaki, T. A study of the effectiveness of supervisory patterns in a Japanese hierarchical organization. *Japanese Psychological Research*, 1965, 7, 151–162.

Nealey, S. M., & Blood, M. R. Leadership performance of nursing supervisors at two organizational levels. *Journal of Applied Psychology*, 1968, 52, 414–422.

Oaklander, H., & Fleishman, E. A. Patterns of leadership related to organizational stress in hospital settings. *Administrative Science Quarterly*, 1964, 8, 520–532.

Pacinelli, R. N. Rehabilitation counselor job satisfaction as it relates to perceived leadership behavior and selected background factors. Unpublished doctoral dissertation. Pennsylvania State University, 1968.

Rambo, W. W. The construction and analysis of a leadership behavior rating form. *Journal of Applied Psychology*, 1958, 41, 409–415.

Rice, L. E., & Mitchell, T. R. Structural determinants of individual behavior in organizations. *Administrative Science Quarterly*, 1973, 18, 56–70.

Rotter, J. B. Generalized expectancies for internal versus external control of reinforcement. *Psychological Monographs,* 1966, 80, (whole No. 609), 1–28.

Schriesheim, C. A., & Bish, J. Toward a leadership theory. Unpublished paper, 1974.

Schriesheim, C., & Kerr, S. Psychometric properties of the Ohio State leadership scales. *Psychological Bulletin.* In press.

Skinner, E. W. Relationships between leader behavior patterns and organizational-situational variables. *Personnel Psychology,* 1969, 22, 489–494.

Soliman, H. M. Hartman, R. I., & Olinger, A. H. Leadership style under conditions of high and low knowledge. *Proceedings of the Fifteenth Annual Midwest Academy of Management Conference,* 1972.

Stinson, J. E., & Johnson, T. W. The path–goal theory of leadership: a partial test and suggested refinement. Unpublished paper, 1973.

Spector, A. J., Clark, R. A., & Glickman, A. S. Supervisory characteristics and attitudes of subordinates. *Personnel Psychology,* 1960, 13, 301–316.

Stogdill, R. M. Personal factors associated with leadership: a survey of the literature. *Journal of Psychology,* 1948, 25, 35–71.

Stogdill, R. M. *Manual for the leader behavior description questionnaire—form XII.* Columbus: Bureau of Business Research, Ohio State University, 1963.

Stogdill, R. M. Validity of leader behavior descriptions. *Personnel Psychology,* 1969, 22, 153–158.

Stogdill, R. M. *Handbook of leadership.* New York: Free Press, 1974.

Stogdill, R. M., & Coons, A. E. (Eds.). *Leader behavior: its description and measurement.* Columbus: Bureau of Business Research, Ohio State University, 1957.

Stogdill, R. M. Scott, E. L., & Jaynes, W. E. *Leadership and role expectations.* Columbus: Bureau of Business Research, Ohio State University, 1956.

Weissenberg, P., & Kavanagh, M. J. The independence of initiating structure and consideration: a review of the evidence. *Personnel Psychology,* 1972, 25, 119–130.

Yukl, G. Toward a behavioral theory of leadership. *Organizational Behavior and Human Performance,* 1971, 6, 414–440.

Path-Goal Theory of Leadership

R. J. House
University of Toronto

T. R. Mitchell
University of Washington

*A*n integrated body of conjecture by students of leadership, referred to as the "Path-Goal Theory of Leadership," is currently emerging. According to this theory, leaders are effective because of their impact on subordinates' motivation, ability to perform effectively, and satisfactions. The theory is called Path-Goal because its major concern is how the leader influences the subordinates' perceptions of their work goals, personal goals, and paths to goal attainment. The theory suggests that a leader's behavior is motivating or satisfying to the degree that the behavior increases subordinate goal attainment and clarifies the paths to these goals.

Historical Foundations

The path-goal approach has its roots in a more general motivational theory called expectancy theory.[1] Briefly, expectancy theory states that an individual's attitudes (e.g., satisfaction with supervision or job satisfaction) or behavior (e.g., leader behavior or job effort) can be predicted from: (1) the degree to which the job, or behavior, is seen as leading to various outcomes (expectancy) and (2) the evaluation of these outcomes (valences). Thus, people are satisfied with their job if they think it leads to things that are highly valued, and they work hard if they believe that effort leads to things that are highly valued. This type of theoretical rationale can be used to predict a variety of phenomena related to leadership, such as why leaders behave the way they do, or how leader behavior influences subordinate motivation.[2]

This latter approach is the primary concern of this article. The implication for leadership is that subordinates are motivated by leader behavior to the extent that this behavior influences expectancies, e.g., goal paths and valences, e.g., goal attractiveness.

Several writers have advanced specific hypotheses concerning how the leader affects the paths and the goals of subordinates.[3] These writers focused on two issues: (1) how the leader affects subordinates' expectations that effort will lead to effective performance and valued rewards, and (2) how this expectation affects motivation to work hard and perform well.

While the state of theorizing about leadership in terms of subordinates' paths and goals is in its infancy, we believe it is promising for two reason. First, it suggests effects of leader behavior that have not yet been investigated but which appear to be fruitful areas of inquiry. And, second, it suggests with some precision the situational factors on which the effects of leader behavior are contingent.

The initial theoretical work by Evans asserts that leaders will be effective by making rewards available to subordinates and by making these rewards contingent on the subordinate's accomplishment of specific goals.[4] Evans argued that one of the strategic functions of the leader is to clarify for subordinates the kind of behavior that leads to goal accomplishment and valued rewards. This function might be referred to as path clarification. Evans also argued that the leader increases the rewards available to subordinates by being supportive toward subordinates, *i.e.*, by being concerned about their status, welfare, and comfort. Leader supportiveness is in itself a reward that the leader has at his or her disposal, and the judicious use of this reward increases the motivation of subordinates.

Evans studied the relationship between the behavior of leaders and the subordinates' expectations that effort leads to rewards and also studied the resulting impact on ratings of the subordinates' performance. He found that when subordinates viewed leaders as being supportive (considerate of their needs) and when these superiors provided directions and guidance to the subordinates, there was a positive relationship between leader behavior and subordinates' performance ratings.

However, leader behavior was only related to subordinates' performance when the leader's behavior also was related to the subordinates' expectations that their effort would result in desired rewards. Thus, Evans' findings suggest that the major impact of a leader on the performance of subordinates is clarifying the path to desired rewards and making such rewards contingent on effective performance.

Stimulated by this line of reasoning, House, and House and Dessler advanced a more complex theory of the effects of leader behavior on the motivation of subordinates.[5] The theory intends to explain the effects of four specific kinds of leader behavior on the following three subordinate attitudes or expectations: (1) the satisfaction of subordinates, (2) the subordinates' acceptance of the leader and (3) the expectations of subordinates that effort will result in effective performance and that effective performance is the path to rewards. The four kinds of leader behavior included in the

Source: Edited and reprinted with permission from *Journal of Contemporary Business* (Autumn, 1974), 81–97. Author affiliation may have changed since article was first published.

theory are: (1) directive leadership, (2) supportive leadership, (3) participative leadership and (4) achievement-oriented leadership. Directive leadership is characterized by a leader who lets subordinates know what is expected of them, gives specific guidance as to what should be done and how it should be done, makes his or her part in the group understood, schedules work to be done, maintains definite standards of performance, and asks that group members follow standard rules and regulations. Supportive leadership is characterized by a friendly and approachable leader who shows concern for the status, well-being, and needs of subordinates. Such a leader does little things to make the work more pleasant, treats members as equals, and is friendly and approachable. Participative leadership is characterized by a leader who consults with subordinates, solicits their suggestions, and takes these suggestions seriously into consideration before making a decision. An achievement-oriented leader sets challenging goals, expects subordinates to perform at their highest level, continuously seeks improvement in performance, *and* shows a high degree of confidence that the subordinates will assume responsibility, put forth effort, and accomplish challenging goals. This kind of leader constantly emphasizes excellence in performance and simultaneously displays confidence that subordinates will meet high standards of excellence.

A number of studies suggest that these different leadership styles can be shown by the same leader in various situations.[6] For example, a leader may show directiveness toward subordinates in some instances and be participative or supportive in other instances.[7] Thus, the traditional method of characterizing a leader as either highly participative and supportive *or* highly directive is invalid; rather, it can be concluded that leaders vary in the particular fashion employed for supervising their subordinates. Also, the theory, in its present stage, is a tentative explanation of the effects of leader behavior—it is incomplete because it does not explain other kinds of leader behavior and does not explain the effects of the leader on factors other than subordinates' acceptance, satisfaction, and expectations. However, the theory is stated so that additional variables may be included in it as new knowledge is made available.

Path-Goal Theory

General Propositions

The first proposition of path-goal theory is that leader behavior is acceptable and satisfying to subordinates to the extent that the subordinates see such behavior as either an immediate source of satisfaction or as instrumental to future satisfaction.

The second proposition of this theory is that the leader's behavior will be motivational, *i.e.*, increase effort, to the extent that (1) such behavior makes satisfaction of subordinate's needs contingent on effective performance and (2) such behavior complements the environment of subordinates by providing the coaching, guidance, support, and rewards necessary for effective performance.

These two propositions suggest that the leader's strategic functions are to enhance subordinates' motivation to perform, satisfaction with the job, and acceptance of the leader. From previous research on expectancy theory of motivation, it can be inferred that the strategic functions of the leader consist of: (1) recognizing and/or arousing subordinates' needs for outcomes over which the leader has some control, (2) increasing personal payoffs to subordinates for work-goal attainment, (3) making the path to those payoffs easier to travel by coaching and direction, (4) helping subordinates clarify expectancies, (5) reducing frustrating barriers, and (6) increasing the opportunities for personal satisfaction contingent on effective performance.

Stated less formally, the motivational functions of the leader consist of increasing the number and kinds of personal payoffs to subordinates for work-goal attainment and making paths to these payoffs easier to travel by clarifying the paths, reducing road blocks and pitfalls, and increasing the opportunities for personal satisfaction en route.

Contingency Factors

Two classes of situational variables are asserted to be contingency factors. A contingency factor is a variable which moderates the relationship between two other variables such as leader behavior and subordinate satisfaction. For example, we might suggest that the degree of structure in the task moderates the relationship between leaders' directive behavior and subordinates' job satisfaction. Figure 1 shows how such a relationship might look. Thus, subordinates are satisfied with directive behavior in an unstructured task and are satisfied with nondirective behavior in a structured task. Therefore, we say that the relationship between leader directiveness and subordinate satisfaction is contingent upon the structure of the task.

FIGURE 1

Hypothetical Relationship between Directive Leadership and Subordinate Satisfaction with Task Structure as a Contingency Factor

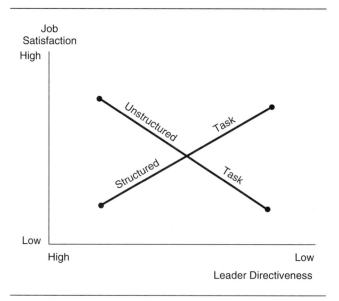

The two contingency variables are (a) personal characteristics of the subordinates and (b) the environmental pressures and demands with which subordinates must cope in order to accomplish the work goals and to satisfy their needs. While other situational factors also may operate to determine the effects of leader behavior, they are not presently known.

With respect to the first class of contingency factors, the characteristics of subordinates, path-goal theory asserts that leader behavior will be acceptable to subordinates to the extent that the subordinates see such behavior as either an immediate source of satisfaction or as instrumental to future satisfaction. Subordinates' characteristics are hypothesized to partially determine this perception. For example, Runyon[8] and Mitchell[9] show that the subordinate's source on a measure called Locus of Control moderates the relationship between participative leadership style and subordinate satisfaction. The Locus-of-Control measure reflects the degree to which an individual sees the environment as systematically responding to his or her behavior. People who believe that what happens to them occurs because of their behavior are called internals; people who believe that what happens to them occurs because of luck or chance are called externals. Mitchell's findings suggest that internals are more satisfied with a participative leadership style and externals are more satisfied with a directive style.

A second characteristic of subordinates on which the effects of leader behavior are contingent is subordinates' perception of their own ability with respect to their assigned tasks. The higher the degree of perceived ability relative to task demands, the less the subordinate will view leader directiveness and coaching behavior as acceptable. Where the subordinate's perceived ability is high, such behavior is likely to have little positive effect on the motivation of the subordinate and to be perceived as excessively close control. Thus, the acceptability of the leader's behavior is determined in part by the characteristics of the subordinates.

The second aspect of the situation, the environment of the subordinate, consists of those factors that are not within the control of the subordinate but which are important to need satisfaction or to ability to perform effectively. The theory asserts that effects of the leader's behavior on the psychological states of subordinates are contingent on other parts of the subordinates' environment that are relevant to subordinate motivation. Three broad classifications of contingency factors in the environment are: the subordinates' tasks, the formal authority system of the organization, and the primary work group.

Assessment of the environmental conditions makes it possible to predict the kind and amount of influence that specific leader behaviors will have on the motivation of subordinates. Any of the three environmental factors could act upon the subordinate in any of three ways: first, to serve as stimuli that motivate and direct the subordinate to perform necessary task operations; second, to constrain variability in behavior. Constraints may help the subordinate by clarifying expectancies that effort leads to rewards or by preventing the subordinates from experiencing conflict and confusion. Constraints also may be counterproductive to the extent that they restrict initiative or prevent increases in effort from being associated positively with rewards. Third, environmental factors may serve as rewards for achieving desired performance, e.g., it is possible for the subordinate to receive the necessary cues to do the job and the needed rewards for satisfaction from sources other than the leader, e.g., co-workers in the primary work group. Thus, the effect of the leader on subordinates' motivation will be a function of how deficient the environment is with respect to motivational stimuli, constraints or rewards.

With respect to the environment, path-goal theory asserts that when goals and paths to desired goals are apparent because of the routine nature of the task, clear group norms, or objective controls of the formal authority systems, attempts by the leader to clarify paths and goals will be both redundant and seen by subordinates as imposing unnecessary, close control. Although such control may increase performance by preventing soldiering or malingering, it also will result in decreased satisfaction (*see Figure 1*). Also with respect to the work environment, the theory asserts that the more dissatisfying the task, the more the subordinates will resent leader behavior directed at increasing productivity or enforcing compliance to organizational rules and procedures.

Finally, with respect to environmental variables, the theory states that leader behavior will be motivational to the extent that it helps subordinates cope with environmental uncertainties, threats from others, or sources of frustration. Such leader behavior is predicted to increase subordinates' satisfaction with the job context and to be motivational to the extent that it increases the subordinates' expectations that their effort will lead to valued rewards.

These propositions and specification of situational contingencies provide a heuristic framework on which to base future research. Hopefully, this will lead to a more fully developed, explicitly formal theory of leadership.

Figure 2 presents a summary of the theory. It is hoped that these propositions, while admittedly tentative, will provide managers with some insights concerning the effects of their own leader behavior and that of others.

Empirical Support

The theory has been tested in a limited number of studies which have generated considerable empirical support for our ideas and also suggest areas in which the theory requires revision. A brief review of these studies follows.

Leader Directiveness

Leader directiveness has a positive correlation with satisfaction and expectancies of subordinates who are engaged in ambiguous tasks and has a negative correlation with satisfaction and expectancies of subordinates engaged in clear tasks. These findings were predicted by the theory and have been replicated in seven organizations. They suggest that when task demands are ambiguous or when the organization procedures, rules and policies are not clear, a leader behaving in a directive manner complements the tasks and the organization by providing the necessary guidance and psychological structure for subordinates.[10] However, when task demands are clear to subordinates, leader directiveness is seen more as a hindrance. . . .

Summary of Path-Goal Relationships

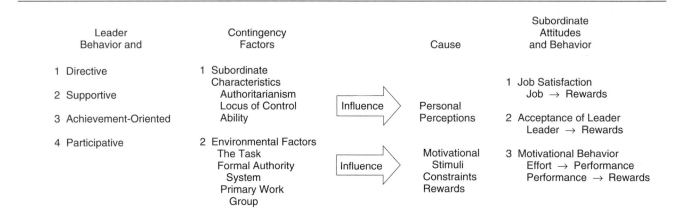

Supportive Leadership

The theory hypothesizes that supportive leadership will have its most positive effect on subordinate satisfaction for subordinates who work on stressful, frustrating or dissatisfying tasks. This hypothesis has been tested in 10 samples of employees,[14] and in only one of these studies was the hypothesis disconfirmed.[15] Despite some inconsistency in research on supportive leadership, the evidence is sufficiently positive to suggest that managers should be alert to the critical need for supportive leadership under conditions where tasks are dissatisfying, frustrating or stressful to subordinates. . . .

Achievement-Oriented Leadership

The theory hypothesizes that achievement-oriented leadership will cause subordinates to strive for higher standards of performance and to have more confidence in the ability to meet challenging goals. A recent study by House, Valency, and Van der Krabben provides a partial test on this hypothesis among white collar employees in service organizations.[16] For subordinates performing ambiguous, nonrepetitive tasks, they found a positive relationship between the amount of achievement orientation of the leader and subordinates' expectancy that their effort would result in effective performance. Stated less technically, for subordinates performing ambiguous, nonrepetitive tasks, the higher the achievement orientation of the leader, the more the subordinates were confident that their efforts would pay off in effective performance. For subordinates performing moderately unambiguous, repetitive tasks, there was no significant relationship between achievement-oriented leadership and subordinate expectancies that their effort would lead to effective performance. This finding held in four separate organizations.

Two plausible interpretations may be used to explain these data. First, people who select ambiguous, nonrepetitive tasks may be different in personality from those who select a repetitive job and may, therefore, be more responsive to an achievement-oriented leader. A second explanation is that achievement orientation only affects expectancies in am-

biguous situations because there is more flexibility and autonomy in such tasks. Therefore, subordinates in such tasks are more likely to be able to change in response to such leadership style. Neither of the above interpretations have been tested to date; however, additional research is currently under way to investigate these relationships.

Participative Leadership

In theorizing about the effects of participative leadership, it is necessary to ask about the specific characteristics of both the subordinates and their situation that would cause participative leadership to be viewed as satisfying and instrumental to effective performance.

Mitchell recently described at least four ways in which a participative leadership style would impact on subordinate attitudes and behavior as predicted by expectancy theory.[17] First, a participative climate should increase the clarity of organizational contingencies. Through participation in decision making, subordinates should learn what leads to what. From a path-goal viewpoint, participation would lead to greater clarity of the paths to various goals. A second impact of participation would be that subordinates, hopefully, should select goals they highly value. If one participates in decisions about various goals, it makes sense that this individual would select goals he or she wants. Thus, participation would increase the correspondence between organization and subordinate goals. Third, we can see how participation would increase the control the individual has over what happens on the job. If our motivation is higher (based on the preceding two points), then having greater autonomy and ability to carry out our intentions should lead to increased effort and performance. Finally, under a participative system, pressure towards high performance should come from sources other than the leader or the organization. More specifically, when people participate in the decision process, they become more ego-involved; the decisions made are in some part their own. Also, their peers know what is expected and the social pressure has a greater impact. Thus, motivation to perform well stems from internal and social factors as well as formal external ones.

A number of investigations prior to the above formulation supported the idea that participation appears to be helpful,[18] and Mitchell presents a number of recent studies that support the above four points.[19] However, it is also true that we would expect the relationship between a participative style and subordinate behavior to be moderated by both the personality characteristics of the subordinate and the situational demands. Studies by Tannenbaum and Alport and Vroom have shown that subordinates who prefer autonomy and self-control respond more positively to participative leadership in terms of both satisfaction and performance than subordinates who do not have such preferences.[20] Also, the studies mentioned by Runyon[21] and Mitchell[22] showed that subordinates who were external in orientation were less satisfied with a participative style of leadership than were internal subordinates.

House also has reviewed these studies in an attempt to explain the ways in which the situation or environment moderates the relationship between participation and subordinate attitudes and behavior.[23] His analysis suggests that where participative leadership is positively related to satisfaction, regardless of the predispositions of subordinates, the task of the subjects appear to be ambiguous and ego-involving. In the studies in which the subjects' personalities or predispositions moderate the effect of participative leadership, the tasks of the subjects are inferred to be highly routine and/or nonego-involving.

House reasoned from this analysis that the task may have an overriding effect on the relationship between leader participation and subordinate responses, and that individual predispositions or personality characteristics of subordinates may have an effect only under some tasks. It was assumed that when task demands are ambiguous, subordinates will have a need to reduce the ambiguity. Further, it was assumed that when task demands are ambiguous, participative problem solving between the leader and the subordinate will result in more effective decisions than when the task demands are unambiguous. Finally, it was assumed that when the subordinates are ego-involved in their tasks, they are more likely to want to have a say in the decisions that affect them. Given these assumptions, the following hypotheses were formulated to account for the conflicting findings reviewed above:

- When subjects are highly ego-involved in a decision or a task and the decision or task demands are ambiguous, participative leadership will have a positive effect on the satisfaction and motivation of the subordinate, *regardless* of the subordinate's predisposition toward self-control, authoritarianism or need for independence.

- When subordinates are not ego-involved in their tasks and when task demands are clear, subordinates who are

not authoritarian and who have high needs for independence and self-control will respond favorably to leader participation, and their opposite personality types will respond less favorably.

These hypotheses were derived on the basis of path-goal theorizing; *i.e.*, the rationale guiding the analysis of prior studies was that both task characteristics and characteristics of subordinates interact to determine the effect of a specific kind of leader behavior on the satisfaction, expectancies and performance of subordinates. To date, one major investigation has supported some of these predictions[24] in which personality variables, amount of participative leadership, task ambiguity, and job satisfaction were assessed for 324 employees of an industrial manufacturing organization. As expected, in nonrepetitive, ego-involving tasks, employees (regardless of their personality) were more satisfied under a participative style than a nonparticipative style. However, in repetitive tasks which were less ego-involving the amount of authoritarianism of subordinates moderated the relationship between leadership style and satisfaction. Specifically, low authoritarian subordinates were *more satisfied* under a participative style. These findings are exactly as the theory would predict; thus, it has promise in reconciling a set of confusing and contradictory findings with respect to participative leadership.

Summary and Conclusions

We have attempted to describe what we believe is a useful theoretical framework for understanding the effect of leadership behavior on subordinate satisfaction and motivation. Most theorists today have moved away from the simplistic notions that all effective leaders have a certain set of personality traits or that the situation completely determines performance. Some researchers have presented rather complex attempts at matching certain types of leaders with certain types of situations, e.g., the articles written by Vroom and Fiedler in this issue. But, we believe that a path-goal approach goes one step further. It not only suggests what type of style may be most effective in a given situation—it also attempts to explain *why* it is most effective.

We are optimistic about the future outlook of leadership research. With the guidance of path-goal theorizing, future research is expected to unravel many confusing puzzles about the reasons for and effects of leader behavior that have, heretofore, not been solved. However, we add a word of caution: the theory, and the research on it, are relatively new to the literature of organizational behavior. Consequently, path-goal theory is offered more as a tool for directing research and stimulating insight than as a proven guide for managerial action.

Notes

[1] T. R. Mitchell, "Expectancy Model of Job Satisfaction, Occupational Preference and Effort: A Theoretical, Methodological and Empirical Appraisal," *Psychological Bulletin* (1974, in press).

[2] D. M. Nebeker and T. R. Mitchell, "Leader Behavior: An Expectancy Theory Approach," *Organization Behavior and Human Performance*, Vol. 11 (1974), pp. 355–367.

[3] M. G. Evans, "The Effects of Supervisory Behavior on the Path-Goal Relationship," *Organizational Behavior and Human Performance*, Vol. 55 (1970), pp. 277–298; T. H. Hammer and H. T. Dachler, "The Process of Supervision in the Context of Motivation Theory," Research Report No. 3 (University of Maryland, 1973); F. Dansereau, Jr., J. Cashman and G. Graen, "Instrumentality Theory

and Equity Theory as Complementary Approaches in Predicting the Relationship of Leadership and Turnover among Managers," *Organization Behavior and Human Performance*, Vol. 10 (1973), pp. 184–200; R. J. House, "A Path-Goal Theory of Leader Effectiveness," *Administrative Science Quarterly*, Vol. 16, No. 3 (September 1971), pp. 321–338; T. R. Mitchell, "Motivation and Participation: An Integration,"

Academy of Management Journal, Vol. 16, No. 4(1973), pp. 160–179; G. Graen, F. Dansereau, Jr. and T. Minami, "Dysfunctional Leadership Styles," *Organizational Behavior and Human Performance*, Vol. 7(1972), pp. 216–236; ———, "An Empirical Test of the Man-in-the-Middle Hypothesis among Executives in a Hierarchical Organization Employing a Unit Analysis," *Organizational Behavior and Human Performance;* Vol. 8(1972), pp. 262–285; R. J. House and G. Dessler, "The Path-Goal Theory of Leadership: Some Post Hoc and A Priori Tests," to appear in J. G. Hunt, ed., *Contingency Approaches to Leadership* (Carbondale, Ill.: Southern Illinois University Press, 1974).

[4] M. G. Evans, "Effects of Supervisory Behavior"; ———, "Extensions of a Path-Goal Theory of Motivation," *Journal of Applied Psychology*, Vol. 59(1974), pp. 172–178.

[5] R. J. House, "A Path-Goal Theory"; R. J. House and G. Dessler, "Path-Goal Theory of Leadership."

[6] R. J. House and G. Dessler, "Path-Goal Theory of Leadership"; R. M. Stogdill, *Managers, Employees, Organization* (Ohio State University, Bureau of Business Research, 1965); R. J. House, A. Valency and R. Van der Krabben, "Some Tests and Extension of the Path-Goal Theory of Leadership" (in preparation).

[7] W. A. Hill and D. Hughes, "Variations in Leader Behavior as a Function of Task Type," *Organizational Behavior and Human Performance* (1974, in press).

[8] K. E. Runyon, "Some Interactions Between Personality Variables and Management Styles," *Journal of Applied Psychology*, Vol. 57, No. 3(1973), pp. 288–294; T. R. Mitchell, C. R. Smyser and S. E. Weed, "Locus of Control: Supervision and Work Satisfaction"; *Academy of Management Journal* (in press).

[9] T. R. Mitchell, "Locus of Control."

[10] R. J. House, "A Path-Goal Theory"; ——— and G. Dessler, "Path-Goal Theory of Leadership"; A. D. Szilagyi and H. P. Sims, "An Exploration of the Path-Goal Theory of Leadership in a Health Care Environment," *Academy of Management Journal* (in press); J. D. Dermer, "Supervisory Behavior and Budget Motivation" (Cambridge, Mass.: unpublished, MIT, Sloan School of Management, 1974); R. W. Smetana, "The Relationship between Managerial Behavior and Subordinate Attitudes and Motivation: A Contribution to a Behavioral Theory of Leadership" (Ph.D. diss., Wayne State University, 1974).

[11] S. E. Weed, T. R. Mitchell and C. R. Smyser, "A Test of House's Path-Goal Theory of Leadership in an Organizational Setting" (paper presented at Western Psychological Assoc., 1974); J. D. Dermer and J. P. Siegel, "A Test of Path-Goal Theory: Disconfirming Evidence and a Critique" (unpublished, University of Toronto, Faculty of Management Studies, 1973); R. S. Schuler, "A Path-Goal Theory of Leadership: An Empirical Investigation" (Ph.D. diss., Michigan State University, 1973); H. K. Downey, J. E. Sheridan and J. W. Slocum, Jr., "Analysis of Relationships Among Leader Behavior, Subordinate Job Performance and Satisfaction: A Path-Goal Approach" (unpublished mimeograph, 1974); J. E. Stinson and T. W. Johnson, "The Path-Goal Theory of Leadership: A Partial Test and Suggested Refinement," *Proceedings* (Kent, Ohio: 7th Annual Conference of the Midwest Academy of Management, April 1974), pp. 18–36.

[12] G. Dessler, "An Investigation of the Path-Goal Theory of Leadership" (Ph.D. diss., City University of New York, Bernard M. Baruch College, 1973).

[13] R. J. House, D. Burrill and G. Dessler, "Tests and Extensions of Path-Goal Theory of Leadership, I" (unpublished, in process).

[14] R. J. House, "A Path-Goal Theory"; ——— and G. Dessler, "Path-Goal Theory of Leadership"; A. D. Szilagyi and H. P. Sims, "Exploration of Path-Goal"; J. E. Stinson and T. W. Johnson, *Proceedings;* R. S. Schuler, "Path-Goal: Investigation"; H. K. Downey, J. E. Sheridan and J. W. Slocum, Jr., "Analysis of Relationships"; S. E. Weed, T. R. Mitchell and C. R. Smyser, "Test of House's Path-Goal."

[15] A. D. Szilagyi and H. P. Sims, "Exploration of Path-Goal."

[16] R. J. House, A. Valency and R. Van der Krabben, "Tests and Extensions of Path-Goal Theory of Leadership, II" (unpublished, in process).

[17] T. R. Mitchell, "Motivation and Participation."

[18] H. Tosi, "A Reexamination of Personality as a Determinant of the Effects of Participation," *Personnel Psychology*, Vol. 23(1970), pp. 91–99; J. Sadler, "Leadership Style, Confidence in Management and Job Satisfaction," *Journal of Applied Behavioral Sciences*, Vol. 6(1970), pp. 3–19; K. N. Wexley, J. P. Singh and J. A. Yukl, "Subordinate Personality as a Moderator of the Effects of Participation in Three Types of Appraisal Interviews," *Journal of Applied Psychology*, Vol. 83(1973), pp. 54–59.

[19] T. R. Mitchell, "Motivation and Participation."

[20] A. S. Tannenbaum and F. H. Allport, "Personality Structure and Group Structure: An Interpretive Study of Their Relationship Through an Event-Structure Hypothesis," *Journal of Abnormal and Social Psychology*, Vol. 53(1956), pp. 272–280; V. H. Vroom, "Some Personality Determinants of the Effects of Participation," *Journal of Abnormal and Social Psychology*, Vol. 59(1959), pp. 322–327.

[21] K. E. Runyon, "Some Interactions between Personality Variables and Management Styles," *Journal of Applied Psychology*, Vol. 57, No. 3(1973), pp. 288–294.

[22] T. R. Mitchell, C. R. Smyser and S. E. Weed, "Locus of Control."

[23] R. J. House, "Notes on the Path-Goal Theory of Leadership" (University of Toronto, Faculty of Management Studies, May 1974).

[24] R. S. Schuler, "Leader Participation, Task-Structure and Subordinate Authoritarianism" (unpublished mimeograph, Cleveland State University, 1974).

How Do You Make Leaders More Effective?
New Answers to an Old Puzzle

F. E. Fiedler
University of Washington

*L*et's begin with a basic proposition: The organization that employs the leader is as responsible for his success or failure as the leader himself. Not that this is a new insight—far from it. Terman wrote in 1904 that leadership performance depends on the situation, as well as on the leader. Although this statement would not be questioned by anyone currently working in this area, it also has been widely ignored. Practically all formal training programs attempt to change the individual; many of them assume explicitly or implicitly that there is one style of leadership or one way of acting that will work best under all conditions. Most military academies, for example, attempt to mold the individual into a supposedly ideal leader personality. Others assume that the training should enable the individual to become more flexible or more sensitive to his environment so that he can adapt himself to it.

Before going further let's define a few terms. I will confine my discussion to *task groups* rather than the organization of which the group is a part. Furthermore, we will assume that anyone who is placed in a leadership position will have the requisite technical qualifications for the job. Just as the leader of a surgical team obviously has to have medical training, so a manager must know the essential administrative requirements of his job. We will here talk primarily about training *as a leader* rather than training as a specialist. The effectiveness of the leader will be defined in terms of how well his group or organization performs the primary tasks for which the group exists. We measure the effectiveness of a football coach by how many games his team wins and not by the character he builds, and the excellence of an orchestra conductor by how well his orchestra plays, not by the happiness of his musicians or his ability as a musicologist. Whether the musicians' job satisfaction or the conductor's musicological expertness do, in fact, contribute to the orchestra's excellence is an interesting question in its own right, but it is not what people pay to hear. Likewise, the performance of a manager is here measured in terms of his department's or group's effectiveness in doing its assigned job. Whether the accomplishment of this job is to be measured after a week or after five years depends, of course, upon the assignment the organization gives the group, and the accomplishments the organization considers important.

When we think of improving leadership, we almost automatically think of training the individual. This training frequently involves giving the man a new perspective on his supervisory responsibilities by means of role playing, discussions, detailed instructions on how to behave toward subordinates, as well as instruction in the technical and administrative skills he will need in his job. A training program might last a few days, a few months, or as in the case of college programs and military academies, as long as four years. What is the hard evidence that this type of training actually increases organizational performance?

Empirical studies to evaluate the effectiveness of various leadership training programs, executive development, and supervisory workshops have been generally disappointing. Certainly, the two field experiments and two studies of ongoing organizations conducted by my associates and me failed to show that training increases organizational performance. . . .

I repeat that these findings are by no means unusual. Empirical studies to determine whether or not leadership training improves organizational performance have generally come up with negative findings. Newport, after surveying 121 large companies, concluded that not *one* of the companies had obtained any scientifically acceptable evidence that the leadership training for their middle management had actually improved performance.

T-group and sensitivity training, which has become fashionable in business and industry, has yielded similarly unsatisfactory results. Reviews of the literature by Campbell and Dunnette and by House found no convincing evidence that this type of training increased organizational effectiveness, and a well-known study at the International Harvester Company by Fleishman, Harris, and Burtt on the effects of supervisory training concluded that the effects of supervisory training in modifying behavior were very short-lived and did not improve performance.

Effect of Experience on Leadership

Let us now ask whether supervisory experience improves performance. Actually, since leadership experience almost always involves on-the-job training, we are dealing with a closely related phenomenon.

Interestingly enough, the literature actually contains few, if any, studies which attempt to link leadership experience to organizational effectiveness. Yet, there seems to be a firmly held expectation that leadership experience makes a leader more effective. We simply have more trust in experienced leaders. We can infer this, for example, from the many regulations that require time in grade before promotion to the next higher level, as well as the many specifications of prior job in hiring executives for responsible positions.

Source: Edited and reprinted by permission of publisher, from *Organizational Dynamics*, 1972, 1, 2, 3–18. Copyright American Management Association, New York. All rights reserved. Author affiliation may have changed since article was first published.

We have already seen that the experienced petty officers and military academy officers did not perform more effectively than did the inexperienced enlisted men, nor did the more experienced officers or petty officers perform better than the less experienced.

In addition, we also analyzed data from various other groups and organizations. These included directors of research and development teams at a large physical research laboratory, foremen of craftshops, general foremen in a heavy machinery manufacturing company, managers of meat, and of grocery markets in a large supermarket chain as well as post office supervisors and managers, and police sergeants. For all these managers we could obtain reliable performance ratings or objective group effectiveness criteria. None of the correlations was significant in the expected direction. The median correlation relating leadership experience to leadership performance for all groups and organizations was −.12—certainly not significant in the positive direction!

To summarize the findings, neither orthodox leadership training nor leadership experience nor sensitivity training appear to contribute across the board to group or organizational effectiveness. It is, therefore, imperative first that we ask why this might be so, and second that we consider alternative methods for improving leadership performance.

The Contingency Model

The "Contingency Model," a recent theory of leadership, holds that the effectiveness of group performance is contingent upon (a) the leader's motivational pattern and (b) the degree to which the situation gives the leader power and influence. We have worked with a leadership motivation measure called the "Esteem for the Least Preferred Co-worker," or LPC for short. The subject is first asked to think of all the people with whom he has ever worked, and then given a simple scale on which he describes the one person in his life with whom he has been able to work *least well*. This "least preferred co-worker" may be someone he knows at the time or it may be someone he has known in the past. It does not have to be a member of his present work group.

In grossly oversimplified terms, the person who describes his least preferred co-worker in relatively favorable terms is basically motivated to have close interpersonal relations with others. By contrast, the person who rejects someone with whom he cannot work is basically motivated to accomplish or achieve on the task, and he derives satisfaction from being recognized as having performed well on the task. The task-motivated person thus uses the task to obtain a favorable position and good interpersonal relations.

Classifying Leadership Situations

The statement that some leaders perform better in one kind of situation while some leaders perform better in different situations is begging a question, "What kinds of situations are best suited for which type of leader?" In other words, how can we best classify groups if we wish to predict leadership performance?

We can approach this problem by assuming that leadership is essentially a work relationship involving power and influence. It is easier to be a leader when you have complete control than when your control is weak and dependent on the good will of others. It is easier to be the captain of a ship than the chairman of a volunteer group organized to settle a school busing dispute. The *job* may be more complex for the navy captain, but *being in the leadership role* is easier for him than for the committee chairman. It is, therefore, not unreasonable to classify situations in terms of how much power and influence the situation gives the leader. We call this "situational favorableness." One simple categorization of groups on their situational favorableness classifies leadership situations on the basis of three major dimensions:

1. *Leader-member relations.* Leaders presumably have more power and influence if they have a good relationship with their members than if they have a poor relationship with them, if they are liked, respected, trusted, than if they are not. Research has shown that this is by far the most important single dimension.

2. *Task structure.* Tasks or assignments that are highly structured, spelled out, or programmed give the leader more influence than tasks that are vague, nebulous, and unstructured. It is easier, for example, to be a leader whose task it is to set up a sales display according to clearly delineated steps than it is to be a chairman of a committee preparing a new sales campaign.

3. *Position power.* Leaders will have more power and influence if their position is vested with such prerogatives as being able to hire and fire, being able to discipline, to reprimand, and so on. Position power, as it is here used, is determined by how much power the leader has over his subordinates. If the janitor foreman can hire and fire, he has more position power in his own group than the chairman of a board of directors who, frequently, cannot hire or fire—or even reprimand his board members.

Using this classification method we can now roughly order groups as being high or low on each of these three dimensions. This gives us an eight-celled classification (Figure 1). This scheme postulates that it is easier to be a leader in groups that fall into Cell 1 since you are liked, have position power, and have a structured task. It is somewhat more difficult in Cell 2 since you are liked, have a structured task, but little position power, and so on to groups in Cell 8 where the leader is not liked, has a vague, unstructured task, and little position power. A good example of Cell 8 would be the disliked chairman of the volunteer committee we mentioned before.

The critical question is, "What kind of leadership does each of these different group situations call for?" Figure 2 summarizes the results of 63 analyses based on a total of 454 separate groups. These included bomber and tank crews, antiaircraft artillery units, managements of consumer cooperative companies, boards of directors, open-hearth shops, basketball and surveying teams, and various groups involved in creative and problem-solving tasks.

The horizontal axis of the graph indicates the "situational favorableness," namely, the leader's control and influence as defined by the eight-fold classification shown in Figure 1. The vertical axis indicates the relationship between the leader's motivational pattern, as measured by the LPC score, and his group's performance. A median correlation above

F I G U R E 1
Cells or "Octants"

	Very Favorable			Intermediate in Favorableness			Unfavorable	
	1	2	3	4	5	6	7	8
Leader-member relations	Good	Good	Good	Good	Poor	Poor	Poor	Poor
Task structure	High	High	Low	Low	High	High	Low	Low
Position power	Strong	Weak	Strong	Weak	Strong	Weak	Strong	Weak

the midline shows that the relationship-motivated leaders tended to perform better than the task-motivated leaders. A correlation below the midline indicates that the task-motivated leaders performed better than the relationship-motivated leaders. Figure 3 shows the predictions that the model would make in each of the eight cells.

These findings have two important implications for our understanding of what makes leaders effective. First, Figure 2 tells us that the task-motivated leaders tend to perform better than relationship-motivated leaders in situations that are very favorable and in those that are unfavorable. Relationship-motivated leaders tend to perform better than task-motivated leaders in situations that are intermediate in favorableness. Hence, both the relationship- and the task-

motivated leaders perform well under some conditions and not under others. It is, therefore, not correct to speak of any person as generally a good leader or generally a poor leader. Rather, a leader may perform well in one situation but not in another. This is also borne out by the repeated findings that we cannot predict a leader's performance on the basis of his personality traits, or even by knowing how well he performed on a previous task unless that task was similar in situational favorableness.

Second, the graph on Figure 2 shows that the performance of a leader depends as much on the situational favorableness as it does on the individual in the leadership position. Hence, the organization can change leadership performance either by trying to change the individual's personality and motiva-

F I G U R E 2

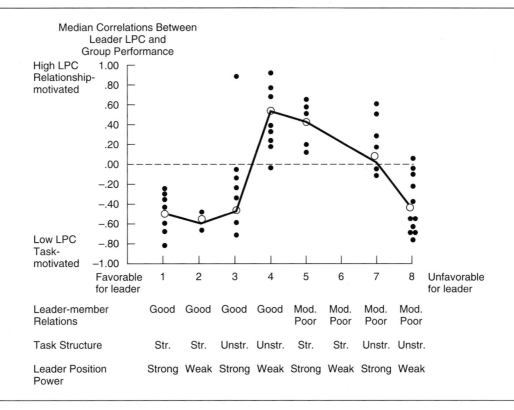

FIGURE 3

Prediction of the Performance of Relationship- and Task-Motivated Leaders

	1	2	3	4	5	6	7	8
Relationship-Motivated High LPC				Good	Good	Some-what better	Some-what better	
Task-Motivated Low LPC	Good	Good	Good					Good

tional pattern or by changing the favorableness of the leader's situation. As we shall see, this is really what training is all about.

Before we go further, we must ask how valid the Contingency Model is. How well does it predict in new situations? There have been at least 25 studies to date that have tested the theory. These validation studies included research on grocery and meat markets, a physical science laboratory, a machinery plant, a hospital, an electronics company, and teams of volunteer public health workers in Central America, as well as various experimentally assembled groups in the laboratory. Of particular importance is a large experiment that used cadets at West Point to test the entire eight cells of the model. This study almost completely reproduced the curve shown on Figure 2. In all studies that were recently reviewed, 35 of the 44 obtained correlations were in the predicted direction—a finding that could have occurred by chance less than one time in 100. An exception is Cell 2, in which laboratory experiments—but not field studies—have yielded correlations showing the relationship-motivated leaders perform better than task-motivated leaders. . . .

To Train or Not to Train

What does all this mean for improving managerial performance, and how can we apply the findings that we have described?

In sum, if we want to improve leadership performance, we can either change the leader by training, or we can change his leadership situation. Common sense suggests that it is much easier to change various aspects of a man's job than to change the man. When we talk about leadership behavior, we are talking about fairly deeply ingrained personality factors and habits of interacting with others. These cannot be changed easily, either in a few hours or in a few days. In fact, as we have seen, not even four years of military academy and 5 to 17 years of subsequent experience enable a leader to perform significantly better on different tasks than someone that has had neither training nor experience.

We have seen that a leader's performance depends not only on his personality, but also on the organizational factors that determine the leader's control and influence,—that is, the "situational favorableness." As we have shown, appropriate training and experience improve situational favorableness. Whether or not they improve performance depends

upon the match between the leader's motivational pattern and the favorableness of the situation. This means that a training program that improves the leader's control and influence may benefit the relationship-motivated managers, but it will be detrimental to the task-motivated managers, or vice versa, depending upon the situation.

The idea that we can improve a leader's performance by increasing the favorableness of his situation is, of course, far from new. A poorly performing manager may be given more authority, more explicit instructions, more congenial co-workers in the hope that it will help him do a better job. Moreover, decreasing the favorableness of the situation in order to improve a manager's performance is also not quite as unusual as it might appear at first blush. If a man becomes bored, stale, or disinterested in his job, a frequent remedy is to transfer him to a more challenging job. As it turns out, "challenging" is just another way of saying that the job is less structured, has less position power, or requires working with difficult people. It is certainly well known that some men perform best under pressure and that they get into difficulty when life is too calm. These are the trouble shooters who are dispatched to branch offices or departments that need to be bailed out.

What, then, can an organization do to increase managerial performance? As a first step, it is necessary to determine which of the managers are task- and which are relationship-motivated. This can be accomplished by means of a short scale. Second, the organization needs to categorize carefully the situational favorableness of its managerial jobs. (Scales are available in Fiedler, F. E., *A Theory of Leadership Effectiveness*, McGraw-Hill, 1967.) Third, the organization can decide on a number of options in its management of executive personnel.

The least expensive and probably most efficient method is to develop a careful program of managerial rotation that moves some individuals from one job to another at a faster rate than it moves others. . . .

A second major option is management training. The problem here is whether to train only some people or all those who are eligible: training a task-motivated manager who is accepted by his group and has a structured task is likely to improve his performance; training a relationship-motivated manager for the same job is likely to make him less effective. The organization would, therefore, be better off if it simply did not train relationship-motivated managers for these particular jobs. On the other hand, the relationship-motivated but not the task-motivated managers should be trained for jobs in which the situational favorableness is intermediate. . . .

Conclusion

As a consequence of our research, we have both discredited some old myths and learned some new lessons.

The old myths:

- That there is one best leadership style, or that there are leaders who excel under all circumstances.

- That some men are born leaders, and that neither training, experience, or conditions can materially affect leadership skills.

The lessons, while more pedestrian and less dogmatic, are more useful. We know that people differ in how they respond to management situations. Furthermore, we know that almost every manager in an organization can perform effectively, providing that we place him in a situation that matches his personality, providing we know how to match his training and experience to the available jobs—and providing that we take the trouble.

Selected Bibliography

The interested reader may wish to consult Fiedler's *A Theory of Leadership Effectiveness*, McGraw-Hill, 1967, which presents a detailed summary of many of his studies as well as a fairly technical description of the theory. A more popular version of the theory is described in a *Harvard Business Review* article entitled, "Engineer the Job to Fit the Manager," September, 1965 and in *Psychology Today*, "Style or Circumstance: the Leadership Enigma," March 1969. A more technical and extensive summary of the work on leadership training will appear shortly in a forthcoming issue of *Administrative Science Quarterly*.

Situational Leadership®

P. Hersey
Center for Leadership Studies, Inc.

Situational Leadership is a practical model designed to help leaders be more effective in their interactions with people. It is based on an interplay among three factors:

1. the amount of guidance and direction a leader gives (similar to task behavior);

2. the amount of socio-emotional support a leader provides (similar to relationship behavior); and

3. the readiness level that followers exhibit in performing a specific task, function, or objective.

According to the Situational Leadership model, there is no one best style of leadership, or way to influence people. The style to be used depends on the readiness level of the people the leader is attempting to influence, as illustrated in Figure 1.

The model displays the interaction of two separate and distinct leadership orientations—task and relationships—appearing on the horizontal and vertical axes:

- *Task behavior* is defined as the extent to which the leader engages in spelling out the duties and responsibilities of an individual or group. These behaviors include telling people what to do, how to do it, when to do it, where to do it, and who is to do it. This is the guidance role of a leader.

- *Relationship behavior* is defined as the extent to which the leader engages in two-way or multi-way communication. The behaviors include listening, facilitating, and supportive behaviors.

The products of this interaction are four leadership styles, one in each of the quadrants shown in Figure 1. Each behavior is plotted from low to high on its axis. This produces four distinct styles:

- Style 1 (Tell): This style demonstrates high degrees of task behavior and low degrees of relationship behavior.

- Style 2 (Sell): This style is characterized by high amounts of both task and relationship behavior.

- Style 3 (Participate): This style uses high amounts of relationship behavior, and low amounts of task behavior.

- Style 4 (Delegate): In this style, low amounts of both task and relationship behavior are used.

Any one of the four styles may prove effective in a given situation. The key (independent) variable that is believed to affect its success lies in the concept of *follower readiness.* This is the extent to which a follower has the ability and willingness to accomplish a specific task. In contrast to personal characteristics (such as traits, values, or age), readiness is a measure of how ready a person is to perform a specific task, function, assignment, or objective that a leader views as important.

In assessing (and developing) follower readiness, a leader must consider two separate components:

- *Ability* (job readiness) is the knowledge, experience, and skill that an individual or group brings to a particular task or activity.

- *Willingness* (psychological readiness) is the extent to which an individual or group has the confidence, commitment, and motivation to accomplish a specific task. These components are interactive; willingness affects not only the use of present ability, but the extent to which competence and ability will grow. Similarly, one's current ability may impact self-assessments of competence, commitment, and motivation.

The combination of low or high levels of ability and willingness produces a continuum of follower readiness. For the sake of discussion and analysis, this continuum can be divided into four levels, each representing a different combination:

- Readiness Level One (R1): The follower is both unable to do the task, and lacks commitment, confidence, and willingness.

- Readiness Level Two (R2): The follower is motivated to make an effort and would try if the leader was there to provide guidance, but lacks current ability to perform well.

- Readiness Level Three (R3): The follower has the capacity to perform the function requested, but is insecure, apprehensive, or unwilling to use that ability.

- Readiness Level Four (R4): The follower has the requisite ability to perform successfully, and also demonstrates the necessary commitment and confidence to do it.

The leader's challenge is to identify follower readiness and then match it with the appropriate leadership style called for by the model. For example, a follower or group at

Copyrighted material. Adopted from Chapter 8, Paul Hersey and Kenneth H. Blanchard. *Management of Organizational Behavior: Utilizing Human Resources,* Englewood Cliffs, N. J.: Prentice-Hall, 1988. Reprinted with permission of the Center for Leadership Studies. All rights reserved. Author affiliation may have changed since article was first published.

FIGURE 1
Situational Leadership®

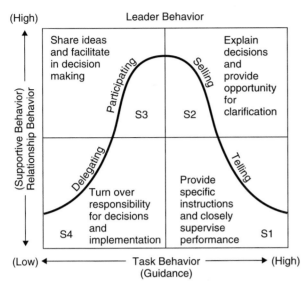

Leader Behavior

(High)

(Supportive Behavior)
Relationship Behavior

Share ideas and facilitate in decision making

Participating

Selling

S3

S2

Explain decisions and provide opportunity for clarification

Delegating

Telling

Turn over responsibility for decisions and implementation

S4

Provide specific instructions and closely supervise performance

S1

(Low) ◄——— Task Behavior ———► (High)
(Guidance)

Follower Readiness

High	Moderate		Low
R4	R3	R2	R1
Able and Willing or Confident	Able but Unwilling or Insecure	Unable but Willing or Confident	Unable and Unwilling or Insecure

Follower Directed ———— Leader Directed

Readiness Level 1 requires a leader to *tell* the person what to do. Guiding, directing, and structuring the work environment are all appropriate. Readiness Level 2 (willing but un-

able) calls for a *selling* approach—providing answers to the questions of what, how, when, where, and who. Although selling focuses on explaining, persuading, and clarifying, it also opens up the possibility of dialogue for the follower to ask questions and receive clarification.

Readiness Level 3 calls for a *participating* style. The leader encourages an able person through supportive communication, and engages in collaborative, facilitating, or committing behaviors, while accenting both task and relationship orientations. Readiness Level 4 needs a *delegating* style. The follower or group is able, confident, and willing, and only needs the opportunity to perform. Although some relationship behavior is still needed, followers need to take responsibility for the objective and implement action on their own. The leader may wish to observe, stand by to respond to requests for assistance, and monitor results.

In addition to specifying the high-probability leadership style for various readiness levels, Situational Leadership also attempts to indicate the probability of success of the other three options for each situation. In order of preference, they appear as follows for each level of follower readiness:

- R1: S1, S2, S3, S4
- R2: S2, S1, S3, S4
- R3: S3, S2, S4, S1
- R4: S4, S3, S2, S1.

The Situational Leadership model has been used in a large number of U.S. companies for several decades, and therefore has considerable face validity. It is a prescriptive approach that tells leaders how to assess their followers and how to respond to that assessment of follower readiness with one of the four defined styles. It is flexible, with no hard and fast rules. It is based on subjective probabilities of success from using each style, in hopes of improving the odds for a productive outcome. Finally, the Situational Leadership model also recognizes that other situational variables may be of equal or greater importance, such as a crisis, time pressures, or the unique nature of the work.

The Case for Directive Leadership

J. P. Muczyk and B. C. Reimann
Cleveland State University

Gerry Gladstone still doesn't know what hit him. After a little over a year as president of Allied Machinery Company, he's out looking for a job again. Things started out so well, too! When Allied's board first offered him the job as president, Gerry was delighted. He had always wanted the opportunity to run his own show. And with his prior experience as the general manager of the Machinery Division of a large conglomerate, he was confident that he could turn the smaller firm around. He felt that he had learned just about everything he needed to know about running a company while rising through the ranks of his previous employer. Moreover, his division had been one of the most profitable in the corporation, and particularly adept in competing against Allied. No wonder Allied's board had high hopes that Gerry would be able to turn their company around.

Unfortunately things haven't worked out quite that way. A year later Allied is still doing quite poorly and hasn't even been able to get its share of the substantial increase in its industry's sales. Why was a manager with a proven record and impeccable credentials unable to work his accustomed magic in his new position? What Gerry found out, much to his chagrin, was that he had been "spoiled" in his previous management positions.

Without fully realizing it, Gerry had come to count on the superior quality subordinates and organizational support systems that had allowed him to leverage his own management talents. He had learned how to make the most of his organization's substantial resources through extensive delegation and employee participation. What's more, his democratic leadership style, which had come quite naturally to an idealistic MBA graduate in the late '60s, was subsequently reinforced by considerable success in this early business career. He had literally come to believe that there was no other way to manage. When Gerry took over as president of Allied, he faced an environment that differed radically from the one to which he had grown accustomed. First of all, most of the managers reporting to him did not have nearly the capabilities or initiative of his former subordinates. They were used to being told what to do and then having the boss follow up closely to make sure they were doing it right. Small wonder that Gerry's participative and delegative style was foreign to these executives and resulted in more confusion than action!

To make matters worse, Allied did not have most of the well-developed support systems, from basic organizational procedures like order processing and inventory control to so-phisticated information systems, that Gerry had learned to use so well. As a result, he was unable to get the kinds of results that had come so naturally in his previous management posts. Without the accustomed guidance and follow-up of their boss, his new subordinates simply failed to carry out their assigned tasks properly or on time. And, lacking any standard procedures and reliable control systems, Gerry didn't discover many of these failures until too late. Instead of the expected improvement in Allied's performance, things went from bad to worse in several critical areas. The board, understandably disappointed with these results, finally asked Gerry to resign.

Why Participative Management May Not Work

While the names are fictitious, the above scenario is not. What's more, similar events are taking place all over the country, in a wide variety of organizational settings. This common scenario illustrates the danger of concluding that the "best" or "excellent" style of leadership is a participative or democratic one. Like Gerry Gladstone, many managers have been forced to face the harsh reality that participative management simply may not work in some situations. Leadership is a two-way street, so a democratic style will be effective only if followers are both willing and able to participate actively in the decision-making process. If they are not, the leader cannot be democratic without also being "directive" and following up very closely to see that directives are being carried out properly.

In spite of its practical importance, direction has not received the attention it deserves in the leadership literature. This slight is due, in part at least, to a common failure to distinguish between the direction and participation dimensions of leadership. Some writers have even implied that direction is the opposite of participation, making directive leadership appear somehow undemocratic and even un-American.

In this article we intend to show that directive leadership is not inconsistent with participation. On the contrary, directiveness may be regarded as a separate dimension of leadership style in its own right—one that complements, but does not negate, participative management. What's more, the combination of the direction and participation dimensions can be helpful in reconciling some of the conflicting theories and research about whether a particular style of leadership is "best" for managers in various situations. The combination

Source: Edited and reprinted with permission from *Academy of Management Executive* 1, 4(1987), 301–11. Author affiliation may have changed since article was first published.

of these two dimensions can also be used to describe four "generic" leadership styles and the circumstances under which each is most likely to be effective. . . .

Participation versus Direction

One explanation for the inconsistent results from leadership research is that the impact of participation may have been confounded in at least some studies by a tendency to regard decision making and execution as one and the same. To appreciate how direction both differs from and complements participation, the act of making a decision needs to be separated from the process of executing it. Participation is associated with making a decision, while direction is concerned with executing a decision once it has been made. Democratic or participative leadership is typically defined in terms of the degree to which employees are involved in significant day-to-day work-related decisions. However, the participation of employees in making decisions is a separate issue from the amount of direction that a leader provides in executing those decisions. Thus, a leader can be participative or democratic by consulting employees during the decision-making phase, yet still be directive by following up closely on progress toward the ends that have been mutually decided on. This is illustrated in the two scales below:

Participation
(Autocratic) Low ———— High (Democratic or participative)

Direction
(Permissive, general supervision) Low ———— High (Directive, close supervision, constant follow-up)

Autocratic leaders take the position that they are paid to make key decisions and the subordinates are compensated for executing those decisions. Thus, subordinates are not involved in decision making under pure autocratic leadership. Democratic leaders, on the other hand, believe in the legitimacy of subordinate involvement in decision making, even though they may retain the authority to make the final decision. Participation does not mean the mere solicitation of inputs from subordinates, which are then ignored. Yet, on occasion, circumstances may dictate that the recommendations of subordinates need to be reversed. At times subordinates may even have to be excluded entirely from a decision. However, a truly participative leader feels obligated to explain to subordinates why their counsel had to be rejected.

Directive behavior is a function of the way the leader delegates the tasks associated with the execution of a decision, once it is made. A nondirective or permissive leader holds followers responsible for results, but leaves them free to execute their tasks in any way they choose. A very directive leader, on the other hand, specifies how subordinates are to accomplish their assignments and then follows up closely on all phases of the actual execution as well as the end results.

It is worth noting that both participation and direction involve aspects of delegation. Participation concerns the degree to which the leader lets subordinates take on some of the responsibility for making decisions about which tasks, projects, or results are to be achieved. Direction reflects the extent to which the leader delegates the responsibility for

choosing the actual means to accomplish the desired tasks, projects, or results. . . .

Which Leadership Style Is "Best"?

A fundamental controversy in the leadership literature revolves around the existence or nonexistence of "one best style of leadership." The normative school supports the notion that the most effective style is generalizable to all leadership situations. In direct contrast, the situational or contingency theorists believe that the effectiveness of a given leadership style is a function of the situation.[11] We feel that these arguments may be largely futile because the two camps have been concerned with important, but entirely different, aspects of leadership. Therefore, we propose a new way of relating and reconciling these apparently different points of view. What emerges from this reconciliation is a set of fresh guidelines for the use of participative and directive leadership behaviors.

Much of the normative research has focused on the three dimensions of consideration, concern for production, and incentive for performance. Furthermore, the normative findings are borne out by the management practices of excellent companies like IBM, 3M, and General Electric. These firms all emphasize sound human relations, high achievement levels, and rewards tied to performance. Therefore, we suggest that managers should earn and maintain high marks on all three of the above dimensions, regardless of the circumstances. That is, high concern for both people and production, coupled with strong incentives for performance, are necessary in any situation that calls for the accomplishment of goals through organized effort.

However, high scores on these three factors are insufficient for the most effective exercise of leadership. In keeping with the view of contingency theorists, these three dimensions need to be augmented by the proper display of participative and directive leader behaviors, as called for by different situations. In other words, the effectiveness of participative and directive leader behaviors depends on the situation in which leadership is to be exercised. Thus, the answer to the question "Which leadership style is best?" is still "It all depends!" However, we can simplify the situational contingencies since we have reduced our critical factors down to the two that are most sensitive to changes in the leadership environment.

Types of Leader Behavior

If leaders are classified as either high or low on participation and direction, we come up with the four sets of leader behaviors illustrated in Exhibit 1. We have labeled the types of leaders exhibiting these four patterns of behavior as follows: (1) the directive autocrat, (2) the permissive autocrat, (3) the directive democrat, and (4) the permissive democrat. We will briefly describe each of these and identify the circumstances under which each type of leader would be most likely to be successful.

The Directive Autocrat

This is the type of leader who makes decisions unilaterally and also supervises the activities of subordinates very

EXHIBIT 1
Types of Leader Behaviors

Degree of Participation in Decision Making:

		Low	High
Amount of Leader Direction:	**High**	Directive Autocrat	Directive Democrat
	Low	Permissive Autocrat	Permissive Democrat

closely. Directive-autocratic leaders would suit situations that require quick action, with no time for extensive employee participation. They would also be effective in an organization or subunit with limited scope or size and with relatively unstructured tasks. The low degree of delegation, coupled with extensive follow up would overburden the leader in larger more complex organizational units. The directive autocrat is particularly well suited to lead new, inexperienced, or under-qualified subordinates. This type of leader may also be required if subordinates are in an adversarial relationship to management, and must be constantly coerced to do their work. However, the directive autocrat must be very knowledgeable in all aspects of the unit's mission and be comfortable in an autocratic role.[12] . . .

The Permissive Autocrat

This type of leader still makes decisions alone, but permits followers a great deal of latitude in accomplishing their delegated tasks. The permissive autocrat would also be well suited for situations calling for quick responses. However, the tasks should be relatively simple and structured, or employees should have good experience, ability, and initiative. While still autocratically inclined, this permissive leader trusts subordinates to carry out their orders without constant follow-up. Or this permissiveness may simply reflect an unwillingness to take the time needed for extensive follow-up.

At first glance, permissiveness and autocracy don't seem to be compatible. After all, what self-respecting autocrat would take the risk of losing control over the activities and outputs of subordinates? Autocratic managers have to be sure that their directives are followed. Therefore, they cannot afford to be permissive unless they have access to some sort of substitute for personal direction. A wide variety of such substitutes can be found, but some of the more common ones include well-defined or routine tasks, technology, incentive systems, professional standards, or a strong corporate culture. . . .

The Directive Democrat

This type of leader invites full participation from subordinates in decision making. However, he or she still supervises employees very closely to make sure they carry out their democratically assigned tasks properly. A directive democrat would be called for when employee involvement is important to the decision process, such as in a very complex undertaking involving many interdependent activities—a situation where a timely response is less important than a technically correct one. The extensive direction would be needed here if employees lack either experience and ability or reliability and initiative. The directive-democratic combination is also appropriate if the leader is predisposed toward sharing decision making authority but doesn't really trust the reliability of subordinates.

Again, the common interpretation of participation seems to conflict with the idea of close supervision and direction. Yet, this combination may well be the most effective of the four generic leadership behaviors in the vast majority of leadership situations. As pointed out earlier, a great many organizations (business or otherwise) lack the people, systems, or resources needed to support extensive delegation. In these types of organizations leaders must be very directive to make up for any shortages in capabilities and initiative among their subordinates. . . .

The Permissive Democrat

In a sense, this is the ideal, "All-American" type of leader, since employees get to participate in decision making as well as enjoy a high degree of autonomy in executing the decision. This kind of leader is exemplified by the popular phrase at Texas Instruments: "Every employee a manager." The permissive democrat is suitable for any organization where employee involvement has both informational and motivational benefits. However, this type of leader behavior requires highly qualified employees, some effective substitute(s) for personal direction and enough time to reach consensus. In addition, the leader must value the democratic process and have trust in subordinates' capabilities, judgment, and motives. . . .

The Leadership Cycle

The fundamental changes that most organizations undergo as they grow raises the question of whether any given leadership style or approach can be suitable for an organization throughout its lifetime. A number of researchers have studied the evolution of organizations through various stages of development and concluded that the appropriate leadership style tends to change as well.[19] Many leaders who were successful in one stage find that their styles are no longer effective in the next. A classic example is Ford Motor Company. Henry Ford I by all accounts was a directive autocrat. He continued to lead in his directive and autocratic manner as the company grew in size and complexity well beyond the limits of one man's absolute governance. The result was the near demise of the company. Ironically, the kind of leadership that was instituted to save Ford Motor was similar to the one adopted in the 1920s by its archrival, General Motors, when it reached about the same stage of organizational evolution.[20]

A more recent example of the dynamics of the leadership cycle is provided by the experience of People Express. Don Burr, founder and CEO of this new airline, was an extraordinarily permissive democrat—quite unlike Henry Ford. In fact, he carried his democratic and permissive leadership behavior to its limit by emphasizing autonomous work groups, constant job rotation, salaries tied to profits, and by giving everyone the title of manager. This highly innovative way of organizing was widely praised and was credited with much of the upstart airline's phenomenal success during its entrepreneurial stage.

However, People Express experienced major difficulties in trying to make it through the next stage of growth. Its explosive expansion naturally increased the organization's complexity, but also made it more and more difficult to find and hire the kind of highly motivated and qualified personnel that made its permissive structure work in the first place. It could no longer afford to keep its treasured, highly participative approach to management and be highly permissive at the same time. Unfortunately, management was reluctant to change what was perceived to have been a fundamental factor in the company's earlier success.[21] The inevitable result was a serious deterioration in performance, culminating in heavy losses and the subsequent takeover by Texas Airlines. Frank Lorenzo, People's new boss, is likely to impose far more directive leadership on the airline as it becomes more formalized. Hopefully this direction will still be combined with the kind of employee participation which has been instrumental in People's past success.

The experience of Robert C. Hazard, Jr., a directive autocrat, can serve as still another illustration. As CEO of Best Western International, Inc., Hazard had achieved great success in bringing the nonprofit motel chain from 800 to 2,597 members between 1974 and 1980. Yet his recent resignation as CEO was greeted with "a collective sigh of relief from Best Western's affiliated hotel owners."[22] His leadership style, immensely successful during the fast growth of Best Western's entrepreneurial and growth stages, became a liability as the organization matured. Hotel managers, now much more concerned with profitability and independence than with rapid growth, apparently began to fret under their CEO's autocratic and directive leadership. Mr. Hazard moved on to renewed success as the CEO of the more entrepreneurial Quality Inns International, Inc.—a former competitor with great ambitions for rapid growth. In the meantime, Best Western International appeared to be very satisfied with its new CEO, Ronald A. Evans, a permissive democrat who was "highly regarded" by hotel affiliates.

Best Western had become a mature, highly formal organization operated by confident and capable personnel. It affiliates both wanted, and could afford, a leader who would be a first among equals and would leave day-to-day operations up to them. Therefore, Best Western could successfully make the transition to a more permissive leader. By contrast, Quality Inns had just gone through a period of decline and just barely avoided bankruptcy. Its hotel affiliates were looking for a strong leader to tell them where to go and how to get there. The most critical difference in leadership requirements here was along the directiveness dimension, and Hazard was just the type of "hands-on" manager needed to accomplish Quality Inns' turnaround.

The experience of BankAmerica constitutes another example of an organization in dire straits turning to a directive autocrat for salvation. Former CEO A. W. "Tom" Clausen, a man so unwilling to listen to others that he was routinely de-

The Leadership Cycle

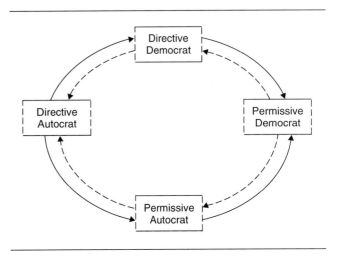

scribed as "the dictator," was rehired as CEO to save the organization when it became the target for a hostile takeover.[23]

Best Western's experience illustrates an extreme case where an autocratic and directive leader was successfully replaced by a democratic and permissive one. However, we feel that this abrupt and extreme type of transition is the exception rather than the rule. The addition of the direction dimension opens up two less direct and less risky paths from the "pure" autocratic and directive behavior in the earlier stages of growth toward the democratic and permissive leadership usually found in more mature and sophisticated organizations. The two paths from directive autocrat to permissive democrat are illustrated in Exhibit 2. The autocratic and directive leader can try to become either more participative or less directive before turning into a permissive democrat. The key to an effective transition in leadership behaviors may be to change only one dimension at a time. . . .

The Real Leadership Challenge

The unbridled enthusiasm for democracy and individual autonomy that pervades the very fiber of our society seems to have blinded many scholars and practitioners to the fact that few organizations can really achieve this ideal state in the workplace. The inescapable fact is that many, many organizations who are less than "excellent" in the caliber of their people and support systems simply can't afford to have their managers be participative without a commensurate dose of direction. That is, in the vast majority of actual leadership situations, democratic behaviors must be tempered with a measure of direction or follow-up to assure that organizational goals are accomplished efficiently and effectively.

Actually, the excellent organizations make their leaders' jobs easy—even routine. The real challenge to leadership is posed by those organizations that lack the resources to facilitate extensive participation and delegation. It is in these tough situations that leaders can be of real value. Instead of directing the organization's abundant resources, leaders must themselves act as resources for their followers.

In particular, those managers who want to encourage employee participation must make every effort to guide and develop their subordinates and follow up on their activities. Failure to do so can result in reduced performance for the organization and, therefore, failure for the manager. Like Gerry Gladstone, the participative manager may delegate himself (or herself) right out of a job!

Notes

[1] See Henry Mintzberg, *The Nature of Managerial Work*, (New York: Harper & Row, 1973).

[2a] A search of only one of Dialog's databases (File B15: ABI/Inform) resulted in 12,025 listings under "leader?" (which would include such references as "leaders" or "leader behavior") and 5,479 under the full designation of "leadership." While many of these references dealt only indirectly with the subject of leadership, the database also goes back only to 1971.

[2] For a good summary of these major leadership theories, see Gary A. Yukl, *Leadership in Organizations*, Englewood Cliffs, NJ: Prentice-Hall, Inc., 1981.

[3] For an excellent discussion about the values and expectations of the generation growing to maturity during the 1960's, and some implications for today's managers, see Joseph A. Raelin, "The '60's Kids in the Corporation: More Than Just 'Daydream Believers,'" the *Academy of Management Executive*, February 1987, pp. 21–30.

[4] Perhaps the most influential book extolling the virtues of participative management in major corporations is *In Search of Excellence* by Thomas J. Peters and Robert H. Waterman (New York: Harper & Row, 1982). Also see Terrence E. Deal and Allen A. Kennedy, *Corporate Cultures* (Reading, Mass: Addison-Wesley, 1982) and William G. Ouchi, *Theory Z* (New York: Avon Books, 1981).

[5] See Jan P. Muczyk and Bernard C. Reimann, "Has Participative Management Been Oversold?" *Personnel*, May 1987, pp. 52–56.

[6] These conflicting results of research on participative management have been well documented by Yukl (note 2) and by E. A. Locke and D. M. Schweiger, "Participation in Decision Making: One more Look," *Research on Organizational Behavior*, 1979, pp. 265–339. For a particularly thorough critique of some of the major studies, see Arlyn J. Melcher, "Participation: A Critical Review of Research Findings," *Human Resource Management*, Summer 1976, pp. 12–21.

[7] See Robert R. Blake and Jane S. Mouton, *The Managerial Grid*, Houston: Gulf Publishing, 1964.

[8] We consider this concern for production variable to be distinct from the Ohio State researchers' "initiating structure" dimension, which deals more explicitly with follow-up or directive behavior. We believe that a permissive leader can be, and often is, high in concern for production through a Management by Objectives type of approach rather than through frequent follow-up and/or coaching.

[9] For the evidence and rationale supporting the importance of creating and maintaining a strong nexus between performance and rewards see the following: Lawler, E. E. "Whatever Happened to Incentive Pay," *New Management*, Vol. 1 (4), 1984, pp. 37–41; Muczyk, J. P. and Hastings, R. E. "In Defense of Enlightened Hardball Management," *Business Horizons*, July/August 1985, pp. 23–29; Muczyk, J. P. "The Strategic Role of Compensation," *Human Resource Planning* (in print).

[10] See M. G. Evans, "The Effects of Supervisory Behavior on the Path-Goal Relationship," *Organizational Behavior and Human Performance*, 1970, 5, pp. 277–298, and Robert J. House, "A Path-Goal Theory of Leader Effectiveness," *Administrative Science Quarterly*, 1971, pp. 321–339.

[11] Blake and Mouton (Endnote 7) exemplify the normative approach, while Fred Fiedler is best known for his situational theory of leadership. (See his articles, "Engineering the Job to Fit the Manager," *Harvard Business Review*, September-October 1965, pp. 115–122, or "The Leadership Game: Matching the Man to the Situation," *Organizational Dynamics*, Winter 1976, pp. 6–16.

[12] Our situational prescriptions for the four generic leadership behaviors are based on the approach taken by Robert Tannenbaum and Warren Schmidt in their classic article, "How to Choose a Leadership Pattern," *Harvard Business Review*, (May/June 1973), pp. 162–80.

[13] See Timothy K. Smith and Laura Landro's article, "Coke's Future: Profoundly Changed, Coca-Cola Co. Strives to Keep on Bubbling," *The Wall Street Journal*, April 24, 1986, p. 1.

[14] Small and medium-size firms typically do not pay as well as large firms. Also, premature promotions are particularly likely in smaller firms, which typically have four or fewer organizational levels (e.g., employees, supervisors, managers or vice-presidents in charge of functional areas, and presidents). Hence, only two promotions will get you a vice-presidency in a small firm. Also, the smaller the firm, the more limited the choices for a given opening. To make matters worse, many small firms (especially privately held or family-owned ones) are loath to go to the external labor market even if they cannot find a qualified internal candidate. Since the vast majority of business firms are of the small and relatively resource-poor variety, most practicing managers face situations with limited support from ideally qualified subordinates or sophisticated systems.

[15] See Carole and Bryant Cushing, "Fitting Managers Into Management," *Financial Executive*, January 1987, pp. 4–5.

[16] See Peters and Waterman or Deal and Kennedy (Endnote 4).

[17] For a detailed discussion of Ronald Reagan's leadership and its impact on Irangate, see Ann Reilly Dowd, "Learning from Reagan's Debacle," *Fortune*, April 27, 1987, pp. 169–172.

[18] Leader behavior was not the only management failure leading to the Irangate scandal, of course. For a perceptive analysis of the broader management issues, see Peter F. Drucker, "Management Lessons of Irangate," *The Wall Street Journal*, March 1987, p. 32.

[19] For some in depth analyses of organizational life cycles see Larry E. Greiner, "Evolution and Revolution as Organizations Grow," *Harvard Business Review*, July/August 1972, pp. 37–46, and Robert E. Quinn and Kim Cameron, "Organizational Life Cycles and Some Shifting Criteria of Effectiveness: Some Preliminary Evidence," *Management Science*, 1983, pp. 33–51.

[20] See Martin J. Gannon, Management: An Integrated Framework, 2nd Ed., Boston, MA: Little Brown & Co., 1982.

[21] See Amanda Bennett, "Airline's Ills Point Out Weaknesses of Unorthodox Management Style," *The Wall Street Journal*, August 11, 1986.

[22] See "Matching Managers to a Company's Life Cycle," *Business Week*, February 23, 1981, p. 62. Also, Jolie Solomon's "Kroger Says Kagler Quit as President Because of Differences With Chairman," *The Wall Street Journal*, October 28, 1986, p. 42 and "Heirs Apparent to Chief Executive Often Trip Over Prospect of Power," *The Wall Street Journal*, March 24, 1987, p. 35.

[23] See Christian G. Hill and Richard B. Schmitt, "Autocrat Tom Clausen Faces Formidable Task to Save BankAmerica," *The Wall Street Journal*, October 17, 1986, p. 1.

[24] Much of the background information about IBM's evolution and management practices was drawn from the following articles in *The Wall Street Journal*, April 7, 1986: "Behind the Monolith: A Look at IBM," by John Marcom, Jr. (p. 15); "IBM, Once a Dictatorship, Is Now a Vast Decentralized Democracy," by Randall Smith (p. 16); and "Working at IBM: Intense Loyalty in a Rigid Culture," by Dennis Keale (p. 17).

[25] See Theodore T. Herbert and Helen Deresky, "Should General Managers Match Their Business Strategies?" *Organizational Dynamics*, Winter 1987, pp. 40–51.

Chapter Six

Followers and the Leadership Process

*I*n the last two chapters several situational factors that might play a role in determining the effectiveness of a particular behavior were considered. For example, followers might find their role clouded by ambiguity, they may experience frustration and the lack of challenge in their work, and some individuals might be more or less capable of exercising self-direction and self-control (possibly as a function of task-based knowledge/expertise and/or personal motivation).

This chapter addresses the role of the follower in the leadership process. In general, there are two significant questions that have been posed by students of leadership: (1) To what extent do "attributes" of the follower serve to moderate the leader behavior-outcome (e.g., satisfaction, performance) relationship? and (2) How does the follower affect/influence the leader? The readings in this chapter will provide insight into this complex part of the leadership process.

As we have seen thus far, students of leadership have sought to understand leadership and the leadership process by focusing primarily on the leader and on how his or her behaviors influence follower attitudes, motivation, behavior, and group effectiveness. Charles N. Greene (1975) calls attention to the fact that the causal arrow between leader behavior and followers may run in the opposite direction, suggesting that *follower performance may shape the amount of consideration and initiating structure behavior exhibited by the leader.* Even if this is true, this observation does not negate the impact that leader behavior (e.g., initiating structure and consideration) has upon subordinate attitudes and performance, but it highlights the notion that *the relationship between leader and follower is a reciprocal relationship.* The idea of a reciprocal relationship (i.e., a two-way influence process) reinforces Murphy's (1941) suggestion that leadership is an interactive and dynamic process, whereby the leader influences the follower, the follower influences the leader, and both are influenced by the context surrounding this leader-follower relationship.

Fillmore H. Sanford (1952) and Gary Yukl (1971), in separate readings, observe that attributes of the follower serve to influence the leadership process. Both authors call attention to the personality traits that the followers carry into the leadership context, suggesting that the followers' personalities shape their reactions to the leader's behaviors.

According to Sanford, leadership can be seen as a relationship between a leader and follower. Therefore, it is important to understand the role of the follower in this relationship if one hopes to understand the total process. Sanford suggests that *the follower's own unique personality* (e.g., needs, abilities, and attitudes) *defines his or her "readiness for leadership."* When placed into a leadership situation, these factors combine to determine the follower's receptivity to a particular leader and his or her personality and leadership style. Those followers with an authoritarian personality tend, for example, to accept leaders who exhibit a strong and directive style of leadership, while those with more of

FIGURE 6.1
The Leader Behavior—Follower Satisfaction Relationship

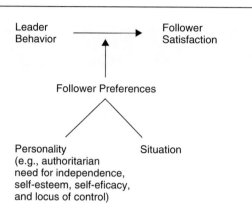

an equalitarian personality tend to accept leaders who exhibit a democratic style of leadership.

Gary Yukl (1971) explores the role of the follower's personality in the leadership equation as he presents a behavioral theory of leadership. As a part of this process, Yukl identifies the conditions under which three different dimensions of leader behavior (i.e., initiating structure, consideration, and decision centralization) are associated with member satisfaction with the leader and their level of productivity.

Yukl carefully presents these three leader behaviors as separate and distinct dimensions and suggests that variation in one dimension does not imply variation on the next. His observation parallels earlier contentions that a production and people emphasis, or initiating structure and consideration behaviors, are not opposite ends of the same continuum. Instead these behaviors are independent of one another, and it is therefore possible for a leader to display either one or both behaviors.

In Yukl's behavioral theory of leadership, consideration and initiating structure stem from the leadership work conducted at The Ohio State University. *Consideration* refers to the degree to which a leader expresses a positive, indifferent, or negative attitude toward a subordinate. A leader high in consideration is friendly, supportive, and considerate. *Initiating structure* is a task-oriented behavior reflecting the leader's concern for productivity (e.g., goal-orientation), making sure that task decisions are made, and exhibiting behaviors that are directed toward making sure that directives are carried out. *Decision centralization* builds upon Lewin, Lippitt, and White's work with democratic, autocratic, and laissez-faire leaders. Specifically, decision centralization refers to the manner in which decisions are made, highlighting the amount of influence exercised by the leader and followers. Thus, decision centralization can range from high subordinate influence to complete leader influence over decisions affecting the group. (The self-assessment presented at the end of this chapter opener provides you with the opportunity to profile yourself around each of these three leader behaviors.)

The degree to which a particular leader behavior produces follower satisfaction is shaped by the follower's personal preferences for that behavior (see Figure 6.1). This statement suggests that not all followers will necessarily like or dislike any particular leader behavior (e.g., initiating structure, decision centralization). Instead, the relationship between leader behavior and follower satisfaction with the leader will be influenced (moderated) by the follower's preferences. Subordinate preferences tend to be shaped by their own personalities, the situation in which they find themselves, and what they believe their leader should be doing at a particular point in time.

Yukl's work, along with that of Vroom (1964),[1] suggests that leader behavior is un-

---

[1] V. H. Vroom, *Work and Motivation* (New York: John Wiley & Sons, 1964).

F I G U R E   6 . 2
The Leader Behavior—Follower Performance Relationship*

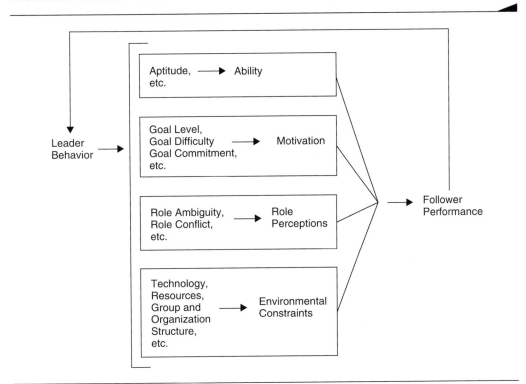

*This model depicts many of the arguments made by Wofford and Spinivaser (1983) in their leader-environment-follower theory of leadership. J. C. Wofford and T. N. Spinivaser, "Experimental Tests of the Leader-Environment-Follower Interaction Theory of Leadership," *Organizational Behavior and Human Performance* 32 (1983), 35–54.

likely to have a direct impact upon follower performance. Instead, if a leader's behavior is going to have an impact upon performance, it must lead to an increase in one or more of the following intermediate (mediating) conditions: the skills/abilities that the follower brings to task performance; follower task motivation (i.e., the effort put forth toward task performance); the accuracy of the perceptions that the followers have in terms of their role requirements; and/or by providing the group with needed information, resources, and cooperation from individuals/groups outside of the work group (see Figure 6.2).

In summary, the literature focused on followers within the leadership context generates several observations that enhance our understanding of this complex mosaic called the leadership process (see Figure 6.3). First, we note that leaders influence followers and followers exercise an influence over the behavior of leaders. Second, this reciprocal relationship is dynamic in nature. Third, followers bring to the leadership situation their personality—skills/abilities, motives (e.g., needs, wants, preferences, expectations), biases, and personal histories. These follower attributes in part determine the effectiveness of a leader's influence attempts (i.e., characteristics of the follower will mediate the leader-outcome relationship).

FIGURE 6.3
The Leadership Process: Followers

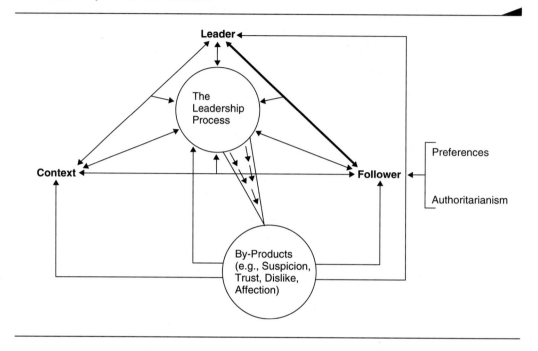

Consideration, and Decision Centralization

Instructions: The questions below ask about your personal leadership orientation. Each item describes a specific kind of behavior, but does not ask you to judge whether the behavior is desirable or undesirable.

READ each item carefully.

THINK about how frequently you engage in the behavior described by the item.

DRAW A CIRCLE around one of the five numerical response codes (1, 2, 3, 4, 5), following each question, that reflects this frequency of behavior.

1. Put suggestions made by people in the work group into operation.

Always	Often	Occasionally	Seldom	Never
1	2	3	4	5

2. Treat all people in the work group as your equal.

Always	Often	Occasionally	Seldom	Never
1	2	3	4	5

3. Back up what people under you do.

Always	Often	Occasionally	Seldom	Never
1	2	3	4	5

4. Reject suggestions for change.

Always	Often	Occasionally	Seldom	Never
1	2	3	4	5

5. Talk about how much should be done.

A Great Deal	Fairly Much	To Some Degree	Comparatively Little	Not at All
1	2	3	4	5

6. Assign people in the work group to particular tasks.

Always	Often	Occasionally	Seldom	Never
1	2	3	4	5

7. Offer new approaches to problems.

Often	Fairly Often	Occasionally	Once in a While	Very Seldom
1	2	3	4	5

(*continued*)

8. Emphasize meeting of deadlines.

A Great Deal	**Fairly Much**	**To some Degree**	**Comparatively Little**	**Not at All**
1	2	3	4	5

Scoring: *Consideration* behavior—Subtract your score to questions 2, 3, and 4 from 6. Next, sum your adjusted response to questions 1, 2, 3, and 4, and divide by 4.

Enter your Consideration score here _____.

Initiating Structure behavior—Sum your response to questions 5, 6, 7, and 8, and divide by 4.

Enter your Initiating Structure score here _____.

Interpretation: A high score (4 and greater) suggests a relatively strong orientation toward consideration-oriented behavior by you as a leader. A low score (2 and less) suggests a relatively weak consideration orientation.

A high score (4 and greater) suggests a relatively weak orientation toward initiating structure-oriented behavior by you as a leader. A low score (2 and less) suggests a relatively strong orientation to initiation of structure behavior.

Source: Sample items from and reprinted with permission: Edwin A. Fleishman's *Leadership Opinion Questionnaire.* (Copyright 1960, Science Research Associates, Inc., Chicago, IL).

Instructions: Many decisions are made that affect activities within your work unit. For each of the following questions indicate how frequently you involve others in making the following decisions, when they are made.

CIRCLE ONE CODE ON EACH LINE.	Never	Seldom	Sometimes	Often	Always
1. How frequently do you allow others to participate in defining personnel (manpower) needs (for example, number of personnel and kinds of skills needed) for the work unit?	1	2	3	4	5
2. How frequently do you allow others to participate in deciding which new job applicants to hire for the unit?	1	2	3	4	5
3. How frequently do you allow others to participate in defining training needs for unit personnel?	1	2	3	4	5
4. How frequently do you allow others to participate in the decision to promote work unit employees?	1	2	3	4	5
5. How frequently do you allow others to participate in making work allocation assignments (defining who does which tasks) for personnel in the work unit?	1	2	3	4	5
6. How frequently do you allow others to participate in making decisions defining the work that you will perform in the work unit?	1	2	3	4	5
7. How frequently do you allow others to participate in defining work schedules (define work quotas) for the work unit personnel?	1	2	3	4	5
8. How frequently do you allow others to participate in establishing performance standards for jobs in the work unit?	1	2	3	4	5
9. How frequently do you allow others to participate in making performance evaluations for the work unit personnel?	1	2	3	4	5
10. How frequently do you allow others to participate in defining work unit policy and procedures (for example, define starting time, personal time off, etc.)	1	2	3	4	5

(continued)

CIRCLE ONE CODE ON EACH LINE.	Never	Seldom	Sometimes	Often	Always
11. How frequently do you allow others to participate in the preparation of the work unit's budget?	1	2	3	4	5
12. How frequently do you allow others to participate in the preparation of annual plans (defining objectives) for the work unit?	1	2	3	4	5

Scoring: Sum your answer to each of the 12 questions, and divide this value by 12.

Interpretation: A high score (4 and greater) indicates a relatively high level of *decision decentralization* (i.e., as a leader you involve others in decision-making processes). A low score (2 and less) indicates a relatively high level of *decision centralization* (i.e., as a leader you do not involve others in decision-making processes).

Source: Modified centralization scale taken from: J. L. Pierce, "Employee Affective Responses to Work Unit Structure and Job Design: A Test of an Intervening Variable," (University of Wisconsin, Madison, Wisconsin: Unpublished doctoral dissertation, 1977).

The Reciprocal Nature of Influence between Leader and Subordinate

C. N. Greene
Indiana University

Researchers and practitioners would agree that leader behavior is an important variable related to organizational effectiveness. Much of the empirical evidence on organizational leadership has come from the numerous field studies investigating the relationships between leadership styles (e.g., initiating structure and consideration) and subordinate performance and satisfaction (see Fleishman, 1973b). The majority of these studies have employed static correlational techniques or have contrasted the leader behavior of high- and low-productivity groups, which do not allow inferences of the direction of causality. To what extent does the leader influence the subordinate? To what extent does the subordinate influence the leader's behavior? Further, to what extent are there reciprocal effects? There is a need for more studies investigating such directional relationships between leader and group behavior (see e.g. Fleishman, 1973a).

Most often, the importance attributed to leader behavior stems from the presumed effect of the leader's behavior on his subordinates' performance and job satisfaction (Likert, 1961). There is evidence that leadership style affects subordinate performance and attitudes. For example, Day and Hamblin (1964) found subordinate performance varied according to the leader's use of punishment and closeness of supervision. More recently, Dawson, Messe, and Phillips (1972) have shown that experimental variation in the leader's consideration and structure produces changes in group behavior, and Jones, Gergen, Gumpert, and Thibaut (1965) have shown that leader attitudes do get translated into group attitudes.

Other studies investigating the possible effects of subordinate performance on leadership style have had mixed results. Jackson (1953) found that supervisors' leadership styles remained unchanged even though the performance characteristics of the different groups they managed varied substantially—thus indicating that subordinate performance did not affect subsequent leader behavior. In contrast, however, Hawthorne, Couch, Haefner, Langham, and Carter (1956), Lowin and Craig (1968), Farris and Lim (1969), and Crowe, Bochner, and Clark (1972) provided evidence that subordinate performance caused changes in leader behavior....

There are sound theoretical bases (a number of which are reviewed by Lowin and Craig, 1968) from which one can argue that subordinate performance and, in addition, subordinate satisfaction can cause the leader to vary his style of leadership. For example, Katz and Stotland (1959) in their "functional view of attitudes" postulate that a person will develop positive attitudes toward objects which are instrumental to the satisfaction of his needs. This proposition can be applied to leader-subordinate relationships to the degree that the organization makes rewards bestowed on the leader contingent upon his subordinates' performance; in such an organization, the leader may develop more positive attitudes toward his high-performing subordinates. The expectation is that the person whose behavior causes another to be positively reinforced will in return by rewarded by the other. A further expectation is that low performance by a subordinate will cause the leader to restrict or to further specify the subordinate's work activities (both are forms of increased initiating structure) in attempting to improve his performance and, further, to express disapproval (a form of reduced consideration). Conversely, the leader would be expected to see little need for structure and thus engage in less structuring behavior with the high-performing subordinate and, further, to show greater approval and concern for the subordinate's own interests (both are forms of increased consideration). Similar predictions can be made about the influence of subordinate satisfaction on leader behavior to the extent that a subordinate's expression of satisfaction with work is perceived as reinforcing to the leader. Of the few studies which have examined such causality questions, none were designed to examine the extent to which causation may be reciprocal. When longitudinal data are obtained, as an alternative to experimental designs, there are means for inferring the strength and direction of causality, without requiring the actual manipulation of variables. Two methods for longitudinal data collection are the cross-lagged panel correlational technique and dynamic correlational analysis.

The purpose of this research was to assess, by means of these two techniques, questions of the direction of causal influence in relationships between leader and follower variables. Does a manager's leadership style (in particular, consideration and structure) have greater effect on his subordinate's performance and satisfaction, or is the opposite direction of causality stronger? Further, to what extent are the relationships reciprocal?

Source: Edited and reprinted with permission from *Journal of Applied Psychology* 60 (1975), 187–193. Copyright (1975) by the American Psychological Association. Author affiliation may have changed since article was first published.

This research was supported by a Graduate School of Business research grant, Indiana University.
The author wishes to thank Ralph M. Stogdill for the useful suggestions he provided during the formulation stage of this research.

Method

Sample

The data were collected from 103 first-line managers and for each manager, two of his immediate subordinates. The sample of first-line managers included: 42 department heads employed at either the corporate headquarters or a regional office of an insurance company; 31 project managers representing the research and engineering functions of a manufacturer of industrial and electronics equipment; and 30 first-line managers employed in the financial and marketing divisions of a chemical products firm. . . .

Consideration and Satisfaction

. . . The "consideration-causes-subordinate satisfaction" coefficients were relatively strong (.40, .34, and .45, for the three respective time periods; all *ps* < .001) and considerably stronger than the S → C cross-lagged coefficients. . . .

In addition, the significant but rather *moderate* dynamic correlations (*rs* extended from .42 to .50, all *ps* < .001) indicate that a third variable and, more likely, several additional variables may have contributed to the covariance between consideration and satisfaction. This particular finding is not surprising, however, since there are other known causes of satisfaction with work. Thus, one interpretation that can be made from these results is that leader emphasis on consideration constitutes one of several likely causes of subordinate satisfaction.

Consideration and Performance

The coefficients provided rather strong indications that subordinate performance *causes* leader emphasis on consideration. The only significant correlations were the P → C cross-lagged coefficients: *rs* = .37, .45, and .33, respectively; all *ps* < .001. All of the remaining correlations, including the C → P cross-lagged coefficients, were low and did not approach significance. These results help confirm the findings of Lowin and Craig's (1968) experiment and, further, can be interpreted as supporting the theoretical proposition that the leader's attitude toward his subordinates, and its expression, is contingent upon their performance. The leader may be expected, for example, to support and show his approval of those subordinates who have positively reinforced him by their good performance and to be less considerate of subordinates who negatively reinforce him by their low performance. . . .

Initiating Structure and Satisfaction

The correlations testing the relationships between leader initiating structure and subordinate work satisfaction, presented in Table 1C, provide little evidence of causality. . . .

Initiating Structure and Performance

The only significant correlations obtained in the cross-lagged analysis of relationships between leader initiating structure and subordinate satisfaction were the moderate, though significant, P → IS cross-lagged coefficients (−.33, −.37, and −.36). Consistent with the theory discussed earlier, the most apparent explanation of these findings (given the negative signs of all of the coefficients) is that low performance by a subordinate caused the leader to engage in more structuring behavior. High subordinate performance, on the other hand, would appear to lead to reduced emphasis on initiating structure. The dynamic coefficients were significant but, as before, too low to exclude the possibility of additional variables affecting the relationships found.

The results concerning the proposition about the moderating effects of consideration were suggested earlier by Fleishman and Harris (1962) who did provide evidence of one such "additional variable." This earlier work by Fleishman and Harris demonstrated that leadership styles may interact so that high emphasis on consideration allows the leader to initiate more structure to achieve organizational objectives. Thus, high turnover and grievances were related to low consideration and high structure. However, supervisors with high consideration could increase structure without adverse effects on grievances and turnover. Supervisors with low structure had high turnover and grievances regardless. Thus, Fleishman and Harris (1962) found consideration to be an important moderator variable of the leader structure-group performance relationship. Cummins (1971) later replicated these results using "quality" as a group output measure. . . .

For leaders perceived to be high on consideration, the "initiating structure-causes-subordinate performance" cross-lagged coefficients were positive, significant, and substantially higher than the corresponding P → IS coefficients. Conversely, significant results in exactly the opposite direction were obtained when the leader was perceived as not emphasizing a high degree of consideration. Here, all of the correlations were negative and the patterns of coefficients rather strongly indicated that performance caused initiating structure, particularly in the low consideration group. While of substantially lesser magnitudes, the negative signs of the IS → P cross-lagged coefficients in the low consideration group are supportive of the contention that high emphasis on structure may be counterproductive when the leader shows little consideration. . . .

Summary

The results of this investigation have provided indications that consideration causes subordinate satisfaction and, conversely, that subordinate performance causes both leader consideration and structure across conditions. However, when the relationship between initiating structure and subordinate performance was moderated by consideration, there was evidence of reciprocal causation. In particular, the results indicate how a leader might positively affect subordinate performance by increased emphasis on both consideration and structure. . . .

References

Campbell, D. T. From description to experimentation: Interpreting trends as quasi-experiments. In C. W. Harris (Ed.), *Problems in measuring change.* Madison: University of Wisconsin Press, 1963.

Crowe, B. J., Bochner, S., & Clark, A. W. The effects of subordinates' behavior on managerial style. *Human Relations*, 1972, *25*, 215–237.

Cummins, R. C. Relationship of initiating structures and job performance as moderated by consideration. *Journal of Applied Psychology*, 1971, *55*, 489–490.

Dawson, J. E., Messe, L. A., & Phillips, J. L. Effect of instructor-leader behavior on student performance. *Journal of Applied Psychology*, 1972, *56*, 369–376.

Day, R. C., & Hamblin, R. L. Some effects of close and punitive styles of supervision. *American Journal of Sociology*, 1964, *69*, 499–510.

Farris, G. F., & Lim, G. F., Jr. Effects of performance on leadership cohesiveness, influence, satisfaction and subsequent performance. *Journal of Applied Psychology*, 1969, *53*, 490–497.

Fleishman, E. A. Overview. In E. A. Fleishman & J. G. Hunt (Eds.), *Current developments in the study of leadership.* Carbondale: Southern Illinois University Press, 1973. (a)

Fleishman, E. A. Twenty years of consideration and structure. In E. A. Fleishman & J. G. Hunt (Eds.), *Current developments in the study of leadership.*

Carbondale: Southern Illinois University Press, 1973. (b)

Fleishman, E. A., & Harris, E. F. Patterns of leadership related to employee grievances and turnover. *Personnel Psychology*, 1962, *15*, 43–56.

Greene, C. N. Causal connections among managers' merit pay, satisfaction, and performance. *Journal of Applied Psychology*, 1973, *58*, 95–100.

Hawthorne, W. W., Couch, A., Haefner, D., Langham, P., & Carter, L. F. The effects of varying combinations of authoritarian and equalitarian leaders and followers. *Journal of Personality and Social Psychology*, 1956, *53*, 210–219.

Jackson, J. M. The effect of changing the leadership of small work groups. *Human Relations*, 1953, *6*, 25–44.

Jones, E. E., Gergen, K. J., Gumpert, P., & Thibaut, J. W. Some conditions affecting the use of ingratiation to influence performance evaluation. *Journal of Personality and Social Psychology*, 1965, *1*, 613–625.

Katz, D., & Stotland, E. A preliminary statement to a theory of attitude structure and change. In S. Koch (Ed.), *Psychology: A study of science* (Vol. 3). New York: McGraw-Hill, 1959.

Lawler, E. E., & Suttle, J. L. A causal correlational test of the need hierarchy concept. *Organizational Behavior and Human Performance*, 1972, *3*, 265–287.

Likert, R. *New patterns of management.* New York: McGraw-Hill, 1961.

Lowin, A., & Craig, J. R. The influence of level of performance on managerial style: An experimental object lesson in the ambiguity of correlational data. *Organizational Behavior and Human Performance*, 1968, *3*, 441–458.

Pelz, D. C., & Andrews, F. M. Detecting causal priorities in panel study data. *American Sociological Review*, 1964, *29*, 836–848.

Simon, H. A. Spurious correlation: A causal interpretation. *Journal of the American Statistical Association*, 1954, *49*, 467–479.

Stogdill, R. M. *Manual for job description and job expectation questionnaire—Form XII.* Columbus: Ohio State University, Bureau of Business Research, 1965. (a)

Stogdill, R. M. *Manual for job description and job expectation questionnaire.* Columbus: Ohio State University, College of Administrative Science, Program for Research in Leadership and Organization, 1965. (b)

Vroom, V. H. A comparison of static and dynamic correlation methods in the study of organizations. *Organizational Behavior and Human Performance*, 1966, *1*, 55–70.

Yee, A. H., & Gage, N. L. Techniques for estimating the source and direction of causal influence in panel data. *Psychological Bulletin*, 1968, *2*, 115–126.

The Follower's Role in Leadership Phenomena

F. H. Sanford

Most psychological researches on leadership have been concerned with the traits of leaders. Psychologists, traditionally, have dealt with the characteristics of individuals and have made available many instruments, such as personality tests, to facilitate thinking in terms of traits. The search for "leadership traits," however, has not been very rewarding. Stogdill's review[1] strongly suggests that some new approach is needed if we are going to make sense out of leadership phenomena. The literature leads us to think either (a) that there are no general "leadership traits" or (b) that if there are, they do not come in such a form as to be properly described in terms of those personality variables which we now can most easily measure.

The present study departs rather drastically from the search for leadership traits. It looks instead at the follower. It starts off with the idea that leadership is a *relation* between leader and follower, as marriage is a relation between husband and wife and friendship a relation between two people. If we want to learn about marriage, we do not study only husbands or only wives. We have to study the relation that exists between them. The same thing holds for friendship or enmity or partnership or leadership. The present study, while based on the notion that leadership is a relation between leader and follower, does not succeed in studying the relation directly. It seeks to learn about the relation by looking at the follower—the heretofore neglected follower—and his role in the relationship.

The follower is always there when leadership occurs. It is he who accepts or rejects leadership. It is he who follows reluctantly or enthusiastically, obediently or creatively. In any situation where leadership occurs, he is there with all his psychological attributes. He brings with him his habits, attitudes, preferences, biases, and deep-lying psychological needs. If we know something about these psychological attributes, we know something about the follower's "readiness for leadership." We know something about the sort of relations he will be inclined to establish with what sort of leaders.

It is probably true, our general notion says, that every individual has his own unique pattern of readiness for leadership. He has learned both general and specific attitudes toward authority and the ways it is exercised. Perhaps he has learned to like strong and directive leadership, exercised by people with all the accoutrements of conventional status. Perhaps he dislikes leaders who are less than six feet tall and has a great antipathy for any female who tries to assume a leadership role. Another individual may have learned, by contrast, to reject any form of autocratic or directive leadership, preferring his leaders to be more human, more sympathetic, and more responsive to the follower.

In any group or in any society we may expect to find a wide variety of learned readinesses for leadership. But any group may have a modal pattern of readinesses that sets it off from other groups. Eventually we may be able to describe the southern or the middle class or the Jewish or the Protestant or the educated or uneducated orientation to leadership. Or we may be able to trace out the American as contrasted with the German or the Samoan pattern of attitudes toward authority in its various forms.

The present paper presents first some specimen data on what may be roughly called the American orientation to leadership. It analyzes followers' responses to some interview items designed to elicit general attitudes about leadership, and it goes on to examine the public's orientation to F. D. Roosevelt as a leader. Then the paper talks about one personality factor in the individual which has something to do with his readiness to follow. . . .

The Follower's Personality as a Factor in Leadership

The foregoing data bear on what we may eventually be able to describe as the "typical" American way of reacting to leadership. We have been working under the general background hypothesis that psychological needs or predispositions of the follower have an important hand in determining both how a leader is perceived and the degree to which he is accepted. The data so far presented tend to fall in line with this hypothesis and lead to tentative statements about some follower needs that are involved in the leader-follower relation.

Source: Excerpts from "The follower's role in leadership phenomena" from *Readings in Social Psychology* by Guy E. Swanson, Theodore M. Newcomb, and Eugene L. Hartley (copyright 1952 and renewed 1980 by Holt, Rinehart and Winston, Inc.), reprinted by permission of the publisher. Author affiliation may have changed since article was first published.

The present paper reports on some of the results from a large-scale study of leadership conducted at The Institute for Research in Human Relations. More detailed accounts appear in the author's book *Authoritarianism and Leadership* (Philadelphia: The Institute for Research in Human Relations, 1950), and in his report "Public Orientation to Roosevelt," *Public Opinion Quarterly*, 1951, XV, 189–216. Permission to reprint certain materials from these sources has been given by The Institute for Research in Human Relations and by Princeton University Press.

The project was supported by the Office of Naval Research, but the publication of assertions growing out of the study does not imply their endorsement by any branch of the Naval Service. John N. Patterson, Barney Korchin, Harry J. Older, Emily L. Ehle, Irwin Rosenstock, Doris M. Barnett, F. Loyal Greer, and Douglas Courtney were collaborators in the over-all project and were direct or indirect contributors to the present report.

But we can come to closer grips with such matters if we can deal with the psychology of the individual follower rather than the psychology of masses of followers.

The plan of the project called for the intensive study of one personality variable which, on the basis of theory, ought to have a great deal to do with the individuals' reactions to leadership. The variable chosen was authoritarianism, and the instrument used to study it was an authoritarian-equalitarian (A–E) scale.[3] . . .

On the basis of theory and existing evidence, we expect that the people who score toward the authoritarian end of the A–E scale will want strong and directive leadership and will accept leadership that "pays off" in material terms. The authoritarian's "bargaining" orientation to authority, his respect for the strong and scorn for the weak, should lead him to accept Roosevelt as a good leader because Roosevelt was strong and because he produced.

The low scorers, on the other hand, tending toward a warmer—and perhaps more rational—relation with people and with authority, should emphasize Roosevelt's humanity or humanitarianism and should take a reasonably objective view of his ability to do his job. Being less deeply concerned with authority relationships, they should not be concerned with the strength-weakness dimension, unless they perceive strength as necessary for the achievement of a social goal, and should judge Roosevelt against a relatively "democratic" frame of reference.

In order to test such hypotheses, the procedure was:

1. To select from our population 80 individuals who were in the B economic group ($5,000 to $10,000 annual income) and who had completed at least a high-school education.

2. To split the 80 into two groups with respect to A–E scores—40 "highs" and 40 "lows."

3. To classify the responses of all 80 individuals with respect to psychologically conceived variables.

4. To examine the tendency, if any, of "highs" and "lows" to respond in accordance with theoretical expectations.

The selection of 80 individuals of approximately the same income group and educational level should succeed in holding relatively constant these demographic variables so that personality variables can show through clearly.

Each response of these 80 individuals was classified according to the following variables:

1. *Emphasis on Function.* The tendency of the respondent to think of Roosevelt's functioning as a leader of a democratic country. "Was an excellent administrator," "chose good advisers."

2. *Material Dependency.* The respondent's emphasis on Roosevelt's "payoff," the material benefits he brought to his followers. "Looked out for the average man," "saved us from depression."

3. *Emphasis on Power.* The emphasis on power and strength of the man; the suggestion that the follower wanted a powerful leader to keep him safe. "He was a pillar of strength in time of need."

4. *Personal Warmth.* The emphasis on F.D.R.'s responsiveness to and fondness for people. "He liked people," "he was a great humanitarian."

The procedure was for three judges, two of whom were trained in psychology, to examine all 80 responses, to discuss each one, then to put in one pile all those agreed upon as clearly expressing the quality under consideration. This was done, of course, in ignorance of the A–E scores of the respondents. By this method all the 80 responses agreed upon as expressing a *concern with function* were separated out. Then the total 80 were shuffled, and those agreed upon as showing *material dependency* were separated, and so on for each of the four variables. It was then possible to compare with chance expectation the frequency of high scorers and low scorers in each pile.

Of the 80 responses, 25 were agreed upon as showing *concern with function.* Theory dictates that those who demonstate this relatively objective concern for the leader's function should be low scorers. The results showed 19 out of the 25 answers in this category were made by people in the low-scoring group. This result is different from chance expectation at the 2-percent level of significance. (The C.R. by the sign test is 2.40.)

Only 6 of these 80 respondents gave responses that were agreed upon as showing clear *material dependency.* (These 80 were all middle- or upper-middle-class people.) We expect from theory that high scorers will give this sort of response. The fact is that five out of the six of those expressing material dependency are high scorers. This difference is suggestive but by no means conclusive since the N is so small.

Thirty-one of the respondents gave responses agreed upon as *emphasizing the leader's power.* We would expect, theoretically, that our high scorers, with their respect for power, would be the ones responding in this category. Eighteen out of the 31 respondents here were high, 13 were low. This result does not differ significantly from chance. One gets the impression, however, that this may be because the low scorers, in a way consistent with personality structure, are regarding Roosevelt's strength as a *means* rather than as an end in itself. In time of stress the equalitarian is perfectly willing to accept the powerful leader whose emergency function is clear. There is reason to believe that while the equalitarian can take power or leave it alone, the authoritarian *needs* it—almost to a neurotic degree. In the reaction to Roosevelt, the low scorers may be expressing admiration for strength when strength was functionally necessary—during a war and a depression when democracy was threatened. The authoritarian may be admiring strength for its own sweet savor. But our present data cannot be used to test these hypotheses.

There were 13 of the 80 responses agreed upon by three judges as expressing admiration for Roosevelt's *warmth and humanitarian qualities.* We would expect our low scorers to predominate in this area. Twelve out of the 13 responses in this category were made by our equalitarians—a result that differs significantly (at better than the 1-percent level) from chance expectation.

These results show with reasonable clarity that personality factors in the follower play a role in determining the orientation to a leader. While authoritarians and equalitarians, as classified by the A–E scale, are almost equal in the frequency with which they express admiration for Roosevelt, they clearly differ in the reasons they give for accepting him as a leader. Authoritarians do not think of him in terms of his social function or in terms of his humanity and warmth. They tend to emphasize his materially beneficial accomplishments.

The low scorers on the A–E scale–the so-called "equalitarians"—clearly see F.D.R.'s concern for people, observe his successful functioning, and show little concern for how he "paid off" in terms of beneficial accomplishments.

Discussion

The study of the follower and an emphasis on the leader-follower relation lead to a way of thinking about leadership that may overcome some of the limitations inherent in a trait approach and that someday may develop into a systematic theory of leadership. It may be worth while here to look at a summary sketch of this way of thinking.

Leadership is a relation. Psychological factors in the follower as well as psychological factors in the leader help determine this relation. The individual follower has his own unique pattern of needs and attitudes that constitute his readiness for leadership. He has problems which the leader must solve. He has learned certain standards whereby he judges the leader's effectiveness. All these factors are there in determining what sort of relation will be established with what sort of leader.

Because all Americans have more-or-less common learning experiences, American followers can be expected to have a more-or-less "typical" way of reacting to authority. And because the relevant learning differs somewhat from one group to another within American society, we might expect the ways of reacting to authority to differ somewhat from one demographic segment of the population to another.

In a concrete leadership situation, the follower's deeply-lying attitudes and needs are present as background determiners of his reaction to the leader, but there are also *situationally determined needs* that arise. The need to achieve a group goal or the need to adjust to here-and-now demands is imposed on the more persistent patterns of needs, making new demands on the leader. In a life-or-death situation, the follower's need for warm approval is likely to be less important than his need to survive. He will thus be less likely to accept the "nice guy" as a leader, more likely to follow the man who appears able to help solve the immediate and pressing problem. It is possible to state this sort of observation as a definite hypothesis: the more psychologically significant the group goal, the greater the follower's emphasis on the leader's competence to assist in achieving that goal. A corollary to the hypothesis is as follows: the more *clearly perceived* the goal, and the more visible is progress toward it, the more follower emphasis there will be on the functional competence of the leader. The converse of each of these hypotheses will also be of interest. In groups where the goal is (*a*) not very important, and (*b*) not very visible, there will be a preference for leaders who meet those persistent psychological needs that are relatively independent of the immediate situation—e.g., the need for warm approval. Certainly in many everyday groups (fraternities, clubs, neighborhood or church organizations, etc.) the preferred leader often seems to be the one who is good at giving psychological structure and satisfaction to garden-variety individuals with standard American social needs. It sometimes happens in these groups, that "nice guy" leaders are by-passed or thrown out when the group comes down with a desire to do a specific and challenging job. Sometimes in such groups we also see "leadership by default." Where the role of the leader is neither very functionally significant nor clearly defined, the individual who desperately wants to be leader is allowed to assume the mantle, whether or not he is a "nice guy."

These are examples of the sort of hypotheses—testable hypotheses—that grow out of the present approach to leadership phenomena.

We can, with profit, start to think about leadership in terms of the follower's needs or problems and their variations from situation to situation. But we still cannot understand leadership without paying close attention to the leader and *his* problems. The leader is as much of an individual as is the follower. His needs, his abilities, obviously are involved in the leader-follower relation. We have built up a picture here of follower's needs creating a demand for leadership of a certain sort. In any situation there will be a pressure to put into the leader's role a person who fits the demand. Formal or informal candidates for the leader's role have their own pressures to exert also. Some people want to be leaders, sometimes desperately so. Some of these will be able, because of their own pattern of needs, to play the leader's role with only one style. Some people are very chronic "nice guys" and cannot meet situational demands for strong and directive authority. Others are chronic authoritarians who may desperately want to dominate others and would be a severe handicap to a group with a strong need for individual initiative and freedom of expression. There are individuals who seek responsibility but who clearly lack the abilities necessary to advance specific group goals. Others will have requisite abilities but do not particularly like to assume responsibility.

Who will become leader will depend on (*a*) the pattern of follower needs and (*b*) the pattern of leader needs and abilities. The leader-follower relation most likely to become established in a free situation—and most likely to persist in either a free situation or one in which leadership is determined from outside—is the relation that is reciprocally rewarding to both follower and leader.

Notes

[1] R. M. Stogdill, "Personal Factors Associated with Leadership: A Survey of the Literature," *J. Psychol.,* 1948, XXV, 35–71.

[2] The sample was actually a modified area sample. Twenty-four four-block areas were selected randomly from census tract data and 40 interviews were taken in 21 of them. By accident 41 were taken in three areas. The sample thus obtained was representative, within a small margin of error, with respect to the usual demographic parameters. The data presented here under the label of "American" are good data for Philadelphia but probably would be somewhat different in other parts of the country. Thus the term "American orientation" must be taken with a large grain of salt.

[3] The most extensive studies of the variable are contained in W. Adorno, E. Frenkel-Brunswik, D. Levinson, and R. N. Sanford, *The Authoritarian Personality* (New York: Harpers, 1950). The A–E scale used in the present study is an adaptation of the F scale described in that volume.

Toward a Behavioral Theory of Leadership[1]

G. Yukl
University of Akron, Ohio

D espite over two decades of extensive leadership re-search, the relation of leader behavior to subordi-nate productivity and satisfaction with the leader is still not very clear. The apparent absence of consistent rela-tionships in the research literature (Sales, 1966; Korman, 1966; Lowin, 1968) may be due in part to several related prob-lems. First, there is a great deal of semantic confusion regarding the conceptual and operational definition of lead-ership behavior. Over the years there has been a proliferation of leader behavior terms, and the same term is often defined differently from one study to the next. Secondly, a great deal of empirical data has been collected, but a theoretical frame-work which adequately explains causal relationships and identifies limiting conditions has not yet emerged. Finally, the research has often failed to include intermediate and situational variables which are necessary in order to under-stand how a leader's actions can affect his subordinates' productivity.

The purpose of this article is to begin the development of a theory which explains how leader behavior, situational variables, and intermediate variables interact to determine subordinate productivity and satisfaction with the leader. In the first section of the article, a system of three distinct and generally applicable leader behavior dimensions will be pro-posed. In the next two sections, these leadership dimensions will be used to develop a discrepancy model of subordinate satisfaction and a multiple linkage model of leader effective-ness. Finally, the extent to which the research literature sup-ports these behavioral models will be evaluated.

Classification of Leader Behavior

Consideration and Initiating Structure

Some early investigators began with a list of very specific leadership activities (e.g., "inspection," "write reports," "hear complaints") and attempted to determine how per-formance of these activities or the amount of time allocated to them related to leader success. Since the number of specific leader activities that are possible is nearly endless, several Ohio State University psychologists attempted to find a few general behavior dimensions which would apply to all types

of leaders. Factor analyses of leadership behavior question-naires were carried out, and two orthogonal factors were found (Hemphill & Coons, 1957; Halpin & Winer, 1957). These factors were called Consideration and Initiating Struc-ture. Consideration refers to the degree to which a leader acts in a warm and supportive manner and shows concern and respect for his subordinates. Initiating Structure refers to the degree to which a leader defines and structures his own role and those of his subordinates toward goal attainment. . . .

Decision-Centralization

A somewhat different approach to the classification of leaders was initiated by Lewin's (1944) theoretical typology of democratic, autocratic, and laissez-faire leaders. Studies following in this tradition have usually focused on the rela-tive degree of leader and subordinate influence over the group's decisions. The various decision-making procedures used by a leader, such as delegation, joint decision-making, consultation, and autocratic decision making, can be or-dered along a continuum ranging from high subordinate in-fluence to complete leader influence. Although a leader will usually allow more subordinate participation and influence for some decisions than for others, the average degree of participation can be computed for any specified set of typ-ical decisions. Heller and Yukl (1969) have used the term "Decision-Centralization" to refer to this average. A high Decision-Centralization score means a low amount of subor-dinate participation. Naturally, a leader is capable of volun-tarily sharing decision making with his subordinates only to the extent that he has authority to make decisions.

Most methods that have been used to measure partici-pation can also be regarded as a measure of Decision-Centralization. Participation and Decision-Centralization have been measured by subordinate ratings of their per-ceived autonomy or influence in decision making, by subor-dinate responses to a questionnaire concerning the leader's decision behavior, and by leader responses to a decision be-havior questionnaire. In some studies the leader's actual decision-making behavior has been experimentally manipu-lated. The term Decision-Centralization was introduced for two reasons. First, this term emphasizes the behavior of the leader rather than the behavior of the subordinates. Second,

Source: Edited and reprinted with permission from *Organizational Behavior and Human Performance* 6 (1971), 414–440. (A revised and expanded version of the model is described in *Leadership in Organizations*, Prentice-Hall, 1994.) Copyright © 1971 by Academic Press, Inc. Author affiliation may have changed since article was first published.

[1] The author is grateful to Ken Wexley and Alexis Anikeeff for their helpful comments.

the definition of Decision-Centralization explicitly encompasses a greater variety of leader decision procedures than does the typical definition of participation (Heller & Yukl, 1969.[2] . . .

A Discrepancy Model of Subordinate Satisfaction with the Leader

In this section, a discrepancy model of satisfaction will be used to explain the relation of the three leadership dimensions to subordinate satisfaction with the leader. Discrepancy or subtraction models of job satisfaction have been proposed by a number of psychologists (Morse, 1953; Schaffer, 1953; Rosen & Rosen, 1955; Ross & Zander, 1957; Porter, 1962; Katzell, 1964; Locke, 1969). In a discrepancy model, satisfaction is a function of the difference between a person's preferences and his actual experience. The less the discrepancy between preferences and experience, the greater the satisfaction. This hypothesis has received some support in the studies cited above, but the evidence is by no means conclusive. In some versions of the discrepancy model, there is a second hypothesis which states that the amount of dissatisfaction with a given discrepancy also depends upon the importance of the needs affecting the preference level. If importance varies from person to person, the discrepancy scores cannot be compared unless first adjusted for importance. Whether such a correction is necessary, and if so, how it should be made appears to be a matter of growing controversy.

Although the discrepancy model appears to be applicable to the analysis of subordinates' satisfaction with their leader, only a few studies have used it for this purpose. In two of these studies (Foa, 1957; Greer, 1961), leadership variables other than Consideration, Initiating Structure, and Decision-Centralization were used. No studies were found which included subordinate preferences for Consideration and Initiating Structure as as moderating variable. The results from studies which have included subordinate preferences for participation in decision-making tend to be consistent with the discrepancy model.

According to the proposed discrepancy model, the shape of the curve relating leader behavior to subordinate satisfaction will vary somewhat depending upon a subordinate's preference level. A preference level will be defined tentatively as a range of leader behavior acceptable to subordinates rather than as a single point on a behavior continuum. Figure 1 shows the theoretical curves for a low, medium, and high preference level. The curves represent the relation for a single subordinate. When the preference levels of group members are relatively homogeneous, the relation between leader behavior and average group satisfaction with their leader will yield a curve similar to that for an individual. However, the more variable the preferences are in a group, the less likely it is that any significant relation will be found between leader behavior and average group satisfaction.

Subordinate preference levels are determined both by subordinate personality and by situational variables (see Figure 2). Preferences can be expected to vary more for Initiating Structure and Decision-Centralization than for Consideration. Except for a few masochists, it is probably safe to assume that subordinates will desire a high degree of considerate behavior by their leaders. As a result, the function

F I G U R E   1

The relation between leader behavior and subordinate satisfaction for a low, medium, and high preference level (PL).

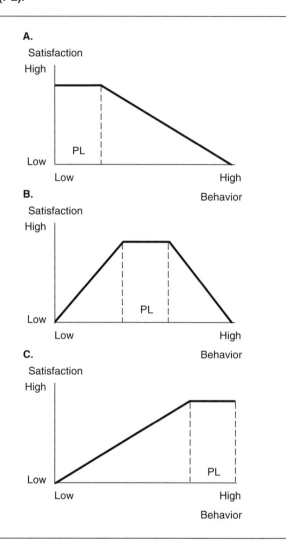

relating Consideration and subordinate satisfaction should resemble curve C in Figure 1.

Preference levels for Decision-Centralization, i.e., the subordinate's desire for participation in decision making, may be partially determined by two personality traits: authoritarianism (Vroom, 1959) and "need for independence" (Trow, 1957; Ross & Zander, 1957; Vroom, 1959; Beer, 1966, p. 51; French, Kay, & Meyer, 1966). Although none of these investigators assessed the relation between a personality measure and expressed behavior preferences, they did find that personality had the expected moderating effect upon the relation between Decision-Centralization and subordinate satisfaction. However, it should be noted that Tosi (1970) was not able to replicate the results of the study by Vroom (1959). The measurement of subordinate preferences in future replications may aid in clearing up the contradiction between these two studies.

The major situational determinant of the preference level

FIGURE 2
A Discrepancy Model of Subordinate Satisfaction with the Leader.

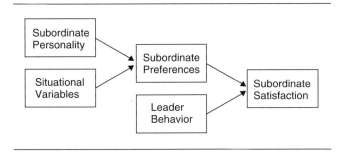

FIGURE 3
A Multiple Linkage Model of Leader Effectiveness.

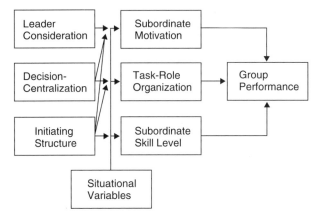

for participation in making a decision is probably the importance of that decision for the subordinate (Maier, 1965, p. 165). When a decision is very important to subordinates, they are likely to prefer as much influence as possible (e.g., joint decision making or delegation). When decisions do not involve matters of importance, consultation or even autocratic decision making is more likely to be preferred. Of course, the more that subordinates trust their leader to make a decision favorable to them, the less need they will feel to participate in order to protect their interests. Also, when the subordinates are committed to group goal attainment or survival and the task or environment favors centralized decision making (e.g., a crisis), then they are likely to expect the leader to make most of the decisions (Mulder & Stemerding, 1963).

Preference levels for Initiating Structure are partially determined by the subordinates' commitment to group goals and their perception of the amount of structuring that is necessary to help the group attain these goals. Subordinates who are indifferent about or hostile toward the goal of maximum productivity are likely to prefer a leader who is not very task oriented in his behavior.

Summary of the Discrepancy Model

The major features of the proposed discrepancy model can be summarized in terms of the following hypotheses:

Hyp 1: Subordinate satisfaction with the leader is a function of the discrepancy between actual leader behavior and the behavior preferences of subordinates.

Hyp 2: Subordinate preferences are determined by the combined effect of subordinate personality and situational variables.

Hyp 3: Subordinates usually prefer a high degree of leader Consideration, and this preference level results in a positive relation between Consideration and subordinate satisfaction.

The discrepancy model in its present form is only a static model representing one-way causality at one point in time. No attempt has been made to include additional complexities such as the effects of leader behavior on subordinate preferences. For example, a leader who gradually allows greater subordinate participation may find that the subordinates' preference for decision-making increases over time. Nor does the model explicitly deal with such other determinants of

subordinate satisfaction with the leader as his intelligence or the feedback effects from successful or unsuccessful group performance. Finally, the influence of various components of the model on leader behavior has also been ignored. For example, subordinate preferences represent one of several sources of role expectations for the leader, and these role expectations interact with other situational variables and leader personality to determine his behavior.

A Multiple Linkage Model of Leader Effectiveness

When a leader is dependent upon his subordinates to do the work, subordinate performance is unlikely to improve unless the leader can increase one or more of the following three intermediate variables: (1) subordinate task motivation (i.e., effort devoted to their tasks), (2) subordinate task skills, and (3) Task-Role Organization (i.e., the technical quality of task decisions).[4] Consideration, Initiating Structure, Decision-Centralization, and various situational variables interact in their effects on these intermediate variables. The intermediate variables interact in turn to determine group performance (see Figure 3).

Consideration, Initiating Structure, and Subordinate Motivation

Consideration and Initiating Structure interact in their effect upon subordinate task motivation. Subordinate task motivation will be highest when the leader is high on both Consideration and Initiating Structure. The ordering of the other combinations is less certain, because the interaction appears to be highly complex and irregular. If leaders were subgrouped according to their Initiating Structures scores, for high structuring leaders there would probably be a positive relation between Consideration and subordinate task motivation. For low structuring leaders, there is some reason to suspect that the relation between Consideration and subordinate motivation is described by an inverted U-shaped curve. In other words, subordinate task motivation can be adversely affected when the low structuring leader is either very supportive and friendly or very hostile and punitive.

There are at least two hypotheses for explaining the interaction between Consideration and Initiating Structure, and it is not yet clear if either or both are correct. From instrumentality theory (Vroom, 1964, p. 220; Galbraith & Cummings, 1967), comes the hypothesis that a leader can improve subordinate performance by being highly considerate to subordinates who make an effort to perform well, while withholding Consideration from subordinates who show little task motivation. In effect, considerate behavior is a reward which is contingent upon the display of certain task-motivated behavior by subordinates.

The "identification" hypothesis proposes that subordinate motivation is a response to previous leader Consideration rather than an attempt to obtain future Consideration. As Consideration increases, subordinate attitudes toward the leader become more favorable, and his influence over the subordinates increases correspondingly. In effect, the considerate leader has greater "referent power" (French & Raven, 1959). However, in order for subordinate loyalty to be translated into task motivation, it is necessary for the leader to communicate a concern for productivity. If the leader is highly considerate but does not stress productivity, the subordinates are likely to feel that they can safely neglect their tasks.

If a leader actually becomes hostile and punitive, it is likely that subordinate task motivation will be adversely affected, regardless of the level of Initiating Structure. Punitive leadership can lead to counteraggression by subordinates in the form of slowdowns and subtle sabotage (Day & Hamblin, 1964).

Decision-Centralization and Subordinate Motivation

Although there is some direct evidence that subordinate participation can result in increased task motivation (Baumgartel, 1956), the nature and relative importance of the psychological processes accounting for the relation and the prerequisite conditions for their occurrence are not yet clear. A number of explanations for the effect of participation on subordinate motivation have been proposed during the last two decades.

Probably the most important of the proposed processes is the possibility that subordinates become "ego-involved" with a decision which they have helped to make. When subordinates identify with a decision, they become motivated to help make the decision successful, if only to maintain a favorable self-concept. However, there may be several limiting conditions for this causal sequence (Strauss, 1964; Vroom, 1964; Lowin, 1968). It is possible that there is some minimal amount of individual influence, actual or perceived, which is necessary before identification will occur. As a group gets larger, the influence of each member over a decision will necessarily decline; thus the size of the group may be one limiting factor. Also, it is not clear whether a person who supports a proposal that is rejected will become committed to the proposal finally selected by the group. Another prerequisite may be the subordinate's perception that the decision process is a test of his decision ability and those skills of his which are used in implementing the decision. In the case where subordinates participate in making decisions unrelated to their tasks, there is no reason to assume that any increased commitment to these decisions will generalize to task decisions. Finally, if responsibility for making decisions is thrust upon subordinates who do not want it or who see it as the legitimate role of the leader, then these subordinates may fail to identify with the decisions (French, Israel, & As, 1960).

Another explanation of the relation between Decision-Centralization and task motivation is that participation facilitates reduction of subordinate resistance to change (Coch & French, 1948). One way this could occur is through direct persuasion. Since the leader is usually not aware of all the subordinates' fears and doubts regarding a proposed change, consultation provides him with an opportunity to uncover these fears and to persuade subordinates that the change will be beneficial rather than harmful. When a leader's proposal involves features which clearly are detrimental to subordinates, mere persuasion is not likely to win their support. However, consultation or joint decision making provides the opportunity for bargaining and agreement on a compromise proposal which the subordinates can support (Strauss, 1964).

When the leader allows his subordinates to make a group decision, the interaction dynamics of the group are yet another possible source of increased task motivation. If the work group is cohesive, its members are subject to direct social pressure to conform to group norms (Schachter, Willerman, Festinger, & Hyman, 1961; Berkowitz, 1954; Seashore, 1954). In addition, the work group may function as a "reference group" for its members (Newcomb, 1965, p. 109). Subordinates who have positive attitudes toward their work group will tend to support group norms, including group decisions made in a legitimate manner. This tendency for member attitudes and behavior to be consistent with reference group norms will occur even in the absence of direct social pressure.

Of course, increased commitment to carry out decisions is not conceptually equivalent to increased task motivation. Subordinates can make task decisions which in effect restrict output or resist change. Subordinate attitudes toward the leader and the organization constitute an important situational variable which moderates the effect of participation upon task motivation. If relations between the leader and the subordinates are very poor, or the subordinates are in opposition to the goal of maximum group performance, then participation in decisions involving production goals, standards, quotas, etc., is not likely to result in increased subordinate task motivation (Strauss, 1964). Since Consideration is an important determinant of subordinate attitudes toward the leader, participation is more likely to be effective if combined with high Consideration than if combined with low Consideration.

Leader Behavior and Subordinate Task Skill

The second way in which leaders can increase group performance is to increase the ability of subordinates to perform their individual tasks. A number of studies (reviewed in Vroom, 1964, p. 197) support Maier's (1965) hypothesis that performance is a function of a person's Motivation × Ability. According to this hypothesis, even highly motivated subordinates will not perform well if they lack the necessary knowledge or skills to carry out their assignments. Therefore, one way for a leader to improve group performance is to correct deficiencies in subordinate task skills and knowledge by means of on-the-job instruction and improved downward communication of task-relevant information. Instruction and communication of this nature are, by definition, elements of Initiating Structure. A more complex analysis of the relation between Initiating Structure and subordinate task skill was beyond the scope of this article.

The Nature of Task-Role Organization

Task-Role Organization refers to how efficiently the skill resources of subordinates are utilized to perform the group's formal tasks. Adequacy of Task-Role Organization depends upon how well job assignment decisions and work method decisions are made. The making of job assignment decisions is usually referred to in industrial psychology as "placement" or "classification." When the jobs of each subordinate are identical and subordinates work independently of each other, it doesn't matter what subordinates are assigned to what jobs. However, when jobs are highly specialized, each job has different skill requirements, and skill differences among subordinates are substantial, then job assignments are an important type of task decision. If work assignments are not made carefully, the skills of some workers will not be fully utilized, while other workers will be placed in jobs which they cannot perform adequately. Furthermore, if the jobs are interdependent, bottlenecks will occur at various points in the flow of work.

Work method decisions are important whenever a task can be performed in many different ways, and some ways are better than others. Work methods and procedures can be designed with the available skills of a particular work group in mind, but it is common practice in industrial engineering to ignore individual differences and develop methods which maximize the efficiency of the typical worker. Decisions about work procedures are not always the responsibility of the leader. In some organizations, work methods are designed by staff specialists or are rigidly prescribed by company or union regulations.

Task-Role Organization was included in the multiple linkage model to account for any variability in group productivity which is not attributable to subordinate motivation, subordinate ability, or to extraneous events such as an improvement in the flow of material inputs, a breakdown in equipment, etc. The identification of Task-Role Organization as a separate variable is analogous to Maier's (1965) distinction between the quality of a decision and group acceptance of the decision. Although Task-Role Organization is an important conceptual component of the multiple linkage model, measurement of this variable is likely to prove troublesome. Any measure of Task-Role Organization will be highly specific to a given set of tasks and subordinates. Within a specific situation, one could attempt to scale the adequacy of job assignment decisions by evaluating the match between job requirements and subordinate skills for all possible combinations of job assignments. Adequacy of work method decisions could be evaluated in several ways. In some situations, the accumulated knowledge of industrial engineering specialists may permit the subjective ranking of various possible work procedures according to their relative efficiency. When objective measures of group performance

(e.g., quantity or quality of output, labor time, errors) are available to use as a criterion of efficiency, then alternative work methods may be experimentally compared. However, it may be difficult to hold task motivation constant, even within a single work group, because job design can affect the intrinsic motivation of workers as well as their efficiency.

Initiating Structure, Decision-Centralization, and Task-Role Organization

Both Initiating Structure and Decision-Centralization appear to be related to Task-Role Organization. By definition, a leader who is high in Initiating Structure will attempt to improve the efficiency of his group. However, simply engaging in structuring behavior does not guarantee that Task-Role Organization will improve. The leader's success depends upon his organizing skills, technical knowledge, and the extent to which he taps the knowledge of his subordinates by allowing them some degree of participation in making task decisions. The relation between Decision-Centralization and Task-Role Organization is moderated by the relative amount of leader and subordinate organizing skills and task knowledge. When the leader is very capable in this respect but the subordinates lack the appropriate talents, then there will be a negative relation between participation and Task-Role Organization. When the subordinates have more relevant knowledge and organizing talent than the leader, we would expect a positive relation between participation and Task-Role Organization. We have already seen that Decision-Centralization can affect the task motivation of subordinates as well as the quality of task decisions. This means that in the situation where there is a negative relation between participation and Task-Role Organization, there may also be a positive relation between participation and subordinate motivation. When such a trade-off dilemma occurs, some intermediate degree of Decision-Centralization will probably be optimal with respect to group performance.

In some situations, the quality of task decisions involves a time dimension. That is, the effectiveness of decisions depends in part upon how quickly they are made (Strauss, 1964; Lowin, 1968). Autocratic decision making is faster than other decision procedures because little communication with subordinates is necessary. Therefore, participation is likely to be negatively related to group performance when rapid decision making is required. The magnitude of this negative relation will be greatest when the leader already has the necessary knowledge and ability to make good decisions, the subordinates are motivated by the urgency of the situation, and the task group is very large. . . .

Review of Related Research

Most studies of the relation between leader behavior and subordinate satisfaction with the leader have not measured subordinate preferences or the personality and situational variables which determine these preferences. Most studies of the relation between leader behavior and group productivity have not included measures of the intermediate and situational variables in the proposed linkage model. The approach typical of most leadership research has been to look for a linear relation between leader behavior and one of the criterion variables. Nevertheless, previous research does provide some direct and some indirect evidence for evaluating the proposed models.

In the following sections of this article, relevant leadership research will be reviewed. The review will include studies dealing with variables which are reasonably similar to those in the proposed discrepancy and linkage models. However, it should be emphasized that in many of these studies, the operational measurement of a variable only approximates the conceptual definition presented in this article. Studies using scales which can be regarded as a measure of leader attitudes (e.g., LPC scale, F scale, Leadership Opinion Questionnaire) rather than leader behavior were not included. Also excluded were studies of general versus close supervision. This leadership dimension, as usually defined, confounds Decision-Centralization with Initiating Structure. Finally, the review does not include studies of emergent leaders in informal groups, studies using children, studies involving an entire organization rather than individual work groups or departments, and studies in which leader behavior is obviously confounded with organizational variables such as the incentive system.

Consideration and Satisfaction

In seven studies of the relation between Consideration and subordinate satisfaction with their leader, Consideration was measured by means of subordinate responses on leader behavior description questionnaires. In five of these studies (Halpin, 1957; Halpin & Winer, 1957; Nealey & Blood, 1968; Yukl, 1969a; Anderson, 1966) there was a strong positive relation between Consideration and subordinate satisfaction. In the remaining two studies (Fleishman & Harris, 1962; Skinner, 1969) there was a significant curvilinear relation between Consideration and two objective measures which reflect subordinate satisfaction, namely turnover and grievances. The curve describing the relation corresponded roughly to curve C in Fig. 1. If subordinate preferences were homogeneous, this curve would represent supporting evidence for the concept of a zone of indifference within which leader behavior does not affect subordinate satisfaction. Below this indifference zone, the relation between Consideration and satisfaction was positive.

In research reported in Likert (1961, p. 17), aspects of Consideration such as "supervisor takes an interest in me and understands my problems" and "supervisor thinks of employees as human beings rather than as persons to get the work done," were related to favorable attitudes on job-related matters. In two laboratory experiments (Day & Hamblin, 1964; Misumi & Shirakashi, 1966) punitive leader behavior (i.e., low Consideration) was associated with low subordinate satisfaction. In another laboratory experiment, Lowin (1969) found a significant positive relation between subordinates' satisfaction and their ratings of leader Consideration, but the difference in satisfaction between high and low Consideration conditions, although in the right direction, was not significant.

Only two studies were found in which a positive relation between Consideration and subordinate satisfaction with the leader did not occur. In a study by Argyle, Gardner, and Cioffi (1958), leader self-reports of punitive behavior did not correlate significantly with subordinate turnover and absences. Pelz (1952) found an interaction between the degree

to which a leader acts as a representative of his subordinates when dealing with higher management (one form of Consideration) and the leader's upward influence in the organization. For leaders with little upward influence subordinates were less satisfied when the leader "went to bat" for them than when he did not go to bat. Presumably the leader representation raised expectations which he could not fulfill, thereby frustrating subordinates. In terms of the discrepancy model, the subordinates' preferences for leader representation are probably lower when it repeatedly causes frustration. Whether the negative effects of unsuccessful representation can completely cancel out the positive effects of other considerate behavior by the leader is not clear. It does not seem likely.

In summary, the research literature indicates that in most situations, considerate leaders will have more satisfied subordinates. Although none of the investigators included subordinate preferences in their analysis, the results are consistent with the discrepancy model if we can make the relatively safe assumption that most subordinates prefer considerate leaders.

Initiating Structure and Satisfaction

A consistent linear relation between Initiating Structure and subordinate satisfaction was not found, even within sets of studies using comparable measures. Unfortunately, none of the studies reviewed included subordinate preferences. Baumgartel (1956), Halpin and Winer (1957), Argyle *et al.* (1958), Misumi and Shirakashi (1966), Lowin (1969), Anderson (1966), and Likert (1961, pp. 16–18) failed to find a significant relation. Halpin (1957) and Yukl (1969a) found positive correlations. Vroom and Mann (1960) found a significant negative correlation between pressure for production and job satisfaction for delivery truck drivers but not for loaders. Nealey and Blood (1968) found a negative correlation between Initiating Structure and subordinate satisfaction for second-level supervisors and a positive correlation for first-level supervisors.

Only three studies were found which examined the possibility of a curvilinear relation between Initiating Structure and subordinate satisfaction. Likert (1955) found that the relation between pressure for productivity and subordinate satisfaction took the form of an inverted U-shaped curve which is similar to curve B in Fig. 1. Fleishman and Harris (1962) and Skinner (1969) found a curvilinear relation between Initiating Structure and both turnover and grievances. Although subordinate preferences were not measured, the relationships in these studies were roughly comparable to curve A in Fig. 1.

Fleishman and Harris also tested for an interaction between Initiating Structure and Consideration. The results of their analysis suggest that Consideration has a greater effect upon subordinate satisfaction than does Initiating Structure. High Consideration leaders could increase Initiating Structure with little accompanying increase in turnover or grievances. Fleishman and Harris provide two possible explanations for this interaction. One explanation is that considerate leaders are more likely to deal with any dissatisfaction caused by high structuring behavior before the dissatisfaction results in official grievances or withdrawal (i.e., turnover). Another explanation is that Consideration affects the way subordinates perceive structuring behavior. In terms of the discrepancy model, subordinates of highly considerate leaders are more likely to have a higher preference level for Initiating Structure because they do not perceive leader structuring as threatening and restrictive.

Decision-Centralization and Satisfaction

Six studies were found which examined the correlation between subordinate satisfaction and participation as perceived either by the leaders or by the subordinates (Baumgartel, 1956; Argyle *et al.*, 1958; Vroom, 1959; Bachman, Smith, & Slesinger, 1966; Yukl, 1969a; Tosi, 1970). In each of these studies evidence was found to support a positive relation between participation and subordinate satisfaction, although within some of the studies, a significant relation was not obtained for every subsample or for every alternative measure of the variables. A significant positive relation was also found in each of five studies in which participation was experimentally manipulated (Coch & French, 1948; Shaw, 1955, Morse & Reimer, 1956; Solem, 1958; Maier & Hoffman, 1962). The results of these studies are generally consistent with the discrepancy model if one can assume that the subordinates preferred a substantial degree of participation.

In those cases where a significant relation between participation and subordinate satisfaction was not found, there was usually some reason to expect that the subordinates preferred a moderate or low amount of participation. In the study by Vroom (1959), a positive correlation occurred for subordinates with a high need for independence but not for subordinates with a low need for independence. Bass (1965, pp. 169–170) and French *et al.* (1960) found that subordinate participation did not result in more favorable attitudes toward a leader unless the subordinates perceived the decision making as a legitimate part of their role. Further evidence for the moderating effect of subordinate preferences can be found in a study by Baumgartel (1956) and in two unpublished studies (Jacobson, 1951; Tannenbaum, 1954) which were reported in Likert (1961, pp. 92–93). In the Tannenbaum study, some subordinates reacted adversely to a sudden substantial increase in participation. Finally, Morse (1953, p. 64) found that, regardless of whether workers made some decisions or none, they reported more intrinsic job satisfaction when the amount of decision making equalled the amount desired than when they were not allowed to make as many decisions as they desired. Although intrinsic job satisfaction is conceptually distinct from satisfaction with the leader, these two variables are probably highly correlated when the leader determines how much responsibility a subordinate has for making task decisions.

Consideration, Initiating Structure, and Productivity

Considering the complexity of the interaction between Consideration and Initiating Structure, it is not surprising that research on the relation between Consideration and productivity does not yield consistent results. In the large majority of studies, there was either a significant positive relation (Katz, Maccoby, Gurin, & Floor, 1951; Argyle *et al.*, 1958; Besco & Lawshe, 1959; Schachter *et al.*, 1961; Kay, Meyer, &

French, 1965) or there was no significant linear relation (Bass, 1957; Halpin, 1957; Rambo, 1958; Day & Hamblin, 1964; Anderson, 1966; Nealey & Blood, 1968; Rowland & Scott, 1968). Lowin (1969) found a positive relation for objectively manipulated Consideration in an experiment but not for subordinate ratings of Consideration. A significant negative relation was found by Halpin and Winer (1957) for aircraft commanders and by Fleishman, Harris, and Burtt (1955, p. 80) for foremen of production departments but not for nonproduction departments. In both of these studies, productivity was measured by superior ratings, and the highest ratings went to leaders low on Consideration but high on Initiating Structure. It is possible that the ratings were influenced more by the raters' task-oriented stereotype of the ideal leader than by actual group performance.

Turning to research on the relation between Initiating Structure and productivity, we again find mixed results. In a number of studies a significant positive relation was reported (Fleishman *et al.*, 1955; Likert, 1955; Halpin & Winer, 1957; Maier & Maier, 1957; Besco & Lawshe, 1959; Anderson, 1966; Nealey & Blood, 1968). For some subsamples in three of these studies, and for leaders studied by Argyle *et al.* (1958), Bass (1957), Halpin (1957), Rambo (1958), and Lowin (1969), a significant relation was not found. In no case was a significant negative relation reported.

It is unfortunate that so few investigators measured intermediate variables or tested for an interaction between Consideration and Initiating Structure. However, the few studies which are directly relevant to the proposed linkage model do provide supporting evidence. In a laboratory experiment in Japan, Misumi and Shirakashi (1966) found that leaders who were both task oriented and considerate in their behavior had the most productive groups. Halpin (1957) found that aircraft commanders were rated highest in effectiveness when they were above the mean on both Consideration and Initiating Structure. Hemphill (1957) obtained the same results for the relation between the behavior of department chairmen in a Liberal Arts College and faculty ratings of how well the department was administered. Fleishman and Simmons (1970) translated the Supervisory Behavior Description into Hebrew and administered this questionnaire to the superiors of Israeli foremen. Proficiency ratings for the foremen were also obtained from their superiors. Once again, the foremen with the best ratings tended to be high on both Consideration and Initiating Structure. Patchen (1962) found that personal production norms (i.e., task motivation) of workers were highest when the leader encouraged proficiency as well as "going to bat" for them. These production norms were related in turn to actual group production. Finally, although he didn't measure Consideration, Baumgartel (1956) found a significant positive relation between subordinate motivation and the concern of research laboratory directors for goal attainment (i.e., Initiating Structure).

Decision-Centralization and Productivity

Seventeen studies were found which examined the relation between Decision-Centralization and group productivity. A significant positive relation between participation and productivity was found by Bachman *et al.* (1966), Coch and French (1948), Fleishman (1965), French (1950), French, Kay, and Meyer (1966), Lawrence and Smith (1955), Likert (1961,

p. 20), Mann and Dent (1954), McCurdy and Eber (1953), Meltzer (1956), and Vroom (1959). Argyle *et al.* (1958) found a positive relation only for departments without piece rates, suggesting that the organizational incentive system, a situational variable, interacts with Decision-Centralization in determining the subordinates' task motivation. Tosi (1970), French *et al.* (1960), and McCurdy and Lambert (1952) failed to find a significant relation between participation and productivity. In two other studies (Shaw, 1955; Morse & Reimer, 1956) a significant negative relation was found. Several of these studies demonstrate that various situational variables can moderate the effects of leader decision behavior on group performance. Nevertheless, the high percentage of studies reporting a positive relation is an indication that some degree of participation leads to an increase in group performance in most situations. However, this generalization is *not* equivalent to concluding "the more participation there is, the greater will be group productivity." For a particular group, there is probably some optimal pattern of decision making which will consist of various amounts of delegation, joint decision making, consultation, and autocratic decision making (Heller & Yukl, 1969). The optimal pattern is likely to involve some intermediate amount of subordinate influence, rather than the greatest possible amount. . . .

Discussions

The discrepancy model and the multiple linkage model provide only the skeleton of a static leadership theory which purposely ignores the additional complexities of feedback loops and circular causality. Much additional research and revision will be necessary to transform the skeleton into a full-fledged dynamic model which permits accurate predictions about leader effectiveness in formal task groups.

Notes

[4]The leader can also improve productivity by obtaining necessary information, resources, and cooperation from other organization members and outside agencies, but this involves leader behavior outside the context of the work group.

References

Anderson, L. R. Leader behavior, member attitudes, and task performance of intercultural discussion groups. *Journal of Social Psychology*, 1966, **69**, 305–319.

Argyle, M., Gardner, G., & Cioffi, F. The measurement of supervisory methods. *Human Relations*, 1957, **10**, 295–313.

Argyle, M., Gardner, G., & Cioffi, F. Supervisory methods related to productivity, absenteeism, and labor turnover. *Human Relations*, 1958, **11**, 23–40.

Bachman, J. G., Smith, C. G., & Slesinger, J. A. Control, performance, and satisfaction: An analysis of structural and individual effects. *Journal of Personality and Social Psychology*, 1966, **4**, 127–136.

Bass, B. M. Leadership opinions and related characteristics of salesmen and sales managers. In R. M. Stogdill and A. E. Coons (Eds.), *Leader behavior: Its description and measurement*. Columbus: Bureau of Business Research, Ohio State University, 1957.

Bass, B. M. *Organizational psychology*. Boston: Allyn & Bacon, 1965.

Baumgartel, H. Leadership, motivations, and attitudes in research laboratories. *Journal of Social Issues*, 1956, **12**, (2), 24–31.

Beer, M. *Leadership, employee needs, and motivation*. Columbus: Bureau of Business Research, Ohio State University, Monograph No. 129, 1966.

Berkowitz, L. Group Standards, cohesiveness, and productivity. *Human Relations*, 1954, **7**, 509–519.

Besco, R. O., & Lawshe, C. H. Foreman leadership as perceived by supervisor and subordinate, *Personnel Psychology*, 1959, **12**, 573–582.

Coch, L., & French, J. R. P. Overcoming resistance to change. *Human Relations*, 1948, **1**, 512–532.

Day, R. C., & Hamblin, R. L. Some effects of close and punitive styles of supervision. *American Journal of Sociology*, 1964, **16**, 499–510.

Fiedler, F. E. *A theory of leadership effectiveness*. New York: McGraw-Hill, 1967.

Fleishman, E. A. A leader behavior description for industry. In R. M. Stogdill and A. E. Coons (Eds.), *Leader behavior: Its description and measurement*. Columbus: Bureau of Business Research, Ohio State University, 1957 (a).

Fleishman, E. A. The Leadership Opinion Questionnaire. In R. M. Stogdill and A. E. Coons (Eds.), *Leader behavior: Its description and measurement*. Columbus: Bureau of Business Research, Ohio State University, 1957 (b).

Fleishman, E. A. Attitude versus skill factors in work group productivity. *Personnel Psychology*, 1965, **18**, 253–266.

Fleishman, E. A., & Simmons, J. Relationship between leadership patterns and effectiveness ratings among Israeli foremen. *Personnel Psychology*, 1970, **23**, 169–172.

Fleishman, E. A., & Harris, E. F. Patterns of leadership behavior related to employee grievances and turnover. *Personnel Psychology*, 1962, **15**, 43–56.

Fleishman, E. A., Harris, E. F., & Burtt, H. E. *Leadership and supervision in industry*. Columbus: Bureau of Educational Research, Ohio State University, Research monograph No. 33, 1955.

Foa, U. G. Relation of worker's expectations to satisfaction with his supervisor. *Personnel Psychology*, 1957, **10**, 161–168.

French, J. R. P. Field experiments: Changing group productivity. In J. G. Miller (Ed.), *Experiments in social process: A symposium on social psychology*. New York: McGraw-Hill, 1950.

French, J. R. P., Israel J., & As, D. An experiment on participation in a Norwegian factory. *Human Relations*, 1960, **13**, 3–19.

French, J. R. P., Kay, E., & Meyer, H. Participation and the appraisal system. *Human Relations*, 1966, **19**, 3–20.

French, J. R. P., & Raven, B. The bases of social power. In D. Cartwright (Ed.), *Studies in social power*. Ann Arbor: Institute for Social Research, University of Michigan, 1959.

Galbraith, J., & Cummings, L. L. An empirical investigation of the motivational determinants of task performance: Interactive effects between instrumentality-valence and motivation-ability. *Organizational Behavior and Human Performance*, 1967, **2**, 237–257.

Gomberg, W. The trouble with democratic management. *Transaction*, 1966, **3**, (5), 30–35.

Greer, F. L. Leader indulgence and group performance. *Psychological Monographs*, 1961, **75**, (12, Whole No. 516).

Gruenfeld, L. W., Rance, D. E., & Weissenberg, P. The behavior of task-oriented (low LPC) and socially-oriented (high LPC) leaders under several conditions of social support. *Journal of Social Psychology*, 1969, **79**, 99–107.

Halpin, A. W. The leader behavior and effectiveness of aircraft commanders. In R. M. Stogdill and A. E. Coons (Eds.), *Leader behavior: Its description and measurement*. Columbus: Bureau of Business Research, Ohio State University, 1957.

Halpin, A. W., & Winer, B. J. A factorial study of the leader behavior descriptions. In R. M. Stogdill and A. E. Coons (Eds.), *Leader behavior: Its description and measurement*. Columbus: Bureau of Business Research, Ohio State University, 1957.

Heller, F., & Yukl, G. Participation, managerial decision-making, and situational variables. *Organizational Behavior and Human Performance*, 1969, **4**, 227–241.

Hemphill, J. K. Leader behavior associated with the administrative reputations of college departments. In R. M. Stogdill and A. E. Coons (Eds.), *Leader behavior: Its description and measurement*. Columbus: Bureau of Business Research, Ohio State University, 1957.

Hemphill, J. K., & Coons, A. E. Development of the leader behavior description questionnaire. In R. M.

Stogdill and A. E. Coons (Eds.), *Leader behavior: Its description and measurement*. Columbus: Bureau of Business Research, Ohio State University, 1957.

Jacobson, J. M. Analysis of interpersonal relations in a formal organization. Unpublished doctoral dissertation, University of Michigan, 1953.

Katz, D., Maccoby, N., Gurin, G., & Floor, L. *Productivity, supervision, and morale among railroad workers*. Ann Arbor: Survey Research Center, University of Michigan, 1951.

Katzell, R. A. Personal values, job satisfaction, and job behavior. In H. Borrow (Ed.), *Man in a World of Work*. Boston: Houghton-Mifflin, 1964.

Kay, E., Meyer, H. H., & French, J. R. P. Effects of threat in a performance appraisal interview. *Journal of Applied Psychology*. 1965, 49, 311–317.

Korman, A. K. Consideration, initiating structure, and organizational criteria—A review. *Personnel Psychology*, 1966, **19**, 349–362.

Lawrence, L. C., & Smith, P. C. Group decision and employee participation. *Journal of Applied Psychology*, 1955, **39**, 334–337.

Lewin, K. The dynamics of group action. *Educational Leadership*, 1944, **1**, 195–200.

Likert, R. Developing patterns in management. *Strengthening management for the new technology*. New York: American Management Association, 1955.

Likert, R. *New patterns of management*. New York: McGraw-Hill, 1961.

Locke, E. A. What is job satisfaction? *Organizational Behavior and Human Performance*, 1969, **4**, 309–336.

Lowin, A. Participative decision-making: A model, literature critique, and prescriptions for research. *Organizational Behavior and Human Performance*, 1968, **3**, 68–106.

Lowin, A., Hrapchak, W. J., & Kavanagh, M. J. Consideration and Initiating Structure: An experimental investigation of leadership traits. *Administrative Science Quarterly*, 1969, **14**, 238–253.

Maier, N. R. F. *Psychology in industry*. Third ed. Boston: Houghton-Mifflin Co., 1965.

Maier, N. R. F., & Hoffman, L. R. Group decision in England and the United States. *Personnel Psychology*, 1962, **15**, 75–87.

Maier, N. R. F., & Maier, R. A. An experimental test of the effects of "developmental" vs. "free" discussions on the quality of group decisions. *Journal of Applied Psychology*, 1957, **41**, 320–323.

Mann, F. C., & Dent, J. The supervisor: Member of two organizational families. *Harvard Business Review*, 1954, **32**, (6), 103–112.

McCurdy, H. G., & Eber, H. W. Democratic vs. authoritarian leadership: A further investigation of group problem-solving. *Journal of Personality*, 1953, **22**, 258–269.

McCurdy, H. G., & Lambert, W. E. The efficiency of small groups in the solution of problems requiring genuine cooperation. *Journal of Personality*, 1952, **20**, 478–494.

McMurray, R. N. The case for benevolent autocracy. *Harvard Business Review*, 1958, **36**, (1), 82–90.

Meltzer, L. Scientific productivity in organizational settings. *Journal of Social Issues*, 1956, **12**, (2), 32–40.

Misumi, J., & Shirakashi, S. An experimental study of the effects of supervisory behavior on productivity and morale in a hierarchical organization. *Human Relations*, 1966, **19**, 297–307.

Morse, N. *Satisfaction in the white-collar job*. Ann Arbor: Institute for Social Research, University of Michigan, 1953.

Morse, N. C., & Reimer, E. The experimental change of a major organizational variable. *Journal of Abnormal and Social Psychology*, 1956, **52**, 120–129.

Mulder, M., & Stemerding, A. Threat, attraction to group and strong leadership: A laboratory experiment in a natural setting. *Human Relations*, 1963, **16**, 317–334.

Nealey, S. M., & Blood, M. R. Leadership performance of nursing supervisors at two organizational levels. *Journal of Applied Psychology*, 1968, **52**, 414–422.

Newcomb, T. H., Turner, R. H., & Converse, P. E. *Social psychology*. New York: Holt, Rinehart, & Winston, 1965.

Newport, G. A. A study of attitudes and leadership behavior. *Personnel Administration*, 1962, **25**, (5), 42–46.

Patchen, M. Supervisory methods and group performance norms. *Administrative Science Quarterly*, 1962, **7**, 275–294.

Pelz, D. C. Influence: A key to effective leadership in the first-line supervisor. *Personnel*, 1952, **29**, 209–217.

Porter, L. W. Job attitudes in management: I. Perceived deficiencies in need fulfillment as a function of job level. *Journal of Applied Psychology*, 1962, **46**, 375–384.

Rambo, W. W. The construction and analysis of a leadership behavior rating form. *Journal of Applied Psychology*, 1958, **42**, 409–415.

Reilly, A. J. The effects of different leadership styles on group performance: A field experiment. Paper presented at the American Psychological Association Convention, Washington, D.C., Sept. 1, 1969.

Rosen, R. A. H., & Rosen, R. A. A. Suggested modification in job satisfaction surveys. *Personnel Psychology*, 1955, **8**, 303–314.

Ross, I.C., & Zander, A. Need satisfactions and employee turnover. *Personnel Psychology*, 1957, **10**, 327–338.

Rowland, K. M., & Scott, W. E. Psychological attributes of effective leadership in a formal organization. *Pesonnel Psychology*, 1968, **21**, 365–378.

Sales, S. M. Supervisory style and productivity: Review and theory. *Personnel Psychology*, 1966, **19**, 275–286.

Sample, J. A., & Wilson, T. R. Leader behavior, group productivity, and rating of least preferred coworker. *Journal of Personality and Social Psychology*, 1965, **1**, 266–270.

Schachter, S., Willerman, B., Festinger, L., & Hyman, R. Emotional disruption and industrial productivity. *Journal of Applied Psychology*, 1961, **45**, 201–213.

Schaffer, R. H. Job satisfaction as related to need satisfaction in work. *Psychological Monograph*, 1953, **67**, (14, Whole No. 364).

Schoenfeld, E. Authoritarian management: A reviving concept. *Personnel*, 1959, **36**, 21–24.

Seashore, S. *Group cohesiveness in the industrial work group*. Ann Arbor: Institute for Social Research, University of Michigan, 1954.

Shaw, M. E. A comparison of two types of leadership in various communication nets. *Journal of Abnormal and Social Psychology*, 1955, **50**, 127–134.

Skinner, E. W. Relationships between leadership behavior patterns and organizational-situational variables. *Personnel Psychology*, 1969, **22**, 489–494.

Solem, A. R. An evaluation of two attitudinal approaches to delegation. *Journal of Applied Psychology*, 1958, **42**, 36–39.

Stanton, E. S. Which approach to management—democratic, authoritarian, or . . .? *Personnel Administration*, 1962, **25** (2), 44–47.

Stogdill, R. M., Good, O. S., & Day, D. R. New leader behavior description subscales. *Journal of Psychology*, 1962, **54**, 259–269.

Stogdill, R. M., Goode, O. S., & Day, D. R. The leader behavior of corporation presidents. *Personnel Psychology*, 1963, **16**, 127–132.

Stogdill, R. M., Goode, O. S., & Day, D. R. The leader behavior of presidents of labor unions. *Personnel Psychology*, 1964, **17**, 49–57.

Strauss, G. Some notes on power equalization. In H. J. Leavitt (Ed.), *The social science of organizations: Four perspectives*. Englewood Cliffs, New Jersey: Prentice-Hall, 1964.

Tosi, H. A re-examination of personality as a determinant of the effects of participation. *Personnel Psychology*, 1970, **23**, 91–99.

Tannenbaum, A. S. The relationship between personality and group structure. Unpublished doctoral dissertation, Syracuse University, 1954.

Trow, D. B. Autonomy and job satisfaction in task-oriented groups. *Journal of Abnormal and Social Psychology*, 1957, **54**, 204–209.

Vroom, V. H. Some personality determinants of the effects of participation. *Journal of Abnormal and Social Psychology*, 1959, **59**, 322–327.

Vroom, V. H. *Work and Motivation*. New York: John Wiley and Sons, 1964.

Vroom, V. H., & Mann, F. C. Leader authoritarianism and employee attitudes. *Personnel Psychology*, 1960, **13**, 125–140.

Woodward, J. *Industrial organization: Theory and practice*. London: Oxford University Press, 1965.

Yukl, G. A. Conceptions and consequences of leader behavior. Paper presented at the annual convention of the California State Psychological Association, Newport Beach, January, 1969 (a).

Yukl, G. A. A situation description questionnaire for leaders. *Educational and Psychological Measurement*, 1969, **29**, 515–518 (b).

Yukl, G. A. Leader LPC scores: Attitude dimensions and behavioral correlates. *Journal of Social Psychology*, 1970, **80**, 207–212.

Chapter Seven

Participative Leadership

T he classic study of leader behavior conducted at the University of Michigan by Kurt Lewin and his students, Ronald Lippitt and Ralph K. White, during 1939 and 1940 stimulated an interest in looking at the relative effectiveness of three leadership styles—authoritarian, democratic, and laissez-faire—on group and individual behavior. Among some of the results from their investigation was the suggestion that leader behavior has a number of different effects on member reactions. Among some of their major observations are the following: (a) laissez-faire and democratic leadership are not the same; (b) democratic leadership can be efficient; (c) greater hostility, aggression, and discontent arise under autocratic than democratic leadership; (d) autocratic leadership produced more dependence and less individuality; (e) there was more group-mindedness and more friendliness under democratic leadership; and (f) groups with democratic leaders were more productive even when the leader was not present.[1]

Following the Hawthorne studies (1927–1933), the work of Lewin and his associates, Eric Trist and Fred Emery's work with sociotechnical systems, the onset of the human relations movement, and the development of the human resource model, there emerged a strong interest in participative leadership practices. This is evident by numerous participative management theories, a myriad of research investigations, the development of a number of employee involvement strategies, and recent organizational efforts to create high-involvement organizations (cf., Lawler, 1992).[2]

In the first reading in this chapter, Stephen M. Sales (1966) provides a review of the theory and empirical observations of the effects associated with authoritarian and democratic dimensions of leader behavior. Sales' observations, when coupled with those stemming from Lewin, Lippitt, and White's work, suggest that absenteeism and turnover may be higher under autocratic leaders than their democratic counterparts, and, as a result, productivity may be lower.

It has been suggested that leader behavior is determined by an interaction between attributes of the leader and characteristics of the situation in which the leadership process unfolds. Recognizing the role of situational differences and their impact upon the leadership process, the question has often been raised about when democratic/participative practices should be employed within the organizational context. In an earlier chapter, House and Mitchell (1974) provided insight into the appropriate conditions for participative management in their path-goal theory of leadership.

---

[1] R. White and R. Lippitt, "Leader Behavior and Member Reaction in Three 'Social Climates.'" In D. Cartwright and A. Zander, eds., *Group Dynamics: Research and Theory* (New York: Harper & Row, 1968), 318–35.

[2] E. E. Lawler III, *The Ultimate Advantage: Creating the High-Involvement Organization* (San Francisco: Jossey-Bass, 1992).

Victor H. Vroom and his associates have worked on the development of a model that addresses the use of participative decision making in the organizational context.[3] In the second reading in this chapter, Vroom (1973) presents a framework that is designed to help managers decide when to use a participative style of leadership vis à vis an autocratic style, and the amount of subordinate involvement that should be employed in a variety of situations. Instead of adopting a style of leadership that is "most comfortable," Vroom suggests that leaders should be flexible in their behavioral approach, analyze each leadership situation, and then select an approach that best fits the situation. This situationally driven decision tree model is designed to prescribe the "best" style of leadership for a given leadership situation. Vroom's work highlights the fact that neither the autocratic nor participative style of leadership is universally the most appropriate. (It is important to note that Vroom's work has been cast as both a leadership and decision-making model. His objective is to provide a model that details the type of leader behavior and the amount of subordinate participation that should be employed in different types of situations.)

Fueled by Frederick Herzberg and Douglas McGregor's criticisms of scientific management, a number of different schools of thought (e.g., human relations, human resource) and theoretical models (e.g., cognitive, affective, contingency) have articulated the processes associated with efficacious participatory practices. While there has been a plethora of empirical studies that have examined participation, questions as to the effectiveness of participation remain equivocal in nature.

In the face of the uncertainty surrounding the effectiveness of participative leadership practices (see the reviews conducted by Locke & Schweiger, 1979; Dachler & Wilpert, 1978; Strauss, 1982),[4] Cotton (1993) observes that the past several decades have been characterized by the adoption of a number of different employee involvement systems (e.g., employee ownership, self-directed work teams, job enrichment, representative participation, quality circles, and quality of work life programs).[5] These involvement systems reflect organizational experimentation with different *forms* of participative leadership at different organizational *levels*—some operating at the team and department level, and others reflecting a top-management orientation toward organizational leadership.

In the third and final reading in this chapter, Katherine I. Miller and Peter R. Monge (1988) discuss the relationship of participation with satisfaction and productivity. They highlight three theoretical models—contingency, affective, and cognitive—to articulate how and why participation might have a favorable relationship with both of these outcomes. Miller and Monge conducted a statistical meta-analytic review of the participation literature, providing a test for each of these three models. They report finding strong support for the affective model, some support for the cognitive model, and no support for the contingency model. They suggest that "participation fulfills needs, fulfilled needs lead to satisfaction, satisfaction strengthens motivation, and increased motivation improves workers' productivity" (Miller & Monge, p. 731).

The self-assessment presented at the end of this chapter can provide you with insight into your human resource/human relations (i.e., Theory Y versus Theory X) orientation. Individuals with a strong Theory Y orientation are more predisposed to, and comfortable with, a participatory leadership orientation.

---

[3] V. H. Vroom and P. H. Yetton, *Leadership and Decision Making* (Pittsburgh, PA: University of Pittsburgh Press, 1973); V. H. Vroom and A. G. Jago, *The New Leadership* (New York: Prentice-Hall, 1973).

[4] H. P. Dachler and B. Wilpert, "Conceptual Dimensions and Boundaries of Participation in Organizations," *Administrative Science Quarterly* 23 (1978), 1–39; E. A. Locke and D. M. Schweiger, "Participation in Decision Making: One More Look," *Research in Organizational Behavior* 1 (1979), 265–339; G. Strauss, "Workers' Participation in Management: An International Perspective," *Research in Organizational Behavior* 4 (1982), 173–265.

[5] J. L. Cotton, *Employee Involvement: Methods for Improving Performance and Work Attitudes* (Newbury Park, CA: Sage, 1993).

Self-Assessment

Participatory Leadership Attitudes

Instructions: In the section below, you will see a series of statements. Please indicate your agreement or disagreement. Use the scale below for each statement.

For example: It is easier to work in cool weather than in hot.

: _____   : _____   : _____   : _____   : _____
Strongly   Agree   Undecided   Disagree   Strongly
Agree   Disagree

If you think it is easier to work in cool weather, put an (X) above "agree"; if you think it is much easier to work in cool weather, put a mark above "strongly agree." If you think it doesn't matter, put a mark over "undecided" and so on. Put your mark in a space, not on the boundaries.

There is no right or wrong answer. It is only your opinion about the statements that follow that matters.

1. The average human being prefers to be directed, wishes to avoid reponsibility, and has relatively little ambition.

: _____   : _____   : _____   : _____   : _____
Strongly   Agree   Undecided   Disagree   Strongly
Agree   Disagree

2. Leadership skills can be acquired by most people regardless of their particular inborn traits and abilities.

: _____   : _____   : _____   : _____   : _____
Strongly   Agree   Undecided   Disagree   Strongly
Agree   Disagree

3. The use of rewards (pay, promotion, etc.) and punishment (failure to promote, etc.) is not the best way to get subordinates to do their work.

: _____   : _____   : _____   : _____   : _____
Strongly   Agree   Undecided   Disagree   Strongly
Agree   Disagree

4. In a work situation, if the subordinates cannot influence me, then I lose some influence on them.

: _____   : _____   : _____   : _____   : _____
Strongly   Agree   Undecided   Disagree   Strongly
Agree   Disagree

5. A good leader should give detailed and complete instructions to his or her subordinates rather than merely giving them general directions and depending upon their initiative to work out the details.

: _____   : _____   : _____   : _____   : _____
Strongly   Agree   Undecided   Disagree   Strongly
Agree   Disagree

(continued)

setting offers advantages that cannot be obtained by individual goal setting.

:_____	:_____	:_____	:_____	:_____
trongly Agree	Agree	Undecided	Disagree	Strongly Disagree

7. A superior should give his or her subordinates only that information which is needed for them to do their immediate tasks.

:_____	:_____	:_____	:_____	:_____
Strongly Agree	Agree	Undecided	Disagree	Strongly Disagree

8. The superior's authority over his or her subordinates in an organization is primarily economic.

:_____	:_____	:_____	:_____	:_____
Strongly Agree	Agree	Undecided	Disagree	Strongly Disagree

Scoring: Four attitudes are being assessed by these 8 questions: (1) attitudes toward belief in the average person's capacities (questions 1 and 2), (2) attitudes toward sharing information (questions 5 and 7), (3) attitudes toward participation (questions 4 and 6), and (4) attitudes toward the nature of supervisory controls (questions 3 and 8).

    For each of the 8 questions, assign:
        5 points for "strongly agree"
        4 points for "agree"
        3 points for "undecided"
        2 points for "disagree"
        1 point for "strongly disagree"

1. Rescore your answer to questions 1, 5, 7, and 8 by subtracting your score from 6.
2. Next, sum your scores for questions 1 and 2, and divide by 2.
3. Sum your scores for questions 5 and 7, and divide by 2.
4. Sum your scores for questions 4 and 6, and divide by 2.
5. Sum your scores for questions 3 and 8, and divide by 2.
6. Finally, sum your final scores as produced in steps 2, 3, 4, and 5 above and divide by 4.

Interpretation: These questions on leadership, according to Haire, Ghiselli, and Porter (1966) are focused upon attitudes that pertain to a somewhat unilateral, autocratic approach to management at one extreme and to a more group-oriented, team, participatory approach at the other. The questions are intended to capture beliefs in "the capacity of subordinates," and views on "the efficacy of participation, of sharing information, and of providing opportunities for internal self-control on the job" (p. 3).

    A high score (4 and greater) for each of the four attitudes and in the aggregate would reflect a "favorable" disposition toward subordinates (followers), their capacities, and their involvement in organizational activities. A score of 2.5 and less might reflect a hesitancy toward the full and active involvement of followers in the leadership context (i.e., a propensity toward self-control as opposed to a participatory style of leadership). The high score might be reflective of McGregor's vision of the Theory Y leader, while the low score is reflective of Theory X.

Source: M. Haire, E. E. Ghiselli, and L. W. Porter, *Managerial Thinking: An International Study* (New York: John Wiley & Sons, 1966).

Supervisory Style and Productivity
Review and Theory[1]

S. M. Sales
University of Michigan

*I*t is widely assumed that employees will work harder for supervisors who employ given styles of supervision than they will for supervisors who use other styles. This supposition clearly underlies much of supervisory training; it is a basic tenet of the writings of Morse (1953), Likert (1961), and many others. However, the theoretical underpinnings of this assumption are often unclearly stated (when they are stated at all); furthermore, the wide variety of studies investigating the validity of this position are rarely fully described. The present article will sketch a theory which accounts for the predicted differential in productivity and will review and evaluate the literature relevant to this theory.

Authoritarianism and Democracy

The styles to be discussed are the authoritarian and democratic dimensions. The distinction between these orientations has often been made in the literature; it will not be extensively elaborated here. Rather, we shall discuss only the major differences between these styles.

Authoritarian supervision, in general, is characterized by the relatively high degree of power wielded by the supervisor over the work group. As contrasted with democratic supervision, both power and all decision-making functions are absolutely concentrated in the person of the authoritarian. Democratic supervision, on the other hand, is characterized by a sharing of power and by participative decision making. Under democratic supervision, the work group becomes in some ways co-equal with the supervisor; responsibility is spread rather than concentrated.

Differential Effectiveness

It is commonly assumed that, with other conditions held constant, employees will produce more under democratic supervision than they would have produced under autocratic supervision. (Such an assumption, of course, lies behind the entire human relations movement.) There is at least one good reason for this prediction. Specifically, the reinforcing value of work performed under democratic supervision should be higher than that of work performed under autocratic supervision.

It is a basic tenet of experimental psychology that high levels of performance will obtain in situations in which the reinforcement is large, whereas low performance levels will occur in those in which the reinforcement is small. In terms of industrial situations, the more reinforcement an employee receives for production, the higher his production should be. (This is, of course, the assumption which underlies incentive systems, although reinforcement is rather narrowly defined in such programs.) Vroom (1962, pp. 26–43) in particular has explored the ramifications of this argument.

The importance of this point for the present consideration is that production is attended by two different levels of need-satisfaction under the two styles of supervision sketched above. Democratic supervision, by allowing subordinates freedom in determining the specific form and content of their work, implicates the personalities of the employees in the tasks they perform. This means that production, under democratic supervision, becomes a means for satisfying the employees' ego-esteem and self-actualization needs (see Maslow, 1954; Argyris, 1957). That is, the "greater opportunity for regulating and controlling their own activities [provided by democratic supervision] . . . should increase the degree to which individuals could express their various and diverse needs and could move in the direction of fully exploiting their potential while on the job" (Morse & Reimer, 1956). Authoritarian supervision, inasmuch as it makes work merely the carrying out of the supervisor's will, reduces the degree to which such need-satisfaction can be derived from production. Therefore, since productivity is less satisfying under autocratic than under democratic supervision, one would expect that workers would be less productive in the former condition than in the latter. (This effect, of course, should be accentuated for those individuals for whom the needs in question are most important.)

It should be noted that the above considerations do not involve between-style differences which rest upon uncontrolled factors (even when such factors might themselves follow from the style variation). For instance, if turnover were higher under one supervisory style than under the other, one would expect that the method resulting in higher turnover would be accompanied by the lower productivity rate (because of lowered effectiveness during learning periods). Factors of this sort would lead to productivity differences

Source: Edited and reprinted with permission from *Personnel Psychology* 19 (1966), 275–86. Author affiliation may have changed since article was first published.

[1] The author wishes to express his appreciation to Dr. Ned A. Rosen of the New York State School of Industrial and Labor Relations, Cornell University, for his constant assistance and encouragement. A grant from the Foundation for Research on Human Behavior, Ann Arbor, Michigan, provided the time necessary for the preparation of this article.

between the supervisory styles; however, such differences would not truly bear upon the question of effectiveness as usually posed. That is, statements about supervisory style center in general about the proposition that employees will work harder for some supervisors than for others. This statement cannot be supported by dependent variable differences which may be shown to result from between-condition variations other than that of supervisory style. The present discussion is concerned solely with productivity differences which follow *directly* from the style of supervision. . . .

Experimental Investigations

The original and best known study in this area is the experiment of Lewin, Lippitt, and White (e.g., Lippitt & White, 1958, pp. 496–510; White & Lippitt, 1962). These investigators employed as subjects thirty ten-year-old boys who met in six groups which ostensibly were recreational clubs. These groups were supervised by adults who had been trained to act in either a democratic, autocratic, or laissez-faire manner. (The last condition is not considered in the present discussion.) Each club was exposed to each of the three styles for six weeks.

The results of this experiment, in terms of productivity, are extremely difficult to establish. When exposed to autocratic supervision[2] the boys spent more time at work than they did under democratic supervision (74% of the total time as opposed to 50% under democratic supervision). However, the "work-mindedness" of the democratically supervised boys appeared to be somewhat higher since under democratic supervision the groups engaged in a slightly larger amount of "work-minded conversation." (There were 63 work-minded remarks per child under the democratic condition, whereas in the autocratic condition this figure fell to 52.) However, *no objective measure of productivity is reported by the authors, and therefore it is impossible to determine accurately which of the two styles evoked the higher production* (a factor often overlooked by reviewers of this study).

McCurdy and Eber (1953) examined supervisory style in an investigation on group problem-solving. In this experiment, three-man groups participated in a task in which the group determined the proper setting of three switches. In the authoritarian condition one subject was given the power to order the others at will, making him an "absolute" supervisor. The other subjects were instructed merely to obey orders. In the democratic condition the instructions emphasized equalitarianism, specifying that each subject could offer suggestions and that no individual could order the others in any way. No differences whatever appeared between the two conditions on a productivity criterion.

Shaw (1955), working with communication networks, also used problem-solving as a dependent variable in an investigation of supervisory style effects. Employing three different "nets," he instructed the subjects assigned to the position with the highest independence score within each structure[3] to behave either in an autocratic manner (e.g., by giving orders) or in a democratic manner (e.g., by making suggestions). Shaw found that the autocratically-supervised subjects (a) required less time to solve the problems, regardless of the communication net in which they were placed, and (b) made fewer errors.

Day and Hamblin (1964) trained a female student to employ "close" and "general" supervisory styles in leading groups of female subjects in an assembly-line task. These researchers found that subjects exposed to close supervision produced less than did subjects exposed to general supervision.

Sales (1964), like Day and Hamblin, replicated an industrial assembly-line setting in the laboratory. In Sales' experiment two male supervisors played democratic and autocratic roles over male and female groups. (Both role and sex of the subordinates were fully counterbalanced in this experiment.) Sales reports no differential effectiveness whatever between the two styles; the productivity means for the two conditions were virtually identical.

Spector and Suttell (1957) report a relevant laboratory study with naval trainees as subjects. These authors trained supervisors to use either "single leadership" or "leadership sharing" styles, patterns which seem to parallel the democratic-autocratic distinction. The task consisted of problems in which team members cooperated in receiving, processing, and recording information. No differences were detected in the productivity of the groups under the two styles.

In the most extensive of the investigations reported in this area, Morse and Reimer (1956) created groups exposed either to democratic or to autocratic supervision by altering the style of supervision used in an on-going industrial setting. In two divisions ("participative treatment") an attempt was made to push down the level of decision making. Supervisors were trained to employ more democratic supervisory methods, and they were given greater freedom of action than previously had been allowed. In two other divisions an "hierarchically controlled treatment" was established by an increase in the closeness of supervision and a movement upward in the level at which decisions were made. The treatments were administered for a year's time to approximately five hundred employees.

Morse and Reimer found that both programs resulted in a significant increase in productivity. This increase was slightly higher for the hierarchically controlled divisions; however, the actual difference between the treatments was quite small.

On balance, then, the experimental studies reviewed above show no consistent superiority of one style over the other in terms of a productivity criterion. Of the six studies for which objective production data are available, one (Day & Hamblin, 1964) reports democratic supervision to be more effective and one (Shaw, 1955) reports authoritarian supervision to be more effective. The other four investigations note no differences of consequence between the two styles.

Survey Investigations

Survey researches applied to the problem discussed herein follow a standard methodology. The supervisory style which exists in each of the work groups in the situation is determined (usually by means of questionnaires administered to the employees), and this variable is then related to productivity. Researchers using this methodology generally have found a clear relationship between style of supervision and work group productivity.

The extensive investigations performed by the Survey Research Center at the University of Michigan during the early 1950's (Katz, Maccoby & Morse, 1950; Katz, Maccoby, Gurin & Floor, 1951; Katz & Kahn, 1951, pp. 146–171) are representative of this approach. In a wide variety of industrial situations (including railway maintenance crews, insurance office staffs, and heavy industry production lines), these authors found (1) that general supervision was associated with high productivity whereas close supervision was associated with low productivity, and (2) that "employee-oriented" attitudes in the supervisor were associated with high productivity whereas "job-oriented" attitudes were associated with low productivity. It is unclear exactly what relationship these independent variables have to the democratic-autocratic dimension; however, it can certainly be assumed that employee-oriented attitudes and general supervision will tend to be associated with democracy (as here used) whereas job-oriented attitudes and close supervision will tend to be associated with authoritarianism. The data of Morse (1953) and Argyle, Gardner, and Cioffi (1957) support these assumptions.

Argyle *et al.* (1958) performed a successful replication of these earlier investigations in a British industrial situation. The authors report that foremen of high-producing work groups tended to use general rather than close supervision and were relatively more democratic in their behavior than were foremen of less productive work groups. Further, the attitudes of the more effective foremen tended to be more "employee-oriented" than those of the less effective foremen. In contrast to experimental findings, therefore, these survey data clearly seem to support the hypothesis that democratic supervision leads to higher production than does authoritarian supervision.

Discussion

The usual explanations offered for the failure of the experimental method to replicate survey findings rest upon either (a) the brevity of the experimental sessions or (b) the peripheral nature of the experimental tasks. It seems to the present author, however, that these explanations are respectively (a) too facile and (b) inadequately elaborated for proper handling of the problem.

Of the two, the "brevity" argument is the more open to attack. Experimental sessions are, of course, of relatively short duration. However, the entire science of experimental social psychology rests upon the assumption that experimental periods are sufficiently lengthy for treatments to "take," an assumption which is supported in every significant finding obtained in an experimental laboratory. To argue that the experiments reviewed here failed to demonstrate predicted productivity differences because of inadequate time periods (especially when these same time periods are sufficient to evoke morale differences—favoring the democratic supervisor—between the groups exposed to the two styles) seems somehow an unscientific and unsatisfactory way of explaining the findings. Furthermore, such an explanation fails to account for the quite small productivity differential which existed between the conditions created by Morse and Reimer in

an experiment which continued over the course of an entire year.

It appears to the author that, rather than looking to brevity, one may best explain the equal experimental effectiveness of the two supervisory styles by concentrating upon the nature of the tasks involved. (This is, of course, the approach incompletely hinted at in the "peripheral nature" argument.) Specifically, it seems that no differences in effectiveness have been found between the two styles *because the tasks employed wholly fail to meet the conditions under which differential productivity was predicted.*

Democratic supervision, it will be remembered, was expected to be the more effective style because of the greater extent to which it makes productivity a means to need-satisfaction. This prediction rests upon the assumption that democratic supervision allows productivity to be a path to the satisfaction of self-actualization and ego-esteem needs, whereas autocratic supervision does not serve such a purpose.

These conditions do not seem to have been generated by the experimental investigations reported above. Democratic supervision, in these experiments, can hardly be seen as allowing the subjects to see production on the task involved as a path to self-actualization. *The thought is virtually absurd.* Regardless of the intent of the investigators, the decisions allowed by the democratic supervisors (e.g., suggesting possible solutions to simple problems) do not seem to implicate the unique personalities of the subjects in their tasks. This seems to have been true even in the Morse and Reimer investigation, for the authors report that "both groups of clerks indicated that their jobs throughout the course of the experiment did not give them a very high degree of self-actualization." To the extent that experimental studies fail to make productivity under democratic supervision a path to significantly greater need-satisfaction than it would be under autocratic supervision, there is no reason to suspect that they should demonstrate democratic supervision to be more effective. Such investigations simply fail to provide the conditions necessary for a test of the hypothesis in question.

It should not be inferred, however, that survey investigations provide a more adequate test of the hypothesis that workers will work harder for democratic supervisors, in spite of the satisfying direction of the findings. There are at least two reasons for approaching the results of these studies with caution, both of which rest upon the fact that spurious variables which clearly affect work group productivity accompany both these styles. To the extent that the effects of such variables cannot be discounted, survey methodology is incapable of offering convincing evidence concerning the relative effort expended by workers exposed to the styles in question.

In the first place, the supervisory styles discussed herein are accompanied by differential turnover and absenteeism (e.g., Mann & Baumgartel, 1953; Morse & Reimer, 1956; Argyle *et al.*, 1958). These effects do contribute to productivity differences between groups exposed to these styles, since the higher absenteeism and turnover evoked by autocratic supervision would lead to a productivity difference favoring democratic supervision. However, such a difference would be irrelevant to the hypothesis that democratic supervision leads directly to more concerted effort on the part of the employees involved. The effects of absenteeism and/or turnover could be removed from the analysis by means of simple statistical techniques, although no survey research known to the author has as yet attempted to do so.

A second consideration lies in the fact that supervisors who naturally affect a democratic style of supervision cannot be assumed to be otherwise similar to those who affect an authoritarian style. In particular, the author feels that democratically oriented supervisors can be expected to be more intelligent than are autocratically oriented supervisors. There are no direct data drawn from industry which bear on this statement. However, the fact that intelligence has clearly been shown to be negatively correlated with measured (*F*-scale) authoritarianism (e.g., Titus & Hollander, 1957), which in turn has been shown to be highly correlated with authoritarian behavior (McGee, 1955), seems sufficient to make the point.

It may be assumed that the intelligence of the supervisor should be of some importance in determining the productivity of the employees under him. The more intelligent supervisor might be expected to diagnose production difficulties more quickly than the less intelligent supervisor, and he might also be expected to take more effective remedial action. Therefore, inasmuch as authoritarian and democratic supervisors are differentiated on intelligence, one might expect them to be differentiated on their skill in dealing with day-to-day production problems. The advantage, of course, would go to the democratic supervisors.

The effect of this predicted difference between the two supervisory populations would be to make the work groups under democratic supervision more productive than those under autocratic supervision. However, as in the case of the different levels of turnover evoked by the two styles, such a finding would *not* necessarily imply that employees worked harder for supervisors affecting the democratic style. Like the effect of absenteeism, the effect of supervisory intelligence could be removed from the analysis by means of proper statistical techniques, but again there has been no survey research which has done so.

Therefore, in neither experimental studies nor survey investigations has an adequate test of the theory sketched above been made. Experimental studies have not created the conditions necessary for such a test; survey research has introduced at least two contaminating variables which render proper interpretation of the observed relationship extremely difficult. Such studies have not *disproved* the theory in question. They simply have not offered the unambiguous evidence administrative science must have in order to evaluate plans of action (e.g., supervisory training) tacitly based on this theory.

This should not be interpreted to mean that such a test cannot be made. Experimental investigations of the sort attempted by Morse and Reimer (1956), *using a technology in which self-actualization could occur under democratic supervision*, would provide an adequate test, as would survey investigations in which the intelligence of the supervisors and the turnover (and/or absenteeism) levels existing in the various work groups were assessed and partialled out of the correlation between the style of the supervisor and the productivity of the subordinates. (Research now in progress is directed toward this latter objective.) Without such conditions, however, the hypothesis that democratic supervision will evoke greater effort from employees than will autocratic supervision cannot truly be either supported or rejected.

Notes

2Only the "submissive reaction" to autocracy will be here considered; the "aggressive reaction" is felt to be a function of the subjects and the situation employed by the investigators.

3The research of Leavitt (1951) clearly suggests that these positions are the ones from which leadership is exercised.

References

Argyle, Michael, Gardner, Godfrey, and Cioffi, Frank. "The Measurement of Supervisory Methods." *Human Relations*, X (1957), 295–313.

Argyle, Michael, Gardner, Godfrey, and Cioffi, Frank. "Supervisory Methods Related to Productivity, Absenteeism, and Labour Turnover." *Human Relations*, XI (1958), 23–40.

Argyris, Chris. *Personality and Organization*. New York: Harper & Brothers, 1957.

Coch, L. and French, J. R. P., Jr. "Overcoming Resistance to Change." *Human Relations*, I (1948), 512–532.

Day, R. C. and Hamblin, R. L. "Some Effects of Close and Punitive Styles of Supervision." *American Journal of Sociology*, LXIX (1964), 499–510.

Katz, D. and Kahn, R. L. "Human Organization and Worker Motivation." In Tripp, L. Reed (Editor), *Industrial Productivity*. Madison, Wisconsin: Industrial Relations Research Association, 1951.

Katz, D., Maccoby, N., Gurin, G., and Floor, Lucretia. *Productivity, Supervision, and Morale Among Railroad Workers*. Ann Arbor, Michigan: Institute for Social Research, 1951.

Katz, D., Maccoby, N., and Morse, Nancy C. *Productivity, Supervision and Morale in an Office Situation*. Part 1. Ann Arbor, Michigan: Institute for Social Research, 1950.

Leavitt, Harold. "Some Effects of Certain Communication Patterns on Group Performance." *Journal of Abnormal and Social Psychology*, XLVI (1951), 16–30.

Likert, Rensis. *New Patterns of Management*. New York: McGraw-Hill, 1961.

Lippitt, R. and White, R. K. "An Experimental Study of Leadership and Group Life." In Maccoby, E. E., Newcomb, T. N., and Hartley, E. L. (Editors), *Readings in Social Psychology*, Third Edition. New York: Holt, Rinehart, & Winston, 1958.

Maslow, A. H. *Motivation and Personality*. New York: Harper & Brothers, 1954.

Mann, F. C. and Baumgartel, H. D. "Absences and Employee Attitudes in an Electric Power Company." Ann Arbor, Michigan: Institute for Social Research, 1953.

McCurdy, H. G. and Eber, H. W. "Democratic Versus Authoritarian: A Further Investigation of Group Problem-Solving." *Journal of Personality*, XXII (1953), 258–269.

McGee, H. M. "Measurement of Authoritarianism and its Relation to Teacher Classroom Behavior." *Genetic Psychological Monographs*, LII (1955), 89–146.

Morse, Nancy C. *Satisfactions in the White-Collar Job*. Ann Arbor, Michigan: Institute for Social Research, 1953.

Morse, Nancy C. and Reimer, E. "The Experimental Change of a Major Organizational Variable." *Journal of Abnormal and Social Psychology*, LI (1956), 120–129.

Sales, Stephen M. "A Laboratory Investigation of the Effectiveness of Two Industrial Supervisory Dimensions." Unpublished MS Thesis, Cornell University, 1964.

Shaw, M. E. "A Comparison of Two Types of Leadership in Various Communication Nets." *Journal of Abnormal and Social Psychology,* L (1955), 127–134.

Spector, Paul, and Suttell, Barbara. *An Experimental Comparison of the Effectiveness of Three Patterns of Leadership Behavior.* Washington, D.C.: American Institute for Research, 1957.

Titus, H. E. and Hollander, E. P. "The California *F*-Scale in Psychological Research: 1950–1955." *Psychological Bulletin,* LIV (1957), 47–65.

Vroom, V. H. "Human Relations Research in Industry: Some Things Learned." In Baristow, Frances (Editor), *Research Frontiers in Industrial Relations Today.* Montreal: Industrial Relations Centre, 1962.

White, Ralph, and Lippitt, R. "Leader Behavior and Member Reaction in Three 'Social Climates.'" In Cartwright, Dorin, and Zander, Alvin (Editors), *Group Dynamics, Research and Theory,* Second Edition. Evanston, Illinois: Row, Peterson, 1962.

A New Look at Managerial Decision Making

V. H. Vroom
Yale University

*A*ll managers are decision makers. Furthermore, their effectiveness as managers is largely reflected in their "track record" in making the "right decisions." These "right decisions" in turn largely depend on whether or not the manager has utilized the right person or persons in the right ways in helping him solve the problem.

Our concern in this article is with decision making as a social process. We view the manager's task as determining how the problem is to be solved, not the solution to be adopted. Within that overall framework, we have attempted to answer two broad sets of questions: What decision-making processes should managers use to deal effectively with the problems they encounter in their jobs? What decision-making processes do they use in dealing with these problems and what considerations affect their decisions about how much to share their decision-making power with subordinates?

The reader will recognize the former as a normative or prescriptive question. A rational and analytic answer to it would constitute a normative model of decision making as a social process. The second question is descriptive, since it concerns how managers do, rather than should, behave.

Toward a Normative Model

About four years ago, Philip Yetton, then a graduate student at Carnegie-Mellon University, and I began a major research program in an attempt to answer these normative and descriptive questions.

We began with the normative question. What would be a rational way of deciding on the form and amount of participation in decision making that should be used in different situations? We were tired of debates over the relative merits of Theory X and Theory Y and of the truism that leadership depends upon the situation. We felt that it was time for the behavioral sciences to move beyond such generalities and to attempt to come to grips with the complexities of the phenomena with which they intended to deal.

Our aim was ambitious—to develop a set of ground rules for matching a manager's leadership behavior to the demands of the situation. It was critical that these ground rules be consistent with research evidence concerning the consequences of participation and that the model based on the rules be operational, so that any manager could use it to determine how he should act in any decision-making situation.

Table I shows a set of alternative decision processes that we have employed in our research. Each process is represented by a symbol (e.g., AI, CI, GII) that will be used as a convenient method of referring to each process. The first letter in this symbol signifies the basic properties of the process (A stands for autocratic; C for consultative; and G for group). The Roman numerals that follow the first letter constitute variants on that process. Thus, AI represents the first variant on an autocratic process, and AII the second variant.

Conceptual and Empirical Basis of the Model

A model designed to regulate, in some rational way, choices among the decision processes shown in Table I should be based on sound empirical evidence concerning the likely consequences of the styles. The more complete the empirical base of knowledge, the greater the certainty with which we can develop the model and the greater will be its usefulness. To aid in understanding the conceptual basis of the model, it is important to distinguish among three classes of outcomes that bear on the ultimate effectiveness of decisions. These are:

1. The quality or rationality of the decision.
2. The acceptance or commitment on the part of subordinates to execute the decision effectively.
3. The amount of time required to make the decision.

The effects of participation on each of these outcomes or consequences were summed up by the author in *The Handbook of Social Psychology* as follows:

The results suggest that allocating problem solving and decision-making tasks to entire groups requires a greater investment of man hours but produces higher acceptance of decisions and a higher probability that the decision will be executed efficiently. Differences between these two methods in quality of decisions and in elapsed time are inconclusive and probably highly variable . . . It would be naive to think that group decision making is always more "effective" than autocratic decision making, or vice versa; the relative effectiveness of these two extreme methods depends both on the weights attached to quality, acceptance and time variables and on differences in amounts of these outcomes resulting from these methods, neither of which is invariant from one situation to another. The critics and proponents of participative management would

Source: Edited and reprinted by permission of publisher *Organizational Dynamics* 3, 1, Copyright 1973. American Management Association, New York. All rights reserved. Author affiliation may have changed since article was first published.

do well to direct their efforts toward identifying the properties of situations in which different decision-making approaches are effective rather than wholesale condemnation or deification of one approach.

We have gone on from there to identify the properties of the situation or problem that will be the basic elements in the model. These problem attributes are of two types: 1) Those that specify the importance for a particular problem of quality and acceptance, and 2) those that, on the basis of available evidence, have a high probability of moderating the effects of participation on each of these outcomes. Table II shows the problem attributes used in the present form of the model. For each attribute a question is provided that might be used by a leader in diagnosing a particular problem prior to choosing his leadership style.

In phrasing the questions, we have held technical language to a minimum. Furthermore, we have phrased the questions in Yes-No form, translating the continuous variables defined above into dichotomous variables. For example, instead of attempting to determine how important the decision quality is to the effectiveness of the decision (attribute A), the leader is asked in the first question to judge whether there is any quality component to the problem.

TABLE I
Types of Management Decision Styles

AI   You solve the problem or make the decision yourself, using information available to you at that time.

AII   You obtain the necessary information from your subordinate(s), then decide on the solution to the problem yourself. You may or may not tell your subordinates what the problem is in getting the information from them. The role played by your subordinates in making the decision is clearly one of providing the necessary information to you, rather than generating or evaluating alternative solutions.

CI   You share the problem with relevant subordinates individually, getting their ideas and suggestions without bringing them together as a group. Then *you* make the decision that may or may not reflect your subordinates' influence.

CII   You share the problem with your subordinates as a group, collectively obtaining their ideas and suggestions. Then *you* make the decision that may or may not reflect your subordinates' influence.

GII   You share a problem with your subordinates as a group. Together you generate and evaluate alternatives and attempt to reach agreement (consensus) on a solution. Your role is much like that of chairman. You do not try to influence the group to adopt "your" solution and you are willing to accept and implement any solution that has the support of the entire group.

(GI is omitted because it applies only to more comprehensive models outside the scope of the article.)

TABLE II
Problem Attributes Used in the Model

Problem Attributes	Diagnostic Questions
A. The importance of the quality of the decision.	Is there a quality requirement such that one solution is likely to be more rational than another?
B. The extent to which the leader possesses sufficient information / expertise to make a high-quality decision by himself.	Do I have sufficient information to make a high-quality decision?
C. The extent to which the problem is structured.	Is the problem structured?
D. The extent to which acceptance or commitment on the part of subordinates is critical to the effective implementation of the decision.	Is acceptance of decision by subordinates critical to effective implementation?
E. The prior probability that the leader's autocratic decision will receive acceptance by subordinates.	If you were to make the decision by yourself, is it reasonably certain that it would be accepted by your subordinates?
F. The extent to which subordinates are motivated to attain the organizational goals as represented in the objectives explicit in the statement of the problem.	Do subordinates share the organizational goals to be attained in solving this problem?
G. The extent to which subordinates are likely to be in conflict over preferred solutions.	Is conflict among subordinates likely in preferred solutions?

Similarly, the difficult task of specifying exactly how much information the leader possesses that is relevant to the decision (attribute B) is reduced to a simple judgment by the leader concerning whether or not he has sufficient information to make a high quality decision.

We have found that managers can diagnose a situation quickly and accurately by answering this set of seven questions concerning it. But how can such responses generate a prescription concerning the most effective leadership style or decision process? What kind of normative model of participation in decision making can be built from this set of problem attributes?

Figure 1 shows one such model expressed in the form of a decision tree. It is the seventh version of such a model that we have developed over the last three years. The problem attributes, expressed in question form, are arranged along the top of the figure. To use the model for a particular decision-making situation, one starts at the left-hand side and

FIGURE 1
Decision Model

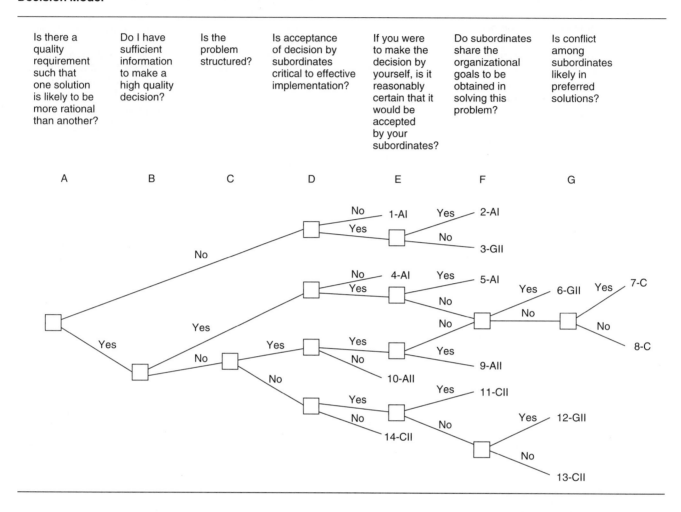

| Is there a quality requirement such that one solution is likely to be more rational than another? | Do I have sufficient information to make a high quality decision? | Is the problem structured? | Is acceptance of decision by subordinates critical to effective implementation? | If you were to make the decision by yourself, is it reasonably certain that it would be accepted by your subordinates? | Do subordinates share the organizational goals to be obtained in solving this problem? | Is conflict among subordinates likely in preferred solutions? |

works toward the right asking oneself the question immediately above any box that is encountered. When a terminal node is reached, a number will be found designating the problem type and one of the decision-making processes appearing in Table I. AI is prescribed for four problem types (1, 2, 4, and 5); AII is prescribed for two problem types (9 and 10); CI is prescribed for only one problem type (8); CII is prescribed for four problem types (7, 11, 13, and 14); and GII is prescribed for three problem types (3, 6, and 12). The relative frequency with which each of the five decision processes would be prescribed for any manager would, of course, depend on the distribution of problem types encountered in his decision making.

Rationale Underlying the Model: The decision processes specified for each problem type are not arbitrary. The model's behavior is governed by a set of principles intended to be consistent with existing evidence concerning the consequences of participation in decision making on organizational effectiveness.

There are two mechanisms underlying the behavior of the model. The first is a set of seven rules that serve to protect the quality and the acceptance of the decision by eliminating alternatives that risk one or the other of these decision outcomes. Once the rules have been applied, a feasible set of de-

cision processes is generated. The second mechanism is a principle for choosing among alternatives in the feasible set where more than one exists.

Let us examine the rules first, because they do much of the work of the model. As previously indicated, the rules are intended to protect both the quality and acceptance of the decision. In the form of the model shown, there are three rules that protect decision quality and four that protect acceptance.

1. *The Information Rule.* If the quality of the decision is important and if the leader does not possess enough information or expertise to solve the problem by himself, AI is eliminated from the feasible set. (Its use risks a low-quality decision.)

2. *The Goal Congruence Rule.* If the quality of the decision is important and if the subordinates do not share the organizational goals to be obtained in solving the problem, GII is eliminated from the feasible set. (Alternatives that eliminate the leader's final control of the decision reached may jeopardize the quality of the decision.)

3. *The Unstructured Problem Rule.* In decisions in which the quality of the decision is important, if the leader lacks the necessary information or expertise to solve the problem by himself, and if the problem is unstructured, i.e.,

he does not know exactly what information is needed and where it is located, the method used must provide not only for him to collect the information but to do so in an efficient and effective manner. Methods that involve interaction among all subordinates with full knowledge of the problem are likely to be both more efficient and more likely to generate a high-quality solution to the problem. Under these conditions, AI, AII, and CI are eliminated from the feasible set. (AI does not provide for him to collect the necessary information, and AII and CI represent more cumbersome, less effective, and less efficient means of bringing the necessary information to bear on the solution of the problem than methods that do permit those with the necessary information to interact.)

4. *The Acceptance Rule.* If the acceptance of the decision by subordinates is critical to effective implementation, and if it is not certain that an autocratic decision made by the leader would receive that acceptance, AI and AII are eliminated from the feasible set. (Neither provides an opportunity for subordinates to participate in the decision and both risk the necessary acceptance.)

5. *The Conflict Rule.* If the acceptance of the decision is critical, and an autocratic decision is not certain to be accepted, and subordinates are likely to be in conflict or disagreement over the appropriate solution, AI, AII, and CI are eliminated from the feasible set. (The method used in solving the problem should enable those in disagreement to resolve their differences with full knowledge of the problem. Accordingly, under these conditions, AI, AII, and CI, which involve no interaction or only "one-on-one" relationships and therefore provide no opportunity for those in conflict to resolve their differences, are eliminated from the feasible set. Their use runs the risk of leaving some of the subordinates with less than the necessary commitment to the final decision.)

6. *The Fairness Rule.* If the quality of decision is unimportant and if acceptance is critical and not certain to result from an autocratic decision, AI, AII, CI, and CII are eliminated from the feasible set. (The method used should maximize the probability of acceptance as this is the only relevant consideration in determining the effectiveness of the decision. Under these circumstances, AI, AII, CI, and CII, which create less acceptance or commitment than GII, are eliminated from the feasible set. To use them is to run the risk of getting less than the needed acceptance of the decision.)

7. *The Acceptance Priority Rule.* If acceptance is critical, not assured by an autocratic decision, and if subordinates can be trusted, AI, AII, CI, and CII are eliminated from the feasible set. (Methods that provide equal partnership in the decision-making process can provide greater acceptance without risking decision quality. Use of any method other than GII results in an unnecessary risk that the decision will not be fully accepted or receive the necessary commitment on the part of subordinates.)

Once all seven rules have been applied to a given problem, we emerge with a feasible set of decision processes. The feasible set for each of the fourteen problem types is shown

T A B L E I I I
Problem Types and the Feasible Set of Decision Processes

Problem Type	Acceptable Methods
1.	AI, AII, CI, CII, GII
2.	AI, AII, CI, CII, GII
3.	GII
4.	AI, AII, CI, CII, GII*
5.	AI, AII, CI, CII, GII*
6.	GII
7.	CII
8.	CI, CII
9.	AII, CI, CII, GII*
10.	AII, CI, CII, GII*
11.	CII, GII*
12.	GII
13.	CII
14.	CII, GII*

*Within the feasible set only when the answer to question F is Yes.

in Table III. It can be seen that there are some problem types for which only one method remains in the feasible set, others for which two methods remain feasible, and still others for which five methods remain feasible.

When more than one method remains in the feasible set, there are a number of ways in which one might choose among them. The mechanism we have selected and the principle underlying the choices of the model in Figure 1 utilizes the number of man-hours used in solving the problem as the basis for choice. Given a set of methods with equal likelihood of meeting both quality and acceptance requirements for the decision, it chooses that method that requires the least investment in man-hours. On the basis of the empirical evidence summarized earlier, this is deemed to be the method furthest to the left within the feasible set. For example, since AI, AII, CI, CII, and GII are all feasible as in Problem Types 1 and 2, AI would be the method chosen. . . .

To summarize everything we learned in the course of this research is well beyond the scope of this paper, but it is possible to discuss some of the highlights. Since the results obtained from the two research methods—recalled and standardized problems—are consistent, we can present the major results independent of the method used.

Perhaps the most striking finding is the weakening of the widespread view that participativeness is a general trait that individual managers exhibit in different amounts. To be sure, there were differences *among* managers in their general tendencies to utilize participative methods as opposed to autocratic ones. On the standardized problems, these differences accounted for about 10 percent of the total variance in the decision processes observed. These differences in behavior between managers, however, were small in comparison with differences *within* managers. On the standardized problems, no manager has indicated that he would use the same decision process on all problems or decisions, and most use all five methods under some circumstances.

Some of this variance in behavior within managers can be attributed to widely shared tendencies to respond to some situations by sharing power and others by retaining it. It makes more sense to talk about participative and autocratic situations than it does to talk about participative and autocratic managers. In fact, on the standardized problems, the variance in behavior across problems or cases is about three times as large as the variance across managers!

What are the characteristics of an autocratic as opposed to a participative situation? An answer to this question would constitute a partial descriptive model of this aspect of the decision-making process and has been our goal in much of the research that we have conducted. From our observations of behavior on both recalled problems and on standardized problems, it is clear that the decision-making process employed by a typical manager is influenced by a large number of factors, many of which also show up in the normative model. Following are several conclusions substantiated by the results on both recalled and standardized problems: Managers use decision processes providing less opportunity for participation (1) when they possess all the necessary information than when they lack some of the needed information. (2) when the problem that they face is well structured rather than unstructured, (3) when their subordinates' acceptance of the decision is not critical for the effective implementation of the decision or when the prior probability of acceptance of an autocratic decision is high, and (4) when the personal goals of their subordinates are *not* congruent with the goals of the organization as manifested in the problem.

So far we have been talking about relatively common or widely shared ways of dealing with organizational problems. Our results strongly suggest that there are ways of "tailoring" one's approach to the situation that distinguish managers from one another. Theoretically, these can be thought of as differences among managers in decision rules that they employ about when to encourage participation. Statistically, they are represented as interactions between situational variables and personal characteristics. . . .

Selected Bibliography

The interested reader may wish to consult *Leadership and Decision-Making* by Vroom and Yetton, which presents a more complete explication of the model, other models dealing with related aspects of the decision-making process, and their use in leadership development. This book will be published in June 1973 by the University of Pittsburgh Press. For another perspective on the normative questions with which this article deals, the leader should consult "How to Choose a Leadership Pattern" by Robert Tannenbaum and Warren Schmidt (*Harvard Business Review,* September 1958). The descriptive questions are explored by Frank Heller in his new book *Managerial Decision-Making* (Tavistock, 1971).

Finally, *Problem-Solving Discussions and Conferences* (McGraw-Hill 1963) by Norman R. F. Maier represents the most useful account of the conference leadership techniques and skills required to implement participative approaches to management.

The reader interested in exploring the approach to managerial training discussed in this article should contact Kepner-Tregoe and Associates, Research Road, P.O. Box 704, Princeton, New Jersey 08540. . . .

Participation, Satisfaction, and Productivity: A Meta-Analytic Review

K. I. Miller

P. R. Monge

I would not think of making a decision by going around the table and then deciding on the basis of how everyone felt. Of course, I like to hear everyone, but then I go off alone and decide. The decisions that are important must be made alone.
— Richard M. Nixon (Schecter, 1972:18–19)

Like Mr. Nixon, most people have strong feelings about the best way to make decisions. However, individuals often disagree about the proper decision-making procedure. Should subordinates be included in decision-making processes, or should managers stand alone as decision makers? Far from being limited to high national offices, the debate over the efficacy of participation in decision making exists throughout government, business, and many academic fields.

There are several reasons for the continuing disagreement on this topic. Moral reasoning regarding participation is often confounded with practical reasoning. Locke and Schweiger (1979) provided several examples of managers and academicians advocating the use of participation on moral grounds, regardless of whether or not it works. In addition, conflicting models of the mechanisms at work in the process of participation lead to confusion over the interpretation of research findings. Finally, in spite of the plethora of empirical research studies investigating participation, when reviewers of the literature draw conclusions on its effectiveness, they invariably still state that "it depends" (Locke & Schweiger; Lowin, 1968; Singer, 1974). Unfortunately, the question of what it depends on has never been clearly answered. To begin to answer this question, we carried out a meta-analytic review of past research on the effects of participation in decision making on satisfaction and productivity.

"One More Look" Revisited

In recent years, several sets of scholars have done wide-ranging reviews of thinking and research on participation in the workplace. For example, Strauss (1982) took an international perspective on workers' participation, and Dachler and Wilpert (1978) looked at the dimensions and boundaries of the participation process. Perhaps the most comprehensive review of empirical research to date, however, is Locke and Schweiger's (1979) "one more look" at participation in decision making, which considered both moral and practical arguments for participation. They reviewed laboratory studies, correlational studies, multivariate field studies, and univariate field studies in which satisfaction and productivity were criterion variables. Locke and Schweiger concluded that little could be said about the effects of participation from multivariate field studies because too many other variables—differences in training, reward systems, education, and so forth—could account for effects often attributed to participation. They did, however, make generalizations based on correlational, laboratory, and univariate field studies.

Locke and Schweiger classified the conclusions of studies as "participation superior," "participation inferior," or "no difference or contextual" (1979: 317). Having found that the results in laboratory, correlational, and univariate field studies were remarkably consistent, they finally concluded: "(1) With respect to the productivity criterion, there is no trend in favor of participative leadership as compared to more directive styles; and (2) with respect to satisfaction, the results generally favor participative over directive methods, although nearly 40 percent of the studies did not find participation to be superior" (Locke & Schweiger, 1979: 316).

Although Locke and Schweiger's review considered well over 50 empirical research reports on participation, their final conclusions seem somewhat anticlimatic—probably for several reasons. First, they used a very gross classification system in considering effects of participation. The categories of superior, inferior, and contextual, though certainly useful, tell us nothing about the strength of participation's effects on satisfaction and productivity. Second, many studies fell into the contextual category, 56 percent for the productivity criterion and 30 percent for the satisfaction criterion. They suggested a number of contextual factors to account for the effectiveness of participation, including two individual factors,

---

Source: Edited and reprinted with permission from *Academy of Management Journal* 29 (1988), 727–53. At the time this article was first published K. I. Miller was affiliated with Michigan State University, and P. R. Monge was affiliated with the University of Southern California.

The preparation of this manuscript was supported by a grant from the National Science Foundation (No. ISI-8412761), Peter R. Monge and Richard V. Farace, coprincipal investigators. The authors wish to express their appreciation to Jim Stiff for his assistance in analysis and to Jim Dillard, Eric Eisenberg, and the anonymous reviewers for their comments on earlier drafts.

knowledge and motivation, and several organizational factors, such as task attributes, group characteristics, and leaders' attributes, but did not go back to the studies reviewed to systematically sort out these contextual effects. Finally, no attempt was made to consider systematic patterns differentiating the studies concluding that participation was superior from those concluding that participation was inferior.

Meta-analysis (Hunter, Schmidt, & Jackson, 1982) can be employed to refine and extend Locke and Schweiger's findings. This method of cumulating results over studies allowed us to summarize numerically the effects of participation on satisfaction and productivity and to take into account artifactual and substantive sources of variance in the individual estimates of effects. Meta-analysis is an improvement over the review methods used by Locke and Schweiger on several counts. It considers the strength of effects between two variables rather than simply counting significant results or levels of probability, thus providing a more accurate representation of cumulated relationships between variables and eliminating the problem of giving a study with a strong effect the same consideration as one with a barely significant effect. Meta-analysis also provides methods for correcting for such systematic, artifactual sources of variance in the estimates of effects as measurement error and restriction in range. Finally, meta-analysis allows for the consideration of both substantive and methodological moderator variables that could account for unexplained variance in estimates of effects. . . .

Thus, we decided that a meta-analysis of this literature would be useful in resolving several of the problems of earlier reviews. In the next section, we discuss the relationships of participation with satisfaction and productivity through the presentation of cognitive, affective, and contingency models of participation. Meta-analysis does not allow for direct tests of these models, but the models enable identification of substantive and methodological variables that could moderate the relationships of participation with satisfaction and productivity.

Participation, Satisfaction, and Productivity

Theorists have advanced a variety of models to account for participation's influence on satisfaction and productivity; each proposes mechanisms through which participation has its effects. We used three types of models—cognitive, affective, and contingency—to highlight differences in these propositions. Each of the three types emphasizes a different explanatory mechanism. The three are not mutually exclusive, however, as many theorists have proposed that cognitive, affect, and contingency variables all play important roles in the participative process.

Cognitive Models of Participative Effects

Cognitive models of participative effects suggest that participation in decision making is a viable strategy because it enhances the flow and use of important information in organizations. Theorists supporting such models (Anthony, 1978; Frost, Wakely, & Ruh, 1974) propose that workers typically have more complete knowledge of their work than management; hence, if workers participate in decision making, decisions will be made with better pools of information. In addition, cognitive models suggest that if employees participate in decision making, they will know more about implementing work procedures after decisions have been made (Maier, 1963; Melcher, 1976). Other scholars (Miles & Ritchie, 1971; Ritchie & Miles, 1970), designating cognitive models as the "human resources" theory of participation, note that such a model is "primarily concerned with the meaningful utilization of subordinates' capabilities and views satisfaction as a by-product of their participation in important organizational decisions" (Ritchie & Miles, 1970: 348).

Cognitive models predict a definite pattern of results in empirical research investigating participation, satisfaction, and productivity. First, because these models consider information to be crucial, increases in productivity are expected to be stronger where workers have good information about decisions to be made. For instance, such models would predict a stronger effect for participation in job design than for participation in companywide policy decisions or experimental discussions. Second, such models do not predict immediate increases in satisfaction as a result of participation in decision making, as it is essentially a knowledge of results that is hypothesized to lead to eventual increases in satisfaction. Third, they do not predict increases in workers' productivity and satisfaction simply from their working in participative work climates or for nondirective leaders. According to cognitive models, increases in productivity and satisfaction are attributable to specific inputs from subordinates on issues in which they are interested and knowledgeable.

Affective Models of Participative Effects

There are several models linking participation to productivity and satisfaction through affective mechanisms. Followers of the "human relations"[1] school of management (Blake & Mouton, 1964; Likert, 1967; McGregor, 1960) adamantly espouse these models, in which the most crucial link is that between participation and workers' satisfaction. These theorists propose that participation will lead to greater attainment of high-order needs, such as self-expression, respect, independence, and equality, which will in turn increase morale and satisfaction. Ritchie and Miles stated that "managers who hold the Human Relations theory of participation believe simply in involvement for the sake of involvement, arguing that as long as subordinates feel they are participating and are being consulted, their ego needs will be satisfied and they will be more cooperative" (1970: 348).

The link between participation and productivity in affective models is less straightforward than that between participation and satisfaction. Essentially, this school proposes that participation will enhance productivity through intervening motivational processes: participation fulfills needs, fulfilled needs lead to satisfaction, satisfaction strengthens motivation, and increased motivation improves workers' productivity. According to French, Israel, and As (1960):

One effect of a high degree of participation by workers in decisions concerning their own work will be to strengthen their motivation to carry out these decisions. This is the major rationale for expecting a relation between participation and production. When management accords the workers participation in any important decision, it implies that workers are intelligent, competent, and valued partners. Thus, participation directly affects such aspects of worker-management relations as the perception of being valued, the perception of common goals, and cooperation. It satisfies such important social needs as the need for recognition and appreciation and the need for independence. These satisfactions and in addition the improvements in their jobs that are introduced through participation lead to higher job satisfaction (1960: 5).

Although several theorists (Locke & Schweiger, 1979; Ritchie & Miles, 1970) feel strongly that scholarly and practical emphasis should be placed on the cognitive effects of participation, researchers in the tradition of McGregor (1960), Likert (1967), and Coch and French (1948) still hold strongly to the importance of participation in providing affective changes in workers. Thus, it is important to consider the predictions of affective models as to the effects of participation on satisfaction and productivity. First, they predict that participation will affect satisfaction in a wide variety of situations. Participation need not be centered on issues of which employees are particularly knowledgeable, for it is the act, not the informational content, of participation that is the crucial mechanism. Second, such models do not predict increases in productivity without initial increases in workers' satisfaction. Finally, affective models suggest that participation will more strongly influence lower-level employees, because managers' higher-order ego needs may well be fulfilled by other aspects of their work.

Contingency Models of Participative Effects

Several theorists suggest that it is not possible to develop models of participative effects that will hold across a wide variety of individuals and situations. Rather, they suggest that participation will affect satisfaction and productivity differently for different people and situations. Scholars have offered a variety of contingency theories centering on personality, particular decision situations, relationships between superiors and subordinates, job levels, and values.

Vroom (1960) was the first to propose that personality might mediate the effects of participation on satisfaction and productivity. Specifically, he suggested that participation will positively influence only employees having personalities with low authoritarianism and high needs for independence. Vroom found some support for his hypotheses, and his work has stimulated other research. However, further studies have provided mixed support for his hypotheses (Abdel-Halim, 1983; Tosi, 1970; Vroom & Mann, 1960).

Vroom was also involved in the major theoretical statement of situational influences on the participation process. Vroom and Yetton (1973), building on the work of Tannenbaum and Schmidt (1958), considered different decision situations and provided rules for deciding the optimal level of participation in decision making. They proposed both rules to protect the quality of decisions and rules to protect their acceptance. Most of the research on this model has been descriptive, drawing on self-reports about how managers behave in different decision situations. However, several normative tests (Vroom & Jago, 1978) have indicated that decisions made within participative modes specified by these rules were more effective than other decisions. Vroom and Yetton's work moves toward an integration of cognitive and affective models of participation. Their contingency rules for protecting the quality of decisions deal with the cognitive portion of participation, and their rules for protecting the acceptance of decisions address its affective components.

Several other theorists have proposed additional variables as intervening in the process of participation. For example, Vroom and Deci (1960) suggested that the types of problems dealt with at various organizational levels influence the appropriateness of participation; it may be less appropriate at low levels, where jobs are routine, and more appropriate at high levels, where jobs involve addressing complex problems. Several scholars (Hulin, 1971; Singer, 1974) have suggested that values mediate the relationship between participation and outcomes, specifically, that many workers may not value participation to the extent that academicians do. Singer further commented, "While the necessity for determining a 'one best' leadership style for the 'composite worker' is understandable from a financial and expediency standpoint, to assume that *all* workers desire participation opportunities is to lack sensitivity to *individual* needs—the antithesis of the humanization that ardent proponents of participation advocate" (1974: 359). Thus, these scholars predicted that participation may only be effective for employees in certain types of organizations—such as research or service organizations, rather than manufacturing organizations—or only for middle- or upper-level employees.

Overview

In sum, *cognitive* models of participation propose that participation leads to increases in productivity through bringing high-quality information to decisions and through increasing knowledge at times of implementation. Such models predict that: (1) The effects of participation on an individual's productivity will be the strongest for decisions that draw on the individual's expertise. (2) There will not be a direct influence of participation on job satisfaction. Rather, the effect of participation on productivity will mediate this effect. (3) Participation in specific decisions is necessary for increases in productivity and satisfaction; working in a participative climate is not adequate.

Affective models suggest that participation will satisfy higher-order needs of workers and that, as these needs are satisfied, workers will be more satisfied with their jobs. Such models predict that: (1) Working in a participative climate is adequate for increasing workers' productivity. It is not necessary that workers participate in decisions on which they have special knowledge. (2) There is no direct link between participation and productivity. Rather, improved attitudes reduce resistance to change and increase motivation through the satisfaction of needs. (3) Participation may provide more noticeable increases in satisfaction for employees who are not having higher-order needs fulfilled from other aspects of their jobs.

Contingency models of participation suggest that no single model of participation is appropriate for all employees in all organizations. Instead, various contingency models predict that: (1) Employees with high needs for independence and personalities with low authoritarianism will be the most positively influenced by participation. (2) Some decisions are more appropriate for participation than others. Appropriateness depends on requirements for the quality or acceptance of a decision (Vroom & Yetton, 1973), or on its complexity. (3) Employees who value participation will be the most positively influenced by it, and these are likely to be higher-level employees, or individuals working in research or service industries.

Methodological Moderators

In addition to the substantive moderators suggested by the cognitive, affective, and contingency models, several methodological moderators might explain variance in findings about the relationships between participation and satisfaction and productivity. According to Schweiger and Leana, "One potential contextual factor that has not been adequately addressed in previous reviews of the PDM [participation in decision making] literature concerns the research environment in which participation has been examined. Just as PDM may be effective for some subordinates and not for others, consistent findings concerning the effects of PDM may depend, at least in part, on the research setting in which PDM is being investigated" (1985: 148). These authors compared studies conducted in laboratory settings with those conducted in field settings. Locke and Schweiger (1979) considered laboratory, correlational, multivariate, and univariate field studies. Neither of these reviews found that research settings moderated the effect of participation on satisfaction and productivity. Schweiger and Leana concluded that "the laboratory is capable of producing findings that are generalizable to the field" (1985: 18). However, both of these reviews used counting or narrative techniques to assess the differences among research reports. It is quite possible that the more stringent requirements of meta-analysis could reveal effects for research setting that were not apparent in these reviews.

Measurement is a second methodological variable that might moderate findings about participative effects. There are many conceptualizations of participation, ranging from delegation, through representative systems, to joint decision making by superiors and subordinates. Following Locke and Schweiger (1979), we defined participation as joint decision making, a definition that does not specify the precise form or content of the participative process, but does exclude delegation. However, this conceptual definition embraces a wide range of operational definitions of participation. Similarly, the concepts of satisfaction and productivity take on many meanings in different research efforts. It is quite possible that this wide range of conceptual and operational definitions has resulted in varying strengths of relationships between participation and satisfaction and productivity.

Methods

Our literature search for relevant research on the effects of participation on satisfaction and productivity included journals in the areas of social psychology, management, organizational behavior, and communication, and several relevant social citation indices. We restricted it to the published literature and to English language journals and books, excluding dissertations and other unpublished research. It is possible that this led us to include more studies with significant results and fewer with nonsignificant results. However, Hunter, Schmidt, and Jackson (1982) did not see this as a serious problem, noting that it is likely that nonsignificant dissertation results may well be attenuated owing to methodological problems. They further stated that, typically, only a very large number of lost studies will make a substantive difference in a meta-analysis.

This literature search identified 106 articles and book chapters on participation. However, many of these were not appropriate for meta-analysis. We eliminated literature reviews and essays that were not based on data (12 articles), 13 data-based articles without quantifiable effect sizes, 5 studies in which participation was the dependent variable, 6 studies whose dependent variables were not appropriate for this meta-analysis, 15 studies lacking clear measures of participation, and 7 studies in which methodological problems[2] posed serious questions about an estimation of effects or whose data came from another study included in the meta-analysis. . . .

Results

Satisfaction

Forty-one estimates of the relationship between participation and satisfaction were considered. After cumulation of estimates of effects, the weighted mean correlation was .34, and the true variance was .0301. A chi-square test showed this variance to be statistically different from 0 ($\chi^2 = 244.27$, $df = 40$, $p < .01$), indicating that moderator variables would reduce the variance in estimates. We first looked at substantive moderators like organizational type, job level, and type of decision. None of these subgroupings proved useful in reducing variance or in differentiating among effect sizes. Hence, we considered methodological moderators.

The first moderator variable that was effective in reducing subgroup variance was type of respondent. We divided the studies into those conducted with nonorganizational participants (students) and those conducted with organizational respondents. The mean weighted correlation for the nonorganizational studies was .38; the true variance among these estimates was negative, hence considered to be 0. The variance in the organizational studies was still significant, so we considered additional moderators.

The organizational studies were divided into those that measured actual participation and those that measured perceived participation. The mean weighted correlation for studies of actual participation was .16; the variance among these estimates was .0035, which is not significantly different from 0 ($\chi^2 = 8.19$, $df = 10$, $p > .05$). However, the variance in studies investigating perceived participation was still significant. We considered one additional moderator to eliminate the remaining variance: whether perceived participation was in reference to specific issues, such as goals, pay plans, or job redesign, or in reference to multiple issues or a general participative climate, evaluated by a question like "In general, how much do you participate in decision making on your job?" The mean weighted correlation for studies concerned with specific issues was .21; the variance among these estimates was .0009. This variance was not significant ($\chi^2 = .78$, $df = 4$, $p > .05$). The mean weighted correlation for studies concerned with multiple issues was .46. The variance among these effect size estimates was .0156. This variance is still significant ($\chi^2 = 88.5$, $df = 19$, $p < .01$). Several other variables (measurement, job level, and organizational type) were considered for further reducing the variance among effect sizes. However, no other moderator variables reduced the variance within subgroups, so the analysis of studies in which satisfaction was the dependent variable ended at this point.

Table 2 presents information regarding the satisfaction subgroups in which variance was reduced to the greatest extent possible. These groups include (1) nonorganizational studies, (2) studies of actual participation, (3) studies of perceived participation in relation to specific issues, and (4) studies of perceived participation in relation to multiple issues. The table provides the studies included in each subgroup, the mean weighted correlations, the observed variance among estimates of effect sizes, the variance among estimates expected from sampling error, the true variance among estimates, and the chi-square value testing whether the variance is statistically different from 0. Figure 1 is a tree diagram of analyses performed with satisfaction as the dependent variable.

All of the subgroup estimates for satisfaction differ significantly from 0, but there is substantial variation in the magnitudes of effects. The strongest effects of participation on satisfaction are found in studies of perceived participation focusing on multiple issues and in the nonorganizational studies. Much smaller effects are found in the studies of perceived participation focusing on single issues and in the studies of actual participation. In three out of four subgroups, the variance has been reduced to what would be expected from sampling error. Because of the reduction in variance and the

sharp differences among subgroups in sizes of effects, it appears that the analyses were successful in partitioning the studies into appropriate subgroups.

Productivity

Twenty-five studies containing estimates of the relationship between participation and productivity were analyzed. After cumulation of effect estimates the weighted mean correlation was .15, and the true variance was .0334. A chi-square test showed this variance differed significantly from 0 ($\chi^2 = 69.47$, $df = 25$, $p < .01$), so we considered moderator variables. Again, substantive moderator variables were considered first. Of these variables, the objects of participation proved to be useful for subgroup analysis. Seven studies investigated the effects of participation in goal setting on productivity. The cumulated mean weighted correlation for studies of goal setting was .11, and the variance among these estimates was 0. However, the variance among other studies was still significant, so we sought additional moderators. Because other substantive moderators did not prove useful, we evaluated methodological moderators. The first methodological moderator used was research setting. The mean weighted correlation for the nine field studies was .27; the variance among these estimates was 0. Hence, no further analyses were necessary on this subgroup. The variance among estimates for the laboratory studies was significant, so we analyzed these further.

The final moderator considered for studies in which productivity was the dependent variable was the manipulation used in the laboratory studies. Four of the studies manipulated leadership style; a research assistant or member of the experimental group had been instructed to be leader and to behave in an authoritarian or democratic style. The correlation between participation and productivity in the studies manipulating leadership style was −.33; the variance among these estimates was .014. This variance was not significant ($\chi^2 = 3.73$, $df = 3$, $p > .05$). The other four studies manipulated the nature of the tasks the groups performed, by placing subjects in assigned or participative task groups. The correlation between participation and productivity in these studies was −.01; the variance among the estimates was 0.

Table 3 presents information regarding the subgroups of studies investigating productivity in which variance was reduced to the greatest extent possible. These groups are (1) studies concerned with participation in goal setting, (2) field studies, (3) laboratory studies in which leadership style was manipulated, and (4) laboratory studies in which the nature of a task was manipulated. The table provides the studies in each subgroup, the mean weighted correlations, the observed variance among estimates of effect sizes, the variance among estimates expected from sampling error, the true variance among estimates, and the chi-square value testing whether the variance differs statistically from 0. Figure 2 is a tree diagram of subgroup analyses performed with productivity as the dependent variable.

As with the satisfaction studies, the mean weighted correlations of the different subgroups differ substantially. The laboratory studies that manipulated the nature of a task show essentially no correlation, and the studies concerned with

FIGURE 1
Tree Diagram of Studies in the Meta-Analysis for Satisfaction as Dependent Variable

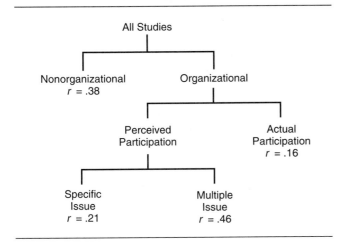

FIGURE 2

Tree Diagram of Studies in the Meta-Analysis for Productivity as Dependent Variable

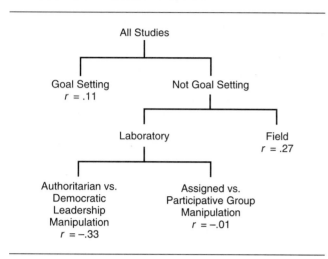

goal setting exhibit a significant, but small, positive correlation. The field studies show a relatively strong positive correlation, and the studies of leadership style exhibit a relatively strong negative correlation. The variance among estimates in these subgroups has been reduced to that attributable to sampling error. The substantially different effect sizes and the reduction in subgroup variance suggest that our partitioning efforts were appropriate and successful.

Discussion

Contingency Models of Participation

This meta-analysis provided no support for any of the contingency predictions discussed. We considered both job type and organizational type as possible moderator variables at all stages of analysis, but there was no reduction of variance in effect sizes through subgroupings on the basis of these variables. Thus, it does not appear that participation is more effective for managers than for lower-level employees, or vice versa. There is also no evidence that research, service, and manufacturing organizations differ in terms of the effectiveness of participation. It was not possible to provide a test of contingency predictions referring to personality, because very few studies provided subgroup analyses considering individuals with different personality types. As mentioned earlier, studies that have considered authoritarianism and need for independence have provided conflicting conclusions.

Finally, it should be noted that the variance in studies of participation in goal setting was reduced to that accountable to sampling error. The correlation between participation in goal setting and productivity was significant, but small ($r = .11$). This result should come as little surprise to those researching goal setting, most of whom have now concluded (e.g., Latham & Marshall, 1982; Latham & Steele, 1983) that participation may have an effect on the levels of goals set, but that it has no effect on productivity if the levels of goals stay the same. Cumulating these results over a variety of research settings adds credence to the generalizability of this conclusion.

Cognitive versus Affective Models of Participation

This meta-analysis provided several tests of the efficacy of cognitive and affective models of participation. First, the findings can be considered in terms of contrasting the effects of participation on satisfaction with the effects of participation on productivity. Affective models predict that participation will have a stronger effect on satisfaction than on productivity, and cognitive models predict the opposite. Second, cognitive models predict that participation will have a stronger influence on productivity and satisfaction for decisions about which employees have specific knowledge. In contrast, affective models predict that working in a participative climate will have the most beneficial effects on workers' attitudes and productivity.

The studies investigating effects of participation other than goal setting on *productivity* exhibited a stronger influence of participation ($r = .27$) than the studies of satisfaction investigating actual participation ($r = .16$) or perceived participation for a single variable ($r = .21$). Of course, comparisons of these effects for different dependent variables should be made with caution, and the differences here are not substantial. However, even the fact that there is a moderately strong effect size for field studies investigating the influence of participation on productivity indicates that cognitive models have some plausibility. Further, the relatively low, but significant, correlations between actual participation and satisfaction and between participation and satisfaction in studies of single issues might lessen confidence in affective models of participation.

However, the data seem more consistent with an affective explanation when we consider studies of participation involving multiple issues. These studies investigated perceived participation and typically used such items as "In general, how participative is your workplace?" or "How much do you generally share in decision making with your supervisor?" After subgroup analysis, some unexplained variance remained in this subgroup, but the mean weighted effect size was .46, much larger than the average correlations in other subgroups of field studies. It appears that working in a participative climate is strongly related to satisfaction at work. This result is in keeping with the human relations school of organizational behavior and with current interest in work climates. In particular, it supports the idea that microclimates (Schneider, 1981), such as a climate for variety, a climate for innovation, or a climate for participation, are related to individual attitudes. However, it is important to consider the structure of this relationship. Does a participative climate cause workers' satisfaction? Does workers' satisfaction help develop a participative climate? Or are these two variables redundant indicators of the same concept? LaFollette and Sims (1975), discussing Johannesson (1973), summarized this dilemma well:

> If it appears as if perceptual climate research is converging upon any domain, job satisfaction seems the likely candidate. Indeed it is hard to imagine how this

possibly could have been avoided. Even if researchers had taken the pains to create new items and had adopted different item formats (which they have not) there remains the psychological problem of divorcing description from feelings. Since descriptions of work situations have been operationally defined as indices of job satisfaction it seems redundant at best to also term such descriptions organizational climate (1975: 257).

Climate has traditionally been defined as a descriptive construct and satisfaction as an affective construct. However, these definitions get muddied operationally if satisfaction is measured through descriptors, as it is in the JDI, or if scales measuring climate include items on attitude. This problem probably is not crucial for the studies in this meta-analysis, because participation involves a specific microclimate, rather than omnibus organizational climate. Thus, it is not likely that measures of participative climate and overall work satisfaction are redundant. In addition, all of these studies considered descriptions of participation rather than attitudes toward participation as the independent variable. Finally, with the exception of studies using the JDI, measures of satisfaction were purely affective. Moreover, results of studies using the JDI were not systematically different from those of studies using other measures of satisfaction.

The question of causality remains: does participation cause satisfaction or does satisfaction cause participation? All of the studies in the multiple-issue subgrouping were correlational, so we cannot answer this question with full confidence. However, we can bring evidence from the literature on climate to bear on this issue. Laboratory research investigating experimentally created social climates (Litwin & Stringer, 1968) found that manipulated climate had an effect on satisfaction. Hand, Richards, and Slocum (1973) found a positive relationship between initial perceptions of climate and subsequent acceptance of self and others. Taylor and Bowers's (1972)[3] cross-lagged panel study of over 284 work groups in 15 different organizations found that "organization climate shows evidence of being more the cause of, than caused by, satisfaction" (1972: 89).

Several concluding comments about the comparison between cognitive, affective, and contingency models of participation are in order. First, there was little support for contingency models of participation, though the lack of measures for several contingency variables could have affected findings. Second, this meta-analysis did not allow for a complete test of the models presented, as we lacked data on several intervening variables in these models, such as upward and downward sharing of information and satisfaction of higher-order ego needs. We would encourage researchers to measure these variables in future investigations of participation. Despite this limitation, some evidence to support both cognitive and affective models of participation emerged. The relatively large correlation between participation and productivity in field studies somewhat supports cognitive models. However, the largest subgroup correlation, between perceived participation and satisfaction, provides greater support for affective models of participation.

Estimates of the effect of participation on *both* satisfaction and productivity appeared in 13 studies. An examination of these studies sheds some light on the relative efficacy of cognitive and affective models: (1) the relationship between participation and satisfaction was stronger than that between participation and productivity in 4 studies (Katzell, Miller, Rotter, & Venet, 1970; Schuler & Kim, 1978; Shaw, 1955; Vroom, 1960), (2) the relationship between participation and productivity was stronger in one study (Ivancevich, 1977), and (3) no significant difference emerged in the other 8 studies. These studies provide somewhat stronger evidence for the relationship between participation and satisfaction than for that between participation and productivity. However, the large number of insignificant differences in this subset precludes our suggesting that this comparison provides strong evidence for either cognitive or affective models.

Research Setting as a Moderator

Several of the strongest moderators were methodological variables; in particular, research setting and type of subject played important roles. For the studies concerned with satisfaction, the variance was zero among investigations involving nonorganizational subjects, all but one of which (Veen, 1972) had a laboratory setting. The weighted correlation for these studies was relatively high ($r = .38$). This effect size was considerably higher than that in studies involving actual participation in organizations ($r = .16$) or perceived participation in reference to a specific issue ($r = .21$).

There are two clear explanations for these results. First, an explanation in terms of internal validity suggests that the high degree of control in laboratories over extraneous variables would make the higher correlation a better indicator of the true relationship between participation and satisfaction. However, an explanation in terms of external validity suggests that college students and laboratory tasks have little in common with real organizational life; hence, field estimates of the effect between participation and satisfaction would be more meaningful. Both arguments undoubtedly have merit. This meta-analysis seems to indicate that there is a relatively high pure effect of participation on satisfaction, but that a host of other organizational influences dilute this effect in field studies investigating actual participation or perceived participation in relation to specific issues.

The effect of research setting in the productivity studies is also striking. Among studies not investigating goal setting, field studies showed a moderately high positive correlation ($r = .27$), and laboratory studies yielded either no correlation (assigned versus participative task manipulation, $r = -.01$) or negative correlations (authoritarian versus democratic leadership manipulation, $r = -.33$). The points of interest here are the sharp differences between laboratory and field studies and the differences in effect sizes for different manipulations.

The substantial difference between field and laboratory studies can probably be attributed to the tasks typically performed in these settings. The laboratory studies typically involved a simple and well-defined manipulated task like turning switches on a control panel or a game of twenty questions; the field studies typically involved participation in naturally occurring, more complex activities, such as pay incentive plans or job design, or participation over a wide gamut of organizational issues. In the laboratory, there usually was a correct answer; there are rarely such guarantees in organizations. Finally, organizational members in field studies had more at stake in the decisions that were made than students in a laboratory.

All of these factors contributed to a higher level of complexity for the organizational participative tasks than for the laboratory participative tasks. Research on small group behavior (Cartwright & Zander, 1960) has suggested that different types of leadership and structure are appropriate for different types of tasks; specifically, that authoritarian leadership and centralized group structure are most appropriate for simple tasks. The studies in this meta-analysis investigating leadership behavior bear this out. Most of the tasks were simple, and authoritarian leadership was more effective in eliciting high levels of productivity. In contrast, the field studies involving complex problems benefited more from participative processes. The lack of effects in the laboratory studies that manipulated the nature of a task is more difficult to interpret. It could be that in laboratory groups without defined leaders, such typical manipulations as assigned or participative groups are not strong enough to elicit effects on productivity. . . .

Conclusions and Future Directions

In spite of these limitations, this research supports some current wisdom about the effects of participation and extends our knowledge of the participative process in organizations in important ways. First, the meta-analysis provides some support for the conclusions reached by Locke and Schweiger (1979). Participation has an effect on both satisfaction and productivity, and its effect on satisfaction is somewhat stronger than its effect on productivity. This meta-analysis allowed us to be more explicit about these effects. As Figures 1 and 2 demonstrate, we can now make quite precise statements about the *magnitude* of the effect of participation

on satisfaction and productivity. In addition, strong evidence exists for a consistent and substantial effect of research setting in these studies, because consideration of this methodological variable considerably reduces the variance among studies. Finally, our analysis indicates specific organizational factors that may enhance or constrain the effect of participation. For example, there is evidence that participative climate has a more substantial effect on workers' satisfaction than participation in specific decisions, and it appears that participation in goal setting does not have a strong effect on productivity.

These conclusions provide some clear avenues for future research. It is important for organizational scholars to conduct research that can specifically test the relationships in the cognitive and affective models. For instance, research contrasting the effects of both participative climate and participation in relation to specific issues on both satisfaction and productivity could lead to an important clarification of the cognitive and the affective processes at work in participative situations. Researchers should also extend our consideration of contingency variables to areas this meta-analysis highlights. For example, the contrast between studies of participative climate and studies of participation in relation to specific issues suggests that organizations with formal systems of participation may differ greatly from organizations in which participativeness is an informal managerial norm. Our investigation (Miller & Monge, 1986) of the Scanlon plan of participative management suggests that this might be the case. Future research could also usefully consider the development of participative systems and norms in organizations over time. Longitudinal research of this nature could help clarify the causal structure of the relationships among participation, satisfaction, and productivity. Finally, the meta-analytic procedure itself could be usefully extended to allow for the testing of relationships that go beyond the simple bivariate level.

Notes

[1] Ritchie and Miles (1970: 348) coined this term in regard to participation in decision making.

[2] The category of methodological problems included a number of studies in which confounding variables or unusual methods made accurate estimation of effects impossible. For instance, the overtime study of Lawler and Hackman (1969) included an outlying data point that made interpretation difficult. In addition, the nonparticipative group in this study had much lower attendance than the participative group to begin with, limiting our confidence in the results. A second example of a methodological problem is Ivancevich's (1976) investigation of goal setting in which both participative and assigned groups went through extensive and active training sessions. In all ways except the actual goal setting, both groups had high levels of participation.

[3] LaFollette and Sims (1975) cited this study.

References

Abdel-Halim, A. A. 1983. Effects of task and personality characteristics on subordinate responses to participative decision making. *Academy of Management Journal*, 26: 477–484.

Abdel-Halim, A. A., & Rowland, K. M. 1976. Some personality determinants in the effects of participation: A further investigation. *Personnel Psychology*, 29: 41–55.

Alutto, J. A., & Acito, F. 1974. Decisional participation and sources of job satisfaction: A study of manufacturing personnel. *Academy of Management Journal*, 17: 160–167.

Alutto, J. A., & Vrenenburgh, D. J. 1977. Characteristics of decisional participation by nurses. *Academy of Management Journal*, 20: 341–347.

Anthony, W. P. 1978. *Participative management.* Reading, Mass.: Addison-Wesley.

Bartlem, C. S., & Locke, E. A. 1981. The Coch and French study: A critique and reinterpretation. *Human Relations*, 34: 555–566.

Baumgartel, H. 1956. Leadership, motivations, and attitudes in research laboratories. *Journal of Social Issues*, 12: 24–31.

Blake, R. R., & Mouton, J. S. 1964. *The managerial grid.* Houston: Gulf.

Carey, A. 1967. The Hawthorne studies: A radical criticism. *American Sociological Review*, 32: 403–416.

Cartwright, D., & Zander, A. 1960. *Group dynamics: Research and theory* (2nd ed.). Evanston, Ill.: Row, Peterson.

Coch, L., & French, J. R. P. 1948. Overcoming resistance to change. *Human Relations*, 1: 512–532.

Dachler, H. P., & Wilpert, B. 1978. Conceptual dimensions and boundaries of participation in organizations. *Administrative Science Quarterly*, 23: 1–39.

Dossett, D. L., Latham, G. P., & Mitchell, T. R. 1979. Effects of assigned versus participatively set goals, knowledge of results, and individual differences on employee behavior when goal difficulty is held constant. *Journal of Applied Psychology*, 64: 291–298.

Falcione, R. L. 1974. Credibility: Qualifier of subordinate participation. *Journal of Business Communication*, 11 (3): 43–54.

Fiman, B. G. 1973. An investigation of the relationships among supervisory attitudes, behaviors, and outputs: An examination of McGregor's Theory Y. *Personnel Psychology*, 26: 95–105.

Fox, W. M. 1957. Group reactions to two types of conference leadership. *Human Relations*, 10: 279–289.

French, J. R. P., Israel, J., & As, D. 1960. An experiment in a Norwegian factory: Interpersonal dimensions in decision-making. *Human Relations*, 13: 3–19.

French, J. R. P., Kay, E., & Meyer, H. H. 1966. Participation and the appraisal system. *Human Relations*, 19: 3–20.

Frost, C. H., Wakely, J. H., & Ruh, R. A. 1974. *The Scanlon Plan for organization development: Identity, participation, and equity.* East Lansing: Michigan State University Press.

Gibb, C. A. 1951. An experimental approach to the study of leadership. *Occupational Psychology*, 25: 233–248.

Glass, G. V., McGaw, B., & Smith, M. L. 1981. *Meta-analysis in social research.* Beverly Hills, Calif.: Sage Publications.

Hand, H. H., Richards, M. D., & Slocum, J. W. 1973. Organizational climate and the effectiveness of a human relations training program. *Academy of Management Journal*, 16: 185–195.

House, R. J., & Dessler, G. 1974. The path goal theory of leadership: Some post hoc and a priori tests. In J. Hunt & L. Larson (Eds.), *Contingency approaches to leadership*: 29–55. Carbondale: Southern Illinois University Press.

Hulin, C. L. 1971. Individual differences and job enrichment: The case against general treatment. In J. R. Maher (Ed.), *New perspectives in job enrichment*: 159–191. New York: Van Nostrand Reinhold Co.

Hunter, J. W., Schmidt, F. L., & Jackson, G. B. 1982. *Meta-analysis: Cumulating research findings across studies.* Beverly Hills, Calif.: Sage Publications.

Ivancevich, J. M. 1974. A study of a cognitive training program: Trainer styles and group development. *Academy of Management Journal*, 17: 428–439.

Ivancevich, J. M. 1976. Effects of goal setting on performance and job satisfaction. *Journal of Applied Psychology*, 61: 605–612.

Ivancevich, J. M. 1977. Different goal setting treatments and their effects on performance and job satisfaction. *Academy of Management Journal*, 20: 406–419.

Jenkins, G. D., & Lawler, E. E. 1981. Impact of employee participation in pay plan development. *Organizational Behavior and Human Performance*, 28: 111–128.

Johannesson, R. E. 1973. Some problems in the measurement of organizational climate. *Organizational Behavior and Human Performance*, 10: 118–144.

Katzell, R. A., Miller, C. E., Rotter, N. G., & Venet, T. G. 1970. Effects of leadership and other inputs on group processes and outputs. *Journal of Social Psychology*, 80: 157–169.

LaFollette, W. R., & Sims, H. P. 1975. Is satisfaction redundant with organizational climate? *Organizational Behavior and Human Performance*, 13: 257–278.

Lanzetta, J. T., & Roby, T. 1960. The relationship between certain group process variables and group problem-solving efficiency. *Journal of Social Psychology*, 52: 135–148.

Latham, G. P., & Marshall, H. A. 1982. The effects of self-set, participatively set, and assigned goals on the performance of government employees. *Personnel Psychology*, 35: 399–404.

Latham, G. P., Mitchell, T. R., & Dossett, D. L. 1978. Importance of participative goal setting and anticipated rewards on goal difficulty and job performance. *Journal of Applied Psychology*, 63: 163–171.

Latham, G. P., & Saari, L. M. 1979. The effects of holding goal difficulty constant on assigned and participatively set goals. *Academy of Management Journal*, 22: 163–168.

Latham, G. P., & Steele, T. P. 1983. The motivational effects of participation versus goal setting on performance. *Academy of Management Journal*, 26: 406–417.

Latham, G. P., & Yukl, G. A. 1976. Effects of assigned and participative goal setting on performance and job satisfaction. *Journal of Applied Psychology*, 61: 166–171.

Lawler, E. E. 1975. Pay, participation and organizational change. In E. L. Cass & F. G. Zimmer (Eds.), *Man and work in society*: 137–149. New York: Van Nostrand Reinhold Co.

Lawler, E. E., & Hackman, J. R. 1969. Impact of employee participation in the development of pay-incentive plans: A field experiment. *Journal of Applied Psychology*, 53: 467–471.

Likert, R. L. 1967. *The human organization.* New York: McGraw-Hill Book Co.

Lischeron, J., & Wall, T. D. 1974. Attitudes towards participating among local authority employees. *Human Relations*, 28: 499–517.

Lischeron, J., & Wall, T. D. 1975. Employee participation: An experimental field study. *Human Relations*, 28: 863–884.

Litwin, G. H., & Stringer, R. A., Jr. 1968. *Motivation and organizational climate.* Boston: Harvard Business School, Division of Research.

Locke, E. A., & Schweiger, D. M. 1979. Participation in decision-making: One more look. *Research in Organizational Behavior*, 1: 265–339.

Lowin, A. 1968. Participative decision making: A model, literature critique, and prescriptions for research. *Organizational Behavior and Human Performance*, 3: 68–106.

Maier, N. R. F. 1963. *Problem solving discussions and conferences: Leadership methods and skills.* New York: McGraw-Hill Book Co.

McCurdy, H. G., & Lambert, W. E. 1952. The efficiency of small human groups in the solution of problems requiring genuine cooperation. *Journal of Personality*, 20: 478–494.

McGregor, D. 1960. *The human side of enterprise.* New York: McGraw-Hill Book Co.

Melcher, A. J. 1976. Participation: A critical review of research findings. *Human Resource Management*, 15 (2): 12–21.

Miles, R. E., & Ritchie, J. B. 1971. Participative management: Quality vs. quantity. *California Management Review*, 13 (4): 48–56.

Miller, K. I., & Monge, P. R. 1986. The development and test of a system of organizational participation and allocation. In M. McLaughlin (Ed.), *Communication yearbook 10*: in press. Beverly Hills, Calif.: Sage Publications.

Mitchell, T. R., Smyser, C. M., & Weed, S. E. 1975. Locus of control: Supervision and work satisfaction. *Academy of Management Journal*, 18: 623–631.

Morse, N. C., & Reimer, E. 1956. The experimental change of a major organizational variable. *Journal of Abnormal and Social Psychology*, 52: 120–129.

Neider, L. L. 1980. An experimental field investigation utilizing an expectancy theory view of participation. *Organizational Behavior and Human Performance*, 26: 425–442.

Obradovic, J. 1970. Participation and work attitudes in Yugoslavia. *Industrial Relations*, 9: 161–169.

Obradovic, J., French, J. R. P., & Rodgers, W. 1970. Workers' councils in Yugoslavia. *Human Relations*, 23: 459–471.

Ritchie, J. B., & Miles, R. E. 1970. An analysis of quantity and quality of participation as mediating variables in the participative decision making process. *Personnel Psychology*, 23: 347–359.

Roberts, K. H., Blankenship, L. V., & Miles, R. E. 1968. Organizational leadership, satisfaction, and productivity. *Academy of Management Journal*, 11: 401–422.

Roethlisberger, F. J., & Dickson, W. J. 1939. *Management and the worker.* Cambridge, Mass.: Harvard University Press.

Runyon, K. E. 1973. Some interactions between personality variables and management styles. *Journal of Applied Psychology*, 57: 288–294.

Schecter, J. 1972. The private world of Richard Nixon. *Time*, 99 (1): 18–19.

Schneider, B. 1981. *Work climates: an interactionist perspective.* Research report No. 81–2, Department of Psychology, Michigan State University, East Lansing.

Schuler, R. S. 1976. Participation with supervisor and subordinate authoritarianism: A path-goal theory reconciliation. *Administrative Science Quarterly*, 21: 320–325.

Schuler, R. S. 1980. A role and expectancy perception model of participation in decision making. *Academy of Management Journal*, 23: 331–340.

Schuler, R. S., & Kim, J. S. 1978. Employees' expectancy perceptions as explanatory variables for effectiveness of participation in decision making. *Psychological Reports*, 43: 651–656.

Schweiger, D. M., & Leana, C. R. 1986. Participation in decision making. In E. A. Locke (Ed.), *Generalizing from laboratory to field settings*: 147–166. Lexington, Mass.: D. C. Heath Co.

Seeborg, I. S. 1978. The influence of employee participation in job redesign. *Journal of Applied Behavioral Science*, 14: 87–98.

Shaw, M. E. 1955. A comparison of two types of leadership in various communication nets. *Journal of Abnormal and Social Psychology*, 50: 127–134.

Singer, J. N. 1974. Participative decision-making about work: An overdue look at variables which mediate its effects. *Sociology of Work and Occupations*, 1: 347–371.

Smith, M. L., & Glass, G. V. 1977. Meta-analyses of psychotherapy outcome studies. *American Psychologist*, 32: 752–760.

Smith, P. C., Kendall, M., & Hulin, C. L. 1969. *The measurement of satisfaction in work and retirement.* Chicago: Rand McNally & Co.

Strauss, G. 1982. Workers' participation in management: An international perspective. *Research in Organizational Behavior,* 4: 173–265.

Tannenbaum, R., & Schmidt, W. 1958. How to choose a leadership pattern. *Harvard Business Review,* 36 (2): 95–101.

Taylor, J. C., & Bowers, D. G. 1972. *Survey of organizations: A machine-scored standardized questionnaire instrument.* Ann Arbor, Mich.: Institute for Social Research.

Torrance, E. P. 1953. Methods of conducting critiques of group problem-solving performance. *Journal of Applied Psychology,* 37: 394–398.

Tosi, H. 1970. A reexamination of personality as a determinant of the effect of participation. *Personnel Psychology,* 23: 91–99.

Veen, P. 1972. Effects of participative decision-making in field hockey training: A field experiment. *Organizational Behavior and Human Performance,* 7: 288–307.

Vroom, V. H. 1960. *Some personality determinants of the effects of participation.* Englewood Cliffs, N.J.: Prentice-Hall.

Vroom, V. H., & Deci, E. L. (Eds.). 1960. *Management and motivation.* Baltimore: Penguin Books.

Vroom, V. H., & Jago, A. G. 1978. On the validity of the Vroom/Yetton model. *Journal of Applied Psychology,* 63: 151–162.

Vroom, V. H., & Mann, F. C. 1960. Leader authoritarianism and employee attitudes. *Personnel Psychology,* 13: 125–140.

Vroom, V. H., & Yetton, P. W. 1973. *Leadership and decision-making.* Pittsburgh, Pa.: University of Pittsburgh Press.

Wexley, K. E., Singh, J. P., & Yukl, G. A. 1973. Subordinate personality as a moderator of the effects of participation in three types of appraisal interviews. *Journal of Applied Psychology,* 58: 54–59.

Yukl, G. A., & Kanuk, L. 1979. Leadership behavior and the effectiveness of beauty salon managers. *Personnel Psychology,* 32: 663–675.

Chapter Eight

Leadership: Substitutes, Neutralizers, and Enhancers

T he previous two chapters suggested that the leadership-outcome relationship is not a simple and direct relationship. The path-goal (House & Mitchell, 1974), behavioral (Yukl, 1971), and contingency theories of leadership (Fiedler, 1974), for example, suggest that there are a variety of situational factors that serve to mediate the leader-outcome relationship. As a consequence, the effectiveness of a particular leader behavior is influenced, for example, by characteristics of the task and the followers.

Influenced by his 1974[1] review of the literature on leader initiating structure and consideration, Steven Kerr concluded that existing evidence did not necessarily support a hypothesis that was implicitly embedded in most situational theories of leadership—namely, that in each and every situation some form of leadership will be effective. Instead, Kerr (1977) argued that there are many individual, task, and organizational factors that may serve as either *substitutes for* or *neutralizers of* a leader's behavior in terms of its impact upon follower satisfaction and performance.

There are two readings in this chapter. The first by Steven Kerr and John M. Jermier (1978) and the second by Jon P. Howell (1990) and his colleagues (David E. Bowen, Peter W. Dorfman, Steven Kerr, and Philip M. Podsakoff), provide insight into the task, follower, and organizational factors that serve as substitutes and neutralizers of leadership. Both readings provide insight into the somewhat startling question "Is leadership necessary?"

The concept "substitute for leadership" suggests that there are factors in the work environment that can take the place of the behavior of a leader. Attributes of the organization, technology, task, and follower can provide the motivation, guidance, reward, and satisfaction needed for effective performance to such a degree that the behaviors of the leader are rendered unimportant. The concept "neutralizer of leadership" suggests that there are work environment factors that *prevent* leaders from acting as they wish or which neutralize the effects of certain acts of leadership.

The organization literature suggests that there are a number of different forces within the work environment that structure the behavior and thinking of organizational members, as well as serve as sources of member motivation and satisfaction. For example, social system design (e.g., organization and work unit), technology, job design, and leader-initiating structure represent four sources of environmental structuring to which group and organizational members are exposed. Looking at the relative contributions of each of these sources of structure on employee attitudes (e.g., satisfaction, job involvement, identification), intrinsic motivation, and behaviors (e.g., performance and absen-

---

[1]S. Kerr, C. Schriesheim, C. Murphy, and R. Stogdill, "Toward a Contingency Theory of Leadership Based upon the Consideration and Initiating Structure Literature," *Organizational Behavior and Human Performance* 12 (1974), 62–82.

teeism), Pierce, Dunham, and Cummings (1984)[2] found that technology, job design, and work unit structure were substitutes for leader-initiating structure. Leader structure had little unique association with employee reactions except when the other sources of environmental structure were weak. In general, the most powerful substitute was found in the design of the member's job.

A recent study by Podsakoff (1993) and his associates revealed that the effects of a number of substitutes (i.e., subordinate, task, and organizational characteristics) had a substantial impact on employee attitudes, perceptions, and performance.[3] Commenting on their findings, they note, "The results of the present research provide strong support for Kerr and Jermier's (1978) suggestion that one reason why leader behaviors account for little variance in employee attitudes, perceptions, and behaviors is that the leader's context, defined in terms of subordinate, task, and organizational characteristics, also has an impact on such criterion measures" (p. 36). Based upon the findings of Podsakoff et al., three conclusions can be tentatively drawn: (a) the substitutes are more important than leader behavior in the determination of job satisfaction, commitment, and role ambiguity; (b) leader behaviors seem to be more important than the substitutes in terms of employee performance; and (c) for role conflict, altruism, attendance, and conscientiousness, the substitutes and leader behaviors were equally influential.

Howell and his colleagues also suggest that there are certain attributes of the organization, task, and follower that actually serve to enhance (magnify) the leader and leadership effects. The concept "leadership enhancers" is similar to Fiedler's (1974) notion of situation favorableness. For example, directive leader behavior, coming from a relatively weak leader in a highly cohesive work group, is likely to be able to benefit from the presence of peer support, work facilitation, and clan control. (The self-assessment at the end of this chapter opener provides you with an opportunity to assess the level of cohesiveness within a work group with which you are associated.)

In the last chapter of this book, you will be introduced by Charles C. Manz (1986) to the concept "self-leadership." The follower (subordinate) who exhibits self-leadership (e.g., self-direction and self-control) engages in behaviors that may render unnecessary the same behaviors stemming from the leader.[4] Building upon the work of Manz, it might be hypothesized that individuals with a strong sense of self (i.e., organization-based self-esteem and generalized self-efficacy) are more likely to have the capacity for self-leadership and serve as a substitute for directive leader behavior. (You can profile yourself with regard to the strength of your own organization-based self-esteem and generalized sense of self-efficacy by turning to the self-assessment at the end of this chapter opener).

Bowers and Seashore (1966) suggested that there are certain behaviors that are important to effective group (team) functioning. In some instances, these behaviors (e.g., support, work and interaction facilitation, goal emphasis) need to be supplied by the leader. They went on to note, however, that it is not necessary that the leader supply these behaviors. These behaviors may find their substitute in one's peers, or one's self, as well as features of the organization, its technology, and the design of jobs. Figure 8.1 provides an expanded view of the leadership process, reflecting the central contributions of this chapter.

[2]J. L. Pierce, R. B. Dunham, and L. L. Cummings, "Sources of Environmental Structuring and Participant Responses," *Organizational Behavior and Human Performance* 33 (1984), 214–42.

[3]P. M. Podsakoff, B. P. Niehoff, S. B. MacKenzie, and M. L. Williams, "Do Substitutes for Leadership Really Substitute for Leadership? An Empirical Examination of Kerr and Jermier's Situational Leadership Model," *Organizational Behavior and Human Decision Processes* 54 (1993), 1–44.

[4]C. C. Manz, "Self-leadership: Toward an Expanded Theory of Self-Influence Processes in Organizations," *Academy of Management Review* 11 (1986), 585–600.

The Role of The Leadership Process: Substitutes, Neutralizers, and Enhancers (S, N, E)

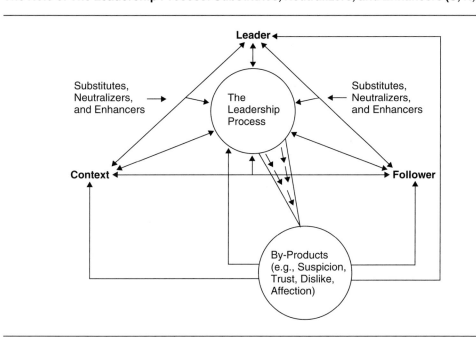

Substitutes for Leadership

Instructions: Turn to Table 2 in the reading by Kerr and Jermier (1978), "Substitutes for Leadership: Their Meaning and Measurement." Thinking in terms of your current job, answer each of the questions posed in Table 2 by employing the following response scale:

> 5 = Almost always true, or almost completely true.
> 4 = Usually true, or true to a large extent.
> 3 = Sometimes true, sometimes untrue, or true to some extent.
> 2 = Usually untrue, or untrue to a large extent.
> 1 = Almost always untrue, or almost completely untrue.

Scoring: For each of the questions in Table 2 with an (R) following the items, subtract your response (i.e., 1–5) from 6. Next, sum your score to each of the items in category 1 and divide by 3. Following this procedure, move to the next category of questions, sum your score to each item and divide by the number of questions in that category. Complete this process for each of the 10 categories.

Interpretation: A high score (4 and greater) indicates a relatively strong presence of that "category" (e.g., ability, experience, training and knowledge; professional orientation; indifference toward organizational rewards; unambiguous, routine, and methodologically invariant tasks) acting as a substitute for leadership within your job.

Group Cohesiveness

Instructions: This questionnaire is concerned with work groups in an organization. Please think of your "work group" as the set of people with whom you work most closely on a day-to-day basis. If you are a member of only one work group, these questions will be easy to answer.

If you are not a member of a work group, think about the individual or set of individuals you deal with most frequently in the performance of your job.

If you are a member of two or more different groups, you will need to decide which *one* group is most important (for example, that you deal with most frequently). Think about one and only one group while answering these questions.

The following statements may or may not describe your work group. How much do you *AGREE* or *DISAGREE* with each statement?

	Strongly Disagree	Disagree	Slightly Dis- agree	Neither Agree nor Disagree	Slightly Agree	Agree	Strongly Agree
1. I feel I am really part of my work group.	1	2	3	4	5	6	7
2. There is confidence and trust among members of my work group.	1	2	3	4	5	6	7
3. This group is extremely attractive to me.	1	2	3	4	5	6	7
4. I look forward to being with the members of my work group each day.	1	2	3	4	5	6	7
5. There is a strong bond holding members of this group together.	1	2	3	4	5	6	7
6. There is a high level of tension among certain members of my work group.	1	2	3	4	5	6	7

(*continued*)

Scoring: Subtract your numeric answer to question 6 from 8. Next, add this adjusted score to your responses to questions 1 through 5, divide the total by 6, and enter your score here _____.

Interpretation: A high score (5.5 and greater) suggests that you perceive a relatively high degree of group cohesiveness. A low score (2.5 and less) is indicative of a relatively low degree of group cohesiveness. As might be hypothesized from the material covered in this chapter, cohesive work groups are extremely likely to provide their members with personal and task support, thereby reducing the importance of (need for) certain leader behaviors.

Source: These are illustrative group cohesiveness items, constructed for this self-assessment. There is no prior validation evidence available.

Self-Assessment

Organization-Based Self-Esteem and Generalized Self-Efficacy

Part I

Instructions: The following questions ask about you and your relationship with an organization.

Please indicate the extent to which you *believe* in each of the following statements by expressing the level of your *Agreement* or *Disagreement*.

	Strongly Disagree	Disagree	Neither Agree Nor Disagree	Agree	Strongly Agree
1. I COUNT around here.	1	2	3	4	5
2. I am TAKEN SERIOUSLY around here.	1	2	3	4	5
3. There is FAITH IN ME around here.	1	2	3	4	5
4. I am TRUSTED around here.	1	2	3	4	5
5. I am HELPFUL around here.	1	2	3	4	5
6. I am a VALUABLE PART OF THIS PLACE.	1	2	3	4	5
7. I am EFFICIENT around here.	1	2	3	4	5
8. I am an IMPORTANT PART OF THIS PLACE.	1	2	3	4	5
9. I MAKE A DIFFERENCE around here.	1	2	3	4	5
10. I am COOPERATIVE around here.	1	2	3	4	5

Part II

Instructions: For each of the following statements, please indicate the degree to which you *agree* or *disagree* with the statement.

	Strongly Disagree	Disagree	Slightly Disagree	Neither Agree nor Disagree	Slightly Agree	Agree	Strongly Agree
1. When I make plans, I am certain I can make them work.	1	2	3	4	5	6	7

(*continued*)

	Strongly Disagree	Disagree	Slightly Disagree	Neither Agree nor Disagree	Slightly Agree	Agree	Strongly Agree
2. One of my problems is that I cannot get down to work when I should.	1	2	3	4	5	6	7
3. If I can't do a job the first time, I keep trying until I can.	1	2	3	4	5	6	7
4. When I set important goals for myself, I rarely achieve them.	1	2	3	4	5	6	7
5. I give up on things before completing them.	1	2	3	4	5	6	7
6. I avoid facing difficulties.	1	2	3	4	5	6	7
7. If something looks too complicated, I will not even bother to try it.	1	2	3	4	5	6	7
8. When I have something unpleasant to do, I stick to it until I finish it.	1	2	3	4	5	6	7
9. When I decide to do something, I go right to work on it.	1	2	3	4	5	6	7
10. When trying to learn something new, I soon give up if I am not initially successful.	1	2	3	4	5	6	7
11. When unexpected problems occur, I don't handle them well.	1	2	3	4	5	6	7
12. I avoid trying to learn new things when they look too difficult for me.	1	2	3	4	5	6	7

	Strongly Disagree	Disagree	Slightly Disagree	Neither Agree nor Disagree	Slightly Agree	Agree	Strongly Agree
13. Failure just makes me try harder.	1	2	3	4	5	6	7
14. I feel insecure about my ability to do things.	1	2	3	4	5	6	7
15. I am a self-reliant person.	1	2	3	4	5	6	7
16. I give up easily.	1	2	3	4	5	6	7
17. I do not seem capable of dealing with most problems that come up in life.	1	2	3	4	5	6	7

Scoring: PART I: Sum your scores to each of the 10 statements and then divide by 10. Enter your score here _____.

PART II: Subtract your scores to questions 2, 4, 5, 6, 7, 10, 11, 12, 14, 16, and 17 from 8. Next, employing your adjusted scores, sum your score for each of the 17 questions, then divide by 17, and enter your score here _____.

Interpretation: PART I: A high score (4 and greater) suggests that you have a relatively high level of organization-based self-esteem. A low score (2 and less) suggests a relatively weak organization-based self-esteem.

PART II: A high score (5.5 and greater) suggests that you have a relatively strong generalized sense of self-efficacy—your belief that you possess the ability to successfully perform in achievement situations. A low score (2.5 and less) suggests that you have relatively strong reservations as they pertain to your ability to perform in achievement situations.

It has been suggested that individuals who have a strong and positive sense of "self," as might be reflected by a high level of organization-based self-esteem and a strong generalized self-efficacy, are more capable of functioning with less leadership support and direction than individuals whose sense of self within the work environment is relatively weak. This becomes particularly true as role conditions become increasingly difficult, conflict-laden, ambiguous, nonsupportive, and overloaded.

Source: J. L. Pierce, D. G. Gardner, L. L. Cummings, and R. B. Dunham, "Organization-Based Self-Esteem: Construct Definition, Measurement, and Validation," *Academy of Management Journal* 32 (1989), 622–48; M. Sherer, J. E. Maddux, B. Mercadante, S. Prentice-Dunn, B. Jacobs, and R. W. Rogers, "The Self-Efficacy Scale: Construction and Validation," *Psychological Reports* 53 (1982), 899–902.

Substitutes for Leadership
Their Meaning and Measurement

Steven Kerr
University of Southern California

John M. Jermier
The Ohio State University

A number of theories and models of leadership exist, each seeking to most clearly identify and best explain the presumedly powerful effects of leader behavior or personality attributes upon the satisfaction and performance of hierarchical subordinates. These theories and models fail to agree in many respects, but have in common the fact that none of them systematically accounts for very much criterion variance. It is certainly true that data indicating strong superior-subordinate relationships have sometimes been reported. In numerous studies, however, conclusions have had to be based on statistical rather than practical significance, and hypothesis support has rested upon the researcher's ability to show that the trivially low correlations obtained were not the result of chance.

Current theories and models of leadership have something else in common: a conviction that hierarchical leadership is always important. Even situational approaches to leadership share the assumption that while the *style* of leadership likely to be effective will vary according to the situation, *some* leadership style will *always* be effective *regardless* of the situation. Of course, the extent to which this assumption is explicated varies greatly, as does the degree to which each theory is dependent upon the assumption. Fairly explicit is the Vertical Dyad Linkage model developed by Graen and his associates (Graen, Dansereau, & Minami, 1972; Dansereau, Cashman, & Graen, 1973), which attributes importance to hierarchical leadership without concern for the situation. The Fiedler (1964, 1967) Contingency Model also makes the general assumption that hierarchical leadership is important in situations of low, medium, and high favorableness, though predictions about relationships between LPC and performance in Octants VI and VII are qualified (Fiedler & Chemers, 1974, p. 82). Most models of decision-centralization (e.g., Tannenbaum & Schmidt, 1958; Heller & Yukl, 1969; Vroom & Yetton, 1973; Bass & Valenzi, 1974) include among their leader decision-style alternatives one whereby subordinates attempt a solution by themselves, with minimal participation by the hierarchical superior. Even in such cases, however, the leader is responsible for initiating the method through delegation of the problem and is usually described as providing (structuring) information.

The approach to leadership which is least dependent upon the assumption articulated above, and which comes closest to the conceptualization to be proposed in this paper, is the Path-Goal Theory (House, 1971; House & Mitchell, 1974). Under circumstances when both goals and paths to goals may be clear, House and Mitchell (1974) point out that "attempts by the leader to clarify paths and goals will be both redundant and seen by subordinates as imposing unnecessary close control." They go on to predict that "although such control may increase performance by preventing soldiering or malingering, it will also result in decreased satisfaction."

This prediction is supported in part by conclusions drawn by Kerr, Schriesheim, Murphy, and Stogdill (1974) from their review of the consideration-initiating structure literature and is at least somewhat consistent with results from a few recent studies. A most interesting and pertinent premise of the theory, however, is that even unnecessary and redundant leader behaviors will have an impact upon leadership satisfaction, morale, motivation, performance, and acceptance of the leader (House & Mitchell, 1974; House & Dessler, 1974). While leader attempts to clarify paths and goals are therefore recognized by Path-Goal Theory to be unnecessary and redundant in certain situations, in no situation are they explicitly hypothesized by Path-Goal (or any other leadership theory) to be irrelevant.

This lack of recognition is unfortunate. As has already been mentioned, data from numerous studies collectively demonstrate that in many situations these leader behaviors *are* irrelevant, and hierarchical leadership (as operationalized in these studies) per se does not seem to matter. In fact, leadership variables so often account for very little criterion variance that a few writers have begun to argue that the leadership construct is sterile altogether, that "the concept of leadership itself has outlived its usefulness" (Miner, 1975, p. 200). This view is also unfortunate, however, and fails to take note of accurate predictions by leadership theorists even as such theorists fail to conceptually reconcile their inaccurate predictions.

What is clearly needed to resolve this dilemma is a conceptualization adequate to explain both the occasional successes and frequent failures of the various theories and models of leadership.

Source: Edited and reprinted with permission from *Organizational Behavior and Human Performance* 22 (1978), 375–403. Author affiliation may have changed since article was first published.

Substitutes for Leadership

A wide variety of individual, task, and organizational characteristics have been found to influence relationships between leader behavior and subordinate satisfaction, morale, and performance. Some of these variables (for example, job pressure and subordinate expectations of leader behavior) act primarily to influence which leadership style will best permit the hierarchical superior to motivate, direct, and control subordinates. The effect of others, however, is to act as "substitutes for leadership," tending to negate the leader's ability to either improve or impair subordinate satisfaction and performance.

Substitutes for leadership are apparently prominent in many different organizational settings, but their existence is not explicated in any of the dominant leadership theories. As a result, data describing formal superior-subordinate relationships are often obtained in situations where important substitutes exist. These data logically ought to be, and usually are, insignificant and are useful primarily as a reminder that when leadership styles are studied in circumstances where the choice of style is irrelevant, the effect is to replace the potential power of the leadership construct with the unintentional comedy of the "Law of the instrument."[1]

What is needed, then, is a taxonomy of situations where we should not be studying "leadership" (in the formal hierarchical sense) at all. Development of such a taxonomy is still at an early stage, but Woodward (1973) and Miner (1975) have laid important groundwork through their classifications of control, and some effects of nonleader sources of clarity have been considered by Hunt (Note 2) and Hunt and Osborn (1975). Reviews of the leadership literature by House and Mitchell (1974) and Kerr *et al.* (1974) have also proved pertinent in this regard and suggest that individual, task, and organizational characteristics of the kind outlined in Table 1 will help to determine whether or not hierarchical leadership is likely to matter.

Conceptual domain of substitutes for leadership. Since Table 1 is derived from previously conducted studies, substitutes are only suggested for the two leader behavior styles which dominate the research literature. The substitutes construct probably has much wider applicability, however, perhaps to hierarchical leadership in general.

It is probably useful to clarify some of the characteristics listed in Table 1. "Professional orientation" is considered a potential substitute for leadership because employees with such an orientation typically cultivate horizontal rather than vertical relationships, give greater credence to peer review

T A B L E   1
Substitutes for Leadership

Characteristic	Will Tend to Neutralize	
	Relationship-Oriented, Supportive, People-Centered Leadership: Consideration, Support, and Interaction Facilitation	**Task-Oriented, Instrumental, Job-Centered Leadership: Initiating Structure, Goal Emphasis, and Work Facilitation**
Of the Subordinate		
1. ability, experience, training, knowledge		X
2. need for independence	X	X
3. "professional" orientation	X	X
4. indifference toward organizational rewards	X	X
Of the Task		
5. unambiguous and routine		X
6. methodologically invariant		X
7. provides its own feedback concerning accomplishment		X
8. intrinsically satisfying	X	
Of the Organization		
9. formalization (explicit plans, goals, and areas of responsibility)		X
10. inflexibility (rigid, unbending rules and procedures)		X
11. highly-specified and active advisory and staff functions		X
12. closely-knit, cohesive work groups	X	X
13. organizational rewards not within the leader's control	X	X
14. spatial distance between superior and subordinates	X	X

processes, however informal, than to hierarchical evaluations, and tend to develop important referents external to the employing organization (Filley, House, & Kerr, 1976). Clearly, such attitudes and behaviors can sharply reduce the influence of the hierarchical superior.

"Methodologically invariant" tasks may result from serial interdependence, from machine-paced operations, or from work methods which are highly standardized. In one study (House, Filley, & Kerr, 1971, p. 26), invariance was found to derive from a network of government contracts which "specified not only the performance requirements of the end product, but also many of the management practices and control techniques that the company must follow in carrying out the contract."

Invariant methodology relates to what Miner (1975) describes as the "push" of work. Tasks which are "intrinsically satisfying" (another potential substitute listed in Table 1) contribute in turn to the "pull" of work. Miner believes that for "task control" to be effective, a force comprised of both the push and pull of work must be developed. At least in theory, however, either type alone may act as a substitute for hierarchical leadership.

Performance feedback provided by the work itself is another characteristic of the task which potentially functions in place of the formal leader. It has been reported that employees with high growth need strength in particular derive beneficial psychological states (internal motivation, general satisfaction, work effectiveness) from clear and direct knowledge of the results of performance (Hackman & Oldham, 1976; Oldham, 1976). Task-provided feedback is often: (1) the most immediate source of feedback given the infrequency of performance appraisal sessions (Hall & Lawler, 1969), (2) the most accurate source of feedback given the problems of measuring the performance of others (Campbell, Dunnette, Lawler, & Weick, 1970); and (3) the most self-evaluation evoking and intrinsically motivating source of feedback given the controlling and informational aspects of feedback from others (DeCharms, 1968; Deci, 1972, 1975; Greller & Herold, 1975). For these reasons, the formal leader's function as a provider of role structure through performance feedback may be insignificant by comparison.

Cohesive, interdependent work groups and active advisory and staff personnel also have the ability to render the formal leader's performance feedback function inconsequential. Inherent in mature group structures are stable performance norms and positional differentiation (Bales & Strodtbeck, 1951; Borgatta & Bales, 1953; Stogdill, 1959; Lott & Lott, 1965; Zander, 1968). Task-relevant guidance and feedback from others may be provided directly by the formal leader, indirectly by the formal leader through the primary work group members, directly by the primary work group members, by staff personnel, or by the client. If the latter four instances prevail, the formal leader's role may be quite trivial. Cohesive work groups are, of course, important sources of affiliative need satisfaction.

Programming through impersonal modes has been reported to be the most frequent type of coordination strategy employed under conditions of low-to-medium task uncertainty and low task interdependence (Van de Ven, Delbecq, & Koenig, 1976). Thus, the existence of written work goals, guidelines, and groundrules (organizational formalization) and rigid rules and procedures (organizational inflexibility) may serve as substitutes for leader-provided coordination under certain conditions. Personal and group coordination modes involving the formal leader may become important only when less costly impersonal strategies are not suitable. . . .

Elaboration of the Construct

Table 1 was designed to capsulize our present knowledge with respect to possible substitutes for hierarchical leadership. Since present knowledge is the product of past research, and since past research was primarily unconcerned with the topic, the table is probably oversimplified and incomplete in a number of respects. Rigorous elaboration of the substitutes construct must necessarily await additional research, but we would speculate that such research would show the following refinements to be important.

Distinguishing between "substitutes" and "neutralizers." A "neutralizer" is defined by Webster's as something which is able to "paralyze, destroy, or counteract the effectiveness of" something else. In the context of leadership, this term may be applied to characteristics which make it effectively *impossible* for relationship and/or task-oriented leadership to make a difference. Neutralizers are a type of moderator variable when uncorrelated with both predictors and the criterion and act as suppressor variables when correlated with predictors but not the criterion (Zedeck, 1971; Wherry, 1946).

A "substitute" is defined to be "a person or thing acting or used in place of another." In context, this term may be used to describe characteristics which render relationship and/or task-oriented leadership not only impossible but also *unnecessary*.[6] Substitutes may be correlated with both predictors and the criterion, but tend to improve the validity coefficient when included in the predictor set. That is, they will not only tend to affect which leader behaviors (if any) are influential, but will also tend to impact upon the criterion variable.

The consequences of neutralizers and substitutes for previous research have probably been similar, since both act to reduce the impact of leader behaviors upon subordinate attitudes and performance. For this reason it is not too important that such summaries of previous research as Table 1 distinguish between them. Nevertheless, an important theoretical distinction does exist. It is that substitutes do, but neutralizers do not, provide a "person or thing acting or used in place of" the formal leader's negated influence. The effect of neutralizers is therefore to create an "influence vacuum" from which a variety of dysfunctions may emerge.

As an illustration of this point, look again at the characteristics outlined in Table 1. Since each characteristic has the capacity to counteract leader influence, all 14 may clearly be termed neutralizers. It is *not* clear, however, that all 14 are substitutes. For example, subordinates' perceived "ability, experience, training, and knowledge" tend to impair the leader's influence, but may or may not act as substitutes for leadership. It is known that individuals who are high in task-related self-esteem place high value upon nonhierarchical control systems which are consistent with a belief in the competence of people (Korman, 1970). The problem is that sub-

TABLE 2

Questionnaire Items for the Measurement of Substitutes for Leadership

(1) Ability, Experience, Training, and Knowledge
—Because of my ability, experience, training or job knowledge, I have the competence to act independently of my immediate superior in performing my day-to-day duties.
—Because of my ability, experience, training or job knowledge, I have the competence to act independently of my immediate superior in performing unusual and unexpected job duties.
—Due to my lack of experience and training, I must depend upon my immediate superior to provide me with necessary data, information, and advice. (R)

(2) Professional Orientation
—For feedback about how well I am performing, I rely on people in my occupational specialty, whether or not they are members of my work unit or organization.
—I receive very useful information and guidance from people who share my occupational specialty, but who are not members of my employing organization.
—My job satisfaction depends to a considerable extent on people in my occupational speciality who are not members of my employing organization.

(3) Indifference toward Organizational Rewards
—I cannot get enthusiastic about the rewards offered in this organization, or about the opportunities available.
—This organization offers attractive payoffs to people it values. (R)
—In general, most of the things I seek and value in this world cannot be obtained from my job or my employing organization.

(4) Unambiguous, Routine, and Methodologically Invariant Tasks
—Because of the nature of the tasks I perform on my job, there is little doubt about the best way to get the work done.
—Because of the nature of the work I do, I am often required to perform nonroutine tasks. (R)

—Because of the nature of my work, at the beginning of each work day, I can predict with near certainty exactly what activities I will be performing that day.
—There is really only one correct way to perform most of my tasks.
—My job duties are so simple that almost anyone could perform them after a little bit of instruction and practice.
—It is so hard to figure out the correct approach to most of my work problems that second-guessers would have a field day. (R)

(5) Task-Provided Feedback Concerning Accomplishment
—After I've done something on my job, I can tell right away from the results I get whether I've done it correctly.
—My job is the kind where you can make a mistake or an error and not be able to see that you've made it. (R)
—Because of the nature of the tasks I perform, it is easy for me to see when I've done something exceptionally well.

(6) Intrinsically Satisfying Tasks
—I get a great deal of personal satisfaction from the work I do.
—It is hard to imagine that anyone could enjoy performing the tasks that I perform on my job. (R)
—My job satisfaction depends to a considerable extent on the nature of the actual tasks I perform on the job.

(7) Organizational Formalization
—Clear, written goals and objectives exist for my job.
—My job responsibilities are clearly specified in writing.
—In this organization, performance appraisals are based on written standards.
—Written schedules, programs, and work specifications are available to guide me on my job.
—My duties, authority, and accountability are documented in policies, procedures, and job descriptions.
—Written rules and guidelines exist to direct work efforts.
—Written documents (such as budgets, schedules, and plans) are used as an essential part of my job.

---

ordinate perceptions concerning ability and knowledge may not be accurate. Actual ability and knowledge may therefore act as a substitute, while false perceptions of competence and unfounded self-esteem may produce simply a neutralizing effect.

"Spatial distance," "subordinate indifference toward organizational rewards," and "organizational rewards not within the leader's control" are other examples of characteristics which do not render formal leadership unnecessary, but merely create circumstances in which effective leadership may be impossible. If rewards are clearly within the control of some other person, this other person can probably act as a substitute for the formal leader, and no adverse consequences (except probably to the leader's morale) need result. When no one knows where control over rewards lies, however, or when rewards are linked rigidly to seniority or to other factors beyond anyone's control, or when rewards are perceived to be unattractive altogether, the resulting influence vacuum would almost inevitably be dysfunctional.

Distinguishing between Direct and Indirect Leader Behavior Effects.   It is possible to conceptualize a *direct effect* of leadership as one which occurs when a subordinate is influenced by some leader behavior *in and of itself.* An *indirect effect* may be said to result when the subordinate is influenced by the *implications* of the behavior for some future consequence. Attempts by the leader to influence subordinates must always produce direct and/or indirect effects or, when strong substitutes for leadership exist, no effect.

This distinction between direct and indirect effects of leader behavior has received very little attention, but its importance to any discussion of leadership substitutes is considerable. For example, in their review of Path-Goal theory, House and Dessler (1974, p. 31) state that "subordinates with high needs for affiliation and social approval would see friendly, considerate leader behavior as an immediate source of satisfaction" (direct effect). As Table 1 suggests, it is conceivable that fellow group members could supply such subordinates with enough affiliation and social approval to

T A B L E 2
(*Continued*)

—There are contradictions and inconsistencies among the written statements of goals and objectives. (R)
—There are contradictions and inconsistencies among the written guidelines and groundrules. (R)

(8) Organizational Inflexibility
—In this organization, the written rules are treated as a bible and are never violated.
—People in this organization consider the rulebooks and policy manuals as general guidelines, not as rigid and unbending. (R)
—In this organization, anytime there is a policy in writing that fits some situation, everybody has to follow that policy very strictly.

(9) Advisory and Staff Functions
—For feedback about how well I am performing, I rely on staff personnel inside the organization, based outside my work unit or department.
—In my job I must depend on staff personnel located outside of my work unit or department to provide me with data, reports, and informal advice necessary for my job performance.
—I receive very useful information and guidance from staff personnel who are based outside my work unit or department.

(10) Closely Knit, Cohesive, Interdependent Work Groups
—For feedback about how well I am performing, I rely on members of my work group other than my superior.
—The quantity of work I turn out depends largely on the performance of members of my work group other than my superior.
—The quality of work I turn out depends largely on the performance of members of my work group other than my superior.
—I receive very useful information and advice from members of my work group other than my superior.
—I am dependent on members of my work group other than my superior for important organizational rewards.

—My job satisfaction depends to a considerable extent on members of my work group other than my superior.

(11) Organizational Rewards Not within the Leader's Control
—On my job I must depend on my immediate superior to provide the necessary financial resources (such as budget and expense money). (R)
—On my job I must depend on my immediate superior to provide the necessary nonfinancial resources (such as file space and equipment). (R)
—My chances for a promotion depend on my immediate superior's recommendation. (R)
—My chances for a pay raise depend on my immediate superior's recommendation. (R)
—My immediate superior has little say or influence over which of his or her subordinates receives organizational rewards.
—The only performance feedback that matters to me is that given me by my immediate superior. (R)
—I am dependent on my immediate superior for important organizational rewards. (R)

(12) Spatial Distance between Superior and Subordinates
—The nature of my job is such that my immediate superior is seldom around me when I'm working.
—On my job my most important tasks take place away from where my immediate superior is located.
—My immediate superior and I are seldom in actual contact or direct sight of one another.

(13) Subordinate Need for Independence
—I like it when the person in charge of a group I am in tells me what to do. (R)
—When I have a problem, I like to think it through myself without help from others.
—It is important for me to be able to feel that I can run my life without depending on people older and more experienced than myself.

---

eliminate dependence on the leader. With other subordinates, however, the key "may be not so much in terms of what the leader does but may be in terms of how it is *interpreted* by his members" (Graen *et al.*, 1972, p. 235). Graen *et al.* concluded from their data that "consideration is interpreted as the leader's evaluation of the member's role behavior . . ." (p. 233). For these subordinates, therefore, consideration seems to have been influential primarily because of its perceived implications for the likelihood of receiving future rewards. In this case the effect is an indirect one, for which group member approval and affiliation probably cannot substitute.

In the same vein, we are told by House and Dessler (1974, pp. 31–32) that:

Subordinates with high needs for achievement would be predicted to view leader behavior that clarifies path-goal relationships and provides goal oriented feedback as satisfying. Subordinates with high needs for extrin-

---

sic rewards would be predicted to see leader directiveness or coaching behavior as instrumental to their satisfaction if such behavior helped them perform in such a manner as to gain recognition, promotion, security, or pay increases.

It is apparent from House and Dessler's remarks that the distinction between direct and indirect effects need not be limited to relationship-oriented behaviors. Such characteristics of the task as the fact that it "provides its own feedback" (listed in Table 1 as a potential substitute for task-oriented behavior) may provide achievement-oriented subordinates with immediate satisfaction (direct effect), but fail to negate the superior's ability to help subordinates perform so as to obtain future rewards (indirect effect). Conversely, subordinate experience and training may act as substitutes for the indirect effects of task-oriented leadership by preventing the leader from improving subordinate performance, but may not offset the direct effects.

T A B L E   8
Substitutes for Leadership: A Theoretical Extension

Characteristic	Will Act as a Substitute for					
	Relationship-Oriented Supportive, People-Centered Leadership (Consideration, Support, and Interaction Facilitation):		Task-Oriented, Instrumental, Job-Centered Leadership (Initiating Structure, Goal Emphasis, and Work Facilitation):		(Other Leader Behaviors . . .)	
	Directly	Indirectly	Directly	Indirectly	Directly	Indirectly
Substitutes						
of the subordinate						
1. ability				X	?	?
3. "professional" orientation	X	X	X	X	?	?
of the task						
5. unambiguous and routine			X	X	?	?
7. provides its own feedback concerning accomplishment			X		?	?
8. intrinsically satisfying	X				?	?
of the organization						
12. closely-knit, cohesive work groups	X		X	X	?	?
Neutralizers						
4. indifference toward organizational rewards		X		X	?	?
13. organizational rewards not within the leader's control		X		X	?	?
⋮						

Identifying Other Characteristics and Other Leader Behaviors. Any elaboration of the substitutes construct must necessarily include the specification of other leader behaviors, and other characteristics which may act as substitutes for leader behaviors. As was mentioned earlier, most previous studies of leadership were concerned with only two of its dimensions. This approach is intuitively indefensible. Richer conceptualizations of the leadership process already exist and almost inevitably underscore the importance of additional leader activities. As these activities are delineated in future research, it is likely that substitutes for them will also be identified.

Table 8 is offered as a guide to research. It portrays a state of increased sophistication of the substitutes construct, assuming future development along lines suggested in this section. Substitutes would be differentiated from neutralizers, and direct effects of leadership empirically distinguished from indirect effects. The columns on the right are intended to represent as-yet-unexplored leader behaviors, and the dotted lines on the bottom indicate the presence of additional characteristics which may act either as neutralizers or as true substitutes for leadership.

Distinguishing between Cause and Effect in Leader Behavior. Another area where the substitutes construct appears to have implications for leadership research concerns the question of causality. It is now evident from a variety of laboratory experiments and longitudinal field studies that leader behavior may result from as well as cause subordinate attitudes and performance. It is possible to speculate upon the effect that leadership substitutes would have on the relative causal strength of superior- and subordinate-related variables. This paper has tried to show that such substitutes act to reduce changes in subordinates' attitudes and performance which are *caused* by leader behaviors. On the other hand, there seems no reason why leadership substitutes should prevent changes in leader behavior which *result* from different levels of subordinate performance, satisfaction, and morale. The substitutes for leadership construct may therefore help to explain why the direction of causality is sometimes predominantly from leader behavior to subordinate outcomes, while at other times the reverse is true.

Specification of Interaction Effects among Substitutes and Neutralizers. From the limited data obtained thus far, it is not possible to differentiate at all among leadership substitutes and neutralizers in terms of relative strength and predictive capability. We have received some indication that the strength of a substitute, as measured by its mean level, is not strongly related to its predictive power. Substitutes for leadership as theoretically important as intrinsic satisfaction, for example, apparently need only be present in moderate amounts (as is the case with the City Police; see Table 6) to have potent substituting effects (see Table 7). Other, less important substitutes and neutralizers might have to be present to a tremendous degree before their effects might be felt. Clearly, the data reported in this study are insufficient to determine at what point a particular substitute becomes important, or at what point several substitutes, each fairly weak by itself, might combine to collectively impair hierarchical leader influence. Multiplicative functions involving information on the strength and predictive power of substitutes for leadership should be able to be specified as evidence accumulates.

Conclusions

The research literature provides abundant evidence that for organization members to maximize organizational and personal outcomes, they must be able to obtain both guidance and good feelings from their work settings. Guidance is usually offered in the form of role or task structuring, while good feelings may stem from "stroking" behaviors,[7] or may be derived from intrinsic satisfaction associated with the task itself.

The research literature does *not* suggest that guidance and good feelings must be provided by the hierarchical superior; it is only necessary that they somehow be provided. Certainly the formal leader represents a potential source of structuring and stroking behaviors, but many other organization members do too, and impersonal equivalents also exist. To the extent that other potential sources are deficient, the hierarchical superior is clearly in a position to play a dominant role. In these situations the opportunity for leader downward influence is great, and formal leadership ought to be important. To the extent that other sources provide structure and stroking in abundance, the hierarchical leader will have little chance to exert downward influence. In such cases it is of small value to gain entree to the organization, distribute leader behavior questionnaires to anything that moves, and later debate about which leadership theory best accounts for the pitifully small percentage of variance explained, while remaining uncurious about the large percentage unexplained.

Of course, few organizations would be expected to have leadership substitutes so strong as to totally overwhelm the leader, or so weak as to require subordinates to rely entirely on him. In most organizations it is likely that, as was true here, substitutes exist for some leader activities but not for others. Effective leadership might therefore be described as the ability to supply subordinates with needed guidance and good feelings which are not being supplied by other sources.

From this viewpoint it is inaccurate to inform leaders (say, in management development programs) that they are incompetent if they do not personally provide these things regardless of the situation. While it may (or may not) be necessary that the organization as a whole function in a "9–9" manner (Blake & Mouton, 1964), it clearly is unnecessary for the manager to behave in such a manner unless no substitutes for leader-provided guidance and good feelings exist.

Dubin (1976, p. 33) draws a nice distinction between "proving" and "improving" a theory and points out that "if the purpose is to prove the adequacy of the theoretical model . . . data are likely to be collected for values on only those units incorporated in the theoretical model. This usually means that, either experimentally or by discarding data, attention in the empirical research is focused solely upon values measured on units incorporated in the theory."

In Dubin's terms, if we are really interested in improving rather than proving our various theories and models of leadership, a logical first step is that we stop assuming what really needs to be demonstrated empirically. The criticality of the leader's role in supplying necessary structure and stroking should be evaluated in the broader organizational context. Data pertaining to both leadership and possible substitutes for leadership (Table 1) should be obtained, and both main and interaction effects examined. A somewhat different use of information about substitutes for leadership would be a "prescreen," to assess the appropriateness of a potential sample for a hierarchical leadership study.

What this all adds up to is that, if we really want to know more about the sources and consequences of guidance and good feelings in organizations, we should be prepared to study these things *whether or not* they happen to be provided through hierarchical leadership. For those not so catholic, whose interest lies in the derivation and refinement of theories of formal leadership, a commitment should be made to the importance of developing and operationalizing a *true* situational theory of leadership, one which will explicitly limit its propositions and restrict its predictions *to those situations* where hierarchical leadership theoretically ought to make a difference.

Notes

[1] Abraham Kaplan (1964, p. 28) has observed: "Give a small boy a hammer, and he will find that everything he encounters needs pounding."

[6] This potentially important distinction was first pointed out by M. A. Von Glinow in a doctoral seminar.

[7] "Stroking" is used here, as in transactional analysis, to describe "any type of physical, oral, or visual recognition of one person by another" (Huse, 1975, p. 288).

References

Bales, R., & Strodtbeck, F. Phases in group problem solving. *Journal of Abnormal and Social Psychology,* 1951, **46,** 485–495.

Bass, B., & Valenzi, E. Contingent aspects of effective management styles. In J. G. Hunt & L. L. Larson (Eds.), *Contingency approaches to leadership.* Carbondale: Southern Illinois Press, 1974.

Blake, R., & Mouton, J. *The managerial grid.* Houston: Gulf, 1964.

Bordua, D., & Reiss, A. Command, control, and charisma: Reflections on police bureaucracy. *American Journal of Sociology,* 1966, **72,** 68–76.

Borgatta, E., & Bales, R. Task and accumulation of experience as factors in the interaction of small groups. *Sociometry,* 1953, **16,** 239–252.

Campbell, J., Dunnette, E., Lawler, E., & Weick, K. *Managerial behavior, performance and effectiveness.* New York: McGraw-Hill, 1970.

Dansereau, F., Cashman, J., & Graen, G. Instrumentality theory and equity theory as complementary approaches in predicting the relationship of leadership and turnover among managers. *Organizational Behavior and Human Performance,* 1973, **10,** 184–200.

DeCharms, R. *Personal causation.* New York: Academic Press, 1968.

Deci, E. Intrinsic motivation, extrinsic reinforcement, and inequity. *Journal of Personality and Social Psychology,* 1972, **22,** 113–120.

Deci, E. *Intrinsic motivation.* New York: Plenum, 1975.

Dubin, R. Theory building in applied areas. In M. Dunnette (Ed.), *Handbook of industrial and organizational psychology.* Chicago: Rand-McNally, 1976.

Fiedler, F. E. A contingency model of leadership effectiveness. In L. Berkowitz (Ed.), *Advances in experimental social psychology.* New York: Academic Press, 1964.

Fiedler, F. E. *A theory of leadership effectiveness.* New York: McGraw-Hill, 1967.

Fiedler, F. E., & Chemers, M. M. *Leadership and effective management.* Glenview, IL: Scott, Foresman, 1974.

Filley, A. C., House, R. J., & Kerr, S. *Managerial process and organizational behavior* (2nd ed.). Glenview, IL: Scott, Foresman, 1976.

Graen, G., Dansereau, F., Jr., & Minami, T. Dysfunctional leadership styles. *Organizational Behavior and Human Performance,* 1972, **7,** 216–236.

Greller, M., & Herold, D. Sources of feedback: A preliminary investigation. *Organizational Behavior and Human Performance,* 1975, **13,** 244–256.

Hackman, R., & Oldham, G. Motivation through the design of work: Test of a theory. *Organizational Behavior and Human Performance,* 1976, **16,** 250–279.

Hall, D., & Lawler, E. Unused potential in R and D labs. *Research Management,* 1969, **12,** 339–354.

Heller, F. A., & Yukl, G. Participation, managerial decision-making, and situational variables. *Organizational Behavior and Human Performance,* 1969, **4,** 227–234.

House, R. J. A path-goal theory of leader effectiveness. *Administrative Science Quarterly,* 1971, **16,** 321–338.

House, R. J., & Dessler, G. The path-goal theory of leadership: Some post hoc and a priori tests. In J. G. Hunt & L. L. Larson (Eds.), *Contingency approaches to leadership.* Carbondale: Southern Illinois University Press, 1974.

House, R. J., Filley, A. C., & Kerr, S. Relation of leader consideration and initiating structure to R and D subordinates' satisfaction. *Administrative Science Quarterly,* 1971, **16,** 19–30.

House, R. J., & Mitchell, T. R. Path-goal theory of leadership. *Journal of Contemporary Business,* 1974, **3,** 81–97.

House, R. J., & Rizzo, J. R. Toward the measurement of organizational practices: Scale development and validation. *Journal of Applied Psychology,* 1972, **56,** 288–296.

Hunt, J. G., & Osborn, R. N. An adaptive-reactive theory of leadership: The role of macro variables in leadership research. In J. G. Hunt & L. L. Larson (Eds.), *Leadership frontiers.* Carbondale: Southern Illinois University Press, 1975.

Huse, E. F. *Organization development and change.* St. Paul: West, 1975.

Kaplan, Abraham. *The conduct of inquiry.* San Francisco: Chandler, 1964.

Kerr, S., Schriesheim, C., Murphy, C. J., & Stogdill, R. M. Toward a contingency theory of leadership based upon the consideration and initiating structure literature. *Organizational Behavior and Human Performance,* 1974, **12,** 62–82.

Korman, A. Toward a hypothesis of work behavior. *Journal of Applied Psychology,* 1970, **54,** 31–41.

Lott, A., & Lott, B. Group cohesiveness as interpersonal attraction: A review of relationships with antecedent and consequent variables. *Psychological Bulletin,* 1965, **64,** 259–302.

McNamara, J. Uncertainties in police work: The relevance of police recruits' backgrounds and training. In D. Bordua (Ed.), *The police: Six sociological essays.* New York: Wiley, 1967.

Miner, J. The uncertain future of the leadership concept: An overview. In J. G. Hunt & L. L. Larson (Eds.), *Leadership frontiers.* Carbondale: Southern Illinois Press, 1975.

Oldham, G. Job characteristics and internal motivation: The moderating effect of interpersonal and individual variables. *Human Relations,* 1976, **29,** 559–570.

Ouchi, W. The relationship between organizational structure and organizational control. *Administrative Science Quarterly,* 1977, **22,** 95–113.

Porter, L., Steers, R., Mowday, R., & Boulian, P. Organizational commitment, job satisfaction, and turnover among psychiatric technicians. *Journal of Applied Psychology,* 1974, **59,** 603–609.

Rizzo, J. R., House, R. J., & Lirtzman, S. I. Role conflict and ambiguity in complex organizations. *Administrative Science Quarterly,* 1970, **15,** 150–163.

Schuler, R., Aldag, R., & Brief, A. Role conflict and ambiguity: A scale analysis. *Organizational Behavior and Human Performance,* 1977, **20,** 111–128.

Stogdill, R. *Individual behavior and group achievement.* New York: Oxford University Press, 1959.

Tannenbaum, R., & Schmidt, W. How to choose a leadership pattern. *Harvard Business Review,* 1958, **36,** 95–101.

Van de Ven, A., Delbecq, A., & Koenig, R. Determinants of coordination modes within organizations. *American Sociological Review,* 1976, **41,** 322–338.

Vroom, V., & Yetton, P. *Leadership and decision making.* Pittsburgh: University of Pittsburgh Press, 1973.

Wherry, R. Test selection and suppressor variables. *Psychometrika,* 1946, **11,** 239–247.

Wilson, O., & McLaren, R. *Police administration* (3rd ed.). New York: McGraw-Hill, 1972.

Woodward, J. Technology, material control, and organizational behavior. In A. Negandhi (Ed.), *Modern organization theory.* Kent: Kent State University, 1973.

Zander, A. Group aspirations. In D. Cartwright & A. Zander (Eds.), *Group dynamics: Research and theory* (3rd ed.). New York: Harper & Row, 1968.

Zedeck, S. Problems with the use of "moderator" variables. *Psychological Bulletin,* 1971, **76,** 295–310.

Reference Notes

[1] Bish, J., & Schriesheim, C. *An exploratory analysis of Form XII of The Ohio State Leadership Scales.* Paper presented at the National Academy of Management Conference, 1974.

[2] Hunt, J. *Different nonleader clarity sources as alternatives to leadership.* Paper presented at the Eastern Academy of Management Conference, 1975.

[3] Schriesheim, C. *The development and validation of instrumental and supportive leadership scales and their application to some tests of path-goal theory of leadership hypotheses.* Unpublished doctoral dissertation, The Ohio State University, 1978.

[4] Wigdor, L. *Effectiveness of various management and organizational characteristics on employee satisfaction and performance as a function of the employee's need for job independence.* Unpublished doctoral dissertation, City University of New York, 1969.

Substitutes for Leadership
Effective Alternatives to Ineffective Leadership

J. P. Howell
New Mexico State University

D. E. Bowen
University of Southern California

P. W. Dorfman
New Mexico State University

S. Kerr
University of Southern California

P. M. Podsakoff
Indiana University

Leadership has been recognized through the ages as a primary means of influencing the behavior of others. Research into the keys to effective and ineffective leadership has also been going on for quite some time. The earliest assumption was that effective leaders possessed particular traits that distinguished them from ineffective leaders. Effective leaders were thought to be dynamic, intelligent, dependable, high-achieving individuals—so, since traits are hard to change, problems caused by poor leadership were considered best solved by *replacing the leader* with someone who possessed more of the key traits. Regrettably, researchers were unable to identify leader traits that systematically improved organizational effectiveness. Yet leader replacement continues to be a very popular tool in the executive toolkit.

Partly in response to the limitations of trait theory, research in the late 1940s began to focus on relationships between leader behaviors and employee performance, in search of behaviors exhibited by effective leaders that were not displayed by those less effective. With this approach, effective leaders need not possess magical traits but, instead, provide strong direction and support while encouraging subordinates to participate in important decisions. This emphasis on leader behaviors still permitted replacement of a weak leader but allowed an additional remedy as well: namely, *changing the leader's behavior* through some form of training. Probably the most disappointing aspect of research on leader behaviors is that no strong, consistent relationships between particular leader behaviors and organizational effectiveness have ever been found. This has not prevented many off-the-shelf training programs from becoming popular, however, nor the marketers of such programs from becoming prosperous.

Situational Theories

By the late 1950s it became evident that an approach was needed that didn't depend on ideal traits and universal behaviors. One answer was "situational theory," which starts with the assumption that there are no traits, and no behaviors, that automatically constitute effective leadership. The key is the fit between a leader's style and the situation the leader faces; thus the leader who is highly effective in one situation may be totally ineffective in another. For instance, although General George Patton led the 3rd Army to outstanding performance in World War II, one could hardly imagine the effective use of his leadership style in Mahatma Gandhi's situation against the British in India.

According to situational theories, effective leaders must correctly identify the behaviors each situation requires and then be flexible enough to exhibit these behaviors. Leaders who are behaviorally inflexible, or who lack the necessary diagnostic skills, must be either trained or replaced—the same remedies identified by researchers of leader traits and behaviors. An alternative is to let the leader alone but *change the situation so that the fit is improved.*

Various situational leadership theories have spawned a large number of intervention strategies, many of them competent and some of them useful. However, an assumption underlies all these theories that is wholly unsupported by the research literature. This assumption is that, though different situations require different leadership styles, in *every* situation there is *some* leadership style that will be effective. It has been shown in numerous studies, however, that circumstances often counteract the potential power of leadership, making it virtually impossible in some situations for leaders to have much impact regardless of their style or how good the fit is between leader and situation.

Source: Edited and reprinted by permission of publisher *Organizational Dynamics* 19, 1. Copyright 1990. American Management Association, New York. All rights reserved. Author affiliation may have changed since article was first published.

Substitutes for Leadership

Fortunately, additional remedies for problems stemming from weak leadership—remedies not articulated in any of the earlier trait, behavioral, or situational approaches—have been identified. Such remedies derive from acceptance of the conclusion, based on the research studies referenced earlier, that many organizations contain "substitutes for leadership"—attributes of subordinates, tasks, and organizations that provide task guidance and incentives to perform to such a degree that they virtually negate the leader's ability to either improve or impair subordinate performance. To the extent that powerful leadership substitutes exist, formal leadership, however displayed, tends to be unproductive and can even be counterproductive. In comparison with situational leadership approaches, research on leadership substitutes focuses on whether subordinates are receiving needed task guidance and incentives to perform without taking it for granted that the formal leader is the primary supplier.

Closely Knit Teams of Highly Trained Individuals

Consider the positive impact of substitutes in the following example. Todd LaPorte, Gene Rochlin, and Karlene Roberts are three researchers studying such highly stressful organizational situations as those involving pilots who land jet fighters on a nuclear carrier and air-traffic controllers who direct traffic into San Francisco. They have found that directive leadership is relatively unimportant compared with the work experience and training of individuals in closely knit work groups. This is particularly evident ". . . in the white heat of danger, when the whole system threatens to collapse. . . . The stress creates a need for competence among colleagues who by necessity develop close working relationships with each other." All such individuals are trained extensively and daily, regardless of their position in the hierarchy, to redirect operations or bring them to an abrupt halt. This can involve ignoring orders from managers who are removed from the front line of action. Here the experience and continuous training of individuals, along with the close relationships among members of a work force, substitute for the manager's directive leadership.

By creating alternate sources of task guidance and incentives to perform, substitutes for leadership may have a temporary negative effect on morale among leaders who perceive a loss of power. However, leadership substitutes can also serve as important remedies where there are organizational problems, particularly in situations where the leader is not the source of the problems or where, if the leader is the source, replacement, training, and improving the leader-situation fit are overly expensive, politically infeasible, or too time-consuming to be considered.

A principal advantage of the substitutes construct is that it identifies a remedy for problems stemming from weak leadership in addition to replacement, training, or situational engineering. The remedy is to intentionally, systematically *create substitutes for hierarchical leadership*. In fact, whereas weak, power-hungry leaders invariably regard substitutes as frustrating and necessarily dysfunctional (when they are aware of them at all), strong leaders understand and are comfortable with the idea that effective results can be achieved when task guidance and incentives to perform emanate from sources other than themselves. When other sources are deficient, the hierarchical superior is in a position to play a dominant role; when strong incentives and guidance derive from other sources, the hierarchical superior has less opportunity, but also less need, to exert his or her influence.

Intrinsic Satisfaction

The degree of intrinsic satisfaction that employees derive from their work task is a strong leadership substitute in a large manufacturer of camping equipment in the western United States. The company produces sleeping bags that range from top-of-the-line light-weight backpackers to low-cost models filled with floor sweepings from a mattress factory. Manufacturing personnel are required to rotate among all the lines, so no one group gains a territorial claim to a particular product. Management reports that for workers on the top-quality down-filled bags, supervisory direction has become relatively unnecessary, yet output and quality typically exceed management expectations. Workers report pride in working on this line and usually solve production problems themselves or with co-workers.

The production of bottom-line bags is very different. Quality problems are commonplace, workers cooperate less to overcome the problems, and workers seem to care little about meeting output or quality standards. The constant supervision required to address these problems raises indirect costs. Consultants observing the various production lines during a typical day report that supervisors slowly gravitate away from high-quality lines toward the lowest-quality lines. Thus the workers' intrinsic satisfaction from producing a high-quality product alleviates the need for most supervisory leadership.

Computer Technology

Edward E. Lawler III has noticed that companies with computer-integrated manufacturing and networked computer systems rely on computers to take over many of the supervisor's leadership functions. Feedback is provided by computerized productivity and quality data; directions for certain tasks are entered into the information system; even error detection and goal setting are incorporated in some interactive systems. When individual workers have access to operating data and to a network that allows them to ask employees at other locations to help solve problems, they become more independent of their managers and arrive at solutions among themselves. Spans of control greater than 100 are not unheard of in these organizations. Computerized information technology is therefore providing a substitute for certain types of managerial leadership.

Effective leadership, then, depends upon a leader's ability to supply subordinates with task guidance and incentives to perform to the extent that these are not provided by other sources. The inverse of this assertion is equally valid. Leadership substitutes can contribute to organizational effectiveness by supplying subordinates with task guidance and incentives to perform that are not being provided by the hierarchical superior. From this perspective it makes sense for a leader or someone above the leader to create substitutes when, for example, the leader must be frequently absent, has a large span of control, or is saddled with time-consuming nonmanagerial duties. Substitutes are also useful when a leader departs before a successor has been identified or there is a need to manage employees who are geographically dispersed or who, as in the following example, are culturally resistant to hierarchical supervision.

Extensive Professional Education

Professional employees may come to their firms with so much formal education that they can perform most work assignments without relying upon technical guidance from their hierarchical superior. Their education also often includes a strong socialization component, instilling in them a desire for autonomous, self-controlling behavior. The result may be that they neither need nor will readily accept a leader's direction. In such instances, professional education and socialization can serve as substitutes for formal leadership. A 1981 study by Jeffrey Ford found that extensive subordinate education acted as a substitute for directive and supportive leadership in a book publishing firm, a branch bank, and a midwestern university.

Using Leadership Substitutes to Solve Organizational Problems

The notion that professional education and socialization can substitute for traditional formal leadership identifies an important potential problem, but it can be turned to advantage if a leader is sensitive to the situation and builds collegial systems of task-related guidance and interpersonal support. This approach can be found in most well-run hospitals and universities, where deliberately designed substitutes for leadership abound.

Thus charges of medical malfeasance are often investigated by peer review teams, and university promotion and tenure decisions depend greatly on assessments by faculty colleagues who lack formal authority. Indeed, many a dean has learned that the same criticism that would be bitterly denied if it came from him or her is grudgingly accepted if the source is a peer-review committee. The trick is to develop norms and structures that consistently produce feedback when feedback is needed, rather than merely an occasional spontaneous outburst when circumstances become intolerable.

Team Approaches

Tracy Kidder's *The Soul of a New Machine* provides an excellent account of how a key manager at Data General utilized subordinates' professional norms and standards as a substitute for leadership to produce a faster computer than the competition's. The company at that time was competitive, highly political, and resource-poor, but the computer-design engineers were young, creative, well trained, and highly motivated. Recognizing the futility of relying on directive leadership and meager financial rewards, the leader obtained work space that encouraged considerable interaction among team members and discouraged interaction outside the team.

He articulated key parameters and project deadlines, stayed out of members' personal disputes, obtained resources for the team, and buffered them from organization politics. Reflecting the attitude of team members, Kidder observes, "They were building the machine all by themselves, without any significant help from their leader."

Task guidance and incentives to perform may derive from a number of sources other than the leader, including organized staff groups, internal and external consultants, and competent peers at all organizational levels. In the Columbus, Ohio, Police Department, the creation of two-person patrol units and field-training officer positions effectively substituted for the guidance and support traditionally provided by hierarchical leaders, thus making time available for them to attend to other tasks. Where one-person patrols without field-training officers were utilized, leader guidance and support continued to be essential. (An ancillary benefit of substituting peer for hierarchical sources of task guidance is that it is often easier for subordinates to admit inadequacies to and request assistance from their co-workers than from their boss.)

High-Ability Independent Workers

Even when subordinates haven't much formal education, ability combined with experience can serve as a substitute for hierarchical leadership. Cummins Engine Company, General Motors Corporation, and Procter and Gamble all have reduced supervisory personnel and managerial overhead by selecting and developing high-ability, independent workers who require little or no supervision. Paul Reeves, a key production foreman for Harmon Auto Parts, taught workers to take over his job by helping them increase their ability and experience so that their responsibilities could also be increased. Each worker voluntarily spent half-days with him—asking questions, discussing his responses and, eventually, helping him perform his duties. When Reeves was promoted, the group continued to operate effectively without a foreman.

In Place of Hierarchical Feedback

Among the most important elements of task guidance is performance feedback. In the absence of feedback, ability to perform cannot be improved and motivation to perform cannot be sustained. Most organizations assign responsibility for feedback to the hierarchical superior, even in cases where the superior works at a physical distance from employees or doesn't know enough about their technical specialties to give them credible feedback.

However, many organizations have come to the realization that feedback from clients and peers, and feedback provided by the task itself, can serve as powerful substitutes for hierarchical feedback. Charles Manz and Hank Sims, two organizational researchers, described the operation of one such feedback system in a nonunion small-parts manufacturing plant. A subsidiary of a large U.S. corporation, the plant was organized around the concept of self-managed work teams from its inception in the early 1970s.

Each team of eight to twelve members is assigned a set of closely related production tasks, and the teams are buffered

EXHIBIT 1

Eleven Managerial Leadership Problems and Effective Coping Strategies*

Leadership Problems	Enhancer/Neutralizer	Substitutes
Leader doesn't keep on top of details in the department; coordination among subordinates is difficult.	Not useful.	Develop self-managed work teams; encourage team members to interact within and across departments.
Competent leadership is resisted through noncompliance or passive resistance.	*Enhancers:* Increase employees' dependence on leader through greater leader control of rewards/resources; increase their perception of leader's influence outside of work group.	Develop collegial systems of guidance for decision making.
Leader doesn't provide support or recognition for jobs well done.	Not useful.	Develop a reward system that operates independently of the leader. Enrich jobs to make them inherently satisfying.
Leader doesn't set targets or goals, or clarify roles for employees.	Not useful.	Emphasize experience and ability in selecting subordinates. Establish group goal-setting. Develop an organizational culture that stresses high performance expectations.
A leader behaves inconsistently over time.	*Enhancers:* These are dysfunctional. *Neutralizer:* Remove rewards from leader's control.	Develop group goal-setting and group rewards.
An upper-level manager regularly bypasses a leader in dealing with employees, or countermands the leader's directions.	*Enhancers:* Increase leader's control over rewards and resources: build leader's image via in-house champion or visible "important" responsibilities. *Neutralizer:* Physically distance subordinates from upper-level manager.	Increase the professionalization of employees.
A unit is in disarray or out of control.	Not useful.	Develop highly formalized plans, goals, routines, and areas of responsibility.
Leadership is brutal, autocratic.	*Enhancers:* These are dysfunctional. *Neutralizers:* Physically distance subordinates; remove rewards from leader's control.	Establish group goal-setting and peer performance appraisal.
There is inconsistency across different organizational units.	Not useful.	Increase formalization. Set up a behaviorally focused reward system.
Leadership is unstable over time; leaders are rotated and/or leave office frequently.	Not useful.	Establish competent advisory staff units. Increase professionalism of employees.
Incumbent management is poor; there's no heir apparent.	*Enhancers:* These are dysfunctional. *Neutralizer:* Assign nonleader duties to problem managers.	Emphasize experience and ability in selecting employees. Give employees more training.

*The suggested solutions are examples of many possibilities for each problem.

from each other by physical space and stores of in-process inventory. Each team prepares its own budgets, makes within-team job assignments, keeps track of quality control statistics and hours worked, and handles member absenteeism and discipline problems. Team members are trained in conducting meetings and in group problem solving. A hierarchical leader is responsible for each team, but this person is not supposed to supply either task guidance or interpersonal support, aside from encouraging self-observation, self-evaluation, and self-reinforcement. Manz and Sims found, in fact, that the most effective teams were those whose leaders

did refrain from providing guidance and support. Leaders of effective teams spent much of their time representing the team to higher management, obtaining resources for the team, training new members, and coaching team members with respect to peer feedback and peer evaluation.

Substitutes by Procedure

The detailed work rules, guidelines, policies, and procedures existing in many organizations also serve to some extent as substitutes for hierarchical leadership by providing impor-

EXHIBIT 2
Creative Strategies for Improving Leadership Effectiveness

Creating Substitutes for Leader Directiveness and Supportiveness	Creating Enhancers for Leader Directiveness and Supportiveness
Develop colleagial systems of guidance: · Peer appraisals to increase acceptability of feedback by subordinates. · Quality circles to increase workers' control over production quality. · Peer support networks; mentor systems.	Increase subordinates' perceptions of leader's influence/expertise: · Provide a visible champion of leader. · Give leader important organizational responsibilities. · Build leader's image through in-house publications and other means.
Improve performance-oriented organizational formalization: · Automatic organization reward system (such as commissions or gainsharing). · Group management-by-objectives (MBO) program. · Company mission statements and codes of conduct (as at Johnson & Johnson).	Build organizational climate: · Reward small wins to increase subordinates' confidence. · Emphasize ceremony and myth to encourage team spirit. · Develop superordinate goals to encourage cohesiveness and high performance norms.
Increase administrative staff availability: · Specialized training personnel. · Troubleshooters for human relations problems. · Technical advisors to assist production operators.	Increase subordinates' dependence on leader: · Create crises requiring immediate action. · Increase leader centrality in providing information. · Eliminate one-over-one approvals.
Increase professionalism of subordinates: · Staffing based on employee professionalism. · Development plans to increase employees' abilities and experience. · Encourage active participation in professional associations.	Increase leader's position power: · Change title to increase status. · Increase reward power. · Increase resource base.
Redesign jobs to increase: · Performance feedback from the task. · Ideological importance of jobs.	Create cohesive work groups with high performance norms: · Provide physical setting conducive to teamwork. · Encourage subordinates' participation in group problem solving. · Increase group's status. · Create intergroup competition.
Start team-building activities to develop group self-management skills such as: · Solving work-related problems on their own. · Resolving interpersonal conflicts among members. · Providing interpersonal support to members.	

tant nonleader sources of task guidance. Researchers Jon Howell and Peter Dorfman found this to be the case in a medium-size hospital, as did Robert Miles and M. M. Petty in county-level social service agencies. This type of leadership substitute can be particularly useful in situations where consistent behavior is imperative. For example, units of a firm increase the firm's legal exposure by acting inconsistently with respect to hiring, firing, leaves of absence, promotions, or other human resources actions. In other instances, such as pricing or purchasing activities, variation may be legal but cost-ineffective. It is quite common in these cases for organizations to install procedures, rules, and guidelines to replace or forestall managerial discretion.

Leadership Neutralizers

Thus far we have discussed only leadership substitutes, whose effect is to make it both less possible and less necessary for leaders to influence subordinate satisfaction and per-

formance, replacing the leader's impact with impact of their own. Leadership "neutralizers" are attributes of subordinates, tasks, and organizations that also interfere with a leader's attempts to influence subordinates. Unlike leadership substitutes, however, neutralizers do not replace the leader's impact over subordinates, but rather create an "influence vacuum" that can have serious negative consequences.

Physical Distances

For example, when subordinates work at a physical distance from their leader, many recommended leadership practices have limited usefulness or are nearly impossible to perform. A case in point is found at Kinko's, which provides professional copying services at widely dispersed locations nationwide. Regional managers at Kinko's are continually frustrated by not being able to provide enough direction, guidance, and personal support for the new store managers because physical distances are too great for much personal

E X H I B I T   3
A Decision Tree for Overcoming Ineffective Managerial Leadership

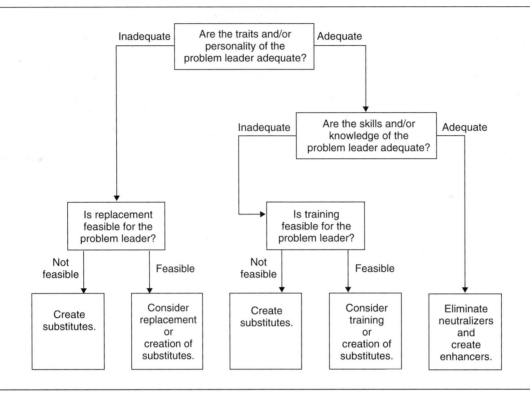

interaction. In other organizations, subordinates and leaders may not share a common time zone; indeed, they may scarcely share the same work day.

Spatial distance will be increasingly important as a potential leadership neutralizer in the future because, as the number of firms with international operations continues to rise, managers will increasingly be required to supervise subordinates across great distances. Furthermore, the growing importance of the U.S. service sector means that more and more employees will be working at home or at their client's work site.

Reward Systems

Organizational reward systems can also be important neutralizers of the hierarchical leadership's effects. Rewards may be awarded strictly according to seniority, for example, or attractive rewards may be unavailable to subordinates. Leaders tend to have little influence on corporate "rebels" because, in part, the rebels are not attracted to the typical rewards available in corporate bureaucracies. Union contracts also may mandate that all employees within a given job classification be paid the same wage rate, and civil service policies may require that promotions be based on objective examinations. In other cases, rewards may be controlled by higher management in ways that prevent the immediate supervisor from exerting influence. This occurs, for example, in firms requiring numerous one-over-one approvals before a salary recommendation takes effect. Other firms permit leaders to influ-

ence the amount of rewards, but their timing is wholly constrained by fiscal periods or employee anniversary dates.

Bypassing Management Structure

A very different type of neutralization occurs when someone at a higher level repeatedly bypasses a level of management to deal directly with that manager's subordinates. Another neutralizer is the continual countermanding by higher management of a leader's orders and instructions. These neutralizers often occur in instances where an organization's founder has finally, reluctantly, hired a subordinate manager to oversee operations and where a union's potential for mischief is so feared that supervisory efforts aimed at maintaining discipline are routinely reversed at higher levels.

Although normally dysfunctional, leadership neutralizers can occasionally be used to advantage. One such occasion occurred in a petrochemical processing firm where, because of his technical expertise and involvement in several critical projects, an interpersonally incompetent director of design engineering could not be replaced. As an interim solution until he could be phased out, his day-to-day contact with employees was sharply curtailed, he was given numerous technical (nonleader) assignments, and his influence over salary and personnel decisions was considerably reduced. In this instance the "influence vacuum" caused by creating leadership neutralizers was deemed preferable to the state of leadership that previously existed.

Leadership Enhancers

Leader "enhancers" are attributes of employees, tasks, and organizations that amplify a leader's impact on the employees. For example, cohesive work groups with strong norms in support of cooperation with management can crystallize ambiguous goals and role definitions, augment overly subtle leader-provided feedback, and otherwise increase the power of weak, inconsistent leaders—for better or for worse. A study of four large hospitals found that development of a culture with strong performance norms greatly enhanced the impact of the head nurse's directive leadership style.

The creation of leadership enhancers makes particular sense when a leader has both the skill to manage effectively and personal goals consonant with organizational objectives but is prevented by one or more neutralizers from being effective. One way to amplify such a leader's power is to alter the organization's reward system. For example, make additional resources available, grant more discretion concerning the distribution of existing resources, or increase subordinates' dependency on the leader for desired physical and financial resources. Another type of enhancement is to give the leader access to key information and prestigious people at high levels—for example, as a member of a visible, prestigious task force. Enhancement in this case derives from connecting the leader to sources of power and important information, as well as from signaling to others that the leader probably has considerable influence with those at the top.

Chapter Nine

Charismatic and Transformational Leadership

*T*he last two decades of the 20th century presented organizations with unparalleled levels of uncertainty, turbulence, rapid change, and intense competition. Many organizations are struggling with the need to manage chaos, to undergo internal cultural change, to reinvent their businesses, to restructure their organizations, to adopt or invent new technologies, to empower organizational members, to reduce organizational boundaries, to discover the path to continuous improvement, and to invent high involvement organization and management systems. In the face of such challenges, the transformational and charismatic leader represents a style of leadership that may be capable of navigating organizations through chaos and into the 21st century.

The current interest in charismatic and transformational leaders brings us back, in part, to a focus on the leader. It provides another perspective on traits of the leader and the "things" that leaders do. Yet, *charisma is relational* in nature. It is not something found solely in the leader as a psychological phenomenon, nor is it totally situationally determined. Instead, charisma is found in the interplay between the leader (his/her traits and behaviors) and the follower (his/her needs, beliefs, values, and perceptions).

Both transformational and charismatic forms of leadership are commonly discussed in terms of the effects that the leader has upon his/her followers and in terms of the relationship that exists between the leader and followers. It has been noted that transformational leaders move and change (fix) things "in a big way," not by offering tokens of inducement, but through the inspiration of others. They are individuals who through personal values, vision, passion, and a commitment to a mission energize and move others.[1]

The famous German sociologist, Max Weber, described the charismatic leader as one who reveals "a transcendent mission or course of action that may not be in itself appealing to the potential followers, but which is acted on because the followers believe their leader is extraordinarily gifted." He or she is described as "supernatural, superhuman or exceptional."[2]

Thus the charismatic leader is described as someone who by the sheer force of personality is capable of having profound effects upon followers. Charismatic leaders generate extremely intense loyalty, passion, and devotion. Followers are inspired and seem to enthusiastically and unquestionably give "blind" obedience to the leader, heeding his or her word almost without hesitation. Their relationship is extremely emotional in nature, producing a profound effect upon the follower's commitment, motivation, and performance.

[1] J. M. Burns, *Leadership* (New York: Harper & Row, 1978).

[2] M. Weber, *The Theory of Social and Economic Organization*, A. M. Henderson and T. Parsons, ed. and trans. (New York: Oxford University Press, 1947), p. 358.

Not only is charismatic leadership seen in terms of the relationship between leader and follower and its effects, but there appear to be several traits possessed and behaviors engaged in by those individuals. Among the most defining characteristics of those leaders who have charisma are a strong sense of self-confidence, a strong conviction of the rightness of their own beliefs and ideals, and dominance (i.e., a strong need for power with a reliance upon referent power as their primary power base). In terms of behaviors, charismatic leaders role-model a set of values and beliefs that they want their followers to internalize, they set high goals and have demanding expectations, they demonstrate confidence in their followers' abilities, and they articulate exciting visions of the future.[3]

In the first two readings in this chapter, Robert J. House (1977), and Jay A. Conger and Rabindra N. Kanungo (1987) provide us insight into charismatic leadership within the organization context. House provides a theoretical explanation of charisma from a psychological perspective. His work gives us insight into how charismatic leadership emerges and its effects in organizations. Building upon the assumption that charismatic leadership emerges from the behavior of the leader, Conger and Kanungo pursue the question, What are the behavioral components that produce the experiences of a charismatic leader?

The distinction between the charismatic and the transformational leader will not be readily apparent. Some authors make no distinction between the two while others conceptualize charisma as one of several attributes that may define the transformational leader. Thus, charismatic leaders by definition are transformational, but not all transformational leaders achieve their transforming effect through the charismatic effects produced by their personalities.

Bernard M. Bass has studied and written extensively about leaders and the leadership process.[4] He contrasts the transactional leader (i.e., that leadership style where something is offered by the leader in exchange for something wanted from the follower) with the transformational leader. Similar to the charismatic leader, the transformational leader, according to Bass, is one who is experienced as engaging in a particular set of behaviors—is a model of integrity and fairness, sets clear goals, has high expectations, encourages, provides support and recognition, stirs the emotions of people, and gets people to look beyond their self-interests and to reach for the improbable. Like the charismatic leader, Bass sees trust, loyalty, and respect as common by-products of this form of leadership. Transformational leaders achieve their results in one or more ways. They may inspire their followers through charisma, they may meet the emotional needs of their followers through individualized consideration, and/or they may intellectually stimulate their followers by stirring within them an awareness of problems, insight into solutions, and the passion to bring about resolution.[5] (We suggest that as a part of your reading and thinking about the role and influence of the transformational leader you reread Smircich and Morgan's (1982) discussion of the management of meaning, which was presented in Chapter One.)

Ronald J. Deluga's (1988) study provides insight into a comparison of transformational and transactional leadership styles. His study suggests that the transformational leader is more effective and has stronger follower satisfaction than that produced by the transactional style of leadership. Philip W. Podsakoff, Scott B. MacKenzie, Robert H. Moorman, and Richard Fetter (1990) also provide an empirical insight into transformational leaders, their behaviors, and the effects they produce. Specifically, they looked at several consequences produced by six behaviors—articulating a vision, providing an appropriate model, fostering acceptance of group goals, high performance expectations, individualized support, and intellectual stimulation—commonly associated with trans-

---

[3] R. J. House, A 1976 Theory of Charismatic Leadership, in J. G. Hunt and K. Rowland, eds., *The Cutting Edge of Leadership* (Carbondale, IL: Southern Illinois University Press, 1976), 189–207.

[4] See for example B. M. Bass, *Bass & Stogdill's Handbook of Leadership: Theory, Research & Managerial Implications* (New York: The Free Press, 1990).

[5] B. Bass. "Leadership: Good, Better, Best." *Organizational Dynamics,* 13(1985), 26–40.

F I G U R E   9 . 1
The Leadership Process

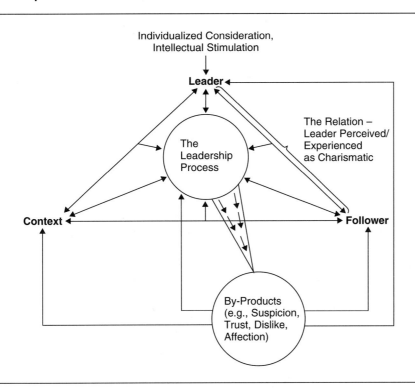

formational leadership. The self-assessment presented at the end of this chapter gives you the opportunity to profile yourself on several of the behavioral dimensions associated with transformational and transactional leader behaviors.

The research conducted by Podsakoff and his colleagues provides insight into the processes through which transformational leadership produces its effects. They observed that trust and satisfaction are common by-products of transformational leadership, and that it is the simultaneous presence of transformational leadership, trust in the leader, and satisfaction that give rise to the follower's engagement in acts of good organizational citizenship behaviors (i.e., the follower's going above and beyond the call of duty to assist the group and members of the group to achieve their goals).

The readings in this chapter provide yet another piece of understanding of the leadership phenomenon (see Figure 1). They remind the reader of the interactive nature of leadership and that a part of the leadership process is relational in nature. Followers see leaders as individuals and experience their acts of leadership. In some instances attributions are made, and some individuals emerge as charismatic leaders for some followers. In addition, some acts of leadership are extremely emotional in nature—powerful experiences—that tend to lift and energize followers, propelling them forward toward the achievement of some potentially tremendous feats. The results are not always positive, as might be witnessed through the acts of Adolph Hitler, James Jones, and, more recently, David Koresh. Each has been described as a leader with charismatic qualities but misguided values.

Self-Assessment

Transformational and Charismatic Leadership

Instructions: Think about a situation in which you either assumed or were given a leadership role. Think about your own behaviors within this context. To what extent does each of the following statements characterize your leadership orientation?

I:	Very Little 1	2	3	A Moderate Amount 4	5	6	Very Much 7
1. Have a clear understanding of where we are going	1	2	3	4	5	6	7
2. Paint an interesting picture of the future for my group	1	2	3	4	5	6	7
3. Am always seeking new opportunities for the organization/group	1	2	3	4	5	6	7
4. Inspire others with my plans for the future	1	2	3	4	5	6	7
5. Am able to get others to be committed to my dreams	1	2	3	4	5	6	7
6. Lead by "doing," rather than simply by "telling"	1	2	3	4	5	6	7
7. Provide a good model for others to follow	1	2	3	4	5	6	7
8. Lead by example	1	2	3	4	5	6	7
9. Foster collaboration among group members	1	2	3	4	5	6	7
10. Encourage employees to be "team players"	1	2	3	4	5	6	7
11. Get the group to work together for the same goal	1	2	3	4	5	6	7
12. Develop a team attitude and spirit among employees	1	2	3	4	5	6	7
13. Show that I expect a lot from others	1	2	3	4	5	6	7

(continued)

I:	Very Little			A Moderate Amount			Very Much
	1	2	3	4	5	6	7
14. Insist on only the best performance	1	2	3	4	5	6	7
15. Will not settle for second best	1	2	3	4	5	6	7
16. Act without considering the feelings of others	1	2	3	4	5	6	7
17. Show respect for the personal feelings of others	1	2	3	4	5	6	7
18. Behave in a manner thoughtful of the personal needs of others	1	2	3	4	5	6	7
19. Treat others without considering their personal feelings	1	2	3	4	5	6	7
20. Challenge others to think about old problems in new ways	1	2	3	4	5	6	7
21. Ask questions that prompt others to think	1	2	3	4	5	6	7
22. Stimulate others to rethink the way they do things	1	2	3	4	5	6	7
23. Have ideas that challenge others to reexamine some of their basic assumptions about work	1	2	3	4	5	6	7
24. Always give positive feedback when others perform well	1	2	3	4	5	6	7
25. Give special recognition when others' work is very good	1	2	3	4	5	6	7
26. Commend others when they do a better-than-average job	1	2	3	4	5	6	7
27. Personally compliment others when they do outstanding work	1	2	3	4	5	6	7
28. Frequently do not acknowledge the good performance of others	1	2	3	4	5	6	7

Scoring: Subtract your response to questions 16, 19, and 28 from 8. There are seven dimension scores to be computed. *Articulate Vision*—Sum your response to questions 1 through 5 and divide by 5. *Provide Appropriate*

Model—Sum your response to questions 6 through 8 and divide by 3. *Foster Acceptance of Goals*—Sum your response to questions 9 through 12 and divide by 4. *High-Performance Expectations*—Sum your response to questions 13 through 15 and divide by 3. *Individual Support*—Sum your response to questions 16 through 19 and divide by 4. *Intellectual Stimulation*—Sum your response to questions 20 through 23 and divide by 4. *Transactional Leader Behaviors*—Sum your response to questions 24 through 28 and divide by 5.

Interpretation: Six basic dimensions of the *transformational* leader are profiled by this self-assessment: articulate vision, provide appropriate model, foster acceptance of goals, high-performance expectations, individual support, and intellectual stimulation. A high score (5.5 and greater) reflects a relatively high behavioral orientation to engage in each of these behaviors. The seventh leadership dimension profiled here reflects your tendency to engage in behaviors characteristic of the *transactional* leader. A high score (5.5 and greater) reflects a relatively strong behavioral orientation to give something to your followers in *exchange* for their giving something to you that as a leader you want (expect) of your followers.

Source: P. M. Podsakoff, S. B. MacKenzie, R. H. Moorman, and R. Fetter, "Transformational Leader Behaviors and Their Effects on Followers' Trust in Leader, Satisfaction, and Organizational Citizenship Behaviors," *Leadership Quarterly* 1, 2 (1990), 107–42.

A 1976 Theory of Charismatic Leadership

R. J. House
University of Toronto

Charisma is the term commonly used in the sociological and political science literature to describe leaders who by force of their personal abilities are capable of having profound and extraordinary effects on followers.[1] These effects include commanding loyalty and devotion to the leader and inspiring followers to accept and execute the will of the leader without hesitation or question or regard to one's self-interest. The term *charisma*, whose initial meaning was "gift," is usually reserved for leaders who by their influence are able to cause followers to accomplish outstanding feats. Frequently, such leaders represent a break with the established order, and through their leadership major social changes are accomplished.

Most writers concerned with charisma or charismatic leadership begin their discussion with Max Weber's conception of charisma. Weber describes as charismatic those leaders who "reveal a transcendent mission or course of action which may be in itself appealing to the potential followers, but which is acted on because the followers believe their leader is extraordinarily gifted" (Weber, 1947, p. 358). Transcendence is attributed implicitly to both the qualities of the leader and the content of his mission, the former being variously described as "supernatural, superhuman, or exceptional (Weber, 1947, p. 358).

Shils (1965) points out that Weber conceived of charismatic leadership as one of the processes through which routinized social processes, norms, and legal rules are changed. Weber distinguished innovators and creators from maintainers and attributed the "gift" of charisma in part to the creative or innovative quality of the leader's goals.

Several writers contend that charismatic leadership can and does exist in formal complex organizations (Dow, 1969; Oberg, 1972; Runciman, 1963; Shils, 1965). Yet despite the profound effects that charismatic leaders are presumed to have on followers' commitment, motivation, and performance, discussions of charisma have been speculative in nature and almost exclusively theoretical. To the knowledge of this writer none of the theoretical notions in the sociological or political science literature have been subjected to empirical test, despite the fact that many of these notions are implicitly testable.

In this chapter the sociological and political science literature on charisma will be reviewed and, where possible, the major assertions in this literature will be restated as propositions in an attempt to make them testable. In addition, selected literature from the discipline of social psychology will be reviewed and propositions which the writer believes are relevant to the concept of charisma will be inferred from the literature.

The outcome of this analysis is a speculative theoretical explanation of charisma from a psychological perspective rather than from a sociological or political science perspective. Hopefully, such an explanation will help us to have greater insight into how charismatic leadership emerges and its effects in modern organizations. Further, it is hoped that such an explanation will provide testable propositions with which to further leadership research.

In the remainder of this presentation the concept of charisma will be examined under the following topics: charismatic effects, characteristics of charismatic leaders, behavior of charismatic leaders, situational factors associated with the emergence and effectiveness of charismatic leaders. While these topics will be addressed separately, they are necessarily intertwined. Thus, at times a discussion of one topic will have implications for the other topics, and reference will be made to such implications.

The Effects of Charismatic Leadership

In the current literature the term charismatic leadership is generally defined and described in terms of the effects of the leader on followers, or in terms of the relationship between leaders and followers. For example Oberg (1972) states that "the test for charisma . . . is the degree of devotion and trust the object (charismatic leader) inspires and the degree to which it enables the individual to transcend his own finiteness and alienation and feel made whole" (p. 22). Tucker (1968) refers to both "charismatic following" and the "charismatic relationship."

> Often times, the relationship of the followers to the charismatic leader is that of disciples to a master, and in any event he is revered by them. They do not follow him out of fear or monetary inducement, but out of love, passionate devotion, enthusiasm. They are not as a rule concerned with career, promotion, salary, or benefice. The charismatic following is a non-bureaucratic group [p. 735].

It appears that most, if not all, writers agree that the effects of charismatic leadership are more emotional than calculative in that the follower is inspired enthusiastically to give

Source: Edited and reprinted with permission from J. G. Hunt and K Rowland (Eds.), *The Cutting Edge of Leadership*. Carbondale, IL: Southern University Press. Author affiliation may have changed since the article was first published.

unquestioned obedience, loyalty, commitment and devotion to the leader and to the cause that the leader represents.

The charismatic leader is also implicitly assumed to be an object of identification by which the followers emulate the leader's values, goals, and behavior. Thus, one of the effects of the charismatic leader is to cause followers to model their behavior, feelings, and cognitions after the leader (Friedrich, 1961). Through the articulation of a transcendent goal the leader is assumed to clarify or specify a mission for the followers. By the leader's expression of self-confidence, and through the exhibition of confidence in followers the leader is also assumed to inspire self-confidence in the followers. Thus the charismatic leader is asserted to clarify followers' goals, cause them to set or accept higher goals, and have greater confidence in their ability to contribute to the attainment of such goals.

Finally, according to the political science and sociological literature on charisma, the charismatic leader is assumed to have the effect of bringing about rather radical change by virtue of beliefs and values that are different from the established order. Thus Oberg (1972) speaks of the "change agent" function of the charismatic leader.

The above review of the effects of charismatic leadership suggests several dependent variables for a theory of charisma. Some of these effects are: follower trust in the correctness of the leader's beliefs, similarity of followers' beliefs to those of the leader, unquestioning acceptance of the leader, affection for the leader, willing obedience to the leader, identification with and emulation of the leader, emotional involvement of the follower in the mission, heightened goals of the follower, and the feeling on the part of followers that they will be able to accomplish, or contribute to the accomplishment of, the mission. This large number of charismatic effects is consistent with Etzioni's definition of charisma as "the ability of an actor to exercise diffuse and intensive influence over the normative (ideological) orientations of other actors" (Etzioni, 1961, p. 203).

The charismatic effects listed above constitute an *initial* list of variables that can be used as preliminary dependent variables for a theory of charisma. While this number of variables lacks parsimony as the defining criteria of a charismatic leader, this list of presumed "charismatic effects" provides a starting point for empiric research on charisma. If one were to identify a number of persons in a population (say military or industrial leaders in a given population) who informed observers (such as superiors or peers) could agree on as being clearly charismatic, it would be possible to identify these leaders' effects by measuring the degree to which their followers responses to them are different from responses of followers of other leaders randomly selected from the same population. The major differences in follower responses could then be clustered into primary groups and scaled. The scores of the followers on these groups could then serve as the basis for a more accurate, complete and parsimonious operational definition of charismatic effects. Leaders who have such effects on followers could be identified in subsequent samples. Such leaders could then be classified as charismatic leaders. Their personality characteristics and behaviors could be compared with those of other leaders (who do not have such effects) to identify characteristics and behaviors which differentiate the charismatic leaders from others. This process of operationally defining charismatic leadership permits one to identify leaders in a population who have the charismatic effects described in the political science and sociological literature and thereby specify an operational set of dependent variables for a theory of leadership.

Some of the above effects have also been the dependent variables in social-psychological research. Specifically, the ability of one person to arouse needs and enhance self-esteem of others, and the ability of one person to serve successfully as a behavioral model for another have been the subject of substantial empirical investigation by psychologists. Later in this chapter we will review this research in an attempt to identify and describe the specific situational factors and leader behaviors that result in such "charismatic" effects.

Defining charismatic leadership in terms of its effects permits one to identify charismatic leaders only after they have had an impact on followers. Such a definition says nothing about the personal characteristics, behaviors, or situational factors that bring about the charismatic effects. This is the scientific challenge that must be addressed if the mysterious quality of charismatic leadership is to be explained and charismatic effects are to be made predictable. We now turn to a discussion of these issues.

Definition of Charismatic Leadership

Throughout this chapter the term charismatic leadership will be used to refer to any leader who has the above "charismatic effects" on followers to an unusually high degree.[2] The operational definition of a given charismatic leader awaits research which will allow one to scale the above specific "charismatic effects." While it is not likely that all charismatic leaders have all of the above "charismatic effects," there are many possibilities that can be examined. For example such effects may be present in a complex interacting manner. Alternatively it may be the sum of, or some absolute level of selected effects that do indeed differentiate charismatic leaders from others.

Characteristics of the Charismatic Leader

Both the literature concerning charismatic leadership and the opinion of laymen seem to agree that the charismatic leader can be described by a specific set of personal characteristics. According to Weber (1947), the charismatic leader is accepted by followers because both the leader and the follower perceive the leader as possessing a certain extraordinary gift. This "gift" of charisma is seldom specified and generally held to be some mysterious quality that defies definition. In actuality the "gift" is likely to be a complex interaction of personal characteristics, the behavior the leader employs, characteristics of followers, and certain situational factors prevailing at the time of the assumption of the leadership role.

The literature on charismatic leadership repeatedly attributes three personal characteristics to leaders who have charismatic effects, namely extremely high levels of self-confidence, dominance, and a strong conviction in the moral righteousness of his/her beliefs.[3] It is interesting to note that three of these characteristics are also attributed to charismatic leaders by laymen as well as by scholars. As a class-room exercise I have on three occasions asked students to form into small groups and to discuss the characteristics of some charismatic leader that they have personally known or to whom they have been exposed. These groups repeatedly described the charismatic leaders that they selected for discussion as possessing dominance, self-confidence, and a strong conviction in their beliefs and ideals.

While the consensus of political science and sociological writers and the results of my own informal experiment are not evidence that leaders who have charismatic effects do indeed possess these characteristics, the argument is certainly subject to an empiric test with self-report measures of personality traits, beliefs, and values.

In addition to the characteristics discussed above it is hypothesized here that leaders who have charismatic effects have a high need to have influence over others. Such a need seems intuitively likely to characterize leaders who have such effects because without such a need they are unlikely to have developed the necessary persuasive skills to influence others and also are unlikely to obtain satisfaction from the leadership role. Uleman (1972) has developed a measure of the need for influence that can be used to test the above hypotheses.

The following proposition summarizes the above discussion:

Proposition 1. Characteristics that differentiate leaders who have charismatic effects on subordinates from leaders who do not have such charismatic effects are dominance and self-confidence, need for influence, and a strong conviction in the moral righteousness of their beliefs.[4]

Behavior of Charismatic Leaders

The sociological and political science literature offer some hints about the behavior of charismatic leaders.

Role Modeling

First it is suggested that leaders who have charismatic effects express, by their actions, a set of values and beliefs to which they want their followers to subscribe. That is, the leader "role models" a value system for the followers. Gandhi constitutes an outstanding example of such systematic and intentional role modeling. He preached self-sacrifice, brotherly love, and nonviolent resistance to British rule. Repeatedly he engaged in self-sacrificing behaviors, such as giving up his lucrative law practice to live the life of a peasant, engaging in civil disobedience, fasting, and refusing to accept the ordinary conveniences offered to him by others.

The importance of the role modeling as a leadership strategy is illustrated by Gandhi's proposed leadership policies for the self-governance of India. "Most important for Gandhi was the example that leaders set for their followers . . . 'No leader of an independent India will hesitate to give an example by cleaning out his own toilet box'" (Collins & LaPierre, 1975, 234–35).

Concerning role modeling, a study by Joestling and Joestling (1972) is suggestive of the effects that a high status role model can have on the self-esteem of observers. Male and female students were asked to rate the value of being a woman. Half of the students were enrolled in the class taught by a qualified female instructor. Twenty-six percent of the women subjects in the class taught by a male thought there was nothing good about being a woman. In contrast only five percent of the women subjects in the class taught by a qualified female had similar negative attitudes toward being a woman.

While role modeling often proves successful, success does not always occur. The question then is what permits a leader to be a successful role model, i.e., to be emulated by the followers.

There is substantial evidence that a person is more likely to be modeled to the extent that that person is perceived as nurturant (i.e., helpful, sympathetic, approving) and as being successful or possessing competence.

There is evidence that role modeling can have profound effects. Behavior resulting from modeling may be very specific such that the individual can be said to imitate or mimic the behavior of the model. Or, the behavior may be more general, taking the form of innovative behavior, generalized behavior orientations, and applications of principles for generating novel combinations of responses (Bandura, 1968).

Bandura (1968) reviews a substantial body of experimental evidence that shows that: (a) model's emotional responses to rewards or punishments elicit similar emotional responses in observers (p. 240); (b) stable changes in the valences (a measure of attractiveness) subjects assign to outcomes and changes in long-standing attitudes often result from the role modeling (pp. 243–44); and (c) modeling is capable of developing generalized conceptual and behavioral properties of observers such as moral judgement orientations and delay-of-gratification patterns of behavior (p. 252).

Of particular significance for the study of leadership are the diverse kinds of attitudes, feelings, and behavior and the diversity of subjects involved in prior studies. Role modeling has been shown to influence the degree to which: (a) undergraduate females learn assertive behavior in assertiveness training program (Young, Rimm & Kennedy, 1973); (b) mentally disturbed patients assume independence in their personal life (Goldstein, Martins, Hubben, Van Belle, Schaaf, Wiersma, & Goedhart, 1973); (c) undergraduates are willing to disclose unfavorable or favorable anxiety related information to others (Sarason, Ganzer & Singer, 1972); (d) personal changes and learning outcomes result from adult *t*-groups (Peters, 1973); (e) individuals are willing to induce punishment (electric shock) to others (Baron, 1971); (f) nurses experience fear of tuberculosis (DeWolfe, 1967); (g) subjects adopt biased attitudes toward minority ethnic groups (Kelman, 1958; Stotland and Patchen, 1961).

Many of the subjects in the above studies were either college students or adults. Thus, the findings are not limited to young children but are also relevant to persons in full-time occupations. Further, the dependent variables are all of significance for effective organizational or group performance. Feelings of fear, willingness to administer punishment, prejudicial attitudes, learning of interpersonal skills, and learning independence are relevant to interpersonal relations within organizations. Similarly, these cognitions and behaviors are relevant to the establishment of trust, to adequacy of communication, and to experiences that are satisfying in organizational life.

Thus it is argued here that role modeling is one of the processes by which leaders bring about charismatic effects. Furthermore, it is likely that the feelings, cognitions and behavior that are modeled frequently determine subordinates' adjustment to organizational life, their job satisfaction, and their motivation to work. With respect to motivation, the above findings suggest that leaders can have an effect on the values (or valences) subordinates attach to the outcomes of their effort as well as their expectations. And, as will be discussed below, leaders can also have an effect on subordinates' self-esteem, and their goal levels. Based on the above review of the literature concerned with role modeling, the following proposition is advanced:

Proposition 2. The more favorable the perceptions of the potential follower toward a leader the more the follower will model: (a) the valences of the leader; (b) the expectations of the leader that effective performance will result in desired or undesired outcomes for the follower; (c) the emotional responses of the leader to work related stimuli; (d) the attitudes of the leader toward work and toward the organization. Here "favorable perceptions" is defined as the perceptions of the leader as attractive, nurturant, successful, or competent.

Image Building

If proposition 2 is valid, then it can be speculated that leaders who have charismatic effects not only model the values and beliefs they want followers to adopt, but also that such leaders take actions consciously designed to be viewed favorably by followers. This speculation leads to the following proposition:

Proposition 3. Leaders who have charismatic effects are more likely to engage in behaviors designed to create the impression of competence and success than leaders who do not have such effects.

This proposition is consistent with the traditional literature on charismatic leadership. Weber (1947) speaks of the necessity of the charismatic leader to "prove" his extraordinary powers to the followers. Only as long as he can do so will he be recognized. While Weber and others have argued that such "proof" lies in actual accomplishments, the above proposition stresses the *appearance* of accomplishments and asserts that charismatic leaders engage in behaviors to gain such an appearance.

Goal Articulation

In the traditional literature on charisma it is frequently asserted that charismatic leaders articulate a "transcendent" goal which becomes the basis of a movement or a cause. Such a goal is ideological rather than pragmatic and is laden with moral overtones. Alternatively, if a movement is already in effect, one behavior of the emergent leader is the articulation of the goal of the movement with conviction and exhortation of the moral rightness of the goal (Tucker, 1968, p. 738).

Examples of such goals are Martin Luther King's "I have a dream," Hitler's "Thousand-year Reich" and his "lebensraum," or Gandhi's vision of an India in which Hindus and Moslems would live in brotherly love independent from British rule.

Berlew (1974, p. 269) states:

The first requirement for . . . charismatic leadership is a common or shared vision for what the future *could be*. To provide meaning and generate excitement, such a common vision must reflect goals or a future state of affairs that is valued by the organizations' members and thus important to them to bring about. . . . All inspirational speeches or writings have the common element of some vision or dream of a better existence which will inspire or excite those who share the author's values. This basic wisdom too often has been ignored by managers.

Thus the following proposition is advanced:

Proposition 4. Leaders who have charismatic effects are more likely to articulate ideological goals than leaders who do not have such effects.

Exhibiting High Expectations and Showing Confidence

Leaders who communicate high performance expectations for subordinates and exhibit confidence in their ability to meet such expectations are hypothesized to enhance subordinates' self-esteem and to affect the goals subordinates accept or set for themselves. Some examples of this kind of charismatic leader behavior are Churchill's statement that England's air defense in World War II was "England's finest hour," Hitler's claim that aryans were "the master race," black leaders' exhortation that "Black is beautiful," and Martin Luther King's prediction that "We shall overcome." All of these statements imply high expectations and confidence in the followers.

There is substantial evidence that the expectation that one can accomplish one's goals is positively related to motivation and goal attainment. Persons with high self-esteem are more likely than persons with low self-esteem to seek higher personal rewards for performance (Pepitone, 1964), and to choose occupations that are congruent with self-perceived traits (Korman, 1966) and self-perceived ability level (Korman, 1967). Further, Korman (1968) has shown experimentally that for high self-esteem subjects there is a positive relationship between task performance and satisfaction, but that no such relationship exists for low self-esteem subjects. Raben and Klimoski (1973) have also shown experimentally that high self-esteem subjects are more likely than low self-esteem subjects to rise to the challenge of doing a task for which they believe they are not qualified. Thus, it is argued here that, to the extent the leader can affect the self-esteem of subordinates, leader behavior will have an effect on the kinds of rewards subordinates seek, their satisfaction with the rewards they obtain, and their motivation to perform effectively.

The effect of leader behavior on subordinate self-esteem has been given little attention in the leadership literature.[5] The assertion that leaders can affect subordinates' self-esteem is derived from two lines of research: research concerning the role-modeling effects and research concerned with reality testing.

We have already argued that through role modeling leaders can have a rather profound effect on subordinates' beliefs. One of these beliefs is self-esteem which is defined by Lawler (1971, p. 107) as the belief that subordinates have with respect to their own general level of ability to cope with and control their environment. It is argued here that subordinates' self-perceptions are likely to be modeled after the leader's perceptions of the subordinates.[6] Thus if the leader communicates high performance expectations and shows confidence in subordinates, they will in turn set or accept a higher goal for themselves and have greater confidence in themselves.[7]

The second line of research suggesting that leaders affect subordinates' self-esteem is that research concerned with "reality testing." In social situations where interpersonal evaluation is highly subjective, individuals tend to "reality test," i.e., to test their notions of reality against the opinions of others (Deutsch & Gerard, 1955; Festinger, 1950). Consequently, to the extent that the leader shows followers that he/she believes them to be competent and personally responsible, the followers are hypothesized also to perceive themselves as competent. This self-perception is hypothesized to enhance motivation, performance, and satisfaction. Some indirect evidence in support of this line of reasoning is found in the results of studies by Berlew and Hall (1966), Stedry and Kay (1966), Korman (1971), Rosenthal and Jacobson (1968), Seaver (1973), and Meichenbaum, Bowers, and Ross (1969). Berlew and Hall (1966) and Stedry and Kay (1966) in field studies both found that individual performance increased as a function of the level of expectation superiors communicated to the individuals. Similarly, Korman (1971) showed in a laboratory study that the performance of students on creative tasks was a direct positive function of the expectations that other college students had for the laboratory subjects. Korman (1971) also showed that ratings of subordinates' performance in two field settings and self-ratings of motivation in three field settings were all significantly correlated with the degree to which subordinates perceived their leaders' practices to reflect confidence in the subordinates.

These findings are consistent with those conducted in educational settings in which the expectations of teachers have been shown to be reflected in the performance of students (Meichenbaum, et al., 1969; Rosenthal & Jacobson, 1968; Seaver, 1973). In these studies teachers were induced to believe that certain students were more competent than others. This belief, or expectancy, on the part of the teacher was shown to be associated with higher student performance. However, there are also studies conducted in educational settings which have failed to demonstrate an effect of teachers' expectancies of students' performance (Anderson & Rosenthal, 1968; Collins, 1969; Conn, Edwards, Rosenthal, & Crowne, 1968); Evans & Rosenthal, 1969; Fiedler, Cohen & Finney, 1971). Seaver (1973) points out that in all of these disconfirming studies and also in the Rosenthal and Jacobson study which is the subject of much controversy, the means of inducing teacher expectations were weak and thus "failure to find expectancy effects may be attributable solely to their failure to induce the desired expectancy in teachers" (p. 341).

If it is assumed that the leader's expectation of subordinates affects the subordinates' self-esteem and their self-esteem in turn affects their performance, then the above studies all provide indirect support for the assertion that leader's expectations affect subordinates' performance.

The *combination* of leader's confidence and high expectations, rather than high expectations alone, should be emphasized here. It is possible that leaders might set high performance standards, thus implying high expectations of subordinates, while at the same time showing low confidence in the subordinates' ability to meet such expectations. An example of this would be the leader who scores high on such questionnaire items as "he needles foremen for production."[8] While such leader behavior may motivate subordinates to strive for high performance in order to avoid punishment, it is also likely to induce fear of failure. Such a state in turn will likely be accompanied by efforts to avoid accountability on the part of the subordinates, strong feelings of dissatisfaction, low acceptance of the leader, and resistance to the leader's influence attempts in the long run.

Thus, while leader expectations are considered to have a significant effect on the reactions of subordinates, high expectations are hypothesized to have a positive effect *only* when subordinates perceive the superior to also have confidence in their (the subordinates') ability to meet such expectations.

Effect on Followers' Goals

In addition to affecting the self-esteem of subordinates, leader expectations and confidence are also hypothesized to affect several important characteristics of the subordinates' goals. In the following paragraphs we review the research concerned with goal characteristics.

In a series of laboratory studies, Locke and his associates (Bryan & Locke, 1967a, 1967b; Locke & Bryan, 1966a, 1966b) have demonstrated that when subjects are given specific goals by the experimenter they perform at significantly higher levels than those given the instruction to "do your best." Two field studies (Mace, 1935; Mendleson, 1971) also offer support for the generalizability of these laboratory findings to natural field settings. Thus, it is argued here that, if laboratory experimenters can influence the goal characteristics of experimental subjects, it seems reasonable that leaders can have similar influence on the goal characteristics of subordinates.

Specific and high expectations of leaders are hypothesized to clarify subordinates' performance goals. Further, it is hypothesized that the more the leader shows confidence in the subordinates' ability to meet goals, the more subordinates are likely to accept them as realistic and attainable.

Specific and high leader expectations are likely to provide a standard against which subordinates can evaluate their own performance. Accordingly, it is hypothesized here that leaders' expectations also serve as a basis on which subordinates may derive feedback. Finally, it is hypothesized that, when the leader's expectations are both high and clear to the subordinate and when the leader shows confidence in the subordinate's ability to meet such expectations, the subordinates will set and/or accept higher goals for themselves than would otherwise be the case, and will have more confidence that they will be able to meet the goals.

The above hypotheses concerning the leaders' effect on followers' self-esteem and goals can be summarized in the following proposition:

Proposition 5. Leaders who simultaneously communicate high expectations of, and confidence in followers are more likely to have followers who accept the goals of the leader and believe that they can contribute to goal accomplishment and are more likely to have followers who strive to meet specific and challenging performance standards.

Motive Arousal Leader Behavior

One explanation for the emotional appeal of the charismatic leader may be the specific content of the messages he communicates to followers. It is speculated here that charismatic leaders communicate messages that arouse motives that are especially relevant to mission accomplishment. For example Gandhi's exhortations of love and acceptance of one's fellow man likely aroused the need for affiliation, a need (or motive) especially relevant to the goal of uniting Hindus, Moslems, and Christians.

Military leaders often employ symbols of authoritarianism and evoke the image of the enemy, thus arousing the power motive, a motive especially relevant to effective combat performance. For example Patton, when addressing infantry recruits, would do so against the background of a large American flag, dressed with medals of his accomplishments, and wearing a shining helmet displaying the four stars indicating the status of general.

Miner's research is relevant to defining some of the conditions under which the arousal of the need for power is associated with successful performance. Miner found that individuals who were high on a projective (sentence completion) measure of the power need were more likely to be successful in hierarchical bureaucratic organizations than individuals low on the power need. These findings did not hold true in egalitarian nonbureaucratic organizations, however (Miner, 1965).

Industrial leaders and leaders of scientists frequently stress excellence of performance as a measure of one's worth, thus arousing the need for achievement, a motive especially relevant to the assumption of personal responsibility, persistence, and pride in high-quality work performance. Varga (1975) has shown that the need for achievement is positively associated with economic and technical performance among research and development project leaders. He has also shown that the need for power is a strong factor contributing to such success when in conjunction with the need for achievement, but a factor making for failure when possessed by leaders low on the need for achievement.

There is some evidence that formally appointed leaders in a laboratory situation are capable of arousing subordinates' need for achievement (Litwin & Stringer, 1968). There is also a substantial amount of evidence that the achievement, affili-

ation, and power needs can be aroused from experimental inductions. For example the need for achievement has been aroused for males by suggesting to subjects that the experimental task is a measure of personal competence, or that the task is a standard against which one can measure his general level of ability (Heckhausen, 1967; McClelland, 1953; McClelland, Clarke, Roby, & Atkinson, 1958; Raynor, 1974).

The need for affiliation has been aroused by having fraternity members rate one another, while all were present, on a sociometric friendship index (Shipley & Veroff, 1952) while at the same time requiring each brother to stand and be rated by the other members of the fraternity on a list of trait adjectives.

The power need has been aroused experimentally by (a) evoking the image of, or reminding one of, an enemy, (b) having subjects observe the exercise of power by one person over another, or (c) allowing subjects to exercise power over another (Winter, 1973). Thus it is hypothesized that needs can be, and often are, similarly aroused by leaders in natural settings. By stressing the challenging aspects of tasks, making group members' acceptance of each other salient to performance appraisal, or talking about competition from others, it is hypothesized that leaders can and frequently do arouse the needs for achievement, affiliation, and power. Further it is hypothesized that, to the extent that such motives are associated with task-required performance, the arousal of these motives will result in increased effectiveness on the part of subordinates. Thus the performance consequence of motive arousal is contingent on the task contingencies. For example, when task demands of subordinates require assumption of calculated risks, achievement oriented initiative, assumption of personal responsibility, and persistence toward challenging goals, the arousal of the need for achievement will facilitate task accomplishment. Further, there is evidence that when subordinates' need for achievement is high, task accomplishment will lead to satisfaction. When subordinates' need for achievement is low, task accomplishment will not be related to satisfaction (Steers, 1975).

When the task demands of subordinates require them to be persuasive, assert influence over or exercise control of others, or be highly competitive or combative, the arousal of the power motive is hypothesized to be related to effective performance and satisfaction. For example, on competitive tasks, or tasks requiring persuasion or aggression, the arousal of the power motive is hypothesized to lead to effective performance.

Finally, when task demands require affiliate behavior, as in the case of tasks requiring cohesiveness, team work, and peer support, the arousal of the affiliative motive becomes highly relevant to performance and satisfaction. An example of such tasks would be tasks that are enriched by assignment of major work goals to groups rather than individuals (Trist & Bamforth, 1951).

These speculations are summarized with the following proposition:

Proposition 6. Leaders who have charismatic effects are more likely to engage in behaviors that arouse motives relevant to the accomplishment of the mission than are leaders who do not have charismatic effects.[9]

Social Determinants of Charismatic Leadership

The sociological literature (Weber, 1947) stresses that charismatic leadership is born out of stressful situations. It is argued that such leaders express sentiments deeply held by followers. These sentiments are different from the established order and thus their expression is likely to be hazardous to the leader (Friedland, 1964). Since their expression is hazardous, the leader is perceived as courageous. Because of other "gifts" attributed to the leader, such as extraordinary competence, the followers believe that the leader will bring about social change and will thus deliver them from their plight.

Thus it can be hypothesized that a strong feeling of distress on the part of followers is one situational factor that interacts with the characteristics and behavior of leaders to result in charismatic effects.

However Shils (1965) argues that charisma need not be born out of distress. Rather, according to Shils, charisma is dispersed throughout the formal institutions of society. Accordingly, persons holding positions of great power will be perceived as charismatic because of the "awe-inspiring" quality of power. Shils' only requirement is that the expression of power must appear to be integrated with a transcendent goal.

The above controversy suggests the hypothesis that leaders are more likely to have charismatic effects in situations stressful for followers than in non-stressful situations. Further it can be hypothesized that persons with the characteristics of dominance, self-confidence, need for influence, and strong convictions will be more likely to emerge as leaders under stressful conditions. Whether or not follower distress is a necessary condition for leaders to have charismatic effects or for persons with such characteristics to emerge as leaders is an empirical question that remains to be tested.

While there is lack of agreement as to whether or not leaders can have charismatic effects under nonstressful situations, all writers do seem to agree that charisma must be based on the articulation of an ideological goal. Opportunity to articulate such a goal, whether in stressful or nonstressful situations, thus can be hypothesized as one of the situational requirements for a person to have charismatic effects. This hypothesis suggests that, whenever the roles of followers can be defined as contributing to ideological values held by the follower, a leader can have some degree of charismatic effect by stressing such values and engaging in the specific behaviors described in the above propositions.

The question then is under what circumstances are roles definable in terms of ideological values. Clearly the roles of followers in political or religious movements can be defined in terms of ideological values. In addition, Berlew (1974) argues that since man seeks meaning in work there are many such ideological values to be stressed in modern formal organizations. Specifically he argues that any of the value-related opportunities listed in Table 22 can have a charismatic effect.

There are some work roles in society which do not lend themselves to ideological value orientation. These are generally the roles requiring highly routine, nonthinking effort in institutions directed exclusively to economic ends. It is hard

TABLE 22

Sources of Meaning in Organizations: Opportunities and Related Values*

Type of Opportunity	Related Need or Value
1. A chance to be tested; to make it on one's own	Self-reliance Self-actualization
2. A social experiment, to combine work, family, and play in some new way	Community integration of life
3. A chance to do something *well*—e.g., return to real craftsmanship; to be really creative	Excellence Unique accomplishment
4. A chance to do something *good*—e.g., run an honest, no rip-off business, or a youth counselling center	Consideration Service
5. A chance to change the way things are—e.g., from Republican to Democrat or Socialist, from war to peace, from unjust to just.	Activism Social responsiblity Citizenship

**Source.*—Berlew, 1974, with permission by Prentice-Hall.

to conceive of clerks or assembly-line workers in profit-making firms as perceiving their roles as ideologically oriented. However the same work when directed toward an ideological goal could lend itself to charismatic leadership. For example in World War II, "Rosie the Riveter" expressed the ideological contribution of an assembly-line worker. And such menial efforts as stuffing envelopes frequently are directed toward ideological goals in political or religious organizations. The following proposition summarizes the above argument:

Proposition 8. A necessary condition for a leader to have charismatic effects is that the role of followers be definable in ideological terms that appeal to the follower.

Summary and Overview

Figure 11 presents a diagramatic overview of the theory presented above. It is hypothesized that leaders who have charismatic effects are differentiated from others by some combination (possibly additive and possibly interactive) of the four personal characteristics shown in the upper right box: dominance, self-confidence, need for influence, and a strong conviction in the moral righteousness of his or her beliefs. Charismatic leaders are hypothesized to employ these characteristics with the following specific behaviors: goal articulation, role modeling, personal image-building, demonstration of confidence and high expectations for followers, and motive arousal behaviors. Goal articulation and personal image-building are hypothesized to result in favorable perceptions of the leader by followers. These favorable perceptions are asserted to enhance followers' trust, loyalty, and obedience to the leader and also to moderate the relation-

F I G U R E   1 1
A model of charismatic leadership. (Dotted lines indicate that favorable perceptions moderate the relationship between leader and follower responses).

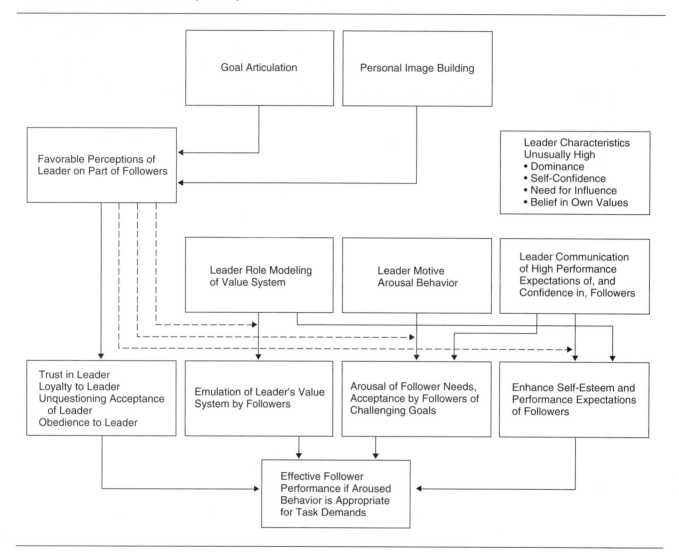

ships between the remaining leader behaviors and the follower responses to the leader. The follower responses are hypothesized to result in effective performance if the aroused behavior is appropriate for their task demands.

Conclusion—Why a 1976 Theory

This chapter presents a "1976" theory of charismatic leadership. The date 1976 is attached to the title to reflect the philosophy of science of the writer. The theory is advanced for the purpose of guiding future research and not as a conclusive explanation of the charismatic phenomenon. As such it includes a set of propositions that are hopefully testable. Admittedly tests of the theory will require the development and valuation of several new scales. However it is hoped that

the propositions are at least presently testable in principle. "A theory that can not be mortally endangered cannot be alive" (cited in Platt, 1964, from personal communication by W. A. H. Rustin).

The results of empiric tests of the theory will undoubtedly require revision of the theory. It is believed by the writer that theories, no matter how good at explaining a set of phenomena, are ultimately incorrect and consequently will undergo modification over time. Thus as MacKenzie and House (1975) have stated, "the fate of the better theories is to become explanations that hold for some phenomena in some limited condition." Or, as Hebb (1969, p. 21) asserts, "A good theory is one that holds together long enough to get you to a better theory."

Hopefully at some future date this theory will have led to a better theory.

Notes

[1] The author is indebted to Hugh J. Arnold, Martin G. Evans, Harvey Kolodny, Stephan J. Motowidlo, John A. Dearness, and William Cooper for their helpful critiques of this chapter. The literature review on which this chapter is based was conducted while the author was visiting professor at Florida International University, April–July, 1975.

[2] This definition would be tautological if the "charismatic effects" were not operationally discovered using two independent operations. However, since the discovery of the "charismatic effects" involves having charismatic leaders identified by one set of observers (peers or superiors) and specification of their effects by an independent set of observers (namely their followers), such a definition avoids the tautological problem.

[3] It is entirely possible that charismatic leaders present themselves as highly confident and as having a strong conviction in the moral righteousness of their beliefs but do not indeed believe in either themselves or their beliefs. Some leaders may thus have charismatic effects because of their ability to *act as though* they have such confidence and convictions. The writer is indebted to Ed Locke for pointing out this alternative hypothesis.

[4] Sashkin, in his commentary on the present chapter, points out that earlier research has shown eminent leaders possess the traits of "intellectual fortitude and integrity of character" and speech fluency (or "capacity for ready communication"). While these traits were not specified in the earlier version of this presentation which Professor Sashkin reviewed, they are not in contradiction to the earlier literature on charismatic leadership and rather consistent with the general description of the charismatic personality advanced in this literature. Thus I would accept these characteristics, along with those in proposition 1, as possible characteristics that differentiate leaders who have charismatic effects from other leaders.

[5] The argument that the enhancement of subordinate self-esteem is an important charismatic effect grew out of earlier conversations between the writer and David E. Berlew. See Berlew (1974) for further elaboration of this argument.

[6] Such modeling, of course, will be a function of the degree to which the subordinate holds favorable perceptions of the leader, as specified in proposition 2.

[7] It is possible that such leader behavior will have a positive effect on subordinates' task-related self-esteem only (i.e., on the subordinates' confidence in their ability to accomplish task goals). It is also possible that such leader behavior will result in enhanced chronic and generalized self-esteem of subordinates. Whether leaders can indeed have such a powerful effect on subordinates' self-perceptions is of course a question that requires empiric investigation.

[8] Fleishman, E. A. *Manual For the Supervisory Behavior Description Questionnaire.* Washington, D.C.: American Institutes for Research, 1972.

[9] The ability of the leader to arouse motives of subordinates is hypothesized to be a function of the degree to which subordinates hold favorable perceptions of the leader, as specified in proposition 2.

Toward a Behavioral Theory of Charismatic Leadership in Organizational Settings

J. A. Conger and R. N. Kanungo
McGill University

Charismatic leadership has been largely overlooked by organizational theorists. In part, the problem can be attributed to the lack of a systematic conceptual framework. Drawing from political science, sociology, and social psychology, this paper addresses the problem by proposing a model linking organizational contexts to charismatic leadership. A series of research hypotheses is offered.

The term *charisma* often is used in political science and sociology to describe a subset of leaders who "by the force of their personal abilities are capable of having profound and extraordinary effects on followers" (House & Baetz, 1979, p. 399). Followers perceive the charismatic leader as one who possesses superhuman qualities and accept unconditionally the leader's mission and directives for action (Willner, 1984). These leaders represent revolutionary social forces, and they are responsible for significant societal transformations (House & Baetz, 1979).

Certain writers contend that charismatic leaders can be found in business firms and other complex formal organizations (Bass, 1985; Berlew, 1974; Berger, 1963; Conger, 1985; Dow, 1969; Etzioni, 1961; House, 1977; Katz & Kahn, 1978; Oberg, 1972; Runciman, 1963; Shils, 1965; Zaleznik & Kets de Vries, 1975). Yet while examples of charismatic business leaders such as John DeLorean and Lee Iacocca are well documented in the press and popular journals (Baker, 1983; Nicholson, 1983; Wright, 1979), they have received little attention as a subject of serious study. For example, only 12 of 5,000 citations reported in Bass' revision of *Stogdill's Handbook of Leadership* (1981) deal with charismatic leadership.

Several reasons are possible for the topic's conspicuous absence from the research literature. First, researchers have shied away from studying charismatic leadership because of its elusive nature and the mystical connotation of the term. Second, without a systematic conceptual framework, researchers often have found it difficult to define and operationalize charisma and to identify the variables that influence its development (Willner, 1984). Third, it is difficult to obtain access to charismatic business leaders.

This paper addresses the second of these problems, and by doing so, alleviates the first. It presents a model linking organizational contexts to charismatic leadership drawing upon research and theory from political science, sociology, social psychology, and existing theories of organizational leadership.

The Literature

Charisma is a Greek word meaning gift. It is used in two letters of St. Paul—Romans, Chapter 12 and 1 Corinthians, Chapter 12—in the Christian Bible to describe the Holy Spirit. Prophecy, ruling, teaching, ministry, wisdom, and healing are among the charismatic gifts described. However, over time the word also came to signify the basis of ecclesiastical organization for the Church itself. The various roles played by members of the Church were determined by gifts of God, rather than by a set of rules or procedures designed by man.

Influenced by this use of charisma to describe a basis for legitimacy, the sociologist Max Weber expanded the concept to include any authority that derives its legitimacy not from rules, positions, or traditions, but from a "devotion to the specific and exceptional sanctity, heroism, or exemplary character of an individual person, and of the normative patterns or order revealed or ordained by him" (Eisenstadt, 1968, p. 46). In addition, Weber ascribed a revolutionary and counternormative quality to charismatic authority: "its attitude is revolutionary and transvalues everything; it makes a sovereign break with all traditional and rational norms" (Eisenstadt, 1968, p. 24).

Weber's conceptualization of charismatic authority, however, is limited by its lack of specificity. For example, he used only generalities to describe a leader's qualities: "[they] comprise especially magical abilities, revelations of heroism, power of the mind and speech" (Etzioni, 1961, p. 12). He identified few behavioral dimensions that might distinguish these individuals from other leaders. Although he described charisma as "a certain quality of an individual personality," he also appears to acknowledge a relational basis for charisma: "It is recognition on the part of those subject to authority which is decisive for the validity of charisma" (Weber, 1947, p. 359).

Political scientists and sociologists have spent several decades examining the phenomenon. Although several have identified specific charismatic attributes such as a transcendent vision and/or ideology (Blau, 1963; Dow, 1969; Marcus, 1961; Willner, 1984), acts of heroism (Willner, 1984), an ability to inspire and build confidence (Dow, 1969; Friedrich,

Source: Edited and reprinted with permission from *Academy of Management Review* 12, 4(1987), 637–47. Author affiliation may have changed since the article was first published.

1961; Marcus, 1961; Willner, 1984), the expression of revolutionary and often "hazardous" ideals (Berger, 1963; Dow, 1969; Friedland, 1961; Marcus, 1961), rhetorical ability (Willner, 1984), and a "powerful aura" (Willner, 1984), much of their work centered on determining the locus of charismatic leadership.

Some (Blau, 1963; Chinoy, 1961; Friedland, 1964; Wolpe, 1968) argued that social and historical contexts were the critical elements in the emergence of charismatic leadership, whereas others (Dow, 1969; Marcus, 1961; Willner, 1984) argued that attributes and relational dynamics between leaders and followers were responsible for the emergence of charisma:

---

it involves a distinct social relationship between the leader and follower, in which the leader presents a revolutionary idea, a transcendent image or ideal which goes beyond the immediate . . . or the reasonable; while the follower accepts this course of action not because of its rational likelihood of success . . . but because of an effective belief in the extraordinary qualities of the leader (Dow, 1969, p. 315).

From in-depth case studies, Willner (1984) concluded that charismatic leadership was neither personality-based nor contextually-determined, but rather the phenomenon was largely relational and perceptual: "It is not what the leader is but what people see the leader as that counts in generating the charismatic relationship" (Willner, 1984, p. 14). Dow (1969) and Willner (1984) found that variations in individual personalities were too great to discern a single charismatic personality type and that the existence of a crisis—previously argued to be necessary for the emergence of charismatic leadership (Chinoy, 1961; Devereux, 1955; Downtown, 1973; Hummel, 1975; Schiffer, 1973)—was "neither a necessary nor a sufficient cause" (Willner, 1984, p. 60).

Among organizational theorists, the topic of charismatic leadership was largely overlooked. Only a handful of theories of charismatic leadership in organizational or business settings have been proposed (Bass, 1985; Bennis & Nanus, 1985; Berlew, 1974; Conger, 1985; Etzioni, 1961; House, 1977; House & Baetz, 1979; Katz & Kahn, 1978; Zaleznik, 1977; Zaleznik & Kets de Vries, 1975). Generally these efforts have been conceptually less sophisticated than their counterparts in political science.

In addition to theoretical works, empirical studies of charismatic (and/or transformational) leadership have been reported by Avolio and Bass (1985), Bass (1985), Conger (1985), House (1985), Howell (1985), Smith (1982), Waldman, Bass, and Einstein (1985), and Yukl and Van Fleet (1982). These studies emphasized the behavioral and psychological attributes of charismatic leadership. Certain personal attributes of charismatic leaders that are identified consistently throughout this literature include vision or appealing ideological goals (Bass, 1985; Berlew, 1974; Conger, 1985; Katz & Kahn, 1978; House, 1977; Zaleznik & Kets de Vries, 1975), behavior that instills confidence (Bass, 1985; Berlew, 1974; House, 1977), an ability to inspire and/or create inspirational activities (Bass, 1985; Berlew, 1974; Conger, 1985; Zaleznik & Kets de Vries, 1975), self-confidence (Bass, 1985; House, 1977;

Zaleznik & Kets de Vries, 1975), dominance (House, 1977; Zaleznik & Kets de Vries, 1975), a need for influence (House, 1977), rhetorical or articulation ability (Conger, 1985), and unconventional and/or counternormative behavior (Conger, 1985; Martin & Siehl, 1983).

In addition, House and Baetz (1979, p. 399) postulated a set of behavioral dimensions that distinguished the followers of charismatic leaders from others. These characteristics include an unquestioning acceptance of the leader by followers, followers' trust in the leader's beliefs, affection for the leader, willing obedience to the leader, emulation of and identification with the leader, similarity of followers' beliefs to those of the leader, emotional involvement of followers in the mission, heightened goals of the followers, and feelings on the part of the followers that they are able to accomplish or contribute to the leader's mission.

Unlike the political science and sociological literature, there appears to be little disagreement over the locus of charismatic leadership; a relational basis for charismatic leadership is widely accepted (Bass, 1985; Berlew, 1974; Conger, 1985; House, 1977; House & Baetz, 1979; Katz & Kahn, 1978; Zaleznik & Kets de Vries, 1975). It is believed that charisma per se is not found solely in the leader and his/her personal qualities but rather is found in the interplay between the leader's attributes and the needs, beliefs, values, and perceptions of his/her followers. Both Katz and Kahn (1978) and House and Baetz (1979) further contended that both the leader and his/her followers must share basic beliefs and values in order to validate the leader's charisma.

Unfortunately, a more unified conceptual framework for understanding the behavioral dimensions of the phenomenon has yet to be presented by organizational theorists. Instead, the literature provides a set of overlapping attributes that identify pieces of the puzzle but lack a structure to explain their relationships. Equally important, there is little or no empirical evidence to support conclusions.

A Behavioral Framework for Studying Charisma

If a deeper understanding of charismatic leadership within organizations is to be obtained, it is important to strip the aura of mysticism from charisma and to deal with it strictly as a behavioral process. Charismatic leadership, like any other form of leadership, should be considered to be an observable behavioral process that can be described and analyzed in terms of a formal model.

The model presented here builds on the idea that charisma is an attributional phenomenon. When members of a group work together to attain group objectives, observations of the influence process within the group help them determine their status. One who exerts maximum influence over other members is perceived as a leader. This role is consensually validated when followers recognize and identify the leader on the basis of interaction with him or her. Charismatic leadership is no exception to this process. Like other kinds of leadership, charisma must be viewed as an attribution made by followers who observe certain behaviors on the part of the leader within organizational contexts. The roles played by a person not only make the person, in the eyes of the followers, a task leader or a social leader, but they also make him or her a charismatic leader or a noncharismatic leader. The leader's observed behavior within the organization can be interpreted by his/her followers as expressions of charismatic qualities. Such dispositional attributes are inferred from the leader's observed behavior in the same way that many personal styles of leadership have been observed previously (Blake & Mouton, 1964; Fiedler, 1967; Hersey & Blanchard, 1977; House, 1971). In this sense, charisma can be considered to be an additional inferred dimension of leadership behavior. As such, it is not an attribution made about an individual because of his or her rank in the organization, but rather it is an attribution made because of the behavior he or she exhibits. Charismatic disposition or leadership style should be subjected to the same empirical and behavioral analysis as participative, task, or people dimensions of leadership have been subjected to in the past.

Behavioral Components of Charisma

If the follower's attribution of charisma depends on observed behavior of the leader, then what are the behavioral components responsible for such attributions? Can these attributions be identified and operationalized in order to develop charismatic qualities among organizational leaders? Table 1 includes a hypothesized description of what the present authors believe to be the essential and distinguishable behavioral components of charismatic leadership.

It is assumed that these components are interrelated and that they differ in presence and intensity among charismatic leaders. These ideas are represented in the following hypothesis.

Hypothesis 1: *The behavioral components of charismatic leadership are interrelated, and as such they form a constellation of components.*

Although all leadership roles involve charting a clear path for group members to achieve a common goal, attribution of charisma to leaders is believed to depend on four variables: the degree of discrepancy between the status quo and the future goal or vision advocated by the leader, the use of innovative and unconventional means for achieving the desired change, a realistic assessment of environmental resources and constraints for bringing about such change, and the nature of articulation and impression management employed to inspire subordinates in the pursuit of the vision. The role of these variables in the development of charisma is discussed below.

Charisma and the Future Vision.   Many theorists see vision as a component of charismatic leadership (Bass, 1985; Berlew, 1974; Blau, 1963; Conger, 1985; Dow, 1969; Katz & Kahn, 1978; House, 1977; Marcus, 1961; Willner, 1984; Zaleznik & Kets de Vries, 1975). Here the word *vision* refers to some idealized goal that the leader wants the organization to achieve in the future. In this paper, it is hypothesized that the nature,

T A B L E   1
Behavioral Components of Charismatic and Noncharismatic Leaders

	Noncharismatic Leader	Charismatic Leader
Relation to Status quo	Essentially agrees with status quo and strives to maintain it	Essentially opposed to status quo and strives to change it
Future Goal	Goal not too discrepant from status quo	Idealized vision which is highly discrepant from status quo
Likableness	Shared perspective makes him/her likable	Shared perspective and idealized vision makes him/her a likable and honorable hero worthy of identification and imitation
Trustworthiness	Disinterested advocacy in persuasion attempts	Disinterested advocacy by incurring great personal risk and cost
Expertise	Expert in using available means to achieve goals within the framework of the existing order	Expert in using unconventional means to transcend the existing order
Behavior	Conventional, conforming to existing norms	Unconventional or counternormative
Environmental Sensitivity	Low need for environmental sensitivity to maintain status quo	High need for environmental sensitivity for changing the status quo
Articulation	Weak articulation of goals and motivation to lead	Strong articulation of future vision and motivation to lead
Power Base	Position power and personal power (based on reward, expertise, and liking for a friend who is a similar other)	Personal power (based on expertise, respect, and admiration for a unique hero)
Leader-Follower Relationship	Egalitarian, consensus seeking, or directive	Elitist, entrepreneur, and exemplary
	Nudges or orders people to share his/her views	Transforms people to share the radical changes advocated

formulation, articulation, and means of achieving this goal can be distinguished from those advocated by other kinds of leaders.

The more idealized or utopian the goal advocated by the leader, the more discrepant it is relative to the status quo. And, the greater the discrepancy of the goal from the status quo, the more likely followers will attribute extraordinary vision to the leader. By presenting an idealized goal to followers, a leader provides a challenge and a motivating force for change. The literature on change in attitude suggests that a maximum discrepant position within the latitude of acceptance puts the greatest amount of pressure on the followers to change their attitudes (Hovland & Pritzker, 1957; Petty & Cacioppo, 1981). Since the idealized goal represents a perspective shared by the followers and promises to meet their hopes and aspirations, it tends to be within the latitude of acceptance in spite of the extreme discrepancy. A leader becomes charismatic when he/she succeeds in changing his/her followers' attitudes to accept the advocated vision. In religion, charisma stems from prophecy; in organizations, charisma stems from advocacy for the future. Failure of either prophecy or advocacy may change the attribution from charisma to madness.

What attributes of charismatic leaders make them successful advocates of their discrepant vision? Research on persuasive communication suggests that in order to be a successful advocate, one needs to be a credible communicator. A leader's credibility could result from projecting an image of being likable, trustworthy, and knowledgeable (Hovland, Janis, & Kelley, 1953; Sears, Freedman, & Peplau, 1985).

It is the shared perspective of the charismatic leader's idealized vision and its potential for satisfying followers' needs that makes the leader likable. Both the perceived similarity between followers and their leader and the perceived potential of the leader to satisfy followers' needs form the basis of their interpersonal attraction (Byrne, 1977; Rubin, 1973). Through this idealized (and therefore discrepant) version of their vision, followers respect their leader and find him or her worthy of identifying with and imitating. Charismatic leaders are not just similar others who are generally liked (as one would find with popular, consensus-seeking leaders), but they are also holders of an idealized vision. Thus, the following hypothesis is advanced.

Hypothesis 2: *Leaders are charismatic when their vision is highly discrepant from the status quo yet remains within a latitude of acceptance for their followers.*

It is important for leaders to be trusted. Generally leaders are trusted when they advocate their position in a disinterested manner and demonstrate a concern for followers' needs rather than their own self-interest (Walster, Aronson, & Abrahams, 1966). However, charismatic leaders make these qualities appear extraordinary. They transform their concern for followers' needs into total dedication and commitment to the common cause they share with followers in a disinterested and selfless manner. They engage in exemplary acts that followers perceive as involving great personal risk, cost, and energy (Friedland, 1964). These personal risks might include: possible loss of finances or career success; the withdrawal of organizational resources; the potential for being fired or demoted; and the loss of formal or informal status, power, authority, and credibility. Lee Iacocca's reduction of his salary to one dollar during his first year at Chrysler (Iacocca & Novak, 1984) and John DeLorean's confrontations with senior management at GM (Martin & Siehl, 1983) are examples of personal risk. The higher the personal cost or sacrifice for the common good, the greater is the trustworthiness of leaders. The more leaders demonstrate that they are prepared to take high personal risks or incur high personal costs for achieving the shared vision, the more they are charismatic in the sense of being worthy of complete trust. This leads to the next hypothesis.

Hypothesis 3: *Charismatic leaders may take on high personal risks, incur high costs, and engage in self-sacrifice to achieve a shared vision.*

Finally, charismatic leaders appear to be experts in their area of influence. Past success may be a condition for the attribution of charisma (Weber, 1947)—for example, Iacocca's responsibility for the Ford Mustang. The attribution of charisma generally is influenced by leaders' expertise in two areas. First, charismatic leaders demonstrate the inadequacy of the traditional technology, rules, and regulations of the status quo as a means of achieving the shared vision (Weber, 1947). Second, the leaders devise effective but unconventional strategies and plans of action (Conger, 1985). Leaders are perceived as charismatic when they demonstrate expertise in transcending the existing order through the use of unconventional means. Iacocca's use of government-backed loans, money-back guarantees on cars, union representation on the board of directors, and advertisements featuring himself are examples of unconventional strategic actions in the automobile industry. Such phenomena lead to the following hypothesis.

Hypothesis 4: *Charismatic leaders demonstrate expertise in transcending the existing order through the use of unconventional or extraordinary means.*

Charisma and Unconventional Behavior. Attribution of charisma to leaders depends on followers' perception of their revolutionary and unconventional qualities (Berger, 1963; Conger, 1983; Dow, 1969; Friedland, 1964; Marcus, 1961). The revolutionary qualities of leaders are manifested in part in their discrepant idealized visions. More important, charismatic leaders engage in innovative behaviors that run counter to the established norms of their organizations, industries, and/or societies while leading their followers toward the realization of their visions. Martin and Siehl (1983) demonstrated this in their analysis of John DeLorean's counternormative behavior at GM. Charismatic leaders are not group facilitators like consensual leaders, but they are active innovators. Their plans and the strategies they use to achieve change, their exemplary acts of heroism involving personal risks, and their self-sacrificing behaviors must be novel, unconventional, and out of the ordinary. Such behavior, when successful, evokes surprise and admiration in followers. Such uncommon behavior also leads to an attribution of charisma in the sense of the possession of superhuman abilities. Thus the following hypothesis is advanced.

Hypothesis 5: *Charismatic leaders engage in behaviors that are novel, unconventional, and counternormative, and as such, involve high personal risk or high probability of harming their own self-interest.*

Charisma and Sensitivity to the Environment.   When a leader loses sight of reality and his or her unconventional behavior fails to achieve its objective, the leader may be degraded from charismatic to ineffective (Friedland, 1964). The knowledge, experience, and expertise of the leader become critical. Charismatic leaders realistically assess environmental resources and constraints affecting their ability to bring about change within their organizations. They are sensitive to both the abilities and emotional needs of followers, and they understand the resources and constraints of the physical and social environments in which they operate. Their innovative strategies and unconventional actions are based on realistic appraisals of environmental conditions. Instead of launching a course of action as soon as a vision is formulated, often leaders prepare the ground or will wait for an appropriate time, place, and the availability of resources. Charisma often fades due to a lack of sensitivity for the environment. The following hypothesis captures this idea.

Hypothesis 6: *Charismatic leaders engage in realistic assessments of the environmental resources and constraints affecting the realization of their visions. They implement innovative strategies when the environmental resource-constraint ratio is favorable to them.*

Charisma and Articulation.   Charismatic leaders articulate their visions and strategies for action through two processes. First, they articulate the context including: (a) the nature of the status quo; (b) the nature of the future vision; (c) the manner through which these future visions, if realized, remove sources of discontent and provide fulfillment of hopes and aspirations of the followers; and (d) plans of action for realizing the vision. In articulating the context, leaders' verbal messages paint positive pictures of the future vision and negative ones of the status quo. The status quo often is presented as intolerable, whereas the vision is presented as the most attractive and attainable alternative in clear, specific terms.

Second, charismatic leaders also communicate their own motivation to lead their followers. Through expressive modes of action, both verbal and nonverbal, the leaders communicate their convictions, self-confidence, and dedication in order to give credibility to what they advocate. Expression of high energy and persistence, unconventional and risky behavior, heroic deeds and personal sacrifices, all communicate the leaders' high motivation and enthusiasm, which then become contagious with their followers. In articulating their motivation to lead, charismatic leaders use a number of impression management techniques. For instance, they use rhetoric by selecting words to reflect assertiveness, confidence, expertise, and concern for followers' needs. These same qualities are also expressed through their dress, appearance, and other forms of body language. Unconventionality in the use of rhetoric and nonverbal forms of communication creates conditions for a dispositional attribution of charisma. These ideas about charismatic leaders' articulation

of context and motivation are contained in the following two hypotheses.

Hypothesis 7: *Charismatic leaders portray the status quo as negative or intolerable and the future vision as the most attractive and attainable alternative.*

Hypothesis 8: *Charismatic leaders articulate their motivation to lead through assertive behavior and expression of self-confidence, expertise, unconventionality, and concern for followers' needs.*

Charisma and the Use of Personal Power.   Influence over followers can stem from different bases of power (French & Raven, 1968). Charismatic influence, however, stems from leaders' personal idiosyncratic power (referent and expert powers) rather than their position power (legal, coercive, and reward powers) legitimated by organizational rules and regulations. Participative consensual leaders also use personal power through consensus seeking. Some nonparticipative organizational leaders also use personal power through their benevolent but directive behavior. However, charismatic leaders differ from both consensual and directive leaders in the use of their personal power. Charismatic personal power stems from the elitist idealized vision, the entrepreneurial advocacy of radical changes, and the depth of knowledge and expertise to help achieve desired objectives. All these personal qualities appear extraordinary to their followers, and they form the basis of charisma. The following two hypotheses state this aspect of charismatic leadership.

Hypothesis 9: *Charismatic leaders' influence on their followers stems from the use of their personal idiosyncratic power (expert and referent) rather than the use of their position power (legal, coercive, and reward) within the organization.*

Hypothesis 10: *Charismatic leaders exert idiosyncratic personal power over their followers through elitist, entrepreneurial, and exemplary behavior rather than through consensus-seeking or directive behavior.*

Charisma and the Reformer Role.   A charismatic leader is seen as an organizational reformer. As Weber (1947) pointed out, charismatic authority is essentially unstable and transitory. Once a new order is institutionalized, charisma fades (Eisenstadt, 1968). Thus charisma is seen in leaders only when they act as agents bringing about radical changes. The attribution is made simply on the basis of actions taken to bring about change or reform. It is not a post facto attribution made after the outcomes of changes are known. Outcomes may, however, reinforce or diminish existing attributions.

From the perspective of change management, leaders should be distinguished from administrators (Zaleznik, 1977). Administrators act as caretakers responsible for the maintenance of the status quo. They influence others through their position power as legitimated by the organization. Leaders, as opposed to administrators, direct or nudge their followers in the direction of an established goal. Charismatic leaders, however, transform their followers (instead of nudging them) and seek radical reforms in them in order to achieve the idealized goal. Thus, charisma can never be perceived either in an administrator (caretaker) role or in a leadership role designed only to nudge the system. This idea is contained in the following hypothesis.

Hypothesis 11: *Charismatic leaders act as reformers or agents of radical changes, and their charisma fades when they act as administrators (caretaker role) or managers (nudging role).*

The Context for Emergence of Charisma. The preceding discussion implies that a need for major transition or change triggers the emergence of a charismatic leader. Sometimes contextual factors are so overwhelmingly in favor of a change that leaders take advantage of them. For instance, when a system is dysfunctional or when it faces a crisis, leaders find it to their advantage to advocate radical change, thereby creating a charismatic image for themselves. In periods of relative tranquility, leaders play a major role in creating the need for change in their followers. They anticipate future change and induce supportive conditions. In any case, context must be viewed as a precipitating factor, sometimes facilitating the emergence of certain behavior in leaders that forms the basis of charisma. As Willner (1984) pointed out regarding political leadership, "preconditions of exogenous social crisis and psychic distress are conducive to the emergence of charismatic political leadership, but they are not necessary" (p. 52). From the point of view of the leader, however, sensitivity to contextual factors is important if he or she is to develop appropriate strategies for change. The following two hypotheses deal with the role of context in the emergence of charisma.

Hypothesis 12: *Contextual factors that cause potential followers to be disenchanted with the prevailing social order, or that cause followers to experience psychological distress, although not a necessary condition for the emergence of charismatic leaders, facilitate such emergence.*

Hypothesis 13: *Under conditions of relative social tranquility and lack of psychological distress among followers, the actions by a leader that foster or support an attribution of charisma facilitate the emergence of that leader as a charismatic leader.*

Implications

In order to demystify charisma, these tentative hypotheses for future testing have been presented. Existing evidence forms the basis of the model, but the specific predictions should be tested.

In the model, charisma is viewed both as a set of dispositional attributions by followers and as a set of leaders' manifest behaviors. The two are linked in the sense that the leaders' behaviors form the basis of followers' attributions. To validate such a framework, two steps are necessary. First, the behavioral and dispositional attributes of charismatic leaders suggested in this framework require independent empirical confirmation. To determine if convergent and discriminant validity exist, a behavioral attribute checklist or questionnaire could be developed including the attributes believed to characterize charismatic leaders as well as those cited in the literature for other forms of leadership. A group of test subjects could identify leaders they perceive as charismatic and as noncharismatic. Respondents then could describe the distinguishing attributes of charismatic and noncharismatic leaders using the checklist. With this format, it would be possible to test whether an attribution of charisma is associated with the attributes described. Second, the discriminant validity of the charismatic leadership construct as described in this paper could be tested by demonstrating that a dependent variable (e.g., followers' trust) is related to charisma in a different way than other leadership constructs.

The model also has direct implications for management. Specifically, if the behavioral components of charismatic leadership can be isolated, it may be possible to develop these attributes in managers. Assuming that charismatic leadership is important for organizational reforms, organizations may wish to select managers on the basis of charismatic characteristics that have been identified. Certain tests such as those already developed to test sensitivity to the environment (Kenny & Zaccaro, 1983) could be administered to potential managerial candidates. The need for such selection procedures may be particularly important for developing countries, where greater levels of organizational change would be necessary in order to adopt new technologies and to transform traditional ways of operating.

References

Avolio, B. J., & Bass, B. M. (1985) *Charisma and beyond.* Paper presented at the annual meeting of the Academy of Management, San Diego.

Baker, R. (1983, March 27) Peripatetic pitchman. *New York Times Magazine,* p. 26.

Bass, B. M. (1981) *Stogdill's handbook of leadership.* New York: Free Press.

Bass, B. M. (1985) *Leadership performance beyond expectations.* New York: Academic Press.

Bennis, W. G., & Nanus, G. (1985) *Leaders.* New York: Harper & Row.

Berger, P. L. (1963) Charisma and religious innovation: The social location of Israelite prophecy. *American Sociological Review,* 28, 940–950.

Berlew, D. E. (1974) Leadership and organizational excitement. *California Management Review,* 17(2), 21–30.

Blake, R. R., & Mouton, J. S. (1964) *The managerial grid.* Houston: Gulf.

Blau, P. (1963) Critical remarks on Weber's theory of authority. *American Political Science Review,* 57, 305–315.

Byrne, D. (1977) *The attraction paradigm.* New York: Academic Press.

Chinoy, E. (1961) *Society.* New York: Random House.

Conger, J. (1985) *Charismatic leadership in business: An exploratory study.* Unpublished doctoral dissertation, Harvard Business School, Boston.

Devereux, G. (1955) Charismatic leadership and crisis. In W. Muensterberger & S. Axelrod (Eds.), *Psychoanalysis and the social sciences* (Vol. 4, pp. 145–157). New York: International University Press.

Dow, T. E., Jr. (1969) The theory of charisma. *Sociological Quarterly,* 10, 306–318.

Downtown, J. V., Jr. (1973) *Rebel leadership.* New York: Free Press.

Eisenstadt, S. N. (1968) *Max Weber: On charisma and institution building.* Chicago: University of Chicago Press.

Etzioni, A. (1961) *A comparative analysis of complex organizations.* New York: Free Press.

Fiedler, F. F. (1967) *A theory of leadership effectiveness.* New York: McGraw-Hill.

French, J. R., Jr., & Raven, B. H. (1968) The bases of social power. In D. Cartwright & A. Zander (Eds.), *Group dynamics* (pp. 259–269). New York: Harper & Row.

Friedland, W. H. (1964) For a sociological concept of charisma. *Social Forces.* 43, 18–26.

Friedrich, C. J. (1961) Political ledership and the problem of the charismatic power. *Journal of Politics,* 23, 3–24.

Hersey, P., & Blanchard, K. H. (1977) *Management of organizational behavior: Utilizing human resources* (4th ed.). Englewood Cliffs, NJ: Prentice-Hall.

House, R. J. (1971) A path-goal theory of leadership effectiveness. *Administrative Science Quarterly,* 321–332.

House, R. J. (1977) A 1976 theory of charismatic leadership. In J. G. Hunt & L. L. Larson (Eds.), *Leadership: The cutting edge* (pp. 189–207). Carbondale, IL: Southern Illinois University press.

House, R. J. (1985) *Research contrasting the behavior and effects of reputed charismatic versus reputed noncharismatic.* Paper presented at the annual meeting of the Administrative Science Association, Montreal.

House, R. J., & Baetz, M. L. (1979) Leadership: Some empirical generalizations and new research directions. In B. M. Staw (Ed.), *Research in organizational behavior* (Vol. 1, pp. 399–401). Greenwich, CT: JAI Press.

Hovland, C. I, Janis, I. L, & Kelley, H. H. (1953) *Communication and persuasion.* New Haven, CT: Yale University Press.

Hovland, C. I., & Pritzker, H. A. (1957) Extent of opinion change as a function of amount of change advocated. *Journal of Abnormal Pscyhology,* 54, 257–261.

Howell, J. M. (1985) *A laboratory study of charismatic leadership.* Paper presented at the annual meeting of the Academy of Management, San Diego.

Hummel, R. P. (1975) Psychology of charismatic followers. *Psychological Reports,* 37, 759–770.

Iacocca, L., Novak, W. (1984) *Iacocca.* New York: Bantam Books.

Katz, D. & Kahn, R. L. (1978) *The social psychology of organizations.* New York: Wiley.

Kenny, D. A. & Zacarro, S. J. (1983) An estimate of variance due to traits in leadership. *Journal of Applied Psychology,* 68, 678–685.

Marcus, J. T. (1961, March) Transcendence and charisma. *Western Political Quarterly,* 14, 236–241.

Martin, J., & Siehl, C. (1983) Organizational culture and counterculture: An uneasy symbiosis. *Organizational Dynamics,* 12(2), 52–64.

Nicholson, T. (1983, February 14) Iacocca shifts into high. *Newsweek,* pp. 101, 64.

Oberg, W. (1972) Charisma, commitment, and contemporary organization theory. *Business Topics,* 20(2), 18–32.

Petty, R. E., & Cacioppo, J. T. (1981) *Attitudes and persuasion: Classic and contemporary approaches.* Dubuque, IA: Brown.

Rubin, Z. (1973) *Liking and loving: An invitation to social psychology.* New York: Holt, Rinehart, & Winston.

Runciman, W. G. (1963) Charismatic legitimacy and one-party rule in Ghana. *Archives Eupreenes de Sociologie,* 4, 148–165.

Schiffer, I. (1973) *Charisma: A psychoanalytic look at mass society.* Toronto: University of Toronto Press.

Sears, D. O., Freedman, L., & Peplau, L. A. (1985) *Social psychology* (5th ed.) Englewood Cliffs, NJ: Prentice-Hall.

Shils, E. A. (1965) Charisma, order, and status. *American Sociological Review,* 30, 199–213.

Smith, B. J. (1982) *An initial test of a theory of charismatic leadership based on responses of subordinates.* Unpublished doctoral dissertation, University of Toronto.

Tucker, R. C. (1968) The theory of charismatic leadership. *Daedulus,* 97, 731–756.

Waldman, D. A., Bass, B. M., & Einstein, W. O. (1985) *Effort, performance and transformational leadership in industrial and military settings.* (Working Paper 85–80). State University of New York at Binghamton, School of Management.

Walster, E., Aronson, D., & Abrahams, D. (1966) On increasing the persuasiveness of a low prestige communicator. *Journal of Experimental Social Psychology,* 2, 325–342.

Weber, M. (1947) *The theory of social and economic organization.* (A. M. Henderson & T. Parsons, Trans.). New York: Oxford University Press.

Willner, A. R. (1968) *Charismatic political leadership: A theory.* Princeton, NJ: Princeton University, Center of International Studies.

Willner, A. R. (1984) *The spellbinders: Charismatic political leadership.* New Haven, CT: Yale University Press.

Wolpe, H. (1968) A critical analysis of some aspects of charisma. *Sociological Review,* 16, 305–318.

Wright, P. J. (1979) *On a clear day you can see General Motors.* New York: Avon Books.

Yukl, G. A. (1981) *Leadership in organizations.* Englewood Cliffs, NJ: Prentice-Hall.

Yukl, G. A., & Van Fleet, D. D. (1982) Cross-situational multimethod research on military leader effectiveness. *Organizational Behavior and Human Performance,* 30, 87–108.

Zaleznik, A. (1977) Managers and leaders: Are they different? *Harvard Business Review,* 55(3), 67–78.

Zaleznik, A., & Kets de Vries, M. F. R. (1975) *Power and the corporate mind.* Boston: Houghton Mifflin.

Relationship of Transformational and Transactional Leadership with Employee Influencing Strategies

R. J. Deluga
Bryant College

Effective leadership implies an understanding of how managers and employees influence one another (Yates, 1985). Of particular importance to the practicing manager is the relationship of leadership style to employee influencing behavior. Could the manager's leadership style encourage constructive or destructive employee influencing? That is, in what ways could this interaction affect such critical organizational outcomes as manager effectiveness and employee satisfaction with the manager? The implications of these influencing dynamics on organizational productivity and employee developmental needs seem apparent. Thus the purpose of this study was to investigate the nature of managerial leadership and employee-influencing systems in a manufacturing environment. Transactional and transformational leadership have been two approaches offering an explanation as to how managers-employees influence one another (Bass, 1981, 1985a; Burns, 1978; Hollander, 1985).

Burns (1978) argues that leadership can be understood best as either a transactional or a transformational process. Transactional leadership suggests that most managers engage in a bargaining relationship with employees (Hollander, 1978). Bass (1981, 1985a) cites contingent reward and management-by-exception as two factors that emerge with transactional leadership. Contingent reward describes the familiar work-for-pay agreement. Employees are told what they need to do to obtain rewards. Management-by-exception characterizes how the manager reacts primarily to employee errors. The manager exerts corrective action only when employees fail to meet performance objectives.

On the other hand, transformational leadership differs from transactional leadership. The transformational manager cultivates employee acceptance of the work group mission. The manager-employee relationship is one of mutual stimulation and is characterized by four factors, including (1) charisma, (2) inspiration, (3) individual consideration, and (4) intellectual stimulation (Bass, 1985a).

First, charisma is the fundamental factor in the transformational process. Charisma is the leader's ability to generate great symbolic power with which the employees want to identify. Employees idealize the leader and often develop a strong emotional attachment (Bass, 1985a).

Closely related to charisma is inspiration. Inspiration describes how the leader passionately communicates a future idealistic organization that can be shared. The leader uses visionary explanations to depict what the employee work group can accomplish. Excited employees are then motivated to achieve organizational objectives (Bass, 1985a).

Third, individual consideration characterizes how the leader serves as an employee mentor. He or she treats employees as individuals and uses a developmental orientation that responds to employee needs and concerns (Bass, 1985a).

Finally, intellectual stimulation describes how transformational leaders encourage employees to approach old and familiar problems in new ways. By stimulating novel employee thinking patterns, employees question their own beliefs and learn creatively to solve problems by themselves (Bass, 1985a).

Transformational and transactional leaders differ in another important respect. The typical manager is a transactional leader who analyzes employee lower-level needs and determines their goals (Zaleznik, 1983). That is, she or he attempts to satisfy the employee's basic wants and works to maintain the organizational status quo. However, the transactional leader also limits the employee's (1) effort toward goals, (2) job satisfaction, and (3) effectiveness toward contributing to organizational goals (Bass, 1985a). Bass (1986) suggests that transactional leadership is acceptable as far as it goes, but fundamentally is a prescription for organizational mediocrity.

Conversely, transformational leaders incorporate and amplify the impact of transactional leadership (Waldman, Bass, & Einstein, 1985). They recognize and exploit those employee higher-level needs that surpass immediate self-interests. By appealing to these elevated needs, the transformational leader motivates employees to perform beyond initial performance goals and objectives (Bass, 1985a; Burns, 1978; Tichy & Devanna, 1986).

Hypotheses

Transactional and transformational leadership theories have contributed to the understanding of manager-employee influencing processes. However, just how manager-employee influencing networks interact has been cited as an underdeveloped research area requiring further methodological exploration (Ansari & Kapoor, 1987; Bass, 1985a; Crowe, Bochner & Clark, 1972; Kipnis, Schmidt, & Wilkinson, 1980; Tichy & Devanna, 1986). Thus the purpose of the study was to com-

Source: Edited and reprinted with permission from *Group and Organization Studies* 13, 4(1988), 456–67. Author affiliation may have changed since article was first published.

pare manager-employee influencing dynamics within the framework of the transformational and transactional leadership approaches.

As expressed in manager-employee influencing relationships, it seems reasonable that managers who have organizational support, multiple sources of power, and control resources valued by employees, and who are perceived to be in a position of dominance (French & Raven, 1959; Podsakoff & Schriesheim, 1985) would display stronger influencing patterns relative to employees. An accelerated managerial ability to influence would seemingly further diminish employees' influencing capability. Following the same mechanism, employees experiencing a favorable power position would likewise display an influencing advantage. Therefore:

H1: Perceived transformational and transactional leadership (manager downward influencing behavior) will be inversely related to reported employee upward influencing behavior.

Transactional leaders were described as engaging in an exchange relationship with employees. As such, it appears plausible that the flow of influencing behavior may constantly fluctuate in response to manager-employee comparative bargaining strength. Managers perceived as transactional would then seem to be more likely targets of employee influencing activity. Therefore:

H2: Perceived transactional leadership will be more strongly inversely related to reported employee upward influencing behavior than transformational leadership.

If in fact transactional leaders are subject to more employee influencing, the less volatile transformational manager-employee influencing behavior may minimize distractions and promote both leader effectiveness and employee satisfaction. Therefore:

H3: Perceived transformational leadership will be more closely associated with reported leader effectiveness and employee satisfaction with the leader than transactional leadership.

In terms of day-to-day managerial implications, the influencing activity predicted for transactional leadership may be organizationally detrimental. Managers and employees may take turns with the carrot and stick as their negotiating positions change. Lingering resentment could further escalate the game playing. For instance, an employee may feel he or she was unfairly denied a much wanted promotion. At a later time, the relative power position could shift in favor of the employee. She or he may then feel compelled to seek revenge by withholding valued skills and knowledge.

On the other hand, the stability predicted for transformational leader-employee influencing behavior could be organizationally advantageous. Both the manager and employees would be jointly working toward shared group goals, rather than being diverted by the urge to repay past slights.

Method

Participants and Procedure

The target population was 400 exempt and nonexempt employees of a manufacturing firm located in a lower-middle-

class multiethnic area of the Northeast. All were nonunion employees. After reading an explanatory page indicating company support and detailing instructions, volunteer employees completed a confidential self-report questionnaire. The questionnaire contained the leadership style and satisfaction with leadership instruments (Part I) as well as the upward influence strategy instrument (Part II). To encourage participation, all employees completing the questionnaire received a free coffee and donut. Also, participants had their names entered into a random drawing for the opportunity to win a day off with pay or a pair of state lottery tickets.

Over five working days, 117 usable questionnaires (29.3%) from 41 males and 76 females were anonymously returned to a box located in the factory cafeteria. Respondents included upper-level managers (23%), middle/entry-level managers (21%), manual laborers (36%), and "other" (20%) who represented the manufacturing (39.87%), international (28%), creative/marketing (31.5%), finance/administration (11.1%), and sales/merchandising (14.8%) departments. . . .

Strategies used by subordinates to influence their superiors were measured by Form M of the Profile of Organizational Influence Strategies (POIS-M) (Kipnis & Schmidt, 1982). The 27-item behavioral-based instruments assess how frequently an employee reports using each of six behavioral strategies directed as a first attempt and, when encountering resistance, as a second attempt toward influencing the manager. The strategies assessed by the POIS-M include:

(1) *Friendliness* is designed to create a favorable impression through flattering or "buttering up" the manager.

(2) *Bargaining* involves exchanging benefits and making deals.

(3) *Reason* is the use of facts and data to support the development of a logical argument.

(4) *Assertiveness* includes the use of a direct and forceful approach.

(5) *Higher authority* is "going over the boss's head" to gain support.

(6) *Coalition* is the mobilization of other employees to collectively influence the manager. . . .

Discussion

The findings appeared to support the hypotheses that perceived managerial downward influencing behavior would be inversely related to reported employee upward influencing behavior. Similarly, the data suggest that as compared to transformational leadership, transactional leadership does promote more influencing activity between managers and employees. Finally, transformational leadership was found to be more closely associated with leader effectiveness and employee satisfaction than was transactional leadership. Therefore, further discussion of these findings seems warranted.

Transactional Leadership

The transactional manager enters into an exchange relationship with employees and reacts primarily only when goals are not met. (Bass, 1985a). It would appear that as employees fall short of expectations, the employee's bargaining position is eroded, while that of the manager is correspondingly strengthened. At the same time, alert employees aware of their own vulnerable position may conclude that influencing attempts would be futile or even professionally harmful. The manager subsequently can use her or his multiple sources of power (French & Raven, 1959; Podsakoff & Schriesheim, 1985), that is, reward and punishment, to control valued outcomes and influence employee performance. The process seems feasible, as previous studies have proposed that employee performance does appear to influence manager behavior (Greene, 1976; Sims, 1977; Sims & Szilagyi, 1978; Szilagyi, 1980).

The volatile process may also operate to the employee's advantage. Due to their own unique sources of power, such as expertise, effort, commitment, and access to valued facilities (Mechanic, 1962; Porter, Allen, & Angle, 1983), employees operating from a position of more relative strength may be able to obtain a greater flow of organizational benefits.

An example of this influencing process can occur when an employee has failed to meet recent sales goals. He or she is obviously in a weak negotiating position and is not likely to succeed in gaining the desired larger office, preferred vacation schedule, or a monetary bonus. In fact, the manager would probably use these desired benefits to influence the employee to reach the sales goals. However, employees may resent this carrot-and-stick approach and seek to retaliate as sales and bargaining strength improve. The retaliation may take the form of unreasonable demands to compensate for perceived slights or even through accepting a position with a competitor. As proposed above, the flow of power and influence may constantly fluctuate as a function of transactional manager-employee comparative power base potency. Associated dysfunctional "game playing" may result in marginal organizational performance.

Transformational Leadership

The findings supported the prediction that relative to transactional manager-employee relationships, transformational manager-employee interactions would exhibit more stable influencing activity. This apparent equilibrium is indicated by these findings in two ways. First, the transformational manager-employee influencing patterns shown in Table 1 appear less volatile. Fewer and less severe inverse relationships are evident. Second, employees reported significantly greater satisfaction with transformational leadership and viewed the approach as more effective (Table 2).

The transformational leader-employee interactions may be more balanced since the manager and satisfied employees both jointly and effectively work toward the organizational mission. Perhaps the vision of a common goal as articulated by the transformational leader has relegated harmful organizational game playing to a subordinate role.

For example, company sales may be plummeting due to the impact of a foreign competitor. The transformational leader emotionally arouses employees to collectively meet the foreign challenge and inspires them to extra effort and greater accomplishment. Employees are not occupied by what they may individually bargain for as a result of the crisis. Rather, employees are motivated to succeed beyond their immediate self-interests and to achieve the goals of organizational survival and prosperity.

Implications

The battles among competing and mutually exclusive interests usually claim a high price in management attention; the focus of an entire organization may be adversely affected by turbulence in the internal balance of power (Selznick, 1957). The major point is that the transformational approach appears to alter destructive influencing networks created by fluctuating manager-employee power differences. In return, the organization will experience dividends in organizational productivity.

Implications for fostering transformationally oriented organizational cultures through training, job and organizational design, and human resource decisions seem clear. Bass (1986) has suggested that training in mentoring and recognizing the varying development needs of employees can promote the transformational factor of individual consideration. Integrative problem-solving, rather than competitive (win-lose) relationships, would advance the transformational factor of intellectual stimulation. Both factors could be learned through the use of scenarios, videotapes of actual situations, and/or role playing. With appropriate feedback, work group productivity would increase. Similarly, organizations facing rapid environmental change would benefit from the flexibility nurtured by transformational leadership at all levels. For example, encouraging transformational leadership through recruiting programs, selection standards, and promotion policies seems likely to attract desirable prospects and retain valued employees.

Future studies might use longitudinal approaches examining how manager-employee influencing networks evolve over time. Perhaps the balance shifts as a function of organizational type, employee group, or internal/external environmental forces. Other investigations could systematically manipulate alternative leadership theories to further illuminate the dynamics of manager-employee influencing behavior.

References

Ansari, M. A., & Kapoor, A. (1987). Organizational context and upward influence tactics. *Organizational Behavior and Human Decision Processes, 40,* 39–49.

Bass, B. M. (1981). *Stogdill's handbook of leadership: A survey of theory and research.* New York: Free Press.

Bass, B. M. (1985a). *Leadership and performance beyond expectations.* New York: Free Press.

Bass, B. M. (1985b). *Multifactor Leadership Questionnaire (Form 5).* Binghamton: University Center, State University of New York.

Bass, B. M. (1986). *Implications of a new leadership paradigm.* Binghamton: School of Management, State University of New York.

Burns, J. M. (1978). *Leadership.* New York: Harper.

Carmines, E. G., & Zeller, R. A. (1979). *Reliability and validity assessment.* Sage University Paper Series on Quantitative Applications in the Social Services, series no. 17. Beverly Hills, CA: Sage.

Crowe, B. J., Bochner, S., & Clark, A. W. (1972). The effects of subordinates' behavior on managerial style. *Human Relations, 25*(3), 215–237.

French, J., & Raven, B. H. (1959). The bases of social power. In D. Cartwright (Ed.), *Studies in social power* (pp. 150–167). Ann Arbor: Institute for Social Research.

Greene, C. N. (1976). A longitudinal investigation of performance-reinforcing behavior and subordinate satisfaction and performance. In S. Sikula & P. Hilgert (Eds.), *Proceedings: Midwest Division of the Academy of Management* (pp. 157–185). St. Louis: Washington University.

Hollander, E. P. (1978). *Leadership dynamics: A practical guide to effective relationships.* New York: Free Press.

Hollander, E. P. (1985). Leadership and Power. In G. Lindzey & E. Aronson (Eds.), *The handbook of social psychology: Vol. II.* (pp. 485–537). New York: Random House.

Kipnis, D., & Schmidt, S. M. (1982). *Profiles of organizational influence strategies (Form M).* San Diego: University Associates.

Kipnis, D., Schmidt, S. M., & Wilkinson, I. (1980). Intraorganizational influence tactics: Explorations in getting one's way. *Journal of Applied Psychology, 65*(4), 440–452.

Mechanic, D. (1962). Sources of power of lower participants in complex organizations. *Administrative Science Quarterly, 7*(3), 349–364.

Podsakoff, P. M., & Schriesheim, C. A. (1985). Field studies and Raven's bases of power: Critique, reanalysis, and suggestions for future research. *Psychological Bulletin, 97*(3), 387–411.

Porter, L. W., Allen, R. W., & Angle, H. L. (1983). The politics of upward influence in organizations. In L. W. Porter & R. W. Allen (Eds.), *Organizational influence processes* (pp. 408–422). Glenview, IL: Scott, Foresman.

Selznick, P. (1957). *Leadership in administration: A sociological interpretation.* Berkeley: University of California Press.

Sims, H. P. (1977). The leader as a manager of reinforcing contingencies: An empirical example and a model. In J. G. Hunt & L. L. Larson (Eds.), *Leadership: The cutting edge* (pp. 121–137). Carbondale: Southern Illinois University Press.

Sims, H. P., & Szilagyi, A. D. (1978). A causal analysis of leader behavior over three different time lags. *Proceedings; Eastern Academy of Management.*

Szilagyi, A. D. (1980). *Causal inferences in leadership: A three time period longtiudinal analysis.* Working paper, University of Houston, Houston, TX.

Tichy, N. M., & Devanna, M. A. (1986) *The transformational leader.* New York: John Wiley.

Waldman, D. A., Bass, B. M., & Einstein, W. O. (1985). *Effort, performance, and transformational leadership in industrial and military service* (Working Paper 85–80). Binghamton: School of Management, State University of New York.

Yates, D. (1985). *The politics of management.* San Francisco: Jossey-Bass.

Zaleznik, A. (1983). The leadership gap. *Washington Quarterly, 6*(1), 32–39.

Transformational Leader Behaviors and Their Effects on Followers' Trust in Leader, Satisfaction, and Organizational Citizenship Behaviors

P. M. Podsakoff and S. B. MacKenzie
Indiana University

R. H. Moorman
West Virginia University

R. Fetter
Indiana University

The search for and identification of those behaviors that increase a leader's effectiveness has been a major concern of practicing managers and leadership researchers alike for the past several decades (cf. Bass, 1981; House, 1971; 1988; House & Baetz, 1979; Stogdill, 1974; Yukl, 1989a; 1989b). Traditional views of leadership effectiveness have focused primarily, although not exclusively, on what Burns (1978) and Bass (1985) have called *transactional* leader behaviors. According to Burns (1978), transactional behaviors are founded on an exchange process in which the leader provides rewards in return for the subordinate's effort.

More recently, however, the focus of leadership research has shifted from one of examining the effects of transactional leadership to the identification and examination of those behaviors exhibited by the leader that make followers more aware of the importance and values of task outcomes, activate their higher-order needs, and induce them to transcend self-interests for the sake of the organization (Bass, 1985; Yukl, 1989a, 1989b). These *transformational* or *charismatic* behaviors[1] are believed to *augment* the impact of transactional leader behaviors on employee outcome variables, because "followers feel trust and respect toward the leader and they are motivated to do more than they are expected to do" (Yukl, 1989b, p. 272). Examples of this new focus on leadership include the work of House, Bass, and others (e.g., Avolio & Bass, 1988; Bass, 1985; Bass, Avolio, & Goodheim, 1987; Bass, Waldman, Avolio, & Bebb, 1987; Bennis & Nanus, 1985; Boal & Bryson, 1988; House, 1977; House, Spangler, & Woycke, 1989; House, Woycke, & Fodor, 1988; Howell & Frost, 1989; Conger & Kanungo, 1987; Shamir, House, & Arthur, 1988; Tichy & DeVanna, 1986). While each of these approaches differs somewhat in the specific behaviors they associate with transformational leadership, all of them share the common perspective that effective leaders transform or change the basic values, beliefs, and attitudes of followers so that they are willing to perform beyond the minimum levels specified by the organization.

Preliminary research on transformational leadership has been rather promising. Some of this research (Bass, 1985; Bennis & Nanus, 1985; Boal & Bryson, 1988; Conger & Kanungo, 1987; House, 1977; House, Woycke, & Fodor, 1988; Howell & Frost, 1989; Kouzes & Posner, 1987; Tichy & DeVanna, 1986) has been primarily conceptual in nature, focusing on the identification of the key transformational behaviors, and the development of theories of their antecedents and consequences. The remainder of this research has focused on empirically testing these conceptual frameworks. Generally speaking, the empirical results have verified the impact of transformational leader behaviors on employee attitudes, effort, and "in-role" performance. For example, Bass (1985) cites a variety of field studies demonstrating that transformational leader behaviors are positively related to employees' satisfaction, self-reported effort, and job performance. Similar results have been reported by Howell and Frost (1989). They manipulated the behavior of leaders in a laboratory setting and found that charismatic leader behaviors produced better performance, greater satisfaction, and enhanced role perceptions (less role conflict) than directive leader behaviors.

Despite these encouraging results, it is important to note that the majority of the empirical research in this area has focused on the impact of transformational leader behaviors on in-role performance and follower satisfaction, rather than "extra-role" performance. While the effects of transformational behaviors on employee in-role performance are interesting, they do not capture the most important effects of transformational leader behaviors. The real essence of transformational leadership is that these leaders "lift ordinary people to extraordinary heights" (Boal & Bryson, 1988, p. 11), and cause followers to "do more than they are expected to do" (Yukl, 1989a, p. 272), and "perform beyond the level of expectations" (Bass, 1985). In other words, as noted by Graham (1988), the most important effects of transformational leaders should be on extra-role performance, rather than in-role performance. Transformational leaders should motivate followers to perform at a level "over and above mechanical compliance with the routine directives of the organization" (Katz & Kahn, 1978, p. 528).

Also surprising, given the theoretical discussions of Bennis and Nanus (1985), Boal and Bryson (1988), and Yukl

Source: Edited and reprinted with permission from *Leadership Quarterly* 1, 2(1990), 107–142. Copyright © 1990 by JAI Press Inc. Author affiliation may have changed since article was first published.

(1989a, 1989b), is that a follower's *trust* in his or her leader has not been given more attention in empirical research as a potential mediator of the effects of transformational leader behaviors on criterion variables. Bennis and Nanus (1985), for example, have suggested that effective leaders are ones that earn the trust of their followers. Similarly, trust in and loyalty to the leader play a critical role in the transformational leadership model of Boal and Bryson (1988). Finally, as noted by Yukl (1989b), one of the key reasons why followers are motivated by transformational leaders to perform beyond expectations is that followers trust and respect them. Indeed, Kouzes and Posner (1987) cite several studies, all of which indicate that the leader characteristics most valued by followers are honesty, integrity, and truthfulness. Thus, trust is viewed as playing an important mediating role in the transformational leadership process.

Another potential mediator of the impact of transformational leader behaviors on extra-role performance, in addition to trust, is employee satisfaction. Organ (1988a, 1988b, in press) has reviewed empirical research which demonstrates that employee job satisfaction is an important determinant of extra-role (e.g., "organizational citizenship") behavior. Moreover, virtually all models of transformational leadership postulate that transformational leaders enhance followers' work attitudes and satisfaction. Thus, when Organ's research on the antecedents of organizational citizenship behaviors (OCBs) is combined with models of the effects of transformational leadership, satisfaction emerges as a potential mediator of the impact of transformational leader behavior on the extra-role performance of followers.

In summary, previous theoretical and empirical research suggests that there is good reason to believe that transformational leader behaviors influence extra-role or organizational citizenship behaviors. There are, however, several potential ways in which this might happen. As shown in Figure 1, one way is for transformational leader behaviors to *directly* influence organizational citizenship behaviors, much in the same way that transactional leader behaviors have been shown to influence in-role performance (e.g., Podsakoff, Todor, & Skov, 1982; Podsakoff, Todor, Grover, & Huber, 1984; Sims & Szilagyi, 1975). This is consistent with Smith, Organ, and Near's (1983) finding that a leader's individualized support behavior, one of the transformational leader behaviors identified by Bass (Avolio & Bass, 1988; Bass, 1985), has a direct effect on some forms of employee citizenship behavior (i.e., conscientiousness).

Another possibility, also depicted in Figure 1, is that transformational leader behaviors influence organizational citizenship behaviors *only indirectly*, through their effects on mediators like followers' trust in their leaders and satisfaction. For example, in addition to documenting the direct effects of leader supportiveness on conscientiousness, Smith et al. (1983) also found that employee satisfaction *mediated* the impact of leader supportiveness on employee altruism. Followers' trust in and loyalty to the leader also has been accorded a similar role in several recent discussions of the transformational leadership process (e.g., Boal & Bryson, 1988; Kouzes & Posner, 1987; Yukl, 1989b). Thus, both followers' trust and satisfaction have been identified as potential mediators of the impact of transformational leader behaviors on followers' citizenship behaviors.

Finally, it is possible that transformational leader behaviors influence followers' citizenship behaviors *both directly* and *indirectly*. Their total effects may, in other words, be due to a combination of direct (unmediated) effects, and indirect effects working through mediators like trust and satisfaction.

The purpose of the present study, therefore, is to examine the effects of transformational leader behaviors on organizational citizenship behaviors, and the potential mediating roles of trust and satisfaction in that process. Measures of transformational leader behaviors, trust, and satisfaction were obtained from 988 exempt employees of a large petrochemical company, and measures of these employees' citizenship behaviors were obtained from their leaders. Structural equation modeling then was used to examine the direct and indirect effects of these behaviors on trust, satisfaction, and citizenship behavior. Moreover, because Bass (Avolio & Bass, 1988; Bass, 1985) argues that the effects of transformational leadership behaviors *augment* or *supplement* the effects of transactional leadership behaviors, we examined the effects of the transformational behaviors in the empirical context of the effects of the principal transactional leader behavior identified by him—contingent reward behavior. . . .

Measures

Transformational Leader Behaviors

Although broadly speaking, the topic of transformational leadership has received a great deal of attention in recent years, our understanding of what is involved in transformational leadership still is somewhat unclear. The one thing that is clear, however, is that transformational leadership is multidimensional in nature. Our review of the extant literature suggests that there are at least six key behaviors associated with transformational leaders:

- *Identifying and Articulating a Vision*—Behavior on the part of the leader aimed at identifying new opportunities for

FIGURE 1

Conceptual relationship between transformational leader behaviors, potential moderators, and organizational citizenship behaviors.

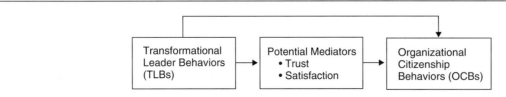

his or her unit/division/company, and developing, articulating, and inspiring others with his or her vision of the future.

- *Providing an Appropriate Model*—Behavior on the part of the leader that sets an example for employees to follow that is consistent with the values the leader espouses.

- *Fostering the Acceptance of Group Goals*—Behavior on the part of the leader aimed at promoting cooperation among employees and getting them to work together toward a common goal.

- *High Performance Expectations*—Behavior that demonstrates the leader's expectations for excellence, quality, and/or high performance on the part of followers.

- *Providing Individualized Support*—Behavior on the part of the leader that indicates that he/she respects followers and is concerned about their personal feelings and needs.

- *Intellectual Stimulation*—Behavior on the part of the leader that challenges followers to re-examine some of their assumptions about their work and rethink how it can be performed.

As shown in Table 2, each of these behaviors has been identified as an important element of the transformational leadership process. There is a great deal of consensus among the researchers on some of these behaviors, but not on others. For example, Identifying and Articulating a Vision has been identified by virtually all of the authors as an important component of the transformational leadership process. Similarly,

T A B L E 2
Behavioral Components of Existing Models of Transformational Leadership

Behavioral Components	House (1977)	Bradford and Cohen (1984)	Bass (1985)	Bennis and Nanus (1985)	Tichy and DeVanna (1986)	Conger and Kanungo (1987)	Kouzes and Posner (1987)
Identify and articulate a vision	Provide an appealing vision	Determine and build a common vision	Charismatic leader behavior*	Management of attention through vision	Recognize a need for change and create a new vision	Advocate an appealing yet unconventional vision	Challenge the process and inspire a shared vision
Provide an appropriate model	Set an example for followers to imitate		Charismatic leader behavior			Take a high personal risk to support the vision	Model the way
Fostering the acceptance of group goals		Build a shared responsibility team		Work to develop commitment and trust	Team build to gain support for new vision		Enable others to act
High performance expectations	Communicate high expectations of follower performance		Inspirational leader behavior				
Provide individualized support			Individualized consideration			Be sensitive to the needs of the followers	
Recognize accomplishments						Behave with confidence and enthusiasm	Encourage the heart
Intellectual stimulation			Intellectual stimulation				
Other	Behave to arouse individual motives	Continuously develop the skills of individuals	Charismatic leader behavior*				

Note: *Bass' (1985) conceptualization of charismatic leadership includes leader vision, as well as respect for the leader and the inspiration and encouragement provided by his or her presence.

Facilitating the Acceptance of Group Goals and Providing an Appropriate Model were identified by at least four different authors as elements of transformational leadership. In contrast, only Bass and his colleagues (Avolio & Bass, 1988; Bass, 1985) argue that Intellectual Stimulation should be considered an aspect of transformational leadership. However, in order to make certain that the domain of transformational leader behaviors was adequately tapped, and that our test of the impact of these behaviors was comprehensive, we chose to include all six of the categories identifed above in the present study. . . .

Aggregate Effects of Leader Behaviors on OCBs

An examination of the aggregate effects of the set of transformational leader behaviors on the set of organizational citizenship behaviors indicates that the effects of these leader behaviors on OCBs are *indirect*, rather than *direct*, in that they are mediated by followers' trust in their leaders. More specifically, our findings generally showed that: (a) transformational leader behaviors had no direct effects on OCBs, (b) transformational leader behaviors influenced both employee trust and satisfaction, and (c) trust influenced OCBs, but employee satisfaction did not. Moreover, it is important to note that these findings are completely independent of the effects of transactional leader behaviors, and also were relatively robust in comparison to the effects of common method biases.

In contrast, the effects of the transactional leader behavior (contingent rewards) on OCBs produced a markedly different pattern. Unlike the transformational leader behaviors, contingent reward behavior had a direct positive impact on both altruism and sportsmanship, but no effect at all on either trust or employee satisfaction. Thus, in contrast to the transformational behaviors, transactional leader behavior influenced OCBs *directly*, rather than indirectly. The fact that these two types of leader behavior appear to influence extra-role performance in very different ways emphasizes the importance of the distinction between transactional and transformational leader behaviors.

One possible explanation for why transactional leader behaviors have direct rather than indirect effects may have to do with the nature of the behaviors themselves. Transactional leader behaviors are ones which are founded on some sort of exchange, or give and take, between the leader and the subordinate. If, as shown by Jackson, Keith, and Schlacter (1983), managers consider both in-role and extra-role behaviors when evaluating employee performance, they may also recognize accomplishments in both of these areas as well. This may cause employees to see the performance of OCBs as a means of obtaining recognition and other forms of rewards, thus motivating them to engage in organizational citizenship behavior.

Individual Effects of Leader Behaviors on OCBs

An examination of the individual level results produced some interesting findings. The standardized estimates suggest that the "core" transformational leader behaviors, individualized support, and intellectual stimulation, were the key determinants of both trust and satisfaction. The "core" transformational behaviors and individualized support both had positive effects, as expected. However, intellectual stimulation was found to have a negative impact on both trust and satisfaction.

One possible explanation for this surprising finding may have to do with the effect of intellectual stimulation on role ambiguity, conflict, and stress. Although intellectual stimulation may produce desirable effects in the long run, it may be that in the short run, leaders who continually urge or exhort followers to search for new and better methods of doing things create ambiguity, conflict, or other forms of stress in the minds of those followers. If the increased task demands produced by a leader's intellectual stimulation behavior increase stress, ambiguity, and conflict, we might expect that followers will express less trust in the leader and engage in fewer OCBs. Indeed, this is consistent with recent research (cf. Cohen, 1980; Motowidlo, Packard, & Manning, 1986) that suggests that stress induced by increased task demands decreases interpersonal sensitivity and helping behavior.

Another possible reason why intellectual stimulation may reduce follower trust and satisfaction may have to do with the destabilizing nature of intellectual stimulation itself. According to Avolio and Bass (1988), intellectual stimulation causes a "cognitive reappraisal of current circumstances," thus possibly reversing an individual's "figure-ground" and leading to a questioning of "old" and perhaps comfortable assumptions.[6] It may be that this process is dissatisfying, and that leaders who continually do this are trusted less because they are perceived as being less predictable and/or dependable.

One additional finding of note is that high performance expectations reduced employee trust. Although it is not immediately obvious why this occurred, it may have to do with the way in which we measured high performance expectations. House (1977) suggests that two aspects of high performance expectations are important. One is that the leader must communicate those expectations to his/her subordinates. The other is that the leader must let them know that he/she is confident they can meet these expectations. In retrospect, our measure seems to do a good job of tapping the former component, but not the latter. It may be natural for an employee to distrust a leader who continually demands high levels of performance without ever expressing any confidence in the employee's ability to achieve those expectations. . . .

Notes

[1]Although there are differences between transformational and charismatic leader behaviors, they are similar in many respects. The principal reason we chose to use the term transformational leadership is that it is broader in the sense that it includes a wider variety of leader behaviors. Thus, unless otherwise indicated in our discussion, we will use the term transformational leadership throughout the paper. . . .

[6]We would like to thank one anonymous reviewer for pointing out this possibility.

References

Alexander, S., & Ruderman, M. (1987). The role of procedural and distributive justice in organizational behavior. *Social Justice Research, 1,* 177–198.

Avolio, B. J., & Bass, B. M. (1988). Transformational leadership, charisma, and beyond. In J. G. Hunt, B. R. Baliga, H. P. Dachler, & C. A. Schriesheim (Eds.), *Emerging leadership vistas* (pp. 29–49). Lexington, MA: Lexington Books.

Bagozzi, R. P. (1978). The construct validity of the affective, behavioral, and cognitive components of attitude by analysis of covariance structures. *Multivariate Behavioral Research, 13,* 9–31.

Bagozzi, R. P. (1980). *Causal models in marketing.* New York: Wiley.

Burnkrant, R. E., & Page, T. J., Jr. (1982). An examination of the convergent, discriminant, and predictive validity of Fishbein's behavioral intention model. *Journal of Marketing Research, 19,* 550–561.

Bass, B. M. (1981). *Stogdill's handbook of leadership* (rev. ed.). New York: Free Press.

Bass, B. M. (1985). *Leadership and performance beyond expectations.* New York: Free Press.

Bass, B. M., Avolio, B. J., & Goodheim, L. (1987). Biography and the assessment of transformational leadership at the world class level. *Journal of Management, 13,* 7–19.

Bass, B. M., Waldman, D. A., Avolio, B. J., & Bebb, M. (1987). Transformational leadership and the falling dominoes effect. *Group and Organization Studies, 12,* 73–87.

Batesman, T. S., & Organ, D. W. (1983). Job satisfaction and the good soldier: The relationship between affect and employee "citizenship." *Academy of Management Journal, 26,* 587–595.

Bennis, W., & Nanus, B. (1985) *Leaders: The strategies for taking charge.* New York: Harper & Row.

Bentler, P. M., & Bonett, D. G. (1980). Significance tests and goodness of fit in the analysis of covariance structures. *Psychological Bulletin, 88,* 588–606.

Boal, K. B., & Bryson, J. M. (1988). Charismatic leadership: A phenomenological and structural approach. In J. G. Hunt, B. R. Baliga, H. P. Dachler, & C. A. Schriesheim (Eds.), *Emerging Leadership Vistas* (pp. 5–28). Lexington, MA: Lexington Books.

Bradford, D. L., & Cohen, A. R. (1984). *Managing for excellence: The guide to developing high performance in contemporary organizations.* New York: Wiley.

Burns, J. M. (1978). *Leadership.* New York: Harper & Row.

Churchill, G. A., Jr. (1979). A paradigm for developing better measures of marketing constructs. *Journal of Marketing Research, 16,* 64–73.

Cohen, S. (1980). Aftereffects of stress on human performance and social behavior: A review of research and theory. *Psychological Bulletin, 88,* 82–108.

Conger, J. A., & Kanungo, R. N. (1987). Toward a behavioral theory of charismatic leadership in organizational settings. *Academy of Management Review, 12,* 637–647.

Cook, J., & Wall, T. (1980). New work attitude measures of trust, organizational commitment and personal need non-fulfillment. *Journal of Occupational Psychology, 53,* 39–52.

Dansereau, F., Jr., Graen, G., & Haga, W. J. (1975). A vertical dyad linkage approach to leadership within formal organizations: A longitudinal investigation of the role-making process. *Organizational Behavior and Human Performance, 13,* 46–78.

Dunham, R. B., Smith, F. J., & Blackburn, R. S. (1977). Validation of the index of organizational reactions with the JDI, the MSQ, and the faces scales. *Academy of Management Journal, 20,* 420–432.

Folger, R. (1977). Distributive and procedural justice: Combined impact of "voice" and improvement on experienced inequity. *Journal of Personality and Psychology, 35,* 108–119.

Folger, R. (1986). Rethinking equity theory. In Bierhof, H. W., Cohen, R. L., & Greenberg, J. (Eds.), *Justice in Social Relations* (pp. 145–162). New York: Plenum.

Folger, R. (1987). Distributive and procedural justice in the workplace. *Social Justice Research, 1,* 143–159.

Folger, R., & Konovsky, M. A. (1989). Effects of procedural and distributive justice on reactions to pay raise decisions. *Academy of Management Journal, 32,* 115–130.

Giffin, K. (1967). The contribution of studies of source credibility to a theory of interpersonal trust in the communication process. *Psychological Bulletin, 68,* 104–120.

Gillet, B., & Schwab, D. P. (1975). Convergent and discriminant validities of corresponding Job Descriptive Index and Minnesota Satisfaction Questionnaire scales. *Journal of Applied Psychology, 60,* 629–631.

Graen, G. (1976). Role making processes within complex organizations. In M. D. Dunnette (Ed.), *Handbook of Industrial and Organizational Psychology* (pp. 1201–1245). Chicago: Rand McNally.

Graen, G., & Cashman, J. (1975). A role-making model of leadership in formal organizations: A developmental approach. J. G. Hunt & L. L. Larson (Eds.), *Leadership frontiers* (pp. 143–166). Kent, OH: Kent State University Press.

Graen, G., & Scandura, T. A. (1987). Toward a psychology of dynamic organizing. L. L. Cummings & B. M. Staw (Eds.), *Research in Organizational Behavior* (Vol. 9, pp. 175–208). Greenwich, CT: JAI.

Graham, J. W. (1988). Chapter 3 commentary: Transformational leadership: Fostering follower autonomy, not automatic followership. In J. G. Hunt, B. R. Baliga, H. P. Dachler, & C. A. Schriesheim (Eds.), *Emerging leadership vistas* (pp. 73–79). Lexington, MA: Lexington Books.

House, R. J. (1971). A path goal theory of leader effectiveness. *Administrative Science Quarterly, 16,* 321–338.

House, R. J. (1977). A 1976 theory of charismatic leadership. In J. G. Hunt & L. L. Larson (Eds.), *Leadership: The cutting edge.* Carbondale, IL: Southern Illinois University Press.

House, R. J. (1988). Leadership research: Some forgotten, ignored, or overlooked findings. In J. G. Hunt, B. R. Baliga, H. P. Dachler, & C. A. Schriesheim (Eds.), *Emerging leadership vistas.* Lexington, MA: Lexington.

House, R. J., & Baetz, M. L. (1979). Leadership: Some empirical generalizations and new research directions. In B. M. Staw (Ed.), *Research in Organizational Behavior* (Vol. 1, pp. 341–423). Greenwich, CT: JAI Press.

House, R. J., Spangler, W. D., & Woycke, J. (1989). *Personality and charisma in the U.S. presidency: A psychological theory of leadership effectiveness.* Working paper, Wharton Business School, University of Pennsylvania.

House, R. J., Woycke, J., & Fodor, E. M. (1988). Perceived behavior and effectiveness of charismatic and non-charismatic U.S. presidents. In Conger, J. & Kanungo, R. (Eds.), *Charismatic Leadership and Management.* San Francisco: Jossey-Bass.

Howell, J. M., & Frost, P. J. (1989). A laboratory study of charismatic leadership. *Organizational Behavior and Human Decision Processes, 43,* 243–269.

Jackson, D. W., Keith, J. E., & Schlacter, J. L. (1983). Evaluation of selling performance: A study of current practices. *Journal of Personal Selling and Sales Management 3,* 43–51.

Joreskog, K. G., & Sorbom, D. (1986). *LISREL IV: Analysis of linear structural relationships by maximum likelihood, instrumental variables and least squares methods* (4th ed.). Mooresville, IN: Scientific Software.

Katz, D., & Kahn, R. L. (1978). *The social psychology of organizations* (2nd ed.). New York: Wiley.

Kouzes, J. M., & Posner, B. Z. (1987). *The Leadership Challenge.* San Francisco: Jossey-Bass.

Kuhnert, K. W., & Lewis, P. (1987). Transactional and transformational leadership: A constructive/developmental analysis. *Academy of Management Review, 12,* 648–657.

Lord, R. G. (1985). An information processing approach to social perceptions, leadership and behavioral measurement in organizations. In L. L. Cummings & B. M. Staw (Eds.), *Research in Organizational Behavior* (Vol. 7, pp. 87–128). Greenwich, CT: JAI Press.

Lord, R. G., Binning, J. F., Rush, M. C., & Thomas, J. C. (1978). The effect of performance cues and leader behavior on questionnaire ratings of leadership behavior. *Organizational Behavior and Human Performance, 21,* 27–39.

Marsh, H. W., Balla, J. R., & McDonald, R. P. (1988). Goodness-of-fit indexes in confirmatory factor analysis: The effect of sample size. *Psychological Bulletin, 103,* 391–410.

McCrae, R. R., & Costa, P. T. (1987). Validation of the five-factor model of personality across instruments and observers. *Journal of Personality and Social Psychology, 52,* 81–90.

Motowidlo, S. J. (1984). Does job satisfaction lead to consideration and personal sensitivity? *Academy of Management Journal, 27,* 910–915.

Motowidlo, S. J., Packard, J. S., & Manning, M. R. (1986). Occupational stress: Its causes and consequences for job performance. *Journal of Applied Psychology, 71,* 618–629.

Nunnally, J. C. (1978). *Psychometric Theory* (2nd ed.). New York: McGraw-Hill.

Organ, D. W. (1988a). *Organizational citizenship behavior: The good soldier syndrome.* Lexington, MA: Lexington Books.

Organ, D. W. (1988b). A restatement of the satisfaction-performance hypothesis. *Journal of Management, 14,* 547–557.

Organ, D. W. (in press). The motivational basis of organizational citizenship behavior. In Staw, B. M.

& Cummings, L. L. (Eds.), *Research in organizational behavior* (Vol. 12). Greenwich, CT: JAI Press.

Phillips, J. S., & Lord, R. G. (1986). Notes on the practical and theoretical consequences of implicit leadership theories for the future of leadership measurement. *Journal of Management, 12,* 31–41.

Podsakoff, P. M., & Organ, D. W. (1986). Self-reports in organizational research: Problems and prospects, *Journal of Management, 13,* 419–441.

Podsakoff, P. M., Todor, W. D., Grover, R. A., & Huber, V. L. (1984). Situational moderators of leader reward and punishment behavior: Fact or fiction? *Organizational Behavior and Human Performance, 34,* 21–63.

Podsakoff, P. M., Todor, W. D., & Skov, R. (1982). Effects of leader performance contingent and non-contingent reward and punishment behaviors on subordinate performance and satisfaction. *Academy of Management Journal, 25,* 812–821.

Puffer, S. M. (1987). Prosocial behavior, noncompliant behavior, and work performance among commission salespeople. *Journal of Applied Psychology, 72,* 615–621.

Rotter, J. B. (1967). A new scale for the measurement of interpersonal trust. *Journal of Personality, 35,* 651–665.

Schmitt, N., & Stults, D. M. (1986). Methodology review: Analysis of multitrait-multimethod matrices. *Applied Psychological Measurement, 10,* 1–22.

Schwab, D. P. (1980). Construct validity in organizational behavior. In L. L. Cummings & B. M. Staw (Eds.), *Research in Organizational Behavior* (Vol. 2, pp. 3–43. Greenwich, CT: JAI Press.

Shamir, B., House, R. J., & Arthur, M. B. (1988). *The transformational effects of charismatic leadership: A motivational theory.* Unpublished Working Paper, The Hebrew University, Jerusalem.

Sims, H. P., Jr., & Szilagyi, A. D. (1975). Leader reward behavior and subordinate satisfaction and performance. *Organizational Behavior and Human Performance, 14,* 426–437.

Smith, C. A., Organ, D. W., & Near, J. P. (1983) Organizational citizenship behavior: Its nature and antecedents. *Journal of Applied Psychology, 68,* 653–663.

Stogdill, R. M. (1974). *Handbook of leadership.* New York: Free Press.

Tichy, N., & DeVanna, M. (1986). *The transformational leader.* New York: Wiley.

Tucker, L. R., & Lewis, C. (1973). The reliability coefficient for maximum likelihood factor analysis. *Psychometrika, 38,* 1–10.

Weiss, D. J., Dawis, R. V., England, G. W., & Lofquist, L. H. (1967). *Manual for the Minnesota Satisfaction Questionnaire* (Minnesota Studies in Vocational Rehabilitation: XXII). Minneapolis: University of Minnesota, Industrial Relations Center Work Adjustment Project.

Widaman, K. F. (1985). Hierarchically nested covariance structure models for multitrait-multimethod data. *Applied Psychological Measurement, 9,* 1–26.

Yukl, G. A. (1989a). *Leadership in organizations* (2nd ed.). Englewood Cliffs, NJ: Prentice-Hall.

Yukl, G. A. (1989b). Managerial leadership: A review of theory and research. *Yearly Review of Management, 15,* 251–289.

Chapter Ten

Leadership and the High Office

Most commonly, reference to leadership focuses upon a group of individuals working together toward the accomplishment of a common goal. Committees, task or project teams, departments (work groups), and self-managed work teams each consist of a relatively small group of individuals. They typify the organizational images that we form when thinking about a leader and his or her followers. But what about the leadership of entire organizations? Is it possible that one individual, who by the sheer force of his or her personality, skills/abilities, and/or behaviors, can create relationships that are powerful enough to move hundreds and thousands of people such that the leader actually makes a significant organizational difference? This chapter focuses on organizational leadership as orchestrated from the upper echelons of the organization.

American organizations have been criticized for being "over managed and under-led." Critics contend that the crisis facing American organizations (e.g., declining rates of productivity increases, deteriorating plants and machinery, lost ground in research and development, lack of competitive responsiveness at home and abroad, and worker discontent) stem from bad management and inept leadership. W. Edwards Deming commented that American management is one thing that this country should not export to a friendly country, since it suffers from many diseases that unless corrected are potentially fatal. Carl Icahn, while president of Trans World Airlines, struck a similar chord when he suggested that the crises facing U.S. corporations are largely the result of inadequate leadership and poor management practices.[1]

A number of organization and leadership scholars suggest that leadership at the small group and lower organizational level is qualitatively different from leadership at the higher organization levels. According to Daniel Katz and Robert L. Kahn (1978), top-level leaders create structures, negotiate with key power brokers in the organization's external environment, make major organizational resource commitments, create vision and formulate organizational strategies, define organizational culture, and articulate major organizational policies. Middle-level leaders interpret and elaborate the visions formulated at the top, and they orchestrate and integrate lower-level organizational activities. Small-group and lower-level leaders, on the other hand, assume responsibility for day-to-day organizational activities through the application of their technical and interpersonal skills.[2] In the high-involvement organization, they work with and lead small groups by serving as mentors, teachers, and as facilitators of the exercise of self- and group-direction and control in the conduct of the group's performance affairs.

---

[1] W. E. Deming, Deming Seminar Sponsored by School of Engineering and Applied Science, San Diego, California, January 24–27 1984; C. Icahn, "What Ails Corporate America—and What Should Be Done?" *Business Week,* October 27, 1986, p. 101.

[2] D. Katz and R. L. Kahn, *The Social Psychology of Organizations,* 2nd ed (New York: Wiley, 1978).

In the first reading in this chapter, Donald C. Hambrick (1989) suggests that if we want to understand why organizations do the things that they do and why they perform the way that they do, it is necessary to look toward those at the helm of the organization—those responsible for strategic leadership. Hambrick provides insight into the definition of strategic leadership, and he differentiates this role from that of a small-group and lower-level organizational leader.

The strategic leader focuses upon: (a) attempting to achieve a fit or alignment between the organization and its external environment, (b) assuming the responsibility for the development of the organization's internal environment into an adaptive system that is aligned with the mission of the organization, (c) understanding and integrating the multifunctional activities of the organization, and (d) achieving its effects through the leadership efforts of others. All of this, of course, tends to be accomplished while embedded in a sea of complexity, uncertainty, and information overload.

There are four major dimensions that tend to characterize strategic leadership. They consist of attributes of the leader (e.g., knowledge, aptitude, personality, values, age, socioeconomic background), what it is that strategic leaders do (e.g., think, create/envision, signal/symbolize), their organizational responsibilities, and how they do it (e.g., speed, politicization, openness, formality). Thus, it is clear that strategic leadership is more than a trait embedded within a particular person; it is also characterized from a behavioral and process perspective.

Donald C. Hambrick and Phyllis A. Mason (1984) present an interesting and unique perspective on leadership—leadership from the upper echelons of the organization that stems from a "group" of individuals acting on behalf of the organization as opposed to the acts, personage, and relationships that derive from a particular individual. There are organizations today that, instead of having an individual serve as the organization's chief executive officer (CEO) and strategic leader, have created the office of the CEO and, through this office, a team of upper-level managers provide organizational leadership. When Louis V. Gerstner, Jr., left RJR Nabisco to take over at IBM, RJR moved two of its executive vice presidents to their newly created "office of the chairman." They were to jointly operate as the chief executive and chairman.

In the second reading, Hambrick and Mason provide insight into the process through which a strategic leader or a dominant coalition can affect the behavior and performance of an entire organization. Their work, in part, reflects the social psychological dynamics of leadership effects.

Hambrick and Mason suggest that organizational performance (e.g., profitability, growth, survival) is significantly affected by the strategic choices made (e.g., product innovation, diversification, acquisitions, administrative complexity, response time), formally and informally, by an organization's dominant decision-making coalition. Strategic decision making (i.e., strategic choice) tends to get exercised amidst a sea of uncertainty and more information (i.e., stimuli) than can be systematically processed. Decision makers, either individuals or groups, bring to the decision context their idiosyncrasies (e.g., values and cognitive bases) that tend to shape, filter, distort, or selectively define the stimuli that will be attended to and frame the interpretation that will be given to these stimuli. It is these idiosyncrasies that ultimately define the strategic choices that get made on the organization's behalf.

Hambrick and Mason provide insight into the role played by several attributes (i.e., age, functional track, career experiences, formal education, socioeconomic background, financial position, and group heterogeneity) that can be employed to describe upper-level organizational leaders and the potential impact that these attributes might have upon different dimensions of the organization's performance. They hypothesize, for example, that a homogeneous top-management leadership team will make a positive contribution to organizational profitability in a stable environment. By contrast, in a turbulent and discontinuous environment, a homogeneous top-leadership team is not equipped to make the same positive contribution to the firm's profitability as that provided by a heterogeneous leadership group.

In the last reading in this chapter, Brian P. Niehoff, Cathy A. Enz, and Richard A. Grover (1990) provide additional insight into the role of transformational leadership (a topic explored in the previous chapter). Specifically, Niehoff and his colleagues found a relationship between top-management (i.e., chief executive officer and the vice president levels) actions (i.e., inspiring a shared vision, modeling the vision, encouraging innovativeness, supporting employee efforts, and allowing for employee influence in decision making) and employee attitudes and perceptions (i.e., job satisfaction, organizational commitment, and role ambiguity). Commitment was, for example, stronger when top management was experienced at inspiring a shared vision and modeling that vision.

According to David V. Day and Robert G. Lord (1988), there are several means by which top-level leaders can affect organizational performance. For example, they suggest several ways that leaders influence and adapt to their external environment (e.g., direct political influence, integration) and promote internal adaptation and exercise internal influence (e.g., use information to shape symbols, determine or influence organizational policies). Implicit in their work is the argument that top-level organizational leaders can work to affect the overall performance of very large social systems.[3]

The purpose of this chapter is to stimulate your thinking about leadership of large and complex social systems.[4] Does it really make sense to think about leadership of an entire organization? While it is common to hear discussions about the leadership of such individuals as Jack Welch at General Electric, Andy Grove of Intel, Bill Gates at Microsoft, Jan Carlzon at Scandinavian Airlines (SAS), and Lee Iacocca while he was with Chrysler, observers should question whether these individuals "really made a difference" or whether their role was merely one of being their organization's public figurehead and symbolic leader.

This chapter focuses your attention on two very important issues. First, Hambrick provides a *definition* of strategic leadership and differentiates it from lower-level organizational leadership. Second, Hambrick and Mason provide insight into the *process* of how the strategic leader and/or the organization's upper-echelon leadership group can have an impact upon the overall behavior and performance of an organization. This leads logically to the subject of attention in the next chapter—"Does leadership really make a difference in terms of organizational performance?"

[3] D. V. Day and R. G. Lord, "Executive Leadership and Organizational Performance: Suggestions for a New Theory and Methodology," *Journal of Management* 14 (1988), 453–64.

[4] Further insight into the role of organizational leadership can be gained by reviewing: R. J. House and M. L. Baetz, "Leadership: Some Empirical Generalizations and New Research Directions," in B. M. Staw ed., *Research in Organizational Behavior* 1 (Greenwich, CT: JAI Press 1979), 341–423; and R. J. House and J. V. Singh, "Organizational Behavior: Some New Directions for I/O Psychology," in M. R. Rosenzweig and L. W. Porter, eds., *Annual Review of Psychology* 38 (Palo Alto, CA: Annuals Reviews, Inc., 1987), 669–718.

Putting Top Managers Back in the Strategy Picture

D. C. Hambrick
Columbia University

*A*t one time, top managers were front and center in the frameworks of the strategy field. The Harvard model (Learned *et al.,* 1961; Andrews, 1971), which served as principal guide for policy thinkers in the sixties and early seventies, emphasized the personal role of senior executives in shaping their firms. This view was not new. Earlier theoretical work by Barnard (1938) and Selznick (1957), for example, had established a rationale for including top managers in analytic investigations of contemporary organizations.

However, as of the early seventies, this theme was essentially lost. Top managers became noticeably absent from writings on strategy, somehow passed over in favor of more technoeconomic factors such as product life cycles, market share, experience curves, portfolio matrices, and industry analysis. Consulting firms all sought their own concise, analytic, quantifiable schemes. Strategy researchers struggled to demonstrate that their domain was as "hard" as any other. Corporations came to think of strategic management as the annual production of glossy three-ring binders and slide shows, rather than the development and cultivation of strategic thinkers.

Now, after almost two decades of relative neglect, the people at the helms of organizations are once again becoming part of the theoretical formulations of strategy and organization researchers (e.g., Kotter, 1982; Hambrick and Mason, 1984; Gupta and Govindarajan, 1984; Miller and Droge, 1986; Gabarro, 1987). The press and politicians have put forth a cry for "leadership" to restore economic vitality to Western countries. Companies are investing unprecedented amounts in management development activities.

That we would return to a focus on top managers was inevitable. Ultimately, they account for what happens to the organization. In the face of the complex, multitudinous, and ambiguous information that typifies the top-management task, no two strategists will identify the same array of options for the firm; they will rarely prefer the same options; if, by remote chance, they were to pick the same options, they almost certainly would not implement them identically. Biases, blinders, egos, aptitudes, experiences, fatigue, and other human factors in the executive ranks greatly affect what happens to companies. This is not to say that managers are weak or sinister, only that they are human and finite. As a result, if we want to explain why organizations do the things they do, or, in turn, why they perform the way they do, we must examine the people at the top. . . .

The study of *strategic leadership* focuses on the people who have overall responsibility for an organization—the characteristics of those people, what they do, and how they do it. The people who are the subjects of strategic leadership research can be individual executives (e.g. CEOs or division general managers), more broadly defined "top-management teams," or other governance bodies (e.g. boards of directors).

I prefer "strategic leadership" because it connotes management of an overall enterprise, not just a small part; and it implies substantive decision-making responsibilities, not only the interpersonal and social dimensions typically associated with the word *leadership* alone. Moreover, as an area of academic study, leadership tends to be equated with a series of inquiries (done in the late 60s and early 70s) into low-level supervisory managers. *Upper echelons,* a term set forth by Phyllis Mason and me (Hambrick and Mason, 1984), has its own limitations in referring primarily to the association between executive characteristics and organizational outcomes, or only a part of the domain of strategic leadership.

Before moving on, it is useful to distinguish the strategic leadership task from the management task at lower, operational levels of the organization. Obviously, the two types share some characteristics, but there are certain features of the top management job which should influence its study (Mintzberg, 1973; Kotter, 1982).

First, the strategic leader is concerned with both the external and internal spheres. A major job is to align the organization with the current and expected external environment—technology, market trends, regulatory forces, competitor actions, and so on. As important, however, is the job of developing an internal organization that has an adaptive capacity and is itself aligned with the strategic thrusts of the firm.

Second, the strategic leader is embedded in ambiguity, complexity, and information overload. There are far more stimuli than can be attended to, stimuli that are often vague, ill-formed, and competing, and that typically have important interconnections which are hard to discern.

A third characteristic of the strategic leadership task is that it is multifunctional—cutting across marketing, operations, finance, and other activities. This means that the strategic leader has a complex integrative task, and it also means that subordinate managers typically possess greater expertise about the components of the enterprise than does the strategic leader. This knowledge asymmetry has important implications for information exchange, reward and control systems, and top team composition.

Finally, the strategic leadership task, in contrast to leading

Source: Edited and reprinted with permission from *Strategic Management Journal* 10 (1989), 5–15. Author affiliation may have changed since the article was first published.

a smaller departmental subunit, largely involves managing through others. With hundreds or thousands of employees, the strategic leader must rely on intermediaries for managing the daily affairs of the enterprise. While it may be a prescriptive ideal for the strategic leader to have a strong personal presence throughout the organization, realistically the job largely entails the "management of managers" who will serve as the leader's conduits and agents.

In advocating the study of top managers, we might be seen as glorifying them. But the strategic leadership perspective does not mean to do that. We do not wish to elevate top managers in any moral, social, or economic sense. Managers are worth studying as much for their flaws and shortcomings as for their achievements. In response to the debate on whether managers, including strategic leaders, matter, our position is: some do, some don't, and a lot more could. There are good and bad managers. Our ultimate aim, as part of the practical tradition of the field of strategy, is to help shift the proportions.

Framework for Mapping Strategic Leadership Research

How does strategic leadership fit into the overall domains of strategy and organization theory? Figure 1 portrays the several theoretical connections that can be drawn from strategic leadership to the other conceptual elements that comprise the strategy researcher's world. With simplification, we can think of three major conceptual elements with which strategy and organization researchers customarily deal, as well as the typical connections theorized among them (dashed lines in

Figure 1). *Settings* are exogenous "givens" which describe the environment (e.g. industry growth rate or concentration ratio) or organization (e.g. size or diversity). *Organizational form and conduct* are a class of characteristics of the firm which researchers either: (1) try to explain on the basis of settings; (2) use in conjunction with settings to explain performance; or (3) use alone to predict performance. In the third case, there may be no important distinction between whether an organizational characteristic (say, diversity) is a setting or form/conduct; however, in the prior two cases the distinction is important, with setting being the more immutable given and form/conduct being the firm's "response" to the setting. Both temporally and causally, then, the direction is from setting to form/conduct. The third customary element in strategy theory is *performance* (effectiveness, efficiency, fulfillment of various stakeholders' needs). Not every inquiry will, or should, encompass organization performance. However, the improvement of organization performance is part of the charter of the field of strategy, setting it apart from other related fields.

If one believes in the potentially influential role of top managers in affecting organizational outcomes, and if one sees top managers as distinct from the outcomes they produce (e.g. they shape structure and are not simply part of the structure), then strategic leadership should be seen as a fourth element in the theoretical framework of the field of strategy. Without getting into many possible multiway interactions and feedback loops, there are six broad classes of inquiry into strategic leadership (the solid numbered lines in Figure 1). We will now inventory these and provide examples (if only a few of each) in existing literature.

FIGURE 1
Fitting Strategic Leadership into the Strategy Framework

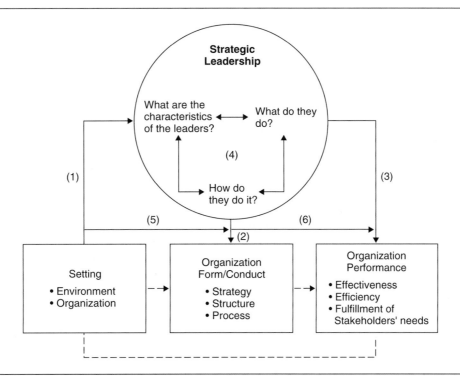

1) Settings Affect Strategic Leadership

Executives do not randomly arrive at the tops of organizations. Whether managerial profiles occur through purposive attempts to align the managerial cadre with environmental requirements, or through political or Darwinian processes, it is important to study why certain people hold executive positions and engage in the behaviors they do. In this case, leadership is a dependent variable.

Examples:

a. A firm's diversification posture affects the mix of functional areas represented on the top-management team (Song, 1982).

b. The age of an industry affects the ages of senior executives within the industry (Pfeffer, 1983).

c. A firm's size affects the chief executive's role behaviors (Mintzberg, 1973).

2) Strategic Leadership Affects Organization Form and Conduct

Most closely aligned with the "upper echelons" perspective (Hambrick and Mason, 1984), this view argues that the organization is a reflection of its top managers. Values, cognitions, and interpersonal dynamics affect ultimate choices.

Examples:

a. The chief executive's personality affects the structure of the organization (Miller and Droge, 1986).

b. The values of the top-management team affect the organization's level of innovation (Hage and Dewar, 1972).

c. Whether a new chief executive comes from inside or outside the organization affects how much organizational change will occur early in his or her tenure (Helmich and Brown, 1972).

d. Executive team tenure affects the firm's strategic decision process (Fredrickson and Iaquinto, in press).

3) Strategic Leadership Affects Organizational Performance

In some cases, specific characteristics of executives can influence performance. As the following examples indicate, the most promising predictors may be relatively direct gauges of executive caliber, such as prior track record.

Examples:

a. The leader's performance in prior positions affects the performance of the organization the leader currently heads (Smith *et al.* 1984; Pfeffer and Davis-Blake, 1986).

b. The scope of a leader's influence affects the likelihood of organizational failure when the leader departs (Carroll, 1984).

4) Certain Aspects of Strategic Leadership (e.g., the Executive's Characteristics) Affect Other Aspects of Leadership (e.g., How the Executive Behaves)

As a conceptual element, strategic leadership consists of many facets or subelements. It is reasonable and important, then, to study how executive dimensions tend to be related to each other.

Examples:

a. Executives' functional backgrounds affect how they perceive and define business problems (Dearborn and Simon, 1958; Walsh, 1988).

b. The degree of demographic dissimilarity within a top-management team affects the rate of member turnover (Wagner *et al.*, 1984).

c. An executive's early upbringing and family situation affect his/her management style and preferences (Collins and Moore, 1970; Kotter, 1982).

5) The Association between Strategic Leadership and Form/Conduct Depends on the Setting

Executive characteristics and behaviors will not have uniform effects in all contexts. Certain settings may enhance or restrict the amount of executive impact (Hambrick and Finkelstein, 1987), or even the direction of executive impact.

Examples:

a. The association between CEO personality and organizational innovation is stronger in small firms than in large firms (Miller *et al.*, 1982).

b. Mayors are able to make more changes in budget categories that have diffuse political constituencies than in those that have concentrated constituencies (Salancik and Pfeffer, 1977).

c. The association between top-team tenure and strategic persistence is greater in high-discretion industries (growing, differentiable, unregulated) than in low-discretion industries (mature, commodity, regulated) (Finkelstein, 1988).

6) The Association between Leadership and Organizational Performance Depends on the Setting

This is the prescriptive contingency perspective, arguing that there is no universally ideal set of executive characteristics or behaviors. Rather, leadership must "fit" the setting in order to yield high performance.

Examples:

a. The association between different types of general manager expertise and organizational performance depends on the strategy of the business (Gupta and Govindarajan, 1984).

b. The association between top management team heterogeneity and organizational performance depends on the dynamism of the environment (Hambrick and Mason, 1984; Hambrick and Brandon, 1988).

c. The association between top-team turnover and subsequent organizational performance depends on prior performance (Tushman *et al.*, 1985).

As noted earlier, more complex multiway interactions can also be studied. But, by and large, the primary focus (sometimes explicit, sometimes implicit) of nearly all strategic leadership research conducted so far can be assigned to the six categories just discussed.

In an attempt to explicate even further what we mean by strategic leadership, it is useful to focus on its discrete elements. Table 1 lists some of the key dimensions of each of the three main components of strategic leadership: What are the characteristics of the leaders? What do they do? How do they do it? The attempt is not to be exhaustive, but only to provide a broad range of illustrative characteristics of leadership that may concern its theorists. Some of the dimensions listed, such as executive tenure and top team heterogeneity, have been used in prior research; however, most others have been given very little attention.

As can be seen, strategic leadership is an expansive domain. It is an area of research that can benefit from such disparate theoretical perspectives as cognitive psychology, social psychology, personality theory, sociology, agency theory, human development theory, information processing, political science, military science, anthropology, game theory, language theory, as well as others. Promising prospects may exist for projects that draw from more than one of these perspectives. Certainly, the most significant projects will be those that relate leadership to other elements of the strategy paradigm: settings, conduct/firm, or performance. Accordingly, multidisciplinary research teams may be critical to the continued development of strategic leadership theory and research. Above all, we must avoid premature closure on any single perspective for studying the people at the upper reaches of organizations. . . .

T A B L E   1
Illustrative Dimensions of Strategic Leadership

What Are the Characteristics of the Leaders?

Demographics	Knowledge
Tenure	Skills
Age	Aptitudes
Functional backgrounds	Personalities
Education	Values
Socio-economic background	Cognitive Styles
Financial wealth	
Ownership position	
Team Heterogeneity	
Team Size	

What Do They Do?

Think
Create/Envision
Decide
Communicate/Interact
Signal/Symbolize
Allocate their time

How Do They Do It?

Speed	Explicitness
Style	Formality
Politicization	Directiveness
Openness	

References

Andrews, K. R. *The Concept of Corporate Strategy.* Dow Jones-Irwin, Homewood, IL, 1971.

Barnard, C. I. *The Functions of the Executive.* Harvard University Press, Cambridge, MA, 1938.

Carroll, G. R. "Dynamics of Publisher Succession in Newspaper Organizations," *Administrative Science Quarterly,* **29,** 1984, pp. 93–113.

Collins, O. and D. Moore. *The Organization Makers.* Appleton-Century-Crofts, New York, 1970.

Dearborn, D. C. and H. A. Simon. "Selective perception: A note on the departmental identifications of executives," *Sociometry,* **21,** 1958, pp. 140–144.

Finkelstein, S. "Managerial orientations and organizational outcomes; the moderating roles of managerial discretion and power," Ph.D. dissertation, Columbia University, 1988.

Fredrickson, J. W. and A. Iaquinto. "Inertia and creeping rationality in strategic decision processes," *Academy of Management Journal,* in press.

Gabarro, J. J. *The Dynamics of Taking Charge.* Harvard Business School Press, Boston, 1987.

Gupta, A. "Contingency perspectives on strategic leadership: Current knowledge and future research directions." In D. C. Hambrick (ed.), *The Executive Effect: Concepts and Methods for Studying Top Managers.* JAI Press, Greenwich, CT, 1988, pp. 141–178.

Gupta, A. K. and V. Govindarajan. "Business unit strategy, managerial characteristics, and business unit effectiveness at strategy implementation." *Academy of Management Journal,* **27,** 1984, pp. 25–41.

Hage, J. and R. Dewar. "Elite values versus organizational structure in predicting innovations." *Administrative Science Quarterly,* **18,** 1973, pp. 279–290.

Hambrick, D. C. "Top Management Teams: Key to Strategic Success," *California Management Review,* **30,** 1987, pp. 88–108.

Hambrick, D.C. and G. Brandon. "Executive Values." In D. C. Hambrick (ed.), *The Executive Effect: Concepts and Methods for Studying Top Managers,* JAI Press, Greenwich, CT, 1988 pp. 3–34.

Hambrick, D. C. and S. Finkelstein. "Managerial discretion: A bridge between polar views of organizations," *Research in Organizational Behavior,* L. Cummings and B. Staw, (eds), JAI Press, 1987, pp. 369–406.

Hambrick, D. C. and P. A. Mason. "Upper echelons: The organization as a reflection of its top managers." *Academy of Management Review,* **9,** 1984, pp. 195–206.

Helmich, D. L. and W. B. Brown, "Successor type and organizational change in the corporate enterprise," *Administrative Science Quarterly,* **17,** 1972, pp. 371–381.

Jensen, M. C. and W. H. Meckling. "Theory of the firm: Managerial behavior, agency costs, and ownership structure," *Journal of Financial Economics,* **3,** 1976, pp. 305–360.

Kets de Vries, M. F. R. and D. Miller. "Neurotic style and organizational pathology," *Strategic Management Journal,* **5,** 1984, pp. 35–55.

Kimberly, J. R. and M. J. Evanisko. "Organizational innovation: The influence of individual, organizational, and contextual factors on hospital adoption of technological and administrative innovations," *Academy of Management Journal,* **24,** 1981, pp. 689–713.

Kotter, J. P. *The General Managers.* Free Press, New York, 1982.

Learned, E. P., C. R. Christensen and K. R. Andrews. *Problems of General Management-Business Policy.* Irwin, Homewood, IL, 1961.

Miller, D. and C. Droge. "Psychological and traditional determinants of structure," *Administrative Science Quarterly,* **31,** 1986, pp. 539–560.

Miller, D., M. F. R. Kets de Vries and J. M. Toulouse. "Top executive locus of control and its relationship to strategy-making, structure and environment," *Academy of Management Journal,* **27,** 1984, pp. 25–41.

Miles, R. E. and C. C. Snow. *Organizational Strategy, Structure and Process.* McGraw-Hill, New York, 1978.

Mintzberg, H. *Power In and Around Organizations.* Prentice-Hall, Englewood Cliffs, NJ, 1983.

Mintzberg, H. *The Nature of Managerial Work,* Harper and Row, New York, 1973 (Chapters 15–17).

Pfeffer, J. "Management as symbolic action: The creation and maintenance of organizational paradigms," *Research in Organizational Behavior,* L. L. Cummings and B. M. Staw (eds), JAI Press, Greenwich, CT, 1981, pp. 1–52.

Pfeffer, J. "Organizational demography." In *Research in Organizational Behavior,* L. L. Cummings and B. W. Staw (eds), Greenwich, CT, JAI Press, 1983, pp. 299–357.

Pfeffer, J. and A. Davis-Blake. "Administrative succession and organizational performance: how administrator experience mediates the succession effect, *Academy of Management Journal,* **29,** 1986, pp. 72–83.

Salancik, G. R. and J. Pfeffer. "Constraints on administrator discretion: The limited influence of mayors on city budgets," *Urban Affairs Quarterly,* **12,** 1977, pp. 475–498.

Selznick, P., *Leadership and Administration.* Row, Peterson, Evanston, IL, 1957.

Smith, J. E., P. C. Carson and R. A. Alexander. "Leadership: It can make a difference," *Academy of Management Journal,* **27,** 1985, pp. 765–776.

Song, J. H. "Diversification strategies and the experience of top executives of large firms," *Strategic Management Journal,* **3,** 1982, pp. 377–380.

Tushman, M. L., B. Virany and E. Romanelli. "Executive succession, strategic reorientations, and organizational evolution," *Technology in Society,* **7,** 1985, pp. 297–313.

Wagner, G. W., J. Pfeffer and C. A. O'Reilly. "Organizational demography and turnover in top management groups," *Administrative Science Quarterly,* **29,** 1984, pp. 74–92.

Walsh, J. P. "Selectivity and selective perception: An investigation of managers' belief structures and information processing," *Academy of Management Journal,* **31,** 1988, pp. 873–896.

Wrapp, H. E. "Good managers don't make policy decisions," *Harvard Business Review,* **45,** September-October 1967, pp. 91–99.

Zaleznik, A. and M. F. R. Kets de Vries. *Power and the Corporate Mind,* Houghton-Mifflin, Boston, MA, 1975.

Upper Echelons

The Organization as a Reflection of Its Top Managers

D. C. Hambrick and P. A. Mason
Columbia University

A question of key importance to organizational theorists is, Why do organizations act as they do? Recently prevailing theories have tended to reify organizations, variously viewing them as purposeful (Pfeffer & Salancik, 1978) or hapless (Hannan & Freeman, 1977) entities. In the field of strategy, explanations of (and prescriptions for) organizational moves have centered on technoeconomic factors (Hambrick, MacMillan, & Day, 1982; Harrigan, 1980; Porter, 1980). Even when strategic "process" is studied, it typically is viewed as flows of information and decisions, detached from the people involved (Aguilar, 1967; Allen, 1979; Bourgeois, 1980; Mintzberg, Raisinghani, & Théorêt, 1976).

This paper argues for a new emphasis in macroorganizational research: an emphasis on the dominant coalition of the organization, in particular its top managers. Organizational outcomes—both strategies and effectiveness—are viewed as reflections of the values and cognitive bases of powerful actors in the organization. It is expected that, to some extent, such linkages can be detected empirically.

Anecdotal evidence in support of this view has always abounded. The popular business press regularly cites linkages between, for example, a chief executive's background in operations and his or her pursuit of a cost-reduction strategy, or between a chief executive's long service in an industry and his or her hesitance to diversify from that industry. . . .

This paper has three primary aims. The first is to propose a model of how upper echelon characteristics may become reflected in organizational outcomes. The second is to review literature that has addressed the upper echelon's perspective. The third is to provide a foundation and stimulus for empirical research into the links between managerial backgrounds and organizational outcomes. To meet this third aim, the paper identifies some major variables of interest, propositions, and methodological suggestions. . . .

Development of the Model

Human Limits on Choice

Theorists of the Carnegie School have argued that complex decisions are largely the outcome of behavioral factors rather than a mechanical quest for economic optimization (Cyert & March, 1963; March & Simon, 1958). In their view, bounded rationality, multiple and conflicting goals, myriad options, and varying aspiration levels all serve to limit the extent to which complex decisions can be made on a techno-economic basis. Generally, the more complex the decision, the more applicable this behavioral theory is thought to be. So, for that class of choices called "strategic"—complex and of major significance to the organization—the behavioral theory is especially apt.

The term "strategic choice" is used here in the same way as it was by Child (1972). It is intended to be a fairly comprehensive term to include choices made formally and informally, indecision as well as decision, major administrative choices (e.g., reward systems and structure) as well as the domain and competitive choices more generally associated with the term *strategy*. Strategic choices stand in contrast to operational choices such as inventory decisions and credit policies, which lend themselves more to calculable solution.

If strategic choices have a large behavioral component, then to some extent they reflect the idiosyncracies of decision makers. As March and Simon (1958) argued, each decision maker brings his or her own set of "givens" to an administrative situation. These givens reflect the decision maker's cognitive base:

1. knowledge or assumptions about future events,

2. knowledge of alternatives, and

3. knowledge of consequences attached to alternatives.

They also reflect his or her values: principles for ordering consequences or alternatives according to preference.

These idiosyncratic givens are in place at the same time the decision maker is being exposed to an ongoing stream of potential stimuli both within and outside the organization. Thus, the givens are always being updated, but, more important for the argument here, the givens serve to filter and distort the decision maker's perception of what is going on and what should be done about it.

As summarized in Figure 1, the situation a strategic decision maker faces is complex and made up of far more phenomena than he/she can possibly comprehend. The decision maker brings a cognitive base and values to a decision, which create a screen between the situation and his/her eventual perception of it.

The perceptual process can be conceptualized by taking a sequential view (Hambrick & Snow, 1977). First, a manager,

Source: Edited and reprinted with permission from *Academy of Management Review* 9 (1984), 193–206.

FIGURE 1
Strategic Choice under Conditions of Bounded Rationality

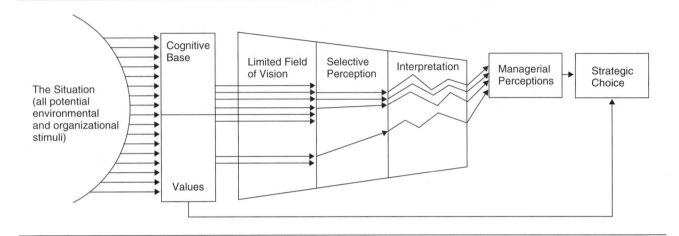

or even an entire team of managers, cannot scan every aspect of the organization and its environment. The manager's *field of vision*—those areas to which attention is directed—is restricted, posing a sharp limitation on eventual perceptions. Second, the manager's perceptions are further limited because one *selectively perceives* only some of the phenomena included in the field of vision. Finally, the bits of information selected for processing are *interpreted* through a filter woven by one's cognitive base and values.

The manager's eventual perception of the situation combines with his/her values to provide the basis for strategic choice. Values are treated here as something that, on the one hand, can affect perceptions (Scott & Mitchell, 1972) but, on the other hand, can directly enter into a strategic choice, because theoretically a decision maker can arrive at a set of perceptions that suggest a certain choice but discard that choice on the basis of values.

Emphasis on Observable Managerial Characteristics

In this paper, primary emphasis is placed on observable managerial characteristics as indicators of the givens that a manager brings to an administrative situation. Examples of such characteristics are age, tenure in the organization, functional background, education, socioeconomic roots, and financial position. In this approach, some important but complex psychological issues are bypassed in favor of an emphasis on broad tendencies that, if empirically confirmed, can be later held up to the psychologist's finer lens. . . .

Unit of Analysis

The limited research that has been done on the linkages between top managers and the strategies they pursue has focused almost entirely on the chief executive, generally in the context of managerial succession (Carlson, 1972; Helmich & Brown, 1972). No such research centering on characteristics of entire top management teams is known to the authors. Although it is true that in most firms the chief executive has

the most power, it still is of interest to study management teams (Bourgeois, 1980; Hambrick, 1981b). An entire team—say, the firm's officers—aligns well with Cyert and March's (1963) appealing, but little-studied, concept of the dominant coalition. At a more practical level, study of an entire team increases the potential strength of the theory to predict, because the chief executive shares tasks and, to some extent, power with other team members.

For example, assume that two firms each have chief executives whose primary functional backgrounds are in production. In Firm A, three of four other key executives also rose primarily through production-oriented careers, even though they now are serving in nonproduction or generalist roles. In Firm B, the mix of executive backgrounds is more balanced and typical—one from production, one from sales, one from engineering, and one from accounting. Knowledge about the central tendencies of the entire top-management teams improves one's confidence in any predictions about the two firms' strategies. Moreover, the study of an entire team has the added advantage of allowing inquiry into dispersion characteristics, such as homogeneity and balance. Group indicators of this latter type are among those included in propositions set forth later. . . .

Development of Propositions

In discussing each of the upper echelon characteristics presented in Figure 2, prior literature will be drawn on, but to some extent speculations will be made because this paper primarily is an attempt to build theory—even more to encourage theory building. The propositions presented should not be taken as the only propositions that could be drawn from past inquiry or reasoning. Rather, they are illustrative and appear to be some of the most supportable and interesting. The propositions are presented as part of the paper's aim to stimulate empirical inquiry into upper echelons.

Age

The association between the age of top executives and organizational characteristics has not been the subject of many studies, but the few that exist yield strikingly consistent results: managerial youth appears to be associated with corporate growth (Child, 1974, Hart & Mellons, 1970). As Child notes, however, it is not possible, with the research designs used, to disentangle the extent to which growth leads to youth or vice versa. A related finding of these studies is that volatility of sales and earnings also is associated with managerial youth. So, what emerges is a picture of youthful managers attempting the novel, the unprecedented, taking risks.

There are three possible explanations for the apparent conservative stance of older executives. The first is that older executives may have less physical and mental stamina (Child, 1974) or may be less able to grasp new ideas and learn new behaviors (Chown, 1960). Managerial age has been negatively associated with the ability to integrate information in making decisions and with confidence in decisions, though it appears to be positively associated with tendencies to seek more information, to evaluate information accurately, and to take longer to make decisions (Taylor, 1975). A second explanation is that older executives have greater psychological commitment to the organizational status quo (Alutto & Hrebiniak, 1975; Stevens, Beyer, & Trice, 1978). Third, older executives may be at a point in their lives at which financial security and career security are important. Their social circles, their spending traits, and their expectations about retirement income are established. Any risky actions that might disrupt these generally are avoided (Carlsson & Karlsson, 1970).

In line with the research and reasoning laid out above, the following propositions might be set forth. (Once again, all propositions should be understood to apply within an industry, but not necessarily across a diverse sample of organizations.)

P 1: *Firms with young managers will be more inclined to pursue risky strategies than will firms with older managers.* Specific forms of risk include unrelated diversification, product innovation, and financial leverage.

P 2: *Firms with young managers will experience greater growth and variability in profitability from industry averages than will firms with older managers.*

Functional Track

Although members of a firm's dominant coalition—especially the chief executive—are presumed to have a generalist's view, each brings to his or her job an orientation that usually has developed from experience in some primary functional area. This functional-track orientation may not dominate the strategic choices an executive makes, but it can be expected to exert some influence. For example, Dearborn and Simon (1958) found that when a group of executives from different functional areas was presented with the same problem (a case study) and asked to consider it from a companywide perspective, they defined the problem largely in terms of the activities and goals of their own areas.

For purposes of building a parsimonious set of propositions, functional tracks have been classified into three categories, the first two of which are based on an open-systems view (Katz & Kahn, 1966) and also align with the functional areas described as key in Miles and Snow's (1978) strategic typology. "Output functions"—marketing, sales, and product R&D—emphasize growth and the search for new domain opportunities and are responsible for monitoring and adjusting products and markets. "Throughput functions"—production, process engineering, and accounting—work at improving the efficiency of the transformation process. These two problem areas are somewhat distinct in their emphasis, and individuals who work within them are likely to develop distinctly different orientations to the firm and its environment (Lawrence & Lorsch, 1967; Miles & Snow, 1978), suggesting the following propositions:

P 3: *There will be a positive association between the degree of output-function experience of top managers and the extent to which the firm emphasizes outputs in its strategy.* Indicators of an output emphasis include product innovation, related diversification, advertising, and forward integration.

P 4: *There will be a positive association between the degree of throughput-function experience of top managers and the extent to which the firm emphasizes throughputs in its strategy.* Indicators of a throughput emphasis include automation, plant and equipment newness, and backward integration.

P 5: *The degree of output-function experience of top managers will be positively associated with growth.*

P 6: *In stable, commodity-like industries, throughput-function experience will be positively associated with profitability.*

P 7: *In turbulent, differentiable industries, out-put function experience will be positively associated with profitability.*

A third functional classification was suggested by Hayes and Abernathy (1980), who documented that major firms are increasingly dominated by executives whose backgrounds are in areas such as law and finance, which are not integrally involved with the organization's core activities. The suggested propositions about executives from these peripheral functions follow from Hayes and Abernathy's concern that such executives pursue strategies that fit with their relative deficiencies in "hands-on" experience:

P 8: *The degree of peripheral-function experience of top managers will be positively related to the degree of unrelated diversification in the firm.*

P 9: *The extent of peripheral-function experience of top managers will be positively related to administrative complexity,* including thoroughness of formal planning systems, complexity of structures and coordination devices, budgeting detail and thoroughness, and complexity of incentive-compensation schemes.

Other Career Experiences

Career experiences other than functional track also can be expected to have a significant effect on the types of actions taken by a manager or an entire top-management team. For example, probably more research has been done on length of service and a related variable, inside versus outside succession, than on any other characteristics of top managers. The primary and consistent conclusion coming from such studies is that chief executives brought in from the outside tend to make more changes in structure, procedures, and people than do chief executives promoted from within (Carlson,

1972; Helmich & Brown, 1972; Kotin & Sharaf, 1967). The behavioral reasons for the changes, as set forth by Carlson (1972), are: less commitment by an outsider to the status quo, a desire to weaken those who resist or resent the new chief executive, and a desire to create new, loyal lieutenants. Of course, outside succession is most likely when the organization is performing poorly, so the corresponding changes may reflect the situation as much as the background of the decision maker.

Executives carry as part of their cognitive and emotional givens the experiences they have had during their careers. Executives who have spent their entire careers in one organization can be assumed to have relatively limited perspectives. If an entire top-management team has risen solely through the organization, it is likely that it will have a very restricted knowledge base from which to conduct its "limited search" (Cyert & March, 1963) when faced with an unprecedented problem such as a deregulation, intensive competition from imports, or a radical technological shift. On the other hand, the in-depth industry familiarity and tested working relationships enjoyed by such a team might serve the organization well in periods of stability (Kotter, 1982). This reasoning leads to the following hypotheses:

P 10: *Years of inside service by top managers will be negatively related to strategic choices involving new terrain, for example, product innovation and unrelated diversification.*

P 11: *For an organization in a stable environment, years of inside service will be positively associated with profitability and growth.*

P 12: *For an organization facing a severe environmental discontinuity, years of inside service will be negatively associated with profitability and growth.*

It is not only whether an executive has worked outside his or her present organization that is of interest. Of even greater relevance is the nature of the industries and companies with which he or she has been involved. For example, an executive who moves from an orderly industry into one in which rivalry is cutthroat may inadvertently allow the firm to fall behind in the unaccustomed hectic race. Or an executive with experience in a firm that tried unsuccessfully to diversify may be dissuaded from attempting diversification in another company. All these conditions are highly situational and, at this point, do not warrant specific propositions. What seems clear, though, is that executives' career experiences partially shape the lenses through which they view current strategic opportunities and problems.

Formal Education

A person's formal educational background may yield rich but complex information. To some degree, education indicates a person's knowledge and skill base. A person educated in engineering generally can be expected to have a somewhat different cognitive base from someone educated in history or law. Beyond that, if it is assumed that most people take seriously their decisions about education, then education serves to some extent as an indicator of a person's values, cognitive preferences, and so on. Granted, people make their educational decisions at a relatively early age, with incomplete information, and they sometimes later transcend those decisions. But, on average, it could be expected that students

enrolled in an English literature curriculum are somewhat different from students enrolled in a business curriculum. Perhaps even students who choose to attend the Harvard Business School are somehow different from those who attended the University of Chicago Business School.

Inclusion of the educational backgrounds of managers in macro-organizational research has been limited primarily to studies attempting to predict innovation. The consistent finding is that level of education (either of the CEO or other central actors) is positively related to receptivity to innovation (Becker, 1970; Kimberly & Evanisko, 1981; Rogers & Shoemaker, 1971). These studies did not consistently include controls for age and so may be masking the tendency toward increased education in recent years. Kimberly and Evanisko examined the type of educational curriculum (administration vs. nonadministration degrees) and found no association with the adoption of organizational innovations. This research suggests the following proposition:

P 13: *The amount, but not the type, of formal education of a management team will be positively associated with innovation.*

One theory of note is that education implies membership in a particular socioeconomic group (Collins, 1971). This theory has been strongly supported by research in England, where class structures are relatively pronounced. Channon (1979) and Stanworth and Giddens (1974), studying two different samples of chief executives in the U.K., each found that about 50 percent of their samples had been educated at Oxford or Cambridge. Channon noted the importance of this background for establishing strong interorganizational ties. It is unlikely that such strong findings would emerge in a U.S. sample, but there may be certain industries in which education, or even certain schools, is deemed important to business success.

It is noted that there has been little research on the effects of formal professional education (the MBA degree in particular) on corporate outcomes. There certainly are plenty of offhand suspicions that MBAs are educated to pursue short-term performance at the expense of innovation and asset building. A contrary view is that the degree does not have any substantive effect in the long run for either the holder or the company, but only serves as a filtering device for matching up individuals and jobs (Pfeffer, 1981a).

The present writers' view is that professional education in management is associated with moderation. MBA candidates by their nature probably are not as innovative or risk-prone as more "self-made" executives (Collins & Moore, 1970); and business schools are not particularly well inclined or equipped (at least to date) to develop innovative or risk-taking tendencies. The analytic techniques learned in an MBA program are geared primarily to avoiding big losses or mistakes. Thus, the following proposition might be set forth:

P 14: *There is no relationship between the amount of formal management education of top managers and the average performance (either profitability or growth) of their firms. However, firms whose managers have had little formal management education will show greater variation from industry performance averages than will firms whose managers are highly educated in management.*

Beyond this tendency toward moderation, professional management education is expected to have an effect on the administrative complexity and sophistication of firms, both because of the types of people who are drawn to business schools, that is, "organizers and rationalizers," and because of the emphasis placed on complex administrative systems in business schools.

P 15: *Firms whose top managers have had substantial formal management education will be more complex administratively than will firms whose managers have had less such training.* Specific forms of administrative complexity include thoroughness of formal planning systems, complexity of structures and coordination devices, budgeting detail and thoroughness, and complexity of incentive-compensation schemes.

Socioeconomic Background

Although the socioeconomic backgrounds of senior executives have been described in some detail (Burck, 1976; Newcomer, 1955; Sturdivant & Adler, 1976), there has been almost no attempt in the organizational literature to relate socioeconomic background to organizational strategy or performance. One reason for the lack of attention to this question may lie in the apparently high degree of homogeneity among socioeconomic backgrounds of executives. In 1975, executives of major U.S. firms were almost exclusively male and white, and predominantly Protestant and Republican. Somewhat more of them came from middle-class families and from the Midwest than was true earlier in this century (Burck, 1976), but they attended largely the same group of prestigious universities as did their predecessors (Sturdivant & Adler, 1976).

Channon (1979) found some relationships between the socioeconomic backgrounds of U.K. executives and the growth strategies of their firms. First classifying firms as entrepreneur-run, family-run, and professionally managed, Channon found companies run by entrepreneurs to be the most widely diversified and to have the highest rate of acquisitions. Then Channon observed that the entrepreneurs themselves were likely to come from relatively humble origins, receive an education through secondary school only, avoid military service (many were refugees from Nazi persecution), and belong to few if any London clubs. At the other extreme were heads of professionally managed firms (lowest acquisition rate) and family-led firms (least diversified), who came from more traditional upper-class English backgrounds: public school, especially Eton; university, usually Cambridge or Oxford; military service, often in famous regiments; and appropriate club membership.

It is not possible to conclude whether it is the form of ownership (e.g., entrepreneurial) or the humble backgrounds of the entrepreneurs that were causally linked to these firms' strategies of growth and diversification. In a clinical study of entrepreneurs, Collins and Moore (1970) concluded that a common pattern is for an entrepreneur from a relatively disadvantaged background to pursue aggressive, often flamboyant strategies, presumably in order to achieve recognition and esteem. These patterns may suggest the following:

P 16: *Firms whose top managers come disproportionately from lower socioeconomic groups will tend to pursue strategies of acquisition and unrelated diversification.*

P 17: *Such firms will experience greater growth and profit variability than will firms whose top managers come from higher socioeconomic groups.*

Financial Position

The relationship between stock ownership of top executives and corporate performance has been studied at length by economists. Findings have been mixed, but they generally favor the conclusion that owner-managed firms do not outperform firms that are managed by nonowners. (See Hay and Morris, 1979 and Kania and McKean, 1976 for summaries.) Inquiry into the issue has been prompted largely by the Berle and Means (1932) thesis that owners have a greater stake in the firm than do nonowners and so will engage in more purely income-seeking behavior. Such reasoning ignores the fact, however, that many nonowner executives derive their entire livelihood from the organization and thus are quite dependent on its continuing health. Because of bonuses and other incentive compensation plans, their income often varies with corporate performance (Lewellyn, 1969; Lewellyn & Huntsman, 1970), and they also run the risk of being fired if firm performance falls off—a risk that owner-managers do not face (James & Soref, 1981; Salancik & Pfeffer, 1980).

It would seem that an improved argument lies in Masson's (1971) suggestion that managerial aspirations are due less to the proportion of a company's shares owned by management than to the proportion of the manager's income that is derived from the firm. Managers—be they owners or not—may be relatively inclined to pursue noneconomic objectives for the focal firm if they have ample income alternatives. This reasoning, when coupled with the available evidence about stock ownership, leads to the following proposition:

P 18: *Corporate profitability is not related to the percent of shares owned by top managers, but is positively related to the percent of their total income that top managers derive from the firm through salaries, bonuses, options, dividends, and so on.*

Group Heterogeneity

Also of relevance is the amount of dispersion, or heterogeneity, within a managerial group. Janis (1972) argued that homogeneity, as manifested in cohesiveness and insularity, leads to inferior decision making. In his view, homogeneity is one of several conditions that bring on groupthink, which amounts to restricted generation and assessment of alternatives. A more two-sided view is offered by Filley, House, and Kerr (1976) in their summary of research on group heterogeneity and performance. They concluded that routine problem solving is best handled by a homogeneous group, and that ill-defined, novel problem solving is best handled by a heterogeneous group in which diversity of opinion, knowledge, and background allows a thorough airing of alternatives. This view may not be at odds with Janis; the decisions he studied were strictly novel, nonroutine problems.

Any discussion of group heterogeneity is aided by a concept drawn from the sociological literature: the cohort. A cohort is a group of individuals that have some relevant date in common: year of birth, year of marriage, entry into the job market, and so on. What categorizes a cohort is the societal experiences that have been imprinted on its members and have helped to shape their values and perceptions.

McNeil and Thompson (1971) looked at the number of cohorts that make up complex organizations and, specifically, at the ratio of older to newer members. The rate at which this ratio changes is a joint function of attrition and the growth or shrinkage of the organization, and it will vary among organizations over time. In organizations undergoing rapid regeneration, the tendency is for members of younger cohorts to move quickly through the hierarchy and become peers, rather than subordinates, of older-cohort members. When this happens, the increased heterogeneity at a given management level increases conflict. Similarly, Pfeffer (1981b) noted that the existence of tenure gaps between cohorts sharpens the difference between them and produces increased conflict.

If the concept of demography can be applied to a total organization, it also can be applied to the organization's dominant coalition. The effects of the homogeneity or heterogeneity of cohort membership and gaps between cohorts would be felt as much in a small group as in a large one. Additionally, if subgroups based on age or organizational tenure can

be considered, then subgroups based on functional track, education, socioeconomic background, and financial position should be considered. As discussed earlier, marketing-oriented people have different outlooks from those with production backgrounds. Professionally trained managers may view situations differently from those without a college degree, and so on. Indeed, for any variable that influences an individual's strategic choice, it can be said that the range of the group's scores on that variable also influences strategic choice through its effects on conflict and the generation of alternatives.

The concepts outlined above suggest many propositions. Three of these are:

P 19: *Homogeneous top-management teams will make strategic decisions more quickly than will heterogeneous teams.*

P 20: *In stable environments, team homogeneity will be positively associated with profitability.*

P 21: *In turbulent, especially discontinuous, environments, team heterogeneity will be positively associated with profitability. . . .*

References

Aguilar, F. J. *Scanning the business environment.* New York: Macmillan, 1967.

Allen, S. A. Understanding reorganization of divisionalized companies. *Academy of Management Journal,* 1979, 22, 641–671.

Alutto, J. A., & Hrebiniak, L. G. Research on commitment to employing organizations: Preliminary findings on a study of managers graduating from engineering and MBA programs. Paper presented at Academy of Management meetings, New Orleans, 1975.

Becker, M. H. Sociometric location and innovativeness: Reformulation and extension of the diffusion model. *American Sociological Review,* 1970, 35, 267–304.

Berle, A. A., Jr., & Means, G. C. *The modern corporation and private property.* New York: Macmillan, 1932.

Boscarino, J. Alcohol abuse among veterans: The importance of demographic factors. *Addictive Behaviors,* 1979, 4, 323–330.

Bourgeois, L. J., III. Performance and consensus. *Strategic Management Journal,* 1980, 1, 227–248.

Buchholz, R. A. The belief structure of managers relative to work concepts measured by a factor analytic model. *Personnel Psychology,* 1977, 30, 567–587.

Buchholz, R. A. An empirical study of contemporary beliefs about work in American society. *Journal of Applied Psychology,* 1978, 63, 219–227.

Burck, C. G. A group profile of the *Fortune* 500 chief executives. *Fortune,* May 14, 1976, pp. 173–177, 308, 311–312.

Carlson, R. O. *School superintendents: Career and performance.* Columbia, Ohio: Merrill, 1972.

Carlsson, G., & Karlsson, K. Age, cohorts and the generation of generations. *American Sociological Review,* 1970, 35, 710–718.

Channon, D. Leadership and corporate performance in the service industries. *Journal of Management Studies,* 1979, 16, 185–201.

Child, J. Organizational structure, environments and performance: The role of strategic choice. *Sociology,* 1972, 6, 1–22.

Child, J. Managerial and organizational factors associated with company performance. *Journal of Management Studies,* 1974, 11, 13–27.

Chown, S. M. The Wesley rigidity inventory: A factor-analytic approach. *Journal of Abnormal and Social Psychology,* 1960, 61, 491–494.

Collins, R. Functional and conflict theories of educational stratification. *American Sociological Review,* 1971, 36, 1002–1019.

Collins, O., & Moore, D. G. *The organization makers.* New York: Appleton-Century-Crofts, 1970.

Cyert, R. M., & March, J. G. *A behavioral theory of the firm.* Englewood Cliffs, N. J.: Prentice-Hall, 1963.

Dearborn, D. C., & Simon, H. A. Selective perceptions: A note on the departmental identification of executives. *Sociometry,* 1958, 21, 140–144.

Filley, A. C., House, R. J., & Kerr, S. *Managerial process and organizational behavior.* Glenview, Ill.: Scott Foresman, 1976.

Frank, R. E., & Greenberg, M. G. Interest-based segments of TV audiences. *Journal of Advertising Research,* 1979, 19(5), 43–52.

Guth, W. D., & Taguiri, R. Personal values and corporate strategies. *Harvard Business Review,* 1965, 43(5), 123–132.

Hall, R. H. *Organizations, structure and process.* 2nd ed. Englewood Cliffs, N. J.: Prentice-Hall, 1977.

Hambrick, D. C. Environment, strategy, and power within top management teams. *Administrative Science Quarterly,* 1981a, 26, 253–275.

Hambrick, D. C. Strategic awareness within top management teams. *Strategic Management Journal,* 1981b, 2, 263–280.

Hambrick, D. C. Environmental scanning and organizational strategy. *Strategic Management Journal,* 1982, 3, 159–174.

Hambrick, D. C., MacMillan, I. C., & Day, D. C.

Strategic attributes and performance of businesses in the four cells of the BCG matrix—A PIMS-based analysis of industrial-product businesses. *Academy of Management Journal,* 1982, 25, 510–531.

Hambrick, D. C., & Snow, C. C. A contextual model of strategic decision making in organizations. In R. L. Taylor, M. J. O'Connell, R. A. Zawacki, & D. D. Warrick (Eds.), *Academy of Management Proceedings,* 1977, 109–112.

Hannan, M. T., & Freeman, J. H. The population ecology of organizations. *American Journal of Sociology,* 1977, 82, 929–964.

Harrigan, K. R. *Strategies for declining businesses.* Lexington, Mass.: Heath, 1980.

Harris, R. G. The potential effects of deregulation upon corporate structure, merger behavior, and organizational relations in the rail freight industry. Draft report. Washington, D.C.: Public Interest Economics Center, 1979.

Hart, P., & Mellons, J. Management youth and company growth: A correlation? *Management Decision,* 1970, 4(2), 50–53.

Hay, D. A., & Morris, D. J. *Industrial economics: Theory and evidence.* Oxford: Oxford University Press, 1979.

Hayes, R. H., & Abernathy, W. J. Managing our way to economic decline. *Harvard Business Review,* 1980, 58(4), 67–77.

Helmich, D. L., & Brown, W. B. Successor type and organizational change in the corporate enterprise. *Administrative Science Quarterly,* 1972, 17, 371–381.

Hornik, J., & Schlinger, J. J. Allocation of time to mass media. *Journal of Consumer Research,* 1981, 7, 343–355.

James, D. R. & Soref, M. Profit constraints on managerial autonomy: Managerial theory and the unmaking of the corporation president. *American Sociological Review,* 1981, 46, 1–18.

Janis, I. L. *Victims of groupthink.* Boston: Houghton Mifflin, 1972.

Kahalas, H., & Groves, D. L. An exploration of graduate business students' values. *Journal of Industrial Psychology,* 1979, 6, 18–24.

Kania, J. J., & McKean, J. R. Ownership, control and the contemporary corporation: A general behavior analysis, *Kyklos,* 1976, 29, 272–291.

Katz, D., & Kahn, R. L. *The social psychology of organizations.* New York: Wiley, 1966.

Kimberly, J. R., & Evanisko, M. J. Organizational innovation: The influence of individual, organizational and contextual factors on hospital adoption of technological and administrative innovations. *Academy of Management Journal,* 1981, 24, 689–713.

Kotin, J., & Sharaf, M. Management succession and administrative style. *Psychiatry,* 1976, 30, 237–248.

Kotter, J. P. *The general managers.* New York: Free Press, 1982.

Lawrence, P. R., & Lorsch, J. W. *Organization and environment.* Homewood, Ill.: Irwin, 1967.

Lewellyn, W. Management and ownership in the large firm. *Journal of Finance,* 1969, 24, 299–322.

Lewellyn, W., & Huntsman, B. Managerial pay and corporate performance. *American Economic Review,* 1970, 60, 710–720.

Lieberson, S., & O'Connor, J. F. Leadership and organizational performance: A study of large corporations. *American Sociological Review,* 1972, 37, 117–130.

McNeil, K., & Thompson, J. D. The regeneration of social organizations. *American Sociological Review,* 1971, 36, 624–637.

March, J. G., & Simon, H. A. *Organizations.* New York: Wiley, 1958.

Masson, R. Executive motivation, earnings and consequent equity performance. *Journal of Political Economy,* 1971, 79, 1278–1292.

Miles, R. E., & Snow, C. C. *Organization strategy, structure and process.* New York: McGraw-Hill, 1978.

Miller, D., Kets de Vries, M. F. R., & Toulouse, J-M. Top executive locus of control and its relationship to strategy-making, structure, and environment. *Academy of Management Journal,* 1982, 25, 237–253.

Mills, C. J., & Bohannon, W. E. Character structure and jury behavior: Conceptual and applied implications. *Journal of Personality and Social Psychology,* 1980, 38, 662–667.

Mintzberg, H., Raisinghani, D., & Théorêt, A. The structure of unstructured decision processes. *Administrative Science Quarterly,* 1976, 21, 246–275.

Newcomer, M. *The big business executive.* New York: Columbia University Press, 1955.

Pfeffer, J. *Power in organizations.* Marshfield, Mass.: Pitman Publishing Inc., 1981a.

Pfeffer, J. Some consequences of organizational demography: Potential impacts of an aging work force on formal organizations. In S. B. Kiesler, J. N. Morgan, & V. K. Oppenheimer (Eds.), *Aging: Social change.* New York: Academic Press, 1981b, 291–329.

Pfeffer, J., & Salancik, G. R. *The external control of organizations.* New York: Harper and Row, 1978.

Porter, M. E. *Competitive strategy.* New York: Free Press, 1980.

Ritchie, R. J., & Beardsley, V. D. A market research approach to determining local labor market availability for non-management jobs. *Personnel Psychology,* 1978, 31, 449–459.

Rogers, E. M., & Shoemaker, P. *Communication of innovations.* New York: Free Press, 1971.

Salancik, G. R., & Pfeffer, J. Constraints on administrator discretion: The limited influence of mayors on city budgets. *Urban Affairs Quarterly,* 1977, 12(4), 475–496.

Salancik, G. R., & Pfeffer, J. Effects of ownership and performance on executive tenure in U.S. corporations. *Academy of Management Journal,* 1980, 23, 653–664.

Schnore, L. F., & Alford, R. R. Forms of government and socioeconomic characteristics of suburbs. *Administrative Science Quarterly,* 1963, 8, 1–17.

Schram, V. R., & Dunsing, M. M. Influences on married women's volunteer work participation. *Journal of Consumer Research,* 1981, 7, 372–379.

Scott, W. G., & Mitchell, T. R. Organization theory: A structural and behavioral analysis. Homewood, Ill.: Irwin, 1972.

Sekaran, U., & Mowday, R. T. A cross-cultural analysis of the influence of individual and job characteristics on job involvement. *International Review of Applied Psychology,* 1981, 30, 51–64.

Stanworth, P., & Giddens, A. An economic elite: A demographic profile of company chairmen. In P. Stanworth & A. Giddens (Eds.), *Elites and power in British society.* Cambridge: Cambridge University Press, 1974, 65–80.

Stevens, J. M., Beyer, J. M., & Trice, H. M. Assessing personal, role, and organizational predictors of managerial commitment. *Academy of Management Journal,* 1978, 21, 380–396.

Sturdivant, F. D., & Adler, R. D. Executive origins: Still a gray flannel world? *Harvard Business Review,* 1976, 54(6), 125–132.

Taylor, R. N. Age and experience as determinants of managerial information processing and decision making performance. *Academy of Management Journal,* 1975, 18, 74–81.

Weick, K. E. *The social psychology of organizing.* Reading, Mass.: Addison-Wesley, 1969.

Weiner, N., & Mahoney, T. A. A model of corporate performance as a function of environmental, organizational, and leadership influences. *Academy of Management Journal,* 1981, 24, 453–470.

Wissema, J. G., Van Der Pol, H. W., & Messer, H. M. Strategic management archetypes. *Strategic Management Journal,* 1980, 1, 37–47.

Zaleznik, A., & Kets de Vries, M. F. R. *Power and the corporate mind.* Boston: Houghton Mifflin, 1975.

The Impact of Top-Management Actions on Employee Attitudes and Perceptions

B. P. Niehoff
Kansas State University

C. A. Enz
Cornell University

R. A. Grover
University of Southern Maine

*I*n recent years, organizational readers in the United States have been inundated with advice and prescriptions regarding ways to overcome the "leadership crisis" and deal with the threat of international competition (e.g., Labich, 1988; Peters & Austin, 1985; Peters & Waterman, 1982; Tichy & Devanna, 1986). In general, the prescriptions focus on changes in the values and culture of the organization through the leadership function as the key to increased productivity and innovation. Specifically, top managers have been advised to develop a vision that reflects the central values of the organization and communicate this vision to employees through words, symbols, and actions (Kouzes & Posner, 1988; Schein, 1985). Leaders have also been told that employees can make important contributions to the performance of the organization and are more likely to do so if they have been delegated some degree of responsibility and influence at the job level (Kouzes & Posner, 1988; Tichy & Devanna, 1986). Finally, innovation is more likely to arise when top management encourages and supports risk taking and new ideas from the employees (Kanter, 1983; Kouzes & Posner, 1988).

Predicted outcomes of "excellence" (Peters & Waterman, 1982), "organizational revitalization" (Tichy & Ulrich, 1984), or "high-performing systems" (Vaill, 1984) suggest achievements in innovation and productivity, but such achievements depend on whether employee attitudes, perceptions, and values have been "transformed" by the actions of top management. The individual efforts necessary to attain high levels of performance are possible only if employees understand and internalize the vision and commit their efforts to its accomplishment. Thus the relationship between top-management actions—such as communicating a vision, encouraging and supporting innovativeness, and allowing decision influence—and organizational excellence should be mediated by the perceived clarity of the vision and the mobilization of member satisfaction with and commitment to the vision (Bennis, 1984; Labich, 1988; Tichy & Devanna, 1986; Vaill, 1984).

Bass's work on "transformational leadership" (Bass, 1985) mirrors the approach of the popular press. He describes two forms of leadership: transactional and transformational. The transactional leader is proficient at obtaining basic levels of compliance from subordinates through behaviors such as "management by exception" and "contingent reward" (Bass, 1985). Transformational leaders, on the other hand, attempt to inspire performance beyond mere compliance. Transformational leaders achieve this by articulating and modeling a vision for the organization, stimulating new ideas from followers, demonstrating concern for individual development through support and recognition, and delegating responsibility to followers for job level decisions (Bass, 1985; Kouzes & Posner, 1988). When compliance is defined as the lowest level of psychological commitment, one can infer that as followers move beyond levels of mere compliance, commitment increases either to levels of identification with the leader or internalization of important organizational values (O'Reilly & Chatman, 1986). As with the popular approach to leadership, key variables in the transformational leadership process are the clarity of the vision and mobilization of follower satisfaction with and commitment to the vision.

Although empirical research on the popular approach is sparse, Bass's work has shown that leaders who exhibit transformational leader behaviors are more likely to be rated as effective than transactional leaders are. Subordinates whose leaders exhibit transformational behaviors also reported the highest levels of extra effort, as well as satisfaction with superiors (Bass, 1985; Hater & Bass, 1988). Bass's research, however, has yet to examine the relationship between the transformational behaviors and employee role clarity and commitment. Given the critical role of these variables in the transformational leadership process, such linkages are worthy of further exploration.

The purpose of this study is to provide a partial test of the approach to organizational leadership underlying both popular (e.g., Peters & Waterman, 1982) and transformational (e.g., Bass, 1985) versions. Our primary concern in this study is the association between top-management actions and employee attitudes and perceptions. Five top-management actions are of importance here: inspiring a shared vision, modeling the vision, encouraging innovativeness, support-

Source: Edited and reprinted with permission from *Groups & Organization Studies* 15 (1990), 337–52. Author affiliation may have changed since article was first published.

ing employee efforts, and allowing for employee influence in decision making (Bass, 1985; Kouzes & Posner, 1988). Employee attitudes and perceptions of importance in this model include organizational commitment, job satisfaction, and role ambiguity. Rather than focus on employee perceptions of the actions of immediate supervisors, as Bass and others have done, this study will focus on employee perceptions of *top-management* actions. Researchers have suggested that more studies examine the impact of top managers (Hambrick & Mason, 1984). For this study, *top management* will refer to the chief executive officer and vice president levels.

Actions of Top Management In Effective Organizations

Inspiring a Shared Vision

Robbins and Duncan (1988) have defined organizational vision as "the shared aspired future state for the organization which identifies the organization's values, sets priorities for goals and objectives, and sets the guidelines or road map by which these goals and objectives will be pursued" (p. 222). Of the three components of vision—identifying values, setting priorities, and setting means for achieving objectives—organizational leaders have the most opportunity to affect the values component (Robbins & Duncan, 1988). Posner, Kouzes, and Schmidt (1985) found that subordinates who perceived senior managers to have effectively communicated a vision for the organization also reported significantly higher levels of satisfaction, commitment, clarity about the organization's values, and productivity.

Bass (1985) found transformational leadership to be composed of three factors: (a) charismatic leadership, (b) intellectual stimulation, and (c) individualized consideration. Charismatic leadership included inspiring a shared vision, as well as role modeling and allowing influence in decision making. This factor is consistently found to be more strongly associated with satisfaction with superior, extra effort, and performance than any other factor (Bass, 1985; Hater & Bass, 1988).

Modeling the Vision

The vision is communicated to employees through verbal and nonverbal means. Top managers' actions provide tangible operationalizations of organizational values and reinforce the importance of such values (Kouzes & Posner, 1988). Visibility is an important part of the process because many of the employees have only limited access to top managers. Instances of contact between the top management and employees are "moments of truth" with regard to the employees' understanding and interpretation of the vision. These moments of truth convey a great deal of information to employees concerning top management's commitment to the vision and, thus, serve a highly symbolic function. Role modeling, then, is a potent vehicle through which the symbolic nature of leadership (Mintzberg, 1973; Pfeffer, 1981) influences employee attitudes, behavior, and perceptions (Bass, 1985). Bass found role modeling, as part of the charisma factor, to be strongly related to satisfaction with superior, extra effort, and performance.

Encouraging Innovativeness

Top management must demonstrate its willingness to challenge the status quo and openly encourage experimentation by employees "in order to find new and better ways of doing things" (Kouzes & Posner, 1988, p. 8). A culture that encourages and rewards risk taking facilitates the innovative process and reflects the value that top management places on employees' ideas. Employees should respond positively to such a culture. Bass's second transformational factor, intellectual stimulation, included behaviors such as the encouragement of new ideas in followers. This factor was found to be strongly associated with employee self-reports of satisfaction with superior and extra effort, as well as ratings of superior effectiveness (Bass, 1985).

Supporting Employee Efforts

As employees make progress toward the vision, organizational leaders should be prepared to demonstrate their appreciation and support for such efforts. Bass's third transformational factor, individualized consideration, included the leader's demonstration of support and recognition of followers' achievements. Research strongly supports a positive relationship between supportive leader behaviors and employee attitudes (Yukl, 1989), and the positive effects of contingent reward practices on attitudes and behaviors in organizational settings are also well-documented (Bass, 1981; Yukl, 1989).

Allowing Employee Influence in Decision Making

Allowing employees input into decisions concerning their jobs has long been recognized as a method for enriching jobs (Hackman & Lawler, 1971) and is generally found to be positively associated with satisfaction, motivation, decision acceptance, and, in some cases, task performance (Miller & Monge, 1986; Wagner & Gooding, 1987). This is the essence of what Peters and Waterman (1982) termed "productivity through people," and demonstrates top-management's interest in developing employees by giving them "a sense of some ownership of decisions of consequence" (Bass, 1985, p. 97). Bass found that allowing decision influence was part of the charisma factor and, thus, strongly related to satisfaction with superior, extra effort, and performance.

Hypotheses

As top management shares and models the vision, employees begin to understand the important organizational values, as well as the efforts necessary to move the organization toward the vision. Top management spurs innovativeness by encouraging risk taking and allowing employees input into decisions concerning their jobs, while also recognizing and supporting their achievements. As they perceive consistency between top management's words and actions, and experience achievement toward the vision, employees internalize the important values, becoming more committed to the vision.

- *Hypothesis 1:* Employees who perceive top management as inspiring a shared vision, modeling the vision, encouraging innovativeness, supporting employee efforts, and allowing decision influence will report greater levels of organizational commitment.

Actions that make employees' tasks more interesting and challenging should have a positive impact on general job satisfaction (Locke, 1976). Top-management actions such as developing and communicating a vision for the organization, allowing influence in decision making, and encouraging innovativeness should accomplish this end. Also, top management's supportiveness of employee efforts should contribute to the intrinsic rewards gained by employees, thus affecting job satisfaction.

- *Hypothesis 2:* Employees who perceive top management as inspiring a shared vision, modeling the vision, supporting employee efforts, encouraging innovativeness, and allowing decision influence will report greater levels of job satisfaction.

Top-management actions that serve to articulate the vision and values of the organization are theorized to have a positive impact on role clarity (Bass, 1985). Thus sharing the vision, modeling the vision, supporting employee efforts, and encouraging risk taking would each act to reduce ambiguities surrounding employees' roles in the organization. Also, as employees are allowed more influence in their jobs, relevant decisions should be more easily understood, thus reducing ambiguity.

- *Hypothesis 3:* Employees who perceive top management as sharing the vision, modeling the vision, encouraging innovativeness, supporting employee efforts, and allowing decision influence will report lower levels of role ambiguity.

Method

Sample

Study participants were 862 employees of a midwestern insurance company. The positions represented in the sample were supervisors ($n = 74$), clerical workers ($n = 398$), field agency mangers ($n = 59$), field agents ($n = 259$), field claims managers ($n = 9$), and field claims representatives ($n = 63$). The supervisors and clerical workers were all located in the home office of the company, whereas the agency and claims personnel were located in separate field offices. Measures of all independent and dependent variables were obtained from each respondent using a survey format. The terms *top management* or *executives* were used in the survey to refer to the chief executive officer and vice presidents of the organization. . . .

Discussion

The results of this study provide support for the notion that employee attitudes and perceptions are strongly associated with top-management actions as prescribed in popular, as well as recent transformational, approaches to organizational leadership. Specifically, actions such as inspiring a shared vision, supporting employee efforts, and allowing influence in decision making were found to be positively related to

organizational commitment and job satisfaction and negatively related to role ambiguity. Top management's encouragement of innovativeness was found to be positively related to commitment and negatively related to role ambiguity, and executive visibility was found to be positively related to commitment.

In the popular and transformational approaches to organizational leadership, the actions of top managers are aimed at clarifying top management's vision for the organization and gaining high levels of employee commitment and satisfaction. These outcomes are hypothesized to positively influence organizational "excellence" or "performance beyond expectations." The present study provides initial support for the linkage between top-management actions and employee attitudinal and perceptual outcomes. Support is the strongest for organizational commitment, a most important variable in the transformational process (Kouzes & Posner, 1988; Tichy & Devanna, 1986).

Neither job satisfaction nor role ambiguity was found to be predicted by top-management visibility. This suggests that the mere presence of executives has little bearing on employees' job-specific attitudes and perceptions. Because employee contact with top management is somewhat limited, it is unlikely that employees depend on such contact for positive effect or role-related information. Regression analysis also revealed that the degree of innovativeness encouraged by top management is not a predictor of job satisfaction, suggesting that employees' jobs can be interesting and challenging without the presence of innovativeness. This is not surprising because many work attributes, including variety, difficulty, and complexity, contribute to the "mental challenge" necessary to influence job satisfaction (Locke, 1976).

An interesting finding concerned the differential effects of top-management actions, depending on the location of the employees (home vs. field offices). Bass posited that transformational leadership may be more effective in certain organizational settings than others, and the present study supported this assertion. Top management's opportunity to maintain visibility was minimal in the field-office subgroup, as reflected in the lack of significant impact of visibility on the commitment of field personnel. Also, the differences in task technology between home-office and field personnel brought about differential impacts for perceptions of decision influence. Because sales and claims personnel are likely to have more autonomy than home-office clerical personnel, decision influence should have more impact on role ambiguity for field- rather than home-office employees. Future research should focus on other potential variables that would limit the effectiveness of top-management actions.

The visibility of top management represents a new variable in the empirical study of transformational leadership. It was found to have a significant, positive impact on commitment in home-office employees. This finding suggests that employee commitment can be influenced by the degree to which executives visibly demonstrate their own commitment to the vision. As measured, however, visibility represents only the physical presence of executives, with no behavioral referent. Thus a narrow interpretation of the finding would be that employee commitment can be positively influenced by the presence of executives in the office. Employees apparently place value on top-management visibility and are more likely to commit themselves to the organization if they perceive top management at work. Further research should focus on refining this aspect of modeling the vision and exploring the role of employee expectations of top management. . . .

Conclusion and Implications

Transformational leadership, whether discussed in the popular press or in academic writings, involves the process of obtaining "extraordinary efforts" from followers, resulting in "excellent" organizations. To accomplish these ends, organizational leaders must first take actions directed at mobilizing the commitment of the followers to the goals, objectives, and values of the organization. Although a preliminary first step, this study does suggest that employee commitment to the organization is strongly influenced by the degree to which employees perceive top management as inspiring a shared vision and modeling that vision. Commitment is also enhanced by allowing employees influence in decision making and supporting them as they progress toward higher levels of performance. Finally, as top management encourages employees to take risks in order to discover new ways of approaching problems, commitment will be gained from the employees, and the innovation process will be greatly facilitated. Similarly, these actions also enhance employee job satisfaction and reduce role ambiguity.

Organizational leadership is a popular issue today, and if indeed a "leadership crisis" exists, there seem to be plenty of "physicians" with the cure. Unfortunately, there is no panacea. The anecdotal evidence provided by the popular press should not be scoffed at but should instead serve to stimulate hypotheses to be tested empirically. This study has linked many popular press notions about leadership to more academic constructs and provided an initial test of some assumed relationships. Future research should focus on testing the causal priorities of the relationships.

References

Bass, B. M. (1981). *Stogdill's handbook of leadership: A survey of theory and research* (rev. ed.). New York: Free Press.

Bass, B. M. (1985). *Leadership and performance beyond expectations.* New York: Free Press.

Bennis, W. (1984). Transformative power and leadership. In T. J. Sergiovanni & J. E. Corbally (Eds.), *Leadership and organizational culture* (pp. 64–71). Urbana: University of Illinois Press.

Brayfield, A. H., & Rothe, H. F. (1951). An index of job satisfaction. *Journal of Applied Psychology, 35,* 307–311.

Cook, T. D., & Campbell, D. T. (1976). The design and conduct of quasi-experiments and true experiments in field settings. In M. D. Dunnette (Ed.), *Handbook of industrial and organizational psychology* (pp. 223–326). Chicago: Rand McNally.

Enz, C. A. (1986). *Power and shared values in the corporate culture.* Ann Arbor, MI: UMI Research Press.

Enz, C. A. (1988). The role of value congruity in intraorganizational power. *Administrative Science Quarterly, 33,* 284–304.

Enz, C. A., & Fryxell, G. E. (1987, August). *The meaning and measurement of organizational value congruity.* Paper presented at the annual meeting of the Academy of Management, New Orleans.

Hackman, J. R., & Lawler, E. E. (1971). Employee reactions to job characteristics. *Journal of Applied Psychology, 55,* 259–286.

Hambrick, D. C., & Mason, P. A. (1984). Upper echelons: The organization as a reflection of its top managers. *Academy of Management Review, 9,* 193–206.

Hater, J. J., & Bass, B. M. (1988). Superiors' evaluations and subordinates' perceptions of transformational and transactional leadership. *Journal of Applied Psychology, 73,* 695–702.

Kanter, R. M. (1983). *The change masters.* New York: Simon & Schuster.

Kouzes, J. M., & Posner, B. Z. (1988). *The leadership challenge: How to get extraordinary things done in organizations.* San Francisco: Jossey-Bass.

Labich, K. (1988, October 24). The seven keys to business leadership. *Fortune,* pp. 58–66.

Lawler, E. E., Seashore, S. E., & Cammann, C. (1975). *Michigan Assessment of Organizations.* Ann Arbor: University of Michigan, Institute for Social Research, Survey Research Center.

Locke, E. A. (1976). The nature and causes of job satisfaction. In M. D. Dunnette (Ed.), *Handbook of industrial and organizational psychology* (pp. 1297–1349). Chicago: Rand McNally.

Margerison, C. (1979). *How to assess your managerial style.* New York: AMACOM.

Miller, K. I., & Monge, P. R. (1986). Participation, satisfaction, and productivity: A meta-analytic review. *Academy of Management Journal, 29,* 727–753.

Mintzberg, H. (1973). *The nature of managerial work.* New York: Harper & Row.

Norusis, M. J. (1988). *SPSS-X advanced statistics guide* (2nd ed.). Chicago: SPSS.

O'Reilly, C., III., & Chatman, J. (1986). Organizational commitment and psychological attachment: The effects of compliance, identification, and internalization on prosocial behavior. *Journal of Applied Psychology, 71,* 492–499.

Peters, T. J., & Austin, N. (1985). *A passion for excellence.* New York: Random House.

Peters, T. J., & Waterman, R. (1982). *In search of excellence: Lessons from America's best run companies.* New York: Harper & Row.

Pfeffer, J. (1981). Management as symbolic action: The creation and maintenance of organizational paradigms. In L. L. Cummings & B. M. Staw (Eds.), *Research in organizational behavior* (Vol. 3, pp. 1–52). Greenwich, CT: JAI Press.

Porter, L. W., Steers, R. M., Mowday, R. T., & Boulian, P. V. (1974). Organizational commitment, job satisfaction, and turnover among psychiatric technicians. *Journal of Applied Psychology, 58,* 603–609.

Posner, B. Z., Kouzes, J. M., & Schmidt, W. H. (1985). Shared values make a difference: An empirical test of corporate culture. *Human Relations Management, 24,* 293–309.

Rizzo, J. R., House, R. J., & Lirtzman, S. I. (1970). Role conflict and ambiguity in complex organizations. *Administrative Science Quarterly, 17,* 150–163.

Robbins, S. R., & Duncan, R. B. (1988). The role of the CEO and top management in the creation and implementation of strategic vision. In D. C. Hambrick (Ed.), *The executive effect: Concepts and methods for studying top management* (pp. 205–233). Greenwich, CT: JAI Press.

Schein, E. H. (1985). *Organizational culture and leadership.* San Francisco: Jossey-Bass.

Tichy, N. M., & Devanna, M. A. (1986). *The transformational leader.* New York: Wiley.

Tichy, N. M., & Ulrich, D. O. (1984). The leadership challenge—A call for the transformational leader. *Sloan Management Review, 25,* 59–68.

Vaill, P. B. (1984). The purposing of high-performing systems. In T. J. Sergiovanni & J. E. Corbally (Eds.), *Leadership and organizational culture* (pp. 85–104). Urbana: University of Illinois Press.

Wagner, J. A., III, & Gooding, R. Z. (1987). Shared influence and organizational behavior: A meta-analysis of situational variables expected to moderate participation-outcome relationships. *Academy of Management Journal, 30,* 524–541.

Yukl, G. A. (1989). *Leadership in organizations* (2nd ed.). Englewood Cliffs, NJ: Prentice-Hall.

Chapter Eleven

Does Leadership Really Make a Difference?

*T*here are few management and organization topics that have generated more interest and research activity, spanning nearly five decades, than the focus on leadership. Thousands of pages in academic books and journals have been devoted to the topic. During the past several years, the popular press has published and sold millions of copies of several dozen books written on the topic of leaders and leadership. Organizations frantically search for that magical leader who can pull the firm together and place it back onto the competitive path. We frequently hear stories about important historical leaders, we attribute organizational successes and failures to the things that our leaders did or failed to do, and at the national level we commonly resurrect dreams of the way it was when certain charismatic leaders were at the nation's helm.

Embedded in and reinforced by this attention is the implicit assumption that leadership is important, that leaders makes a difference, and that positive group and organizational effects are produced by leaders and the leadership process. Our preoccupation with leaders and the leadership process makes the following question appear to hinge upon the absurd—Does leadership really make a positive difference? The readings contained in this chapter are intended, in part, to address and stimulate your thinking about this issue.

Not everyone agrees on the answer to this question. Instead, the question, Does leadership make a difference? has produced a debate among a number of leadership scholars. James R. Meindl and his colleagues (Sanford B. Ehrlich and Janet M. Dukerich, 1985) have argued that as a society we have developed romantic notions about leaders and leadership.[1] In the process, observers make attributions that suggest that "the successful turnaround" was due to the new CEO and that the "losing season" was due to the coach's inability to bring out the talent of his or her team.

Joining the leadership debate are the contextualists and constructionists. The "contextualists" (e.g., Richard Hall, 1977; Jeffrey Pfeffer and Gerald R. Salancik, 1978) argue that situations generally place such strong constraints upon organizational leaders that it is virtually impossible for them to be able to significantly affect the behavior of the organization and its final level of performance.[2] The "social constructionists" contend that much of our understanding about leaders and leadership stems from socially provided information (e.g., Calder, 1977; Meindl, Ehrlich, and Dukerich, 1985; Meindl, 1990).[3] Echoing this debate, James Meindl and his colleagues note that "as observers of

---

[1] J. R. Meindl, S. B. Ehrlich, and J. B. Dukerich, "The Romance of Leadership," *Administrative Science Quarterly* 30 (1985), 78–102.

[2] R. H. Hall, "Organizations: Structure and Process," 2nd ed. (Englewood Cliffs, NJ: Prentice-Hall 1977); J. Pfeffer and G. R. Salancik, *The External Control of Organizations: A Resource Dependence Perspective* (New York: Harper and Row, 1978).

[3] B. J. Calder, An Attribution Theory of Leadership, in B. M. Staw and G. R. Salancik eds., *New Directions in Organizational Behavior* (Chicago: St. Clair, 1977) 179–204; J. R. Meindl, "On Leadership: An Alternative to the Conventional Wisdom," *Research in Organizational Behavior* 12 (1990), 159–203.

and as participants in organizations, we may have developed highly romanticized, heroic views of leadership" (p. 79). These heroic views paint unrealistic pictures about what it is that leaders do, what they are able to accomplish, and the general effects they have on our lives.

Along with Chao C. Chen, Meindl (1991) has argued that much of what people have come to believe about leaders and leadership is the result of what others have told them. This romantic love affair with leaders results in stories that make effective leadership a socially constructed reality.[4] While these socially constructed and heroic views of leadership may be dramatically overestimated and removed from what is reality, Meindl and his colleagues note that this romantic relationship may be very important by helping to sustain followership—a phenomenon that produces significant contributions to the needs and goals of social systems, without which they would surely wither and die.

In an attempt to provide support for the argument that leadership does *not* make a difference, several scholars have looked at the leadership succession literature in an attempt to see if changes in organizational leadership are associated with significant gains (losses) in organizational performance. Two studies are frequently drawn upon in an attempt to support the view that leadership does not make a significant difference in terms of organizational performance. Stanley Lieberson and James F. O'Connor (1972) compared the impact of leadership relative to environmental and organizational influences in 167 organizations operating in 13 different industries. They concluded their study by suggesting that organizational performance was influenced more significantly by environmental factors than by those in top organizational leadership roles.[5] In addition, Gerald Salancik and Jeffrey Pfeffer (1977) in their study of the performance of city governments concluded that changes from mayor to mayor were minor and unlikely to bring about major organizational changes.[6]

Others take the position that leadership *does* make a difference. In the popular press, management authors Tom Peters and Nancy Austin (1985) suggested that top-level leadership is an extremely important part of the process associated with the development and maintenance of excellent organizations.[7] There are also a number of organizational scholars who hold similar views (e.g., Robert J. House, 1988; Day and Lord, 1988).[8] Summarizing evidence from field-based longitudinal studies of the effects of lower organizational leadership and those conducted in the laboratory setting, House (1988) notes that there is an abundance of evidence demonstrating significant leadership effects in the areas of: level of effort expended, adaptability to change, performance under change conditions, level of group turnover, absenteeism, group member performance, decision acceptance, quality of decisions made, and the amount of follower learning from leadership training efforts (p. 347).

Very few scientific investigations have been conducted with a focus on the leadership effects produced by middle-level and upper-level organizational leaders. House cites evidence of leaders producing changes in organizational structure. In addition, House's interpretation of the evidence from the Lieberson and O'Connor study suggests that 31 percent of the variance in organizational net profit on sales over a 20-year time period could be directly attributed to changes in the top leadership of the companies participating in this study (p. 347–48).

[4]C. C. Chen and J. R. Meindl, "The Construction of Leadership Images in the Popular Press: The Case of Donald Burr and People Express," *Administrative Science Quarterly* 36 (1991), 521–51.

[5]S. Lieberson and J. F. O'Connor, "Leadership and Organizational Performance: A Study of Large Corporations," *American Sociological Review* 37 (1972), 117–30.

[6]G. R. Salancik and J. Pfeffer, "Constraints on Administrator Discretion: The Limited Influence of Mayors on City Budgets, *Urban Affairs Quarterly* 12 (1977), 475–98.

[7]T. Peters and N. Austin, *A Passion for Excellence: The Leadership Difference* (New York: Random House 1985).

[8]R. J. House, "Leadership Research: Some Forgotten, Ignored, or Overlooked Findings," in J. G. Hunt, B. R. Baglia, H. P. Dachaler, and C. A. Schriesheim eds., *Emerging Leadership Vistas* (Lexington, MA: D. C. Heath 1988); D. V. Day and R. G. Lord, "Executive Leadership and Organizational Performance: Suggestions for a New Theory and Methodology," *Journal of Management* 14 (1988), 453–64.

According to House, the research evidence, "when viewed collectively, demonstrates unequivocally that leadership can potentially influence significant variables related to organizational effectiveness and individual member satisfaction. However, there have also been longitudinal and experimental studies that show that leader behavior has little or no effect on subordinates' performance. Further, there are several studies that show that leader behavior is *caused* by the performance of subordinates" (p. 348).

The readings in this chapter focus attention on two important leadership issues. The first concerns the implicit notion that leadership does not make a difference in terms of organizational performance. The second issue concerns the implicit notion that the effects of leadership *are* essentially positive in nature.

Point—Leadership Is but a Mirage; It Really Does Not Make a Difference

In the first reading, Jeffrey Pfeffer (1977) questions the implicit assumption that leadership is causally related to the performance of organizations. He challenges common thinking about leadership by raising several significant questions. First, Pfeffer raises issues regarding the definition of leadership. He contends that there remains a great deal of ambiguity surrounding the meaning that is attached to the term, and that the concept of leadership is essentially redundant with other important organizational constructs such as influence, social power, and authority. As a result it is difficult to know whether leadership is needed and whether it is leadership or other factors that account for the differences in organizational performance. Pfeffer also calls attention to the fact that there remains a considerable amount of confusion that surrounds the behaviors that leaders actually engage in and whether or not these behaviors have any significant and meaningful relationship with other organizational outcomes. While Pfeffer's first question focused on the ambiguity of the leadership construct, his second question is concerned with whether or not leadership has any discernible effects on organizational outcomes. He suggests that there is very little evidence that the effects attributable to leadership are large in nature. He also argues that there are so many organizational constraints placed upon the behavior of all leaders that it should not be surprising that they are rendered incapable of producing any profound organizational effects. Third, Pfeffer argues that leadership is perceived to be an important and powerful force because we generally like to have a focus for the assignment of causal attributions. It is difficult, for example, to assign the functions of leadership—task accomplishment and group maintenance—to a large number of individuals whose interactions and relationships are left to chance. Instead, comfort is found in reducing causal uncertainty by directing cause and effect attributions toward a single point of focus—a leader. Thus, *leaders are important social constructions.* They are symbols, and, hence, targets for our attributions. They serve as scapegoats for our failures and heroes around which members of a group can rally in celebration of their collective accomplishments.

Counterpoint—Leadership Really Does Make a Difference

The Dark Side of Leadership

While it is common to think in terms of leaders and their positive (or presumed positive) effects—Lee Iacocca's turnaround of Chrysler, Steve Jobs' creation of Apple and Macintosh, Jack Welch's reinvention of General Electric, and Norman Schwartzkopf and Colin Powell's victorious strategies during Operation Desert Storm—not all of our leadership stories are positive in nature. The names of individuals such as David Koresh, Adolph Hitler, and James Jones serve to remind us that there can also be a negative side of leadership.

In the second reading in this chapter, Jay A. Conger (1990) discusses the dark side of leadership. He suggests that there are those leaders who have lost touch with reality and those who use their position of leadership for their own personal gains. In both instances negative consequences for the group and/or organization are common by-products. In this reading Conger explores the questions, How do leaders produce such negative outcomes, and why? Conger takes the position that leadership can make a significant difference. Unfortunately, however, this difference is not always positive in nature.

The Positive Side of Leadership

Consistent with most of our thinking, as noted by Pfeffer (1977), leadership is generally cast as making a difference. In the previous reading Conger (1990) provided insight into problems that can be associated with leadership. Now we turn to the positive difference that leadership can make in terms of organizational performance.

David V. Day and Robert G. Lord (1988) argue that there is ample evidence to indicate that top-level leadership is significantly related to organizational performance. There are instances where leadership has accounted for 45 percent of the variance in organizational performance. In one study of 167 corporations in 13 industries over a two-year time period, it was found that top-level leadership accounted for 7.5 percent of the variance in net income. While 7.5 percent might be seen as a relatively small proportion, 7.5 percent of several hundreds of millions of dollars translates into a very significant amount of money.

The effects of executive leadership may be *direct* in their impact upon both the external and internal environments of the organization. In addition, many of the effects of leadership are *indirect* in nature. In many instances, for example, top-level leaders create the culture of the organization, which in turn impacts upon the strength of commitment displayed by members throughout the organization. The philosophical orientation of top-level management has also been seen as indirectly affecting the success of employee involvement programs (e.g., management-by-objectives) and the degree to which employee ownership systems have resulted in the creation of psychological ownership and employee performance (e.g., citizenship) behaviors.[9]

In sum, a review and analysis of the research literature revolving around the question Does leadership make a difference to organizational performance? led Alan Berkeley Thomas (1988) to conclude that "it is evident that it will require very considerable additional research before we can offer a general assessment of the impact of leadership on organizational performance."[10] In addition, the observations offered by House (1988) suggest that the contingency models of leadership best represent our understanding of whether or not leadership really does or does not make a significant difference. It is clear that at times the answer to this question may well be yes—leaders and the leadership process make a difference (directly or indirectly). At other times the effects of leadership may be neutralized or substituted for by other forces operating within the organization (group) and/or its environment. Finally, it should be noted that the effects of leadership, when produced, are *not* always positive in nature.

[9]R. Rodgers and J. E. Hunter, "Impact of Management by Objectives on Organizational Productivity," *Journal of Applied Psychology* 76 (1991) 322–36; L. Van Dyne, J. L. Pierce, and L. L. Cummings, "Employee Ownership: Empirical Support for Mediated Relationships." Presented at the eighth annual conference of the Society for Industrial and Organizational Psychology, Symposium on Psychological Ownership: Individual and Organizational Consequences, San Francisco, 1993.

[10]A. B. Thomas, "Does Leadership Make a Difference to Organizational Performance," *Administrative Science Quarterly* 33 (1988), 388–400.

The Ambiguity of Leadership

J. Pfeffer
University of California, Berkeley

*L*eadership has for some time been a major topic in social and organizational psychology. Underlying much of this research has been the assumption that leadership is causally related to organizational performance. Through an analysis of leadership styles, behaviors, or characteristics (depending on the theoretical perspective chosen), the argument has been made that more effective leaders can be selected or trained or, alternatively, the situation can be configured to provide for enhanced leader and organizational effectiveness.

Three problems with emphasis on leadership as a concept can be posed: (*a*) ambiguity in definition and measurement of the concept itself; (*b*) the question of whether leadership has discernible effects on organizational outcomes; and (*c*) the selection process in succession to leadership positions, which frequently uses organizationally irrelevant criteria and which has implications for normative theories of leadership. The argument here is that leadership is of interest primarily as a phenomenological construct. Leaders serve as symbols for representing personal causation of social events. How and why are such attributions of personal effects made? Instead of focusing on leadership and its effects, how do people make inferences about and react to phenomena labelled as leadership (5)?

The Ambiguity of the Concept

While there have been many studies of leadership, the dimensions and definition of the concept remain unclear. To treat leadership as a separate concept, it must be distinguished from other social influence phenomena. Hollander and Julian (24) and Bavelas (2) did not draw distinctions between leadership and other processes of social influence. A major point of the Hollander and Julian review was that leadership research might develop more rapidly if more general theories of social influence were incorporated. Calder (5) also argued that there is no unique content to the construct of leadership that is not subsumed under other, more general models of behavior.

Kochan, Schmidt, and DeCotiis (33) attempted to distinguish leadership from related concepts of authority and social power. In leadership, influence rights are voluntarily conferred. Power does not require goal compatibility—merely dependence—but leadership implies some congruence between the objectives of the leader and the led. These distinctions depend on the ability to distinguish voluntary from involuntary compliance and to assess goal compatibility. Goal statements may be retrospective inferences from action (46, 53) and problems of distinguishing voluntary from involuntary compliance also exist (32). Apparently there are few meaningful distinctions between leadership and other concepts of social influence. Thus, an understanding of the phenomena subsumed under the rubric of leadership may not require the construct of leadership (5).

While there is some agreement that leadership is related to social influence, more disagreement concerns the basic dimensions of leader behavior. Some have argued that there are two tasks to be accomplished in groups—maintenance of the group and performance of some task or activity—and thus leader behavior might be described along these two dimensions (1, 6, 8, 25). The dimensions emerging from the Ohio State leadership studies—consideration and initiating structure—may be seen as similar to the two components of group maintenance and task accomplishment (18).

Other dimensions of leadership behavior have also been proposed (4). Day and Hamblin (10) analyzed leadership in terms of the closeness and punitiveness of the supervision. Several authors have conceptualized leadership behavior in terms of the authority and discretion subordinates are permitted (23, 36, 51). Fiedler (14) analyzed leadership in terms of the least-preferred-co-worker scale (LPC), but the meaning and behavioral attributes of this dimension of leadership behavior remain controversial.

The proliferation of dimensions is partly a function of research strategies frequently employed. Factor analysis on a large number of items describing behavior has frequently been used. This procedure tends to produce as many factors as the analyst decides to find, and permits the development of a large number of possible factor structures. The resultant factors must be named and further impression is introduced. Deciding on a summative concept to represent a factor is inevitably a partly subjective process.

Literature assessing the effects of leadership tends to be equivocal. Sales (45) summarized leadership literature employing the authoritarian-democratic typology and concluded that effects on performance were small and inconsistent. Reviewing the literature on consideration and initiating structure dimensions, Korman (34) reported relatively small and inconsistent results, and Kerr and Schriesheim (30) reported more consistent effects of the two dimensions. Better results apparently emerge when moderating factors are taken into account, including subordinate personalities (50),

Source: Edited and reprinted with permission from *Academy of Management Review* 2, 1 (1977), 104–12. Author affiliation may have changed since article was first published.

and situational characteristics (23, 51). Kerr et al. (31) list many moderating effects grouped under the headings of subordinate considerations, supervisor considerations, and task considerations. Even if each set of considerations consisted of only one factor (which it does not), an attempt to account for the effects of leader behavior would necessitate considering four-way interactions. While social reality is complex and contingent, it seems desirable to attempt to find more parsimonious explanations for the phenomena under study.

The Effects of Leaders

Hall asked a basic question about leadership: Is there any evidence on the magnitude of the effects of leadership (17, p. 248)? Surprisingly, he could find little evidence. Given the resources that have been spent studying, selecting, and training leaders, one might expect that the question of whether or not leaders matter would have been addressed earlier (12).

There are at least three reasons why it might be argued that the observed effects of leaders on organizational outcomes would be small. First, those obtaining leadership positions are selected, and perhaps only certain, limited styles of behavior may be chosen. Second, once in the leadership position, the discretion and behavior of the leader are constrained. And third, leaders can typically affect only a few of the variables that may impact organizational performance.

Homogeneity of Leaders

Persons are selected to leadership positions. As a consequence of this selection process, the range of behaviors or characteristics exhibited by leaders is reduced, making it more problematic to empirically discover an effect of leadership. There are many types of constraints on the selection process. The attraction literature suggests that there is a tendency for persons to like those they perceive as similar (3). In critical decisions such as the selections of persons for leadership positions, compatible styles of behavior probably will be chosen.

Selection of persons is also constrained by the internal system or influence in the organization. As Zald (56) noted, succession is a critical decision, affected by political influence and by environmental contingencies faced by the organization. As Thompson (49) noted, leaders may be selected for their capacity to deal with various organizational contingencies. In a study of characteristics of hospital administrators, Pfeffer and Salancik (42) found a relationship between the hospital's context and the characteristics and tenure of the administrators. To the extent that the contingencies and power distribution within the organization remain stable, the abilities and behaviors of those selected into leadership positions will also remain stable.

Finally, the selection of persons to leadership positions is affected by a self-selection process. Organizations and roles have images, providing information about their character. Persons are likely to select themselves into organizations and roles based upon their preferences for the dimensions of the organizational and role characteristics as perceived through these images. The self-selection of persons would tend to work along with organizational selection to limit the range of abilities and behaviors in a given organizational role.

Such selection processes would tend to increase homogeneity more within a single organization than across organizations. Yet many studies of leadership effect at the work group level have compared groups within a single organization. If there comes to be a widely shared, socially constructed definition of leadership behaviors or characteristics which guides the selection process, then leadership activity may come to be defined similarly in various organizations, leading to the selection of only those who match the constructed image of a leader.

Constraints on Leader Behavior

Analyses of leadership have frequently presumed that leadership style or leader behavior was an independent variable that could be selected or trained at will to conform to what research would find to be optimal. Even theorists who took a more contingent view of appropriate leadership behavior generally assumed that with proper training, appropriate behavior could be produced (51). Fiedler (13), noting how hard it was to change behavior, suggested changing the situational characteristics rather than the person, but this was an unusual suggestion in the context of prevailing literature which suggested that leadership style was something to be strategically selected according to the variables of the particular leadership theory.

But the leader is embedded in a social system, which constrains behavior. The leader has a role set (27), in which members have expectations for appropriate behavior and persons make efforts to modify the leader's behavior. Pressures to conform to the expectations of peers, subordinates, and superiors are all relevant in determining actual behavior.

Leaders, even in high-level positions, have unilateral control over fewer resources and fewer policies than might be expected. Investment decisions may require approval of others, while hiring and promotion decisions may be accomplished by committees. Leader behavior is constrained by both the demands of others in the role set and by organizationally prescribed limitations on the sphere of activity and influence.

External Factors

Many factors that may affect organizational performance are outside a leader's control, even if he or she were to have complete discretion over major areas of organizational decisions. For example, consider the executive in a construction firm. Costs are largely determined by operation of commodities and labor markets; and demand is largely affected by interest rates, availability of mortgage money, and economic conditions which are affected by governmental policies over which the executive has little control. School superintendents have little control over birth rates and community economic development, both of which profoundly affect school system budgets. While the leader may react to contingencies as they arise, or may be a better or worse forecaster, in accounting for variation in organizational outcomes, he or she may account for relatively little compared to external factors.

Second, the leader's success or failure may be partly due to circumstances unique to the organization but still outside his or her control. Leader positions in organizations vary in terms of the strength and position of the organization. The choice of a new executive does not fundamentally alter a market and financial position that has developed over years and affects the leader's ability to make strategic changes and the likelihood that the organization will do well or poorly. Organizations have relatively enduring strengths and weaknesses. The choice of a particular leader for a particular position has limited impact on these capabilities.

Empirical Evidence

Two studies have assessed the effects of leadership changes in major positions in organizations. Lieberson and O'Connor (35) examined 167 business firms in 13 industries over a 20-year period, allocating variance in sales, profits, and profit margins to one of four sources: year (general economic conditions), industry, company effects, and effects of changes in the top executive position. They concluded that compared to other factors, administration had a limited effect on organizational outcomes.

Using a similar analytical procedure, Salancik and Pfeffer (44) examined the effects of mayors on city budgets for 30 U.S. cities. Data on expenditures by budget category were collected for 1951–1968. Variance in amount and proportion of expenditures was apportioned for the year, the city, or the mayor. The mayoral effect was relatively small, with the city accounting for most of the variance, although the mayor effect was larger for expenditure categories that were not as directly connected to important interest groups. Salancik and Pfeffer argued that the effects of the mayor were limited both by absence of power to control many of the expenditures and tax sources, and by construction of politics in response to demands from interests in the environment.

If leadership is defined as a strictly interpersonal phenomenon, the relevance of these two studies for the issue of leadership effects becomes problematic. But such a conceptualization seems unduly restrictive and is certainly inconsistent with Selznick's (47) conceptualization of leadership as strategic management and decision making. If one cannot observe differences when leaders change, then what does it matter who occupies the positions or how they behave?

Pfeffer and Salancik (41) investigated the extent to which behaviors selected by first-line supervisors were constrained by expectations of others in their role set. Variance in task and social behaviors could be accounted for by role-set expectations, with adherence to various demands made by role-set participants a function of similarity and relative power. Lowin and Craig (37) experimentally demonstrated that leader behavior was determined by the subordinate's own behavior. Both studies illustrate that leader behaviors are responses to the demands of the social context.

The effect of leadership may vary depending upon level in the organizational hierarchy, while the appropriate activities and behaviors may also vary with organizational level (26, 40). For the most part, empirical studies of leadership have dealt with first-line supervisors or leaders with relatively low organizational status (17). If leadership has any impact, it should be more evident at higher organizational levels or where there is more discretion in decisions and activities. . . .

The Attribution of Leadership

Kelley conceptualized the layman as:

> an applied scientist, that is, as a person concerned about applying his knowledge of causal relationships in order to *exercise control* of his world (29, p. 2).

Reviewing a series of studies dealing with the attributional process, he concluded that persons were not only interested in understanding their world correctly, but also in controlling it.

> The view here proposed is that attribution processes are to be understood not only as a means of providing the individual with a veridical view of his world, but as a means of encouraging and maintaining his effective exercise of control in that world (29, p. 22).

Controllable factors will have high salience as candidates for causal explanation, while a bias toward the more important causes may shift the attributional emphasis toward causes that are not controllable (29, p. 23). The study of attribution is a study of naive psychology—an examination of how persons make sense out of the events taking place around them.

If Kelley is correct that individuals will tend to develop attributions that give them a feeling of control, then emphasis on leadership may derive partially from a desire to believe in the effectiveness and importance of individual action, since individual action is more controllable than contextual variables. Lieberson and O'Connor (35) made essentially the same point in introducing their paper on the effects of top-management changes on organizational performance. Given the desire for control and a feeling of personal effectiveness, organizational outcomes are more likely to be attributed to individual actions, regardless of their actual causes.

Leadership is attributed by observers. Social action has meaning only through a phenomenological process (46). The identification of certain organizational roles as leadership positions guides the construction of meaning in the direction of attributing effects to the actions of those positions. While Bavelas (2) argued that the functions of leadership, such as task accomplishment and group maintenance, are shared throughout the group, this fact provides no simple and potentially controllable focus for attributing causality. Rather, the identification of leadership positions provides a simpler and more readily changeable model of reality. When causality is lodged in one or a few persons rather than being a function of a complex set of interactions among all group members, changes can be made by replacing or influencing the occupant of the leadership position. Causes of organizational actions are readily identified in this simple causal structure.

Even if, empirically, leadership has little effect, and even if succession to leadership positions is not predicated on ability or performance, the belief in leadership effects and meritocratic succession provides a simple causal framework and a justification for the structure of the social collectivity. More importantly, the beliefs interpret social actions in terms that indicate potential for effective individual intervention or control. The personification of social causality serves too many uses to be easily overcome. Whether or not leader behavior actually influences performance or effectiveness, it is important because people believe it does.

One consequence of the attribution of causality to leaders and leadership is that leaders come to be symbols. Mintzberg (39), in his discussion of the roles of managers, wrote of the symbolic role, but more in terms of attendance at formal events and formally representing the organization. The symbolic role of leadership is more important than implied in such a description. The leader as a symbol provides a target for action when difficulties occur, serving as a scapegoat when things go wrong. Gamson and Scotch (15) noted that in baseball, the firing of the manager served a scapegoating purpose. One cannot fire the whole team, yet when performance is poor, something must be done. The firing of the manager conveys to the world and to the actors involved that success is the result of personal actions, and that steps can and will be taken to enhance organizational performance.

The attribution of causality to leadership may be reinforced by organizational actions, such as the inauguration process, the choice process, and providing the leader with symbols and ceremony. If leaders are chosen by using a random number table, persons are less likely to believe in their effects than if there is an elaborate search or selection process followed by an elaborate ceremony signifying the changing of control, and if the leader then has a variety of perquisites and symbols that distinguish him or her from the rest of the organization. Construction of the importance of leadership in a given social context is the outcome of various social processes, which can be empirically examined.

Since belief in the leadership effect provides a feeling of personal control, one might argue that efforts to increase the attribution of causality to leaders would occur more when it is more necessary and more problematic to attribute causality to controllable factors. Such an argument would lead to the hypothesis that the more the *context* actually affects organizational outcomes, the more efforts will be made to ensure attribution to *leadership*. When leaders really do have effects, it is less necessary to engage in rituals indicating their effects. Such rituals are more likely when there is uncertainty and unpredictability associated with the organization's operations. This results both from the desire to feel control in uncertain situations and from the fact that in ambiguous contexts, it is easier to attribute consequences to leadership without facing possible disconfirmation.

The leader is, in part, an actor. Through statements and actions, the leader attempts to reinforce the operation of an attribution process which tends to vest causality in that position in the social structure. Successful leaders, as perceived by members of the social system, are those who can separate themselves from organizational failures and associate themselves with organizational successes. Since the meaning of action is socially constructed, this involves manipulation of symbols to reinforce the desired process of attribution. For instance, if a manager knows that business in his or her division is about to improve because of the economic cycle, the leader may, nevertheless, write recommendations and undertake actions and changes that are highly visible and that will tend to identify his or her behavior closely with the division. A manager who perceives impending failure will attempt to associate the division and its policies and decisions with others, particularly persons in higher organizational positions, and to disassociate himself or herself from the division's performance, occasionally even transferring or moving to another organization.

Conclusion

The theme of this article has been that analysis of leadership and leadership processes must be contingent on the intent of the researcher. If the interest is in understanding the causality of social phenomena as reliably and accurately as possible, then the concept of leadership may be a poor place to begin. The issue of the effects of leadership is open to question. But examination of situational variables that accompany more or less leadership effect is a worthwhile task.

The more phenomenological analysis of leadership directs attention to the process by which social causality is attributed and focuses on the distinction between causality as perceived by group members and causality as assessed by an outside observer. Leadership is associated with a set of myths reinforcing a social construction of meaning which legitimates leadership role occupants, provides belief in potential mobility for those not in leadership roles, and attributes social causality to leadership roles, thereby providing a belief in the effectiveness of individual control. In analyzing leadership, this mythology and the process by which such mythology is created and supported should be separated from analysis of leadership as a social influence process, operating within constraints.

References

Bales, R. F. *Interaction Process Analysis: A Method for the Study of Small Groups* (Reading, Mass.: Addison-Wesley, 1950).

Bavelas, Alex. "Leadership: Man and Function," *Administrative Science Quarterly* 4 (1960), pp. 491–98.

Berscheid, Ellen, and Elaine Walster. *Interpersonal Attraction* (Reading, Mass.: Addison-Wesley, 1969).

Bowers, David G., and Stanley E. Seashore. "Predicting Organizational Effectiveness with a Four-Factor Theory of Leadership," *Administrative Science Quarterly* 11 (1966), pp. 238–63.

Calder, Bobby J. "An Attribution Theory of Leadership," in *New Directions in Organizational Behav-*ior, ed. B. Staw and G. Salancik (Chicago: St. Clair Press, 1976).

Cartwright, Dorwin C., and Alvin Zander. *Group Dynamics: Research and Theory*, 3d ed. (Evanston, Ill.: Row, Peterson, 1960).

Cole, Jonathan R., and Stephen Cole. *Social Stratification in Science* (Chicago: University of Chicago Press, 1973).

Collins, Barry E., and Harold Guetzkow. *A Social Psychology of Group Processes for Decision Making* (New York: Wiley, 1964).

Collins, Randall. "Functional and Conflict Theories of Stratification," *American Sociological Review* 36 (1971), pp. 1002–19.

Day, R. C., and R. L. Hamblin. "Some Effects of Close and Punitive Styles of Supervision," *American Journal of Sociology* 69 (1964), pp. 499–510.

Domhoff, G. William. *Who Rules America?* (Englewood Cliffs, N.J.: Prentice-Hall, 1967).

Dubin, Robert. "Supervision and Productivity: Empirical Findings and Theoretical Considerations," in *Leadership and Productivity*, ed. R. Dubin, G. C. Homans, F. C. Mann, and D. C. Miller (San Francisco: Chandler Publishing, 1965), pp. 1–50.

Fiedler, Fred E. "Engineering the Job to Fit the Manager," *Harvard Business Review* 43 (1965), pp. 115–322.

Fiedler, Fred E. *A Theory of Leadership Effectiveness* (New York: McGraw-Hill, 1967).

Gamson, William A., and Norman A. Scotch, "Scapegoating in Baseball," *American Journal of Sociology* 70 (1964), pp. 69–72.

Granovetter, Mark. *Getting a Job* (Cambridge, Mass.: Harvard University Press, 1974).

Hall, Richard H. *Organizations: Structure and Process* (Englewood Cliffs, N.J.: Prentice-Hall, 1972).

Halpin, A. W., and J. Winer. "A Factorial Study of the Leader Behavior Description Questionnaire," in *Leader Behavior: Its Description and Measurement*, ed. R. M. Stogdill and A. E. Coons (Columbus, Ohio: Bureau of Business Research, Ohio State University, 1957), pp. 39–51.

Hargens, L. L. "Patterns of Mobility of New Ph.D.'s among American Academic Institutions," *Sociology of Education* 42 (1969), pp. 18–37.

Hargens, L. L., and W. O. Hagstrom. "Sponsored and Contest Mobility of American Academic Scientists," *Sociology of Education* 40 (1967), pp. 24–38.

Harrell, Thomas W. "High Earning MBA's," *Personnel Psychology* 25 (1972), pp. 523–30.

Harrell, Thomas W., and Margaret S. Harrell. "Predictors of Management Success." *Stanford University Graduate School of Business, Technical Report No. 3 to the Office of Naval Research.*

Heller, Frank, and Gary Yukl. "Participation, Managerial Decision Making, and Situational Variables," *Organizational Behavior and Human Performance* 4 (1969), pp. 227–41.

Hollander, Edwin P., and James W. Julian. "Contemporary Trends in the Analysis of Leadership Processes," *Psychological Bulletin* 71 (1969), pp. 387–97.

House, Robert J. "A Path Goal Theory of Leader Effectiveness," *Administrative Science Quarterly* 16 (1971), pp. 321–38.

Hunt, J. G. "Leadership-Style Effects at Two Managerial Levels in a Simulated Organization," *Administrative Science Quarterly* 16 (1971), pp. 476–85.

Kahn, R. L., D. M. Wolfe, R. P. Quinn, and J. D. Snoek. *Organizational Stress: Studies in Role Conflict and Ambiguity* (New York: Wiley, 1964).

Karabel, J., and A. W. Astin. "Social Class, Academic Ability, and College 'Quality'," *Social Forces* 53 (1975), pp. 381–98.

Kelley, Harold H. *Attribution in Social Interaction* (Morristown, N.J.: General Learning Press, 1971).

Kerr, Steven, and Chester Schriesheim. "Consideration, Initiating Structure and Organizational Criteria—An Update of Korman's 1966 Review," *Personnel Psychology* 27 (1974), pp. 555–68.

Kerr, S., C. Schriesheim, C. J. Murphy, and R. M. Stogdill, "Toward a Contingency Theory of Leadership Based upon the Consideration and Initiating Structure Literature," *Organizational Behavior and Human Performance* 12 (1974), pp. 62–82.

Kiesler, C., and S. Kiesler. *Conformity* (Reading, Mass.: Addison-Wesley, 1969).

Kochan, T. A., S. M. Schmidt, and T. A. DeCotiis. "Superior-Subordinate Relations: Leadership and Headship," *Human Relations* 28 (1975), pp. 279–94.

Korman, A. K. "Consideration, Initiating Structure, and Organizational Criteria—A Review," *Personnel Psychology* 19 (1966), pp. 349–62.

Lieberson, Stanley, and James F. O'Connor. "Leadership and Organizational Performance: A Study of Large Corporations," *American Sociological Review* 37 (1972), pp. 117–30.

Lippitt, Ronald. "An Experimental Study of the Effect of Democratic and Authoritarian Group Atmospheres," *University of Iowa Studies in Child Welfare* 16 (1940), pp. 43–195.

Lowin, A., and J. R. Craig. "The Influence of Level of Performance on Managerial Style: An Experimental Object-Lesson in the Ambiguity of Correlational Data," *Organizational Behavior and Human Performance* 3 (1968), pp. 440–58.

Mills, C. Wright. "The American Business Elite: A Collective Portrait," in *Power, Politics, and People*, ed. C. W. Mills (New York: Oxford University Press, 1963), pp. 110–39.

Mintzberg, Henry. *The Nature of Managerial Work* (New York: Harper and Row, 1973).

Nealey, Stanley M., and Milton R. Blood. "Leadership Performance of Nursing Supervisors at Two Organizational Levels," *Journal of Applied Psychology* 52 (1968), pp. 414–42.

Pfeffer, Jeffrey, and Gerald R. Salancik. "Determinants of Supervisory Behavior: A Role Set Analysis," *Human Relations* 28 (1975), pp. 139–54.

Pfeffer, Jeffrey, and Gerald R. Salancik. "Organizational Context and the Characteristics and Tenure of Hospital Administrators," *Academy of Management Journal* 20 (1977).

Reed, R. H., and H. P. Miller. "Some Determinants of the Variation in Earnings per College Men," *Journal of Human Resources* 5 (1970), 117–90.

Salancik, Gerald R., and Jeffrey Pfeffer. "Constraints on Administrator Discretion: The Limited Influence of Mayors on City Budgets," *Urban Affairs Quarterly,* in press.

Sales, Stephen M. "Supervisory Style and Productivity: Review and Theory," *Personnel Psychology* 19 (1966), pp. 275–86.

Schutz, Alfred. *The Phenomenology of the Social World* (Evanston, Ill.: Northwestern University Press, 1967).

Selznick, P. *Leadership in Administration* (Evanston, Ill.: Row, Peterson, 1957).

Spaeth, J. L., and A. M. Greeley. *Recent Alumni and Higher Education* (New York: McGraw-Hill, 1970).

Thompson, James D. *Organizations in Action* (New York: McGraw-Hill, 1967).

Vroom, Victor H. "Some Personality Determinants of the Effects of Participation," *Journal of Abnormal and Social Psychology* 59 (1959), pp. 322–27.

Vroom, Victor H., and Phillip W. Yetton. *Leadership and Decision Making* (Pittsburgh: University of Pittsburgh Press, 1973).

Warner, W. L., and J. C. Abbeglin. *Big Business Leaders in America* (New York: Harper and Row, 1955).

Weick, Karl E. *The Social Psychology of Organizing* (Reading, Mass.: Addison-Wesley, 1969).

Weinstein, Alan G., and V. Srinivasan. "Predicting Managerial Success of Master of Business Administration (MBA) Graduates," *Journal of Applied Psychology* 59 (1974), pp. 207–12.

Wolfle, Dael. *The Uses of Talent* (Princeton: Princeton University Press, 1971).

Zald, Mayer N. "Who Shall Rule? A Political Analysis of Succession in a Large Welfare Organization," *Pacific Sociological Review* 8 (1965), pp. 52–60.

The Dark Side of Leadership

J. A. Conger
McGill University

*I*n recent years, business leaders have gained great popularity: Lee Iaccoca and Steven Jobs, for example, have stepped into the limelight as agents of change and entrepreneurship. But though we tend to think of the positive outcomes associated with leaders, certain risks or liabilities are also entailed. The very behaviors that distinguish leaders from managers also have the potential to produce problematic or even disastrous outcomes for their organizations. For example, when a leader's behaviors become exaggerated, lose touch with reality, or become vehicles for purely personal gain, they may harm the leader and the organization.

How do leaders produce such negative outcomes—and why? Three particular skill areas can contribute to such problems. These include leaders' strategic vision, their communications and impression-management skills, and their general management practices. We will examine each to discover its darker side.

Problems with the Visionary Leader

As we know, the 1970s and 1980s brought tremendous changes in the world's competitive business environment. Previously successful organizations that had grown huge and bureaucratic were suddenly faced with pressures to innovate and alter their ways. Out of these turbulent times came a new breed of business leader: the strategic visionary. These men and women, like Ross Perot of Electronic Data Systems and Mary Kay Ash of Mary Kay Cosmetics, possessed a twofold ability: to foresee market opportunities and to craft organizational strategies that captured these opportunities in ways that were personally meaningful to employees. When their success stories spread, "vision" became the byword of the 1980s. Yet though many of these leaders led their organizations on to great successes, others led their organizations on to great failures. The very qualities that distinguished the visionary leader contained the potential for disaster.

Generally speaking, unsuccessful strategic visions can often be traced to the inclusion of the leaders' personal aims that did not match their constituents' needs. For example, leaders might substitute personal goals for what should be shared organizational goals. They might construct an organizational vision that is essentially a monument to themselves and therefore something quite different from the actual wishes of their organizations or customers.

Moreover, the blind drive to create this very personal vision could result in an inability to see problems and opportunities in the environment. Thomas Edison, for example, so passionately believed in the future of direct electrical current (DC) for urban power grids that he failed to see the more rapid acceptance of alternating power (AC) systems by America's then-emerging utility companies. Thus the company started by Edison to produce DC power stations was soon doomed to failure. He became so enamoured of his own ideas that he failed to see competing and, ultimately, more successful ideas.

In addition, such personal visions encourage the leader to expend enormous amounts of energy, passion, and resources on getting them off the ground. The higher their commitment, the less willing they are to see the viability of competing approaches. Because of the leader's commitment, the organization's investment is also likely to be far greater in such cases. Failure therefore will have more serious consequences.

Fundamental errors in the leader's perceptions can also lead to a failed vision. Common problems include (1) an inability to detect important changes in markets (e.g., competitive, technological, or consumer needs); (2) a failure to accurately assess and obtain the necessary resources for the vision's accomplishment; and (3) a misreading or exaggerated sense of the needs of markets or constituents. For example, with a few exceptions like the Chrysler minivan, Lee Iacocca inaccurately believed that automobile style rather than engineering was the primary concern of automotive buyers. At Chrysler, he relied on new body styles and his charisma to market cars built on an aging chassis (the K car) developed in the late 1970s. The end result was that, after several initial years of successful sales, Chrysler's sales plunged 22.8% in 1987. Today, the future of Chrysler looks equally cloudy.

Ultimately, then, the success of a leader's strategic vision depends on a realistic assessment of both the opportunities and the constraints in the organization's environment and a sensitivity to constituents' needs. If the leader loses sight of reality or loses touch with constituents, the vision becomes a liability. Visions may fail for a wide variety of reasons; Exhibit 1 outlines some of the more significant ones. We will examine several of these categories and illustrate them with the experiences of some prominent business leaders.

Making the Leader's Personal Needs Paramount

As mentioned, one of the most serious liabilities of a visionary leader occurs when he or she projects purely personal needs and beliefs onto those of constituents. A common ex-

Source: Edited and reprinted with permission of the publisher, from *Organizational Dynamics* (Autumn 1990), 44–55. Copyright © 1990 American Management Association, New York. All rights reserved. Author affiliation may have changed since article was first published.

EXHIBIT 1
The Sources of Failed Vision

The vision reflects the internal needs of leaders rather than those of the market or constituents.

The resources needed to achieve vision have been seriously miscalculated.

An unrealistic assessment or distorted perception of market and constituent needs holds sway.

A failure to recognize environmental changes prevents re-direction of the vision.

ample is the inventor with a pet idea who acquires sufficient resources to initiate a venture that fails to meet the market's needs. When a leader's needs and wishes diverge from those of constituents, the consequences can be quite costly.. . . .

Becoming a "Pyrrhic Victor"

In the quest to achieve a vision, a leader may be so driven as to ignore the costly implications of his strategic aims. Ambition and the miscalculation of necessary resources can lead to a "Pyrrhic victory" for the leader. The term "Pyrrhic victory" comes from an incident in Ancient Greece: Pyrrhus, the King of Epirus, sustained such heavy losses in defeating the Romans that despite his numerous victories over them, his entire empire was ultimately undermined. Thus the costs of a "Pyrrhic" victory deplete the resources that are needed for future success.

In this scenario, the leader is usually driven by a desire to expand or accelerate the realization of his vision. The initial vision appears correct, and early successes essentially delude or weaken the leader's ability to realistically assess his resources and marketplace realities. The costs that must be paid for acquisitions or market share ultimately become unsustainable and threaten the long-term viability of the leader's organization. . . .

Chasing a Vision before Its Time

Sometimes a leader's perceptions of the market are so exaggerated or so significantly ahead of their time that the marketplace fails to sustain the leader's venture. The organization's resources are mobilized and spent on a mission that ultimately fails to produce the expected results. In this case, the leader is perhaps too visionary or too idealistic. He or she is unable to see that the time is not ripe, so the vision goes on to failure or, at best, a long dormancy. . . .

Two other factors may play important roles. In their own excitement over an idea, leaders may fail to adequately test-market a new product or service or fail to hear naysayers or overlook contrary signs from the environment. Again, because of successes in other projects (Lipp had had several outstanding ones), they may delude themselves into believing they know their markets more accurately than they actually do. Or their spellbinding ability to lead may not be backed up by an adequate understanding of marketplace trends.

How Leaders Come to Deny Flaws in Their Visions

All three of these cases share certain characteristics that cause leaders to deny the flaws in their visions. Often, for example, leaders will perceive that their course of action is producing negative results, yet they persist. Why this happens can be explained by a process called "cognitive dissonance," which prevents the leader from changing his course. Simply put, individuals act to keep the commitments they have made because failing to do so would damage their favorable perceptions of themselves. For example, studies have found that executives will sometimes persist in an ineffective course of action simply because they feel they have committed themselves to the decision. This same process, I suspect, occurs with leaders.

Others in the organization who tend to become dependent on a visionary leader may perpetuate the problem through their own actions. They may idealize their leader excessively and thus ignore negative aspects and exaggerate the good qualities. As a result, they may carry out their leader's orders unquestioningly—and leaders may in certain cases encourage such behavior because of their needs to dominate and be admired. The resulting sense of omnipotence encourages denial of market and organizational realities. The danger is that leaders will surround themselves with "yes people" and thus fail to receive information that might be important but challenging to the mission. Their excessive confidence and the desire for heroic recognition encourages them to undertake large, risky ventures—but because of their overreliance on themselves and their cadre of "yes people," strategic errors go unnoticed. Bold but poorly thought-out strategies will be designed and implemented. The leader's vision, in essence, becomes a vehicle for his or her own needs for attention and visibility.

Finally, problems with "group-think" can occur where the leader's advisors delude themselves into agreement with the leader or dominant others. In such a case, decision making becomes distorted, and a more thorough and objective review of possible alternatives to a problem are all but precluded. This is especially true of groups that are very cohesive, highly committed to their success, under pressure, and possessing favorable opinions of themselves—common characteristics in the organizations of powerful and charismatic leaders. When group-think occurs, the opinions of the leader and advisors with closely allied views come to dominate decision making. Doubts that others might have are kept hidden for fear of disapproval. It is more important "to go along to get along" rather than to consider contrary viewpoints. . . .

Manipulation through Impression Management and Communication Skills

Because some leaders are gifted at communicating, it may be quite easy for them to misuse this ability. For instance, they may present information that makes their visions appear more realistic or more appealing than the visions actually are. They may also use their language skills to screen out problems in the larger environment or to foster an illusion of control when, in reality, things are out of control. Exhibit 2 highlights a number of these possible problem areas. . . .

EXHIBIT 2

Potential Liabilities in the Leader's Communications and Impression Management Skills

Exaggerated self-descriptions.

Exaggerated claims for the vision.

A technique of fulfilling stereotypes and images of uniqueness to manipulate audiences.

A habit of gaining commitment by restricting negative information and maximizing positive information.

Use of anecdotes to distract attention away from negative statistical information.

Creation of an illusion of control through affirming information and attributing negative outcomes to external causes.

EXHIBIT 3

Potential Liabilities of a Leader's Management Practices

Poor management of people networks, especially superiors and peers.

Unconventional behavior that alienates.

Creation of disruptive "in group/out group" rivalries.

An autocratic, controlling management style.

An informal/impulsive style that is disruptive and dysfunctional.

Alternation between idealizing and devaluing others, particularly direct reports.

Creation of excessive dependence in others.

Failure to manage details and effectively act as an administrator.

Attention to the superficial.

Absence from operations.

Failure to develop successors of equal ability.

When leaders rely greatly on their impression management skills in communicating, they do themselves a disservice. For instance, research in impression management indicates not only that one's self-descriptions are effective in deceiving an audience, but also that they may deceive the presenter as well. This is especially true when an audience reinforces and approves of the individual's image. Such positive responses encourage leaders to internalize their own self-enhancing descriptions. Especially when exaggeration is only moderate, leaders tend to internalize and believe such claims. So DeLorean may ultimately have come to believe in his own responsibility for the Pontiac GTO.

Considerable research has also been performed on people who are ingratiators—people who play to their audiences by telling them what they want to hear. Two particular tactics that I suspect charismatic leaders use to ingratiate themselves with their audiences are to (1) fulfill stereotypes and (2) create an image of uniqueness.

Research shows that if individuals behave in ways that fulfill the positive stereotypes of an audience they are more likely to interact successfully with them. This can be achieved by espousing the beliefs, values, and behaviors associated with the stereotype and appearing as the stereotype is expected to look. . . .

Anecdotal information may be used by the leader not only to influence decision makers' choices, but also to increase their confidence in a choice. The sheer amount of information the leader provides may act to build overconfidence. Various studies of decision making indicate that more information apparently permits people to generate more reasons for justifying their decisions and, in turn, increases the confidence of others in the decisions. Leaders might also create an illusion of control by selectively providing information that affirms they are in control and attribute failures or problems to external causes. All of these tactics may be used by leaders to mislead their direct reports and their investors.

Management Practices That Become Liabilities

The managerial practices of leaders also have certain inherent liabilities. Some leaders are known for their excessively impulsive, autocratic management style. Others become so

disruptive through their unconventional behavior that their organizations mobilize against them. Moreover, leaders can at times be poor at managing their superiors and peers. In general, some of the very management practices that make leaders unique may also lead to their downfall.

Leaders' liabilities fall into several categories: (1) the way they manage relations with important others, (2) their management style with direct reports, and (3) their thoroughness and attention to certain administrative detail. Typical problems associated with each of these categories are shown in Exhibit 3. We will start with the first category: managing relations with important others.

Managing Upwards and Sideways

Some leaders—particularly charismatic leaders in large organizations—seem to be very poor at managing upwards and sideways. Because they are usually unconventional advocates of radical reform, they may often alienate others in the organization, including their own bosses. The charismatic leader's unconventional actions may trigger the ire of forces within the organization which then act to immobilize him or her. Leaders' aggressive style may also alienate many potential supporters and ultimately leave them without sufficient political support for their ambitious plans. This problem is common when charismatic leaders are brought in from the outside; their radically different values and approaches may alienate the rest of the organization.

This kind of situation occurred at General Motors when Ross Perot was made a board member. Once on the board, Perot became one of the company's most outspoken critics. As an entrepreneur, he was quite naturally accustomed to running his own show, and after his company, Electronic Data Systems (EDS), merged with GM, he insisted that any changes made in EDS procedures be cleared through him. His style and outspokenness were so much at odds with the General Motors culture that the company offered Perot $700 million in stock to step down from the board—an offer he finally accepted.

A second problem related to managing relations within large organizations is the tendency of certain leaders to cultivate a feeling of being "special" among members of their operating units. This practice is often accompanied by a corresponding depreciation of other parts of the corporation. In short, the leader creates an "us versus them" attitude. Although this heightens the motivation of the leader's group, it further alienates other groups that may be important for resources or political support. Steven Jobs did this with the MacIntosh division at Apple Computer. Even though the company's Apple II Computer provided the profits, Jobs consistently downplayed that division's importance. He essentially divided the company into two rivals. He was fond of telling people in the MacIntosh division, "This is the cream of Apple. This is the future of Apple." He even went so far as telling marketing managers for Apple II that they worked for an outdated, clumsy organization. Jobs's later departure from Apple stemmed in part from morale problems he created within the company by using this tactic.

In another case, the charismatic president of a division in a large corporation used as his group's emblem a mascot symbol of the TV cartoon character Roadrunner. (In the cartoons, Roadrunner was particularly adept at outwitting a wily coyote.) To him, his division managers were the "roadrunners" who were smarter and faster than the corporate "coyotes" who laid roadblocks in their path. He also had a habit of ignoring corporate staff requests for reports or information, and he returned their reports with "STUPID IDEA" stamped on the front cover. Although such behaviors and tactics fostered a sense of camaraderie and aggressiveness within the charismatic leader's division, they were ultimately detrimental both to the leader and to the organization. In this case, the executive eventually stepped down from the organization.

Relationships with Subordinates

Highly directive and visionary leaders are often described as autocratic. Jobs, for example, has been described as dictatorial. I suspect that in many cases the vision is such a personification of the leader that he or she becomes obsessed about its perfection or implementation. Leaders' natural impatience with the pace of the vision's achievement exacerbates the problem and encourages them to be more hands-on, more controlling.

There also appears to be, at times, an impulsive dynamic at work in the way leaders manage—and at such times they will override subordinates' suggestions or insights. Again, this occurs especially in relation to accomplishing the vision. DeLorean is described as increasing his production of the DeLorean car by 50% in the belief that his product would become an overnight sensation. Production went to an annual rate of 30,000 cars. This was done in spite of market research that showed total annual sales of between 4,000 and 10,000 cars. A company executive lamented, "Our figures showed that this was a viable company with half the production. If the extravagance had been cut out of New York, we could have broken even making just 6,000 cars a year. But that wasn't fast enough for John. First he had to build his paper empire in the stock market. A creditable success was not enough for him" (ibid., pg. 282).

Steven Jobs is known to have darted in and out of operations causing havoc: "He would leap-frog back and forth among various projects, dictating designs, with little or no knowledge of whether or not the technology even existed to make his ideas work" (L. Butcher, *Accidental Millionaire*, Paragon House, 1988, pp. 140–141).

Another potential problem can arise from a style of informality when managing the hierarchy of an organization—this is especially true of charismatic leaders. Advantages of this style are that leaders are highly visible, approachable, and able to react quickly to issues and problems. The drawback is that they often violate the chain of command by going around direct reports and thus undercut their direct reports' authority. If a particular project or idea interests them, they do not hesitate to become involved, sometimes to the detriment of the project managers' responsibilities. DeLorean would drop in on his engineers to suggest what seemed trivial ideas. One company engineer said: "He came in one day to say we should hook into the cooling system and make a little icebox for a six-pack of beer behind behind the driver's seat. Or, another time, he told us to work on a sixty-watt radio speaker that could be detached and hung outside the car for picnics" (H. Levin, ibid., pg. 267).

Administrative Skills

Some visionary leaders are so absorbed by the "big picture" that they fail to understand essential details—except for "pet" projects in which they became excessively involved. Iaccoca, for instance, turned over most of the day-to-day operations to others as he became increasingly famous. As a result, he lost touch with new model planning. He himself admitted: "If I made one mistake, it was delegating all the product development and not going to a single meeting" (ibid., pg. 267). A DeLorean executive complained "He [John DeLorean] just didn't have time for the details of the project. But attention to detail is everything" (ibid., p. 267). Then, too, leaders may get so caught up in corporate stardom that they become absentee leaders. Again, Iaccoca is an example. His success at Chrysler led to his becoming a best-selling author, a U.S. presidential prospect, and the head of the $277 million fund-raising campaign for the Statue of Liberty—all of which distracted him from the important task of leading Chrysler.

Because these individuals are often excited by ideas, they may at times be poor implementors. Once an idea begins to appear as a tangible reality, I suspect they feel the need to move on to the next challenge, thereby leaving subordinates scrambling to pick up the pieces. Furthermore, because some leaders have high needs for visibility, they gravitate toward activities that afford them high people contact and recognition. Such activities are generally not performed at a desk while paying careful attention to the details.

Succession Problems

A true leader is usually a strong figure and, as noted, often one upon whom subordinates develop dependencies. Thus it is difficult for others with leadership potential to develop fully in the shadow of such leaders. For while they may actively coach their subordinates, I suspect that it is extremely difficult for them to develop others to be leaders *of equal power*. Leaders simply enjoy the limelight too much to share it, so when they ultimately depart, a leadership vacuum is created. Moreover, under charismatic leadership authority may be highly centralized around the leader—and this is an arrangement that, unfortunately, weakens the authority structures that are normally dispersed throughout an organization.

It's clear that many of the qualities of a strong leader have both a positive and a negative face. That's why the presence of leaders entails risks for their direct reports, their organi-

zations, and at times their societies. They must be managed with care. The negatives, however, must always be weighed in light of the positives. For companies and society, the need for organizational change and strategic vision may be so great that the risks of confrontation, unconventionality, and so on may seem a small price to pay. It is also possible that organizations and educational institutions can train, socialize, and manage future leaders in ways that will minimize their negative qualities.

Selected Bibliography

For an in-depth look at the psychological dynamics of the dark side of leaders, we recommend *The Neurotic Organization* (Jossey-Bass, 1984) by Manfred Kets de Vries and Danny Miller and "Personality, Culture, and Organization" (*The Academy of Management Review*, April 1986), also by Manfred Kets de Vries and Danny Miller.

Works that provide an informative treatment on the topic of impression management include *The Presentation of Self in Everyday Life* (Doubleday-Anchor, 1959) by Erving Goffman and *Impression Management* (Brooks/Cole, 1980) by B. R. Schlenker. Books and articles that deal more systematically with the issue of commitment to a course of action as well as communicating information are *A Theory of Cognitive Dissonance* (Row, Peterson, 1957) by L. Festinger; Charles R. Schwenk's "Information,

Cognitive Bias, and Commitment to a Course of Action" (*The Academy of Management Review*, April 1986); Barry Staw's "Knee Deep in the Big Muddy: A Study of Escalating Commitment to a Chosen Course of Action" (*Organizational Behavior and Human Performance*, June 1976); and "The Escalation of Commitment to a Course of Action" (*The Academy of Management Review*, October 1981). The definitive work on group-think is *Victims of Group Think* (Houghton Mifflin, 1972), by I. L. Janis.

Readers wishing more depth on the individual case studies of leaders should consult the following sources. For Edwin Land and the SX-70 camera, see G. W. Merry's Polaroid-Kodak Case Study (Harvard Business School, 1976) and P.C. Wensberg's *Land's Polaroid* (Houghton Mifflin, 1987).

Several articles on Robert Campeau include "Buy-Out Bomb" (*Wall Street Journal*, Jan. 11, 1990), Kate Ballen's "Campeau Is on a Shopper's High" (*Fortune*, Aug. 15, 1988), and Eric Berg's "Is Campeau Himself Bankrupt?" (*New York Times*, Feb. 2, 1990). Two interesting sources on John DeLorean are Michael Daly's "The Real DeLorean Story" (*New York*, Nov. 8, 1982) and Hill Levin's *Grand Delusions* (Viking Press, 1983). *Accidental Millionaire* (Paragon House, 1988) by Lee Butcher presents a darker-side view of Steven Jobs. Two articles on the home banking industry and its slow takeoff are Efrem Sigel's "Is Home Banking for Real?" (*Datamation*, Sept. 15, 1986) and Laura Zinn's "Home Banking Is Here—If You Want It" (*Business Week*, Feb. 29, 1988).

Executive Leadership and Organizational Performance

Suggestions for a New Theory and Methodology

D. V. Day and R. G. Lord
University of Akron

The literature regarding executive leadership is paradoxical: Popular thinking (e.g., Peters & Austin, 1985) emphasizes the importance of top-level leadership in establishing "excellent" organizations, but many academic publications assert that executive leadership is an inconsequential determinant of organizational performance (e.g., Meindl & Ehrlich, 1987; Meindl, Ehrlich, & Dukerich, 1985; Pfeffer, 1977). These contrasting positions also have conflicting implications for practice and the development of leadership theory. The benefits of changing leaders or developing theories of executive leadership are bolstered by popular writers, but are undercut by the pessimistic conclusions of academic researchers. Both the popular and academic positions require more careful evaluation. We will scrutinize the arguments and data used by academicians to conclude that top-level leaders have minimal impact on performance. Others (Aupperle, Acar, & Booth, 1986) have recently evaluated the claims of popular writers such as Peters.

Succession studies have often been used by academicians to evaluate the impact of leadership on organizational performance. There are a number of factors that must be considered to interpret properly the results of succession studies. Neglecting these factors leads to erroneous conclusions, which is what has occurred with two widely cited succession studies, Lieberson and O'Connor (1972) and Salancik and Pfeffer (1977). Their misinterpreted results have been used as evidence by researchers arguing that leadership does not directly affect organizational outcomes (e.g., Meindl et al., 1985, p. 78). Even organizational scientists who have argued that leadership *substantially affects* performance have cited these two studies as providing contrary evidence (e.g., Gupta, 1986, pp. 227–228). We believe, however, that proper interpretation of existing succession studies indicates that top-level leaders have a direct and significant effect on their company's performance.

Therefore, one goal of this paper is to assess comprehensively the problems in interpreting succession findings. Our purpose is to help determine whether leadership affects organizational performance and to emphasize the importance of top-level leadership as a topic worthy of its own theory and specific methodology. The plan of this paper is to (a) closely examine the conceptual and empirical basis of claims that leadership is not an important determinant of organizational performance, and (b) offer suggestions for developing a theory of executive leadership that is relevant to understanding *how* top-level leaders directly and significantly affect organizational performance.

Studies of Executive Succession

Statements that top-level leaders have minimal effects on an organization's performance (e.g., Brown, 1982; Meindl et al., 1985; Tsui, 1984) are based on a very small database—usually entirely on the Lieberson and O'Connor (1972) and Salancik and Pfeffer (1977) studies and with occasional reference to studies of athletic teams. These studies have used succession as the methodology for showing the minimal impact of leadership. Because these are the principal sources of empirical support cited by researchers claiming that leaders have little effect on organizational performance, they are carefully evaluated in this section.

In a study of 167 corporations in 13 industries over a time-period of 20 years, Lieberson and O'Connor (1972) analyzed changes in sales, earnings, and profit margin associated with the succession of the president or chair of the board. They compared succession effects with year, industry, and company influences by apportioning performance variance to these sources. Their findings are summarized in Table 1. They found that leadership (administration) accounted for far less of the performance variance than either industry or company. With no lag time, the range of effect for leadership was from 6.5% of sales to 15.2% of profit margin. From these data, Lieberson and O'Connor, followed by a host of other researchers, have stressed the importance of environmental rather than leadership factors in explaining performance. However, even with no lag-time and size confounds, leadership accounted for 7.5% of the variance in net income. This translates into a substantial amount of money to most organizations, which makes leadership at upper organizational levels worthy of their (and our) consideration. If one looks at profit margins, which are not confounded with size, leadership explains 32% of the variance with a 3-year time lag. This latter result indicates a very dramatic effect of executive leadership on organizational performance.

The influence of mayors on two income and eight expenditure variables was the focus of Salancik and Pfeffer (1977).

Source: Edited and reprinted with permission from *Journal of Management* 14 (1988), 453–64. Author affiliation may have changed since article was first published.

A shorter version of this paper was presented at the Academy of Management 46th Annual Meeting, Chicago, 1986.

The authors wish to thank Ken Carson, Laura Kollar, Jim Phillips, and two anonymous reviewers for their helpful comments.

T A B L E   1
Executive Succession Studies

Lieberson & O'Connor (1972)

	Variance Explained		
Variables	**Sales**	**Net Income**	**Profit Margin**
Year	.031	.017	.018
Industry	.230	.186	.285
Company	.648	.677	.226
Administration			
(No lag)	.065	.075	.152
(3-year lag)	.063	.069	.317

Salancik & Pfeffer (1977)

	Variance Explained		
Budget Category	**City**	**Year**	**Mayor**
Income	.908	.025	.056
Property tax			
revenues	(.860)	(.018)	(.049)
General debt	.805	.067	.100
	(.563)	(.035)	(.242)
Expenditures	.792	.072	.099
Median for all			
expenditures	(.591)	(.025)	(.191)

Note: Nonparenthesized figures computed in total dollars. Parenthesized figures computed as proportions of total city budget.

Thirty U.S. cities were examined during the years 1951–1968, with a total of 172 different mayors included in the analysis. They examined the relative effects of city, year, and mayor on the multiple dependent variables of property tax revenues; general debt; and eight expenditure variables (e.g., police, fire, highways, etc.). When the budget variables were computed in *total dollars*, the effects of the mayor variable was limited to around 10% (see Table 1); however, these results are misleading due to the large, but theoretically trivial, contribution of city size. When the budget variables were computed as *proportions of the total city budget* to control for size effects, the mayoral effect was over 24%. The mayoral effect on property tax revenues remained stable when size was controlled, decreasing a modest .7%. This is expected due to the direct influence that voters have over their taxes. Mayoral effects on median expenditures increased from 9.9% to 19.1% when city size was controlled.

Two other studies of executive succession are commendable for attempting to account for numerous methodological problems. Weiner and Mahoney (1981) examined the effects of CEO changes in a sample of 193 manufacturing companies over a 19-year period. By effectively controlling for size and order effects, they found that the CEO had substantial impact on some major organizational variables. For example, stewardship (i.e., leadership) explained 43.9% of the profitability (profit/assets) variance and also accounted for 47% of the variance in stock prices. In a study using a sample of Methodist ministers, Smith, Carson, and Alexander (1984) attempted to assess the impact of effective leaders on organizational performance. They differentiated effective from other leaders to determine whether leadership status had any incremental effect on organizational performance. Despite the large amount of variance accounted for by the control variable of the church's performance in the minister's first year of service (median $R^2 = .701$), the leadership status variable (effective/other) added significantly to the prediction for all five relevant performance variables. This study is also commendable for the attention given to potential confounds, such as ensuring the serial independence of all variables, correcting for inflation, and examining effects over extended time lags.

In short, with appropriate methodological corrections, these four studies indicate much larger leadership effects than implied by most of the literature. Although leadership does not explain all of the variance in organizational outcomes, such effects certainly are not trivial. . . .

Conclusions from Current Literature

The results of research on the impact of changes in top-level leaders (e.g., Lieberson & O'Connor, 1972; Salancik & Pfeffer, 1977; Smith et al., 1984; Weiner & Mahoney, 1981), when properly interpreted and methodologically sound, show a consistent effect for leadership succession explaining 20% to 45% of the variance in relevant organizational outcomes. This finding has been largely overlooked in contemporary organizational theory on leadership.

Interestingly, this conclusion is consistent with much of the popular literature that stresses the importance of executive leadership in determining organizational performance. It underscores the practical and theoretical need for a systematic theory of executive leadership. Such a theory should address two main domains—individual differences in leadership ability and the mechanisms by which executive leaders impact on organizational performance. By individual differences we mean those dispositional factors that differentiate high ability leaders from low ability leaders. Such knowledge has obvious practical implications for selecting executive leaders; however, it goes beyond the scope of this study.

The second domain centers on the mechanisms by which executives affect organizational performance. We need a theory specifying what top-level leaders do that impacts on performance. Such a theory should also differentiate executive leadership from mere executive behavior. This type of theory would have profound implications for executive training, and it would also require that leadership be integrated with organizational theory.

We will focus on this need for a theory of executive leadership in the remainder of this article by discussing appropriate methodologies for investigating top-level leadership and by identifying some of the factors such a theory should address.

Implications for a Theory of Executive Leadership

Although the topic of executive leadership has been discussed extensively in the popular press and in historical accounts of specific organizations (e.g., Chandler, 1962), it has not been a major concern of leadership researchers or theorists. Their focus has been primarily lower-level leadership. We strongly urge researchers and theorists interested in leadership to consider upper levels of management as an important practical domain that needs theoretical and research attention. We believe the opportunity exists for the development of innovative and practically relevant leadership theory and research.

Commendably, some researchers have adopted a top-level focus. For example, Miller and Toulouse (1986) have investigated the effect of chief executive personality on corporate strategy and structure; Bourgeois (1985) reported that how accurately top-level management teams perceived the environment was positively related to the economic performance of their organization; and Donaldson and Lorsch (1983) undertook an in-depth study of executive decision making. Additional research using top-level executives is desired but, more importantly, an underlying theory that can integrate research findings would establish executive leadership as a distinct area of study. It is premature to stay what a theory of executive leadership should be. We can, however, provide recommendations as to how such a theory should be developed.

Problems to Avoid

We think that the major problem to avoid is confusing levels or units of analysis in the development of leadership theory. Theories or empirical findings developed at lower levels do not necessarily apply to executive levels. In particular, there are two major problems in applying theories or results from studies of lower-level leadership to upper levels of an organization. First, leadership at lower levels is qualitatively different than upper-level leadership. Katz and Kahn (1978), Mintzberg (1973), and others have noted the qualitatively different nature of managerial and leader roles across levels.[2] According to Katz and Kahn (1978) leaders at the top echelons of organizations create organizational structure, formulate policy, and develop corporate strategies. Middle-level leaders interpret and elaborate structure, policy, and strategy, and lower-level leaders use technical knowledge, rewards, and sanctions to administer existing structure. Applying leadership theories developed at low levels to explain leadership at upper levels assumes a construct isomorphism across levels that is probably not true. Also, theories developed at lower levels may provide theoretical blinders (see Greenwald, Pratkanis, Leippe, & Baumgardner, 1986, for a general discussion of this issue), keeping researchers from discovering more appropriate perspectives when they focus on upper-level leadership.

A second problem to avoid centers around a predominant focus on style rather than substance in relation to leadership. Factors like the analytic and perceptual ability of leaders, their intelligence and experience, or the capacity to differentiate good from bad decisions are not incorporated into frameworks that focus only on style. For example, much leadership work has focused on the narrow question of how the dimensions of Consideration and Initiating Structure relate to performance. A theory of executive leadership needs a much broader conceptual and methodological foundation. . . .

Where to Look for Theory

We suspect that ideas relevant to theories of executive leadership will be found in very different sources or disciplines than are ideas relevant to lower-level leadership. Lower-level leadership theories seem to be based primarily on ideas borrowed from the social, motivational, and cognitive areas of psychology. We think more macro sources are appropriate for theories of executive-level leadership. In other words, leadership and organizational theory need to be integrated. Current developments in such areas as organizational culture, power and politics in organizations, systems theory, strategic management, and organizational evolution all interface with the problem of developing a theory of executive-level leadership.

An adequate coverage of all these topics is beyond the scope of this paper. As an illustration of this approach, however, we can provide a list of potential means by which executive leaders could impact on organizational performance. Table 2 is a list of such potential means that is organized within a systematic framework based on external/internal and direct/indirect dimensions.

Executive Leadership and Organizational Performance

Many of the factors listed in Table 2 have obvious relations to the theoretical areas mentioned above. They are based on the general framework provided by open-systems theory (Katz & Kahn, 1978). Because open systems must interact with their environment, it follows that leaders can affect organizational performance by actions that operate on the *external* environment, such as exerting influence on government to change taxation or regulation policy, or they can operate on the *internal* environment to influence factors such as operating costs or product quality. Leadership theorists (Pfeffer, 1981) have also noted that leaders can impact on organizational outcomes through either *direct* means, such as formulating appropriate corporate level strategy, or by *indirect* means, such as effectively managing the symbols that help build commitment of employees to an organization. Direct means often involve the application of influence and/or political power applied either externally or internally. For example, changing regulatory policy requires substantial political influence in government or regulatory agencies. Similarly, reducing costs often involves tough decisions that require internal power to implement. Indirect means such as creating and maintaining a favorable public image often require that top executives be effective symbols or good communicators. Similar skills applied internally may be crucial in creating an organizational climate and culture that motivates and retains employees.

An issue that should be addressed is whether altering factors such as corporate strategy, internal organization, or production technology reflect top-level leadership or is better conceptualized simply as executive decision making. We believe the construct of leadership is crucial to changes affecting the above factors, for rarely does a single individual have the authority to unilaterally make such changes. Instead, changes require the agreement of management teams. Attaining such agreement often requires the application of so-

T A B L E   2
Potential Means by Which Top-Level Leaders Can Affect Organizational Performance

| Target | Objective | Tactics | |
		Direct	Indirect
A. INFLUENCING EXTERNAL ENVIRONMENTS			
1. Government policy (e.g., regulation, taxation, trade)	Change policy to reduce uncertainty or increase resources	Direct political influence	Political influence via other groups (e.g., unions, suppliers)
2. Acquiring resources and maintaining boundaries	Increase stability	Horizontal or vertical integration	Create favorable public image or opinion
	Reduce competition	Promote entry barriers and noncompetitive pricing	Enhance image of organization or product
B. ADAPTING TO EXTERNAL ENVIRONMENTS			
1. Choice of markets or environments	Increased stability and munificence	Strategic planning	Influence top mgt's schemas; select those with similar schemas
2. Management and production system	Fit with environment and strategy	Organizational design	Guide top mgt's labelling of environments
C. INTERNAL INFLUENCE AND ADAPTATION			
1. Subsystem organization and management	Rationalization and integration	Definition and functional specification of roles	Shape top mgt's schemas of organizing; select those with similar schemas
	Coordination and appraisal	Design and implementation of mgt. information systems	Use information as sign and symbol
2. Productivity	Increase org. efficiency	Reduce capital or personnel costs	Strengthen productivity norms
3. Quality	Increase product quality	Increase quality control	Strengthen quality norms
4. Organizational climate and culture	Increase motivation and commitment of employees	Determine or influence organizational politics	Enhance participative decision making norms; symbolism of CEO

Note. For each objective there are additional tactics, however, space limitations prohibit their inclusion in this table.

cial influence that goes beyond one's formal position. Such influence falls within common definitions of leadership as being an influence increment going beyond the formal powers associated with one's office (Katz & Kahn, 1978). Increments in influence are particularly necessary for implementing externally focused means to affect organizational performance.

The link between leadership and major changes in organizations is also underscored by recent work on organizational evolution. Tushman and Romanelli (1985) argue that organizations cycle through periods of relative stability and periods of radical reorientations and change. Though reorientations are often precipitated by external factors, they argue that executive leadership is often critical in both overcoming internal resistance to change and in guiding the reorientation. Moreover, how effectively top-level leaders manage such reorientations is a crucial determinant of organizational performance. Chandler's (1962) historical accounts of the development of organizations makes a similar point. He argues that executive leaders have a large impact in shaping strategic choices and notes that dramatic changes in

strategies and structures often occur only when top executives also change.

A complement to theories of organizational evolution is the work done on the impact of executive leader's problem-solving style and cognitive schemas. For example, Dutton and Jackson (1987) argue that the nature of leaders' cognitive categories help them interpret trends in their organization or environment, thereby narrowing the range of actions they may consider. The same situation could be interpreted as a "threat" or as an "opportunity" depending on how it was categorized by leaders. These different interpretations affect leaders' processing of information as well as social processes involving communication and persuasion. Such work shows how the cognitive processes and schemas of executive leaders affect the more macro strategic choices they consider. Work in areas such as individual differences in decision making needs to be integrated with the more macro topics previously mentioned to explain how top-level leaders impact on organizational performance. Also, this cognitively oriented work could be developed to help explain many of the indirect effects noted in Table 2.

Conclusions

We have argued that the academic literature on leadership has tended to neglect the topic of executive leadership largely because a few key articles have been widely misinterpreted.[3] We carefully reexamined those articles and the requirements to interpret succession studies. Based on this examination, we concluded that *executive* leaders do have a substantial impact on organizational performance. This conclusion illustrates the practical and theoretical need for more attention to the topic of executive-level leadership.

Although it is beyond the scope of this article to present such a theory, we provided several methodological recommendations pertinent to developing such a theory. Specifically, confusion over levels of analysis should be avoided, new methodologies should be seriously considered, and very different theoretical bases should be explored. We also offered some preliminary ideas on *macro*-level organizational theories that are relevant to executive leadership. Further, we suggested that such a theory could be organized along the internal/external and direct/indirect dimensions, and we used these dimensions to organize a list of potential means by which executive-level leaders could impact on organizational performance. Finally, we noted that these macro topics should be integrated with micro-level work demonstrating how the schemas and implicit theories of executives affect their strategic judgments and activities.

We think that such a theoretical area would have a natural link with work on leadership succession, for it specifies many potential means by which succession can impact on organizational performance, helping to explain why some changes in executive leaders have little impact on performance whereas other changes have profound and lasting ramifications. If developed further, such a theory would have practical importance as well, for it would have clear implications for training and selecting executive-level leaders. We think the topic of executive leadership offers a challenging and exciting opportunity for both leadership and management theorists. We hope that future researchers in these areas give this topic increased attention.

Notes

[2]We thank the anonymous reviewer who brought several of these studies to our attention.

[3]This topic also may have been overlooked due to the inherent difficulties involved with research using executive samples as well as to the micro-level orientation of most leadership researchers.

References

Aupperle, K.E., Acar, W., & Booth, D.E. (1986). An empirical critique of "In search of excellence": How excellent are the excellent companies? *Journal of Management, 12*, 499–512.

Bourgeois, L.J. III (1985). Strategic goals, perceived uncertainty, and economic performance in volatile environments. *Academy of Management Journal, 28*, 548–573.

Brown, M.C. (1982). Administrative succession and organizational performance: The succession effect. *Administrative Science Quarterly, 27*, 1–16.

Carroll, G.R. (1984). Dynamics of publisher succession in newspaper organizations. *Administrative Science Quarterly, 29*, 93–113.

Chandler Jr., A.D. (1962). *Strategy and structure: Chapters in the history of the industrial enterprise.* Cambridge, MA: M.I.T.

Donaldson, G., & Lorsch, J.W. (1983). *Decision making at the top: The shaping of strategic direction.* New York: Basic Books.

Dutton, J.E., & Jackson, S.E. (1987). The categorization of strategic issues by decision makers and its links to organizational action. *Academy of Management Review, 12*, 76–90.

Greenwald, A.G., Pratkanis, A.R., Leippe, M.R., & Baumgardner, M.H. (1986). Under what conditions does theory obstruct research progress? *Psychological Review, 93*, 216–229.

Gupta, A.K. (1986). Matching managers to strategies: Point and counterpoint. *Human Resource Management, 25*, 215–234.

Jones, M.B. (1974). Regressing group on individual effectiveness. *Organizational Behavior and Human Performance, 11*, 426–451.

Katz, D., & Kahn, R.L. (1978). *The social psychology of organizations* (2nd ed.). New York: Wiley.

Lieberson, S., & O'Connor, J.F. (1972). Leadership and organizational performance: A study of large corporations, *American Sociological Review, 37*, 117–130.

Meindl, J.R., & Ehrlich, S.B. (1987). The romance of leadership and the evaluation of organizational performance. *Academy of Management Journal, 30*, 91–109.

Meindl, J.R., Ehrlich, S.B., & Dukerich, J.M. (1985). The romance of leadership. *Administrative Science Quarterly, 30*, 78–102.

Miller, D., & Toulouse, J. (1986). Chief executive personality and structure in small firms. *Management Science, 32*, 1389–1409.

Mintzberg, H. (1973). *The nature of managerial work.* New York: Harper & Row.

Peters, T., & Austin, A. (1985). *A passion for excellence: The leadership difference.* New York: Random House.

Pfeffer, J. (1981). Management as symbolic action: The creation and maintenance of organizational paradigms. In L.L. Cummings & B.M. Staw (Eds.), *Research in organizational behavior* (Vol. 3, pp. 1–52). Greenwich, CT: JAI Press.

Pfeffer, J. (1977). The ambiguity of leadership. *Academy of Management Review, 2*, 104–112.

Pfeffer, J., & Davis-Blake, A. (1986). Administrative succession and organizational performance: How administrator experience mediates the succession effect. *Academy of Management Journal, 29*, 72–83.

Salancik, G.R., & Pfeffer, J. (1977). Constraints on administrator discretion: The limited influence of mayors on city budgets. *Urban Affairs Quarterly, 12*, 475–498.

Smith, J.E., Carson, K.P., & Alexander, R.A. (1984). Leadership: It can make a difference. *Academy of Management Journal, 27*, 765–776.

Tsui, A.S. (1984). A role set analysis of managerial reputation. *Organizational Behavior and Human Performance, 34*, 64–96.

Tushman, M.L., & Romanelli, E. (1985). Organizational evolution: A metamorphosis model of convergence and reorientation. In L.L. Cummings & B.M. Staw (Eds.), *Research in organizational behavior* (Vol. 7, pp. 171–222). Greenwich, CT: JAI Press.

Weiner, N., & Mahoney, T.A. (1981). A model of corporate performance as a function of environmental, organizational, and leadership influences. *Academy of Management Journal, 24*, 453–470.

Chapter Twelve

Emerging Perspectives on Leadership

*O*ur attempt to understand leadership makes us appreciate the complexity of the leadership mosaic. Images of a leader and leader-follower interactions, while appearing simple and straightforward, have proven to be multidimensional, complicated, and complex in nature.

As a social phenomenon, leadership has sparked a great deal of interest over the past several decades. Hundreds have thought about, observed, and studied it, and many have written about the topic. Their efforts have provided the opportunity to personally acquire a deeper insight into, and a richer understanding about, leaders and the leadership process.

This venture, however, is far from over. There is not yet a grand theory of leadership. There are conflicting answers to many previously raised questions. There are many other questions that either have not been asked or seriously examined. The designs and methodologies that guide our inquiry, extract data, and frame our observations need improvement. Many inconclusive, inconsistent, and conflicting observations need to be resolved. There is much yet to be learned.

Our quest to understand leadership has been complicated further by the emergence of a "new kind of organization." Up to this point in time, the study of leadership has generally unfolded in the control-oriented organization. Accompanying the emergence of the hypercompetitive environment, organizations are scrambling to reinvent themselves.

According to Richard L. Daft and Arie Y. Lewin (1993), the old paradigm of organizational form was one that "strives for mass production efficiencies, hierarchical organization, and bureaucratic structures that provide central control over activities divided into small parts."[1] The emerging paradigm appears to have as its "premise the need for flexible, learning organizations that continuously change and solve problems through interconnected coordinated self-organizing processes."[2] Characteristics of the new organization, according to Daft and Lewin, are flatter hierarchies, internal boundarylessness, permeable external boundaries, empowered employees, involvement, decentralization of decision making and problem solving, greater capacity for ambiguity and risk taking, capacity for self-renewal and self-organizing, and self-integrating coordination mechanisms.

This paradigm shift has significant implications for leaders and the nature of the leadership process. Building upon the situational theories of leadership (see Chapter 5), as the nature and character of the organization (i.e., the leadership context) changes, so too will the type of leadership needed. Thus, it is important to ask: What type of leadership

---

[1] R. L. Daft and A. Y. Lewin, "Where Are the Theories for the 'New' Organizational Forms?" *Organization Science* 4, 4 (1993).

[2] Ibid.

does this new organizational arrangement demand? Is it possible that our old leadership paradigm belonging to the control-oriented organization will be totally inappropriate for the 21st century organization? What *is* the new leadership paradigm?

Since the "emerging organization" has not yet arrived, it is difficult to know what the new and effective leadership paradigm will look like. Daft and Lewin provide several clues, however. Leadership with control will in all likelihood be replaced by leadership without traditional forms of control. Daft and Lewin suggest that the new paradigm will use the "intangible qualities of vision, culture, shared values, and information to set premises and imprint ideas throughout the organization."[3] Influence over the way people frame problems, think about, organize, and solve problems will replace top-down organizational directiveness. Leadership will consist of vision and intellectual stimulation. The exact nature and form of this new leader and leadership process await full articulation. We challenge you to think about and work on the design of the new paradigm.

The readings in this chapter provide two different and emerging perspectives on leadership. In the first reading, Charles C. Manz (1986) provides a look at "self-leadership." The second and final reading is by Peter M. Senge (1990). Senge provides his insight into the leader's new world. The challenge of leading the 21st century organization will be astronomical. As students of leadership today and leaders of tomorrow, your challenge will be to discover the new leadership paradigm. The challenge is indeed awesome, yet one that can be extremely challenging, exhilarating, and fun.

In Conclusion

We hope that your *understanding* of leadership has been expanded. We hope that your *interest* in both leadership and its study has been enhanced. We hope that your *insight* into yourself within the leadership context has been enriched. We hope that you have gained some insight into the leadership challenge that awaits you. We hope that the *care and attention* you will bring to your own future exercise of leadership has been heightened. If those goals are attained for you and others, our organizations, society, and the world will benefit greatly.

[3] Ibid.

Self-Leadership
Toward an Expanded Theory of Self-Influence Processes in Organizations

C. C. Manz
University of Minnesota

*R*ecently, significant attention has been devoted to a previously neglected aspect of organizational behavior—the influence organization members exert over themselves. This "new" managerial focus has emerged primarily from the social learning theory literature (Bandura, 1977a) and related work in self-control (Bandura, 1969; Cautela, 1969; Goldfried & Merbaum, 1973; Kanfer, 1970; Mahoney & Arnkoff, 1978, 1979; Mahoney & Thoresen, 1974; Thoresen & Mahoney, 1974). In the organization literature, this process generally has been referred to as self-management (Andrasik & Heimberg, 1982; Luthans & Davis, 1979; Manz & Sims, 1980; Marx, 1982; Mills, 1983).

This paper, stimulated by the earlier work, proposes an expanded and more comprehensive theory of the self-influence of organization members. First, the fundamental importance, and the need for greater integration, of the self-influence processes into organizational theories are discussed. Second, an overview of conceptualization of self-management thus far in the organization literature is presented. It is argued that while these treatments are useful, they provide an incomplete view of self-influence; therefore, an expanded "self-leadership" perspective is proposed that emphasizes purposeful leadership of self toward personal standards and "natural" rewards that hold greater intrinsic motivational value. Implications for theory, research, and practice are discussed.

Recognizing Self-Control Systems

Organizations impose multiple controls of varying character on employees. Tannenbaum (1962), for example, argued that "organization implies control" (p. 237). Lawler and Rhode (1976) pointed out that control systems try to exert influence by identifying appropriate behavior, providing means to monitor behavior that is taking place, and coordinating, rewarding, and punishing this behavior. One view suggests that the control process involves applying rational, manageable, control mechanisms (work standards, appraisal and reward systems, etc.) to influence employees through external means to assure that the organization achieves its goals.

An alternative view, however, shifts the perspective of the control system-controllee interface significantly. Simply stated, this perspective views each person as possessing an internal self-control system (Manz, 1979; Manz, Mossholder, & Luthans, in press). Organizational control systems in their most basic form provide performance standards, evaluation mechanisms, and systems of reward and punishment (Lawler, 1976; Lawler & Rhode, 1976). Similarly, individuals possess self-generated personal standards, engage in self-evaluation processes, and self-administer rewards and punishments in managing their daily activities (Bandura, 1977a; Mahoney & Thoresen, 1974; Manz & Sims, 1980). Even though these mechanisms take place frequently, in an almost automatic manner, this makes them no less powerful.

Furthermore, while organizations provide employees with certain values and beliefs packaged into cultures, corporate visions and so forth, people too possess their own systems of values, beliefs, and visions (however vague) for their future. In addition, the counterparts of organizational rules, policies, and operating procedures are represented internally in the form of behavioral and psychological scripts (Abelson, 1981; Gioia & Poole, 1984; Schank & Abelson, 1977) or "programs" (Carver & Scheier, 1982) held at various levels of abstraction.

The point is—organizations provide organizational control systems that influence people but these systems do not access individual action directly. Rather, the impact of organizational control mechanisms is determined by the way they influence, in intended as well as unintended ways, the self-control systems within organization members. This logic is portrayed graphically in Figure 1.

While this perspective is not new, an analysis of theory and research in the field reveals that it has not been well integrated into organizational management. The literature does include cognitive mediation of external stimuli (e.g., social learning theory views—Davis & Luthans, 1980; Manz & Sims, 1980; attributed causes to observed physical actions—Feldman, 1981; Green & Mitchell, 1979; Mitchell, Green, & Wood, 1981; Mitchell, Larson, & Green, 1977; Staw, 1975) but does not adequately recognize the self-influence system as a focal point (rather than a mediator) for enhanced understanding and practice of organizational management. The perspective shown in Figure 1, on the other hand, suggests that the self-influence system is the ultimate system of control. In addition, it suggests that this internal control system must receive significant attention in its own right before

Source: Edited and reprinted with permission from *Academy of Management Review* 11 (1986), 585–600. Author affiliation may have changed since article was first published.

The author thanks the participants in "The Not For Prime Time Workshop" for their helpful comments on an earlier draft of this paper.

FIGURE 1

The Organizational and Self-control Systems.

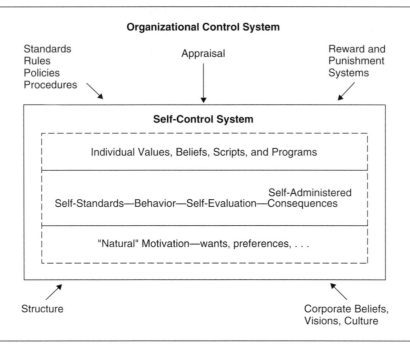

maximum benefits for the organization and employee are realized.

Recent work on cybernetic (control) theory provides a useful perspective for making concrete the nature of employee self-regulating systems (Carver & Scheier, 1981, 1982). Based on the negative feedback loop, Carver and Scheier (1981) present an insightful view of self-regulating processes involving: (a) input perceptions of existing conditions, (b) comparison of the perception with an existing reference value (standard), (c) output behaviors to reduce discrepancies from the standard, and (d) a consequent impact on the environment. From this view, an employee attempting to achieve a given production standard would operate within a closed loop of control aimed at minimizing deviations from standards in existing performance. Unless an environmental disturbance of some kind occurred, this self-regulating process theoretically could occur indefinitely.

Carver and Scheier (1981, 1982) further speculated, based on the work of Powers (1973a, 1973b), that standards emerge from a hierarchical organization of control systems. That is, standards for a particular control system loop (X units of production) derive from superordinate systems of control. Thus, an employee working to achieve a minimum deviation from a production standard at one level may serve higher level systems aimed at higher level standards (meeting job responsibilities, being a conscientious employee, being a good person).

From an organizational perspective, recognizing and facilitating employee self-regulating systems pose a viable and more realistic view of control than views centered entirely on external influence. In addition, overreliance on external controls can lead to a number of dysfunctional employee behaviors: "rigid bureaucratic behavior" (performance of only those behaviors that are rewarded by the control system), inputting of invalid information into management information systems, and so forth (Camman & Nadler, 1976; Lawler, 1976; Lawler & Rhode, 1976).

It is instructive at this point to address current views of employee self-management and then to present an expanded self-leadership view of self-regulatory processes.

Employee Self-Management

Most relevant treatments of self-management to date focused on strategies designed to facilitate behaviors targeted for change (e.g., Andrasik & Heimberg, 1982; Luthans & Davis, 1979; Manz & Sims, 1980). This work generally reflects the view that behaviors are not performed for their intrinsic value but because of their necessity or because of what the performer will receive for his/her performance. A widely recognized definition of self-control, one that illustrates this view, is: "A person displays self-control when in the relative absence of immediate external constraints (performs without external assistance) he or she engages in behavior whose previous probability has been less than that of alternatively available behaviors (a less attractive behavior but one that is implied to be more desirable)" (text added) (Thoresen & Mahoney, 1974, p. 12).

Several specific self-management strategies can be identified. Mahoney and Arnkoff (1978, 1979) provided a useful array of strategies that were applied in clinical contexts. These include: self-observation, self-goal setting, cueing strategies, self-reinforcement, self-punishment, and rehearsal. Much of the employee self-management literature has centered on adaptations of these self-control strategies for addressing management problems (Andrasik & Heimberg, 1982; Luthans &

Davis, 1979; Manz & Sims, 1980, 1981). Luthans and Davis (1979) provided descriptions of cueing strategy interventions across a variety of work contexts. Physical cues such as a wall graph to chart progress on target behaviors and a magnetic message board were used to self-induce desired behavioral change in specific cases. Manz and Sims (1980) explicated the relevance of the broader range of self-control strategies, especially as substitutes for formal organizational leadership. Self-observation, cueing strategies, self-goal setting, self-reward, self-punishment, and rehearsal were each discussed in terms of their applicability to organizational contexts. Andrasik and Heimberg (1982) developed a behavioral self-management program for individualized self-modification of targeted work behaviors. Their approach involved pinpointing a specific behavior for change, observing the behavior over time, developing a behavioral change plan involving self-reward or some other self-influence strategy, and adjusting the plan based on self-awareness of a need for change.

In terms of cybernetic self-regulating systems (Carver & Scheier, 1981, 1982), these employee self-management perspectives can be viewed as providing a set of strategies that facilitate behaviors that serve to reduce deviations from higher level reference values that the employee may or may not have helped establish. That is, the governing standards at higher levels of abstraction (cf., Powers, 1973a, 1973b)—for example, what it means to be a good employee based on organizational or professional values—can remain largely externally defined even though lower level standards to reach the goals may be personally created. Mills (1983) argued that factors such as the normative system and professional norms can exercise just as much control over the individual as a mechanistic situation in which the performance process is manipulated directly. The implication is that, unlike the perspective suggested in Figure 1, the aims of the "self-managed employee" can be, in actuality, externally controlled by existing higher level external standards.

This view is consistent with arguments that employee self-control is perhaps more an illusion than a reality (Dunbar, 1981) and that self-managed individuals are far from loosely supervised or controlled (Mills, 1983). In addition, it has been argued that self-management strategies themselves are behaviors that require reinforcement in order to be maintained (Kerr & Slocum, 1981; Manz & Sims, 1980; Thoresen & Mahoney, 1974). Because of this dependence on external reinforcement, it could be argued that the self-management approach violates Thoresen and Mahoney's (1974) definition cited earlier, ". . . in the relative absence of immediate external constraints . . ." in the long run. That is, while *immediate* external constraints or supports may not be required, *longer-term* reinforcement is. Again, self-management is subject to external control.

Toward a Broader View of Self-Influence Processes

In developing a broader perspective, self-influence should be viewed as more than a set of strategies designed to facilitate employee behaviors that help meet standards. For some individuals, being "less controlled" (not meeting socially based standards) may represent active self-controlled choice.

In addressing the question, "What is truly self-controlled behavior?" one can become immersed in metaphysical arguments on the nature of free-will (cf., Dennett, 1984). Rychlak (1979) suggested that the crucial concern is a telic one—that is, the underlying reason one is performing the behavior. For example, is the individual performing because he/she wants to or because of a belief that he/she "should"? Interestingly, Marx (1982) suggested management of one's "should/want ratio" (p. 439) as a self-control strategy for avoiding becoming overburdened with activities that must be done ("shoulds") relative to those that one likes to do ("wants").

Following this line of reasoning, the differences between self-management and external control can become clouded depending on the perspective adopted. Consider a person who truly wants to deal with a problem behavior to achieve a freely chosen personal standard, but despite systematic persistent use of self-management strategies does not succeed. In such a case, calling on another person or organization to establish constraints for his/her behavior (i.e., giving up "self-management") may be the most effective means to achieve a personal goal. Again, Thoresen and Mahoney's (1974) definition of self-control is violated. Yet, acting on the environment to produce constraints may be the most viable avenue for exercising self-influence in such cases.

Schelling (1980) addressed a host of internal struggles (e.g., inducing over withholding on income taxes to assure a surplus of personal funds later), all of which exemplify relying on external constraints to exercise "self-command." Bandura's (1977a, 1978) notion of reciprocal determinism, which recognized an interdependent relationship between one's behavior and the environment, is useful here. That is, acting on the environment to cause it to influence or control one's behavior in a personally desired way can be a legitimate form of self-influence (albeit one step removed). Indeed, self-constraints (e.g., lack of confidence, inadequate ability) can sometimes produce greater limitations on one's freedom to behave than rigid external controls.

The question "Who is more or less self-controlled, the person who uses self-management to achieve standards imposed by someone else or the person who chooses externally controlled situations to achieve personally chosen standards?" illustrates the heart of this discussion. The position taken in this paper is that true self-leadership is based on the personal meaningfulness and "ownership" of the individual's governing standards. Invoking external influence to achieve personally chosen standards is a legitimate form of self-leadership. Self-imposing self-management strategies to reach externally defined and personally undesired standards, however, is a form of "self-management" that masks external control.

Toward a Theory of Self-Leadership

In this section, a self-leadership view is proposed. Here, self-leadership is conceptualized as a comprehensive self-influence perspective that concerns leading oneself toward performance of naturally motivating tasks as well as managing oneself to do work that must be done but is not naturally motivating. It includes the self-management of immediate behaviors and in addition, similar to the notion of "double loop learning" (Argyris, 1982a, 1982b), it challenges the appropriateness of operating standards that govern the employee self-influence system as the reasons for the behavior. Three critical elements of self-leadership that distinguish it and contribute to our understanding of self-influence beyond the previous work include: (a) that it allows for addressing a wider range (higher level) of *standards* for self-influence, (b) that it more fully incorporates the role of *intrinsic work motivation,* and (c) that it suggests some additional *strategies* for employee self-control. Each of these elements is discussed below.

Standards for Self-Influence

A standard establishes a target or goal for performance and can serve a primary controlling function. Locke, Shaw, Saari, and Latham (1981) pointed out that goals direct attention, mobilize effort, increase persistence, and motivate strategy development. Thus, when goals or standards are established by an external source, they can serve as a significant external influence or control mechanism.

The ability of standards to influence employees is based in part on knowledge of one's progress in meeting the standards that is received from external sources. Thus, external feedback can have an impact on employee self-control. Ilgen, Fisher, and Taylor (1979) indicated that excessive external feedback can place external limits on self-influence. They suggested that in order to shift to an internal locus of control in persons, the frequency of feedback (from external sources) likely will need to be changed (reduced) to allow increased self-monitoring. Despite its importance a systematic review of the role of feedback in employee influence is beyond the scope of the current discussion (cf., Taylor, Fisher, & Ilgen, 1984).

Consequently, the focus here is on the standards themselves. The position taken is that a self-leadership view facilitates a broader higher-level perspective on individuals' guiding standards than does the existing work on employee self-management. Figure 2 illustrates a philosophical difference between the concepts of self-management and self-leadership relating to this issue. The figure relies on a cybernetic control system perspective of self-influence (Carver & Scheier, 1981, 1982). The aim of this system is to reduce deviations from operating standards which are defined hierarchically by increasingly abstract perceptions about the relation between work and self. Conceptually, self-management can be viewed as a set of strategies that aids employees in structuring their work environment, in establishing self-motivation, and so forth, that facilitates appropriate behaviors for achieving minimal deviations from primarily lower-level behavioral standards. Self-leadership, on the other hand, encompasses self-management behavior, but it is also concerned with leading the self-influence system at superordinate levels.

Self-management, for example, might be exercised by establishing a performance self-goal/standard of calling on six customers daily in order to meet sales quotas, and then providing a self-reward each day for meeting this goal. Self-leadership, on the other hand, allows for self-leading of the higher level standards that provide the reasons for the self-managed behaviors—e.g., "Why does one want to meet a sales quota . . . be a good salesperson or be in sales at all . . . be a conscientious provider for one's family . . . be a good person?"

A central distinction between self-management and the proposed self-leadership perspective is a difference in focus.

F I G U R E   2
A Cybernetic Control System View of the Role of Self-Management and Self-Leadership.

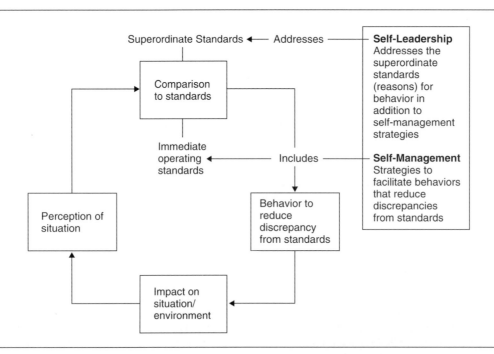

Self-management is largely concerned with a set of behavioral and cognitive strategies that reflect a rational view of what people ought to be doing—for example, stop smoking (Thoresen & Mahoney, 1974), finish a report (Luthans & Davis, 1979), reduce nonproductive informal conversations (Manz & Sims, 1980). Self-leadership goes beyond this to place significant emphasis on the intrinsic value of tasks. While employee self-management theorists likely would recognize the relevance of intrinsic motivation factors for self-management, the existing focus in the literature on strategies that facilitate "appropriate" behaviors tends to distract potential developments in this vein. The self-leadership view proposed here is intended to stimulate a broader view of self-influence that includes the important role of the intrinsically appealing aspects of work ("natural" rewards) and how important these aspects are in defining why behavior is performed.

Intrinsic Motivation in Self-Regulation

Self-management emphasizes rewards that are separate from the task and that are received for its completion (e.g., self-praise, external recognition, and rewards). A broader self-leadership view explicitly recognizes rewards that result from performing activities themselves. These can be described as "natural" rewards (Manz, 1983a, 1983b) because they are a natural part of the task performance process and derive from natural intrinsic responses. Self-leadership goes beyond self-management to address redefining one's tasks and one's relationship with and/or perception of tasks so that desired performance results from a natural motivational process. Particular emphasis is taken from the intrinsic motivation literature (cf., Deci, 1971, 1975a; Deci & Ryan, 1980) and especially, cognitive evaluation theory (Deci, 1975a, 1975b).

Cognitive evaluation theory, based on the work of White (1959) and de Charms (1968), was founded on the assumption that behavior is caused by internal states (Deci, 1975b). Although the validity of cognitive evaluation theory has not received universal support (e.g., Farr, 1976; Farr, Vance, & McIntyre, 1977; Phillips & Lord, 1980; Scott, 1975), an impressive body of evidence has been gathered in its support both from Deci and his colleagues (Benware & Deci, 1975; Deci, 1971, 1975a; Deci, Nezlek, & Sheinman, 1981; Deci & Ryan, 1980) and from others (Calder & Staw, 1975; Daniel & Esser, 1980; Greene & Lepper, 1974; Kruglanski, Alon, & Lewis, 1972; Lepper & Greene, 1975; Lepper, Greene, & Nisbett, 1973). Thus, while this view is subject to potential arguments, for example from more functional viewpoints (Scott, 1975), this assumption as part of a broader view of behavioral causes is accepted here. Notably, social learning theory relies on a reciprocal determinism view in which behavior is caused by internal states as well as external influences, and each of these three components (behavior, internal processes, and external forces) influences each other in a reciprocal fashion (Bandura, 1978). This comprehensive reciprocal determinism view is the assumptive framework upon which conceptual development is based in this paper.

In cognitive evaluation theory (Deci, 1975a), an individual's *feelings of self-determination and competence* are central to the experience of intrinsic motivation. Specifically, rewards that increase these intrinsic outcomes will increase intrinsic motivation. Deci (1975a) suggested that the natural inclination to pursue feelings of competence and self-determination leads to a behavioral pattern. This pattern includes a search for reasonable challenges and an expenditure of effort to overcome these challanges. The logic is that by overcoming such challenges, feelings of competence and self-control will be enhanced.

In a similar vein, Bandura (1977a, 1977b, 1982) viewed individual self-efficacy perceptions as central to social learning theory. He pointed out that perceived self-efficacy will influence the amount of effort and persistence expended in the face of adversity. Bandura (1977b, 1982) also indicated that the strongest contributor to positive self-efficacy perceptions is one's personal performance history.

In performance appraisal, Bernardin and Beatty (1984) suggested that the tendency of raters to be lenient in their evaluations may stem from a perception of a low personal capability (low self-efficacy) to cope with the likely negative reaction of the ratee. They suggested training to assess rater efficacy perceptions followed by training to allow raters to experience mastery of progressively difficult rating tasks. This approach was designed to facilitate increases in rater self-efficacy perceptions which were assumed to result in more accurate evaluations by raters. Again, a greater sense of competence is linked to one's willingness and motivation to perform a task.

By combining the work of Deci and the literature on self-efficacy, it could be concluded that an important aspect of self-influence is the process of establishing intrinsic motivation by enhancing one's feelings of competence and self-control (more generally one's perceptions of self-efficacy). Furthermore, a primary objective of self-leadership practice should be to enhance self-efficacy perceptions which are reciprocally related to performance. That is, enhanced self-efficacy should lead to higher performance through its impact on effort and persistence. A history of higher performance in turn will have a positive impact on future self-efficacy perceptions (Bandura, 1977b).

In addition to feelings of competence and self-control, a third intrinsic motivation factor, the task performer's *feelings of purpose,* is addressed. This additional component is consistent with literature emphasizing the importance of purpose and belief in one's work for fostering task performance. Examples of this are provided in the Japanese management literature (Hatvany & Pucik, 1981a, 1981b; Ouchi, 1981a, 1981b; Ouchi & Jaeger, 1978; Pascale & Athos, 1981; Sullivan, 1983), work that emphasizes the importance of shared vision (e.g., a corporate philosophy) (Hatvany & Pucik, 1981a; Ouchi & Price, 1978), and the job characteristic "task significance" addressed in the job design literature (Hackman & Oldham, 1975). The essential idea is that a reason (purpose) for doing one's work that extends beyond the rewards, reprimands, and so forth, is important. The shared values component of the recently proposed McKinsey "7 S's" approach for characterizing organizations is consistent with this latter phenomenon (Pascale & Athos, 1981; Peters & Waterman, 1982).

One view suggests that feelings of purpose most probably result from worthwhile contributions to something or someone other than oneself (i.e., altruism) (Manz, 1983a). In this sense, "external" corporate philosophies or visions can foster internal purpose if they are defined in an altruistic fashion. It may be that this altruistic component is coupled with an egoistic motive (e.g., altruistic egoism, Selye, 1974). On the other hand, evidence has been gathered suggesting that altruism is part of human nature apart from "selfish" ends (Hoffman, 1981). One American production plant that has displayed highly motivated and committed workers, for example, has as its motto "people helping people" (Manz, 1983b). Examination of Japanese organizations often reveals a similar concern for purposeful (altruistic) ends.

Strategies for Self-Leadership Practice

Self-leadership, with its emphasis on the intrinsic motivational aspects of work, suggests several strategies that can complement existing self-management strategies (cf., Andrasik & Heimberg, 1982; Manz & Sims, 1980). These additional strategies are based on employees wanting to, rather than feeling they should, perform task behaviors.

Work Context Strategies.   Briefly, one self-leadership approach involves choosing, to the extent possible, work environments that enhance the natural impact of the physical work setting on performance. A long-distance runner who chooses to run in pleasant surroundings as opposed to a conventional quarter-mile track uses this approach. In addition, a sense of *competence* can result from successfully navigating new, challenging terrain. Feelings of *self-determination* are enhanced by the runner's control over running routes, and the positive health benefits (*purpose*) are provided to the runner as well. Together these elements stemming from a chosen desirable work context should have a positive impact on motivation and performance.

A subtle, yet no less powerful, aspect of the work context involves social psychological elements such as group norms, corporate values, and existing interpersonal employee interaction patterns. Two more global concepts that have received significant attention in the literature are: organizational climate (e.g., Field & Abelson, 1982; Hellriegel & Slocum, 1974; Schneider, 1975) and corporate culture (e.g., Deal & Kennedy, 1982; Marshall, 1982; Pettigrew, 1979). Again, an individual is using a work context self-leadership strategy by choosing and working to create a social psychological work context that contributes to natural enjoyment of task performance.

Task Performance Process Strategies.   Another approach for exercising self-leadership is to build natural rewards into the *process* of performing, that is, to focus on *how* the task is performed. The challenge for the self-leading individual is to discover what activities provide him/her with "natural" rewards and then to build these activities into the task process, where possible.

A manager, for example, may have a choice regarding whether to explain a new work procedure to a subordinate through a memo or face-to-face communication. If documentation is not essential, a manager might choose oral communication because he/she finds the task process to be more enjoyable (more naturally rewarding). These kinds of work

process choices that continually arise become the base from which self-leadership can be exercised. If an individual can establish a reasonable level of self-awareness regarding what kinds of activities he/she enjoys and perform work consistent with these preferences (where this is possible without jeopardizing performance), self-leadership is enhanced.

An open-ended search for activities that provide natural rewards would be difficult and highly inefficient. Fortunately, the three natural reward elements: feelings of competence, self-control, and purpose, can guide in identifying and building activities into one's work. In essence, the process becomes a self-performed job analysis and job redesign, within the limits of one's job specifications (although these too might be negotiated and modified). While an expanded view of cognitive evaluation theory is suggested here as a flexible and general basis for self-initiated job redesign, other theoretical views could be used to provide some specific alternative strategies. A self-initiated job characteristics approach (e.g., Hackman & Oldham, 1975; Sims, Szilagyi, & Keller, 1975) to job redesign might be one way of exercising self-leadership within these broad guidelines. In this approach, individuals use their discretion to define certain aspects of the performance process to establish enhanced natural motivation potential for work performance.

Other types of self-leadership strategies could be identified beyond those centered on the work context or process discussed above. For example, choice of a vocational field or a particular job position in itself can represent a powerful self-leadership strategy with considerable potential for affecting the intrinsic enjoyment and motivation derived from work. Another important type of self-leadership strategy focuses on management of thought processes, the subject of the following discussion.

Self-Leadership of Thought Patterns.   Perhaps the ultimate goal of self-leadership practice should be to enhance the effectiveness of employees in managing their own thought patterns. For example, in addition to systematically managing one's own behavior or altering the physical context or the process by which work is performed, one can manage his/ her mental representation of the work. In a sense, the job is redesigned mentally rather than physically.

Any job holds both desirable and undesirable elements for a performer. To the extent that one's mental energy is focused on unpleasant aspects of the work (fatigue, pressure, uncertainty, etc.) the work process likely will be experienced unfavorably. On the other hand, if desirable elements (challenge, learning, variety, etc.) become the focus of one's mental energy, the potential for motivation can be established. This view holds obvious similarities to popularized notions such as the power of "positive thinking" (Peale, 1956). There exists more than a little merit, however, to the notion that an existing reality is more in the mind of the beholder than in any physical sense (e.g., Beck, 1970; Ellis, 1970; Meichenbaum, 1974).

Leadership approaches that center on managing meaning and vision (Berlew, 1979; House, 1977) incorporate parallel logic. Berlew (1979) discussed an essentially charismatic approach to leadership that provides employees with, among other things, "common vision" (e.g., purpose) and the opportunity for organization members to "feel stronger and more in control of their own destinies" (a sense of competence and self-control) (p. 347). The logic of self-leadership of thought is similar except that the worker takes an active part in mentally establishing worthwhile states for himself/herself.

Recent applications of the schema concept to organizational behavior (e.g., Gioia & Poole, 1984; Hastie, 1981; Langer, 1978; Taylor & Crocker, 1981), derived from a schema-based, information-processing view (e.g., Graesser, Woll, Kowalski, & Smith, 1980), make it apparent that such mental functioning, that has been characterized as being "automatic," almost "thoughtless," goes beyond descriptive power. That is, if consistent (similar to habitual) ways of processing information develop (e.g., relying on stereotypes—Hamilton, 1979), individuals need not be passive subjects but can and frequently do experience these thought processes in a "thoughtful" way (Gioia & Manz, 1985; Gioia & Poole, 1984). By actively self-managing mental activity (schemas or otherwise) desired thought patterns can be pursued.

It is beyond the scope of this paper to address a detailed analysis of how this can be achieved. It has been suggested elsewhere (Manz, 1983a), however, that desired thought patterns might be developed by managing internal verbalizations or self-talk (Meichenbaum & Cameron, 1974), imagery (Bandura, 1969; Cautela, 1966, 1967, 1971; Mahoney, 1974), and one's belief systems (Ellis, 1975; Ellis & Whiteley, 1979). A general illustrative example could be a conscious effort to increase mental energy devoted to work elements that provide natural reward value over those that do not. The objective is to foster the development of new thought patterns that aid rather than hinder motivation and performance.

Overall, it has been argued that a broader self-influence view (self-leadership) recognizes not only strategies for self-managing behaviors to meet existing standards, but also addresses the higher-level standards (reasons for behavior) themselves. Thus, self-leadership concerns itself with self-leading ongoing self-influence (cybernetic) systems. An important aspect of this self-leadership process centers on "natural" rewards that foster intrinsic motivation to more fully integrate "wants" with "shoulds" in establishing a more comprehensive view of employee self-influence. In particular, the theoretical view developed here suggests that intrinsic motivation derived from feelings of competence, self-control, and purpose is an important component of self-leadership.

Self Leadership: Some Implications for Theory and Practice

Some distinctions have been drawn between existing employee self-management perspectives and a more comprehensive self-leadership view. Self-leadership is conceptualized as a process that encompasses behaviorally focused self-management strategies and further addresses self-regulation of higher-level control standards to more fully recognize the role of intrinsic motivation. Such an expanded view poses significant implications for both theory and practice.

It suggests the existence of at least three self-influence perspectives. The first, labeled here as employee *self-regulation*, consists of an ongoing cybernetic control process aimed at reducing deviation from existing standards that are arranged hierarchically. Usually, self-regulation in the short run occurs automatically and adjustments are made to help reduce discrepancies from established reference points. Control can be anchored to the existing external (e.g., organization) control system where self-regulation serves as a process to satisfy this system.

Employee self-management consists of a set of self-management strategies that are designed to facilitate behaviors that help meet standards. In the immediate time period (i.e., negative feedback loop) these standards may be established by the self-managed individual (e.g., a self-set goal of X units of output on a given day). The self-management strategies (including self-set goals), however, tend to serve as mechanisms for reducing deviation from standards in higher-level control loops (meet job specifications, be a "good" employee, etc.). The focus is on behaviors to facilitate performance of what "should" be done.

The *self-leadership* perspective proposed in this paper represents a broader view of self-influence. This view includes self-management strategies to foster functional behaviors for meeting standards; it also addresses how appropriate or how desirable the standards are themselves. In addition, the self-leadership view goes beyond a behavioral focus to more fully recognize the importance of intrinsic motivation. Recognition of individual "wants," in addition to "shoulds," is viewed as a legitimate aspect of self-influence. The self-leadership view more accurately reflects the concept of free will as an issue of why behavior is performed, not just whether it is personally chosen, by addressing the legitimacy of governing standards and the intrinsic based "wants" of the individual. . . .

Conclusions

The recent attention to self-influence processes has challenged researchers and practitioners to rethink many of their fundamental assumptions regarding organizational research and practice. Indeed, employee self-control should be viewed as a central element of important organizational processes such as leadership, control, and management in general. The employee self-management literature, however, typically has centered on a set of behaviorally focused strategies that tend to divert attention away from, or overlook, the reasons the behavior is being self-managed.

A more comprehensive self-leadership perspective has been proposed to more fully address the higher-level standards/reasons that employee self-influence is performed and to suggest self-influence strategies that allow the intrinsic value of work to help enhance individual performance. Further research and theoretical development is needed to address several central elements of self-influence—for example, the derivation of personal standards at multiple hierarchical levels, human thought patterns, self-influence strategies that build motivation into target behaviors—that have been neglected in the employee self-management literature. This paper is intended to be a first step in advancing the existing literature toward such a broader self-leadership perspective.

References

Abelson, R. P. (1981) Psychological status of the Script Concept. *American Psychologist*, 36, 715–729.

Andrasik, F., & Heimberg, J. S. (1982) Self-management procedures. In L. W. Frederikson (Ed.), *Handbook of organizational behavior management* (pp. 219–247). New York: Wiley.

Argyris, C. (1964) *Integrating the individual and the organization.* New York: Wiley.

Argyris, C. (1982a) *Reasoning, learning and action: Individual and organizational.* San Francisco: Jossey-Bass.

Argyris, C. (1982b) The executive mind and double-loop learning. *Organizational Dynamics*, 11, 5–22.

Bandura, A. (1969) *Principles of behavior modification.* New York: Holt, Rinehart, and Winston.

Bandura, A. (1977a) *Social learning theory.* Englewood Cliffs, NJ: Prentice-Hall.

Bandura, A. (1977b) Self-efficacy: Towards a unifying theory of behavioral change. *Psychological Review*, 84, 191–215.

Bandura, A. (1978) The self system in a reciprocal determinism. *American Psychologist*, 33, 344–358.

Bandura, A. (1982) Self-efficacy mechanism in human agency. *American Psychologist*, 37, 122–147.

Beck, A. T. (1970) Cognitive therapy: Nature and the relation to behavior therapy. *Behavior Therapy*, 1, 184–200.

Benware, C., & Deci, E. L. (1975) Attitude change as a function of the inducement for espousing a pro-attitudinal communication. *Journal of Experimental Social Psychology*, 11, 271–278.

Berlew, D. E. (1979) Leadership and organizational excitement. In D. A. Kolb, I. M. Rubin, & J. M. McIntyre (Eds.), *Organizational psychology: A book of readings* (pp. 343–356). Englewood Cliffs, NJ: Prentice-Hall.

Bernardin, H. J., & Beatty, R. W. (1984) *Performance appraisal: Assessing human behavior at work.* Boston: Kent Publishing Co.

Calder, B. J., & Staw, B. M. (1975) The self-perception of intrinsic and extrinsic motivation. *Journal of Personality and Social Psychology*, 35, 599–605.

Camman, C., & Nadler, D. (1976) Fit control systems to your managerial style. *Harvard Business Review*, 54(1), 65–72.

Carver, C. S., & Scheier, M. F. (1981) *Attention and self-regulation: A control theory approach to human behavior.* New York: Springer-Verlag.

Carver, C. S., & Scheier, M. F. (1982) Control theory: A useful conceptual framework for personality—social, clinical, and health psychology. *Psychological Bulletin*, 92, 111–135.

Cautela, J. R. (1966) Treatment of compulsive behavior by covert sensitization. *Psychological Record*, 16, 33–41.

Cautela, J. R. (1967) Covert sensitization. *Psychological Reports*, 20, 459–468.

Cautela, J. R. (1969) Behavior therapy and self-control: Techniques and implications. In C. M. Franks (Ed.), *Behavior therapy: Appraisal and status* (pp. 323–340). New York: McGraw-Hill.

Cautela, J. R. (1971) *Covert modeling.* Paper presented at the Association for the Advancement of Behavior Therapy, Washington, DC.

Daniel, T. L., & Esser, J. K. (1980) Intrinsic motivation as influenced by rewards, task interest, and task structure. *Journal of Applied Psychology*, 65, 566–573.

Davis, T. R. V., & Luthans, F. (1980) A social learning approach to organizational behavior. *Academy of Management Review*, 5, 281–290.

Deal, T. E., & Kennedy, A. A. (1982) *Corporate cultures.* Reading, MA: Addison-Wesley.

deCharms, R. (1968) *Personal causation: The internal affective determinants of behavior.* New York: Academic Press.

Deci, E. L. (1971) Effects of externally mediated rewards on intrinsic motivation. *Journal of Personality and Social Psychology*, 18, 105–115.

Deci, E. L. (1975a) *Intrinsic motivation.* New York: Plenum.

Deci, E. L. (1975b) Notes on the theory and metatheory of intrinsic motivation. *Organizational Behavior and Human Performance*, 15, 130–145.

Deci, E. L., Nezlek, J., & Sheinman, S. (1981) Characteristics of the rewarder and intrinsic motivation of the rewardee. *Journal of Personality and Social Psychology*, 40, 1–10.

Deci, E. L., & Ryan, R. (1980) The empirical exploration of intrinsic motivational processes. In L. Berkowitz (Ed.), *Advances in experimental social psychology* (Vol. 13, pp. 39–80). New York: Academic Press.

Dennett, D. C. (1984) *Elbow room: The varieties of free will worth wanting.* Cambridge, MA: The MIT Press.

Dunbar, R. L. M. (1981) Designs for organizational control. In W. Starbuck & P. Nystrom (Eds.), *Handbook of organizations* (pp. 85–115). New York: Oxford University Press.

Ellis, A. (1970) *The essence of rational psychotherapy: A comprehensive approach to treatment.* New York: Institute for Rational Living.

Ellis, A. (1975) *A new guide to rational living.* Englewood Cliffs, NJ: Prentice-Hall.

Ellis, A., & Whiteley, J. M. (Eds.) (1979) *Theoretical and empirical foundations of rational emotive therapy.* Monterey, CA: Brooks/Cole.

Farr, J. L. (1976) Task characteristics, reward contingency, and intrinsic motivation. *Organizational Behavior and Human Performance*, 16, 294–307.

Farr, J. L., Vance, R. J., & McIntyre, R. M. (1977) Further examination of the relationship between reward contingency and intrinsic motivation. *Organizational Behavior and Human Performance*, 20, 31–53.

Feldman, J. M. (1981) Beyond attribution theory: Cognitive processes in performance evaluation. *Journal of Applied Psychology*, 66, 127–148.

Field, R. H. G., & Abelson, M. A. (1982) Climate: A reconceptualization and proposed model. *Human Relations*, 35, 131–201.

Gioia, D. A., & Manz, C. C. (1985) Linking cognition and behavior: A script processing interpretation of vicarious learning. *Academy of Management Review*, 9, 449–459.

Goldfried, M. R., & Merbaum, M. (Eds.) (1973) *Behavior change through self-control.* New York: Holt, Rinehart, and Winston.

Graesser, A. C., Woll, S. B., Kowalski, D. J., & Smith, D. A. (1980) Memory for typical and atypical actions in scripted activities. *Journal of Experimental Psychology*, 6, 503–515.

Green, S. G., & Mitchell, T. R. (1979) Attributional processes of leaders in leader-member interactions. *Organizational Behavior and Human Performance*, 23, 429–458.

Greene, D., & Lepper, M. R. (1974) Effects of extrinsic reward on children's subsequent intrinsic interest. *Child Development*, 45, 1141–1145.

Hackman, J. R., & Oldham, G. R. (1975) Development of the job diagnostic survey. *Journal of Applied Psychology*, 60, 159–170.

Hamilton, D. L. (1979) A cognitive-attributional analysis of stereotyping. In L. Berkowitz (Ed.), *Advances in experimental social psychology* (Vol. 12, pp. 53–84). New York: Academic Press.

Hastie, R. (1981) Schematic principles in human memory. In E. T. Higgins, C. P. Herman, and M. P. Sanna (Eds.), *Social cognition* (Vol. 1, pp. 39–88). Hillsdale, NJ: Erlbaum.

Hatvany, N., & Pucik, V. (1981a) An integrated management system: Lessons from the Japanese experience. *Academy of Management Review*, 6, 469–480.

Hatvany, N., & Pucik, V. (1981b) Japanese management practices and productivity. *Organizational Dynamics*, 9, 5–21.

Hellriegel, D., & Slocum, J. W., Jr. (1974) Organizational climate: Measures, research and contingencies. *Academy of Management Journal*, 17, 255–280.

Hoffman, M. L. (1981) Is altruism part of human nature? *Journal of Personality and Social Psychology*, 40, 121–137.

House, R. J. (1977) A 1976 theory of charismatic leadership. In J. G. Hunt & L. L. Larson (Eds.), *Leadership: The cutting edge* (pp. 189–207). Carbondale, IL: Southern Illinois University Press.

Ilgen, D., Fisher, C., & Taylor, M. S. (1979) Consequences of individual feedback on behavior in organizations. *Journal of Applied Psychology*, 64, 349–371.

Kanfer, F. H. (1970) Self-regulation: Research, issues and speculations. In C. Neuringer & J. L. Michael (Eds.), *Behavior modification in clinical psychology* (pp. 178–220). New York: Appleton-Century-Crofts.

Kerr, S., & Slocum, J. W., Jr. (1981) Controlling the performance of people in organizations. In W. Starbuck & P. Nystrom (Eds.), *Handbook of organizations* (pp. 116–134). New York: Oxford University Press.

Kruglanski, A. W., Alon, S., & Lewis, T. (1972) Retrospective misattribution and task enjoyment. *Journal of Experimental Social Psychology*, 8, 493–501.

Langer, E. J. (1978) Rethinking the role of thought in social interaction. In J. H. Harvey, W. J. Ickes, & R. F. Kidd (Eds.), *New directions in attribution research* (Vol. 2, pp. 35–58). Hillsdale, NJ: Erlbaum.

Lawler, E. E. (1976) Control systems in organizations. In M. D. Dunnette (Ed.), *Handbook of industrial and organizational psychology* (pp. 1247–1291). Chicago: Rand-McNally.

Lawler, E. E., & Rhode, J. G. (1976) *Information and control in organizations.* Pacific Palisades, CA: Goodyear.

Lazarus, R. S. (1956) Subception: Fact or artifact? a reply to Eriksen. *Psychology Review, 63,* 343–347.

Lepper, M. R., & Greene, D. (1975) Turning play into work: Effects of adult surveillance and extrinsic rewards on children's intrinsic motivation. *Journal of Personality and Social Psychology, 31,* 479–486.

Lepper, M. R., Greene, D., & Nisbett, R. E. (1973) Undermining children's intrinsic interest with extrinsic rewards: A test of the overjustification hypothesis. *Journal of Personality and Social Psychology, 28,* 129–137.

Locke, E., Shaw, K., Saari, L., & Latham, G. (1981) Goal setting and task performance: 1969–1980. *Psychological Bulletin, 90,* 125–152.

Luthans, F., & Davis, T. (1979) Behavioral self-management (BSM): The missing link in managerial effectiveness. *Organizational Dynamics, 8,* 42–60.

Mahoney, M. J. (1974) *Cognition and behavior modification.* Cambridge: Ballinger.

Mahoney, M. J., & Arnkoff, D. B. (1978) Cognitive and self-control therapies. In S. L. Garfield & A. E. Borgin (Eds.), *Handbook of psychotherapy and therapy change* (pp. 689–722). New York: Wiley.

Mahoney, M. J., & Arnkoff, D. B. (1979) Self-management: Theory, research and application. In J. P. Brady & D. Pomerleau (Eds.), *Behavioral medicine: Theory and practice* (pp. 75–96). Baltimore: Williams and Williams.

Mahoney, M. J., & Thoresen, C. E. (Eds.) (1974) *Self-control: Power to the person.* Monterey, CA: Brooks/Cole.

Manz, C. C. (1979) Sources of control: A behavior modification perspective. *Proceedings: Eastern Academy of Management, 82*–88.

Manz, C. C. (1983a) *The art of self-leadership: Strategies for personal effectiveness in your life and work.* Englewood Cliffs, NJ: Prentice-Hall.

Manz, C. C. (1983b) Improving performance through self-leadership. *National Productivity Review, 2,* 288–297.

Manz, C. C., & Angle, H. L. (1985) *Does group self-management mean a loss of personal control? Triangulating on a paradox.* Paper presented at the annual meeting of the National Academy of Management, San Diego.

Manz, C. C., Mossholder, K. W., & Luthans, F. (in press) An integrated perspective of self-control in organizations. *Administration and Society.*

Manz, C. C., & Sims, H. P., Jr. (1980) Self-management as a substitute for leadership: A social learning theory perspective. *Academy of Management Review, 5,* 361–367.

Manz, C. C., & Sims, H. P., Jr. (1981) Vicarious learning: The influence of modeling on organizational behavior. *Academy of Management Review, 6,* 105–113.

Marshall, J. (1982) Organizational culture: Elements in its portraiture and some implications for organization functioning. *Group and Organization Studies, 7,* 367–384.

Marx, R. D. (1982) Relapse prevention of managerial training: A model for maintenance of behavior change. *Academy of Management Review, 7,* 433–441.

McGregor, D. (1960) *The human side of the enterprise.* New York: McGraw-Hill.

Meichenbaum, D. (1975) Self-instructional methods. In F. H. Kanfer & A. P. Goldstein (Eds.), *Helping people change.* (pp. 357–391). New York: Pergamon.

Meichenbaum, D., & Cameron, R. (1974) The clinical potential of modifying what clients say to themselves. In M. J. Mahoney & C. E. Thoresen (Eds.), *Self-control: Power to the person* (pp. 263–290). Monterey, CA: Brooks/Cole.

Mills, P. K. (1983) Self-management: Its control and relationship to other organizational properties. *Academy of Management Review, 8,* 445–453.

Mitchell, T. R., Green, S. G., & Wood, R. E. (1981) An attributional model of leadership and the poor performing subordinate: Development and validation. In B. Staw & L. Cummings (Eds.), *Research in organizational behavior* (Vol. 3, pp. 197–234). Greenwich, CT: JAI Press.

Mitchell, T. R., Larson, J. R., & Green, S. G. (1977) Leader behavior, situational moderators and group performance: An attributional analysis. *Organizational Behavior and Human Performance, 18,* 254–268.

Ouchi, W. G. (1981a) *Theory Z: How American business can meet the Japanese challenge.* Reading: MA: Addison-Wesley.

Ouchi, W. G. (1981b) Organizational paradigms: A commentary of Japanese management and theory Z organizations. *Organizational Dynamics, 10,* 36–43.

Ouchi, W. G., & Jaeger, A. M. (1978) Type Z organization: Stability in the midst of mobility. *Academy of Management Review, 3,* 305–313.

Ouchi, W. G., & Price, R. L. (1978) Hierarchies, clans and theory Z: A new perspective on organizational development. *Organizational Dynamics, 7,* 25–44.

Pascale, R. T., & Athos, A. G. (1981) *The art of Japanese management.* New York: Simon and Schuster.

Peale, N. V. (1956) *The power of positive thinking.* New York: Spire Books.

Peters, T. J., & Waterman, R. H., Jr. (1982) *In search of excellence: Lessons from America's best run companies.* New York: Harper & Row.

Pettigrew, A. M. (1979) On studying organizational cultures. *Administrative Science Quarterly, 24,* 570–581.

Phillips, J. S., & Lord, R. G. (1980) Determinants of intrinsic motivation: Locus of control and competence information as components of Deci's cognitive evaluation theory. *Journal of Applied Psychology, 65,* 211–218.

Powers, W. T. (1973a) *Behavior: The control of perception.* Chicago: Aldine.

Powers, W. T. (1973b) Feedback: Beyond behaviorism. *Science, 179,* 351–356.

Rychlak, J. F. (1979) *Discovering free will and personal responsibility.* New York: Oxford University Press.

Schank, R. C., & Abelson, R. P. (1977) *Scripts, plans, goals and understanding.* Hillsdale, NJ: Erlbaum.

Schelling, T. C. (1980) The intimate contest for self-command. *The Public Interest,* No. 60, 94–118.

Schneider, B. (1975) Organizational climates: An essay. *Personnel Psychology, 28,* 447–479.

Scott, W. E., Jr. (1975) The effects of extrinsic rewards on intrinsic motivation. A critique. *Organizational Behavior and Human Performance, 15,* 117–129.

Selye, H. (1974) *Stress without distress.* New York: Signet.

Sims, H. P., Jr., Szilagyi, A. D., & Keller, R. (1975) The measurement of job characteristics. *Academy of Management Journal, 19,* 195–212.

Staw, B. M. (1975) Attribution of the "causes" of performance: A general alternative interpretation of cross-sectional research on organizations. *Organizational Behavior and Human Performance, 13,* 414–432.

Sullivan, J. G. (1983) A critique of theory Z. *Academy of Management Review, 8,* 132–142.

Taylor, M. S., Fisher, C. D., & Ilgen, D. R. (1984) Individuals' reactions to performance feedback in organizations: A control theory perspective. In K. Rowland & G. Ferris (Eds.), *Research in personnel and human resources management,* (Vol. 2, pp. 81–124). JAI Press.

Taylor, S. E., & Crocker, J. (1981) Schematic bases of social information processing. In E. T. Higgins, C. P. Herman, & M. P. Zanna (Eds.), *Social cognition* (Vol. 1, pp. 89–134). Hillsdale, NJ: Erlbaum.

Tannenbaum, A. (1962) Control in organizations: Individual adjustment and organizational performance. *Administrative Science Quarterly, 1,* 236–257.

Thoresen, C. E., & Mahoney, M. J. (1974) *Behavioral self-control.* New York: Holt, Rinehart, and Winston.

White, R. W. (1959) Motivation reconsidered: The concept of competence. *Psychology Review, 66,* 297–333.

The Leader's New Work
Building Learning Organizations

P. M. Senge
Massachusetts Institute of Technology

H uman beings are designed for learning. No one has to teach an infant to walk, or talk, or master the spatial relationships needed to stack eight building blocks that don't topple. Children come fully equipped with an insatiable drive to explore and experiment. Unfortunately, the primary institutions of our society are oriented predominantly toward controlling rather than learning, rewarding individuals for performing for others rather than for cultivating their natural curiosity and impulse to learn. The young child entering school discovers quickly that the name of the game is getting the right answer and avoiding mistakes—a mandate no less compelling to the aspiring manager.

"Our prevailing system of management has destroyed our people," writes W. Edwards Deming, leader in the quality movement.[1] "People are born with intrinsic motivation, self-esteem, dignity, curiosity to learn, joy in learning. The forces of destruction begin with toddlers—a prize for the best Halloween costume, grades in school, gold stars, and on up through the university. On the job, people, teams, divisions are ranked—reward for the one at the top, punishment at the bottom. MBO, quotas, incentive pay, business plans, put together separately, division by division, cause further loss, unknown and unknowable."

Ironically, by focusing on performing for someone else's approval, corporations create the very conditions that predestine them to mediocre performance. Over the long run, superior performance depends on superior learning. A Shell study showed that, according to former planning director Arie de Geus, "a full one-third of the Fortune '500' industrials listed in 1970 had vanished by 1983."[2] Today, the average lifetime of the largest industrial enterprises is probably less than *half* the average lifetime of a person in an industrial society. On the other hand, de Geus and his colleagues at Shell also found a small number of companies that survived for seventy-five years or longer. Interestingly, the key to their survival was the ability to run "experiments in the margin," to continually explore new business and organizational opportunities that create potential new sources of growth.

If anything, the need for understanding how organizations learn and accelerating that learning is greater today than ever before. The old days when a Henry Ford, Alfred Sloan, or Tom Watson *learned for the organization* are gone. In an increasingly dynamic, interdependent, and unpredictable world, it is simply no longer possible for anyone to "figure it all out at the top." The old model, "the top thinks and the local acts," must now give way to integrating thinking and acting at all levels. While the challenge is great, so is the potential payoff. "The person who figures out how to harness the collective genius of the people in his or her organization," according to former Citibank CEO Walter Wriston, "is going to blow the competition away."

Adaptive Learning and Generative Learning

The prevailing view of learning organizations emphasizes increased adaptability. Given the accelerating pace of change, or so the standard view goes, "the most successful corporation of the 1990s," according to *Fortune* magazine, "will be something called a learning organization, a consummately adaptive enterprise."[3] As the Shell study shows, examples of traditional authoritarian bureaucracies that responded too slowly to survive in changing business environments are legion.

But increasing adaptiveness is only the first stage in moving toward learning organizations. The impulse to learn in children goes deeper than desires to respond and adapt more effectively to environmental change. The impulse to learn, at its heart, is an impulse to be generative, to expand our capability. This is why leading corporations are focusing on *generative* learning, which is about creating, as well as *adaptive* learning, which is about coping.[4]

The total quality movement in Japan illustrates the evolution from adaptive to generative learning. With its emphasis on continuous experimentation and feedback, the total quality movement has been the first wave in building learning organizations. But Japanese firms' view of serving the customer has evolved. In the early years of total quality, the focus was on "fitness to standard," making a product reliably so that it would do what its designers intended it to do and what the firm told its customers it would do. Then came a focus on "fitness to need," understanding better what the customer wanted and then providing products that reliably met those needs. Today, leading edge firms seek to understand and meet the "latent need" of the customer—what customers might truly value but have never experienced or would never think to ask for. As one Detroit executive commented recently, "You could never produce the Mazda Miata solely from market research. It required a leap of imagination to see what the customer *might* want."[5]

Generative learning, unlike adaptive learning, requires

Source: Reprinted from "The Leader's New Work: Building Learning Organizations," by P. M. Senge, *Sloan Management Review*, (32, 1, 1990) by the Sloan Management Review Association. All rights reserved. Author affiliation may have changed since article was first published.

new ways of looking at the world, whether in understanding customers or in understanding how to better manage a business. For years, U.S. manufacturers sought competitive advantage in aggressive controls on inventories, incentives against overproduction, and rigid adherence to production forecasts. Despite these incentives, their performance was eventually eclipsed by Japanese firms who saw the challenges of manufacturing differently. They realized that eliminating delays in the production process was the key to reducing instability and improving cost, productivity, and service. They worked to build networks of relationships with trusted suppliers and to redesign physical production processes so as to reduce delays in materials procurement, production set up, and in-process inventory—a much higher-leverage approach to improving both cost and customer loyalty.

As Boston Consulting Group's George Stalk has observed, the Japanese saw the significance of delays because they saw the process of order entry, production scheduling, materials procurement, production, and distribution *as an integrated system.* "What distorts the system so badly is time," observed Stalk—the multiple delays between events and responses. "These distortions reverberate throughout the system, producing disruptions, waste, and inefficiency."[6] Generative learning requires seeing the systems that control events. When we fail to grasp the systemic source of problems, we are left to "push on" symptoms rather than eliminate underlying causes. The best we can ever do is adaptive learning.

The Leader's New Work

"I talk with people all over the country about learning organizations, and the response is always very positive," says William O'Brien, CEO of the Hanover Insurance companies. "If this type of organization is so widely preferred, why don't people create such organizations? I think the answer is leadership. People have no real comprehension of the type of commitment it requires to build such an organization."[7]

Our traditional view of leaders—as special people who set the direction, make the key decisions, and energize the troops—is deeply rooted in an individualistic and nonsystemic worldview. Especially in the West, leaders are *heroes*—great men (and occasionally women) who rise to the fore in times of crisis. So long as such myths prevail, they reinforce a focus on short-term events and charismatic heroes rather than on systemic forces and collective learning.

Leadership in learning organizations centers on subtler and ultimately more important work. In a learning organization, leaders' roles differ dramatically from that of the charismatic decision maker. Leaders are designers, teachers, and stewards. These roles require new skills: the ability to build shared vision, to bring to the surface and challenge prevailing mental models, and to foster more systemic patterns of thinking. In short, leaders in learning organizations are responsible for *building organizations* where people are continually expanding their capabilities to shape their future—that is, leaders are responsible for learning.

Creative Tension: The Integrating Principle

Leadership in a learning organization starts with the principle of creative tension.[8] Creative tension comes from seeing clearly where we want to be, our "vision," and telling the truth about where we are, our "current reality." The gap between the two generates a natural tension (see Figure 1).

Creative tension can be resolved in two basic ways: by raising current reality toward the vision, or by lowering the vision toward current reality. Individuals, groups, and organizations who learn how to work with creative tension learn how to use the energy it generates to move reality more reliably toward their visions.

The principle of creative tension has long been recognized by leaders. Martin Luther King, Jr., once said, "Just as Socrates felt that it was necessary to create a tension in the mind, so that individuals could rise from the bondage of myths and half truths . . . so must we . . . create the kind of tension in society that will help men rise from the dark depths of prejudice and racism."[9]

Without vision there is no creative tension. Creative tension cannot be generated from current reality alone. All the analysis in the world will never generate a vision. Many who are otherwise qualified to lead fail to do so because they try to substitute analysis for vision. They believe that, if only people understood current reality, they would surely feel the motivation to change. They are then disappointed to discover that people "resist" the personal and organizational changes that must be made to alter reality. What they never grasp is that the natural energy for changing reality comes from holding a picture of what might be that is more important to people than what is.

But creative tension cannot be generated from vision alone; it demands an accurate picture of current reality as well. Just as King had a dream, so too did he continually strive to "dramatize the shameful conditions" of racism and prejudice so that they could no longer be ignored. Vision without an understanding of current reality will more likely foster cynicism than creativity. The principle of creative ten-

F I G U R E   1
The Principle of Creative Tension

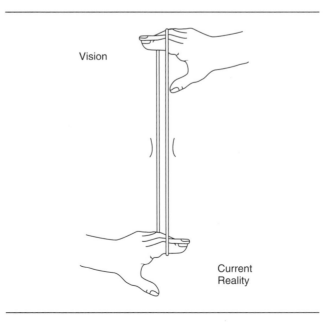

Vision

Current Reality

sion teaches that *an accurate picture of current reality is just as important as a compelling picture of a desired future.*

Leading through creative tension is different than solving problems. In problem solving, the energy for change comes from attempting to get away from an aspect of current reality that is undesirable. With creative tension, the energy for change comes from the vision, from what we want to create, juxtaposed with current reality. While the distinction may seem small, the consequences are not. Many people and organizations find themselves motivated to change only when their problems are bad enough to cause them to change. This works for a while, but the change process runs out of steam as soon as the problems driving the change become less pressing. With problem solving, the motivation for change is extrinsic. With creative tension, the motivation is intrinsic. This distinction mirrors the distinction between adaptive and generative learning.

New Roles

The traditional authoritarian image of the leader as "the boss calling the shots" has been recognized as oversimplified and inadequate for some time. According to Edgar Schein, "Leadership is intertwined with culture formation." Building an organization's culture and shaping its evolution is the "unique and essential function" of leadership.[10] In a learning organization, the critical roles of leadership—designer, teacher, and steward—have antecedents in the ways leaders have contributed to building organizations in the past. But each role takes on new meaning in the learning organization and, as will be seen in the following sections, demands new skills and tools.

Leader as Designer

Imagine that your organization is an ocean liner and that you are "the leader." What is your role?

I have asked this question of groups of managers many times. The most common answer, not surprisingly, is "the captain." Others say, "The navigator, setting the direction." Still others say, "The helmsman, actually controlling the direction," or, "The engineer down there stoking the fire, providing energy," or, "The social director, making sure everybody's enrolled, involved, and communicating." While these are legitimate leadership roles, there is another which, in many ways, eclipses them all in importance. Yet rarely does anyone mention it.

The neglected leadership role is the *designer* of the ship. No one has a more sweeping influence than the designer. What good does it do for the captain to say, "Turn starboard 30 degrees," when the designer has built a rudder that will only turn to port, or which takes six hours to turn to starboard? It's fruitless to be the leader in an organization that is poorly designed.

The functions of design, or what some have called "social architecture," are rarely visible; they take place behind the scenes. The consequences that appear today are the result of work done long in the past, and work today will show its benefits far in the future. Those who aspire to lead out of a desire to control, or gain fame, or simply to be at the center of the action, will find little to attract them to the quiet design work of leadership.

But what, specifically, is involved in organizational design? "Organization design is widely misconstrued as moving around boxes and lines," says Hanover's O'Brien. "The first task of organization design concerns designing the governing ideas of purpose, vision, and core values by which people will live." Few acts of leadership have a more enduring impact on an organization than building a foundation of purpose and core values.

In 1982, Johnson & Johnson found itself facing a corporate nightmare when bottles of its best-selling Tylenol were tampered with, resulting in several deaths. The corporation's immediate response was to pull all Tylenol off the shelves of retail outlets. Thirty-one million capsules were destroyed, even though they were tested and found safe. Although the immediate cost was significant, no other action was possible given the firm's credo. Authored almost forty years earlier by president Robert Wood Johnson, Johnson & Johnson's credo states that permanent success is possible only when modern industry realizes that:

- service to its customers comes first;
- service to its employees and management comes second;
- service to the community comes third; and
- service to its stockholders, last.

Such statements might seem like motherhood and apple pie to those who have not seen the way a clear sense of purpose and values can affect key business decisions. Johnson & Johnson's crisis management in this case was based on that credo. It was simple, it was right, and it worked.

If governing ideas constitute the first design task of leadership, the second design task involves the policies, strategies, and structures that translate guiding ideas into business decisions. Leadership theorist Philip Selznick calls policy and structure the "institutional embodiment of purpose."[11] "Policy making (the rules that guide decisions) ought to be separated from decision making," says Jay Forrester.[12] "Otherwise, short-term pressures will usurp time from policy creation."

Traditionally, writers like Selznick and Forrester have tended to see policy making and implementation as the work of a small number of senior managers. But that view is changing. Both the dynamic business environment and the mandate of the learning organization to engage people at all levels now make it clear that this second design task is more subtle. Henry Mintzberg has argued that strategy is less a rational plan arrived at in the abstract and implemented throughout the organization than an "emergent phenomenon." Successful organizations "craft strategy" according to Mintzberg, as they continually learn about shifting business conditions and balance what is desired and what is possible.[13] The key is not getting the right strategy but fostering strategic thinking. "The choice of individual action is only part of . . . the policymaker's need," according to Mason and Mitroff.[14] "More important is the need to achieve insight into the nature of the complexity and to formulate concepts and world views for coping with it."

Behind appropriate policies, strategies, and structures are effective learning processes; their creation is the third key design responsibility in learning organizations. This does not absolve senior managers of their strategic responsibilities.

Actually, it deepens and extends those responsibilities. Now, they are not only responsible for ensuring that an organization have well-developed strategies and policies, but also for ensuring that processes exist whereby these are continually improved.

In the early 1970s, Shell was the weakest of the big seven oil companies. Today, Shell and Exxon are arguably the strongest, both in size and financial health. Shell's ascendance began with frustration. Around 1971 members of Shell's "Group Planning" in London began to foresee dramatic change and unpredictability in world oil markets. However, it proved impossible to persuade managers that the stable world of steady growth in oil demand and supply they had known for twenty years was about to change. Despite brilliant analysis and artful presentation, Shell's planners realized, in the words of Pierre Wack, that they "had failed to change behavior in much of the Shell organization."[15] Progress would probably have ended there, had the frustration not given way to a radically new view of corporate planning.

As they pondered this failure, the planners' view of their basic task shifted: "We no longer saw our task as producing a documented view of the future business environment five or ten years ahead. Our real target was the microcosm (the 'mental model') of our decision makers." Only when the planners reconceptualized their basic task as fostering learning rather than devising plans did their insights begin to have an impact. The initial tool used was "scenario analysis," through which planners encouraged operating managers to think through how they would manage in the future under different possible scenarios. It mattered not that the managers believed the planners' scenarios absolutely, only that they became engaged in ferreting out the implications. In this way, Shell's planners conditioned managers to be mentally prepared for a shift from low prices to high prices and from stability to instability. The results were significant. When OPEC became a reality, Shell quickly responded by increasing local operating company control (to enhance maneuverability in the new political environment), building buffer stocks, and accelerating development of non-OPEC sources—actions that its competitors took much more slowly or not at all.

Somewhat inadvertently, Shell planners had discovered the leverage of designing institutional learning processes, whereby, in the words of former planning director de Geus, "Management teams change their shared mental models of their company, their markets, and their competitors."[16] Since then, "planning as learning" has become a byword at Shell, and Group Planning has continually sought out new learning tools that can be integrated into the planning process. Some of these are described below.

Leader as Teacher

"The first responsibility of a leader," writes retired Herman Miller CEO Max de Pree, "is to define reality."[17] Much of the leverage leaders can actually exert lies in helping people achieve more accurate, more insightful, and more *empowering* views of reality.

Leader as teacher does *not* mean leader as authoritarian expert whose job it is to teach people the "correct" view of reality. Rather, it is about helping everyone in the organization, oneself included, to gain more insightful views of current reality. This is in line with a popular emerging view of leaders as coaches, guides, or facilitators.[18] In learning organizations, this teaching role is developed further by virtue of explicit attention to people's mental models and by the influence of the systems perspective.

The role of leader as teacher starts with bringing to the surface people's mental models of important issues. No one carries an organization, a market, or a state of technology in his or her head. What we carry in our heads are assumptions. These mental pictures of how the world works have a significant influence on how we perceive problems and opportunities, identify courses of action, and make choices.

One reason that mental models are so deeply entrenched is that they are largely tacit. Ian Mitroff, in his study of General Motors, argues that an assumption that prevailed for years was that, in the United States, "Cars are status symbols. Styling is therefore more important than quality."[19] The Detroit automakers didn't say, "We have a *mental model* that all people care about is styling." Few actual managers would even say publicly that all people care about is styling. So long as the view remained unexpressed, there was little possibility of challenging its validity or forming more accurate assumptions.

But working with mental models goes beyond revealing hidden assumptions. "Reality," as perceived by most people in most organizations, means pressures that must be borne, crises that must be reacted to, and limitations that must be accepted. Leaders as teachers help people *restructure their views of reality* to see beyond the superficial conditions and events into the underlying causes of problems—and therefore to see new possibilities for shaping the future.

Specifically, leaders can influence people to view reality at three distinct levels: events, patterns of behavior, and systemic structure.

Systemic Structure
(Generative)
↓
Patterns of Behavior
(Responsive)
↓
Events
(Reactive)

The key question becomes *where do leaders predominantly focus their own and their organization's attention?*

Contemporary society focuses predominantly on events. The media reinforces this perspective, with almost exclusive attention to short-term, dramatic events. This focus leads naturally to explaining what happens in terms of those events: "The Dow Jones average went up sixteen points because high fourth-quarter profits were announced yesterday."

Pattern-of-behavior explanations are rarer, in contemporary culture, than event explanations, but they do occur. "Trend analysis" is an example of seeing patterns of behavior. A good editorial that interprets a set of current events in the context of long-term historical changes is another example. Systemic, structural explanations go even further by addressing the question, "What causes the patterns of behavior?"

In some sense, all three levels of explanation are equally true. But their usefulness is quite different. Even explanations—who did what to whom—doom their holders to a reactive stance toward change. Pattern-of-behavior explanations focus on identifying long-term trends and assessing their implications. They at least suggest how, over time, we can respond to shifting conditions. Structural explanations are the most powerful. Only they address the underlying causes of behavior at a level such that patterns of behavior can be changed.

By and large, leaders of our current institutions focus their attention on events and patterns of behavior, and, under their influence, their organizations do likewise. That is why contemporary organizations are predominantly reactive, or at best responsive—rarely generative. On the other hand, leaders in learning organizations pay attention to all three levels, but focus especially on systemic structure; largely by example, they teach people throughout the organization to do likewise.

Leader as Steward

This is the subtlest role of leadership. Unlike the roles of designer and teacher, it is almost solely a matter of attitude. It is an attitude critical to learning organizations.

While stewardship has long been recognized as an aspect of leadership, its source is still not widely understood. I believe Robert Greenleaf came closest to explaining real stewardship, in his seminal book *Servant Leadership*.[20] There, Greenleaf argues that "the servant leader *is* servant first. . . . It begins with the natural feeling that one wants to serve, to serve *first*. This conscious choice brings one to aspire to lead. That person is sharply different from one who is leader first, perhaps because of the need to assuage an unusual power drive or to acquire material possessions."

Leaders' sense of stewardship operates on two levels: stewardship for the people they lead and stewardship for the larger purpose or mission that underlies the enterprise. The first type arises from a keen appreciation of the impact one's leadership can have on others. People can suffer economically, emotionally, and spiritually under inept leadership. If anything, people in a learning organization are more vulnerable because of their commitment and sense of shared ownership. Appreciating this naturally instills a sense of responsibility in leaders. The second type of stewardship arises from a leader's sense of personal purpose and commitment to the organization's larger mission. People's natural impulse to learn is unleashed when they are engaged in an endeavor they consider worthy of their fullest commitment. Or, as Lawrence Miller puts it, "Achieving return on equity does not, as a goal, mobilize the most noble forces of our soul."[21]

Leaders engaged in building learning organizations naturally feel part of a larger purpose that goes beyond their organization. They are part of changing the way businesses operate, not from a vague philanthropic urge, but from a conviction that their efforts will produce more productive organizations, capable of achieving higher levels of organizational success and personal satisfaction than more traditional organizations. Their sense of stewardship was succinctly captured by George Bernard Shaw when he said,

---

This is the true joy in life, the being used for a purpose you consider a mighty one, the being a force of nature rather than a feverish, selfish clod of ailments and grievances complaining that the world will not devote itself to making you happy.

New Skills

New leadership roles require new leadership skills. These skills can only be developed, in my judgment, through a life-long commitment. It is not enough for one or two individuals to develop these skills. They must be distributed widely throughout the organization. This is one reason that understanding the *disciplines* of a learning organization is so important. These disciplines embody the principles and practices that can widely foster leadership and development.

Three critical areas of skills (disciplines) are building shared vision, surfacing and challenging mental models, and engaging in systems thinking.[22]

Building Shared Vision

How do individual visions come together to create shared visions? A useful metaphor is the hologram, the three-dimensional image created by interacting light sources.

If you cut a photograph in half, each half shows only part of the whole image. But if you divide a hologram, each part, no matter how small, shows the whole image intact. Likewise, when a group of people come to share a vision for an organization, each person sees an individual picture of the organization at its best. Each shares responsibility for the whole, not just for one piece. But the component pieces of the hologram are not identical. Each represents the whole image from a different point of view. It's something like poking holes in a window shade; each hole offers a unique angle for viewing the whole image. So, too, is each individual's vision unique.

When you add up the pieces of a hologram, something interesting happens. The image becomes more intense, more lifelike. When more people come to share a vision, the vision becomes more real in the sense of a mental reality that people can truly imagine achieving. They now have partners, co-creators; the vision no longer rests on their shoulders alone. Early on, when they are nurturing an individual vision, people may say it is "my vision." But, as the shared vision develops, it becomes both "my vision" and "our vision."

The skills involved in building shared vision include the following:

Encouraging Personal Vision. Shared visions emerge from personal visions. It is not that people only care about their own self-interest—in fact, people's values usually include dimensions that concern family, organization, community, and even the world. Rather, it is that people's capacity for caring is *personal*.

Communicating and Asking for Support. Leaders must be willing to continually share their own vision, rather than being the official representative of the corporate vision. They also must be prepared to ask, "Is this vision worthy of your commitment?" This can be difficult for a person used to setting goals and presuming compliance.

Visioning as an Ongoing Process.   Building shared vision is a never-ending process. At any one point there will be a particular image of the future that is predominant, but that image will evolve. Today, too many managers want to dispense with the "vision business" by going off and writing the Official Vision Statement. Such statements almost always lack the vitality, freshness, and excitement of a genuine vision that comes from people asking, "What do we really want to achieve?"

Blending Extrinsic and Intrinsic Visions.   Many energizing visions are extrinsic—that is, they focus on achieving something relative to an outsider, such as a competitor. But a goal that is limited to defeating an opponent can, once the vision is achieved, easily become a defensive posture. In contrast, intrinsic goals like creating a new type of product, taking an established product to a new level, or setting a new standard for customer satisfaction can call forth a new level of creativity and innovation. Intrinsic and extrinsic visions need to coexist; a vision solely predicated on defeating an adversary will eventually weaken an organization.

Distinguishing Positive from Negative Visions.   Many organizations only truly pull together when their survival is threatened. Similarly, most social movements aim at eliminating what people don't want: for example, antidrugs, antismoking, or antinuclear arms movements. Negative visions carry a subtle message of powerlessness: people will only pull together when there is sufficient threat. Negative visions also tend to be short term. Two fundamental sources of energy can motivate organizations: fear and aspiration. Fear, the energy source behind negative visions, can produce extraordinary changes in short periods, but aspiration endures as a continuing source of learning and growth.

Surfacing and Testing Mental Models

Many of the best ideas in organizations never get put into practice. One reason is that new insights and initiatives often conflict with established mental models. The leadership task of challenging assumptions without invoking defensiveness requires reflection and inquiry skills possessed by few leaders in traditional controlling organizations.[23]

Seeing Leaps of Abstraction.   Our minds literally move at lightning speed. Ironically, this often slows our learning, because we leap to generalizations so quickly that we never think to test them. We then confuse our generalizations with the observable data upon which they are based, treating the generalizations *as if they were data*. The frustrated sales rep reports to the home office that "customers don't really care about quality; price is what matters," when what actually happened was that three consecutive large customers refused to place an order unless a larger discount was offered. The sales rep treats her generalization, "customers care only about price," as if it were absolute fact rather than an as-

sumption (very likely an assumption reflecting her own views of customers and the market). This thwarts future learning because she starts to focus on how to offer attractive discounts rather than probing behind the customers' statements. For example, the customers may have been so disgruntled with the firm's delivery or customer service that they are unwilling to purchase again without larger discounts.

Balancing Inquiry and Advocacy.   Most managers are skilled at articulating their views and presenting them persuasively. While important, advocacy skills can become counterproductive as managers rise in responsibility and confront increasingly complex issues that require collaborative learning among different, equally knowledgeable people. Leaders in learning organizations need to have both inquiry *and* advocacy skills.[24]

Specifically, when advocating a view, they need to be able to:

- explain the reasoning and data that led to their view;
- encourage others to test their view (e.g., Do you see gaps in my reasoning? Do you disagree with the data upon which my view is based?); and
- encourage others to provide different views (e.g., Do you have either different data, different conclusions, or both?).

When inquiring into another's views, they need to:

- actively seek to understand the other's view, rather than simply restating their own view and how it differs from the other's view; and
- make their attributions about the other and the other's view explicit (e.g., Based on your statement that . . . ; I am assuming that you believe . . . ; Am I representing your views fairly?).

If they reach an impasse (others no longer appear open to inquiry), they need to:

- ask what data or logic might unfreeze the impasse, or if an experiment (or some other inquiry) might be designed to provide new information.

Distinguishing Espoused Theory from Theory in Use.
We all like to think that we hold certain views, but often our actions reveal deeper views. For example, I may proclaim that people are trustworthy, but never lend friends money and jealously guard my possessions. Obviously, my deeper mental model (my theory in use), differs from my espoused theory. Recognizing gaps between espoused views and theories in use (which often requires the help of others) can be pivotal to deeper learning.

Recognizing and Defusing Defensive Routines.   As one CEO in our research program puts it, "Nobody ever talks about an issue at the 8:00 business meeting exactly the same way they talk about it at home that evening or over drinks at the end of the day." The reason is what Chris Argyris calls "defensive routines," entrenched habits used to protect ourselves from the embarrassment and threat that come with exposing our thinking. For most of us, such defenses began to build early in life in response to pressures to have the right answers in school or at home. Organizations add new levels of performance anxiety and thereby amplify and exacerbate this defensiveness. Ironically, this makes it even more difficult to expose hidden mental models, and thereby lessens learning.

The first challenge is to recognize defensive routines, then to inquire into their operation. Those who are best at revealing and defusing defensive routines operate with a high degree of self-disclosure regarding their own defensiveness (e.g., I notice that I am feeling uneasy about how this conversation is going. Perhaps I don't understand it or it is threatening to me in ways I don't yet see. Can you help me see this better?)

Systems Thinking

We all know that leaders should help people see the big picture. But the actual skills whereby leaders are supposed to achieve this are not well understood. In my experience, successful leaders often *are* "systems thinkers" to a considerable extent. They focus less on day-to-day events and more on underlying trends and forces of change. But they do this almost completely intuitively. The consequence is that they are often unable to explain their intuitions to others and feel frustrated that others cannot see the world the way they do.

One of the most significant developments in management science today is the gradual coalescence of managerial systems thinking as a field of study and practice. This field suggests some key skills for future leaders:

Seeing Interrelationships, Not Things, and Processes, Not Snapshots.   Most of us have been conditioned throughout our lives to focus on things and to see the world in static images. This leads us to linear explanations of systemic phenomenon. For instance, in an arms race each party is convinced that the other is *the cause* of problems. They react to each new move as an isolated event, not as part of a process. So long as they fail to see the interrelationships of these actions, they are trapped.

Moving beyond Blame.   We tend to blame each other or outside circumstances for our problems. But it is poorly designed systems, not incompetent or unmotivated individuals, that cause most organizational problems. Systems thinking shows us that there is no outside—that you and the cause of your problems are part of a single system.

Distinguishing Detail Complexity from Dynamic Complexity.   Some types of complexity are more important strategically than others. Detail complexity arises when there are many variables. Dynamic complexity arises when cause and effect are distant in time and space and when the consequences over time of interventions are subtle and not obvious to many participants in the system. The leverage in most management situations lies in understanding dynamic complexity, not detail complexity.

Focusing on Areas of High Leverage.   Some have called systems thinking the "new dismal science" because it teaches

that most obvious solutions don't work—at best, they improve matters in the short run, only to make things worse in the long run. But there is another side to the story. Systems thinking also shows that small, well-focused actions can produce significant, enduring improvements, if they are in the right place. Systems thinkers refer to this idea as the principle of "leverage." Tackling a difficult problem is often a matter of seeing where the high leverage lies, where a change—with a minimum of effort—would lead to lasting, significant improvement.

Avoiding Symptomatic Solutions.   The pressures to intervene in management systems that are going awry can be overwhelming. Unfortunately, given the linear thinking that predominates in most organizations, interventions usually focus on symptomatic fixes, not underlying causes. This results in only temporary relief, and it tends to create still more pressures later on for further, low-leverage intervention. If leaders acquiesce to these pressures, they can be sucked into an endless spiral of increasing intervention. Sometimes the most difficult leadership acts are to refrain from intervening through popular quick fixes and to keep the pressure on everyone to identify more enduring solutions.

While leaders who can articulate systemic explanations are rare, those who *can* will leave their stamp on an organization. One person who had this gift was Bill Gore, the founder and long-time CEO of W.L. Gore and Associates (makers of Gore-Tex and other synthetic fiber products). Bill Gore was adept at telling stories that showed how the organization's core values of freedom and individual responsibility required particular operating policies. He was proud of his egalitarian organization, in which there were (and still are) no "employees," only "associates," all of whom own shares in the company and participate in its management. At one talk, he explained the company's policy of controlled growth: "Our limitation is not financial resources. Our limitation is the rate at which we can bring in new associates. Our experience has been that if we try to bring in more than a 25 percent per year increase, we begin to bog down. Twenty-five percent per year growth is a real limitation; you can do much better than that with an authoritarian organization." As Gore tells the story, one of the associates, Esther Baum, went home after this talk and reported the limitation to her husband. As it happened, he was an astronomer and mathematician at Lowell Observatory. He said, "That's a very interesting figure." He took out a pencil and paper and calculated and said, "Do you realize that in only fifty-seven and a half years, everyone in the world will be working for Gore?"

Through this story, Gore explains the systemic rationale behind a key policy, limited growth rate—a policy that undoubtedly caused a lot of stress in the organization. He suggests that, at larger rates of growth, the adverse effects of attempting to integrate too many new people too rapidly would begin to dominate. (This is the "limits to growth" systems archetype explained below.) The story also reaffirms the organization's commitment to creating a unique environment for its associates and illustrates the types of sacrifices that the firm is prepared to make in order to remain true to its vision. The last part of the story shows that, despite the self-imposed limit, the company is still very much a growth company.

The consequences of leaders who lack systems thinking

skills can be devastating. Many charismatic leaders manage almost exclusively at the level of events. They deal in visions and in crises, and little in between. Under their leadership, an organization hurtles from crisis to crisis. Eventually, the worldview of people in the organization becomes dominated by events and reactiveness. Many, especially those who are deeply commited, become burned out. Eventually, cynicism comes to pervade the organization. People have no control over their time, let alone their destiny.

Similar problems arise with the "visionary strategist," the leader with vision who sees both patterns of change and events. This leader is better prepared to manage change. He or she can explain strategies in terms of emerging trends and thereby foster a climate that is less reactive. But such leaders still impart a responsive orientation rather than a generative one.

Many talented leaders have rich, highly systemic intuitions but cannot explain those intuitions to others. Ironically, they often end up being authoritarian leaders, even if they don't want to, because only they see the decisions that need to be made. They are unable to conceptualize their strategic insights so that these can become public knowledge, open to challenge and further improvement.

New Tools

Developing the skills described above requires new tools—tools that will enhance leaders' conceptual abilities and foster communication and collaborative inquiry. What follows is a sampling of tools starting to find use in learning organizations.

Systems Archetypes

One of the insights of the budding, managerial systems-thinking field is that certain types of systemic structures recur again and again. Countless systems grow for a period, then encounter problems and cease to grow (or even collapse) well before they have reached intrinsic limits to growth. Many other systems get locked in runaway vicious spirals where every actor has to run faster and faster to stay in the same place. Still others lure individual actors into doing what seems right locally, yet which eventually causes suffering for all.[25]

Some of the system archetypes that have the broadest relevance include:

Balancing Process with Delay. In this archetype, decision makers fail to appreciate the time delays involved as they move toward a goal. As a result, they overshoot the goal and may even produce recurring cycles. Classic example: Real estate developers who keep starting new projects until the market has gone soft, by which time an eventual glut is guaranteed by the properties still under construction.

Limits to Growth. A reinforcing cycle of growth grinds to a halt, and may even reverse itself, as limits are approached. The limits can be resource constraints, or external or internal responses to growth. Classic examples: Product life cycles that peak prematurely due to poor quality or service, the growth and decline of communication in a management team, and the spread of a new movement.

Shifting the Burden. A short-term "solution" is used to correct a problem, with seemingly happy immediate results. As this correction is used more and more, fundamental long-term corrective measures are used less. Over time, the mechanisms of the fundamental solution may atrophy or become disabled, leading to even greater reliance on the symptomatic solution. Classic example: Using corporate human resource staff to solve local personnel problems, thereby keeping managers from developing their own interpersonal skills.

Eroding Goals. When all else fails, lower your standards. This is like "shifting the burden," except that the short-term solution involves letting a fundamental goal, such as quality standards or employee morale standards, atrophy. Classic example: A company that responds to delivery problems by continually upping its quoted delivery times.

Escalation. Two people or two organizations, who each see their welfare as depending on a relative advantage over the other, continually react to the other's advances. Whenever one side gets ahead, the other is threatened, leading it to act more aggressively to reestablish its advantage, which threatens the first, and so on. Classic examples: Arms race, gang warfare, price wars.

Tragedy of the Commons.[26] Individuals keep intensifying their use of a commonly available but limited resource until all individuals start to experience severely diminishing returns. Classic examples: Sheepherders who keep increasing their flocks until they overgraze the common pasture; divisions in a firm that share a common salesforce and compete for the use of sale reps by upping their sales targets, until the salesforce burns out from overextension.

Growth and Underinvestment. Rapid growth approaches a limit that could be eliminated or pushed into the future, but only by aggressive investment in physical and human capacity. Eroding goals or standards cause investment that is too weak or too slow and customers get increasingly unhappy slowing demand growth and thereby making the needed investment apparently unnecessary or impossible. Classic example: Countless once-successful growth firms that allowed product or service quality to erode, and were unable to generate enough revenues to invest in remedies.

The Archetype template is a specific tool that is helping managers identify archetypes operating in their own strategic areas (see Figure 2).[27] The template shows the basic structural form of the archetype but lets managers fill in the variables of their own situation. For example, the shifting the burden template involves two balancing processes ("B") that compete for control of a problem symptom. The upper, symptomatic solution provides a short-term fix that will make the problem symptom go away for a while. The lower, fundamental solution provides a more enduring solution. The side effect feedback ("R") around the outside of the diagram identifies unintended exacerbating effects of the symptomatic solution, which, over time, make it more and more difficult to invoke the fundamental solution.

Several years ago, a team of managers from a leading consumer goods producer used the shifting the burden archetype in a revealing way. The problem they focused on was

F I G U R E   2
"Shifting the Burden" Archetype Template

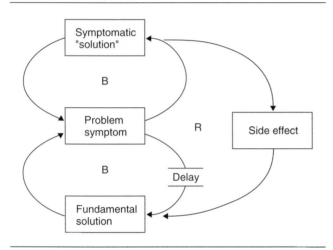

In the "shifting the burden" template, two balancing processes (B) compete for control of a problem symptom. Both solutions affect the symptom, but only the fundamental solution treats the cause. The symptomatic "solution" creates the additional side effect (R) of deferring the fundamental solution, making it harder and harder to achieve.

financial stress, which could be dealt with in two different ways: by running marketing promotions (the symptomatic solution) or by production innovation (the fundamental solution). Marketing promotions were fast. The company was expert in their design and implementation. The results were highly predictable. Product innovation was slow and much less predictable, and the company had a history over the past ten years of product-innovation mismanagement. Yet only through innovation could they retain a leadership position in their industry, which had slid over the past ten to twenty years. What the managers saw clearly was that the more skillful they became at promotions, they more they shifted the burden away from product innovation. But what really struck home was when one member identified the unintended side effect: the last three CEOs had all come from advertising function, which had become the politically dominant function in the corporation, thereby institutionalizing the symptomatic solution. Unless the political values shifted back toward product and process innovation, the managers realized, the firm's decline would accelerate—which is just the shift that has happened over the past several years.

Charting Strategic Dilemmas

Management teams typically come unglued when confronted with core dilemmas. A classic example was the way U.S. manufacturers faced the low-cost, high-quality choice. For years, most assumed that it was necessary to choose between the two. Not surprisingly, given the short-term pressures perceived by most managements, the prevailing choice was low cost. Firms that chose high quality usually perceived themselves as aiming exclusively for a high quality, high price market niche. The consequences of this perceived

either-or choice have been disastrous, even fatal, as U.S. manufacturers have encountered increasingly international competition from firms that have chosen to consistently improve quality *and* cost.

In a recent book, Charles Hampden-Turner presented a variety of tools for helping management teams confront strategic dilemmas creatively.[28] He summarizes the process in seven steps:

Eliciting the Dilemmas.   Identifying the opposed values that form the "horns" of the dilemma, for example, cost as opposed to quality, or local initiative as opposed to central coordination and control. Hampden-Turner suggests that humor can be a distinct asset in this process since "the admission that dilemmas even exist tends to be difficult for some companies."

Mapping.   Locating the opposing values as two axes and helping managers identify where they see themselves, or their organization, along the axes.

Processing.   Getting rid of nouns to describe the axes of the dilemma. Present participles formed by adding "ing" convert rigid nouns into processes that imply movement. For example, central control versus local control becomes "strengthening national office" and "growing local initiatives." This loosens the bond of implied opposition between the two values. For example, it becomes possible to think of "strengthening national services from which local branches can benefit."

Framing/Contextualizing.   Further softening the adversarial structure among different values by letting "each side in turn be the frame or context for the other." This shifting of the "figure-ground" relationship undermines any implicit attempts to hold one value as intrinsically superior to the other, and thereby to become mentally closed to creative strategies for continuous improvement of both.

Sequencing.   Breaking the hold of static thinking. Very often, values like low cost and high quality appear to be in opposition because we think in terms of a point in time, not in terms of an on-going process. For example, a strategy of investing in new process technology and developing a new production-floor culture of worker responsibility may take time and money in the near term, yet reap significant long-term financial rewards.

Waving/Cycling.   Sometimes the strategic path toward improving both values involves cycles where both values will get "worse" for a time. Yet, at a deeper level, learning is occurring that will cause the next cycle to be at a higher plateau for both values.

Synergizing.   Achieving synergy where significant improvement is occurring along all axes of all relevant dilemmas. (This is the ultimate goal, of course.) Synergy, as Hampden-Turner points out, is a uniquely systemic notion, coming from the Greek *syn-ergo* or "work together."

"The Left-Hand Column": Surfacing Mental Models

The idea that mental models can dominate business decisions and that these models are often tacit and even contradictory to what people espouse can be very threatening to managers who pride themselves on rationality and judicious decision making. It is important to have tools to help managers discover for themselves how their mental models operate to undermine their own intentions.

One tool that has worked consistently to help managers see their own mental models in action is the "left-hand column" exercise developed by Chris Argyris and his colleagues. This tool is especially helpful in showing how we leap from data to generalization without testing the validity of our generalizations.

When working with managers, I start this exercise by selecting a specific situation in which I am interacting with other people in a way that is not working, that is not producing the learning that is needed. I write out a sample of the exchange, with the script on the right-hand side of the page. On the left-hand side, I write what I am thinking but not saying at each stage in the exchange (see sidebar).

The left-hand column exercise not only brings hidden assumptions to the surface, it shows how they influence behavior. In the example, I make two key assumptions about Bill: he lacks confidence and he lacks initiative. Neither may be literally true, but both are evident in my internal dialogue, and both influence the way I handle the situation. Believing that he lacks confidence, I skirt the fact that I've heard the presentation was a bomb. I'm afraid that if I say it directly, he will lose what little confidence he has, or he will see me as unsupportive. So I bring up the subject of the presentation obliquely. When I ask Bill what we should do next, he gives no specific course of action. Believing he lacks initiative, I take this as evidence of his laziness; he is content to do nothing when action is definitely required. I conclude that I will have to manufacture some form of pressure to motivate him, or else I will simply have to take matters into my own hands.

The exercise reveals the elaborate webs of assumptions we weave, within which we become our own victims. Rather than dealing directly with my assumptions about Bill and the situation, we talk around the subject. The reasons for my avoidance are self-evident: I assume that if I raised my doubts, I would provoke a defensive reaction that would only make matters worse. But the price of avoiding the issue is high. Instead of determining how to move forward to resolve our problems, we end our exchange with no clear course of action. My assumptions about Bill's limitations have been reinforced. I resort to a manipulative strategy to move things forward.

The exercise not only reveals the need for skills in surfacing assumptions, but that we are the ones most in need of help. There is no one right way to handle difficult situations like my exchange with Bill, but any productive strategy revolves around a high level of self-disclosure and willingness to have my views challenged. I need to recognize my own leaps of abstraction regarding Bill, share the events and reasoning that are leading to my concern over the project, and be open to Bill's views on both. The skills to carry on such

The Left-Hand Column: An Exercise

Imagine my exchange with a colleague, Bill, after he made a big presentation to our boss on a project we are doing together. I had to miss the presentation, but I've heard that it was poorly received.

Me: How did the presentation go?

Bill: Well, I don't know. It's really too early to say. Besides, we're breaking new ground here.

Me: Well, what do you think we should do? I believe that the issues you were raising are important.

Bill: I'm not so sure. Let's just wait and see what happens.

Me: You may be right, but I think we may need to do more than just wait.

Now, here is what the exchange looks like with my "left-hand column":

What I'm Thinking	What Is Said
Everyone says the presentation was a bomb.	**Me:** How did the presentation go?
Does he really not know how bad it was? Or is he not willing to face up to it?	**Bill:** Well, I don't know. It's too early to say. Besides, we're breaking new ground here.
	Me: Well, what do you think we should do? I believe that the issues you were raising are important.
He really is afraid to see the truth. If he only had more confidence, he could probably learn from a situation like this.	**Bill:** I'm not so sure. Let's just wait and see what happens.
I can't believe he doesn't realize how disastrous that presentation was to our moving ahead.	**Me:** You may be right, but I think we may need to do more than just wait.
I've got to find some way to light a fire under the guy.	

conversations without invoking defensiveness take time to develop. But if both parties in a learning impasse start by doing their own left-hand column exercise and sharing them with each other, it is remarkable how quickly everyone recognizes their contribution to the impasse and progress starts to be made.

Learning Laboratories: Practice Fields for Management Teams

One of the most promising new tools is the learning laboratory or "microworld": constructed microcosms of real-life settings in which management teams can learn how to learn together.

The rationale behind learning laboratories can best be explained by analogy. Although most management teams have great difficulty learning (enhancing their collective intelligence and capacity to create), in other domains team learning

Learning at Hanover Insurance

Hanover Insurance has gone from the bottom of the property and liability industry to a position among the top 25 percent of U.S. insurance companies over the past twenty years, largely through the efforts of CEO William O'Brien and his predecessor, Jack Adam. The following comments are excerpted from a series of interviews Senge conducted with O'Brien as background for his book.

Senge: Why do you think there is so much change occurring in management and organizations today? Is it primarily because of increased competitive pressures?

O'Brien: That's a factor, but not the most significant factor. The ferment in management will continue until we find models that are more congruent with human nature.

One of the great insights of modern psychology is the hierarchy of human needs. As Maslow expressed this idea, the most basic needs are food and shelter. Then comes belonging. Once these three basic needs are satisfied, people begin to aspire toward self-respect and esteem, and toward self-actualization—the fourth- and fifth-order needs.

Our traditional hierarchical organizations are designed to provide for the first three levels, but not the fourth and fifth. These first three levels are now widely available to members of industrial society, but our organizations do not offer people sufficient opportunities for growth.

Senge: How would you assess Hanover's progress to date?

O'Brien: We have been on a long journey away from a traditional hierarchical culture. The journey began with everyone understanding some guiding ideas about purpose, vision, and values as a basis for participative management. This is a better way to begin building a participative culture than by simply "letting people in on decision making." Before there can be meaningful participation, people must share certain values and pictures about where we are trying to go. We discovered that people have a real need to feel that they're part of an enobling mission. But developing shared visions and values is not the end, only the beginning.

Next we had to get beyond mechanical, linear thinking. The essence of our jobs as managers is to deal with "divergent" problems—problems that have no simple answer. "Convergent" problems—problems that have a "right" answer—should be solved locally. Yet we are deeply conditioned to see the world in terms of convergent problems. Most managers try to force-fit simplistic solutions and undermine the potential for learning when divergent problems arise. Since everyone handles the linear issues fairly well, companies that learn how to handle divergent issues will have a great advantage.

The next basic stage in our progression was coming to understand inquiry and advocacy. We learned that real openness is rooted in people's ability to continually inquire into their own thinking. This requires exposing yourself to being wrong—not something that most managers are rewarded for. But learning is very difficult if you cannot look for errors or incompleteness in your own ideas.

What all this builds to is the capability throughout an organization to manage mental models. In a locally controlled organization, you have the fundamental challenge of learning how to help people make good decisions without coercing them into making *particular* decisions. By managing mental models, we create "self-concluding" decisions—decisions that people come to themselves—which will result in deeper conviction, better implementation, and the ability to make better adjustments when the situation changes.

Senge: What concrete steps can top managers take to begin moving toward learning organizations?

O'Brien: Look at the signals you send through the organization. For example, one critical signal is how you spend your time. It's hard to build a learning organization if people are unable to take the time to think through important matters. I rarely set up an appointment for less than one hour. If the subject is not worth an hour, it shouldn't be on my calendar.

Senge: Why is this so hard for so many managers?

O'Brien: It comes back to what you believe about the nature of your work. The authoritarian manager has a "chain gang" mental model: "The speed of the boss is the speed of the gang. I've got to keep things moving fast, because I've got to keep people working." In a learning organization, the manager shoulders an almost sacred responsibility: to create conditions that enable people to have happy and productive lives. If you understand the effects the ideas we are discussing can have on the lives of people in your organization, you will take the time.

---

is the norm rather than the exception—team sports and the performing arts, for example. Great basketball teams do not start off great. They learn. But the process by which these teams learn is, by and large, absent from modern organizations. The process is a continual movement between practice and performance.

The vision guiding current research in management learning laboratories is to design and construct effective practice fields for management teams. Much remains to be done, but the broad outlines are emerging.

First, since team learning in organizations is an individual-to-individual and individual-to-system phenomenon, learning laboratories must combine meaningful business issues with meaningful interpersonal dynamics. Either alone is incomplete.

Second, the factors that thwart learning about complex business issues must be eliminated in the learning lab. Chief among these is the inability to experience the long-term, systemic consequences of key strategic decisions. We all learn best from experience, but we are unable to experience the consequences of many important organizational decisions. Learning laboratories remove this constraint through system dynamics simulation games that compress time and space.

Third, new learning skills must be developed. One constraint on learning is the inability of managers to reflect insightfully on their assumptions, and to inquire effectively into each other's assumptions. Both skills can be enhanced in a learning laboratory, where people can practice surfacing assumptions in a low-risk setting. A note of caution: It is far easier to design an entertaining learning laboratory than it is to have an impact on real management practices and firm traditions outside the learning lab. Research on management simulations has shown that they often have greater entertainment value than educational value. One of the reasons appears to be that many simulations do not offer deep insights into systemic structures causing business problems. Another reason is that they do not foster new learning skills. Also, there is no connection between experiments in the learning lab and real life experiments. These are significant problems that research on learning laboratory design is now addressing.

Developing Leaders and Learning Organizations

In a recently published retrospective on organization development in the 1980s, Marshall Sashkin and N. Warner Burke observe the return of an emphasis on developing leaders who can develop organizations.[29] They also note Schein's critique that most top executives are not qualified for the task of developing culture.[30] Learning organizations represent a potentially significant evolution of organizational culture. So it should come as no surprise that such organizations will remain a distant vision until the leadership capabilities they demand are developed. "The 1990s may be the period," suggest Sashkin and Burke, "during which organization development and (a new sort of) management development are reconnected."

I believe that this new sort of management development will focus on the roles, skills, and tools for leadership in learning organizations. Undoubtedly, the ideas offered above are only a rough approximation of this new territory. The sooner we begin seriously exploring the territory, the sooner the initial map can be improved—and the sooner we will realize an age-old vision of leadership:

The wicked leader is he who the people despise. The good leader is he who the people revere. The great leader is he who the people say, "We did it ourselves."

—Lao Tsu

References

[1] P. Senge, *The Fifth Discipline: The Art and Practice of the Learning Organization* (New York: Doubleday / Currency, 1990).

[2] A. P. de Geus, "Planning as Learning," *Harvard Business Review*, March–April 1988, pp. 70–74.

[3] B. Domain, *Fortune*, 3 July 1989, pp. 48–62.

[4] The distinction between adaptive and generative learning has its roots in the distinction between what Argyris and Schon have called their "single-loop" learning, in which individuals or groups adjust their behavior relative to fixed goals, norms, and assumptions, and "double-loop" learning, in which goals, norms, and assumptions, as well as behavior, are open to change (e.g., see C. Argyris and D. Schon, *Organizational Learning: A Theory-in-Action Perspective* (Reading, Massachusetts: Addison-Wesley, 1978).

[5] All unattributed quotes are from personal communications with the author.

[6] G. Stalk, Jr., "Time: The Next Source of Competitive Advantage," *Harvard Business Review*, July–August 1988, pp. 41–51.

[7] Senge (1990).

[8] The principle of creative tension comes from Robert Fritz' work on creativity. See R. Fritz, *The Path of Least Resistance* (New York: Ballantine, 1989) and *Creating* (New York: Ballantine, 1990).

[9] M. L. King, Jr., "Letter from Birmingham Jail," *American Visions*, January–February 1986, pp. 52–59.

[10] E. Schein, *Organizational Culture and Leadership* (San Francisco: Jossey-Bass, 1985).

Similar views have been expressed by many leadership theorists. For example, see:

P. Selznick, *Leadership in Administration* (New York: Harper & Row, 1957);

W. Bennis and B. Nanus, *Leaders* (New York: Harper & Row, 1985); and

N. M. Tichy and M. A. Devanna, *The Transformational Leader* (New York: John Wiley & Sons, 1986).

[11] Selznick (1957).

[12] J.W. Forrester, "A New Corporate Design," *Sloan Management Review* (formerly *Industrial Management Review*), Fall 1965, pp. 5–17.

[13] See, for example, H. Mintzberg, "Crafting Strategy," *Harvard Business Review*, July–August 1987, pp. 66–75.

[14] R. Mason and I. Mitroff, *Challenging Strategic Planning Assumptions* (New York: John Wiley & Sons, 1981), p. 16.

[15] P. Wack, "Scenarios: Uncharted Waters Ahead," *Harvard Business Review*, September–October 1985, pp. 73–89.

[16] de Geus (1988).

[17] M. de Pree, *Leadership Is an Art* (New York: Doubleday, 1989) p. 9.

[18] For example, see T. Peters and N. Austin, *A Passion for Excellence* (New York: Random House, 1985) and J. M. Kouzes and B. Z. Posner, *The Leadership Challenge* (San Francisco: Jossey-Bass, 1987).

[19] I. Mitroff, *Break-Away Thinking* (New York: John Wiley & Sons, 1988), pp. 66–67.

[20] R.K. Greenleaf, *Servant Leadership: A Journey into the Nature of Legitimate Power and Greatness* (New York: Paulist Press, 1977).

[21] L. Miller, *American Spirit: Visions of a New Corporate Culture* (New York: William Morrow, 1984), p. 15.

[22] These points are condensed from the practices of the five disciplines examined in Senge (1990).

[23] The ideas below are based to a considerable extent on the work of Chris Argyris, Donald Schon, and their Action Science colleagues:

C. Argyris and D. Schon, *Organizational Learning: A Theory-in-Action Perspective* (Reading, Massachusetts: Addison-Wesley, 1978);

C. Argyris, R. Putnam, and D. Smith, *Action Science* (San Francisco: Jossey-Bass, 1985);

C. Argyris, *Strategy, Change, and Defensive Routines* (Boston: Pitman, 1985); and

C. Argyris, *Overcoming Organizational Defenses* (Englewood Cliffs, New Jersey: Prentice-Hall, 1990).

[24] I am indebted to Diana Smith for the summary points below.

[25] The system archetypes are one of several systems diagramming and communication tools. See D.H. Kim, "Toward Learning Organizations: Integrating Total Quality Control and System Thinking" (Cambridge, Massachusetts: MIT Sloan School of Management, Working Paper No. 3037-89-BPS, June 1989).

[26] This archetype is closely associated with the work of ecologist Garrett Hardin, who coined its label: G. Hardin, "The Tragedy of the Commons," *Science*, 13 December 1968.

[27] These templates were originally developed by Jennifer Kemeny, Charles Kiefer, and Michael Goodman of Innovation Associates, Inc., Framingham, Massachusetts.

[28] C. Hampden-Turner, *Charting the Corporate Mind* (New York: The Free Press, 1990).

[29] M. Sashkin and W.W. Burke, "Organization Development in the 1980s" and "An End-of-the-Eighties Retrospective," in *Advances in Organization Development*, ed. F. Masarik (Norwood, New Jersey: Ablex, 1990).

[30] E. Schein (1985).

PART II

Beyond the Theory and into the Practice of Leadership

The first 12 chapters have been devoted to a historical sampling of the empirical and conceptual literature on leadership and the leadership process. However, there are many other sources of learning about leadership, and these should not be overlooked. In particular, this section provides a glimpse into three domains that can be viewed as practitioner reflections and reports, analytical opportunities, and experiential exercises.

Practitioner Reflections and Reports

*A wide range of leaders (especially CEOs) have taken the initiative to think about, and report their insights into, what made them successful. Examples include Jack Welch at GE, Andy Grove at Intel, Max DePree at Herman Miller, Harvey Mackay at Mackay Envelope, Mary Kay Ash at Mary Kay Cosmetics, John Sculley at Apple, Ricardo Semler at Semco, Steven Jobs at NeXt, Harold Geneen at ITT, David Kearns at Xerox, and Donald Petersen at Ford Motor Company. (In other cases, independent authors have provided biographies of corporate leaders, such as Bill Gates at MicroSoft, Jack Welch at GE, or Ted Turner at TBS and other ventures). In addition, scholars (such as Warren Bennis, John Kotter, Burt Nanus, John Gardner, and Noel Tichy) and consultants (such as William Byham and Stephen Covey) have observed leaders in action and shared their observations and conclusions in the form of books written for the practitioner market. These portraits are often rich in an-*ecdotal information and contemporary illustrations, although sometimes lacking the broader data basis of well-designed studies. Nevertheless, we have included a sampling of brief synopses of a few of these books in this section as a way to introduce the reader to this set of materials.*

Analytical Opportunities

It is a well-established fact that people learn in different ways. One fruitful approach is through the analysis of cases and (shorter) incidents. These provide opportunities to sift through information, identify key issues, determine the applicability of relevant theories, and suggest appropriate action plans. Cases and incidents, properly guided by a discussion leader, make it possible for the analyst to engage in both deductive (application of principles) and inductive (development of tentative generalizations) thinking. Also, because they are drawn from actual circumstances, they provide a sense of realism to the study of the leadership process. A number of cases and incidents are included to provide an opportunity for learning through analysis and application of concepts.

Experiential Exercises

An oft-quoted phrase (attributed to Confucius and others) suggests that "I hear and I forget, I see and I remember, I do and I understand." This forms the basic rationale for learning some things through experience. Structured experiential exercises typically involve the participants in either a physical activity or in generating some relevant individual or group data. The group is then invited to engage in a retrospective discussion of what took place or what the "data" mean (in the context of lead-ership theories). The process of active involvement serves as a powerful incentive to "see" abstract concepts take on meaning and shape realistic personal agendas for the future. Again, we have included a small sample of experiential exercises to stimulate such personalized learning.

Contemporary Perspectives

Summaries of "Popular" Leadership Books

Leadership—Myths and Realities

R. Bellingham and B. Cohen

Summary prepared by: Deanna Bourget

*A*ll myths hold some truth. It is important, however, for leaders to separate truth from myth and to learn to what extent these myths are alive and well in their organizations. The realities, if recognized, can stimulate changes for these leaders and challenge them to self-improvement.

Leadership—Myths and Realities explores 10 myths and their associated realities. Business leaders need to accept the realities as a foundation for all other actions.

1. What do leaders invest in?

Myth: Leaders invest with financial capital and treat people as financial objects. People are seen as overhead or as a cost that can be reduced if needed. Consideration of the people and their needs is ignored.

Reality: Leaders invest in human and information capital. Organizations realize that people are important to the success of the organization. Moral standards have to be improved. (As Kant suggested, act in a way that you always treat people, never simply as a means but always at the same time as an end.) Financial capital is no longer viewed as the most important source of economic productivity gain. If employees are given authority and responsibility, they will think about their jobs and be prepared to contribute to their organization and to their clients.

2. How do leaders make decisions?

Myth: Leaders are risk takers. There is risk in implementing new, creative ideas, but risk taking is not the key factor. Six conditions limit the value of risk taking: (1) people do not understand the mission; (2) the organization is too future-oriented; (3) the organization is weak on follow-through; (4) people are punished for failures; (5) people are encouraged to take risks without training; and (6) people think risk taking means going it alone. Risk taking involves the chance of failure.

Reality: Leaders think creatively. A leader is thorough in deciding how to go about things and uses the input of others. Leaders do the right thing; therefore, risks must be calculated. Employees need to brainstorm, to open their minds, generate ideas, develop useful ideas, commit to a direction, and then modify the alternatives. Creative thinking requires that time be put aside for considering alternatives, which will usually result in success.

3. How do leaders relate to employees?

Myth: Leaders manage by walking around (MBWA). The idea behind MBWA was to get in touch with the employees and be able to solve problems more effectively. Employees may have felt more an important part of the process, but MBWA did not necessarily improve effectiveness. Other factors must be considered in order for leaders to use MBWA and relate constructively.

Reality: Leaders relate constructively. They need to know more about the job so they know what behavior and performance to look for. Otherwise, walking around will be unproductive. Also, the one walking around must listen. To hear is one thing, but to really listen is the key. Further, employees want clear, noncontradictory answers when they ask questions. Leaders need to know the answers or find the answers, but never just give any answer. Lastly, leaders must maintain open-mindedness. If managers are not secure enough to hear differing points of view or complaints from employees, then they are unlikely to change resentful or bitter feelings that may exist among employees. MBWA works when people know how to relate to each other. Communication is important to create effective relations with employees. Four communication skills that should be mastered are gathering information, demonstrating understanding, getting one's viewpoint across, and negotiating.

4. What role do leaders play in change?

Myth: Leaders manage change. A leader must do more than just understand, accept, and then change. Managing change means that nothing is done until an event occurs and there are no other alternatives. If a change is quickly made because of an unplanned event, then chaos and mistakes are likely to occur.

Reality: Leaders initiate strategic changes. They should initiate change by anticipating a change, mobilizing, and then acting. In the initiation of change, circumstances often start the process, but the leaders communicate the course of action, analyze any possible conflicts, and gather input before making the final decision of how to take action.

5. How are leaders involved in training?

Myth: Leaders develop people through training. Most management experts agree that constant training is required

---

R. Bellingham and B. Cohen, *Leadership—Myths and Realities* (Amherst, MA: Human Resource Development Press, Inc, 1989).

if everyone must contribute ideas and work together with less supervision. The previous myths led to training people to think, relate, and plan. Organizations sought to make greater investments in training, and this created enormous pressure to make training work. Training does increase the *likelihood* of success, but the individuals themselves make the training a success.

Reality: Leaders create an environment that nurtures personal development. Employees must learn the skills needed to be able to communicate and avoid conflicts with other employees. Employees who want to learn and improve will be able to do so when placed in a nurturing environment. If they are encouraged to improve for their own benefit, they will be productive and learn through training. Training programs need to focus on specific skills that an employee can apply to his or her needs, instead of just providing concepts and research information that relate to the job. Also, employees need to actually utilize these skills in a simulated situation where they are given the chance to test the skills they are learning in a safe environment where errors are expected and encouraged. In this type of learning experience, employees can explore and grow to understand what they are learning. Then results can be measured by how successful employees are in transferring their learning to the work situation. An organization's culture is the most powerful training tool, and if these skills are not supported by their culture, they will be quickly lost.

6.   What do leaders emphasize?

Myth: Leaders emphasize product quality, not what customers want. Organizations can produce a better product, but is it what the customer desires? If quality and customer needs are not considered, there will be fewer people willing to help with the process and fewer people willing to purchase the product.

Reality: Leaders emphasize product, process, people, and customer benefits. People involved in the process of the product and the people buying the product are very important. Quality must be defined and measured according to the customer's benefit.

7.   How can a leader motivate?

Myth: Leaders motivate employees. All organizations believe motivation is a primary concern. A primary concern is how to get an employee to want to do what needs to be done. Employees take certain actions that falsely support the myth: reducing time requirements, increasing pay and benefits, training meant to increase commitment, and demonstrations to show employees that companies care about them as people.

Reality: Leaders free exemplars. To have exemplary performers, an employer must have individuals whose values match those of the corporation. Employees are then motivated to high levels of performance because their personal values match the corporate values. Also, when rewards are tied to values and performance, when achievable performance is perceived, and when the organization builds its

team around exemplars, motivational efforts work. Exemplars go beyond doing just what they have to; there are no limits. Therefore, in reality there are three ways to increase motivation within any organization: encourage employees to achieve even higher levels of productivity; provide training in systematic processing skills; and free productive exemplary performance.

8.   How do leaders make decisions?

Myth: Leaders always seek consensus. Throughout history, many writers have concluded that consensus was important, along with emphasizing people and their ideas. However, consensus-oriented management sometimes results in everyone getting less than what they want. Also, individuals are reluctant to reopen the plan for debate after a "group decision" has been made.

Reality: Leaders make fine discriminations on how to lead. In actuality, an effective leader knows how to determine what decision process to use. There are five decision types: tell, sell, test, consult, or join. The employees should be informed exactly what type of decision the leader has made. When a "tell" decision is made, the employees are told that the manager has an idea that needs to be implemented. The manager acknowledges that not everyone may agree, but there are no other alternatives—period. A "selling" decision occurs where the manager feels he or she has a good idea and wants to persuade employees to agree. For a "testing" decision, the manager tries out the possible solution on employees to see if it would work and also to see what inputs they have. In a "consulting" decision, a manager may be having a difficult time making a decision. He or she would ask employees for input before making a final decision. Finally, a manager may decide to "join" with employees on a decision. Since the manger has no specific idea of what to decide, he or she may even allow the group of employees to make the final decision. Clearly, leaders are working constantly on the correct way to answer questions. Also, leaders are deciding which questions are to be addressed at that particular time in the organization's life.

9.   How do leaders deal with time?

Myth: Leaders minimize time. This myth assumes that leadership takes few skills and that performance management issues can be taken care of quickly. Three conditions limit the value of minimizing time through simple solutions. *Condition #1:* Acting as if it is the only tool in your bag. *Condition #2:* Management does not care about people. *Condition #3:* Communication norms block the effect of good intentions.

Reality: Leaders do the right things right. Leaders need a broad range of functional skill applications to manage performance and people. Thinking, relating, and planning skills make leaders effective. An effective leader communicates and innovates at all levels of the organization and knows how to manage time and prioritize decisions. The primary task is to support others; therefore, customer responsiveness is the drive.

10.   What is a leader's role in wellness programs?

Myth: Leaders support individual wellness programs. This flawed myth implies that an individual wellness program has lasting results. This idea presents a limited vision. Employees raise their expectations without being provided any broad, meaningful support for success.

Reality: Leaders develop healthy organizational cultures. Wellness programs work only in a healthy organization. They can succeed with programs that examine and modify organizational behaviors that have an effect on employee health instead of programs that only modify the health behaviors of individuals. Wellness programs should be used to promote healthy development instead of just preventing illness, and they must be improved to include all levels of employees and not just senior management. Also, these programs must provide useful information that demonstrates that what is conducted is useful to the employee's needs within the organization. The benefits of a healthy organizational culture with productive programs include reduction in absenteeism, increase in morale, and increase in productivity. A healthy culture influences the health of employees, and the resultant improvements in morale and absenteeism influence the organization's success.

The assumptions of 10 myths need to be challenged by the realities. Hopefully, leaders will take the challenge and improve the productivity of the employees and maximize the profitability of the organization. Myths are part of the past, and it is time to put them there. Leaders have to invest in their people; they must share the same goals and have shared values. Leaders must listen to what others have to say and show they are open to other people's ideas. They need to establish an open and understanding environment so people learn through training, customers are given what they want, and employees can initiate solutions and become truly motivated. Leaders do need to make some decisions on their own, but when they need help, they must openly seek input from others. Finally, leaders must support employees and honestly believe in their shared goals and how to reach them. Together, they can strive for success.

On Becoming a Leader

W. Bennis

Summary prepared by: Kari Johnson

What things are important for people who are in positions of leadership or for anyone who wants to improve their leadership skills? Warren Bennis answered this question by examining what real people have accomplished in order to become a leader, and how they did it. These people range from CEOs, to writers, to heads of record and movie companies. All offer their own story of what they believe makes a leader successful, how they gained a position of leadership, or what must be done to become a leader. These examples are important because they show successes, failures, and (most importantly) that *it is possible for an average person to become a leader.*

Bennis poses an initial question, Where have all the leaders gone? He argues that leaders of today do not have the same qualities and influence that leaders of the past had. He cites many historic leaders that influenced their followers and challenged them to become better and stronger people than they were: Franklin D. Roosevelt, Winston Churchill, Albert Einstein, Mahatma Ghandi, John and Robert Kennedy, and Martin Luther King, Jr. Today's leaders, by contrast, are viewed as "endangered species"—corporate heads, city and state officials, and university presidents.

The essential ingredients in effective leadership include a guiding vision, passion, integrity, trust, and curiosity. It is important for leaders to create a *vision* for the future because it guides them (and others) to have the strength and ambition to reach their goals. Successful leaders also have a sense of *passion* for what they are doing. They love striving to gain more knowledge, advance in their vocation, and add to their professionalism. The next two ingredients, integrity and trust, are intertwined with each other. *Integrity* is based on self-knowledge, candor, and maturity. Self-knowledge is important because until leaders know their strengths and weaknesses and know what it is that they want to achieve, it is not possible for them to achieve. Successful leaders never lie to themselves or to others about their strengths or weaknesses, and they work to overcome these weaknesses. Candor is a key to self-knowledge, and it is based on honesty and a devotion to one's values. Maturity is an important component of integrity because the leader has had many experiences from which he or she has been able to learn. *Trust* ties into the ingredient of integrity because integrity is "the basis of trust." Successful leaders trust and respect their followers and in return are trusted and respected by them. *Curiosity* and the ability to take risks are important in leadership because the leader wants to learn new things and is willing to take risks and try to do things to accomplish his or her goals. True leaders are not worried about failing, and they know that one can learn from his or her failures.

Bennis also discusses the differences between managers and leaders. He believes that managers and leaders have different qualities and behaviors. Leaders are people who master the context of the situation while managers are simply people who surrender to the situation. Other examples of the differences between leaders and managers include:

1. Managers administer; leaders innovate.

2. Managers ask how and when; leaders ask what and why.

3. Managers have short-range views; leaders have long-range perspectives.

4. Managers imitate; leaders originate.

Unlike managerial skills, leadership skills cannot be taught. Each person must learn for him- or herself the ingredients that go into shaping a leader. These ingredients are as diverse as the leaders themselves.

Leaders must grasp a wide understanding and knowledge of two major themes: themselves and their world. *Self-knowledge* is important because knowing yourself means "separating who you are and who you want to be from what the world thinks you are and wants you to be." Self-knowledge enables you to freely express yourself and your ideas, to take charge of your life and the situations you are in, and to decide what you want to accomplish in your life. Bennis discusses four key lessons for contributing to self-knowledge:

1. You are your own best teacher. Modes of self-learning include role taking, validation, personal growth, scientific learning, emulation, and practical accomplishment.

2. Accept responsibility. It is important to accept responsibility for a situation and run with it. Make the most of each situation you are in.

3. You can learn anything you want to learn. Learning is not only knowledge and expertise; it involves understanding the world as you see it and then acting on your understanding.

4. True understanding comes from reflecting on your experiences. It is important to ask questions like What really happened? Why did it happen? What did it do to me? What did it mean to me? in order to reach a true understanding of yourself and your life.

Self-knowledge is critically important to leaders because when they have the knowledge and understanding of who they are, where they are at in their lives, and what they want to achieve in the future, they will be able to decide what is

W. Bennis, *On Becoming a Leader* (Reading, MA: Addison-Wesley Publishing Company, Inc., 1989).

best for them and choose how to lead their lives so that they can achieve their own personal goals.

It is vitally important for leaders to have *knowledge of the world around them* because the world and the situations the person is in play a large role in shaping his or her life. There are three ways that people are able to innovatively learn about the world around them: anticipation, participation, and listening to the people around them. It is essential that people learn to become active participants and work to create new ideas rather than becoming passive—which demonstrates the ideas of both anticipation and participation. It is also possible to gain knowledge and understanding about the world through friends and mentors, travel, culture, and work. Even the ability to learn from one's mistakes can be extremely helpful to people because errors show what not to do and why not to do it.

Bennis argues that we need to have stronger leaders in our society because we live in a changing world. He presents a set of 10 characteristics that will help future leaders as they seek to change and create new organizations.

1. *Leaders manage the dream.* All leaders have the ability to create a vision for the future and are able to translate that vision into reality.

2. *Leaders embrace error.* Leaders welcome an atmosphere where there are opportunities to take risks. Leaders do not think of risks as a chance to fail—instead, it is a chance to learn.

3. *Leaders encourage reflective backtalk.* Leaders like to hear criticisms, encouragement, or ideas from other people that are close to them.

4. *Leaders encourage dissent.* Leaders like to have people around them that have opposite views because it gives them the opportunity to hear the other side of the situation.

5. *Leaders understand the Pygmalion effect in management.* Leaders expect the best from people but at the same time are realistic in their expectations of other people. Leaders' expectations of others and the way they treat them determine their followers' behaviors and performance.

6. *Leaders possess the Nobel Factor.* Real leaders are optimistic, full of hope for the future, and have faith in themselves and the people around them.

7. *Leaders have the* Gretzky Touch. Like Wayne Gretzky on ice, leaders are able to know where the organization is going and are able to anticipate changes.

8. *Leaders see the long view.* Leaders have patience and look at things in the long-term perspective.

9. *Leaders understand stakeholder symmetry.* Leaders realize that they must take into consideration all other people's points of view when those people have a stake in the organization.

10. *Leaders create strategic alliances and partnerships.* Leaders of today (and in the future) realize that they must create partnerships with other organizations in order to be successful.

Visionary Leadership

B. Nanus

Summary prepared by: Tiffany Sherman

V isionary Leadership presents a step-by-step description of how leaders can develop and implement the right vision for their organizations. Nanus introduces the main message: "There is no more powerful engine driving an organization toward excellence and long-range success than an attractive, worthwhile, and achievable vision of the future, widely shared"(3). The rest of the book represents the necessary steps in the development and implementation of a leader's vision.

An organization's vision is "a realistic, credible, attractive future for your organization"(8). It states a direction the organization should go in the future that is more acceptable for the organization than the current direction. A vision is an idea or image for a better future that calls for the resources and skills of the organization in order to make it happen. The vision is not only important in the beginning of an organization, but throughout its entire life cycle. It is a guide to help people understand what the organization stands for and where it needs to go.

Nanus explains the characteristics of leadership and what it takes to be an effective leader in today's changing business environment. He characterized leaders as people who "take charge, make things happen, dream dreams, and then translate them into reality"(10). He describes effective leaders and the job of visionary leaders as possessing four roles: direction setter, change agent, spokesperson, and coach. Also, to make a vision work in an organization, a leader needs to attract the attention of the people within the organization and persuade them to believe and follow a common goal or vision. A vision attracts commitment and motivates people, creates meaning, establishes standards for excellence, and connects the present with the future.

What are the common properties for effective visions? They are appropriate for the organization and the time, they set standards of excellence and contemplate high ideals, they clarify the purpose and direction, they inspire enthusiasm and commitment, they are easily understood, they reflect the uniqueness of the organization, and they are ambitious. Overall, vision is the initial step in the strategy formulation process. The process of developing a vision involves learning about the organization itself and its industry, including the organization's major constituencies into the vision process, keeping an open mind when exploring the options for a new vision, and encouraging input from many sources in the development of the vision.

There are four major steps in the development process for an organization's vision. First of all, a leader needs to assess the current situation of the organization by determining the organization's mission, its value to society, its position in the industry, how it operates within the industry, and what it takes for its success. After assessing these factors, leaders need to conduct a "Visionary Audit," which includes determining the current vision if one does exist, identifying where the organization is headed if it stays with its current vision, discovering if the key people in the organization know where the organization is headed, and determining if the current operation of the business supports the current direction.

The second step is to evaluate how the organization currently operates by identifying the values of the organization, its strengths and weaknesses, and its current strategy. After assessing the operation, the scope of the vision needs to be identified and understood throughout the organization. The organization and the leader need to identify the important stakeholders of the organization such as suppliers, customers, and competitors. One must know what their interests and expectations of the organization are, and what threats or opportunities they possess that would harm or benefit the business. After considering the stakeholders, the leader must narrow the vision to fit the organization by creating its boundaries, such as time, geographical area, and social constraints that would affect the vision's success.

The third step in the development process is to consider the vision context. This is an important step because in order for the vision to be successful, it must fit not only with the internal environment, but more importantly, with the external environment and the possible future changes that could occur. These changes need to be anticipated, studied, and evaluated for their implications. A time horizon must be established to look at future events that could occur that would alter the outcome of the vision. Within this time horizon, leaders need to determine possible situations, their outcomes, and then evaluate these outcomes to determine which ones have the greatest potential impact on the organization. After identifying key possible outcomes, leaders should try to determine their probability of occurring and draw possible scenarios of these situations and the implications that would affect the organization.

The fourth step deals with the final vision choice. There are several properties that must exist in order for a vision to be the right one: it must be future-oriented, utopian, and appropriate for the organization; it must reflect high ideals, clarify a purpose, inspire enthusiasm, and be unique. In making the final vision choice, leaders need several abilities to bring a vision together: to be flexible, to recognize situations, to clarify the differences and similarities between situations, and to come up with new ideas. After leaders have chosen a vision, their next step is to map out possible paths to take in achieving the vision. Finally, if the chosen vision happens

B. Nanus, *Visionary Leadership* (San Francisco: Jossey-Bass, 1992).

not to be as successful as initially hoped, alternative visions are important. They can be used as back-up plans in case changes occur in the future that would make the current vision unacceptable.

How does a leader implement a vision? Effective leaders implement a vision by assuming four key roles: spokesperson, change agent, coach, and direction setter. For each of these, effective leaders are responsible for communicating the vision to the organization, showing them how it can be effective and more successful than the current vision, and developing a strategy that is achievable by the organization. Once the strategy is created, the leader assigns tasks and responsibilities to people in the organization so that everyone works together as a team, using the right resources to achieve a common goal. Nanus sums visionary leadership into an equation that can prove to be effective: Shared Purpose + Empowered People + Appropriate Organizational Changes + Strategic Thinking = Successful Visionary Leadership. This equation highlights all of the primary elements for a successful vision for the organization.

Leaders also need to know how to change the visionary direction if it becomes necessary during the process of implementing the vision. It is always important to monitor and evaluate the progress of the vision and to keep searching for new ways to improve the vision that will ultimately improve the organization. Leaders are advised to continue learning new things, to be aware of the constantly changing world that could affect the future of their organization, and to allow others to contribute their thoughts in developing a new vision. In effect, leadership (and visioning) is a continuous process that influences the operation and success of organizations. Although it is important for leaders to *have* the idea or image, they must allow others in the organization to *contribute* in its development and implementation.

Principle-Centered Leadership

S. R. Covey

Summary prepared by: Jacklyn Twining and Linda Nordland

This book deals with the principles of effective leadership, focusing on a principle-centered leadership/management style. The basic idea of this style is to train people in terms of the principles of the organization so that the day-to-day crises can be handled at lower levels of the organization instead of bogging down top executives' time. In other words, "I teach them correct principles, and they govern themselves." As a result, higher management has more time to spend planning and organizing.

Principle-centered leadership is basing, or centering, people's lives and organizations around certain "true north" principles that are universal in nature and inviolate. These principles operate whether or not people and organizations recognize them or obey them.

A paradigm shift has occurred in the way people think and do things. This shift involves four fundamental dimensions: security, guidance, wisdom, and power. People are encouraged to concentrate on these dimensions and not on other centers of their lives such as money, spouse, and work.

Principle-centered leadership is a new paradigm. There are four levels of principle-centered leadership, and each has a key principle. The outermost level is organizational, and its key principle is alignment within the organization. The next level is managerial and its key is empowerment. The next level is interpersonal and its key is trust. The innermost level is personal and its key is trustworthiness.

Covey has isolated eight characteristics of people who are principle-centered leaders: (1) they continuously learn by reading and training; (2) they are service-oriented, seeing life as a mission instead of a career; (3) they radiate positive energy by being happy, cheerful, positive, and upbeat; (4) they believe in other people and see the difference between behavior and potential; (5) they lead balanced lives and are active socially, intellectually, and physically; (6) they see life as an adventure by asking questions and getting involved; (7) they are synergistic, and they are change catalysts; (8) they exercise for self-renewal by exercising the four dimensions of human personality.

Stephen R. Covey also provides a short review of another of his books, *The Seven Habits of Highly Effective People.* These seven habits include: thinking with a win/win attitude instead of a win/lose attitude; seeking to understand oneself before seeking for others to understand you; using effective willpower and self-control; beginning with the end result in mind, rather than looking for a quick and easy answer; being proactive instead of reactive; synergizing with one's life, both personal and organizational; participating in continuous improvement of one's body and mind.

Based on natural principles and laws, people cannot have wealth without work, pleasure without conscience, knowledge without character, business without ethics, science without humanity, religion without sacrifice, or politics without principle. But the way people *use* these principles and natural laws varies. There are three types of power: coercive, utility, and principle-centered. True principle-centered power occurs when leaders are trusted, respected, and valued by their followers. In order to achieve any principle-centered power, one must keep the lines of communication open so that misperceptions do not create credibility problems. One must listen and understand and assume good faith in organizations and relationships.

But many organizations still face many problems: lack of shared vision and values, lack of a strategic path, poor alignment, wrong or inappropriate style, low trust among staff, and lack of minimal integrity. These problems can be dealt with through principle-centered leadership (PCL). People are the number one aspect of PCL. Self, style, skills, shared vision, structure and systems, strategy and streams are all also important effects of PCL. PCL paradigm characteristics include dealing with the whole instead of the parts of the whole.

This book is a collection of articles written for *Executive Excellence* magazine. Implementing the ideas presented by Dr. Covey can produce positive results in the areas of quality and productivity as well as an increased appreciation of relationships, both personal and professional. This appreciation can lead to a life that is more fulfilling, well rounded, and effective.

S. R. Covey, *Principle-Centered Leadership* (New York: Summit Books, 1991).

On Leadership

J. W. Gardner

Summary prepared by: Brett Vake

On Leadership addresses our crisis of leadership in society as well as in business. Gardner conducted interviews with hundreds of contemporary leaders in an intensive five-year field study of organizations. He explored leadership as it is practiced, or malpracticed, in America today. Gardner looked beyond the customary cries for charisma to the elements of motivation, shared values, social cohesion, and institutional renewal.

Gardner has served six presidents of the United States in various leadership capacities. He was secretary of Health, Education, and Welfare, chairman of Common Cause, co-founder of Independent Sector, and president of the Carnegie Foundation for the Advancement of Teaching. He has served as director of several major U.S. corporations. His diverse background provided him with a wide variety of experience with various types and styles of leadership.

Gardner defines leadership as "the process of persuasion or example by which an individual (or leadership team) induces a group to pursue objectives held by the leader or shared by the leader and his or her followers"(p. 1). The interaction between leaders and followers or constituents indicates that communication and influence flow in both directions. It is this process that leaders shape and by which they are shaped. Because of this process, there are many kinds of leaders that form to fit the makeup of the group or the setting. Leaders must institutionalize their leadership, meaning that they must bring others into the decision process in order to influence or support the decision of the leader (group consensus).

Leadership must address several tasks, including envisioning goals, affirming values, regenerating values, motivating, managing, achieving workable unity, establishing trust, explaining, serving as a symbol, representing the group, and renewing. The important thing about these tasks is that they can not be treated as a shopping list of individual things a leader must do; rather, an effective leader is always doing several tasks simultaneously.

Gardner next addresses the interaction between leaders and followers. He states, "Leaders are almost never as much in charge as they are pictured to be; followers are almost never as submissive as one might imagine"(p. 23). He adds, "the state of mind of followers is a powerful ingredient in explaining the emergence of the charismatic leader"(p. 23). These statements mean that good constituents tend to produce good leaders and that *leadership is conferred by followers.* This relationship is based on trust, communication, multilevel dialogue, perceptions, and other miscellaneous factors.

Many attributes are prominent in successful leaders. They include:

- Physical vitality and stamina.
- Intelligence and judgment-in-action.
- Willingness to accept responsibilities.
- Task competence.
- Understanding of followers and their needs.
- Skill in dealing with people.
- Need to achieve.
- Capacity to motivate.
- Courage, resolution, steadiness.
- Capacity to win and hold trust.
- Capacity to manage, decide, and set priorities.
- Confidence.
- Ascendance, dominance, and assertiveness.
- Adaptability, flexibility of approach.

Not all of these would necessarily define a leader in various contexts and settings. Not only do the attributes matter, but how they correlate with the context of the situation determines what makes a good or bad leader. The probability is greater than chance, however, *that leaders in one situation will be leaders in another situation.*

Leaders need to understand and use their power. According to Gardner, "power is simply the capacity to bring about certain intended consequences in the behavior of others" (p. 55). It is important to define who leaders and power holders are and who they aren't. Gardner says that "leaders always have a measure of power, but many power holders have no trace of leadership." Gardner goes on to discuss the various sources of power leaders have at their disposal. He then poses three important questions about leaders and power: What sources do they use? How do they exercise power? To what ends do they exercise it? By answering these questions, observers determine whether to admire or trust such people.

Gardner addresses the breakdown of the community as a factor in the failure of leadership. If leaders cannot find for their followers any base of shared values, principled leadership becomes almost impossible. Gardner proposes a list of "ingredients" of a community that would make it real. They include:

- Wholeness incorporating diversity.

J. W. Gardner, *On Leadership* (New York: The Free Press, 1990).

- Shared culture.
- Good internal communication.
- Caring, trust, and team work.
- Group maintenance and government.
- Participation and the sharing of leadership tasks.
- Development of young people.
- Links with the outside world.

A good community finds a balance between individuality and group obligation. This allows for a sense of group, yet allows for individual creativity to enhance the group setting. Skill in the building and rebuilding of community is offered as one of the highest and most essential leadership skills. Five skills are critically important for a leader in this time. They are:

- Agreement building.
- Networking.
- Exercising nonjurisdictional power.
- Institution building.
- Flexibility.

Gardner talks about the loss of shared values in organizations and suggests that leaders of these organizations need to discover that continuous renewal is required to keep the system operating efficiently. Continuous renewal is necessary to renew and interpret values, liberate energies, reenergize forgotten goals, develop new understandings leading to new solutions, and foster the release of human possibilities. Steps toward renewal include the release of talent and energy, reassignment, motivation, diversity and dissent, internal and external communication, reorganization, and the visible future.

The leader's task includes motivating others to accomplish the goals that are laid out for them. Anything a person will expend effort for can be a source of motivation. These forces can be family loyalties, money, security, beliefs, recognition, and so on. To truly motivate people, leaders must look at the needs of the people and try to satisfy those needs to a reasonable extent. These needs can be expressed, unexpressed, individual, or group related. These followers not only have needs, but they have duties or obligations to the organization to accomplish specified goals.

One important task of leadership is to revitalize those shared beliefs and values and to draw upon them as sources of motivation for the completion of the requirements of the group. The leader must move followers toward their commitments. The impact the leader has is partly derived from performance and partly from who he or she is and what he or she represents as a person.

In summary, *On Leadership* expressed several ideas that are becoming a normal part of every leader's workday. The ideas that Gardner has as far as renewing the society to accept diversity and creating an atmosphere of group relatedness is a step that many leaders in organizations today are facing. Gardner identified the leader's desired attributes and contexts in which various attributes play a more important role and concluded that they are situational. He examined power, how that power is used, and the effects it has on the people affected by that leader. Gardner ends his book with a question that every person should try to answer: Does the leader believe in the followers?

Applications

Case Studies & Experiential Exercises

C A S E

Alvis Corporation

Kevin McCarthy was the manager of a production department in Alvis Corporation, a nonunion firm that manufactures office equipment. After taking a management course that stressed the benefits of participative management, Kevin believed that these benefits could be realized in his department if his workers were allowed to participate in making some decisions on matters that affected them. He selected two decisions for his experiment in participative management.

The first decision involved vacation schedules. Each summer the workers get two weeks vacation, but no more than two workers can go on vacation at the same time. In prior years, Kevin had made this decision himself. He would first ask the workers to indicate their preferred dates; then he considered how the work would be affected if different people were out at the same time. It was important to make sure that vacations were planned in a way to ensure adequate staffing for all the essential operations performed by the department. When more than two workers wanted the same time period and they had similar skills, he usually gave preference to the workers with the highest productivity.

The second decision involved production standards. Sales had been increasing steadily over the past few years, and the company had recently installed some new equipment to increase productivity. The new equipment would allow Kevin's department to produce more with the same number of workers. The company had a pay-incentive system in which workers received a piece rate for each unit produced above a standard amount. Separate standards existed for each type of product, based on an industrial engineering study conducted a few years earlier. Top management now wanted to readjust the production standards to reflect the fact that the new equipment made it possible for the workers to earn more without working any harder. The savings from higher productivity were needed to pay for the new equipment.

Kevin called a meeting of his 18 workers an hour before the end of the work day. He explained that he wanted them to discuss the two issues and make recommendations. Kevin figured that the workers might be inhibited about participating in the discussion if he were present, so he left them alone to discuss the issues. Besides, Kevin had an appointment to meet with the quality control manager. Quality problems had increased after the new equipment was installed, and the industrial engineers were studying the problem in a attempt to determine why quality had gotten worse rather than better.

When Kevin returned to his department just at quitting time, he was very surprised to learn that the workers recommended keeping the standards the same. He had assumed they knew the pay incentives were no longer fair and that they would set a higher standard. The spokesman for the group explained that their base pay had not kept up with inflation, and the higher incentive pay merely restored their real income to prior levels.

On the vacation issue, the group was deadlocked. Several of the workers wanted to take their vacations during the same two-week period and could not agree on who should go. Some workers argued that they should have priority because they had more seniority, while others argued that priority should be based on productivity, as in the past. Since it was quitting time, the group concluded that Kevin would have to resolve the dispute himself. After all, wasn't that what he was being paid for?

Questions

1. Were the two decisions suitable ones for a group decision? Explain your answer.

2. What mistakes did Kevin make in the way he used a group decision-making procedure for the two decisions?

3. What issues of implementation and timing are involved in making these decisions in an effective manner? Describe how Kevin should have handled each decision.

4. Evaluate how appropriate these decisions were for introducing participation into Kevin's department.

Source: Reprinted from G. Yukl, Leadership in Organizations (Prentice Hall, 1994) with permission.

Sam Perkins

*D*r. Sam Perkins, a graduate of the Harvard University College of Medicine, was engaged in the private practice of internal medicine for 12 years. Fourteen months ago, he was persuaded by the governor to give up private practice to be director of the State Division of Human Services.

After one year as director, Perkins recognized he had made little progress in reducing the considerable inefficiency in the Division of Human Services. Employee morale and effectiveness seemed even lower than when he assumed the position. He realized his past training and experiences were of a clinical nature with little exposure to effective leadership techniques. Perkins decided to research literature published on the subject of leadership available to him at a local university.

Perkins soon realized that management scholars are divided on the question of what constitutes effective leadership. Some feel that leaders are born with certain identifiable personality traits that make them effective leaders. Others feel a leader can learn to be effective by treating subordinates with a personal and considerate approach and by giving particular attention to the subordinate's need for good working conditions. Still others emphasize the importance of developing a style of leadership characterized by either authoritarian, democratic, or laissez-faire approaches. Perkins was confused further when he learned there are a growing number of scholars who advocate that effective leadership is contingent on the situation, and a proper response to the question of what constitutes effective leadership is that it "depends on the situation."

Since a state university was located nearby, Perkins contacted its College of Business Administration dean. The dean referred him to the director of the college's Management Center, Professor Joel McCann. Discussions between Perkins and McCann resulted in a tentative agreement that the Management Center would organize a series of leadership training sessions for the State Division of Human Services. Before agreeing on the price tag for the leadership conference, Perkins asked McCann to prepare a proposal reflecting his thoughts on the following:

Questions

1. How will the question of what constitutes effective leadership be answered during the conference?

2. How will the lack of congruence among leadership researchers be resolved or reconciled?

3. What will be the specific subject content of the conference?

4. Who will the instructors be?

5. What will be the conference's duration?

6. How can the conference's effectiveness be evaluated?

7. What policies should the State Division of Human Services adopt regarding who the conference participants should be and how they should be selected? How can these policies be best implemented?

Source: Reprinted with permission from Champion/James, "Effective Leadership," *Critical Incidents in Management*, (Homewood, IL: Richard D. Irwin, Inc.)

C A S E

A Different Style of Leadership

*I*n my new position as Systems Engineer with BBG Industries, my initial assignment was in the Glass Research and Development Automations Section. My immediate supervisor, Al Sirroco, was given the mission of providing computer services for laboratory personnel and production, thus bridging the gap between data processing and process control. With a background in chemical engineering and computer sciences, Al was instrumental in pioneering the powerful and beneficial use of the computer as an aid to scientists and engineers. Utilizing a rented time-shared terminal, results were obtained that maximized calculation thruput and accuracy, thus providing concise historical records so vital in the research environment. Upper management was very impressed by Al's initial success in the realm of automation. The formation of the automation section was concrete evidence that management encouraged further growth in this field for BBG Industries.

Al faced the basic problem of obtaining group cohesiveness and coordination in order to build it into an effective organization. People in our group had diverse backgrounds, including a Ph.D. in mathematics, computer operators with high school diplomas, electrical engineers, and operations research personnel.

To overcome possible communications barriers among members of such a diverse unit, informal group meetings were held once a month. During such meetings each member could openly expound upon any problems requiring clarification, without any fear of retaliation. These staff meetings created an air of openness and relaxation of the status differences caused by differences in rank in our group. Each member had ample opportunity to make an informal presentation of what he or she was contributing to the group effort. Talk about work often spilled over to talk about personal life; the net effect was to produce a feeling of togetherness. After awhile one got the impression that any group member would help any other member with any kind of problem. One weekend, five of us helped bail out Tim, a computer operator, whose basement flooded in a rainstorm.

Our group obtained its first real surprise about Al's approach to managing people following a once-in-a-lifetime incident. An unfortunate situation occurred at the computer center which required the immediate dismissal of a key senior analyst. Although quiet and seemingly introverted, the analyst was held in high esteem because of his diligence and his record of accomplishment. Everyone in the group wondered what violation necessitated such drastic action on Al's part.

Rumors spread that perhaps the systems analyst had been engaged in sabotage, physical attack upon a fellow worker, criminal activity, drug abuse, or maybe a combination of several of these. The day after the incident, Al summoned the group into his office for an important announcement. He informed us that the extreme dedication to job performance shown by this systems analyst had caused him to suffer a nervous breakdown. Al maintained that it was necessary for his safety and the safety of the group for this man to be immediately separated from the company.

Evidence to corroborate Al's explanation was discovered when the individual's desk was cleaned out. A note was found buried beneath some papers in one of the drawers. His writings reflected several approaches to suicide. Al instigated efforts and received approval for the analyst to undergo psychiatric help immediately at the company's expense. In addition, severance pay of six month's salary was granted to him, and the company agreed to help him find future employment once his condition improved.

Al's explanation and the suicide note seemed to satisfy everyone's curiosity. However, several weeks later the real cause for the dismissal of the systems analyst surfaced via the company grapevine. One night when the analyst was working late, the only other employee in the building was a female computer operator. While she was walking down the aisle between the office and the computer equipment, he unzipped his pants, exposing himself. Upset by the incident, the computer operator reported the analyst's exhibitionism to her father, a manager in the laboratory. The father demanded retaliation and subsequent criminal prosecution.

Al's handling of the situation was unique and the termination of the systems analyst placated the father. By firing the analyst, the operator was spared the embarrassment of confronting him again at work. Yet, a couple of people in the group felt that Al's handling of the situation was bizarre. Irv, a mathematician, expressed it this way:

"Al sure is cool under pressure, but he's also quite a moralist. Sure, the poor guy exposed himself once that we know of. We cannot estimate the probability that he would expose himself again given the same circumstances. Maybe the father who complained so bitterly was really just jealous of the systems analyst. Worst of all, I question the value of Al making up a phony story just to bury the incident. If we fired everybody in this company who displayed a little deviant behavior once in their lives, we would probably have a pretty thin workforce."

Al's approach to leadership can also be understood in his handling of overtime work. Many times crucial projects required extended periods of late hours in order to meet critical deadlines. For exempt professionals, the lab rule stipulated that no compensation would be given, regardless of the time expended in discharging one's responsibilities.

Al informally modified the rule for his group. The term

Source: Reprinted with permission from Andrew J. DuBrin (Robert E. Gmitter researched and wrote this case, with the exception of several editorial changes); *Casebook of Organizational Behavior*, Copyright 1977, Pergamon Press.

"E-Time," for earned time, could be accumulated by each member for extra hours worked. This was an honor system with responsibility left entirely to the individual. Earned time could be cashed in by trading it for time off with pay when the project load lessened. Al's policy minimized the long, arduous hours of extended toil and promoted excellent group morale.

Al strived constantly to support individual accomplishments and to foster creativity in the glass industry. The Director of Research required a monthly meeting to discuss his group's progress, concepts, improvements, and future goals. Although key projects were mandatory in the agenda, voluntary participation and the initiation of topics were allowed at these important meetings. Each member of the group was encouraged by Al to make his contribution.

Al's impact upon people can be illustrated in his dealings with Kiwabi, a senior mathematician in the group. Kiwabi was advised to present a radical technique for the regression analysis of process data which reduced the time and amount of data, yet maintained qualitative accuracy. His brief presentation in the limelight impressed upper management and paved the way toward Kiwabi obtaining a fully paid leave of absence to obtain his Ph.D.

A study I had made of various computer systems for process control, as to their power and cost, was scheduled by Al for one of these meetings. My presentation led to future study of this same topic, which verified my findings. Not only was my career as a systems engineer brightened because of it, but the company benefited by obtaining more efficient computer systems with the latest technology at the maximum return upon investment. I honestly believe that without Al's prodding and guidance this study would not have come to fruition.

Supplementing our exposure at meetings, Al would circulate, via interlab memos, accomplishments and proposals of his personnel. By this mechanism, all pertinent managers and head scientists were made aware of the existence of group members. It also provided a first-rate opportunity for interface with groups requiring our supportive capabilities in the field of automation.

Al also scheduled trips to the plants to introduce us, explain our function, and relate our specialties. Plant associates could depend upon our expertise to assist them with problems. One such problem solved by our group was the correct depositing of raw materials, such as sand and dolomite, into holding bins. Predetermined amounts of raw material are required for each raw batch composition of glass before heating. The existing manual method had caused production upset due to the wrong ingredients in the bins. An automated, batch unloading protection system was designed, developed, and implemented by our group.

You can understand Al's comprehensive approach to managing people only by sampling the kind of things he did for people. Al would arrange trips for us to other companies, such as Mead Paper, to exchange technological applications and broaden our knowledge of automation. Al also encouraged a few of us to write articles for trade journals, and even provided help in this area. On the basis of these efforts a couple of us have achieved some national recognition.

Al had a keen sense of the ever-persistent technological changes taking place in the world of automation. To maintain the group's expertise, Al would submit a list of appropriate courses relevant to each individual's background. Participation and attendance at symposia and conferences were integrated into the work schedule. One of Al's pet projects was to get us involved in the Process Control Workshop at Purdue University. The Workshop consisted of international representation dedicated to standardization of the principles of process control automation.

For my money, Al is a top manager. But not everybody agrees with me. One of the skeptics in our groups said, "If Al walked into my office at 4:30 and reminded me to brush my teeth because it was good for me, I wouldn't be surprised. It would fit his leadership style."

Questions

1. Evaluate Al Sirroco's handling of the systems analyst problem. What would you have done if you were the supervisor?

2. What style of leadership do you prefer? Would you want a leader like Al? Discuss the pro and cons.

Donny Is My Leader

Breaking in Harvey

The first day I joined the team, Donny asked me how far I was going to run. The team had a goal of running two miles every Monday, Wednesday, and Friday morning, at a fair pace—about eight minutes a mile—on an inside track with 18 laps to the mile. I said I'd try for one mile and a half, a distance I had occasionally managed to complete jogging by myself. I ran at the tail end of the team and did, in fact, run the mile and a half. At the end of a mile and a half, Donny turned and shouted back to me from his place at the front of the group, "Ok, Harvey, that's enough!" And I stopped.

When the others finished, Donny came over and congratulated me. He told me I'd run well. He suggested I try adding three more laps next time, stay at that level for a while, and then add another three until I reached the 36 laps or two-mile objective of the team.

The "team" is a very informal collection of people with no formally appointed leader. Donny, however, is referred to as the coach. The team has existed for a while with a small, hard core and with others who come and go. The regulars comprise Donny, who always runs on the right side of the "pacer," who is almost always "Choc," and Herb, who runs about fourth and takes over as leader when Donny is away. Barrie generally runs third and sometimes sets the pace but is sort of an irregular regular since he occasionally forsakes the group for a squash game or gets in late after a hard night. Harry and Larry are two recent regulars. Larry always runs last and Harry runs just ahead of me. There are three or four others who occasionally join us. On some mornings we are as few as four running. On other mornings there are nine running.

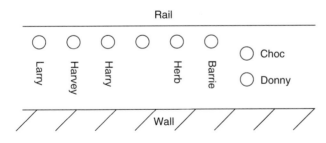

My second day was a beautiful, warm morning and we ran outside. I quit after a mile and a quarter. Harry quit after a mile. No one said anything to us about the running—neither good nor bad.

My third day and my big mistake! I vowed to run one mile and 12 laps to myself, 3 better than my previous inside run. At the end of the 11th lap of the second mile, since I still had

a little left in me, I sprinted the last lap, passing everyone. I'd noticed that all the finishers usually sprinted for the last one or two laps. However, when he was done, Donny came over and severely castigated me. How could I possibly have sprinted? If I could sprint, I must have had some strength left in me and therefore I could have gone for several more laps; in fact, I might even have been able to finish the two miles. He verbally lashed out at me several times both on the track and back down in the locker room. The others joined in, though in a more teasing mode. They said that next time I was not only going to run the two miles, but they would make me set the pace.

Soon after this occurrence, Harry became the culprit and the victim of Donny's wrath. We did each lap in about 28 seconds. Donny was the timekeeper. He shouted out the time for the first lap and for the first mile, and he counted out every second lap each time we passed the starting point (where a wall clock was mounted). Donny constantly encouraged us to keep going. Herb and Larry did so too. They called out milestones, "Three-quarters done!" or "Two-thirds done!" or "Five laps to go!" Near the end of the run, they kept up a steady stream of comments to urge those of us who were struggling to keep going and to try to finish the distance. On this particular day, at the end of the first lap, Harry said, "Hey, we're going too fast! We did it in 20 seconds." It was a bad day. Quite a few of us didn't finish. Donny was angry. He took it out on Harry repeatedly. He said that Harry's statement was incorrect and, furthermore, it had discouraged several of the team members, making them—including me—quit. He carried on all the way down to the locker room, in the showers, and even into the next running day.

Weigh-In

Once a month, Donny had us weigh in. At that time, we set our objectives for how much weight we would lose by the next weigh-in. He made a big occasion out of it, talking about it several days before, advising us to begin to fast a few days before, and culminating with a rather ceremonious act on the day of the weigh-in.

Stepping out to the scale, he asked each person to announce his objective, then weighed him and made a large fanfare about those who had achieved their objective and those who hadn't. We were put into two groupings: those who'd reached target and those who had not. Each one who didn't was publicly castigated, in humour, and asked to reset goals for the next weigh-in. The successful ones were not pressed.

The next running day after the weigh-in, there was a great

Source: Kolodny, H. F. & House, R. J., "Donny is My Leader: A Case Study of Leadership," *The Organizational Behavior Teaching Journal,* vol. VI, Issue 2, 1981, 51–56, Copyright 1981 The Organizational Behavior Teaching Society. Reprinted by permission of Sage Publications, Inc.

ceremony. Herb received a jersey on which was printed "Doctor D's Track Team." Choc had had them made up and kept them in his locker waiting for the appropriate occasion to have one handed out. Herb was the only one to be awarded. He had not only consistently run the distance, but he had also made his weight target. Donny let us all know that he wasn't going to be generous about giving the others out—even though they were all ready and printed. Only consistent demonstrations of performance across several fronts would merit a "Doctor D's Track Team" jersey.

Challenging the Leader

Larry usually ran in last place with the team. One summer he broke his ankle playing baseball, and he didn't run with us for most of the year. Then he started running again, sometimes joining us for short periods, sometimes running before or after us, sometimes faster for short spurts, though usually slower. He was slowly getting back in top shape.

Then one day he took his usual position at the rear as we were starting. After the first few laps, Donny had not called out the number of laps, and Larry chose to call them out loudly. Someone kibitzed and said that wasn't his job. I chipped in jokingly and said that I liked it when Larry called the laps. It was like old times again, I said, having Larry back. Larry kept calling the laps out as we completed them, and Donny, up front, said nothing.

Then Larry lost count somewhere around the eighth or ninth lap. I shouted to Donny, up front, to tell us where we were but he wouldn't answer. Because I feel lost when I don't know what I've run, I asked a few more times, "Would someone please say where we are?" Donny didn't answer. Then, after a while, in a loud voice, he said, "Strictly for Harvey, that was one mile we just passed." The next mile, he gave us two counts, one at the half mile and one at the end of the second mile. Normally he would count out every two laps (i.e. nine times a mile). In the third mile, he gave us three counts.

At the end of the run, he muttered something about "Teaching you guys respect the hard way."

Tinkertoy Construction

Task:	A sighted group leader instructs blindfolded subordinates in putting together a Tinkertoy structure.
Group Size:	Groups of 4 to 6 persons each.
Materials Needed:	One set of basic Tinkertoys for each group (or only one, if a demonstration group is to be used.) One blindfold for each participant. One picture of the structure to be built for each leader.
Time Required:	Approximately one hour.
Procedure:	Divide the class into groups. Ask each group to designate a leader for the exercise. All other members—the subordinates—are then asked to put on blindfolds. Once all subordinates are blindfolded, a picture of the structure to be built is handed to the leader of each group. Leaders are told that they may do anything they wish to get their subordinates to build the structure, except to remove the blindfolds or to touch the Tinkertoys themselves.
Discussion Questions:	1. Does the structure look like you expected it to look? How is it different?
	2. What did your leader do that was helpful?
	3. What did your leader do that was not helpful?
	4. What feelings did you have during, or following, this exercise?
	5. What lessons for leadership can you derive from this experience?
	6. What are the implications of, and relevant insights from, your readings about leadership?

Source: Cindy P. Lindsay and Cathy A. Enz, "Resource Control and Visionary Leadership: Two Exercises," *Journal of Management Education,* 15, no. 1, February 1991, pp. 127–35.

Structure for Blindfold Leadership Exercise*

Source: Cindy P. Lindsay and Cathy A. Enz, "Resource Control and Visionary Leadership: Two Exercises," *Journal of Management Education* 15, no. 1, February 1991, pp. 127–35.

Choosing a Leader

Task: Class members select a leader and examine that person's life, significant contributing events, and leadership behaviors.

Group Size: Members work as individuals initially, then combine their efforts in a group and all-class discussion.

Materials Needed: None.

Time Required: Approximately one hour in class.

Procedure: Assign class members this task:

"Examine the life of an individual whom you believe exemplifies the role of leader. This can be anyone, famous or not, past or present, industry or government, public or private, known to you personally or through the media. Some attention ought to be devoted to the chronology of events in the person's life. However, the bulk of your work should be directed at producing in-depth sociopsychological understanding. Pay attention to *how* the events and circumstances of the person's life affected the ultimate leadership self."

Discussion Questions:
1. Did your choice of leader come from:
   a. Public figures (current or historical)?
   b. Persons known from work?
   c. Family members?
   d. Personal acquaintances?
2. What factors do you think account for the class's observed distribution of choice from question 1?
3. Explore, in small groups, the leaders selected. What leadership qualities and characteristics are consistently represented there?
4. What can you learn about yourself as a leader from your choice of a leader to write about?

Source: David I. Sommers, "The Choice of a Leader to Write About is Not a Random Event," *Journal of Management Education,* August 1991, pp. 359–61.

Characteristics of Superior Leaders

Task:	Rank-order a set of leader characteristics on an individual and group basis, comparing the results to those from a broad sample of top-level managers.
Group Size:	Groups of 3 to 5 persons each.
Materials Needed:	One ranking sheet for each member.
Time Required:	Approximately one hour.
Procedure:	Distribute copies of the "Leader Characteristics" form to each class member. Ask them to rank-order the items from 1 to 10 according to which traits they most admire in leaders (1 being highest). Then form them into small discussion groups, and have them develop a group-based ranking of the items from 1 to 10. Finally, allow them to score themselves (both individually and as a group) against the responses of 2,600 top-level managers.
Discussion Questions:	1. Which characteristics of leaders seem to be most admired by class members? Why?
	2. What traits seem to be missing from this list?
	3. How do these results compare to the research literature on leadership traits?
	4. Why might your individual ranking differ from that of the top-level managers?
	5. In a later book, Kouzes and Posner make a compelling argument that leader credibility is the most important ingredient contributing to their success (in the eyes of subordinates). Which factors in the list of 10 might be components of credibility?

Source: Data drawn from James M. Kouzes and Barry Z. Posner, *The Leadership Challenge* (San Francisco: Jossey-Bass, 1988), p. 17.

Self-Assessment

Leader Characteristics

Directions: Rank-order from 1 to 10 (1=highest, 10=lowest) the following characteristics according to the degree that you admire a leader who exhibits them. Place your results in column 2. Do the same in column 4 when you are assigned to a group and reach a consensus on the ranking. Then your instructor will share the results from a study that you can insert in column 3 and use to compare your data with.

Trait	1	2 (Ind.)	Columns 3	4 (Grp.)	5
Ambitious	_____	_____	_____	_____	_____
Caring	_____	_____	_____	_____	_____
Competent	_____	_____	_____	_____	_____
Determined	_____	_____	_____	_____	_____
Forward-looking	_____	_____	_____	_____	_____
Honest	_____	_____	_____	_____	_____
Imaginative	_____	_____	_____	_____	_____
Inspiring	_____	_____	_____	_____	_____
Loyal	_____	_____	_____	_____	_____
Self-controlled	_____	_____	_____	_____	_____

Leader-Subordinate Friendships (LSF)

Task: Participants complete the LSF questionnaire, share and tabulate results, and discuss their implications.

Group Size: Groups of 3 to 5 persons.

Materials Needed: One copy of the questionnaire for each participant. One transparency master for tabulating results.

Time Required: Minimum of one hour, depending on depth of discussion desired.

Procedure: Distribute a copy of the LSF questionnaire to each participant, and allow a few minutes for its completion. Using a show of hands for each question and response category, tabulate the results (preferably using a visual display, such as the chalkboard or a transparency). Then lead the group in a discussion of the following questions.

Discussion Questions:

1. What does *friendship* mean to you?
2. Can leaders and subordinates be friends on the job and still maintain an effective work environment?
3. What skills contribute to friendships?
4. What are the risks of these friendships?
5. Can LSFs substitute for other leader behaviors?
6. How friendly should a leader be with followers?
7. What are the organizationally desirable consequences of leader-subordinate friendships?
8. Is it possible that LSF would prevent objective appraisal of subordinate performance?
9. How can one obtain the benefits of LSFs without incurring the drawbacks?
10. How does LSF relate to a leader's source of power?

Source: Robert R. Taylor, Susan C. Hanlon, and Nancy G. Boyd, "Can Leaders and Subordinates Be Friends? A Classroom Approach for Addressing An Important Managerial Dilemma," *Journal of Management Education*, February 1992, pp. 39–55.

Leader-Subordinate Friendship Questionnaire

Please respond to the following statements according to your level of agreement: SA—strongly agree; A—agree; N—neutral; D—disagree; SD—strongly disagree. Circle the appropriate letters.

1.	Managers should not try to maintain friendships with subordinates.	SA	A	N	D	SD
2.	It is possible to maintain friendships with subordinates without damaging one's effectiveness as a leader.	SA	A	N	D	SD
3.	As for myself, it works best if I do not try to be friends with my subordinates.	SA	A	N	D	SD
4.	Maintaining friendships with subordinates actually can make one a better leader.	SA	A	N	D	SD
5.	There is a certain skill associated with maintaining leader-subordinate friendships and still being an effective leader: Some managers have it and some don't.	SA	A	N	D	SD
6.	Friendships between leaders and subordinates are a natural consequence growing out of close physical proximity and considerable interpersonal contact.	SA	A	N	D	SD
7.	If a manager wants to maintain a friendship with one subordinate, then he or she must try to maintain friendship relationships with all subordinates.	SA	A	N	D	SD
8.	If a manager is going to maintain friendship relationships with subordinates at all, it might be a good idea to tie those relationships to performance (i.e., the better the performer, the more you encourage a friendship relationship with that subordinate).	SA	A	N	D	SD
9.	Maintaining friendships with subordinates gives a manager more information on which to base business decisions.	SA	A	N	D	SD
10.	Maintaining friendships with subordinates facilitates a manager's ability to motivate subordinates.	SA	A	N	D	SD
11.	The closer the leader-subordinate friendship, the greater the likelihood the subordinate will feel free to disagree with the boss.	SA	A	N	D	SD
12.	Maintaining leader-subordinate friendships gives the subordinate more power to influence the leader.	SA	A	N	D	SD
13.	It is generally not a good idea for subordinates to have the power to influence their bosses.	SA	A	N	D	SD
14.	The closer the friendship relationship between leader and subordinate, the greater the likelihood that the leader will feel free to give the negative performance feedback when a subordinate is doing poorly.	SA	A	N	D	SD
15.	The closer the leader-subordinate friendship, the less likely it is that a leader will give a subordinate a negative mark on a formal performance appraisal.	SA	A	N	D	SD
16.	Being a considerate manager or leader is the same as maintaining a friendship relationship with subordinates.	SA	A	N	D	SD
17.	It is easier for staff area managers to maintain leader-subordinate friendships than it is for production or line area managers.	SA	A	N	D	SD
18.	It is easier for an upper-level manager (a vice president for instance) to maintain leader subordinate friendships with his or her immediate subordinates than it is for a lower-level manager or supervisor.	SA	A	N	D	SD

19. What do you see as the major benefits, if any, of a manager maintaining friendships with subordinates?
    1.
    2.
    3.
    4.

20. What do you see as the major drawbacks, if any, of a manager maintaining friendships with subordinates?
    1.
    2.
    3.
    4.

21.	In general the benefits of maintaining leader subordinate friendships outweigh the drawbacks.	SA	A	N	D	SD

Leader-Subordinate Friendship Tally

| Question | Responses | | | | |
	SA	A	N	D	SD
1					
2					
3					
4					
5					
6					
7					
8					
9					
10					
11					
12					
13					
14					
15					
16					
17					
18					
21					

Leadership (Locker-Room) Talks

Task:
Class members are assigned a topic (see Table 1). Each member prepares and delivers a concise talk on the assigned topic, followed by class and instructor critiques of the effectiveness of the talk and the leadership dimensions demonstrated. The objective is to demonstrate the importance of, and develop, each student's confidence, willingness, and readiness to play an inspirational leadership role.

Group Size:
Any number (overlapping assignments to topics are possible).

Time Required:
Two minutes per student, plus critique time.

Procedure:
1. Explain the objectives of the exercise to the class.
2. Indicate the types of locker-room talk topics and how they fit into the classification scheme.
3. Assign topics and dates of presentations.
4. Cue the class members to act as real audiences, reacting as they might to the situation and the comments made by the speaker.
5. Call for two-minute talks, using a student timekeeper to cue the speaker when 15 seconds remains.
6. Call for comments from the class about the quality and effectiveness of the speeches, as well as the various dimensions of leadership displayed.

Discussion Questions:
1. What are the primary objectives of locker-room talks by leaders?
2. What are the primary abilities that need to be demonstrated by each speaker in these settings?
3. What are characteristics of feedback to the speakers that will be most constructive?
4. How do you handle hostility? Distrust? Apathy?

Source: Richard G. Linowes, "Filling a Gap in Management Education: Giving Leadership Talks in the Classroom," *Journal of Management Education*, 1992, pp. 6–24.

T A B L E   1

Topics for the Leadership Talks and a Classification of Each

Topic Number	Topic Description	Topic Number	Topic Description
1.	Taking charge of an established group The speaker is a manager now newly assigned to a group that has worked together under other managers for some time.	7.	Reprimanding unacceptable behavior The speaker is calling to task certain individuals who have failed to perform up to required levels.
2.	Announcing a new project The speaker is announcing a new undertaking to members of his or her department and is calling on all to rally behind the effort.	8.	Calming a frightened group of people The speaker is endeavoring to restore peace and confidence to those who now panic in the face of distressing business developments.
3.	Calling for better customer service The speaker is motivating all employees to be as attentive and responsive to the customer as possible.	9.	Addressing a challenging opposition The speaker is presenting some heartfelt belief to a critical, even hostile, audience.
4.	Calling for excellence and high-quality work The speaker is motivating all employees to perform their jobs with a commitment to meeting the highest possible standards.	10.	Mediating opposing parties The speaker is calling for reconciliation between two groups bitterly opposed on some key issue.
5.	Announcing the need for cost reductions The speaker is requesting that everyone look for ways to cut expenditures and immediately begin slashing spending.	11.	Taking responsibility for error The speaker is the figurehead spokesman for an institution that has produced some unfortunate result affecting the audience.
6.	Commending for a job well done The speaker is extolling a group of people who have worked very hard for an extended period to produce outstanding results.	12.	Petitioning for special allowances The speaker is presenting the case for an institution seeking certain rights that must be authorized by some external body.

	Individual	Group	Institution

Task oriented	Taking responsibility
	    Taking charge of an established group
	    Introducing a new project
	    Taking responsibility for error[a]
		Shaping behavior
		    Commending for a job well done
		    Reprimanding unacceptable behavior
			Forging a direction
			    Calling for better customer service
			    Calling for excellence and high-quality work
			    Announcing the need for cost reductions

Emotional/values oriented	Taking a stand
	    Addressing a challenging opposition
		Building cohesion
		    Calming a frightened group of people
		    Mediating opposing parties
			Representing the firm
			    Taking responsibility for error[a]
			    Petitioning for special allowances

[a] This topic is suitable for both Taking Responsibility and Representing the Firm.

Follow the Leader

Task:	Students are assigned to read biographical materials on well-known leaders and identify their relationship with their followers.
Group Size:	Any number.
Time Required:	Approximately one class session per leader studied.
Procedure:	Divide the class into study groups. Following prior reading, lecture, or discussion on "followership" factors in leader effectiveness, assign (or allow choice in selection) one major leader (e.g., Lee Iacocca, Martin Luther King, Jr., Adolph Hitler, Eleanor Roosevelt, Mary Cunningham) per group. Provide the group with appropriate references documenting the leaders' lives, from which they may draw their analyses. Ask each group to identify:

1. The ways in which the leader they studied influenced his/her followers.
2. The influence of the followers on the leader studied.
3. How characteristics of their own and their followers' personalities affected the leader's success.

Discussion Questions:	

1. Was your chosen leader successful?
2. Would you have willingly followed that leader?
3. What kinds of facts about the leader studied did you use to make your argument?
4. What kinds of facts about the leader studied did you omit in making your argument?
5. What leadership theories are relevant to your understanding of this leader, and how?
6. What characteristics of their followers' personalities (e.g., skills/abilities, needs, wants, preferences, expectations, biases, and personal histories) affected the leader's success?

Suggested Leader References

Cunningham, M., and F. Schumer. *Powerplay: What Really Happened at Bendix.* New York: Fawcett Gold Medal, 1984.

Garrow, D. J. *Bearing the Cross: Martin Luther King, Jr., and the Southern Christian Leadership Conference.* New York: William Morrow, 1986.

Hitler, A. *Mein Kampf.* Boston: Houghton Mifflin, 1927.

Iacocca, L., with W. Novak. *Iacocca: An Autobiography.* New York: Bantam, 1984.

Lacey, R. *Ford: The Men and the Machine.* Boston: Little, Brown, 1986.

Langer, W. C. *The Mind of Adolph Hitler.* New York: New American Library, 1972.

Roosevelt, E. *The Autobiography of Eleanor Roosevelt.* Boston: G. K. Hall, 1984.

Sloan, A. *The Bendix-Martin Marietta War.* New York: Dow-Jones, 1977.

Youngs, J. W. T. *Eleanor Roosevelt: A Personal and Public Life.* Boston: Little Brown, 1985.

Source: Clayton P. Alderfer, "Teaching Personality and Leadership: A Course on Followership," *OBTR* 12 no. 4, (1987–88), pp. 12–33.

Leadership through Film: Power and Influence

Task: Students view a "popular" video (full-length movie) and analyze it for illustrations of various sources and applications of power. This draws on Bandura's concept of vicarious (observational) learning.

Group Size: Assignments can be made at three levels: total class, small group, or individual.

Materials Needed: VCR/TV and selected video, if a single, common stimulus is desired for total-class discussion.

Time Required: Approximately two hours to view an entire film, plus subsequent discussion time.

Procedure:
1. Choose a video that is rich in demonstration of a leader's use of power and influence. Many prime examples exist, such as *Dead Poets' Society, Watership Down, Aliens, A Few Good Men, The Magnificent Seven.*
2. Show the video to the class. (Alternatively, allow each class member to select the video of his or her choice to view and on which to create a report.)
3. Ask each member to prepare a written paper that thoroughly discusses leadership and power.

Discussion Questions:
1. *Who* has power in the video, *why* do they have that power, and *how* did they acquire it?
2. What was the *source* of that power (e.g., expert, legitimate, referent)?
3. How did they *use* their power (e.g., to make a legitimate request, to gain compliance, or persuade or inspire)?
4. What were the positive/negative *effects* of that power on the followers?
5. Alternatively, how could they have influenced their followers?

Sources: Adapted from various reports by Timothy Serey, Claudia Harris , Kermith V. Harrington, and Ricky W. Griffin.